BLOODY
SHAMBLES

BLOODY SHAMBLES

VOLUME TWO
THE DEFENCE OF SUMATRA TO THE FALL OF BURMA

Christopher Shores and Brian Cull with Yasuho Izawa

GRUB STREET · LONDON

Published by
Grub Street
The Basement
10 Chivalry Road
London SW11 1HT

Maps by Jeff Jefford

A catalogue record for this book is available from the British Library

ISBN 0 948817 67 4

Edited by John Davies

Typeset by BMD Graphics, Hemel Hempstead

Printed and bound in Great Britain by
Biddles Ltd, Guildford and King's Lynn

The Authors would like to thank the following people:

RICHARD SLATER for his assistance in compiling Chapter 1;
GERRIE ZWANENBERG and ROBERT BROOKES
for their assistance in compiling Chapters 4, 6 and 8.

CONTENTS

FOREWORD AND ACKNOWLEDGEMENTS

As with other volumes in the series, this two-part work has seen more than 20 years of research to bring it to its conclusion in the form now before the reader. Great assistance was received from Gerrie Zwanenberg, Peter Boer and Gerard Cassius on Dutch operations, and from William N. Hess, Robert Brooks, and latterly, from Richard Slater on US activities, particularly in the Philippines and Java.

Above all, however, the book has reached ultimate fruition due to the devotion to the project of Brian Cull, to whom the other authors owe a great debt of gratitude. His determination and singleness of purpose in tracking down the surviving fighter pilots and the bomber crews of the RAF, RAAF and RNZAF who served in the area, enabled a full picture to be constructed over the years, the completeness of which totally belies the absolute inadequacy of the few official records that exist. We believe the results speak for themselves: without his efforts, this account would have been but a poor shadow of its present form, if it had been completed at all.

While not every detail of Japanese operations could be discovered, for obvious reasons, the extent of the information provided by Yasuho Izawa, from sources long believed in the West not to exist, allowed a far more balanced view to be provided than has previously been possible.

Of the many ex-aircrew who helped and encouraged, several stand out particularly. Sadly, some of these have passed away before we were able to present for their approval the results of the labours that they did so much to aid and sustain. Notable amongst them must be Peter Bingham-Wallis, whose long-standing support and enthusiasm was of the highest order, and who introduced us to numerous others. It is the authors' greatest regret that Peter did not live to see the book he was so keen should be published. Guy Marsland and Wg Cdr 'Bunny' Stone DFC, also come into this category, which is deeply regretted, as does Mowbray Garden DFC.

Special thanks are due to: Jimmy Parker DFC, of 232/242 Squadron, who made available to the authors private memoirs covering his period with the squadron; to Air Vice-Marshal E.C. Gartrell DFC, RNZAF, of 232/242 Squadron in providing an account of the squadron's latter days in Java; to Gordon Dunn RCAF, of 232/242 Squadron — a friend for nigh on 20 years; to George Mothersdale of 243 Squadron, who was instrumental in piecing together that squadron's history; to Rex Weber DFC, RNZAF, of 243 Squadron for the loan of his diary; to Geoff Fisken DFC, RNZAF, of 243 Squadron for his many informative letters; to Wg Cdr Albert Lewis DFC, of 261 Squadron for

Ceylon operations details.

Thanks also to Peter Ballard RNZAF, of 4 AACU (Anti-Aircraft Co-operation Unit) for his commendable endeavours in reconstructing the unit's history; to Grp Capt Herb Plenty DFC, RAAF, for providing a copy of his privately-produced book, and additional material; to Graeme McCabe RAAF, of 100 Squadron for the extract from his book; to Air Vice-Marshal Bob Bateson CB, DSO, DFC, for background material on 211 Squadron; to Bill Miller of the 84 Squadron Association for information and contacts; to Dave Russell of 84 Squadron for the loan of his unpublished memoirs; to Alex Kelly RAAF, of 36 Squadron for assistance in tracing survivors of the Endau operation; to Grp Capt Alex Jardine of 205 Squadron for copies of the squadron's records and loan of photographs; to the late Air Vice-Marshal S.F. Vincent DFC, Terence O'Brien of 53 Squadron, and Hugh Popham for permission to quote from their respective books.

Amongst the Burma veterans contacted in addition to Messrs Bingham-Wallis, Marsland and Stone, thanks are extended to Grp Capt Jimmy Elsdon OBE, DFC, whom the authors met at a 136 Squadron reunion (and to whom we also offer our condolences on the loss of his son during the recent Gulf War); thanks also to the late Grp Capt Barry Sutton DFC; Wg Cdr 'Bush' Cotton DFC, RAAF, Ken Hemingway and Hedley Everard DFC, RCAF, for permission to quote from their respective books; to Sqn Ldr Jack Storey DFC, RAAF, for the loan of diary, personal notes and photographs; to 'Tex' Barrick for agreeing to be interviewed on our behalf by our American friend, Pete Clausen.

The list of other contributors is long; apart from those mentioned above, others who have helped in a variety of way are listed herewith:

Air Marshal Sir Harold Maguire KCB, DSO, OBE; Grp Capt H.S. Darley DSO; Mr John Maltby (son of the late Air Vice-Marshal Sir Paul Maltby).

232/242 Squadron
Air Commodore Eric Wright DFC, DFM; Henry Nicholls; John Fleming RCAF; Tom Young RAAF; James Sandeman Allen DFM; Fred Margarson; Ken Holmes; Ivan Julian DFC, RNZAF (via Paul Sortehaug); Ian Newlands RNZAF; Tom Watson DFC, RCAF; Bill Lockwood RCAF; Sqn Ldr Norman Welch; Mrs Ida Blake (widow of Jimmy King DFC); Mrs Mary Armitage (sister of the late Wg Cdr R.E.P. Brooker DSO, DFC); Miss Barbara McKechnie (sister of the late John McKechnie RCAF); Mr George Leetham (brother of the late Joe Leetham RCAF); Mrs Katarine Fitzherbert (mother of the late Mike Fitzherbert DFC).

258 Squadron
Wg Cdr James Thomson; Art Sheerin RAAF; Ambrose Milnes; Bert Lambert; Terence Kelly (author of *Hurricanes Over The Jungle* and *The Battle for Palembang*); Doug Nicholls DFC; Jim Dobbyn BEM (brother of the late Harry Dobbyn RNZAF); John Macnamara (brother of the late Graham Macnamara); John Vibert RNZAF; Wg Cdr R.S. Peacock-Edwards (son of the late Spencer Peacock-Edwards DFC); Leslie J. Cristy.

243 Squadron
Rex Weber DFC, RNZAF (via Paul Sortehaug); Terry Marra RNZAF; Mrs Hilda Mumyard (mother of the late Noel Sharp DFC, RNZAF); Mrs Gillian Howell (widow of the late Wg Cdr F.J. Howell DFC); the Wipiti family via Paul Sortehaug and Mrs Joyce Richardson (re the late Bert Wipiti DFM, RNZAF);

the Kronk family via Paul Sortehaug (re the late Charles Kronk RNZAF); Bill 'Paddy' Moulds.

488 Squadron
Jim MacIntosh RNZAF; Harry Pettit RNZAF; Peter Gifford RNZAF; John McKenzie RNZAF.

21/453 Squadrons
G.M. Sheppard RAAF; Geoff Angus RAAF (via Russell Guest); Wg Cdr T.A. Vigors DFC.

67 Squadron
Wg Cdr Bob Milward DFC; Jack Brandt MBE, DFC; the late Ed Beable RNZAF; and, via the services of Paul Sortehaug: Vic Bargh DFC, RNZAF, Gordon Williams DFM, RNZAF, Graham Sharp DSO, RNZAF and Keith Rutherford DFC, RNZAF.

84 Squadron
Mrs Erica Hills (sister of the late Grp Capt John Jeudwine DSO, OBE, DFC); Bill Miller; Eric Oliver; Bob Bennett; Hayes Harding BEM; Archie Wakefield; the distinguished author John Wyllie DFC; Allan Ross RAAF; Frank Cameron RAAF; Ken Lister; George Milson; 'Butch' Finning; Mrs Rosemary Marcon (daughter of the late Maurice Holland).

211 Squadron
Allan Richardson; Bill Baird; the late Tom Henderson; Athol Snook RAAF; George Dunbar; Bill Sykens.

The Survivors of Endau (Aircrew of 36 and 100 Squadrons)
Alex Kelly RAAF; Basil Gotto; Tom Lamb; Richard Allanson DFC; 'Skip' Glowrey RAAF; Peter Atherton RAAF; Charles MacDonald RAAF; Keith Minton DFM, RNZAF; John Smith RAAF; Graeme McCabe RAAF; Harry Lockwood; the late Elwood Cummins RAAF.

Others
Air Commodore 'Spud' Spurgeon DFC, RAAF, of 8 RAAF Squadron; Ray Blunden, Fred McKeever RAAF, and Tom Wright of 4 AACU (via Peter Ballard); Don Pearson DFC, and the family of the late Charles Wareham DFM, RNZAF, of 4 PRU (via Paul Sortehaug); Bill Annand RNZAF, Ray Hemus RNZAF, Abe Moritz RAAF, John Victorsen RAAF, Jack Fellowes RAAF, and Bill McGechie RNZAF, of 'W' Flight; Donald Jackson, Alex Brown and George Dewey RAAF, of 34 Squadron; Don Purdon RAAF, of 60 Squadron; Stan Fielding of 62 Squadron; Les Hayton and the late Grp Capt Tom Burne DSO, AFC, of 53 Squadron; Ian Thomas (son of the late James Thomas of 53 Squadron); Les Patrick of 59 Squadron; the late Frank Hood RNZAF (for loan of diary via Paul Sortehaug); Jim Pickering AFC, ADU ferry pilot; Frank Wilding, Ken Bunting and Viv Jacobs of 136 Squadron; Grp Capt Frank Carey DFC (2 bars), DFM; Eric Batchelar, Lee Hawkins DSO, DFC and Guy Underwood of 135 Squadron; Maj John Viney SAAF, of 113 Squadron.

A number of Fleet Air Arm personnel have been contacted, mainly with regard to operations at Ceylon, and we offer our thanks to these: Capt P.E.I. Bailey, Cdrs John Sykes, Jack Smith and Barry Nation; the late Lt Cdr Gerry Woods DSC; Bill Anderson, Michael Hordern, Roy Hinton, Laurie Brander, Gordon Dixon, Bert Holt and Norman Lauchlan; also to Lt Cdrs Clem Bateman and Bill Crozer for their detailed accounts of Walrus operations from *Prince of Wales* and *Repulse*, respectively; to Norman Hollis of 205 Squadron.

Thanks also to John Havers for the use of information appearing in an article written by him on the Burma Volunteer Air Force; to Don Leate, honorary Historian of 84 Squadron for his assistance and interest; to Flt Lt P.L. Jordan, RNZAF, for photographs of 261 Squadron in Ceylon (a unit with which he served); Lt Cdr T. Brander, DSC, for his reminiscences; Gurney Smead for additional information relating to the evacuation and subsequent sinking of *Pinnace 54* during the exodus from Singapore.

Help from Dutch pilots was generously forthcoming from R.A.D. Anemaet and Pieter Tideman, while 'Link' Laughlin of the AVG also provided reminiscences.

Much assistance and encouragement has been forthcoming from old friends 'down under', especially Paul Sortehaug of New Zealand, who was prominent in contacting survivors (or kin) of aircrew who served with 67,243 and 488 Squadrons; many of the photographs used relating to these squadrons were supplied by Paul. Ian Primmer and Russell Guest in Australia have assisted with regard to RAAF personnel, whilst fellow-Australian and author, Lex McAulay, has supplied photographs and invaluable documents; our thanks also to Bob Piper, RAAF Historical Section, to the late Allan Blythe RAAF, and Bill Panckridge.

As with our previous books, we offer our thanks to Louis Tortell of Malta and Stuart Bickel MSc, for reproducing many of the photographs used; and to old friends Bruce Lander and Eddie Pearson for their practical assistance; to Flt Lt Andy Thomas for the loan of many previously unpublished photographs from his own collection; to fellow authors Ray Sturtivant, Norman Franks, Roy Humphreys, L.J. 'Robbie' Robertson and Bjorn Olsen for their help.

Thanks also to the staff of the Public Record Office, London, for their assistance; to Air Historical Branch of the Ministry of Defence — in particular Mr R.C.M. King — to J. David Brown of the Naval Historical Branch, and to the Bury St Edmunds Public Library, for obtaining hard-to-find books; to the Public Archives Canada; the RNZAF Historical Section; the RAAF Historical Section.

Our US contributor, Richard Slater, wishes to record his gratitude to the following veterans of the Philippines: Samuel Grashio; George Armstrong; Joseph Moore; Raymond Patenaude; Arthur Reynolds; John Brownewell; Ny Blanton; C.C. Montgomery; Bob Jones and Thomas Page.

Brian Cull also wishes to extend his sincere thanks to John and Sylvia Macnamara, with whom he stayed on his research trip to Rhodesia (now Zimbabwe), and to the hospitality and assistance received when he visited John Wyllie DFC, Terence O'Brien, George Mothersdale, Les Patrick and Allan Richardson in more recent times; gratitude as ever goes to Jack Lee and last, but not least, Brian wishes to offer his sincere thanks to Val, without whose help and encouragement these books would not have been completed on time.

No work of this nature is complete without the assistance of other historians and authors, and in this regard we were greatly helped by Frank Olynyk's recently prepared victory claim lists, particularly that relating to the American Volunteer Group. Autobiographies by two of the Group's pilots, Charles R. Bond and Robert T. Smith also helped, as did John Lundstrom's monumental *The First Team* in regard to US Naval operations.

As indicated in Volume One, appendices and a bibliography relating to both volumes appear at the rear of this one.

Christopher F. Shores, Brian Cull and Yasuho Izawa
London, Bury St Edmunds and Tokyo

ADDENDUM AND ERRATUM TO VOLUME ONE

One advantage of a two-volume history is that corrections and additions to the first volume can be incorporated in the second. Firstly, we draw attention to the fact that the captions to the photographs on pages 265 and 266 of Volume One have been transposed; Sgt 'Ketchil' Bargh and his victim appear on the latter page, whilst Capt Fujio Sakaguchi's Ki 27 is illustrated on the former.

On several occasions in Volume One regrettably we used the wrong Christian names for a number of New Zealand personnel, for which our apologies:

Page 6: (67 Squadron) Geoff Sharp (not Graham); Ken Rutherford (not Keith).
Page 293: Vern Meaclem (not Vic).
Page 315: Gordon Bonham (not Graham).
Page 338: Vin Arthur (not Vic).

After publication of Volume One, William H. Bartsch's excellent new book *Doomed at the Start* (Texas A & M University Press) appeared, covering in great detail the activities and operations of the USAAF fighters in the Philippines. From this certain corrections are required to Chapter 5 of Volume One, as follows:

Page 166: Lt F.O. Roberts had not run out of fuel when he crash-landed in the sea — his P-40 had been hit by Zeros.
Page 168: 2/Lt George Ellstrom was not killed on his parachute; he died in hospital subsequently, due to shock and internal injuries. 2/Lt Richard L. Root was also killed on 8 December, not on 10th (as recorded on Page 178); he and 2/Lts Andrew F. Webb and John F. O'Connell were all killed on the ground during the attack.
Page 178: Lt Don Steele and 2/Lt Krieger each claimed A6Ms shot down, although the latter may have been classified as a 'probable'. Lt Varian K. White and Lt Milt Woodside were also shot down and baled out. P-40 losses in the engagement therefore appear to have been nine shot down and three crash-landed, while claims for A6M Zeros seem to have totalled eight.
Page 185: It was recorded that 1/Lt Robert T. Hanson claimed a seaplane shot down on 12 December. He and Grant Mahony had been undertaking a strafing mission in the Legaspi area, when Hanson spotted a large four-engined flyingboat attempting to take off under cover of

fire from a destroyer. It was this aircraft that he claimed to have destroyed, subsequently strafing the destroyer as well. Next day he was hit by a fragment during a bombing raid on Nicholls Field and was mortally wounded, dying shortly afterwards.

Page 188: The lone P-40 seen and claimed probably destroyed by pilots of the Tainan Kokutai's 4th Chutai, would seen to have been that in which 1/Lt Walt Coss was undertaking a reconnaissance sortie. He reported being attacked by two fighters, following which he baled out over the Caygayan River. He was strafed several times after falling into the water, but escaped unharmed, returning on foot.

Page 192: Late on 19 December six P-35As were moved to Clark Field, where they were loaded with six 30lb fragmentation bombs each. Next morning before dawn they took off to attack a schoolhouse where Japanese troops were known to be billetted. The attack was a success, but later as the aircraft returned from Clark to Manila, Lt Steve Crosby became engaged with a Ki 27 fighter, which he pursued. He did not see the wingman, who shot his aircraft down in flames, although he was able to bale out safely.

Page 193: Ki 27 pilots of the 50th Sentai claimed two US fighters shot down, one of which was that flown by Lt Wagner, which actually escaped with damage. Lt Shepherd's P-40 was also hit and returned with some 200 bullet holes in it, having to be written off after he had landed safely.

Page 195: It was reported that attacks were made on the Japanese landings in Lamon Bay. Four P-35As had been moved to Clark, undertaking the first attack from here around midday. During this attack one Zero was claimed shot down — probably the Tainan Ku aircraft flown by NAP 1/C Toshio Kikuchi, lost in this area at this time. Lt Marshall Anderson's P-35A was shot up and he crash-landed on return to Nicholls, whilst Lt LaMar Gillett just made it back to Clark with the tail and rear fuselage of his aircraft damaged. These were undoubtedly the aircraft claimed shot down by the *Mizuho* F1Ms. About an hour later four P-40s attacked with fragmentation bombs, but AA hit 2/Lt James Rowland's aircraft and he force-landed in Laguna Bay on return, swimming to safety.

Page 196: There were three further claims made by US fighter pilots during the last week of December. On 26th Lt William Dyess claimed a single-engined bomber south of Lingayen Gulf during the early morning, whilst half an hour later Lt George Kiser claimed a fighter tentatively identified as a Navy 96 (A5M) over Alabat Island. Over Lingayan Gulf again two days later on 28th, Dyess claimed an Army 97 fighter (Ki 27).

Doomed at the Start is warmly recommended as additional reading for greater detail of US fighter operations and personalities in the Philippines. The book identifies a number of US pilots more precisely, several of whom are mentioned in Volume One, although one or two missed being included in the index.

Corrections to the index:

Name	Unit	Page
Alder, 1/Lt Glen M.	20th Pursuit Squadron	178
Benson, 2/Lt Gordon S.	17th Squadron	178
Hobrecht (*not* Holbrecht), 2/Lt Forrest M.	17th Squadron	178
Kiser (*not* Kizer), 2/Lt George E.	17th Squadron	
Mulcahy, 2/Lt Lowell J. (*not* Tod)	20th Squadron	
Newman, 2/Lt Robert W.	3rd Squadron	183
Phillips, 2/Lt James A.	17th Squadron	178
Root, 2/Lt Richard L.	3rd Squadron	178
Roberts, 1/Lt Fred O. Jr	3rd Squadron	166

Additions to index:

Anderson, 1/Lt Marshall J.	20th Squadron	
Coss, 1/Lt Walter L.	17th Squadron	
Crosby, 2/Lt Stephen H.	17th Squadron	
Gillett, 2/Lt R. LaMar	17th Squadron	
O'Connell, 2/Lt John F.	3rd Squadron	
Steele, 2/Lt Donald D.	3rd Squadron	
Webb, 2/Lt Andrew F.	3rd Squadron	
White, 2/Lt Varian K.	20th Squadron	
Woodside, 2/Lt Milton H.	20th Squadron	

Sqn Ldr T.P.M. Cooper-Slipper, DFC, has confirmed that he did indeed claim two bombers shot down over Singapore on 22 January 1942 (Page 335). On Page 357 we reported that he departed Singapore medically unfit soon thereafter. He advises:

> "I was only in hospital for a few days with a bad stomach, caused by driving into a Chinese carrying two cans of 'you-know-what' on a pole over his shoulder. One can came through the windshield of the station wagon, and I collected it! During the final days in Singapore I took most of the remaining airmen and pilots to the docks where we managed to secure passage to Palembang in the *Whang Pu*.

Grp Capt 'George' Darley has also provided a detailed account of his role in the organisation of the fighter defences in Malaya, Singapore, Burma and Sumatra, and this has been included in full in this Volume as an appendix.

Japanese Aircraft and Unit Designations; Dutch Unit Designations

Several reviewers of Volume One made it clear that some readers find the identification of the various Japanese aircraft types difficult without use of the Allied wartime codenames by which they became familiar throughout the United States and United Kingdom. A brief description of Japanese and Dutch air unit structures was also suggested as a welcome addition. Both are therefore provided here.

Aircraft Nomenclature

Fighters	Codename	Alternative Designation based on year of Design in the Japanese Calendar
Army		
Nakajima Ki 27	Nate	Type 97 fighter
Nakajima Ki 43 Hayabusa	Oscar	Type 01 fighter
Nakajima Ki 44 Shoki	Tojo	Type 02 fighter
Navy		
Mitsubishi A5M	Claude	Type 96 carrier fighter
Mitsubishi A6M Reisen	Zero or Zeke	Type 0 carrier fighter

Bombers and Reconnaissance Aircraft

Army		
Mitsubishi Ki 21	Sally	Type 97 medium bomber
Kawasaki Ki 48	Lily	Type 99 light bomber
Mitsubishi Ki 30	Ann	Type 97 light bomber
Mitsubishi Ki 46	Dinah	Type 100 reconnaissance
Mitsubishi Ki 15	Babs	Type 97 reconnaissance
Mitsubishi Ki 51	Sonia	Type 99 reconnaissance
Tachikawa Ki 36	Ida	Type 98 reconnaissance
Navy		
Mitsubishi G3M	Nell	Type 96 attack bomber
Mitsubishi G4M	Betty	Type 01 attack bomber
Aichi D3A	Val	Type 99 dive-bomber
Nakajima B5N	Kate	Type 97 torpedo-bomber
Mitsubishi C5M	Babs	Type 98 reconnaissance
Flyingboats and Floatplanes (Navy)		
Kawanishi H6K	Mavis	Type 97 flyingboat
Mitsubishi F1M	Pete	Type 0 observation seaplane
Nakajima E8N	Dave	Type 95 reconnaissance seaplane
Aichi E13A	Jake	Type 0 reconnaissance seaplane
Transports (Army)		
Mitsubishi Ki 57	Topsy	Type 100 transport

UNIT STRUCTURES

Japanese unit structures were not directly comparable with the British and US squadron system. They were closer to Luftwaffe, Regia Aeronautica and Armee de l'Air structures.

Army

The basic unit was the Shotai (Flight or Section) usually of three aircraft. Three or four Shotai formed a Chutai (Squadron or Company), two or more Chutai forming a Sentai. This was the main operating unit, similar to a Luftwaffe Gruppe. Three or four Shotai (usually of a variety of aircraft types) were controlled by a Hikodan (Wing or Brigade). Two-four Hikodan would comprise a Hikoshidan (Division), two or three Hikoshidan forming a Kokugun (Air Force). As stated, Sentai usually operated as a complete unit, incorporating a Headquarters Shotai, or Chutai. A certain number of Independent Chutai were employed from time to time, either for operational testing of new aircraft types, or as direct army support units.

Navy
The basic Navy units were again the Shotai and Chutai, which were similar in size and composition to Army units. However, so far as land-based elements were concerned the normal operating unit was the Kokutai, which was rather larger than the Army Sentai, and might contain up to five Chutai. Pairs of Chutai formed Datai within the Kokutai. Typically, fighter Kokutai were larger in aircraft numbers than bomber Kokutai, and frequently included a number of reconnaissance aircraft on strength, which undertook navigation for the fighters on longer penetration missions. Several Kokutai, again usually of different types, were grouped on an area basis with Air Flotillas. For carrier service, autonomous Air Groups were formed for each vessel, including fighters, dive and torpedo bombers. These were not usually numbered, but carried the name of their parent carrier.

DUTCH UNITS
Army Air Force
As with the Japanese Army Air Force, unit organisation was similar, but not identical to other European air forces. The VliegtuigGroep (VlG) was the basic unit, each Groep including two (fighter) or three (bomber and reconnaissance aircraft) Afdeling, which were smaller than a British or American squadron – effectively a large flight, which could on occasion operate independently. For identification purposes the Afdeling number within the Groep prefixed the Groep number, the former being written as an Arabic numeral, the latter in Roman style. Hence the second Afdeling of III Groep would be identified as 2-VlG-III.

Navy
In order to provide wide coverage of the large area which had to be patrolled, Naval aircraft generally operated in small, semi-autonomous sections of three, known as GroepVliegtuigen (GVT), which were numbered consecutively.

ENDAU
It had been our intention originally to include the Chapter detailing the actions over the landings at Endau on the east coast of Malaya in Volume One, since chronologically they occured prior to the fall of Singapore, and involved units based there. They should have been located between Chapters 8 and 9 in that volume, following Page 346. However space and publishing considerations (paper had originally been acquired for a 400 page book only!) required that this Chapter should be held back for inclusion in Volume Two, the reasons being beyond the authors' control. Because of this, the Endau Chapter is not numbered, and readers may wish to consider it as effectively forming an addendum to the first volume.

CHRONOLOGY OF MAJOR EVENTS
(Volumes 1 and 2)

Date	Event	See Vol 1 Chapter No
1941 8 Dec	Initial invasion of Malaya	2
	Major air attack on Philippines airfields	5
	Landing on Bataan Island, north Philippines	5
	First air raid on Singapore	2
	First air raid on Wake Island	2
	First air raid on Hong Kong	2
10 Dec	HMS *Prince of Wales* and *Repulse* sunk by air attack	3
	Second major air attack on Philippines bases	5
	Landing by Japanese forces at Vigan and Appari, north Luzon	5
11 Dec	Invasion of Wake Island repulsed	4
12 Dec	British forces retreat onto Hong Kong Island	4
	Japanese forces land at Legaspi, southern Luzon	5
16 Dec	In Malaya Japanese forces reach Butterworth and land on Penang Island	4
	Japanese forces land at Miri, Sarawak	6
19 Dec	Japanese forces land on Hong Kong Island	4
20 Dec	Japanese forces land at Davao, Mindanao, southern Philippines	5 & 6
22 Dec	Japanese forces land in Lingayen Gulf, western Luzon	5
23 Dec	Dutch flyingboats launch major raid on Davao	6
	First major air raid on Rangoon, Burma	7
	Wake Island invaded	4
24 Dec	Japanese land in Lamon Bay, south-east Luzon	5
25 Dec	Hong Kong surrenders	4
	Japanese forces land at Kuching, southern Sarawak	6
	Japanese occupy Jolo Island, southern Philippines	6
	Second major air raid on Rangoon	7
26 Dec	Perak, Malaya, falls	8
27 Dec	General MacArthur declares Manila an open city	5
28 Dec	Ipoh, Malaya, falls	8
1942 1 Jan	US forces in the Philippines begin withdrawing onto the Bataan Peninsula	3 (Vol 2)
2 Jan	Japanese occupy Kuantan, eastern Malaya	8
3 Jan	First reinforcement convoy reaches Singapore	4 & 8
4 Jan	Japanese air raid on Rabaul, New Britain	6

Date	Event	See Chapter No
	Japanese forces land at Gasmata, southern New Britain	4 (Vol 2)
9 Feb	First major air raid on western Java	4 (Vol 2)
	Japanese complete occupation of Celebes	4 (Vol 2)
10 Feb	Japanese complete occupation of Borneo at Bandjermassin	4 (Vol 2)
13 Feb	Evacuation of Singapore begun	9
	Invasion fleet seen off Sumatra	2 (Vol 2)
14 Feb	Invasion of Sumatra begins with paratroop landings at Palembang	2 (Vol 2)
15 Feb	Singapore surrenders	2 (Vol 2)
16 Feb	Evacuation of southern Sumatra begins	2 (Vol 2)
	Convoy heading for Bali from Darwin, Australia, bombed and all vessels damaged and turn back.	5 (Vol 2)
18 Feb	Heavy air attack on eastern Java	6 (Vol 2)
19 Feb	Heavy air attack on western Java	6 (Vol 2)
	Major air raid by carrier-borne aircraft on Darwin	5 (Vol 2)
	Japanese forces land on Bali and Timor by air and sea	5 & 6 (Vol 2)
20 Feb	USS *Lexington* air group on approach to attack Rabaul, intercepts and destroys Japanese air attack, then withdraws	5 (Vol 2)
	British forces in Burma withdraw behind Sittang River	7 (Vol 2)
22 Feb	Convoy and carrier USS *Langley* leave Fremantle for Java	6 (Vol 2)
25 Feb	Heavy air raid on Rangoon area	7 (Vol 2)
27 Feb	Allied naval forces try to intercept invasion fleet heading for Java; Battle of Java Sea follows – five Allied cruisers and six destroyers lost	6 (Vol 2)
	USS *Langley* found and sunk by air attack	6 (Vol 2)
28 Feb	After dark, naval engagement in Sunda Strait fought	6 (Vol 2)
1 Mar	Japanese forces from Borneo invade eastern Java	8 (Vol 2)
	Japanese forces from Indo-China invade western Java	8 (Vol 2)
2 Mar	RAF and AVG withdraw from Rangoon area to Magwe, Akyab and Loiwing	7 (Vol 2)
3 Mar	Air attack on flying boats in Broome harbour, Australia	8 (Vol 2)
4 Mar	General Sir Harold Alexander takes over command in Burma	9 (Vol 2)
5 Mar	Java virtually sealed off from outside world	8 (Vol 2)
8 Mar	Java surrenders	8 (Vol 2)
	Rangoon falls	7 (Vol 2)
	Invasion force approaches Lae, New Guinea	10 (Vol 2)
12 Mar	Medan, northern Sumatra, captured by invasion force from Singapore	11 (Vol 2)
21 Mar	Heavy air raid on Magwe, Burma	9 (Vol 2)
22 Mar	Second heavy raid on Magwe cripples Allied air power in Burma	9 (Vol 2)
23 Mar	Andaman Islands in Indian Ocean occupied by Japanese	9 (Vol 2)
	Akyab, Burma, heavily raided for first time	9 (Vol 2)

Date	Event	See Chapter No
27 Mar	Final major air raid on Akyab	9 (Vol 2)
30 Mar	Toungoo, Burma, falls	9 (Vol 2)
2 Apr	Prome, Burma falls	9 (Vol 2)
3 Apr	Heavy air raid on Mandalay, Burma	9 (Vol 2)
	Japanese open offensive on Bataan Peninsula, Philippines	3 (Vol 2)
5 Apr	Major carrier air attack on Colombo harbour, Ceylon; cruisers HMS *Dorsetshire* and *Cornwall* sunk	10 (Vol 2)
	Japanese air raid on Calcutta, India	10 (Vol 2)
6 Apr	Heavy air and naval attacks on shipping in Bay of Bengal and off east coast of India	10 (Vol 2)
8 Apr	Heavy air raid on Loiwing, Burma	9 (Vol 2)
9 Apr	Carrier air attack on Trincomalee harbour, Ceylon; aircraft carrier HMS *Hermes* and other warships sunk	10 (Vol 2)
	US forces on Bataan Peninsula surrender	3 (Vol 2)
10 Apr	Japanese forces land on Cebu, southern Philippines	3 (Vol 2)
12 Apr	RAF bombers operate from Indian bases for first time	9 (Vol 2)
16 Apr	Japanese forces land on Panay and Negros, southern Philippines	3 (Vol 2)
17 Apr	Japanese take Yenangyaung, Burma	9 (Vol 2)
29 Apr	Japanese forces land on western Mindanao, Philippines	3 (Vol 2)
	Japanese capture Lashio, Burma; Chinese Army gives up Loiwing and retreats into China as does AVG. RAF to India	9 (Vol 2)
1 May	Mandalay falls	9 (Vol 2)
3 May	Japanese land at Zamboanga and Del Monte, Mindanao	3 (Vol 2)
	Bhamo falls in Burma	9 (Vol 2)
4 May	Akyab evacuated	9 (Vol 2)
5 May	Japanese forces invade Corregidor Island fortress	3 (Vol 2)
6 May	Corregidor surrenders	3 (Vol 2)
8 May	Myitkyina, Burma, falls	9 (Vol 2)
10 May	Mindanao surrenders	3 (Vol 2)
12 May	Kalewa, Burma falls	9 (Vol 2)
16 May	Bohol and Cebu, southern Philippines, surrender	3 (Vol 2)
20 May	General Alexander's forces reach Imphal and complete retreat from Burma	9 (Vol 2)
22 May	Lt Col Tateo Kato lost in combat with RAF Blenheim off Akyab	9 (Vol 2)
26 May	Leyte, southern Philippines, surrenders	3 (Vol 2)
3 Jun	Negros, southern Philippines, surrenders	3 (Vol 2)
9 Jun	Samar, southern Philippines, surrenders	3 (Vol 2)

ENDAU — THE GALLANT 72

Vildebeest K4176 of 36 Squadron, seen here prior to being camouflaged, was shot down over Endau. *(Authors' collection)*

In Chapter 9 of Volume One, brief mention is made of the RAF's attack against the Japanese convoy approaching Endau, which occurred on 26 January 1942. Herewith follows the full story of that day's gallant but tragic operations.

From the Singapore Strait, a motorable road ran as far north-east as Endau, also serving Mersing — located on the coast a few miles to the south — and the airfields at Kluang and Kahang in Central Johore. The British, established on the line of the Mersing river, were hoping to hold a line Mersing-Kluang-Batu Pahat. Japanese forces first made contact with the Mersing defences on 22 January.

Endau is situated on the estuary mouth of the Endau river, providing a satisfactory harbour. It was obvious to the British Command that an early Japanese attempt could be expected to land supplies here to prepare the forces in the area for their part in the final 'push' on Singapore, and to bring in supplies to allow the Kahang and Kluang airfields to be put into use as soon as they were captured. It was also believed that troops were about to be landed at Endau for the purpose of engaging the Australians down the coast at Mersing; this was not to be the case. The main force of Australians had by now withdrawn further down the coast in accordance with III Corps orders. The rearguard defenders at

Mersing had already been assaulted and overwhelmed by Colonel Koba's Detachment from the 18th Division, which had skilfully and silently outflanked the strongly-fortified coastal defences — which comprised concrete pillboxes surrounded by barbed-wire entanglements — and pressed home an attack entirely from the rear, at the same time simulating an attack from the sea.

While most RAF activity was directed towards western Johore, where severe fighting around Batu Pahat was underway, some of the Hudsons still remaining in Singapore had kept a regular watch on the approaches to Endau. At 0745 on the 26th two Hudson crews of 1 RAAF Squadron spotted a convoy some 20 miles north-east of Endau, heading south; this had originally been reported the previous evening, in failing light, by a Catalina from Singapore. The RAAF crews reported sighting two transports of about 10,000 tons each, two cruisers, twelve destroyers, and three barges, but each time they tried to pass this information by R/T to Air HQ, it was jammed. At the same time both Hudsons were attacked by three Japanese fighters, identified as two 'Navy 96s' and a 'Navy 0'; these were in fact Ki 27s from 12th Flying Battalion.

Following a short engagement during which strikes were claimed on two of the fighters by the Hudson gunners (Sgt R.N.B. Gayfer in Flt Lt D.W. Colquhoun's A16-21 and Sgt H.H. Rodgers in A16-54 flown by Flt Lt O.M. Diamond), both reconnaissance aircraft escaped into cloud and returned to base separately, A16-21 having been holed in several places. It was not until the first aircraft landed at Singapore at 0920 therefore, that a report of the sightings was received by Air HQ.

The only striking force available on Singapore were the Vildebeests and

Vildebeest K6402, OE-J, dropping a torpedo during an exercise shortly before the outbreak of hostilities. This aircraft is typical of those flown by 36 Squadron crews at Endau. *(35 Squadron Records via A. Thomas)*

Albacores of 36 and 100 Squadrons, and nine RAAF Hudsons. The two RAF squadrons were thus ordered to prepare as many aircraft as possible for an attack, but most had been operating against motor transport in southern Johore during the night; a dozen Vildebeests and three Albacores had been active in the Muar and Batu Pahat areas, while three others had bombed Kuala Lumpur. Seven of the Vildebeests had later carried out a second mission to Batu Pahat. The crews were tired; the aircraft had to be prepared, refuelled and rearmed. It was clear that no early attack could be made. This was unfortunate because Air Vice-Marshal C.W.H. Pulford (AOC Far East Command), a former Naval officer, was a keen exponent of the torpedo-bomber, and a torpedo attack on the vessels at sea might have achieved some success — at least against the all-important transports. However it was likely that the ships would be anchored in the shallow waters of the estuary by the time an attack could be made, and the aircraft were therefore each armed instead with three 500 lb armour-piercing bombs.

Meanwhile 225 Bomber Group in Sumatra was ordered to despatch all available bombers, and ABDA Command was contacted with a request that USAAF B-17s from Java should also be sent to attack the ships (in the event four B-17s were sent to Sumatra, but arrived too late to join in the attacks at Endau, raiding Kuala Lumpur airfield instead on the 28th).

Total available RAF strength for these operations was:

36 Squadron	9 Vildebeests and 3 Albacores	at Seletar
100 Squadron	12 Vildebeests	at Seletar
1 RAAF Squadron	4 Hudsons	at Sembawang
8 RAAF Squadron	5 Hudsons	at Sembawang
232 (P) Squadron	9 Hurricanes	at Seletar
21/453 Squadron	6 Buffaloes	at Sembawang
243/488 Squadron	6 Buffaloes	at Sembawang
62 Squadron	6 Hudsons	at Palembang
27 Squadron	5 Blenheims Is	at Palembang

The first attack was to be made by the Hudsons and a dozen Vildebeests, nine of which were drawn from 100 Squadron and three from 36 Squadron; take-off was planned for 1350. One of the observers, Tasmanian Sgt Graeme McCabe, later wrote:

> "There were a number of tired, old, young men grouped around their Squadron Leader in the operations room. They were tired because most of them had been on two bombing missions the night before, and they were old for war makes men that way. They were wondering and apprehensive, for as day followed day the invading Japanese, backed by powerful air cover, were remorselessly advancing along the road to Singapore.
>
> "The fliers sitting on the table and huddled on the floor between navigation equipment and paracute packs were drawn from every corner of the British Commonwealth. The babble of sound ceased abruptly as the Commanding Officer read the operational instructions for the afternoon strike. I was half listening to the even tones of the Squadron Leader and also to the pleasant, murmuring note of the bees buzzing through the tropical flowers outside, while intermittently through the hot air could be heard the shrill cries of the Tamils as they sweated on the aerodrome, filling in the bomb holes of the morning raid."

Squadron Leader I.T.B. Rowland (CO of 100 Squadron), who was to lead the Vildebeest strike, outlined the plan of attack, which called for dive-bombing in flight formation from 3,000 feet, with the transports as the obvious targets. The Vildebeest crews were therefore of the mistaken opinion that their task was to prevent a seaborne invasion. Rowland finished the briefing with the warning that Japanese fighters were expected to be encountered. McCabe continued:

> "Most eyes were following the navigation officer as he pencilled in the names of the crews on the big blackboard. 36 men would be selected for the operation, and as we had slightly more men than that, some lucky ones would be free to go back to bed. I rather hoped my name would not be on the board (I think nearly all were hoping the same), but it was."

It had been intended that 4 AACU's lone Shark should accompany the strike but, perhaps fortunately for Sgt A.R.P. Saul and his gunner, it developed an engine defect. From the dispersal area at Seletar the Vildebeests were taxied over to the marshalling point, and one by one they lumbered down the take-off strip. Those first off circled round the airfield until the whole formation had become airborne. Sqn Ldr Rowland was at the head of the leading section, Flt Lt John Tillott following to starboard with his three aircraft, Flt Lt John Wilkins on the port side, with Flg Off Basil Callick bringing up the rear in the box, with his section of three 36 Squadron aircraft (see Table 1).

Flt Lt Mowbray Garden of 243 Squadron was ordered at the last moment to muster all his unit's Buffaloes and rendezvous with the Vildebeests over an island north-east of Singapore. His orders were to "escort them to where they are going and bring them back." He was given no indication of the destination or target! He accordingly led off his mixed flight of six Buffaloes — four of 243 Squadron and two of 488 Squadron — and found the Vildebeests flying at 1,000 feet in close formation, at about 90 mph. Garden commented:

> "This made them rather difficult to escort as we had to use a lot of petrol going backwards and forwards and around them to use up our excess speed."

A little way behind and somewhat higher came the nine RAAF Hudsons, escorted by six Australian-flown Buffaloes of 21/453 Squadron and nine Hurricanes of 232 Squadron, the latter led by Sqn Ldr Peter Brooker.

Over Endau and the task force, nine Ki 27s of 11th Sentai's 2nd Chutai, and ten Ki 27s of 1st Sentai (led by Capt Takejiro Koyanagi) were in the air, together with a lone pre-production Ki 44 of the service test unit, 47th Independent Fighter Chutai, flown by the commanding officer, Capt Yasuhiko Kuroe. The British formation approached the area at about 1500 hours. The weather was overcast, with cloud up to 4,000 feet, then reasonably clear sky up to about 10-12,000 feet, above which was more cloud.

As the formation of Vildebeests and Buffaloes droned on towards the target area, their crews may have seen a small native prahu hugging the coastline about 50 miles south of Mersing. Certainly the four occupants of the southward-bound prahu, Flt Lt Herb Plenty and his crew of the Hudson shot down two days earlier (see Volume One, Chapter 8) observed the attacking force:

> "Four o'clock that afternoon brought a steady droning of many aircraft engines. Flying at 4,000 feet in neat battle formation, nine Hudsons emerged through a wide gap in the clouds. Above the Hudsons we watched a meagre escort of six Brewsters weaving solicitously.

TABLE 1

Crews — 1st Raid:

+

Sqn Ldr I.T.B. Rowland
Sgt C.J.S. Borras
Sgt J.F. Gibson

+	+
Flg Off G.S. Forbes	Sgt D.B.S. Lee, RNZAF
Sgt C.J. MacDonald, RAAF	Sgt G.W. McCabe, RAAF
Sgt J. Grant	Sgt M.B. Proven, RAAF

+

Flt Lt J.D. Tillott
Plt Off J.E. Morrison
Sgt S.D. Birdsall

+	+
Flg Off R.R. Lamb	Flt Lt C.N. Gardiner, RNZAF
Sgt A.R. Cooper, RAAF	Plt Off E.C. Eckersley, RAAF
Sgt K. Connolly	Sgt J. Hardy

+

Flt Lt J.T. Wilkins
Plt Off W. Chisholm, RAAF
Sgt F.G. Brooker

+	+
Flg Off B.A. Gotto	Flg Off G.G. Tayler
Sgt B.A. Toohey, RAAF	Sgt J. Allen
Sgt J.D. Barnes, RAAF	Sgt N. McArthur, RAAF

+

Flg Off B.B. Callick
Plt Off F.N. Bird, RAAF
Sgt B.J. Mann, RAAF

+	+
Plt Off R.C. Barclay, RNZAF	Sgt R.J. Reid, RNZAF
Plt Off F.E. Cummins, RAAF	Sgt J.J. Green, RAAF
Sgt W. Rowell	Sgt J.W. Holmes, RAAF

"A few minutes later we saw, further north, 12 ancient Vildebeest biplanes lumbering through the air at a slow 100 mph, the protective cover being a few Brewsters also."

The Vildebeests flew up the Endau estuary through a bank of cloud, emerging from this to see the black hulks of the two Japanese transports — *Kanbera Maru* and the larger *Kansai Maru* — lying a couple of miles offshore; behind them were two warships identified as cruisers although in fact only the light cruiser *Sendai* was present. A little further out the seven destroyers of the escorting 3rd Destroyer Flotilla could be seen, whilst five minesweepers and six smaller craft skittered around. Landing craft carrying elements of the 96th Airfield Battalion and its signals unit, as well as aviation stores, fuel and bombs, were making their way to the shore. As the biplanes approached, flashes from the decks of the warships showed that the gunners had spotted them, but they managed to hold formation until the defending fighters descended on them. Flt Lt Garden, the Buffalo leader commented:

"Quite soon the air was full of broken and crashing Vildebeests and parachutes, meanwhile what seemed to me to be an enormous force of 'Zeros' (*sic*) was descending on us from the sun in one long line-astern formation. I waited for the first one and jinked at the last moment and he went below me. I rolled over on my back and shot him down from upside down. I set him on fire and he crashed. However I made the mistake of watching the results of my handiwork that split second too long and I was hammered by the next one, which blew a large hole in the right hand side of my aircraft and wrecked all the electric switches which operated the guns and gunsight, and other controls as well."

Owing to the damage inflicted on his aircraft, Garden could not get the Buffalo to fly above 500 feet, although he was able to return safely to Kallang, where he found that one bullet had gone through the carburettor. Garden's No 2, Sgt Rex Weber, wrote in his diary:

"Mowbray led me out of a cloud right into the midst of six fighter 97s in the immediate vicinity, with myriads of enemy fighter aircraft all about. I didn't know which way to turn — I had one fighter blazing away on my tail, one to the side, and one coming down on me from directly above.
"Actually, I have no idea what I did. For one moment I tried to attack, but decided I had better find cover, and soon I was scooting for clouds, which seemed miles away. Just about this time my motor cut and I had visions of being a prisoner of war. Imagine my joy when she picked up, but at the same time I was feeling a coward for keeping in cover and deserting the 'beests. However, when I got back I found I had indeed been lucky — my plane was riddled and the cause of the engine trouble was a bullet in the carburettor system."

The other Buffaloes were also damaged, including W8231 flown by Sgt Geoff Fisken:

"A piece of cannon shell must have bounced off my armour plating and I was struck in my hip; it wasn't much at the time, just a piece of shrapnel sticking out. I did not know until when I landed — I never even felt it at the time. I pulled it out with a pair of pliers. The doctor strapped it up with antiseptic gauze and plaster. There were 22 bullet and shrapnel holes in my aircraft."

Another of the Buffalo pilots, Plt Off Terry Marra — although his fighter had been damaged during the initial contact — was able to attack one Japanese fighter which he was convinced was a Messerschmitt Bf 109 (!), claiming this probably destroyed. This may have been Kuroe's Ki 44 (which however, was not damaged in the action) or a Hurricane — although none were lost — as these had now arrived on the scene, together with the RAAF Hudsons and Buffaloes.
   Meanwhile, the leading section of biplane bombers were trying to drive home their attack, as Sgt Charles MacDonald, Flg Off Jock Forbes' navigator in K2922, recalled:

"We flew directly to Mersing then along the coast in broken cloud until we suddenly emerged at about 2,000 feet at Endau. I had, by this time, fused the bombs ready for Jock Forbes to release. I was looking over the starboard side of the cockpit when I saw Sgt Lee's aircraft slipping off towards the sea. At the same time Sqn Ldr Rowland's aircraft appeared to explode in mid-air, apparently receiving a direct hit by ack-ack.

"Everything then happened so quickly it was difficult to comprehend, but I have a vivid recollection of the scene below. There were two cruisers and about five destroyers and two large transports all with guns blazing away at us. Jock Forbes was completely unperturbed, aimed at the larger transport and our six bombs hit the side of the ship.

"Jock then flew towards the shore with his fixed Vickers gun blazing away at the barges taking troops ashore together with the Brewster Buffaloes which, instead of escorting our aircraft, were strafing the barges plying between the transports and the shore. I believe our bombs seriously damaged the transport as we were the only Vildebeest in the vicinity but there was no way of telling at the time.

"We flew on, crossed the shore and assessed the damage to our aircraft and found it had been badly shot about on the port side with most of the struts between the two wings missing and petrol streaming from punctured tanks like a fine mist. Jock Grant had been shot through the leg but was blazing away with his Lewis gun. I got quite a shock when I found I could not use my left hand as a bullet had made a mess of my forearm which in the excitement I had not noticed. Jock Forbes had not been wounded but was having tremendous difficulty keeping the aircraft in the air. We had to fly straight and level with little chance to manoeuvre as the port wings were just hanging on.

"A 'Zero' (*sic*) fired a couple of bursts at us but could not get down to our speed, but a Navy 96 did and despite Jock Grant's efforts we finally crashed on the road leading from Endau to Mersing. It was a controlled crash in a cutting which prevented any head-on collision with trees. The two Jocks were truly gallant airmen. As there were Japanese soldiers on the road and bullets flying everywhere, we got out of the aircraft as quickly as possible and as I came out facing the jungle kept going at pretty much the same speed. The last I saw of either of them was Jock Grant at the side of the road and Jock Forbes surrounded by Japs as he tried to make his escape. Jock Grant was killed where he lay and I heard much later on that Jock Forbes was captured and executed."

There were no survivors from Sqn Ldr Ian Rowland's K6379, which crashed into the sea; it was with this section that Sgt McCabe was flying in Sgt Bruce Lee's aircraft (K6386), which was also shot down:

"As we ran to the target Lee climbed slightly to the shelter of a fleecy cloudbank and Proven was already firing his gun. We came out again dead above the convoy, and as the nose tilted to go into a power dive we received a short burst from a Jap. The aircraft was holed in several places, but none of us was hit, and Lee again ascended slightly and manoeuvred for position. But he was to manoeuvre for the last time.

"I was lying face downwards with the bomb hatch open, and with my hands on the switches as we came out again to attack, when, with the sudden noise

Vildebeest K2922 of 100 Squadron, seen here prior to being camouflaged, was shot down over Endau. *(Authors' collection)*

like rain on a tin roof, another fighter gave us a straddling five-second burst. Proven was killed at his gun, the fuselage was like a colander.

"My parachute pack had been hit and was billowing around the floor. I had been wounded through the right arm near the shoulder, and three bullets had furrowed along the back of my right hand. The aircraft was smoking and out of control. I stood up and saw Lee, sprawled over the stick; he had taken a burst through the helmet. The Vildebeest was spiralling down and we were still directly above the ships which were blazing away."

Although dazed and hurt, McCabe was able to crawl into the front cockpit, pull the dead pilot's hands away from the joystick and endeavour to head the aircraft away from the ships. He succeeded in coaxing it for several miles on a south-easterly course, parallel to the coast, but with smoke pouring from the damaged engine it eventually stalled into the sea. McCabe floated to the surface to find the aircraft's rubber dinghy had fortuitously broken loose, had inflated, and awaited his presence. He estimated that he was about two miles out to sea and could see and hear the battle raging a few miles up the coast. Feeling conspicuous in the dinghy, he inflated his Mae West and, in spite of his wound, struck out for the shore.

Flt Lt Wilkins' section escaped the worst of the aerial assault and the trio succeeded in making low-level dive-bombing attacks on a transport, Wilkins reporting that one of his bombs appeared to go down the funnel of the vessel but without exploding; this was apparently the *Kanbera Maru*, which was hit several times. His aircraft was only slightly damaged. Wilkins' No 2, Flg Off Basil Gotto in K6380, escaped the initial onslaught and selected a target:

"I gave her full throttle and pulled steeply up and to the left and could see my salvo burst right under the stern of the vessel (probably the *Kanbera*

Maru), the white foam of the explosion touching the bomb burst parallel to the length of the ship, and each one about 10 yards from her side, so we certainly should have done some damage. I was approaching cloud when a noise to port attracted my attention. This must have been machine gun fire because a Jap fighter apparently dived on us from the beam. I saw no damage to my machine.

"He passed underneath us and I could look down into his machine and see the pilot. Here I realised that if I shoved the nose down and wheeled hard over to starboard I could bring my front gun to bear. I would have to give up my idea of reaching the cloud, and if I missed my position would be very bad. After consideration I decided to stick to my original intention of reaching the cloud."

The seaward section meantime had come under attack, three Ki 27s engaging Flt Lt John Tillott's aircraft, forcing it down to sea level and then chasing it towards the coast; Tillott's gunner, Sgt Steve Birdsall, put up a gallant fight, as his subsequent combat report revealed:

"We dived down to sea level. On the first attack I let them come pretty close (50-60 yards) and I gave the leading machine a burst of about 50 rounds in its belly as it broke away. I saw pieces fall from it and I never saw it again. The second machine destroyed my wireless gear and blew away part of my right thigh. I had finished the pan of ammo by this time."

The Ki 27s closed in again and riddled K6390, the stricken aircraft crashing into a mangrove swamp. Tillott was killed, and Plt Off Morrison, the observer, severely wounded. Birdsall, barely able to walk, trudged into the jungle to seek help. The other two aircraft of Tillott's section escaped serious damage.

The 36 Squadron section of three Vildebeests (those in the box) did not escape the onslaught. Plt Off Bob Barclay's K6387 came under attack before reaching the transports and his gunner, Sgt Bill Rowell, was killed; the observer, Plt Off Elwood Cummins, noted:

"Arrived Endau — recognised target — and made mid level bomb attack with near-miss result. As we turned for home we saw close above a 'Zero' (*sic*) fighter, which swept after a Hurricane. Soon the 'Zero' dived on our tail; Sgt Rowell fired our Vickers gun whilst Plt Off Barclay varied course, height, speed, using sparse clouds to confuse the enemy.

"A second 'Zero' joined the attack — our plane was raked by bullets and my right shin was bloodied by a slight nick. Our gun was not firing and I noticed it swinging unattended. Through the aircraft tunnel I saw Rowell slumped on the floor and crawled back to him. His chest was bullet-torn and blood-saturated. No breathing observable, nor movement.

"I stood astride the body, pulled the gun into position, and fired as the 'Zeros' attacked. As it was prone to do, the gun jammed (twice) although I was able to clear it, and continued to use it in short bursts. Aiming was difficult with our plane's weaving.

"I noticed we were flying very low — over trees, then sea. I saw a thin stream from starboard wing like smoke, but which was probably fuel from a punctured tank. Suddenly I was tossed about, and found myself upside down under water. I pushed downwards from the gunnery well and struggled up to the surface. No sign of the 'Zeros'.

"To my relief Plt Off Barclay appeared above the front of the aircraft and swam back to join me. He said that as the plane was almost beyond control, he had deliberately ditched it. I told him of Rowell's early wounding, and described his state and apparent instant death. Now, some 15 minutes later, with his body under water within the inverted plane — about 150 yards from shore — with no medical aid likely, we decided any attempt to aid Rowell would be futile in the circumstances. We left the plane and swam and waded to the beach."

As the Vildebeest crews were fighting for their lives, the Hudsons and their escort became involved in a series of frantic fights. The Hudsons were intercepted just before reaching the target; Flt Lt John O'Brien's aircraft (A16-23), flying in the centre of the closely packed formation of nine aircraft, was engaged by the leading fighter of an estimated 50 (!) which jumped them from above. An indication of the mayhem that could be caused by fighter attack is evident from O'Brien's subsequent report:

"With his first burst he killed my wireless operator (Sgt E.J.J. Silk), who was on one of the side guns, and also killed my second pilot (Flg Off David Hughes) who was sitting alongside me. My second pilot was killed by a bullet through the head, which afterwards struck me on the shoulder, knocking me over the controls, and lodging underneath my badges of rank on my shirt. The bullet when it struck was apparently almost spent."

The stunned pilot regained consciousness in time to pull the aircraft out of a steep dive, and managed to fly back to Sembawang in company with another damaged machine, Flt Lt S.C. Bothroyd's A16-37, which also had been shot-up by fighters. Flg Off Peter Gibbes, flying A16-28, sighted a motor vessel through

Left: Plt Off Bob Barclay, RNZAF, pilot of 36 Squadron, who was shot down over Endau. *(via Paul Sortehaug)*. Right: Plt Off Elwood Cummins, RAAF observer of 36 Squadron, also shot down over Endau. *(Mrs Veneta Cummins)*

a break in the clouds — presumably *Kanbera Maru* — and attacked immediately, obtaining two direct hits and two near misses:

> "Several bodies and articles that looked like soldiers' equipment, kit bags and the like, came hurtling up towards our aircraft. Slowly and grotesquely they revolved, like something in space, before plunging back towards the sea. But that was all. 'Zeros' (*sic*) swept in, firing and giving us no chance to ponder the scene or check the ship's ultimate fate."

His aircraft was then considerably damaged by machine gun fire, as was the other 1 RAAF Squadron Hudson, A16-54 flown by Flt Lt Ken Smith, who had bombed a concentration of troops and some M/T seen near Mersing before being engaged by another Ki 27. The five Hudsons from 8 RAAF Squadron all returned safely, although two or three were shot-up but without injuries to any of the crews. When Flt Lt Phil Parry's aircraft was attacked by a fighter, his gunner, Sgt Neil Menzies, reported that after he had returned fire it had fallen away into a rubber plantation.

Meanwhile, the six 21/453 Squadron Buffaloes were also involved in hectic combats, during which three were damaged, including that flown by Flg Off Geoff Sheppard, who claimed one fighter shot down, as he recalled:

> "Earlier in the campaign a few of us had noticed that the Japanese, whenever they attacked, carried out a stall-turn and came down on us as they were always above. We thought it could be a good idea to attack any individual while at the top of a stall turn.
>
> "In my case I probably carried out the silliest manoeuvre by a pilot who lived to tell the tale. Six Japanese fighters went into orbit above me and one of them started a stall-turn to come down on me. They would have been probably 2,000 and possibly 3,000 feet above us. I had put my nose down slightly, got a speed of 350 mph on the clock and I attacked in a vertical climb and he blew up on fire only feet from me.
>
> "Obviously this put me in a silly position with the other five aircraft, as I was out of speed and, indeed, between the climb and the recoil action of my guns, the aircraft stalled and I went into a violent spin, which probably saved me. I spun for something like 8,000 feet, with hard left rudder and two hands on the stick, to get the aircraft out of the spin.
>
> "Finally I did get out of the spin close to the ground, and dived for a cloud with the remaining Japanese on my tail. Even though I was side-slipping I was shot through the canopy, wings and petrol tank, but I got away. I had 126 holes in my aircraft when I landed back at Sembawang."

Two more Ki 27s were claimed shot down in the melee, one by the Buffalo leader, Flt Lt Bert Grace, who also claimed a second damaged, the other by Sgt Ross Leys. Although they did not see their victims actually crash, their claims were apparently 'confirmed' by virtue of their impressions of the flying altitude of the Japanese aircraft when last seen! Flg Off Barrie Hood's Buffalo was targeted for attack by one determined Japanese pilot, a burst of fire hitting his seat and port fuel tank. Hood dived his aircraft for cloud and headed for Singapore, landing safely despite inflamed eyes from petrol fumes which had invaded his cockpit.

By this time Sqn Ldr Brooker's Hurricanes had also become involved in a series of dogfights, the sky appearing to the pilots to be full of Japanese fighters and burning Vildebeests. Brooker selected the nearest Ki 27 while other pilots chased after the surviving Vildebeests, hoping to give them some protection. Plt Off Jimmy Parker saw a fighter pursuing one of the biplanes and dived to attack; he later wrote:

> "The plane skidded wildly as I pulled out of my dive and I didn't have time to line up the 'Zero' (*sic*) properly. I pulled up to come round again and found a fixed undercart monoplane going straight into the air and on the point of stalling.
>
> "My speed had dropped considerably and I had the plane properly under control so that I was able to hit the Jap with several seconds fire during which it remained in the same attitude before falling off under my nose.
>
> "I pulled round in a sharp turn but could not see it where I anticipated and instead I found it coming at me from behind when I straightened out. I panicked madly, pushed the stick forward, was saved by my straps from going through the roof of the cockpit and broke right down to the ground before pulling up towards the cloud several thousand feet away.
>
> "However I found I'd left the Jap behind and so I came down again in another shallow dive to take on a 'Zero' chasing a Vildebeest almost towards me. They both turned further towards me and I turned inside them so that I was able to rake the 'Zero' at close range with a short burst, and he was unable to bring his guns to bear either on the biplane or on myself.
>
> "I didn't hope to have destroyed him in such a fraction of a second but we had met only just above the trees, and when I looked back, he was burning there, and the Vildebeest still airborne. On our return to Seletar the Vilde-beest pilot, who had been only a few feet away from my chattering guns, confirmed this very lucky kill."

Whilst the air battle raged to the north, Flt Lt Plenty and his Hudson crew in the prahu continued to edge their way closer to Singapore. They heard the sounds of exploding bombs and waited anxiously for some indication of what had occurred:

> "Then aircraft began appearing from northward; firstly, a lone Brewster, flying close to the coast and at a height of about 500 feet, passed overhead; next came two Brewsters flying slightly higher; these were followed by three Hurricanes, flying independently; and a lone Hudson flew southward, one mile inland.
>
> "We remarked that not even one Vildebeest appeared on the return flight. Actually a few, very few, did return via a route further inland and out of our view. A second Hudson, flying low, passed within a quarter of a mile of us, and then turned back to circle us. We waved excitedly, hoping they would recognize us and that a rescue boat would be sent from Singapore next day. As the Hudson circled we noted that it bore A16-37; through the open cockpit window I recognized the pilot, Flt Lt Stu Bothroyd."

Recognition was not mutual however, for Bothroyd and his crew decided that the occupants of the prahu were Malays, sunburnt as they were and without air force caps.

All Hurricanes returned safely. Whilst the aircraft were being refuelled and re-armed the pilots related accounts of their combats; consequently, six of their opponents were assessed to have been destroyed: Sqn Ldr Brooker, Plt Off

Parker, Flt Lt Edwin Taylor and Sgt Henry Nicholls claimed one each, while Plt Off 'Dizzy' Mendizabal added a probable, but the 'star turn' was Sgt Ron Dovell. He claimed two destroyed and reported:

> "I got over the target area and dived steeply to meet a batch of about 12 fighters spread out all over the shop. My number one dived in and split up two of them. One came up again, and as he was on top of a turn I gave him a short burst. Flames came from the engine, and he went down with his aircraft blazing."

Dovell then climbed rapidly and came across another Ki 27:

> "I must have surprised him, because he made no attempt to get away. I gave him a long burst, and he went down in an absolutely vertical spin from low altitude. He couldn't have had a hope."

Admist all the confusion amongst the scattered cloud, there had clearly been much overclaiming by both sides. While Capt Kuroe in the Ki 44 had remained above to observe and report results, the 11th Sentai Ki 27s, which had attacked first, claimed two Hudsons, two biplanes, five Buffaloes and two Hurricanes shot down, one Hudson, one biplane and one Hurricane probable, and three more biplanes crash-landed. In return one Ki 27 was reported to have been damaged. The 1st Sentai claimed six biplanes shot down and a Catalina flying-boat probable — possibly a Dutch aircraft which had stumbled into the arena — although no reports of such a combat or loss have been found. Lt Mizotani of the 1st Sentai was shot down although he managed to bale out safely.

Back at Singapore a second strike was prepared with all haste. Nine Vilde-beests, of which two were 100 Squadron machines — none of which had taken part in the first attack — and three Albacores were to participate; each aircraft was armed with six 250 lb bombs and Sqn Ldr R.F.C. Markham, 36 Squadron's commander, was to lead them off from Seletar at 1615 hours, personally flying at the head of the Albacore section (see Table 2).

All serviceable fighters were ordered to escort the strike force and, as soon as the nine Hurricanes had been readied for flight, Sqn Ldr Brooker went over to 36 Squadron's flight office to discover their flight plan, only to find that the bombers had already taken off! He was then called to Air HQ to report on the earlier attack, so ordered Flt Lt Taylor to lead the escort in his place.

Eight instead of nine Hurricanes therefore prepared to take off, some 40 minutes after the Vildebeests had set out, but Flt Lt Taylor's aircraft refused to start; Plt Off Parker took over the lead of the other three 'A' Flight aircraft (Plt Off Mendizabal, Sgts Mark Porter and Ken Holmes), and three from 'B' Flight (Sgts Dovell, Nicholls and John Fleming). Thus only seven Hurricanes, together with the only four Buffaloes that could be made serviceable, sped after the bombers, which reached Endau at 1730, where ten 1st Sentai Ki 27s and two 47th Chutai Ki 44s attacked them. Over the target area, the skies were clear and devoid of cloud. With no fighter protection or cloud cover, a feeling of impending doom must have been prevalent amongst the crews, their pilots struggling to hold formation as they strove to reach the transports. Sgt Alex Kelly, gunner in Flt Sgt Peck's Albacore (T9184) recalled:

> "I remember that as we neared Endau we had a clear sky with Markham away out in front and Fleming lagging far behind. We were engaged by a

TABLE 2

Crews — 2nd Raid:

+

Sqn Ldr R.F.C. Markham
Flt Sgt H.F. Hicks, RAAF
Flt Sgt J.B. Seaton

+	+
Flt Sgt G.B.W.Peck	Sgt A.H.M. Fleming, RNZAF
Flt Sgt C.H. Lockwood, RAAF	Sgt J.H. Henderson, RAAF
Sgt H.A. Kelly, RAAF	Sgt N.S. Gill, RAAF

+

Flt Lt G.S. Richardson
Flt Sgt B.V. Harris
Sgt J. Lockhart, RAAF

+	+
Flt Sgt E. Lyall	Sgt T.S. Tanner, RNZAF
Flt Sgt E.C. Nodrum, RAAF	Plt Off A.E. Turner, RAAF
Flt Sgt O. Haggan	Sgt G.S. Howis, RAAF

+

Flt Lt B.B. Willmott
Flt Sgt G. Ewen, RCAF
Sgt P.C. Hay, RAAF

+	+
Sgt D.L. Buchanan, RNZAF	Sgt H.K. Minton, RNZAF
Plt Off W.S. Bengsston, RAAF	Plt Off T.C. McKeller, RAAF
Sgt I.R. Jones, RAAF	Sgt T. Woods

+

Flt Lt R.J. Allanson
Plt Off B. Glowrey, RAAF
Sgt R.S. Hornabrook, RAAF

+	+
Flt Lt I.W. Hutcheson	Plt Off T.R. Lamb
Plt Off V.L. Ryan, RAAF	Sgt H.A.H. Mills
Sgt J.H.P. Smith, RAAF	Sgt G.A.L. Sharp, RAAF

Jap fighter. On the second pass George (*Flt Sgt Peck*) took evasive action whilst I was firing and I was thrown onto the floor of the machine and knocked out.

"When I came around, the supposedly self-sealing petrol tank was holed and petrol was gushing into the back cabin. My leg was cut slightly — I think from metal bits off the machine. The intercom was smashed so we couldn't speak to George. The machine was diving steeply so Harry (Flt Sgt Lockwood, the observer) baled out and I followed.

"I must have passed out again or hit something going out as all I can remember of the fall was leaving the aircraft. I can't even remember pulling the cord. My next recollection was standing on the ground amongst tall timber with my parachute about me."

Before baling out, Harry Lockwood had tried to plug the hole in the fuel tank but was soon in danger of being overcome by fumes; of the exciting few minutes' action he recalled:

"We were at about 10,000 feet. Our formation of Vildebeests and Albacores broke and it was each man for himself. I saw at least three aircraft falling in flames in the first two minutes over the target. I saw two or three aircraft get their bombs away but I don't think they had time to do much conventional bomb aiming. Then a Jap latched onto us, he was right on our tail, so close that I swear I could see his spectacles behind his flying goggles. Alex Kelly's bullets I could see were bouncing off the Jap's engine cylinders and cowling.

"At the same time another Jap came up underneath us and his cannon shells ripped through the floor of our aircraft and split open the fuel tank between myself and George Peck. The tear must have been about three feet long from the floor to the centre of the tank. Fuel spilled out into the cabin from the aircraft like a stream of steam. I tried to stop the flow with our gas masks that we carried, but they both fell inside the tank, so big was the split. The aircraft was in a steep spiral dive, radio was out, and I think we both thought (Kelly and I) that we were going in. We couldn't contact anyone by radio, even George, so, at about 3,000 feet I took my 'chute and opened the door and baled out. After a few seconds I saw Alex behind me.

"A few things concerned me as I left the aircraft. Firstly, my skin was smarting agonisingly from my petrol soaked clothing, and splinter wounds on my legs were painful, and thirdly, I got a terrific crack on the forehead as the hook on my chute harness passed my head as the chute opened. A particularly nasty Jap in a 'Zero' (*sic*) followed me down so closely firing his front guns, that I instinctively drew up my legs as he flew under me, and I remember feeling more apprehensive of being incinerated by his tracer than being hit by a bullet."

In the meantime however, Flt Sgt Peck had managed to fly the badly damaged Albacore back to Seletar, where he was somewhat surprised to discover his crew had baled out. His aircraft was the only Albacore to return; Sqn Ldr Markham's X9106 was shot into the sea with the loss of all aboard following a low-level attack on the *Kanbera Maru*, and Sgt Andy Fleming's machine (T9135) crashed on the beach in shallow water, three to four miles north of Teloksari, near

Flg Off Basil Callick and Flt Lt George Richardson, two pilots of 36 Squadron involved in the Endau operation; Richardson was killed, together with his crew. (*J. Brandt*)

Top: Sgt Alex Kelly, air gunner of 36 Squadron, who baled out over Endau and was taken prisoner. *(H.A. Kelly)*. Above: Sqn Ldr R.F.C. Markham, popular and respected commander of 36 Squadron, killed at Endau. *(J. Brandt)*. Opposite: Three of the RAAF Vildebeest observers of 36 Squadron who were in action over Endau. Left to right: Sgt Jack Green, Sgt Jack Henderson (killed) and Sgt Eric Nodrum (killed). *(H.A. Kelly)*

Endau. The 30 year-old New Zealander and his Australian crew were killed.

Flt Lt George Richardson's 'A' Flight section of Vildebeests was annihilated, Richardson and his crew perishing when K4168 was shot into the sea, as were the other two aircraft with the loss of all aboard. Sgt Tom Tanner, another New Zealander, and his Australian crew died in K6392, while Flt Sgt Ernie Lyall and his crew were lost in the dual-control trainer, K4599. A number of bodies from these aircraft were later recovered from the sea, taken to Singapore, and interred in Kranji Cemetery.

'B' Flight fared little better, the leader's aircraft (K4188) coming under attack from a number of Ki 27s, their gunfire killing both the Canadian observer, Flt Sgt George Ewen, and the Australian gunner, Sgt Philip Hay, while Flt Lt Bernard Willmott (the pilot) was wounded in the foot. With his aircraft out of control, Willmott managed to extricate himself from the cockpit and baled out into the sea, from where he was later picked up by one of the destroyers rushed to the area. Sgt Keith Minton, piloting K4176, remembered:

> "We were immediately attacked by 10 to 20 (*sic*) Ki 27s — saw Sgt Buchanan and then Flt Lt Willmott being attacked by two Ki 27s half rolling on top. Shouting a warning on the R/T, I screwed left with Paddy Woods firing on a Jap attacking our tail — last communication from Flt Lt Willmott was: 'Dive bomb independently — go!'
>
> "Selecting salvo I dived straight down for two transports — luckily a direct hit aft of funnel on one, confirmed by Paddy Woods. Continued dive to water level, and with warnings and directions from Woods, managed to avoid further Ki 27s and destroyer fire-power, until receiving a hit from a destroyer bow gun, which hit us in the engine area, causing us to ditch after engine malfunction a few minutes down the coast, east of Mersing."

Vildebeest OE-B (possibly K4176) of 36 Squadron. *(H.A. Kelly)*

The third aircraft of this section, K4167 flown by yet another New Zealander, Sgt 'Buck' Buchanan, survived the attack, albeit badly damaged. A burst of gunfire from an attacking Ki 27 hit the port petrol tank, wounding the pilot in the calf of his left leg and the Australian observer, Plt Off Stew Bengsston, in the left forearm. Buchanan intended to put down at Kluang on the return flight, but then decided against this as it was feared that the airfield might be in Japanese hands. When the damaged machine was eventually landed at Seletar, it was found that one 500 lb bomb had hung up on the bombrack.

Although all three Vildebeests of Flt Lt Allanson's section got back to Seletar, each aircraft returned with a wounded gunner aboard. Plt Off Tom Lamb later reported:

"We put our noses down and I headed flat out for the beach at 160 knots. Its a wonder the old crate (*K6382*) didn't fall apart. The squadron commander ordered individual attacks. We were attacked repeatedly but managed to avoid any vital hits, although it was disconcerting to see rows of holes appearing all over the place in the fabric, and hear the twang of parting wires.

"At one time I could see four machines going down in flames, three Vildebeests and one Japanese, and five parachutes in the sky. It was impossible to reach the target ship and immediately I was over the beaches, which were seething with troops, I dropped my bombs individually and continued in vicious skids over the treetops.

"My air gunner, Sgt Gil Sharp, had his left knee shot away, but was certain he got the aircraft which hit him, as it fell away in flames. The navigator laid Sgt Sharp in the tunnel and took over the guns, firing continually, and eventually the attacks ceased. Unfortunately, the gunner had to have his leg amputated."

"Neither Mills (*Sgt Henry Mills, the observer*) nor I received a scratch, although the poor old Vildebeest came in for a lot of punishment. It was riddled with holes and many bracing wires, both inter-strut and internal, were severed. It has always remained a mystery to me how it kept flying, bearing in mind the extreme stresses I subjected it to each time we were attacked. When we got back to Seletar, and after examination, I was told it was a write-off."

Flt Lt Allanson's aircraft (K4179) also came under attack, pilot and gunner (Sgt Hornabrook) both suffering superficial wounds; Allanson reported later:

"There were 50 or more holes in my aircraft and a vast number of tiny holes down most of my left side, as a result of an explosive bullet having hit my intercom switch, just alongside me. Although the switch had been smashed, the circuit had not been broken and I (most fortunately) still had contact with my crew. My observer (Plt Off Glowrey) did not panic and gave me a truly excellent running commentary upon the movements of the enemy fighters, so that with the vastly superior manoeuvrability of a biplane, it had not been difficult for me to avoid further damage.

"On my return to base I went, as was my duty, to the Squadron Ops room for debriefing. Our Ops Officer started to question me but I was so dammed angry that I told him that it was nothing less than a 'bloody shambles'. I added that I would tell Command AHQ myself. And I did. For I was just about certain who it was who had ordered those two suicidal sorties."

Flt Lt Hutcheson's machine (K6376) returned badly shot-up with both members of his crew wounded; the observer, Plt Off Vic Ryan, had suffered only slight wounds, but his gunner, Sgt John Smith, was more seriously hurt, as he recalled:

> "We were attacked from above. One bullet cut away my goggles and I was also hit in my left foot, the bullet nicked the side of my big toe. We weren't very high and I could see Japs on the beach, I was having a great time shooting at them when Victor (*Ryan*) called out: 'Watch your tail'. We had two fighters closing in on us. I started shooting at them when I was hit in the face. The force of the blow knocked me out of the cockpit, and left me dangling on my monkey strap.
>
> "About this time Hutchy dive bombed something, and as we were diving I kept grabbing the barrel of the Lewis — it was pretty hot. Anyway we pulled out of the dive and Victor clambered up the tunnel from his cockpit and pulled me back in — a great feeling! My intercom plug had been pulled out and I had no idea what was going on. Victor pulled me into the tunnel and went back to the gun. My head was numb but my foot was hurting like anything. Anyway after we had been flying for a while the gun started shooting again. I remember thinking 'Oh God not again'. After a couple of bursts it stopped.
>
> "We got back to Seletar. I was pulled out of the plane. At this time I couldn't see anything. I was loaded onto a stretcher and taken up to what I assume was the station hospital. They took off my helmet and put a dressing on, and then asked me if I'd been hit anywhere else. I told them about my foot and they took off my flying boot and sock and dressed my toe. I was loaded into an ambulance in the top bunk, all I wanted to do was drink water and everytime I had a drink I was sick all over Gil Sharp in the lower bunk who had his right leg shot off. After a couple of air raids we got to Alexandria Hospital in Singapore although at the time I didn't know where I was or what had happened to my eye.
>
> "I didn't know what really had happened to me — I thought I had lost both eyes. I was blind for quite a while. When I was hit I got about 17 pieces of metal in my head, one bit being behind my left eye. They operated and took a lot of metal out."

The victorious Japanese fighter pilots again overestimated the size of the bomber formation when, for the second time, they reported meeting 15-18 biplanes, and claimed 14 shot down; two victories were credited to the two Ki 44 pilots, believed to have been Capts Kuroe and Susumu Jimbo, the latter probably responsible for shooting down Sgt John Fleming's Hurricane (BG828); the Canadian reported:

> "On this last trip of the day I immediately attacked three fixed-undercarriage Japs attacking a Vildebeest who was making a bomb run on one of the ships — I think a freighter. The three scattered and I saw a bomb strike at the waterline of the ship — as I broke away from this attack I was struck by fire from a 'Zero' (*sic*) I think. Oil pressure collapsed — managed to fly south for about 20 miles before the engine seized, abandoning the aircraft at low level over the beach just north of Mersing."

Fleming believed that he had probably shot down one of the Ki 27s before his own aircraft was attacked; his was the only Hurricane lost in this skirmish.

Another of those involved was Jimmy Parker, who wrote:

"I suppose we reached the Vildebeests about a minute after the 'Zeros' (*sic*) did and they had managed to retain their formation on the way in with their bombs. We came down flat out with throttles wide open, as I'd instructed my sergeants before we left, and we attacked, climbed and attacked again, with aircraft all over the lower sky and the Vildebeests scattering after they'd dropped their loads.

"I made quarter attacks on fighters trailing the bomber formation and they generally broke off this shooting to turn towards me. I thought my shots hit one or two at longish range but was moving too fast to hit them with short, close bursts. The 'Zeros' broke off to engage us in dogfights but for the short time of the engagement the speed remaining from our initial dives was too great for them and they could only take snap shots. One big Canadian, Fleming, decided to fight it out with them and was shot down."

Sgt Henry Nicholls claimed his second victory of the day and Sgt Dovell two more. He chased one fighter to within a few feet of the treetops, where he reported shooting it down, and then chased a second, which went down apparently out of control; it was believed by witnesses to have crashed into the jungle. In fact while several 1st Sentai fighters were damaged in this engagement, none seem to have been lost. Two of the British fighters strafed barges and small boats near the *Kansai Maru*, causing a number of casualties.

The final attack was made a little later by six of the newly-arrived Hudson IIIs of 62 Squadron from Palembang, led by Flt Lt Terence O'Brien. Escorting warships opened fire as they closed in at low level on the transports, the lead aircraft flying through waterspouts thrown up by exploding shells. The Hudsons attacked in pairs, as noted by O'Brien:

"Close by the shore ahead was a little rocky islet about which a number of aircraft were swirling at low level. RAF biplanes and Japanese 'Zeros' (*sic*) engaged in conflict; there was no sign of any Hurricane fighter escort. The ships were behind the off-shore islet, and it was only when we came curving over the top of it that we saw them in line half a mile away. Just above our height were two Vildebeests moving so slowly they seemed suspended in the sky. We were so close I could see the helmeted gunner standing in the rear cockpit firing at one of the many 'Zeros' darting about the whole area."

O'Brien released his bombs from low level, only just avoiding colliding with the stern mast of his intended target, the Hudson sustaining some damage from return fire. By skilful handling of his machine he was able to fly back to Sembawang, where he carried out a safe landing on trimming tabs only. Here he was congratulated for saving the aircraft instead of abandoning it, and was recommended for an immediate DFC (which did not materialize however).

Six Ki 27s from the 1st Sentai had taken off from Kuantan on the approach of the Hudsons and gave chase, their pilots reporting engaging three of the bombers, although they had great difficulty in catching these, and were only able to claim one probable. Their fire was more effective than they realized however. One Hudson radioed Singapore that the turret gunner had probably shot down two of the attacking fighters (not in fact the case), but this and another of the bombers failed to reach base, one crashing about a mile east of Sembawang, the other near the Naval Dockyard. Plt Off Tom Waters, in

AE602, and his companion, Plt Off Francis Matson (V9224), together with their respective crews, all perished. An eye-witness recalled:

> "They had no escort and I am not aware of how many there were but I do remember two of them coming back to Singapore right at dusk. Both were obviously very badly shot-up, were flying in a crab-like fashion and both crashed over the island — I believe their casualties were extremely high."

An hour and a half before dusk Wg Cdr John Jeudwine was ordered to lead off five Blenheim Is — 27 Squadron machines — from Palembang, each crewed by 84 Squadron personnel, to attack the convoy; 84's own aircraft were currently undergoing 40-hour inspections. Owing to delays in bombing-up, the Blenheims had got only as far as Singapore when darkness fell, and Jeudwine ordered his formation to land at Sembawang. Sgt Dave Russell, Jeudwine's air gunner, recalled:

> "Jeudwine ordered Geoff (*Sgt Bell, the navigator*) and me to bale out over Sembawang after he'd made several awfully ham-fisted attempts to land in the dark. We both refused point-blank to do so, and he spent another hair-raising half-an-hour nervously attempting to get down. I suspected that he'd never ever had to land a Blenheim at night but, of course, he wasn't going to admit that. His actual landing was atrocious."

The decision to abort the mission and land at Sembawang turned out to be very fortunate for the 84 Squadron formation, for it transpired that the oil consumption of two of the aircraft was so heavy that their engines would probably have seized on the return flight from the target area — supposing the flight had avoided interception and possible annihilation in the first place!

During the late afternoon the destroyers *Thanet* and *Vampire* left Singapore to make a night attack on the ships at Endau. On nearing the location however, two Japanese 'destroyers' were sighted, *Vampire* firing two of her three torpedoes at one which was in fact the minesweeper *W-4*; both missiles missed. The two destroyers continued on course for the site of the landings until two more hostile destroyers were sighted and engaged, the Allied warships firing their remaining torpedoes, albeit in vain. There were now three Japanese destroyers — *Shirayuki*, *Fubuki* and *Asagiri* — as well as the light cruiser *Sendai* and minesweeper *W-1* closing in, and soon *Thanet* was badly damaged. *Vampire* tried to screen her with smoke, but the Royal Navy ship was disabled and stopped, then sank soon afterwards. A number of the crew reached the shore, where some joined forces with survivors of the downed torpedo-bombers.

With the conclusion of aerial engagements, Air HQ was under the totally inaccurate impression that the attacks on the Japanese convoy had been quite successful, even if costly. Direct hits on both transports had been reported by the surviving bomber crews, while a total of 13 fighters had been claimed shot down, with five more reported as probably destroyed. Considerable equipment was also believed to have been destroyed and many Japanese troops killed. The actual results were almost negligible. Although the transport *Kanbera Maru* had indeed suffered a number of direct hits, which killed eight of her crew, she was not sunk, and *Kansai Maru* was only slightly damaged[1].

---

[1] *Kanbera Maru* was later sunk by US aircraft off the Solomon Islands on 14 November 1942; *Kansai Maru* fell victim to a US submarine north of the Admiralty Islands on 18 September 1943.

The cost however, was far from negligible; ten Vildebeests, two Albacores, two Hudsons and a Hurricane were totally lost, two further Vildebeests were written off (Lamb's and Hutcheson's), with at least ten more aircraft damaged. In 36 and 100 Squadrons alone, 38 aircrew had not returned, including both commanding officers, although eight survivors would make their respective ways to Singapore, two of them wounded; two others would be taken prisoner. In the aircraft that did return were a further six wounded crewmen.

One of the returning survivors was Sgt Charles MacDonald, Flg Off Forbes' navigator, who had been the only one of his crew to escape from the crash-landed Vildebeest:

All five depicted above were RAAF members of 100 Squadron Vildebeest crews who participated in the Endau operation. Left to right, rear: Sgt Gil Sharp (wounded), Sgt Maurice Proven (killed), Sgt Norm McArthur, Sgt Charles MacDonald (shot down), Sgt Brian Toohey. *(H.A. Kelly)*

"I could hear the Jap soldiers calling to each other and I went further into the jungle and later hid under a fallen tree completely covered by fallen leaves and other debris.

"My watch had also suffered and had stopped at 3.20 pm. My emergency kit was still in my belt and as things quietened down I was able to make a tourniquet with my handkerchief and a piece of stick, then bind up my wound with bandages from the kit. I stayed in my hiding place all night rearranging the tourniquet several times, but by morning I was so weak I could hardly stand let alone walk. Both knees were cut and had bled quite a lot but they were more or less superficial although extremely stiff and painful.

"My left arm was completely useless and I stayed in the vicinity all Tuesday and from the jungle could see the road quite clearly. The aircraft had been manhandled to the side of the road and Jock Grant's body lay beside it. I returned to my hiding hole and early Wednesday morning I was fit enough to start walking south, keeping parallel to the road but staying in the jungle. I was only in shirt, shorts, and flying boots and had been eaten alive by mosquitos and various other small insects. At nightfall I came to a small deserted village, managed to find some bananas and slept in a hut overnight.

"Thursday morning I felt much better, found some more bananas, a pine-apple and a coconut, drank water from a nearby creek, cut-up the pineapple with an old parang I had found, and waited my opportunity to cross the road and head seawards. This I did and slept Thursday night in another deserted kampong and although I was feeling better and had stopped bleeding, noticed my hand was starting to go black and gangrenous. Friday morning I walked until lunchtime and whilst trying to open a coconut with the parang was surprised by a group approaching me from the south. One of them was quite fair but they were very British, bedraggled and reasonably fit.

"They were English sailors from *Thanet* which, with the Australian destroyer *Vampire*, had been sent up to attack the vastly superior Japanese task force. The *Thanet* was leading into Endau Bay and was immediately sunk. The few survivors managed to get ashore but had no idea where they were and were most pleased to meet me, all of us with the general idea of getting back to Singapore and safety."

This they eventually did.

The injured Sgt Birdsall, survivor of Flt Lt Tillott's aircraft had encountered some Malays during his trek through the jungle for help, but by the time they reached the scene of the crash the observer had died. Birdsall later met-up with other survivors of the day's actions and later still was picked up by the coaster *Lee Sang* and taken to Singapore.

After half an hour or so in the sea, all three of Sgt Minton's crew reached the rocks ashore and started walking down the coast. Next day they came across a small fishing boat complete with sail and oar, and continued their journey by this means, eventually encountering the gunboat HMS *Sylvia*; this took them up river to Sedili Besar, from where they were transported by truck to Singapore, reaching Seletar on the evening of 29th. Their return was warmly greeted by their colleagues and the new commanding officer, Flt Lt Allanson, who had been promoted to lead 36 Squadron on the death of Sqn Ldr Markham.

Sgt Harry Lockwood, who had baled out of Flt Sgt Peck's Albacore, came down in a tree one mile inland. Although his back was injured, he escaped capture and headed south. He later joined forces with six British sailors, survivors from *Vampire* and *Thanet*, reaching Mersing with them aboard a Carley raft. Here, he recalled:

"Leaving the party on the beach, I walked across the tennis courts and up to the foyer of the Rest House. At the top of the steps I opened the door and to my horror saw a group of Jap officers sitting around a table in the foyer. I don't know who was the more surprised. Of course I took off down the steps and through the gates of the tennis courts to cross to the beach. As I ran the Japs were following me firing their small arms and I rather stupidly was firing back over my shoulder, haphazardly, with my revolver upside down. Anyway, why I don't know, but while I went through the gates of the courts, they ran around the outside, which was further, so I widened the gap and shouted to the boys on the raft to push off which they did when they saw what was happening. They were in about ten feet of water when they dragged me on board. Shots were fired after us but no one was hit. I think the surprise confused them.

"I found that was hard to live down with the others as I was so sure and they were trusting in me that the Aussies were there. Anyway, they weren't and that was that."

The party sailed on for several more days until picked up by a cargo vessel (*Lee Sang*) near the Limas islands and were transported to Singapore.

Sgt Alex Kelly, the air gunner from the same machine, was not so fortunate. It took him two days to get clear of the jungle where he had landed, between Mersing and Endau; he was in bad shape, without food or water, when he blundered into a Japanese encampment during the night. Fortunately these were second-line troops and they took him prisoner; he was taken to the guardhouse at Endau where, a few days later, he was joined by Flt Lt 'Spud' Spurgeon, the Australian Hudson pilot who had been shot down on the 24th (see Volume One, Chapter 8).

Another survivor of the action who failed to get back was Sgt McCabe, from Sgt Lee's crew. After swimming to the shore following his aircraft crashing into the sea, he met some Chinese who looked after him until his wounds healed, but he was evenually betrayed by Malays and handed over to a Japanese patrol. Fortunately he still had on his air force clothing, which undoubtedly saved him from being executed, and he was later taken to Changi POW camp.

The two survivors of K6387, Plt Offs Barclay and Cummins, both got back to Singapore following many adventures; they had reached the shore following the ditching, as related by the latter:

"We thought ourselves still north of Mersing, which we hoped was still held by Australian troops, so made off southwards along lightly vegetated coast. We waded through a small brackish creek, then came to a house — old and empty — with no food in it. After an hour or so, the way was blocked by mangrove swamp. We took to the sea, wading around the boggy tree-line to waist-high depth. Slow progress around a wide bay. Finally the mangroves ceased and we returned to the beach, then saw houses ahead.

"Near the first house two persons appeared ahead, walking across the road; they saw us, stopped, then went on. In the early dusk light their dress indicated Japanese or Malays — the enemy? We watched warily from shrub cover before continuing. We entered one of the empty houses; no food, but found water and drank. We slept on the floor throughout the night. At dawn (day 2) we walked on — sculled across the Mersing River on a tiny discarded boat — then over an open area to the welcome shelter of a rocky headland. Here we came upon small group (eight to ten) of RN sailors from a vessel (*Thanet*) sunk near Endau a day earlier. We shared their life-boat emergency rations. We then joined them in their boat, sharing rowing throughout the day. That evening, we pulled to shore by a fisherman's tumbledown hut, and slept there, very tired.

"Day 3. Rowed through day and night, dining frugally in the boat, during changes of oarsmen. Mid morning (day 4) a ship was sighted coming from the north. We rowed out and waved our shirts; we were seen and the ship swung in to meet us, took all on board, and continued southwards.

"It was a coastal freighter of about 1,000 tons with a Chinese crew and British officers. On around south-east of Cape Sepang. Exhausted and sore, we all slept. Then west to Singapore, and berthed mid morning (day 5)."

The missing Hurricane pilot, Sgt John Fleming, also made his way back to Singapore. His aircraft had crashed and caught fire about 20 yards from where he landed after baling out. Observing six Japanese soldiers about 500 yards away, he ran down the beach to a swamp, where he hid until nightfall. Having noted a Japanese guard on the bridge crossing the Mersing River, he was forced to swim, this taking almost five hours; when he finally reached high ground, he fell asleep but was awoken by the sounds of gunfire, and witnessed the battle out to sea between the naval forces.

At daybreak Fleming found it necessary to use the beach to continue his trek southwards as the jungle was inpenetrable. It was the afternoon of the following day when he met a dozen survivors of the sunken *Thanet*, including two or three badly wounded. They had a whaleboat and he fell in with these. After further adventures, during which time the party was joined by other naval survivors, and two or three of the shot down Vildebeest aircrew, all were eventually picked up by a freighter in the channel leading to Singapore harbour.

By the evening of the 27th Flt Lt Plenty's Hudson crew in the prahu had reached Bukit Chunang, on the south-eastern tip of the Malayan peninsula, the location of the radar station (AMES 511); with the retreat to Singapore in full flow, this station had been partly dismantled and removed, and there remained only a skeleton staff of six RAF men, who were also awaiting evacuation. The four Australian airmen, delighted at reaching relative safety, were provided with food and beds for the night. Next morning as they were about to continue their journey, an RN longboat — from a minesweeper anchored a mile out — arrived to evacuate the RAF men, Plenty's crew gratefully accepting a lift back to Singapore.

On arriving at Seletar the returning Australians were awaiting transport back to Sembawang, when they were approached by an RAF Group Captain, who commented:

> "Oh! Flight Lieutenant. You colonial chaps can never seem to remain spick and span when the going is a trifle tough. Get yourselves a good clean up and in short time, too!"

Air Vice-Marshal P.C. Maltby, from Air HQ, visited the survivors of the Vildebeest squadron, congratulated them on the results of their attacks, and assured them that they would never again have to undertake a similar daylight mission. The crews had earlier been promised that they would not be ordered to fly day sorties, but the desperate situation had forced Air HQ to take desperate measures.

Had such gallantry occured nearer home, a plethora of decorations, including perhaps a Victoria Cross or two, would have been announced for the actions performed on this day. As it was, both deceased squadron commanders received posthumous Mentions in Despatches, while Sgt Keith Minton and his WOp/AG, Sgt Paddy Woods, would each be awarded a DFM, specifically for this action, as was 232 Squadron's Sgt Ron Dovell for his four claims.

Chapter 1

THE DEFENCE OF SUMATRA AND
THE EXODUS FROM SINGAPORE
8 December 1941-16 February 1942

Sumatra's position, partially to the west of Malaya, saved it from air attack during the opening weeks of the war. Not until the Japanese advance down the Malayan peninsula brought their forces into closer proximity with the northern tip of the island, across the Malacca Strait, did any air activity of note commence.

The main airfield was sited at Pangkalanbenteng (known to the RAF as P.1), about five miles north of Palembang town. It had been developed for civil use and was well-known to the Japanese. Based there were three Glenn Martins of 1-VlG-II's third 'patrouille', together with three older WH-1 bombers — known as 'WH-1 Patrouille'; the flight was placed under the control of the Dutch Navy and the task of its crews was to carry out maritime reconnaissance patrols.

Before the end of December the Martins of 2-VlG-I would be withdrawn from Borneo to P.1, causing severe congestion, while more aircraft, including fighters, arrived at the airfield to carry out protection patrols for the many convoys making for Singapore. A second airfield had been created some 20 miles south of Palembang, in a natural clearing within the jungle at Praboe-moelih, and was known (to the RAF) as P.2; to this airfield the bombers were now diverted, while the fighters remained at P.1. Two smaller airfields were located at Djambi, about 120 miles north-west of P.1, and at Lahat, about 50 miles south-west of P.2.

While the main airfields were situated in the south, around the major town and oil refinery at Palembang, there were others in this inhospitable country, which was clad in thick and inpenetrable jungle. These were situated at Pakan Baroe, well inland from the Malacca Strait, opposite Malacca itself, but lati-tudinally slightly to the south of Singapore. The landing ground and its general facilities were not very modern, although the Dutch worked hard to extend the runways and improve conditions. Stationed there were two 'patrouilles' of 1-VlG-II, comprising six Glenn Martin bombers, which carried out frequent patrols northwards and over the Malayan Straits. Further north, on the east coast, was Medan, while in the far north at Lho'nga, there was a small landing strip and — just off the coast — the island of Sabang, used by both British Overseas Airways and Qantas as a refuelling stop for their flyingboats.

Towards the end of December it was decided to form another flight of the Malayan Volunteer Air Force, this to be based in the East Indies and, consequently, 2 Detached Flight came into existence at Pakan Baroe, manned by personnel under Flt Lt J.H. Nixon. Thus, in the second week of January, a mixed force of five Tiger Moths and Avro Cadets were transferred from Singapore, together with a detachment of ten pilots and observers, and six ground staff. The solitary Miles Hawk ('31') would later join the Flight, but this crashed on landing at Pakan Baroe; the pilot, Sgt F.W. Roe, survived although his passenger, Colonel Burdett of the Australian Red Cross, was killed.

The Flight was quartered in a newly erected and only partly finished Dutch military camp; recalled Sgt H.F. Frederiksen:

'Food was supplied by the Dutch, consisting chiefly of rice and curry, bread and coffee, supplemented by supplies from Singapore.

"The intention of using aircraft based at Pakan Baroe was greatly hampered by the short range of the machines at the Flight's disposal. Flights were carried out roughly every other day to and from Singapore, carrying passengers and mail. Apart from these routine flights, a considerable amount of reconnaissance work was done, the area covered being chiefly the Siak and Kampar rivers, and the ground and coastline between them.

"A rather amusing, but pretty ineffective system of air raid warning had been devised by some inventive Hollanders. On the field, within shouting distance of the Duty Pilot's hut, was a tall ladder affair with a lookout post under an umbrella. When the umbrella man saw or heard an aircraft approaching, he shouted to the Duty Pilot, and it was then up to the latter to decide whether the aircraft was friendly or otherwise, and whether to sound the alarm or not. However, the troops of the ground defences usually heard the noise long before we did."

Early attacks on Sumatra were made by bombers of the JNAF, which had staged through Northern Malaya whilst on long-range sea searches, looking for Allied convoys or warships. On 28 December however, 18 Ki 48s of the 75th Sentai from Sungei Patani, escorted by seven Ki 43s of the 59th Sentai, attacked Medan, where a KNILM DC-3 (PK-ALN) was soon ablaze although there were no casualties. The Japanese crews claimed one large and three small aircraft destroyed — the latter possibly Tiger Moths and Jungmanns of the local flying club — as well as an ammunition dump and a hangar. Another serious loss occurred next day at Sabang when British Overseas Airways' Short S.23 Empire flyingboat *Cassiopeia* (G-ADUX), which had been engaged in ferrying fuel and supplies to the RAF's staging post, sank. It was believed that as the 'boat attempted to take off it struck some debris. Although it floated for a short while, water flooded into the passenger cabin and despite a frantic rescue bid by First Officer Blunt, all four passengers drowned.

With the sighting of a Japanese invasion force heading for Tarakan, Borneo, on 10 January (see Volume One, Chapter 6), the Dutch immediately decided to despatch the two flights of Glenn Martins of 1-VlG-II from Pakan Baroe to Samarinda II airfield where, as fate would have it, the detachment would be annihilated within a few days.

The next serious raid on Sumatra occurred on 16 January, when bombers from the 75th and 90th Sentais, again escorted by 59th Sentai Ki 43s, attacked Medan, where one aircraft was destroyed on the airfield. The bombers returned in force next day, 32 Ki 21s of the 12th Sentai raiding Pakan Baroe at 1125, where five aircraft were claimed burned and a warehouse destroyed; escorting Ki 43s of the 64th Sentai also strafed buildings and aircraft. It was the turn of JNAF to continue the series of attacks the following day, three of six Mihoro Ku G3Ms which were searching the Malacca Strait, bombing Sabang. The Navy bombers returned next day, when six G3Ms again bombed the island, also attacking merchant vessels in the Strait.

The RAF, with the agreement of the Dutch, set up 225 (Bomber) Group at Palembang on 18 January, under the command of Grp Capt A.G. Bishop. The Dutch army agreed to supply ground defence for the Sumatran airfields, but possessed no AA guns; ABDA Command consequently allotted six heavy guns and six Bofors to P.1 and P.2, and four of each for the defence of the oil refinery complex. However, the ships carrying ammunition for these guns were sunk during the course of subsequent air raids and as a result, the guns were able to offer sporadic fire only, as ammunition had to be rigidly conserved at all times!

The newly established 225 Group was set up to operate two Blenheim IV squadrons — 84 and 211 — imminently due to arrive from the Middle East, each unit having set out with complements of 24 aircraft.

While fighter squadrons — Hurricanes and Kittyhawks — from the Middle Eastern battle fronts could not be spared, the situation regarding bombers was somewhat different. There remained in Egypt in late 1941, a substantial number of units equipped with Blenheim IVs, which had been involved in daylight operations for many months. Supplies of American light bombers of better performance were beginning to reach the area in appreciable numbers, while the Blenheim itself had become rather too vulnerable to the latest generation of German fighters to continue in this role.

Not ideally suited for night operations, the Blenheim was, consequently, the one type of aircraft which could be released without undue detriment, and subsequently at the end of the year 84 Squadron was taken off operations over the Western Desert, and prepared for despatch to the Far East. Whilst a number of the crews remained with the squadron, others were posted away. Amongst those arriving to bring the unit up to strength were a number of RAAF crews, mostly inexperienced youngsters straight from OTUs, while Wg Cdr J.R. Jeudwine arrived to take command.

211 Squadron, which had been based in the Sudan for some time, acting as a Blenheim Operational Training Unit, was also brought up to strength to return to action on the new front. Many of the aircrews posted to this unit were also RAAF personnel straight from East African or Rhodesian flying schools, without the benefit of operational experience — and were "fed in to learn their trade on the job." However, a number of operationally-experienced pilots were posted in to bolster the squadron; Sqn Ldr K.C.V.D. Dundas (a Canadian), Flt Lt J.D.W.H. Clutterbuck and Flt Lt K. Linton had flown Blenheims during the ill-fated Greek campaign, and Plt Offs G.A. Mockridge and A. Devenish, RAAF, arrived from Malta, while in Wg Cdr R.N. Bateson, the unit received a daring, experienced and resolute commanding officer. He had commanded 113 Squadron on Blenheims during late 1940 and had then been promoted to Acting Wg Cdr and, in November 1941, was posted to 270 (Bomber) Wing as Wg Cdr Flying and SASO. Shortly before being posted to command 211 Squadron in early January 1942, he was temporarily blinded by a small Italian booby trap-type bomb, which contained acid, and had been dropped during a night raid:

Blenheim IV of 211 Squadron: aircraft 'Q' on the way to the Far East. *(W. Baird via A. Thomas)*

"Unfortunately, I stepped on one outside my tent with unpleasant results. Luckily my full washbasin was near and I was able to quickly wash most of it off — but was temporarily blinded. I was flown to Cairo for treatment and classified 'unfit to fly'.

"After daily treatment my eyes improved — my posting to command 211 Squadron had come through, so I went to Helwan where the squadron was reforming, and unofficially flew a Blenheim with my new and trusting crew to see if I could cope — my depth perception was poor but I coped."

The ground echelon of each squadron would travel by sea, and would include spare aircrew members. The first elements to depart Heliopolis (Egypt) on 14 January however, were six aircraft of 84 Squadron, led by Flt Lt J.V.C. Wyllie in T2249, who recalled:

"I led the first flight — of what the *Egyptian Gazette*, in a banner headline, called an 'Air Armada' which was supposed, according to the briefing officer, to be a top secret move — of aircraft out of Egypt.

"Lost one of the Blenheims at Sharjah, when the pilot hit his tail wheel on one of the 60 gallon drums marking the aerodrome perimeter. Was the first to be misled by a map reference error of aerodrome at Kutarajah. Was almost out of fuel and had prepared for other aircraft to make landings in paddy fields when we spotted the aerodrome. Sent up aircraft to circle aerodrome to guide in the next flight."

The other three flights, each of six aircraft, followed as and when the machines were fully serviceable, leaving at daily intervals, except the last, which got away on 18th; the second flight was led by Sqn Ldr A.K. Passmore in V6133, the third by Wg Cdr Jeudwine in V6093, and the final flight by Sqn Ldr T. James in Z9732. One aircraft of the CO's flight (Z9723) was flown by Sgt George Sayer, an experienced and much-travelled Australian, who had previously served with a Hurricane unit in the Desert before transferring to Blenheims, operating these against the Italians in Abyssinia. On returning to the Middle East he had been sent to the UK, from where he was posted to Russia for a short period of time, returning to the UK and then back to the Middle East!

Two aircraft of the second flight force-landed in northern India en route, whilst others were delayed at various locations; the main route followed was Habbaniya-Shaibah-Bahrein-Sharjah-Karachi-Calcutta-Toungoo-Rangoon-Lho'nga-Medan (or Pakan Baroe)-Palembang, although the original destination was to have been Singapore. Each aircraft was fitted with a 55 gallon overload fuel tank, carried in the bomb bay, and each carried two passengers (ground-crew) besides the aircrew. The stage Rangoon to Lho'nga was via the Andamans and Nicobars, but BURGROUP had little information to impart regarding Sumatran airfields; although details of Lho'nga's exact location were sent to Rangoon by signal from Sumatra, apparently no notice was taken of it, and subsequent faulty briefing would cause the loss of at least two Blenheims.

Turret gunner's view taken by Plt Off Fred Joerin of 211 Squadron during the flight from Habbaniya to Palembang, in January. *(Authors' collection)*

On the arrival of the first formation at Lho'nga, where briefing was expected for the final stage to Singapore, orders were received that the Blenheims were to proceed to Palembang; no maps of the area were available to the crews, but eventually a small motoring map of Sumatra was procured! Owing to the small size of Lho'nga, aircraft only took on sufficient fuel to enable them to reach Medan, where they were to top up for the flight to Palembang (see Table 3). It was not only the RAF which used the North Africa-India-Burma-Sumatra

Table 3		
84 Squadron — 24 Blenheims departed Middle East		

No 1 Flight departed Heliopolis 14/1/42:

T2249	Flt Lt J.V.C. Wyllie	Z6375	Flg Off A.M. Gill
	Sgt D.G.C. Argent		Sgt C.R. Craddock
	Sgt A.W.G. Wakefield		Sgt J.F. Ellis

Table 3 (Continued)

Z6373	Flg Off G.W. Milson Plt Off R.D. Millar, RNZAF Sgt W. Proctor	V6182	Flg Off B. Fihelly, RAAF Sgt T. Gomm Sgt E. Oliver (changed aircraft at Habbaniya)
Z9543	Plt Off M.S. Macdonald, Plt Off G. Maurice Sgt W. Miller (force-landed on arrival)	V5422	Plt Off J.H. Goldfinch, RAAF Plt Off D.J. Hawke, RAAF Sgt Winchester (did not reach Sumatra)

No 2 Flight departed Heliopolis 15/1/42:

V6133	Sqn Ldr A.K. Passmore Plt Off S.G. Turner Plt Off C.P.L. Streatfield (aircraft left at Medan)	Z9577	Sgt H.H. Hough Sgt D.R. Hooper, RAAF Sgt G. Hirst, RAAF (force-landed at Lho'nga)
R3733	Sgt A.W. Pedler, RAAF Sgt M. Roberts, RAAF Sgt Morris, RAAF (crew did not reach Sumatra)	Z9586	Sgt D.J. MacKillop Sgt J. King Sgt Morris
Z9709	Sgt K. Lister Sgt A.G.A. Sherrott Sgt R. Pile	Z5887	Sgt W.N.P. Cosgrove, RAAF Flt Sgt L.E. Small Sgt H. Harding (changed aircraft at Habbaniya)

No 3 Flight departed Heliopolis 16/1/42:

V6093	Wg Cdr J.R. Jeudwine Sgt G.G. Palmer Sgt D. Russell	V6092	Flt Lt M.K. Holland Sgt F.R. Cameron, RAAF Sgt R.C.H. Bennett
Z9602	Sgt N.S. Geappon, RAAF Sgt D.J. Gosbell, RAAF Sgt J.R. Reid, RAAF	Z9726	Sgt J.M. Hyatt, RAAF Sgt G. Mutton, RAAF Sgt D.E. Irvine, RAAF
Z9723	Sgt G.W. Sayer, RAAF Sgt G.G. Bell Sgt A.H. Ross, RAAF	Z7799	Sgt A.C. Longmore, RAAF Sgt A.G. Nourse, RAAF Sgt S.C. Thompson, RAAF

No 4 Flight departed Heliopolis 18/1/42:

Z9732	Sqn Ldr T. James Sgt K.S.R. Dicks Sgt A.Mc. Blackburn (aircraft left at Pakan Baroe)	Z6282	Sgt C.N.M. Thomson Sgt P.S. Gardner Sgt P.A. Gardner
Z7904	Sgt W.G. Young, RAAF Sgt W.H. Duigan, RNZAF Sgt W.J. Davey, RAAF	V5872	Sgt R.A. Headland, RAAF Sgt H.C. Odgers, RAAF Sgt J.M. Farrer, RAAF (did not reach Sumatra)
Z7886	Sgt S. Owen Sgt E.R. Watkins Sgt J.K. Pritchard, RAAF (aircraft left at Pakan Baroe)	V6128	Sgt S.J. Prentice, RAAF Sgt Engall, RAAF Sgt Thomas, RAAF (did not reach Palembang)

route in an endeavour to replenish its losses for, on the 11th, three LB-30 heavy bombers of the US 7th Bomb Group reached Malang in Java — the first of a dozen LB-30s and 39 B-17Es of this unit which were on their way from the United States. The LB-30 was an export version of the four-engined B-24 Liberator, which had been ordered by the British and modified to RAF standards, but which had been taken over by the USAAF on the outbreak of war (these aircraft incidentally retained their RAF serial numbers). The first three to reach Malang were flown by Maj A.A. Straubel (AL609), Lt J.E. Dougherty (AL535) and Lt H. Wade (AL612). Two B-17Es arrived at P.1 next day, together with another LB-30 (AL576), followed by another two B-17Es on the 15th. By the end of the month a further 12 B-17Es and one LB-30 (AL570) would have staged through P.1 en route for Malang.

Seven B-17Es of the 19th Bomb Group were flown over to P.1 from Malang on the 14th, in readiness for a raid next morning on Sungei Patani airfield in Northern Malaya. At 0830 the bombers took-off but two returned early, one due to engine trouble, the other having become separated from the main formation. Maj Cecil E. Combs (41-3061) successfully led the others to the target area in Northern Malaya, the crews reporting bombs falling on hangars and buildings, following which a number of fires were seen; in fact little damage was caused. Indeed, reconnaissance next day by aircraft from the MVAF failed to reveal any evidence of bombing! The big bombers landed at Lho'nga airstrip, on the northern tip of Sumatra, following a seven and a half hour flight. They returned to Malang next morning, from where four more B-17Es flew to P.1 for servicing. On arrival, Lt William J. Bohnaker's aircraft (41-3064) overshot and crashed; the crew survived, shaken but unhurt.

The crew of a reconnaissance Ki 46 of the 81st Sentai, flying from one of the newly-acquired Northern Malayan airfields on the morning of the 21st, spotted eight large aircraft (probably Hudsons and Blenheims) and four four-engined types (obviously B-17s but including Liberator AL574/0 of 108 Squadron from the Middle East, which was delivering important ground personnel and spares for 84 Squadron) at P.1, the Japanese crew also reporting new construction work taking place. On receipt of this news, the JAAF's 3rd Air Division began making

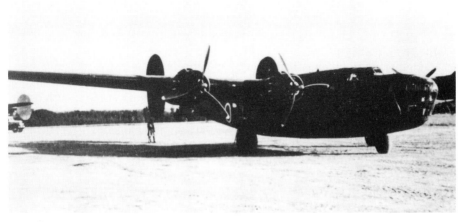

Liberator II of 108 Squadron (AL574 '0') on the way to Palembang to deliver personnel and spares for 84 Squadron. *(G.W.S. Challen via A. Thomas)*

plans for an attack by units of the 7th Flying Battalion. Meanwhile, a detachment of Mihoro Ku bombers at Sungei Patani continued its series of attacks on Sabang and Labuhan harbour. It was probably aircraft from this kokutai which accounted for two small armed traders operating off the east coast of Sumatra during the day, the coasters *Larut* and *Raub* both falling victim to bombing attacks.

The Japanese plans coincided with the take-over of command at Palembang by the RAF, as aircraft began to pour across to P.1 from Singapore. The surviving Blenheim units — 27, 34 and 62 Squadrons — moved first. Nine B-17Es from Malang arrived at P.1 during the day to collect bombs, 2/Lt C.W. Hughes' 41-2419 crash-landing; the aircraft was sufficiently damaged to be rendered irreparable, and was abandoned to be stripped of all usable parts.

At 0900 on the morning of the 23rd, the first serious raid against P.1 developed, 27 Ki 21s from the 98th Sentai bombing the airfield at 1209, their crews claiming two aircraft destroyed on the ground; one of these was Hudson A16-86 of 1 RAAF Squadron, which was non-operational, having been damaged in an earlier accident, whilst the other was a Glenn Martin of 2-VlG-II. The Liberator of 108 Squadron was near missed although not damaged, but bomb splinters struck AC2 Partington as he was leaving the aircraft, and he died in hospital that night.

As the Japanese bombers departed for the return flight, they were attacked by a reported 16 'Curtiss P-36 fighters', which kept up the pursuit for some 50 minutes. These were in fact the ten Hawk 75As of Lt Max van der Poel's 1-VlG-IV. The Dutch pilots claimed at least two of the bombers damaged but their attack was much more effective than they believed however, for 14 of the bombers were hit and three crewmen wounded. The bombers' gunners, in return, optimistically claimed three of the attackers shot down, and two more probably so! Only the aircraft flown by 2/Lt A.J. Marinus suffered any serious damage and force-landed at P.1 after the engagement, with a bullet in the engine; two other Hawks received slight damage.

The first four Blenheims of 84 Squadron reached P.1 during the afternoon; two more would arrive next day, three more on the 26th (one of which, Z7799 flown by Sgt Alf Longmore, was slightly damaged on landing when its wingtip clipped a stationary Hurricane), followed by another on the morrow. On arrival at P.1 all Blenheim crews were ordered to fly south to P.2, which was to be their base of operations. Whilst the ground staff were to remain at P.2, all aircrews were billeted in Maria School, an evacuated girls' school in Palembang itself, on the road leading to P.1.

A number of Blenheims had already effectively been lost to the squadron. Plt Off M.S. Macdonald had become separated from his flight on approaching Palembang, and eventually force-landed Z7971 in a swamp at the mouth of the Loempo River, about 100 miles beyond P.1; the crew and passengers spent an extremely uncomfortable night on their aircraft in a thunderstorm. Wet through and covered with slime, they were also tormented by mosquitoes; fortunately however, at least the aircraft did not sink beneath the surface! They were rescued by natives at dawn, and after a public bath, were taken in boats to Toeloeng Selapan, which took three days and nights; from here they were driven by car to Kajoeagoeng, thence to Palembang. As the airmen were generally taller than the average Sumatran, and all were carrying some Indian four-sided coins, the first report Wg Cdr Jeudwine received that they were safe was that some "tall men with big feet and square money" had been picked up!

By now the first flight of 211 Squadron Blenheims had departed Helwan (Egypt), also initially destined for Singapore. They were led by Wg Cdr Bob Bateson in Z9649, who recalled:

"Our first leg was Helwan to Habbaniya, but bad sandstorms forced us to land at LG44, alongside the Iraq oil pipeline. From LG44 we flew to Habbaniya, where we remained overnight, and checked and refuelled the aircraft. Then to Mularrak Island (Bahrein), then to Sharjah; remained overnight in the fort. To Karachi and remained overnight after thorough check and refuelling. To Allahabad — 800 yards sandstrip; refuelled from cans, then pressed on to Calcutta (Dum Dum airfield).

"To Toungoo — a small outpost airfield surrounded by jungle. Here the Medical Officer grabbed me and put me in bed, having found I had a temperature of 102°. After two nights, he reluctantly restored my flying category! At this stage I can't remember how many aircraft were still with me. We were pressing hard to get to our destination, as news from the Far East was bad. Our aircraft were beginning to develop faults.

"On arrival at Rangoon, war hysteria was very apparent and air attack was anticipated at any time. I was informed that Singapore was no longer a viable base but could we make Sumatra? I decided we could if the head-wind was less than 10 knots. Our route would pass near the Andaman and Nicobar islands, on which there was a small airstrip suitable only for crash-landing a Blenheim. Since the tribes on the islands were suspected to be cannibals, the alternative to those in trouble was only marginally better than ditching and meeting sharks!

"After some trouble getting refuelled, I led an open formation (to conserve fuel) of Blenheims heading for the airstrip at Lho'nga. All went well until we arrived, when all the ground defences opened up on us. We landed safely, very short of fuel, but I seem to recollect that one aircraft was damaged. Apparently no message was received from Rangoon of our departure, and Japanese aircraft had already carried out minor raids. We remained overnight. Lho'nga very pleased to see us go to reduce the risk of air attack. Landed Pakan Baroe for fuel, then on to P.1 — again, not expected. After reporting in and quickly briefed on the local situation, we were sent to P.2."

The other three flights followed closely, led by Sqn Ldr Dundas (Z7699), Flt Lts Clutterbuck (Z7521) and Linton; their misfortune was to match that suffered by 84 Squadron. One aircraft had crash-landed in a dust storm soon after take-off from Helwan, while another crashed at Sharjah, and two others developed engine trouble. Such was the tailback of aircraft heading for the Far East — Burma and Singapore — that aircraft from different units often travelled in convoy, hence Clutterbuck found himself at one time leading a flight of six Hurricanes from Calcutta to Toungoo, then a flight of three Blenheims, including one from 84 Squadron flown by Sgt H.H. Hough (Z9577), from Rangoon to Lho'nga.

On arrival at Rangoon Clutterbuck had been given an incorrect map reference for Lho'nga, and unwittingly led his flight a good many miles down the west coast of Sumatra, in search of the landing ground; the location referred to by the given map reference was actually a rugged spot up in the hills, some 30 miles

Left: 211 Squadron's illustrious commanding officer, WG Cdr R.N. 'Bob' Bateson, DFC. *(Author's collection)*. Right: Flg Off Harry Siddell (rear) and Sgt Les Patrick of 59 Squadron. *(R.L. Patrick)*

south of Lho'nga! By now short of fuel, Clutterbuck turned back and, with just a few gallons remaining, fortuitously spotted a landing ground, which turned out to be Lho'nga. His two companions exhausted their fuel before the airfield could be reached, both being obliged to force-land in paddy-fields. Although none of those aboard the two machines was hurt, neither Blenheim was recoverable (see Table 4).

A few Hudsons were still struggling along the route to Sumatra from the west, one of which — AE506 of 59 Squadron, flown by Flg Off Harry Siddell — approached Sabang island on the morning of the 23rd, in time for the crew to see a departing Japanese floatplane, which had just attacked a Dutch ship in the harbour, as recalled by Sgt Les Patrick aboard the Hudson:

> "We arrived just after a ship sent to evacuate the Dutch civil population had been bombed in the harbour. We had a glimpse of the Japanese aircraft which cleared off when we showed up."

On landing, the Hudson crew found half a dozen rather peeved airmen — the refuelling party — anxious to get away from their undefended outpost. Patrick continued:

> "The airmen at the field were there for refuelling and servicing of transit aircraft, and were wondering how they were to be relieved."

The crews of the old Glenn Martins of 'WH-1 Patrouille', operating out of P.2, continued to fly reconnaissance and protection patrols during this period, but following the loss of Sgt H. van den Berg's M-510 when it ditched near the coast of Billiton Island on the 25th, the remaining two machines were withdrawn to Tjililitan (Java). Meanwhile, the Martins of 2-VlG-I had been transferred to Semplak.

On the 26th the Endau landings occurred in Malaya (see opening chapter).

Table 4

211 Squadron — 18 Blenheims reached Sumatra

Known crews:

1	Z9649	Wg Cdr R.N. Bateson Sgt P. Dennis Sgt W. Baird	10	?	Plt Off G.A. Mockridge Sgt R.D. Mohr, DFM, RAAF Sgt C.G. Sharley
2	Z7699	Sqn Ldr K.C.V. Dundas Plt Off C.R. Ritchie, RAAF Sgt J.B. Keeping, RAAF	11	?	Plt Off Greenwood Sgt R.E.D. Arnold, RAAF Sgt A. Hare, RAAF
3	Z7521	Flt Lt J.D. Clutterbuck Sgt H.G. Newstead Plt Off F.C. Joerin	12	?	Wt Off Logan Sgt N.R. Jeans, RAAF Sgt T. Williams, RAAF
4	?	Flt Lt K. Linton Sgt H. Offord Sgt R.L. Crowe	13	Z7913	Sgt A.T. Bott, RAAF Sgt J.N. Lynas, RAAF Sgt H.J. Lamond, RAAF
5	?	Flg Off G.G. Mackay, RAAF Plt Off N.H. Oddie, RAAF Plt Off J.H. Payne, RAAF	14	Z7589	Sgt G.M. Steele, RAAF Sgt S.K. Menzies, RAAF Sgt G.H. Gornall, RAAF
6	?	Plt Off D.L. Chalmers Plt Off T.T. McInerney, RAAF Sgt G.M. Kendrick	15	?	Sgt J.A. Burrage, RAAF Plt Off D.M. Stewart, RAAF Sgt M.D. McDonald, RAAF
7	Z7855	Plt Off B.L. West, RAAF Flt Sgt G. Chignell Sgt Kite	16	?	Unknown Sgt D. Curran, RAAF Unknown
8	Z9660	Plt Off E.P. Coughlan Sgt A. Cummins, RNZAF Sgt A.P. Richardson	17	?	Unknown Sgt T. Bell, RAAF Unknown
9	Z7974	Plt Off A. Devenish, RAAF Sgt J.O. Penry, RAAF Plt Off J. Ensell	18	?	Unknown Sgt A.R. Travers, RAAF Unknown

Other Blenheims known to have been on the strength of 211 Squadron included L9336, Z7795 and Z9815.

The five crews of 84 Squadron which were to have taken part in the attack on the transports were retained at Singapore; next day (27th) Sgt George Sayer volunteered to fly a reconnaissance sortie up the eastern coast of Malaya, to establish whether a further convoy was on its way. Nothing untoward was sighted, Sayer returning in the dark and landing safely at Sembawang. Meanwhile, the Blenheims of the 84 Squadron detachment were kept at readiness to continue Singapore's strike against the Endau landings, but in the event were not called on until shortly after midnight on the 28th, when Wg Cdr Jeudwine led two others to bomb Kuantan aerodrome; despite thick cloud from almost ground level up to 5,000 feet, which made the target very difficult to find, all released their bombs either through gaps or from underneath the cloud, and returned safely to Sembawang, from where they proceeded to P.2 the following day. Of his brief visit to Singapore, Jeudwine made these damning observations:

> "While at Sembawang some very illuminating glimpses were obtained of the conditions in Singapore Island. There were a number of craters on the aerodrome, but no effort was being made to fill in these craters or clear up any debris; in fact, the most remarkable thing about the station was the absence of personnel during daylight hours.
>
> "The explanation was: the Japanese were sending three raids a day against the island, the first raid coming over about 1000 hours. At about 0930 hours, the yellow warning would be broadcast round the camp, whereupon the great majority of the personnel, officers included, left the camp and hid in the rubber, most of them remaining there all day. There was no system of spotters and insufficient slit trenches round the camp. Native labour, of course, was almost unobtainable, but no effort was being made to get the airmen to repair damage or dig trenches.
>
> "We were all extremely tired, being still unused to the heat and high humidity; we carried away a poor impression of the morale of the people with whom we had come into contact."

While Jeudwine and his flight were in Singapore with the Blenheim IFs, two of the unit's Mark IVs had been taken by Hudson pilots of 62 Squadron to carry out a reconnaissance. One of the pilots had not previously flown a Mark IV, and on approaching Tengah to land, crashed and wrote-off the machine, much to Jeudwine's irritation when he was informed of this on his return to P.2.

By the 27th, the carrier HMS *Indomitable* had reached a position a little to the south of Christmas Island (see Volume One, Chapters 4 and 9), and there the Hurricane pilots of 232 and 258 Squadrons were informed by Wg Cdr J.D. Urie, RAF officer in charge of the operation (codenamed Operation 'Opponent'), that they were to fly off to Batavia. The 48 Hurricanes were to go in three flights, each of 16 aircraft, the first to be led by Sqn Ldr James Thomson of 258 Squadron, at 0900. First off however, were sections of the carrier's own Sea Hurricanes of 880 Squadron, which were to undertake standing patrols to prevent any potential 'snoopers' from coming too close. One pair of Naval fighters — flown by Lt D.B.F. Fiddes and Sub Lt H. Popham — was vectored onto an aircraft plotted on the ship's radar, which turned out to be an unannounced Catalina from Tanjong Priok; this was FV-N of 205 Squadron, flown by Sqn Ldr Alex Jardine, which was carrying out an anti-submarine patrol; the flyingboat was also required to act as 'lifeboat' for the Hurricane delivery, in case any were obliged to ditch en route. Unbeknown to Jardine and his crew, this flight was nearly their last, as Hugh Popham, the Sea Hurricane pilot, recorded:

> "Brian (*Fiddes*) and I were sent off on our first operational interception with our stomachs doing somersaults and our thumbs on the gun button — and that was one Catalina flyingboat that nearly didn't get home."

A pair of Blenheims of 34 Squadron had been sent from Batavia to lead the Hurricanes in, but bad weather and low cloud prevented them from finding the ship; similarly, a second pair from the same unit also failed to make contact, and not until shortly before 1600 did the guides arrive in the form of two 84

Squadron Blenheims, flown by Flt Lts Wyllie and Holland; the former recalled:

"The other pilots had all tried to fly directly to a moving dot in the Indian Ocean. There was one obvious feature they had all missed. Christmas Island was no more than 50 or 60 miles from the point from which we were expected to find our target.

"I decided, in discussing the exercise with Doug Argent (*the navigator*), to fly first to the island where we could get a good fix and proceed from there. We found the carrier right on station and 12 Hurricanes were flown off and we led them back to base.

"The next day we led them on to Singapore. One Sergeant in our ground crew made a killing out of our little trip. He took bets from all the other squadron's ground crew that we would come back with the planes!"

The first take-off from the heaving deck of a carrier had been a traumatic experience for most of the Hurricane pilots. The Navy had demonstrated a quite insulting lack of confidence in the RAF's ability to get off without smashing something, by protecting every conceivable piece of equipment with great baulks of timber! There was, however, a distinct reluctance to be among the first to take off, since these aircraft appeared to have a substantially shorter run than those ranged at the furthest end of the deck. The Flight Deck Officer solved this dilemma somewhat brutally, stamping his foot on a spot about mid-way down the deck, and announcing:

"First or last, you'll all bloody well take off from here!"

This alarmed everyone, as even the formation leaders had to taxi forward a few yards to this spot before commencing take-off! One of the first flights did almost crash into the sea, but thereafter the 200 mile flight was uneventful.

After the delayed departure of the first flight it was clearly too late for any further take-offs that day, but next morning at 1000 the remainder of 258 Squadron and the first batch of 232 Squadron flew off, led by Sqn Ldr Llewellin. They were followed later in the day by the final 16, all flown by 232 Squadron pilots, with Flt Lt Julian at their head. These two flights did not land at Batavia's Kemajoran airfield without event however. The 232 Squadron machine flown by Sgt Gordon Dunn overshot when the airspeed indicator failed, and the Hurricane ground looped into a pile of crushed stone, badly damaging the starboard wing and wheel; Dunn was not hurt. As Sgt Ian Newlands came in to land, he found that his brakes failed to function, and in an effort to avoid the wreck of Dunn's aircraft, he collided with that of 2/Lt Neil Anderson; the South African received injuries which necessitated his removal to Batavia hospital. One other machine was slightly damaged on landing, tipping onto its nose when it struck a soft patch.

258 Squadron boasted three American pilots amongst its number; a fourth, Plt Off Don Geffene[1], had been with the unit at Gibraltar, but had crash-landed his Hurricane in neutral Spanish Morroco, and had been interned. Next morning (29th), the advance contingent of 258 Squadron flew to Sumatra, led by Sqn Ldr Thomson, and was guided by two Blenheims. On landing at P.2, a further Hurricane was damaged due to soft patches on the airfield's grass surface. After

---

[1] Plt Off Geffene, on release from internment, joined 30 Squadron and was posted to Ceylon; he was killed in action on 5 April 1942 in defence of that island (see Chapter 10).

refuelling, the remaining 15 Hurricanes flew on to Singapore, arriving at Seletar during the early evening.

The rest of the Hurricanes were prevented by bad weather from leaving Kemajoran until next day, when they, too, flew to P.2, where one further machine snapped off its propeller in a landing accident. On the last day of the month, four from each squadron were led to Singapore by another pair of Blenheims. To add to the confusion of a confusing campaign, there were now two 232 Squadrons in the East Indies!

The Americans had meanwhile mounted a further raid on the Malayan mainland on the 28th, five B-17Es flying to P.1 from Malang for the operation. Their target was Kuantan airfield but instead they attacked Kuala Lumpur, which was reached by four of the five aircraft during the early afternoon, after they had overflown Kuantan in heavy cloud; from the latter airfield two 1st Sentai Ki 27s were at once scrambled to intercept, whilst the 2nd Chutai of the 11th Sentai began taxying for take-off from Kuala Lumpur. They were too late, for bombs fell amongst them, setting one aircraft on fire, badly damaging three more, and causing lesser damage to another six. Two men were killed and 27 wounded; the 47th Independent Chutai was reduced to a single Ki 44, and the 11th Sentai to a single chutai. One of those killed was Wt Off Zenzaburo Ohtsuka of the 11th, a pilot who had been credited with 22 victories against the Russians during the Nomonhan Incident in 1939. The two intercepting Ki 27s were unable to catch the big bombers.

Pilots of 258 Squadron at RAF Debden prior to their departure for the Far East.
Front row, left to right: Plt Off Fletcher (did not go); Plt Off D. Geffene, RCAF (US) (reached Ceylon); Plt Off A.D.M. Nash; Plt Off G.C.S. Macnamara (Rhod); Flg Off H.A. Dobbyn, RNZAF; Flt Lt D.J.T. Sharp, RNZAF; Sqn Ldr J.A. Thomson; Station Commander, RAF Debden; Station Adjutant, RAF Debden; Flt Lt V.B. de la Perrelle (NZ); Plt Off B.A. McAlister, RNZAF; Plt Off C. Campbell-White, RNZAF; Plt Off C. Kleckner, RCAF (US); Plt Off N.L. McCulloch; Plt Off A.H. Milnes; Plt Off R.L. Cicurel, RCAF (US).
Back row, left to right: Plt Off J.A. Campbell (US); unknown; Sgt H. Lambert; Sgt A. Sheerin, RAAF; Sgt P.T.M. Healy; Sgt Gallagher (reached Ceylon); Sgt N.H. Scott, RCAF; Sgt C.T.R. Kelly; Sgt R.B. Keedwell, RCAF; Sgt Miller (reached Ceylon); Sgt D.B.F. Nicholls; Sgt K.A. Glynn; Sgt D. Gregory (reached Ceylon) *(Sqn Ldr A.H. Milnes)*

With ABDA Command unaware of the damage the B-17Es had inadvertently caused at Kuala Lumpur, Maj Combs was ordered to make a further attempt to bomb Kuantan airfield. In the light of the earlier failure to locate this base, Combs requested help from the RAF, and Flt Lt Don Jackson of 34 Squadron accompanied the B-17 crew on a flight from P.1 to the Malayan airfield. An attack was later carried out by the bombers, when some damage was claimed to the hangar area and runways.

Next afternoon (30th), Wg Cdr Jeudwine led six Blenheims of 84 Squadron to Medan, where they were to refuel in preparation for a night attack on a Japanese submarine base which had been set up in Penang harbour; one was obliged to return owing to faulty petrol feed. The attack was carried out without observed results and all aircraft returned safely to Medan that night. Here a scratch meal and beds were provided for the crews, who flew back to P.2 the next morning.

With the arrival from Singapore of Air Commodore H.J.F. Hunter to take command of 225 (Bomber) Group, and Air Commodore S.F. Vincent to take over 226 (Fighter) Group, the RAF force available in Sumatra by 31 January was as shown in Table 5.

Of the 18 Hudsons of 59 Squadron that had departed England in early January, seven only would eventually reach Palembang, those captained by:

AE488 Sqn Ldr P. Garrard, DFC	AM945 Flg Off R. Richards
AM952 Flg Off T.D. Boyce	AE506 Flg Off H.H. Siddell
AM937 Plt Off J.F.P. Fitzgerald	AE553 Plt Off A.R. Wilson
AE511 Plt Off E.G. O'Kelly	

Table 5

226 Fighter Group

232 Squadron	17 Hurricanes	(of which one was damaged)
258 Squadron	4 Hurricanes	(of which one was damaged)

225 Bomber Group

1 RAAF Squadron	16 Hudson IIs	(many of which were overdue for inspection and major service)
8 RAAF Squadron	6 Hudson IIIs	(just arriving from Singapore and not ready for operations)
59 Sqn Detachm't	7 Hudson IIIs	(arriving from UK; would be attached to 8 RAAF Sqn.)
34 Squadron	6 Blenheim IVs	(most in poor condition)
62 Squadron	10 Hudson IIIs	(ex 53 Squadron aircraft and crews)
	5 Blenheim Is	(in very poor condition)
27 Squadron	3 Blenheim IFs	(in very poor condition)
84 Squadron	10 Blenheim IVs ⎫	(most in need of inspection and repairs after flight
211 Squadron	4 Blenheim IVs ⎭	from Middle East)

Attached:

2 Detached Flt., MVAF	3 Tiger Moths 2 Cadets	at Pakan Baroe

Six of the remaining Hudsons had crashed en route with the loss of at least four crews, while the other five got only as far as Burma. The most serious of the accidents involved AE491 and AE539, which were lost over the Mediterranean, AM946 off the coast of Spain and V9126, which crashed at Malta. It was intended that the surviving aircraft and crews would be absorbed into 8 RAAF Squadron.

Sunday, 1 February

Two hours after midnight five Hudsons of 1 RAAF Squadron, which had earlier ferried over from P.2, set out from Medan to carry out an attack on Alor Star. The formation was broken up by adverse weather before reaching the Malayan coast, and only two aircraft reached the target together, the others delivering individual attacks. A number of hits were claimed on hangars and other buildings, on metalled roads and runways. No enemy aircraft or anti-aircraft fire were encountered, nor were any aircraft observed on the airfield.

The Blenheims were out again during the night. Five aircraft of 84 Squadron, led by Wg Cdr Jeudwine, were joined by one of 34 Squadron (flown by Flt Lt Jackson) for an attack on Singora in Thailand, landing at Medan en route to refuel. The crews reported bombing buildings and stores on a spit of land north of the aerodrome, the only opposition coming from warships at sea off the coast. All arrived back at Medan after a four and a half hour flight.

Monday, 2 February

2ll Squadron flew its first operational sortie early in the morning, Plt Off E.P. Coughlan and his crew in Z9660 carrying out a reconnaissance off Kota Radja, searching for a reported aircraft carrier; nothing was seen. Coughlan, a genial Irishman from Dublin, was then ordered to proceed to P.1. However, no maps of Sumatra were available but a Dutch airman produced a newspaper in which was a very small map of the East Indies! On studying this, Sgt Archie Cummins, Coughlan's experienced New Zealand navigator, announced that he was confident that he could find Pakan Baroe and P.1, which he did without too much trouble.

During the day Japanese aircraft bombed and strafed the 1,461-ton coaster *Katong* in the Banka Straits, after which it sank with all aboard except the master and four members of his crew. A second freighter which had departed Singapore during the day, en route for Calcutta, was bombed during the hours of darkness. Fires broke out aboard the *Norah Moller* (4,434 tons) which could not be controlled, and the vessel was abandoned next morning off Nangka Point in the Banka Strait; 17 of the crew were lost.

It was the turn of the Hudsons again on the night of 2nd/3rd, three aircraft setting out from Medan to attack Singora. On taking off, Flg Off Gibbes (A16-42) experienced an engine failure when at 150 feet. With a full bomb load which he could not jettison, Gibbes managed to carry out a flat circuit and landed back safely in the dark. The remaining aircraft, led by Flt Lt John Douglas, proceeded to the target which was satisfactorily bombed.

While the bombing force was beginning to appear reasonably effective — if small — the situation of 226 (Fighter) Group was less convincing. The two composite squadrons, 232 and 258, were composed mainly of pilots straight from OTUs — though slightly better trained than the members of Singapore's original Buffalo units. The ground crews found the tool kits which had arrived to be

---

deficient, and the aircraft did not enjoy the considerable benefit of having VHF R/T fitted, or any direction-finding equipment for homing purposes. All aircraft were of the Mark IIB variety, armed with 12 Browning .303 machine guns. Having regard to the already-obvious light construction of the opposing machines, the four outer guns were removed from the wings of all Hurricanes to lighten the aircraft. The spare Brownings were to be used for additional AA defence, but had not been provided with mounts — which a local contractor was manufacturing — by the time attacks started in earnest.

Tuesday, 3 February

Early in the month 232 Squadron and the part of 258 Squadron still in Sumatra, had moved from P.2 to P.1 to undertake convoy patrols over the Banka Strait. The latter airfield was still guarded only by a few Dutch troops with four Bofors guns. There was one Dutch-manned Operations Room with an unreliable telephone line, and few other facilities except for a relatively efficient chain of observer posts. 232 Squadron's first patrols were made on the morning of the 3rd over Convoy BM-12, part of which — five transports including the 16,909-ton *Empress of Asia* and the slightly larger *Felix Roussel* (17,083 tons) — were on their way to Singapore, with an escort provided by the cruiser *Danae* and two destroyers. During the day, the convoy was attacked by 18 bombers, which were opposed only by the ships' anti-aircraft defences, the Hurricanes failing to make contact; only minor damage resulted from a number of near-misses.

Meanwhile, other transports of the convoy docked at Batavia (Java), aboard which were a batch of Hurricane pilots, about 40 mainly completely inexperienced Commonwealth NCOs (see Table 6). They were commanded by a Battle of Britain veteran, Wg Cdr H.J. Maguire, and arrived under the grandiose title of 266 Wing; it had been intended that they would replace losses within the existing units, but the rapid deterioration in the fortunes of the Allies would prevent this happening.

The Japanese bombers enjoyed greater success when they attacked the 4,958-ton *Loch Ranza* off Palembang during the day. The master managed to beach his burning vessel, following which it blew up; five of his crew were killed and two others died later in hospital. A British tanker, the 6,121-ton *Pinna* was also bombed while in convoy; she did not sink but drifted helplessly. Next morning she was again bombed and set on fire, running aground in a minefield off Lingga Island, with the loss of 20 of her crew. Two small Dutch coasters were also caught by Japanese bombers during the day — the 1,937 *Van Lansberge* sustained heavy damage by bombing, and was then torpedoed and sunk by the Japanese submarine *I-55*, 20 of her crew perishing. Further north the smaller *Togian* (979 tons) was sunk with the loss of all aboard.

Wednesday, 4 February

A black-painted Liberator dropped into P.1 in the early hours of the morning, carrying the ABDA commander, General Sir Archibald Wavell, who was on his way back to Australia after his brief visit to Singapore. Further arrivals at P.1 during the morning were six Moths of 'A' Flight, MVAF, from Singapore, en route for Batavia via Djambi. When Grp Capt Bishop of 225 Group heard of their arrival he informed the unit's commander, Flt Lt J.C. Cooke, that the Flight was to remain at P.1, as there was work available suited to light aircraft.

Table 6

266 Fighter Wing

Fighter pilot reinforcements aboard *City of Canterbury* are believed to have included the following:

Wg Cdr H.G. Maguire

Plt Off G.D. Binsted
Plt Off R.L. Cicurel
Plt Off K. Dawson-Scott

Sgt F. Bidewell	Sgt P. Brown
Sgt W. Collins	Sgt D.J.B. Isdale
Sgt A.D. Jack	Sgt R.S. Ambrose, RAAF
Sgt W.J. Belford, RAAF	Sgt K. Boyd, RAAF
Sgt K. Collins, RAAF	Sgt R.A. Dickson, RAAF
Sgt G. Gratton, RAAF	Sgt H.L. Hargreaves, RAAF
Sgt H.V. Hobbs, RAAF	Sgt A. Martin, RAAF
Sgt S. Munroe, RAAF	Sgt C.E. Sharp, RAAF
Sgt J. Souter, RAAF	Sgt F. Williams, RAAF
Sgt W.H.J. Williams, RAAF	Sgt K.J. Wylie, RAAF
Sgt F.N. Hood, RNZAF	Sgt H. Jensen, RNZAF
Sgt N.G. Packard, RNZAF	Sgt J.G. Vibert, RNZAF
Sgt E.R. Worts, RNZAF	Sgt D. Jones, RNZAF
Sgt W.H. James, RCAF	Sgt W.H. Monsell, RCAF
Sgt H.P. Low, RCAF	Sgt R.C. Smith, RCAF

However, attempts to requisition a Moth and a Piper Cub of the South Sumatran Flying Club, also based at P.1, came to no avail as Cooke was advised by their civilian owners that they would only be handed over on condition that they would not be flown in any danger area!

The main tasks allotted to the Flight were twofold, involving regular dawn river patrols by pairs of aircraft, when searches were made for unusual activity which might suggest Japanese infiltration — and a passenger and mail service to P.2 and Lahat. The inaugural flight to Lahat almost ended in disaster, as the impending arrival of the Moth had not been advised to the authorities; hence, the pilot arrived to find the airfield covered with obstructions, although he skilfully managed a landing between them, only to be accosted by an irate sentry. He learned later that only the hasty intervention of the Station Commander, Wg Cdr C.H. Noble, had prevented the aircraft being fired upon by the Dutch soldiers!

That evening, at about 1700 hours, there was notification from Group HQ that Japanese parachutists were likely to be dropped over Palembang that night. Accordingly, pickets were posted, machine gun posts manned, and all available officers and men at P.1 were armed either with sub-machine guns or rifles, while aircrew on the station were not allowed to return to Palembang town. In the early hours of the morning the siren was sounded, as an attack was thought to be imminent. Action stations were ordered, and several Blenheims had their port engines started in order that their hydraulically operated gun turrets would function — but it was a false alarm! A similar state of alarm existed at P.2 and, here too, Blenheim gunners manned their turrets, as 211 Squadron's Sgt Allan 'Jock' Richardson commented, "we became the ground defence!"

Earlier that evening Richardson and fellow WOp/AG, Sgt Roy 'Dicky' Crowe, had fallen foul of 84 Squadron's CO, Wg Cdr Jeudwine, upon whom the strain of events was obviously beginning to have a telling effect; Richardson recalled:

> "We were desperate to get new accumulators for one of 211's Blenheims, and we knew that there was a crashed Blenheim on the airfield, so we went to retrieve what appeared to be 'spare' accumulators from it.
>
> "We had just got them loose when a Blenheim taxied up beside us and stopped. The pilot stood up through his open hatch and ordered us to replace the accumulators, and although we explained the situation, and tried a little logical persuasion, the pilot — who was no other than Wg Cdr Jeudwine, pulled out his revolver, and pointed out emphatically that the batteries were the property of 84 Squadron, then threatened that he would shoot us to protect his squadron's equipment! We put them back smartly!"

Thursday, 5 February

During the morning Flt Lt O'Brien of 62 Squadron flew from P.2 to P.1, where he embarked Lt General Sir John Laverak (O/C 1st Australian Corps) and two of his staff, who were keen to survey the Banka Island area, where it was assumed (correctly) that any Japanese Sumatra-bound seaborne invasion force would attempt landings. As the Hudson climbed away from the airfield with its VIP passengers, it was joined by four Hurricanes which were to provide escort. However, before the coast was reached, the Hurricanes broke away and returned to P.1, leaving the Hudson to carry on alone. In the event the three-hour sortie was free of mishap and was carried out to the General's apparent satisfaction.

Following the various moves to and from Singapore, by the evening Palembang housed 18 Hurricanes of 258 Squadron, 11 of 232 (P) Squadron, plus four more attached to this unit from 488 Squadron, and a few unserviceable Buffaloes. In Singapore at this time were about 20 more Hurricanes, of which 14 were serviceable, and perhaps half a dozen Buffaloes. At Kemajoran airfield (Batavia), four more of 232 Squadron's aircraft were under repair, but a further 39 Hurricanes were in the process of being uncrated and assembled, these having just arrived aboard the latest convoy.

Yet another B-17E arrived at P.1 during the day, its crew fatigued following the long flight from Mingaladon (Burma). Before departing after refuelling, Lt W.J. Prichard picked up 2/Lt C.A. Gibson, who had been salvaging parts from the abandoned 41-2419, the machine which had crashed on the airfield two weeks earlier. The crew of a Japanese reconnaissance aircraft flying over Palembang reported six large and up to 50 medium-sized aircraft on the airfield; on receipt of this information an attack was planned for the morrow.

Friday, 6 February

Consequently, at first light, 23 Ki 48 bombers of the 75th and 90th Sentais, together with 18 Ki 43s of the 64th and 14 of the 59th, began taking off from Ipoh and Kahang, but heavy cloud and adverse weather conditions prevented a rendezvous. The 75th and 64th Sentais did manage to join up, but the other units made their way towards the target area individually. The former units arrived first at about 1100, but found low cloud obscuring the area, the Ki 48s diverting their attack to Banka Island instead. The 64th's fighters were able to penetrate the cloud however, and as they appeared over the airfield, Flt Lt Vic de la Perrelle of 258 Squadron was heard to exclaim:

"There you are! Our Hurris from Singapore!"

The Japanese pilots were not to achieve much on this occasion, claiming only one aircraft burned, five probably destroyed and five damaged — all on the ground — before they were forced to break off the attack due to cloud. Maj Tateo Kato, the 64th Sentai's leader, reported:

"Steering to the north below cloud layers, I spotted a runway. Started firing at once. Although there were many planes on the ground, I could not pierce through the clouds, which were hanging low. Accordingly, after smashing two enemy planes, I decided to return."

15 minutes later the other units arrived but, like the 75th, the light bombers of the 90th turned away to Banka. The 59th Sentai pilots had meanwhile encountered a pair of 211 Squadron Blenheims, part of a flight of six such machines acting as escort to the convoy heading for Singapore. At the briefing by a Staff Intelligence officer, the Blenheim crews had been informed:

"You will decoy enemy Naval units and beat off enemy air attacks!"

The two intercepted aircraft were swiftly despatched to watery graves, one falling in flames; none of the six Australian airmen survived from Sgt A.T. Bott's Z7913 or Sgt G.M. Steele's Z7589. One Blenheim of another pair, Plt Off Coughlan's Z9660, was also attacked, fighters making two passes, but the pilot was able to evade and escape. Coughlan's gunner, Sgt Jock Richardson, recalled:

"For a period it was uneventful, until a formation of six Jap bombers escorted by nine fighters passed above and to the south of us, almost on the same track as we were flying. Only one fighter broke off from this formation but it made determined attacks and then went off after his unit. We suffered no damage.

"Almost at the end of this five hour sortie formations again passed over us, with the same number of fighters but this time in the opposite direction to us. Two fighters broke off and made a series of attacks before rejoining their formation. Again we suffered no damage."

Although only the two Blenheims were lost, the jubilant Japanese pilots claimed three shot down, and the probable destruction of another. One of the bombers was almost certainly credited to Sgt Maj Hiroshi Onozaki. The 59th Sentai formation continued to Palembang, where they found the clouds already clearing, and as they went into the attack, met a number of British aircraft in the air.

Six Hurricanes of 258 Squadron were just returning from a patrol and engaged the raiders, while other Hurricanes of both units had scrambled following the initial attack. While some Ki 43s swooped down to strafe, others took on the Hurricanes. Pilots on the ground sheltered where they could, some firing their revolvers at the low-flying raiders; Flg Off Ting Macnamara later recorded:

"The fight took place at less than 1,500 feet, just off the aerodrome. How the aircraft whirled and twisted, their engines now snarling, now wailing, guns blazing — they looked for all the world like a pack of dogs all fighting each other!"

It was over swiftly, the Japanese pilots claiming five Hurricanes shot down and three more probably destroyed. They also claimed to have destroyed three more Blenheims and a Hudson on the ground. Amongst the casualties suffered on the airfield during the attack was Plt Off Keith Dawson-Scott, a replacement pilot posted to 258 Squadron from 266 Wing, who was killed. In return only a single 'confirmed' claim was submitted by Plt Off Reg Bainbridge of 232 Squadron, though a second was claimed damaged by the combined fire of Plt Offs Ambrose Milnes, Doug Nicholls and Jock McCulloch of 258 Squadron.

Amidst the burning aircraft — including two Buffaloes — and debris littering the airfield, the remaining Hurricanes came in to land, one at a time. Sgt Dick Parr's aircraft (BG678) had been hit in the cockpit area, an explosive shell striking the throttle and severing the little finger of the South African's left hand. With great difficulty, and in much pain, he succeeded in landing his damaged aircraft, having first carefully placed his severed finger in his shirt pocket! He was rushed to Palembang Emergency Hospital.

A second Hurricane crash-landed on the airfield, a total write-off, although the Canadian pilot, Sgt Nelson Scott, was unhurt. Two more Hurricanes failed to return, while Blenheim Z6282 of 84 Squadron, flown by Sgt C.N.M. Thomson, which was on its way back from Medan was hit and damaged as it approached to land; the gunner, Sgt P.A. Gardner, had seen the fighters but had believed them to be Hurricanes, having spotted some of the latter shortly before the attack. Unable to use his guns because the Blenheim was going in to land, Gardner was hit in the thigh, although Thomson was able to make a good landing despite damaged elevators.

Of the two missing 258 Squadron Hurricanes, the wreckage of Plt Off Cardell Kleckner's aircraft was later found in the jungle; the body of the American pilot was recovered and buried in Palembang Cemetery. The other, piloted by Plt Off Campbell-White, crashed deep in the jungle. The New Zealander returned four days later, weak, shaken but unhurt by his experience, having been aided considerably by natives; he was eventually driven back to Palembang by the Dutch army.

Further bad news arrived during the day, when Flg Off Gibbes of 1 RAAF Squadron left P.2 at 0620 in A16-42 to reconnoitre the Anambas, where Intelligence reported much Japanese activity. En route, in the vicinity of Metak Island, the Hudson was intercepted by up to ten fighters, but these were evaded. Arriving over the Anambas, Flg Off Tony Jay, the observer, was able to make a sketch of the harbour and indicate the positions of the nine ships seen. Unable to reach Palembang due to shortage of fuel, Gibbes headed for Kallang, where he reported directly to Air Vice-Marshal Pulford. The Hudson returned to Palembang next day, leading a further evacuating Buffalo.

Saturday, 7 February
Early during the morning one of the ubiquitous Ki 46 reconnaissance planes of the JAAF was over Palembang again, the crew confirming many aircraft on the airfield, resulting in a further attack being launched during the late afternoon.

Before the raid materialized however, three transit B-17Es from the Middle East, departed for Bandoeng. A total of 31 Ki 43s from both fighter sentais accompanied six 90th Sentai light bombers to P.1, where insufficient warning of the impending raid was received. Consequently the last Hurricanes were still moving down the runway when the first bombs began to explode, although all the fighters escaped damage at this stage. It seems that the 90th Sentai formation may have included some of the unit's Ki 30s as well as Ki 48s, for single-engined aircraft with fixed undercarriages were identified, incorrectly recognized by the defenders as fighters.

As the Hurricane pilots struggled to gain altitude, the Japanese fighters tore into them, claiming no less than ten shot down, plus five probables; Sgt Maj Hiroshi Onozaki of the 59th Sentai almost certainly claimed at least one of the four credited to his unit, while pilots of 64th Sentai claimed a further six, including one each by Lt Yohei Hinoki and Sgt Akeshi Yokoi, while another was shared by Capt Katsumi Anma, Lt T. Endo and Sgt Maj Yoshito Yasuda. The unit's 3rd Chutai strafed the airfield, claiming ten aircraft destroyed and six damaged, while 59th Sentai pilots also claimed a 'Lockheed' shot down, and a second probably destroyed. The 'Lockheed' was obviously Flt Lt Linton's Blenheim of 211 Squadron returning from a reconnaissance sortie, which was attacked as it was approaching to land. Ken Linton — who had flown with 84 Squadron during the Greek campaign of the previous year, when his aircraft had been shot down by an Italian CR 42 fighter — was fatally wounded; his air gunner, Sgt Dicky Crowe (who had been shot down on two previous occasions, once in Greece and again in Syria) baled out at low altitude, as recalled by his close friend, Jock Richardson:

> "The Blenheim went out of control, low down over the swamps not far from P.2. The navigator, Sgt Harry Offord, was either wounded or still trying to help the pilot, and Dicky — knowing all was lost — baled out at about 300-500 feet above the jungle swamps. He was badly torn and bruised, descending at high speed through the trees with only a partially opened parachute.
>
> "It was assumed at the squadron that all three were lost, but three days later we heard that someone with Dicky's description had been brought in by natives in a very bad state, not certain who he was, and who was in hospital in Palembang town.
>
> "We knew that we would have to evacuate P.2 sometime, so Bill Baird and I managed to make our way to Palembang and we forcibly removed Dicky to P.2. Later we learned that Sgt Offord had also been rescued from the crashed plane, and was so badly injured that he was put on a hospital ship."

Meanwhile, the 90th Sentai crews released their bombs over an estimated 14 aircraft on the airfield, reporting that four of these were set on fire. Losses to the RAF during the attack were heavy, six Blenheims — including three unservice-able machines of 84 Squadron (V6133, Z6282 and Z7799) — two of 211 Squadron and one of 34 Squadron, plus three Hurricanes, were burnt out on the ground; the Flying Club's Piper Cub (PH-ZSV) was also destroyed in this raid, while one of 'A' Flight's Moths received a bullet through a main spar, rendering it unserviceable. A further 11 Hurricanes, a Buffalo and a Hudson were damaged; this latter machine, an aircraft of 62 Squadron, had only just

Sgt Roy 'Dickie' Crowe, 211 Squadron WOP/AG. *(Flt Lt A.R. Richardson)*

landed after a flight from Pakan Baroe, where Flt Lt Tom Burne[1] had delivered supplies:

> "I landed (at P.1) in the middle of a Jap raid. The upshot was a bomb beside the aircraft, and a shattered right leg, which was amputated two days later. That was the inglorious end to my Far East campaign."

Air Commodore Vincent and his SASO, Wg Cdr Ron Barclay, found themselves caught in the open, as the latter recalled:

---

[1] Flt Lt Burne eventually returned to the UK and was the recipient of an artifical leg; he later remustered on fighters, and in 1944 joined 41 Squadron on Spitfires. On 24 February, 1945, he was severely wounded in the chest whilst on a sweep over Germany, but succeeded in flying back to base, a feat for which he was awarded a well-deserved DSO.

"P.1 was a very easy target and I remember Air Commodore Vincent and myself flattening ourselves in the sticky orange-coloured mud in the middle of the airstrip, while a Japanese rear-gunner casually sprayed the field."

The Hurricanes had again suffered, as noted by Vincent:

"Once again the warning came late, and once again the inexperienced pilots found the Japanese more than a match."

Plt Off Doug Nicholls of 258 Squadron was amongst those who managed to get airborne; he pulled into a steep climb soon after take-off and climbed up under the rear flight of bombers, which were at about 1,000 feet. He opened fire on one, which began to smoke and shed pieces, but was driven off by fighters. Once clear of the airfield, he climbed to 6,000 feet and became involved in a 'hide-and-seek' dogfight amongst the clouds. Eventually, his aircraft was hit and the cockpit filled with smoke and coolant, obliging him to bale out about 30 miles west of Palembang, injuring his legs as he crashed through the treetops and landed in a swamp. He had come down in an abandoned rubber plantation and although he managed to get to dry land, there was no sign of recent habitation. After several days of wandering, he was found by a search party of Dutch and Indonesian soldiers, finally reaching Palembang a full week later!

Two more 258 Squadron Hurricanes had been badly shot up, both pilots being obliged to crash-land on the airfield, Plt Off Mick Nash surviving his second such landing in a week, albeit suffering from shock. The other pilot, Canadian Sgt Roy Keedwell, was not so lucky. Having been wounded in the leg, he managed to nurse his damaged aircraft back to Palembang, but then collided with a burning Blenheim. The Hurricane burst into flames, and Keedwell had great difficulty getting out of the cockpit. Sgt Sheerin was amongst those who rushed to his aid, helping to drag him clear, but not before the wounded pilot had received extensive burns to his face, legs and arms. Taken to the Dutch hospital at Palembang, Keedwell appeared to hold his own for 24 hours, but secondary shock then set in, and he died during the afternoon of 10th.

Some measure of success was obtained by Plt Off 'Red' Campbell, who claimed a 'Zero' (sic) shot down, one of three Ki 43s which attempted to engage him:

"As one opened fire, I did a 180° turn — during which he scored several hits on me — and fired head-on. As I came on top, I could see part of his engine cowling ripping away."

The Ki43 crashed on the perimeter of the airfield, as witnessed by Plt Off Bill Lockwood of 232 Squadron:

"I had to take-off in the face of strafing Navy '0's, lying on the ground beside my Hurricane until I had a reasonable opportunity of getting off. As I lined up on the runway to take-off, an '0' fell in flames at the end of the runway."

Another fighter was claimed by Plt Off Milnes, who reported watching his victim catch fire and dive in a graceful arc into the jungle; he also claimed a 'Type 97' fighter damaged, while Sgt Scott reported damaging another; these were possibly Ki 30 light bombers. The Japanese admitted the loss of two of their aircraft including the Ki 43 flown by Sgt Maj Choichi Okuyama of the 64th Sentai.

Whilst the fighting was raging over Palembang, two more of 258 Squadron's Hurricanes returned from a convoy patrol, and were at once set upon by a dozen Ki 43s; Sgt Ken Glynn failed to return and was presumed shot down, while Plt Off Jock McCulloch was chased into the clouds and became lost. He subsequently ran out of fuel and crash-landed in a swamp near a river, his aircraft coming down not far from the wreck of another Hurricane, which had crashed upside-down, and was believed to have been Glynn's aircraft; the pilot was dead. Using his collapsible rubber dinghy, the Scot made his way downstream and eventually spotted a canoe moored on the river bank. Unable to find the owner, he pinned a ten guilder note to a nearby tree and made off in the canoe. After paddling for some time he met some natives who took him to their chief at a nearby village where, to his amazement, he was offered ice cold beer from a refrigerator in the chief's house! For two days, until he was rescued, he dined on European foods and slept in the biggest and most luxurious bed he had ever seen!

Sgt Maj Choichi Okuyama of the 64th Sentai about to take-off in his Ki 43 from an airfield in Southern Malaya, for the attack on Palembang on 7 February, from which he did not return. Behind his fighter is a Nakajima Ki 27.

Pakan Baroe had also been subjected to an attack earlier in the day, Ki 27s of the 11th Sentai claiming one Lockheed burned, plus another and three Blenheims damaged. The defenders reported that about 16 bombers came over, but that heavy cloud up to about 3,000 feet caused the bombs to fall mainly in adjacent paddy-fields, terrifying some farmers. Then about five or six fighters swooped down, strafing aircraft and buildings, before the bombers made a second run, pattern-bombing the wireless station, the camp and the aerodrome area. A Dutch Lodestar was burnt out and two Glenn Martins of 1-VlG-II badly damaged, as were two abandoned 84 Squadron Blenheims; one of these was Sgt Stan Owen's Z7886, he and his crew having been stranded at Pakan Baroe for two weeks after their machine had became unserviceable. A MVAF Tiger Moth and a Club Cadet ('33') of 2 Detached Flight were also irreparably damaged, whilst an oil dump was set on fire and about a dozen personnel were killed and twice that number wounded. Two RAF doctors — a Wing Commander and a Pilot Officer, both of whom had just disembarked from a transit aircraft as the raid commenced — were amongst the casualties.

Dutch colonial troops gallantly returned fire with automatic small-arms, claiming strikes on at least two of the low-flying fighters; reports were later received that two of these had crash-landed in swamps, 50 miles to the south. MVAF aircraft sent out to locate these alleged wrecks were not successful. However, as there were apparently no Japanese losses as a result of this raid, it seems likely that the report of two aircraft having crashed actually referred to the losses from the Palembang raid.

The other bomb-damaged Blenheim — Z9709 in which Sqn Ldr Tom James and his crew had arrived the previous day — had crashed whilst landing, although the crew was unhurt. This particular aircraft had been ferried as far as Mingaladon by Sgt Ken Lister, having been nursed from the Middle East with faulty flaps. On arrival at Mingaladon, Lister required urgent attention to a troublesome wisdom tooth, first reporting that his aircraft also required urgent treatment:

> "I had the wisdom tooth extracted and was given the rest of the day off. The following morning we went out to the airfield, and to my horror, I saw that my aircraft was not there. The aircraft that was there (Z9732) had a burst tailwheel, and the crew had transferred into my aircraft and taken off for Pakan Baroe.
>
> "I took the aircraft that had been left (its tailwheel having been replaced) and followed the route to Pakan Baroe, wondering what might have happened, and on arrival my worst fears were confirmed. There was a crashed aircraft just short of the runway and, on landing, I was informed that it was the aircraft which I had nursed all that way."

With no chance of their Blenheims being repaired, Sqn Ldr James and Sgt Owen, together with their crews, set out by road for Padang on the south coast. On arrival there some days later, they evacuated aboard a departing warship.

At last some anti-aircraft defences arrived for the main Palembang airfields, one battery with 3.7-inch guns, and one with Bofors, although there was as yet no ammunition for the latter! Eight 3.7s were sent to P.1, four to P.2 and four to the Pladjoe refinery, while six Bofors went to P.1 and four each to the other two locations. It was, however, now becoming impossible for Singapore to continue controlling the units on Sumatra and, in consequence, their direction passed to ABDAIR. Orders were at once issued that no further reconnaissance sorties were to be flown, all multi-engined aircraft being required to concentrate on bombing.

As night fell, nine Blenheims, including some from 84 Squadron, were despatched in bad weather to attack the convoy spotted the previous day forming up in the Anambas. Results of the attack were not observed, but the raid was not considered a success owing to the adverse climatic conditions which prevailed. A few Hudsons were also sent off from P.2 to seek and attack the convoy, as recalled by Sgt Arnold Longworth, observer aboard Flg Off Bob Richards' AM945/R of the 59 Squadron Flight:

> "We made a shaky take-off from the sodden grass runway and headed east, dodging tropical thunder clouds on the way. Needless to say we saw nothing of any fleet in spite of a long search. On our way back our electricity supply slowly weakened, which meant that the radio was useless. My navigation light packed up eventually and, after a struggle to see my chart, maps and

calculations or courses on my log, I had to use my petrol lighter to see anything.

"We at last picked up the coast of Sumatra, by which time I was using the spark from the flint in my lighter for momentary looks at the map. More by good luck than good map reading I picked up the river to Palembang. The weather was atrocious, but recognising the point where the town of Palembang should be, we flew the course and time that would put us over P.2. No flare path, no recognition signals, no flares, no hope of landing."

After some discussion with his crew, when baling out was one option suggested — and rejected — Richards agreed to attempt a ditching just off the coast. This was skilfully achieved, although the crew soon discovered, to their dismay, that the aircraft had belly-landed on mud flats covered by about three feet of water. Sgt Karl Holden, the airgunner, jumped into the sea to steady the aircraft's inflatable raft, only to find himself trapped in the mud, and had to be hauled aboard by the others. The crew decided to remain aboard the aircraft until daylight but, when the tide started to flow, they scrambled into the comparative safety of their dinghy and started to head for the coast.

Sunday, 8 February
Shortly after dawn the airmen were rescued by native fishermen and were taken to a nearby village, where they remained until a Dutch police launch arrived hours later, and transported them to the lightship on the approaches leading to the Moesi River. Following a night and day spent aboard the vessel, the police launch returned and took them aboard. Palembang was finally reached after an absence of four days, during which they had been posted "Missing", and cables sent to their respective families accordingly!

For the third day in succession the JAAF attacked Palembang, although this time the 25 Ki 43s and 17 light bombers of the 90th Sentai arrived in the morning; the bomber crews claimed nine aircraft burned on the ground, many of them aircraft hit during previous raids, although at least one operational Blenheim was destroyed; Air Commodore Vincent wrote:

"I was with a group of officers trying to move a Hudson which had had both tyres punctured by splinters while being refuelled from a tanker. The tanker was ablaze and we were endeavouring to save the aeroplane. We succeeded in this, but a Blenheim fully 500 yards away was also on fire.

"I had driven past the Blenheim in my car shortly before, and having noticed it was bombed up, ordered everyone away. The bombs exploded with a tremendous roar, and an airman standing beside me gave a cry of pain, for a bomb splinter had come that great distance and pierced his wrist, and was protruding on both sides."

The Japanese fighter pilots reported meeting four Hurricanes, each sentai claiming one shot down. Only two Hurricanes were actually in the air as the raiders approached, Flt Lt Taylor and Sgt Sam Hackforth unhesitatingly engaging these; it was believed that each probably gained a victory before they were overwhelmed. Taylor's aircraft (BE115) was then seen approaching the airfield, low and fast, pursued by a Ki 43. The Hurricane performed a tight turn, the pursuer almost on top of it, the pilot snapping off short bursts of machine gunfire. The two aircraft completed one and a half full circles, the Ki 43 easily maintaining its position on the tail of the Hurricane. With a final burst, the Japanese pilot — who was himself under fire from the ground defences — pulled up into the clouds, leaving a mortally wounded Taylor to crash into some trees on the edge of the airfield. Meanwhile, Hackforth's aircraft (BE219) was under attack by five Ki 43s and he was last seen being chased away from the airfield with two fighters on either side and one on his tail. He too was killed when his aircraft crashed into the jungle.

The loss of these two 232 Squadron pilots was a severe blow, for they were both among the more successful. Sam Hackforth had been credited with at least four victories; within a day or so of his death, the squadron received notification of his commission. Edwin Taylor, although relatively inexperienced in combat on arrival in Singapore, had nonetheless led his flight with conspicuous success and was personally credited with at least six victories; the award of a DFC would be promulgated the following August.

When some of the pilots accompanied ground staff to retrieve Taylor's body from the wreck, they discovered that although the aircraft had been hit many times, his death had resulted from the fact that he had been out-turned in vertically-banked turns, so that bullets had come over the top of the armour plating into his back and head. Their conclusion was that if he had flown straight, or had made only slight turns, he would doubtless have been shot down, but the armour would have kept his body protected and he would, probably, have survived.

This was to be the last attack on the Palembang area for several days, but the defences were now very short of fighters. An opportune visit to P.1 by Air Vice-Marshal Sir Richard Peirse, Commander-in-Chief Allied Air Forces, ABDA, permitted Air Commodore Vincent to plead his case for more fighters, spares, AA guns and ammunition. A promise was made to hasten the despatch of new Hurricanes being erected at Batavia and, during the day, seven pilots were flown from P.1 to Tjililitan by Dutch Lodestar, to collect the first of these.

Monday-Thursday, 9-12 February

Next day (9th), further reinforcement fighter pilots arrived at P.1, having travelled from Batavia by boat to Oosthaven, then by rail and lorry to the airfield; one of the new arrivals, Sgt Frank Hood, a New Zealander, commented:

> "Very wild country. City rambling and very Eastern. Very little money and issue grub lousy. Lots of air activity. No kites for us."

Despite the losses, the command infrastructure for the defences continued to flow in to Palembang. Headquarters staff and ground personnel of 242, 258 and 605 Squadrons reached 226 Group from Java on 10th, their good morale having a rejuvenating effect on the ex-Singapore men, some of whom were failing to stand up to the bombing. Other new arrivals at P.1 included seven of 232 Squadron's Hurricanes from Singapore, led by Sqn Ldr Brooker, while next day Air Vice-Marshal Maltby, the commander of WESTGROUP, also arrived from Singapore to assume control. Unable, however, to find a suitable headquarters location on the island, he and Air Commodore Staton would move on to Java a few days later.

The newly-arrived Sqn Ldr Brooker was briefed to lead off all available Hurricanes at midday on 10th, but one taxied into the MVAF's remaining

Dragon Rapide ('19'), which was being refuelled following a flight from Batavia; the twin-engined biplane sustained extensive damage to its starboard main-plane, which, under the circumstances prevailing, was deemed irreparable. The Hurricane formation meanwhile, had seen nothing of note, while two pilots were forced to return early, sick and dizzy due to a shortage of oxygen bottles in their aircraft; owing to this serious shortage, one flight was not able to climb above 18,000 feet.

Whilst Blenheim stragglers were still arriving from the Middle East, both the 84 and 211 Squadron commanders had effectively now given up hope of receiving their full complements of aircraft. To date, 17 Blenheims of 84 Squadron had reached Palembang, while 211 Squadron's total was one less at 16; of this total, at least eight had already been lost. One of the last 84 Squadron machines to arrive at P.2 was that flown by Sgt Bill Cosgrove, he and his crew having had an extremely eventful journey. Soon after take-off from Habbaniya, the Blenheim had suffered engine trouble and force-landed at Ramadi, from where the crew were picked up by armoured car and taken back to Habbaniya. Cosgrove was then ferried by flyingboat to Heliopolis to collect a replacement aircraft, which he flew back to Habbaniya to pick up his crew.

At last Cosgrove was able to head eastwards, but on arrival at Dum Dum airfield, Calcutta, this aircraft became unserviceable. Whilst awaiting repairs, he was approached by Sqn Ldr John Tayler for a lift to Sumatra; Tayler, one of 84 Squadron's flight commanders, had been receiving medical treatment when the squadron departed Egypt, and had flown to Calcutta aboard a flying-boat. With his aircraft repaired, Cosgrove set out for Sumatra, which was reached uneventfully, as recalled by his gunner, Sgt Hayes Harding:

> "On arrival at Lho'nga we saw the small runway, only about 600 yards long and surrounded on three sides by mountains. Prevailing winds were from the mountains, so take-off was either with a following wind and over the sea, or the normal into the wind — that, of course, entailed flying towards the mountains.
>
> "Rather a dilemma — the crew before us decided to take-off into the sea, and did just that — they did not get off the ground and ended up in about six feet of sea, but no one was hurt.
>
> "Cosgrove decided to take-off into the wind, and we made it. However, I swear I could count the blades of grass as we banked around, and I was sure we would not make it. I felt sure our time had come — and not even on an op!"

That night (9th/10th) Flt Lt Holland of 84 Squadron was ordered to investigate the area around the Lingb Light, in the Straits, where the previous night an unidentified aircraft — presumed to have been Japanese — had been sighted; on this occasion nothing untoward was seen. Meanwhile, Wg Cdr Bateson (Z9649) led off three 211 Squadron Blenheims for an attack on Kluang airfield, across the Malacca Strait, in central Malaya. On arrival over the airfield in stormy conditions at 0600, anti-aircraft fire was found to be accurate, while night fighters were reported to be active. Sqn Ldr Ken Dundas' aircraft (Z7699) was shot down by AA fire, he and his crew perishing in the crash. The leader's airgunner, Sgt Bill Baird, recalled:

> "We had no time to substitute Browning belts — the daylight selection being three ball bullets, one incendiary, one tracer, three ball, one armour

piercing, one tracer — and instructions were issued to hold fire, otherwise our position would be obvious.

"The night fighters were out over Kluang and we saw them alright, as those we were supposed to see had on their lights. The lethal ones did not! This was the first time I experienced a loop the loop, as Wg Cdr Bateson took superb evasive action."

The loss of the highly experienced Dundas — a seemingly fearless Canadian — was a severe blow to the already severely depleted unit; he was another veteran of the Greek campaign, during which he had been awarded a DFC. A tribute was paid to Dundas by one of the squadron's armourers, Cpl Tom Henderson:

"His death was a hard blow to we longer serving members, who held him in great esteem as an officer and a truly great man. In earlier and happier days, this officer gave me hours and hours of his time, preparing me as a more plausible candidate for the highly desirable state of Sergeant pilot."[1]

A Hudson crew finally located the Japanese convoy, reporting a force north of Banka Island, comprising one battleship, three or four cruisers, eight destroyers and 25-30 transports. In fact, the force comprised two light cruisers and eight destroyers as close escort for 22 transports, with a covering force of five cruisers, eight destroyers and the light aircraft carrier *Ryujo*; embarked on the carrier were a dozen A5M fighters, under the command of Lt Takahide Aioi (a five-victory 'ace' of the fighting in China), and a hikotai of B5N single-engined bombers.

As a result of the latest sighting, a further all-out attack on the Japanese convoy was called for on the night of 11th/12th. All available Blenheims — 23 machines — drawn from all four squadrons, were to attack the convoy, while 11 Hudsons were to raid Kluang airfield, in a further attempt to suppress enemy air activity. Reported Wg Cdr Jeudwine:

"The Station Commander (*Group Captain J.P.J. McCauley*) insisted on the flare-path being controlled from the Watch Office, which had the only telephone on the aerodrome, so that any notification of an impending air raid could be sent by runner to the officer i/c flare-path. In addition, his scheme was for each aircraft in turn to taxi to the take-off position, and switch off. The officer i/c flare-path would then listen for any possible Japanese reconnaissance aircraft, and if none were heard, give the pilot a 'green'! The pilot would then start his engines, which was the sign for the flare-path (hurricane lamps) to be lit, and the aircraft would take-off.

"Apart from the impracticability of stopping and restarting the engines of Blenheim aircraft, ordered to take-off at two minute intervals, with the flare-path starting from the Watch Tower, the last two flares were hidden by a hump in the aerodrome, and the airman in charge of the lamps could not see when to light them. Consequently, aircraft were liable to come over the brow of the hill and have no guide for the rest of their run. Any slight deviation to either side pointed the aircraft at a belt of trees.

---

[1] Tom Henderson did eventually achieve his ambition, becoming a Lancaster bomber pilot in the UK later in the war.

"The Station Commander had insisted on this arrangement as he had been convinced by experience at his last station (*Sembawang*), that this was the only way to avoid accidents."

Take-off commenced shortly after midnight; the first six bomb-laden Blenheims struggled to get airborne, but then disaster struck, as graphically recalled by Flt Lt Wyllie of 84 Squadron:

"The last flare came up . . . another 50 or 100 yards and there would be just that much more speed that would add safety to the climb away. And then, unexpectedly, the aircraft checked, almost as if he — the pilot — had touched the brake lever by mistake. It was only momentary but it threw the tail up . . . the soft mud created a suction under the wide tyres but the Blenheim became airborne.

"His undercarriage took some of the topmost boughs, even as it began to retract. Then the noise . . . as if a whole world built of tin was being ripped and torn apart by the savagery of giant hands . . . The Blenheim burst into flames, only the air gunner managing to extract himself from the wreck."

The 211 Squadron aircraft (Z7521) broke in half, the rear section, with the airgunner trapped in the turret, being found some 20 yards from the blazing wreck. The pilot and his observer, Flt Sgt H.G. Newstead, perished, while the gunner, Swiss-born Plt Off Fred Joerin, survived with broken ribs.

A second machine from 211 Squadron, the CO's Z9649 — on this occasion being flown by Plt Off B.L. West, RAAF — almost immediately followed Clutterbuck's aircraft into the trees, crash-landing near the other, but fortunately not bursting into flames. An onlooker, Sgt Ray Wheatley of 8 RAAF Squadron, dashed over to the smouldering wreck. Finding the hatch jammed, he forced his way into the cockpit and unstrapped West, who was injured; he then went on to the aid of the injured observer, Sgt Gordon Chignell, and

Left: Sqn Ldr Ken Dundas, an experienced Canadian flight commander of 211 Squadron. *(Authors' collection)*. Right: Swiss-born Plt Off Fred Joerin, WOp/AG of 211 Squadron, who survived a Blenheim crash at Palembang on the night of 11/12 February. *(Authors' collection)*

helped both him and the gunner, Sgt Kite, to safety. Within minutes the bombs of the first Blenheim exploded, demolishing both aircraft. Wheatley, who had displayed similar heroism whilst serving in Singapore, would later be awarded the George Medal for his unselfish actions, the most recent of which undoubtedly saved the lives of the Blenheim crew.

As Sgt Sayer prepared to take off he was apparently aware that all was not well, and called for his air gunner, Sgt Ross, to come forward to reduce the weight at the rear of the aircraft. Even then the crew could hear the brush of the trees as the Blenheim struggled to clear them. On return from the sortie, a small branch was removed from the aircraft.

A third Blenheim, Z9726 of 84 Squadron flown by Sgt Joe Hyatt, which also struck the trees on take-off, turned to come in to land again but hit the Orderly Room building. The aircraft crashed in flames near 1 RAAF Squadron's dispersal area, and fires and exploding bombs endangered some of the unit's Hudsons awaiting take-off; these were quickly taxied out of harm's way. Sgt Hyatt and his observer, Sgt George Mutton, were killed in the crash, while the gunner, Sgt D.E. Irvine, was badly injured but was not found until daylight, and then only by good fortune. The rear section of the Blenheim, including the turret, had broken away in the crash and had 'disappeared' into the jungle about half a mile from the main wreckage; it was located by chance as two airmen walked along a track towards the Mess. On inspecting the wreckage, they were astounded to find the seriously injured airman. Irvine was hastily extricated and taken away for treatment, and eventually made a recovery from his injuries.

Next in line for take-off was Plt Off Macdonald's aircraft, in which Sgt Bill Miller was the gunner, who recalled:

> "I was ready for the take-off. Macdonald was revving up and ready for the off. To be quite truthful, to see three Blenheims go in was quite a bad one. I was chatting to Macdonald and we thought it must be sabotage."

Despite these tragic accidents, the Hudsons commenced take-off, but some of the remaining Blenheim crews were stood down. Of the Blenheims airborne, one was obliged to return early and force-landed back at P.2. The others — led by Wg Cdr Jeudwine — encountered heavy tropical thunderstorms on the way to the Anambas, to find the target area itself covered by low clouds. Bombs were released but the crews were unable to see any results. One of the pilots was Flt Lt Wyllie:

> "I had followed Clutterbuck down the field on take-off with less than 100 feet to spare between the flaming wreck and my own aircraft.
> "After being spotted, the convoy had up-anchored and moved off. So we flew 1,000 miles round trip to no purpose. With no second pilot, well over six hours' flying was a testing flight, especially when it was to no purpose, and at least five hours of it on instruments because it was dark."

The Hudson crews believed that they had fared somewhat better, all (four of 1 RAAF Squadron, two from its sister unit, and five of 62 Squadron) reaching Kluang; claims were submitted by the returning crews for hits on hangars and other buildings. Heavy AA fire was endured and night fighters were seen, although no interceptions were reported. On the return flight, Flt Lt J.M.H. Lockwood (in A16-21 of 1 RAAF Squadron) discovered that three of his bombs had not released, so he flew back to Kluang, arriving just as dawn was breaking, and aimed his bombs at a hangar. Despite the claims, Japanese reports speak of only two or three aircraft actually reaching the vicinity of the airfield, where no damage occurred.

Throughout this period, Hurricanes continued to patrol over shipping in the Banka Straits, which was evacuating personnel from Singapore. During one such mission on the 12th, Plt Off John McKechnie of 232 Squadron was obliged to crash-land BG768 in the jungle due to a violent storm; he wrote:

"I crashed in the Sumatran jungle, suffering rather a bad concussion and a fractured wrist, and damaging one eye. However, when I eventually got out of my plane, which was upside down, I managed to make my way through swamps to a river, and then got picked up by a Dutch destroyer and taken to the Palembang hospital."

That evening Air Vice-Marshal Maltby paid P.2 a visit, and gave assembled aircrews a lecture about the "pernicious habit of looking over one's shoulder". He vowed that there would be no evacuation and that everyone from pilots to cooks would fight to the last, emphasising that "this was to be an effort to retrieve the good name of the Air Force, which had been lost in Singapore." One of those on the receiving end of the lecture was Wg Cdr Jeudwine, who wrote:

"A talk of this nature was an excellent thing as the morale of the personnel who had come from Malaya and Singapore was extremely low, but it must be confessed that a lot of the effect was lost as the AVM had only just arrived from Singapore, and had no conception of the conditions under which we were operating, which precluded shaving every day and keeping our buttons polished."

Others noted — with the lecture over — that the Air Vice-Marshal then evacuated himself and his staff to a relatively safer and more comfortable haven in Java, as recalled by Sgt Ken Lister:

"By the end of the day we were a pretty dirty, scruffy lot. The Air Vice-Marshal did nothing but carry on about what a disgrace we looked and how it was necessary to maintain a high degree of smartness, with well-polished shoes and buttons. My only thoughts were that his knife-edge creases and spotless uniform would have looked a sorry mess if he had to do the jobs that I had done that day.

"He certainly did nothing at all to boost the morale of what was a gathering of very experienced aircrew, many of whom had operational experience in Europe, Greece and North Africa. Having had his say, our great leader flew off, never to be seen (by me) again."

Friday, 13 February

At last some of the replacement Hurricanes at Tjililitan were ready, the seven pilots of 232 and 258 Squadron being ordered to prepare for the flight to Palembang. Joined by Wg Cdr H.J. Maguire (ex 266 Wing), who was to lead the formation to P.1, they took off at dawn. At about the same time, a dozen Hurricanes were off from P.1 seeking six Japanese 'flyingboats' reported by the Dutch HQ to have alighted near the north-east coast of Banka Island; these were in fact F1M floatplanes from the seaplane tenders *Kamikawa Maru* and

Left: Sgt Ray Wheatley, RAAF, was awarded the George Medal for rescuing the crew of a crashed Blenheim at Palembang. *(Grp Capt H.C. Plenty)*. Right: Sgt Henry Nicholls of 232 Squadron, who was heavily engaged and shot down on 13 February. He subsequently made his way out of the jungle to reach Oosthaven. *(H.T. Nicholls)*

Sagara Maru, which had been detached to operate from the island, at Muntok; the island had by now largely been evacuated by Europeans and natives alike.

A careful search was made by the Hurricanes, but nothing was to be seen, and Sqn Ldr Brooker led them back to Palembang, low on fuel. They had just landed when the JAAF returned to the attack, 29 Ki 43s from the 59th and 64th Sentais, with seven Ki 48s, approaching. At this moment, the seven reinforcement Hurricanes from Java arrived overhead; almost out of fuel, some were forced to land at once, but Wg Cdr Maguire and Sgt Henry Nicholls remained above to try and give some protection, and these two at once attacked the incoming raiders. Maguire became involved with two Ki 43s, and in the confusion, one of these opened fire on the other; he later commented:

> "I claimed one 'Zero' (*sic*), although I am pretty sure he was first damaged by his own No 2 — possibly over-excited."

Nicholls also fired at this machine, which he saw crash at the end of the runway, then engaged another, which he believed also crashed into the jungle. He was attacked by a third fighter, and his engine was hit, obliging him to bale out at 600 feet, a few miles to the south of the airfield. Suffering from shock, the Cornishman was picked up by a group of natives, who took him down river to a Dutch missionary, from where he eventually made his way to Oosthaven; in the meantime he was posted missing.

Another of the reinforcement Hurricanes, that flown by Sgt Nelson Scott, was on its landing approach with flaps and undercarriage down, when two Ki 43s dived onto its tail. One opened fire, hitting the Hurricane's engine and slightly wounding the Canadian pilot in the arm. He pulled up the heavily smoking aircraft and baled out at 700 feet, coming down in the jungle, not far from the airfield. He was able to walk back, arriving about an hour after the attack.

Flg Off Macnamara was following Scott but managed to avoid the Japanese fighters by side-slipping. One of his pursuers, flown by Lt Masabumi Kunii of the 64th Sentai, attempted to pull out of his dive; however the wings of his aircraft folded up and it crashed into the jungle, where it burst into a ball of flames. Watching Japanese pilots believed Kunii had shot down the Hurricane before his crash, but in fact Macnamara was able to land his undamaged aircraft safely, as did the other four ferry pilots, although one aircraft had suffered slight damage.

The wreck of the 59th Sentai Ki 43 which had crashed at the end of the runway was later inspected by, amongst others, Wg Cdr Ron Barclay, who noted that the lack of armour plate had been mainly responsible for the pilot's death; he was riddled with bullets from head to seat. With the Hurricanes so engaged, the Japanese bomber crews were able to gain a number of successes when they attacked shipping in the river. The minesweeper HMS *Hua Tong* was sunk whilst both the steamer *Hosang* and another requisitioned minesweeper, HMS *Klias*, were damaged.

While the bombing and strafing was underway, three more Hurricanes from 'A' Flight of 232 Squadron were prepared for take-off and, during a lull, were scrambled — climbing into cloud. They were followed a few minutes later by Sqn Ldr Brooker at the head of several more fighters, which began a hide-and-seek fight amongst the low clouds. Of this action Sgt Sandeman Allen (Z5667/T) reported:

> "I was separated, and attacked, in error, 24 'Navy 0s' (*sic*) guarding the bombers. I was credited with two 'Zeros', and one bomber probable."

Sqn Ldr Brooker claimed a second bomber for his sixth personal victory of the war (four of which had been credited prior to his arrival at Singapore). Several other Japanese aircraft were claimed damaged, including a Ki 48 by Sgt Ken Holmes; he reported seeing his victim fall away with one engine stopped before he was forced to break away. One of the Hurricanes (BG693) failed to return, Plt Off Leslie Emmerton last being seen at low level over the treetops, being pursued by several Ki 43s; he was killed.

When the raid began, one unserviceable Hurricane had been taken into the air by Plt Off Tom Watson to prevent it being strafed:

> "It had no air pressure so I had no brakes and my guns would not fire. I was several miles from P.1 when I was attacked by six or seven 'Zeros' (*sic*), and all I could do was run for it. My whole plane was shot-up, wings, fuselage, engine and instrument panel, and I had the uncomfortable feeling of hearing or feeling the Japanese machine gun bullets hitting my armour plate.
>
> "With engine smoking, I headed for P.1 and the cover of our own anti-aircraft fire. My engine conked out but I was able to land; fortunately the undercarriage came down OK. I had no brakes and rambled on past the end of the runway, the plane a complete write-off."

During this attack the Japanese pilots claimed three Hurricanes shot down, plus two more probables and four large aircraft on the ground. In return they reported the loss of three aircraft during the raid; at least two Ki 43s are known to have failed to return, the other loss therefore may have been a Ki 48, possibly the aircraft claimed by Brooker, or by he and Sandeman Allen jointly.

Early in the morning a lone Japanese fighter attacked Lho'nga airfield, on the northern tip of Sumatra, inflicting little damage although one abandoned Blenheim was hit. By now, one of the last Hudson stragglers from the UK had reached this airfield, the pilot of which was Plt Off Les Hayton of 53 Squadron. Aboard this aircraft was a second crew, commanded by Plt Off Tony Ayris, whose 59 Squadron Hudson (AE517) had crashed on take-off at Allahabad, effectively stranding the crew there until the arrival of Hayton, who recalled:

"I had delays in Gibraltar and Malta, where my aircraft (V9180) had been damaged in a Stuka raid; again delayed at Cairo, Habbaniya and Dum Dum, where we arrived on 31 January. The radio was u/s and it was not until a complete radio was received from Bombay where a Hudson of 59 Squadron had crashed, that we were able to continue to Magwe, Rangoon and Lho'nga, arriving on the 13 February.

"It was at Lho'nga that we were ordered to search for enemy shipping coming up the straits from Singapore. They could not have been far away as we had a raid on the airfield by a single 'Zero' (*sic*) that morning."

Hayton and crew were to remain at Lho'nga for a few days before being ordered to return to Burma, taking with them Ayris and his crew.

The rest of the day would see sections of Hurricanes kept at readiness at P.1, from where there were scrambles although no further attacks developed. During the afternoon, two sections again went out to look for the flyingboats, but once more nothing was seen; a violent storm was encountered over Banka, which broke up the formation. That evening the defenders witnessed 14 Hurricanes take to the air together. The 258 Squadron Engineer Officer, Flg Off R. Tudor Jones, assisted by Flg Off John David, his 243 Squadron counterpart, and the ground crews had performed herculean tasks in makeshift hangars on the boundary of the airfield, to make so many fighters serviceable. Much cannibaliz-ation of badly damaged aircraft had taken place to enable others to be made good.

Wg Cdr Maguire led this formation out to look for the Japanese convoy now reported approaching Sumatra. Again the aircraft flew into a severe storm, and although navigation lights were switched on, some aircraft became separated. One flight from 232 Squadron, led by Sgt Sandeman Allen, was severely buffeted and forced away from the airfield, with the result that two of these Hurricanes eventually crash-landed. Both pilots survived, although 2/Lt Neil Dummett, SAAF, suffered injuries and shock, while Sgt Fred Bidewell, one of the new arrivals, was shaken but otherwise unhurt.

The afternoon saw Wg Cdr Bateson at the head of half a dozen 211 Squadron Blenheims, also searching for the approaching Japanese convoy. This was not located however, and on returning to P.2 at dusk, the Blenheims ran into the same storm over Southern Sumatra, resulting in aircraft becoming separated; only four landed at P.2, while one aircraft was reported down in the sea near Banka Island; the pilot of this, Plt Off Doug Chalmers, and his gunner, Sgt G.M. Kendrick, were able to scramble into their dinghy, but the observer, Plt Off T.T. McInerney, an Australian, was lost. Chalmers, who was temporarily blinded, and Kendrick reached a small island where survivors of a sunken ship were met, and from here were later picked up by a passing vessel. The other Blenheim was also presumed to have crashed into the sea[1], with the loss of Flg Off G.G. Mackay, RAAF, and his all-Australian crew (Plt Offs N.H. Oddie and J.K. Payne).

Catalinas of 205 Squadron, currently operating out of Oosthaven harbour, also carried out search patrols for Japanese convoys, Flt Lt Hugh Garnell and his crew of Y52/W making a sighting about 20-30 miles off the Sumatran coast. Garnell decided to attack and dived from low cloud across the lines of ships and a number of near-misses were observed. Heavy AA fire was experienced from the escorting warships although the Catalina was not hit.

Meanwhile, Hudsons of 8 RAAF Squadron were also carrying out reconnaissance sorties; Flt Lt Plenty noted:

> "Flew AM937 on recce during which we sighted carrier *Ryujo*, which was also suspected of being in the area by another recce — A16-37 flown by David Colquhoun — when he was attacked by Navy 96 fighters."

With these latest sighting reports to hand, AHQ ordered a strike to be carried out and, during the late afternoon, Flg Off E.J. Henry (AE521) led off five Hudsons of 62 Squadron. At about 1730 hours, shortly before dusk, they came across a number of warships, which put up a heavy and accurate barrage; the leader reported:

> "Although we were right down on the deck and doing about 145 knots, one salvo actually landed in the middle of the formation, which fortunately at this moment was in a very broad vic. My turret gunner reported that the other aircraft completely disappeared in a cloud of spray, but they all came through untouched, although one side gunner received a wetting. The formation then pulled up and attacked in a shallow dive. Each aircraft singled out a ship."

Attacks were made on the warships as well as transports, crews reporting possible hits on a cruiser and a destroyer, and near misses on a number of transports. Sgt Jim Thomas, WOp/AG aboard Plt Off Tony Oldworth's Hudson, noted:

> "Attacked Jap convoy — three cruisers, four destroyers, two supply ships — no results seen, too much AA and evasive action. What a shambles! 250 lb GP bombs on armoured vessels!"

All the aircraft survived the attack and returned safely to P.2 despite encountering heavy storms en route. A flarepath consisting of 44 gallon drums of petrol was laid out and all got down without mishap.

Exodus from Singapore — Friday-Monday, 13-16 February

Meanwhile, off the eastern coast of Sumatra, hundreds of evacuees and escapees from Singapore, including women and children, were losing their lives. By the evening of the 13th it was estimated that about 3,000 people had officially been ordered away from Singapore during the preceding few days, whilst as many as 5,000 more had departed by whatever means they could find — gunboats, motor launches, coasters, tugs, harbour launches, yachts, dinghies, tongkans (sailing barges) and sampans — many of these vessels not even seaworthy.

Japanese Naval aircraft — G3Ms and G4Ms from the Mihoro, Genzan and

---

[1] In fact the Blenheim crashed in a swamp about 30 miles south-west of the airfield, where the wreck was to remain undiscovered for over 25 years.

Wooden dummy Buffalo, which must have appeared most convincing to attacking Japanese aircrew.

Kanoya Kokutais, together with F1M floatplanes operating from Muntock and B5Ns from *Ryujo* — were now very active against the shipping leaving Singapore, though little effort was made to interfere with vessels carrying supplies towards the island, presumably as it was considered these would be of immense use to the occupying forces.

The smaller vessels headed for Sumatra, the larger ones making for Batavia — some made it, many did not. Most of those which left Singapore in this period failed to reach freedom — many were shipwrecked amongst the numerous islands south of Singapore, where many died: some were rescued and others were captured. Exact figures will never be known but in excess of 70 steamers and smaller craft were believed to have been sunk, wrecked, abandoned or beached, with civilian and service personnel losses put at between 2,000 and 5,000 (see Table 7 for list of vessels known to have been lost during this period, and Table 8 for list of JNAF claims against these vessels).

A number of senior officials also decided the time was right to leave, including Grp Capt R.L. Nunn, commander of the MVAF and head of the Public Works Department; his request to evacuate had been refused by Lt General A.E. Percival (GOC Malaya) although this did not prevent him from joining his wife aboard a departing ship. Percival did however order Air Vice-Marshal Pulford and Rear-Admiral E.J. Spooner (Rear-Admiral, Malaya) to leave; Pulford's last words to his boss were:

> "I suppose you and I will be held responsible for this, but God knows we
> did our best with what little we had been given."

They and their staffs departed that evening aboard an RAF Fairmile launch, *ML310*. Owing to obstructions and debris in the channel leading from Keppel Harbour, the launch (skippered by Lt J.H. Bull, RNVR, and carrying 44 crew and passengers) ran aground on Takong Reef (just outside the harbour) and was only able to get free on the tide at 0600 next morning. She headed for the Durian Straits at full speed so as not to be caught on the open seas in daylight, and by 1000 had anchored close inshore at Penju, at Sugi Banah island, where she was camouflaged with palm fronds to protect her from prying eyes. That evening the launch continued heading southwards, crossing 35 miles of open sea before two cruisers and two destroyers were observed approaching from the Banka Strait. Lt Bull turned the launch, hoping to retrace his course, but just then five floatplanes appeared, one of which swept down and released two bombs which fell some distance away. *ML310* countered with machine gunfire but then one of the destroyers opened fire, the first shells straddling the launch as it reached the shelter afforded by Lalang Island.

All passengers were landed safely on neighbouring Tjebia Island, whilst Bull and his crew remained on the launch as the destroyer closed in. As it hove to, a motor boat was to put out from it and headed for the shore, two officers and 15 marines boarding *ML310*. Although they wrecked all instruments, electrical and radio fittings and parts of the engines, they did not harm any of the crew, and departed again as quickly as they had arrived. It was hoped that the launch might be repairable but this proved not to be the case. Following a search of the island, a native prahu was discovered — in need of repair — and on the 20th, Lt Bull, two ratings and two Javanese fishermen set out in this to get help. After three days and nights edging down the eastern coast of Sumatra, and then three days (and two nights) crossing the Sunda Strait to Java, they sighted five Allied warships anchored off Merak, and were picked up by a motor launch from an RAN corvette.

When it was learned that the two senior officers were alive on Tjebia, the US submarine *S-39* — which was in the area — was ordered to attempt a rescue of the stranded party. The submarine's commander, Lt James W. Coe, later reported that he had put a search party on the island but that no survivors could be located despite a thorough search. One can only assume that the island visited by *S-39* was not in fact Tjebia. On learning subsequently of Pulford's and Spooner's fate, Vice-Admiral C.E.L. Helfrich (Commander-in-Chief, NEI Navy) commented that had he known of their plight he would have ordered Dutch submarine *K-XIV* — which was also in the area — to effect a rescue.

There was a severe shortage of food on Tjebia, which was rife with malaria, and one by one the survivors were stricken. One of the first to succumb was Air Vice-Marshal Pulford, who died on 10 March. It was later stated that he had kept his loaded revolver by his side, determined that the Japanese should never capture him alive. Rear-Admiral Spooner died about five weeks later, and by the time a Japanese search party arrived towards the end of May to round up survivors, a further 15 had perished, one more dying in hospital on arrival at Singapore.

Meantime, other ships and craft attempted to avoid a similar fate by various means — luck playing a not inconsiderable part. One of these, the small Dutch freighter *Phrontis*, which had earlier arrived at Singapore with six crated Glenn Martins secured to her decks, had departed again with these crates intact, it having proved impossible to unload them. Lashed above the crates, covered with a tarpaulin, was the fuselage of another Glenn Martin which had been slightly damaged in a crash landing at Singapore. When the freighter anchored off a small island at daybreak, volunteers disembarked to cut foliage with which to camouflage the conspicuous crates. She eventually reached Batavia safely.

Another of the vessels crowded with servicemen was the old 4,799-ton freighter *Derrymore*, which was also loaded with ammunition and was carrying six Hurricanes in packing cases amongst her cargo. She had departed Keppel Harbour the previous evening and during the hours of daylight had escaped damage when attacked by bombers, but at 2102 she was hit by two torpedoes fired by the Japanese submarine, *I-55*.

Only nine of the 200 airmen embarked were lost, and the old vessel sank about 90 minutes later, allowing time for the majority to take to liferafts. One party reached a small nearby island, from where they were rescued three days later by the Dutch minesweeper *Cheribon*. Amongst those who had been aboard was Sgt Matt O'Mara of 453 Squadron who, despite two broken ribs, managed to get onto a raft and was rescued after 19 hours at sea by the Australian minesweeper *Ballarat*; also on this raft was Sgt Fred Nash, a WOp/AG on the strength of 4 AACU. The minesweeper also picked up the injured Plt Off John Gorton of 232 Squadron and about 20 others from a smaller raft, half of whom had clung to its sides thoughout the ordeal. Sgt Charlie Wareham, late of 4 PRU, was another survivor of the sinking.

The former Yangtse river steamer *Li Wo*, skippered by Lt T.S. Wilkinson, RNR, had departed Singapore with many passengers on board in addition to her crew. Although repeatedly attacked from the air she had escaped damage, but in the morning ran into part of the Palembang invasion force. Despite the fact that the *Li Wo* was armed with only an old 4-inch gun — for which there were fewer than 40 shells — and two machine guns, Wilkinson decided to attack the nearest transport, which his gunner soon hit, setting it on fire. For an hour-and-a-half the little steamer came under fire from one of the escorting cruisers, and when seriously damaged and with no chance of escaping, Wilkinson decided to ram the damaged transport. *Li Wo* sank and there were only ten survivors; Wilkinson[1] was amongst the 92 who perished, as was a RNZAF pilot, Sgt Ian McDonald.

One small group of departing vessels included *Hung Jao* (a former Hong Kong customs craft), *Kuala* (carrying many women and children) and *Giang Bee* (with many wounded aboard), steaming in convoy and heading for Rengat, on the Indragiri River in Sumatra. At about 1000 the first bombers appeared in the brilliantly clear sky, and *Kuala* was hit almost straight away; she sank not far from Pompong Island, 150 survivors reaching shore including Grp Capt Nunn (late of the MVAF) and his wife. *Giang Bee* was also hit, *Hung Jao* going to her aid despite coming under strafing attack by low-flying bombers. About 70 survivors from *Giang Bee* were taken aboard before she sank, over 220 others being reported missing. Many hours later, as *Hung Jao* progressed slowly towards the mouth of the Indragiri, a voice from the darkness of the water was heard to politely enquire: "Going my way?". The enquirer was Harry Puckridge, DFC, a WWI flying ace turned planter, who was one of the few survivors of another sunken vessel, the minesweeper *Chengteh*, which had been blown out of the water earlier in the day. Of his experience, Puckridge later commented:

> "A mixed party of Army and RAF personnel — 11 officers and 85 other ranks — were on the Yangste River ship when bombs caused heavy casualties among the officers on the top deck and lesser casualties below. One other officer and myself escaped with slight flesh wounds whilst the remainder of the officers were either killed or seriously wounded."

---

[1] In 1946, when the story became fully known, Lt Tom Wilkinson was posthumously awarded the Victoria Cross.

Puckridge and the other officer tended the wounded as best they could but, following a second attack, it was obvious that *Chengteh* was sinking rapidly. He and a few others jumped into the sea, some scrambling aboard a lifeboat which Puckridge was unable to reach, although he did manage to gain a hold on a nearby Carley float:

> "I saw three men getting onto a small outboard motor boat. The ship then dipped its nose and it finally sank nose first. The motor boat must have capsized, possibly due to the suction of the sinking ship. One lifeboat was 150 yards in front of where the ship sank but my float was drifting away at a fair speed.
>
> "I was picked up at 2000 that night, some three miles from the lifeboat, and about 15 miles from an island in the Banka Straits. The lifeboat was picked up four days later."[1]

There had been approximately 40 RAF men amongst the 100 crew and passengers aboard *Chengteh*, about half of whom escaped in the only undamaged lifeboat, the proper complement of which was 22. After almost being swamped in heavy weather, they reached land near the mouth of a river a few days later, but found no fresh water. Ten of the survivors died before rescue came the following day. The Naval officer in charge of the party later commended two airmen in particular — AC2 F. Brown and AC2 C.T. Welsh — whom, he reported, never faltered throughout the ordeal and had set a magnificent example, for which each was awarded a BEM.

Meanwhile *Hung Jao*, having disgorged her passengers at Rengat, departed again in company with *Sungei Pinang*, a small coaster, to pick up survivors stranded on the many islands, but the latter was herself soon attacked and sunk. *Hung Jao* reached Pulau Singkep safely, where the crew commandeered five junks to search the nearby islands. Several hundred survivors were rescued and conveyed to Singkep, and a further 90 were taken to Rengat.

Following aerial attack, when about half of those on board the gunboat *Grasshopper* were killed, the vessel was beached on a small, uninhabited island (Sebayer) where it caught fire and blew up. Amongst the survivors were six Japanese airmen prisoners who had been shot down over Singapore, of whom one survivor wrote:

> "The Japanese prisoners were magnificent. All pretence of guarding them was dropped and they went around calmly and efficiently helping the wounded."

Two of the pregnant women passengers gave birth on the beach, both baby boys being delivered safely by the gunboat's coxswain, after whom they were both named by their grateful mothers! Another survivor was 'Judy', the ship's dog (a pointer). Little food was salvaged from the wreck but no water, and the island was searched in vain until 'Judy' discovered a fresh spring. After several days a passing Chinese junk picked up the stranded party and took them to the Sumatran eastern coast. Endeavouring to reach Padang on the western coast, from where they hoped to be evacuated, the survivors ran into Japanese troops

---

[1] Sqn Ldr H.V. Puckeridge later operated the Jungle Training School at Ceylon, as part of the Escape Group of MI.9

Japanese personnel inspect abandoned Buffalo AN196, WP-N, late of 243 Squadron, at Kallang, Singapore. *(64th Sentai Assoc; RAF Museum via A. Thomas)*

and were captured, including 'Judy'.[1]

Another victim of air attack was the small steamer *Vyner Brooke*, which sank off the Sumatran coast. Amongst the 240 crew and passengers on board were 65 members of the Australian Nursing Service, a dozen of whom were either killed during the attack, or drowned. Of the survivors, 22 nurses and a number of wounded men, in a leaking liferaft, reached Banka Island. A party of Japanese soldiers intercepted them almost immediately and dragged away the wounded, bayoneting them to death. The nurses were then ordered to walk into the sea, where they were all shot, the bodies being left where they fell. One, Sister Vivian Bullwinkel, feigned death after being wounded and later managed to crawl from the scene of carnage, into nearby jungle. After a few days she was forced to give herself up owing to pain and hunger. Thus, only 32 of the 65

---

[1] 'Judy' accompanied the party into captivity, and following many escapades and narrow escapes from death, survived to be liberated in 1945. She was awarded the Dickin Medal (the animal VC) for services to POWs, in helping to maintain morale among fellow prisoners.

nurses survived the journey from Singapore and of these, eight would die later in prison camps.

During the afternoon of the 15th, one of the Air-Sea-Rescue launches (*HSL 105*) which had departed Singapore with AHQ staff on board, including Air Commodore C.O.F. Modin, Grp Capt E.B. Rice (former AOC 224 Group), Wg Cdr R.A. Chignell (former OC Kallang) and Sqn Ldrs Wilf Clouston and Frank Howell, former commanders of 488 and 243 Squadrons respectively, was attacked seven times in the Banka Strait. A direct bomb hit after about 20 minutes severely damaged the craft, a splinter instantly killing the popular and respected Chignell; his body was put over the side. One other passenger was wounded and the craft caught fire. The crew and passengers were picked up by two small steamers — *Rentau* and *Relau* — but both were intercepted and captured at dawn, all aboard becoming prisoners (Grp Capt Rice died in a prison camp in 1943).

Unserviceable Hurricane IIb on an airfield occupied by the 64th Sentai. *(64th Sentai Assoc)*

One of the last to leave Singapore was none other than the commander of the Australian troops, Lt General H. Gordon Bennett, who had decided his services would be of better use elsewhere. Departing without informing Lt General Percival of his impending action, he and two of his staff officers set out to find means of escape. A small sampan was located in the harbour, the three Australians joining eight civilians aboard this; some way out into the harbour a tongkan was commandeered, the Chinese captain reluctantly agreeing to take the party to Sumatra; seven swimming soldiers — obviously also deserters — were picked up, and the craft set sail at 0100. By daybreak it was realised that the tongkan was in fact heading back towards Singapore, at which the captain and his crew were locked in a hold, and one of the evaders took over control. Slow progess was made until, on the 19th, a launch was sighted and hailed to stop. Gordon Bennett and his two aides transferred to this and reached Djambi by the evening of the 21st.

After resting there for the night, Gordon Bennett's party set off by car for

Padang (a three day drive), where contact with General Sir Archibald Wavell (C-in-C ABDA Command) was made by phone. Wavell agreed to send a Dutch Lodestar to collect them, this arriving at Padang after dark on the 24th. On arrival at Batavia they were driven to Bandoeng, only to find that Wavell and his staff had already departed for India! Heading for Tjilatjap instead, Gordon Bennett was frustrated to find that he could not officially obtain passage to Australia aboard a departing Qantas flyingboat, although the captain of *Coriolanus* (VH-ABG), Capt L.R. Ambrose, turned a blind eye to him and his aides stowing away on board! Gordon Bennett was not received favourably on his arrival in Australia, particularly when details of his unauthorised escape became known, and he was not offered another operational command.

Table 7			
Vessels Lost Trying to Escape from Singapore, 13-17 February:			
13 February:			**killed/missing**
HMM/L *Andrew*	launch	last seen Rengat	?
SS *Derrymore*	steamer	torpedoed	21
HMS *Giang Bee*	auxiliary	bombed & sunk	223
HMM/L *Kulit*	launch	missing	?
Merula	tanker	bombed & sunk	42
HMM/L *Pengail*	launch	missing	?
SS *Redang*	steamer	naval gunfire	58
SS *Subadar*	steamer	bombed & sunk	many
HMS *Siang Wo*	auxiliary	bombed & beached	1
SS *Sui Wo*	boom ship	bombed & sunk	?
HMS *Shun An*	auxiliary	missing	?
HMS *Scorpion*	gunboat	bombed & damaged; sunk by naval gunfire	115
14 February:			
HMS *Chengteh*	minesweeper	bombed & sunk	68
HMS *Dragonfly*	gunboat	bombed & sunk	135
HMS *Grasshopper*	gunboat	bombed & beached	165
HMS *Kuala*	auxiliary	bombed & sunk	50
HMS *Kung Wo*	minelayer	bombed & abandoned	1
HMS *Li Wo*	auxiliary	naval gunfire	92
HMS *Sin Aik Lee*	auxiliary	missing	?
Manvantara	tanker	bombed & sunk	?
HMM/L *Osprey*	launch	abandoned	0
HMS *Shu Kwang*	auxiliary	bombed & sunk	20
Pengawal	tug	bombed & sunk	?
St Breock	tug	bombed & sunk	1
St Just	tug	bombed & sunk	?
Wo Kwang	tug	missing	?
HMS *Tien Kwang*	auxiliary	bombed & sunk	?
Vyner Brooke	coaster	bombed & sunk	353
SS *Sungei Pinang*	steamer	bombed & sunk	?
HMS *Lipis*	armed trader	missing	?
HMS *Trang*	auxiliary	bombed & abandoned	?

Table 7 (Continued)

15 February:

Blumut	tug	captured Banka	0
HMS *Fuh Wo*	minesweeper	beached/blown up	0
HMM/L *Hung Jao*	launch	scuttled Rengat	0
HMS *Malacca*	minelayer	scuttled Rengat	0
HMS *Mata Hari*	auxiliary	captured Banka	0
HMM/L *Pahlawan*	launch	captured Banka	2
HMM/L *Penghambat*	launch	missing	?
HMM/L *Peningat*	launch	missing	?
Tingarro	yacht	captured Rengat	0
Ying Ping	tug	naval gunfire	57
HMM/L *311*	launch	naval gunfire	58
HMM/L *433*	launch	naval gunfire	71
HMM/L *310*	launch	beached Tjibea	0
HMM/L *105*	ASR launch	bombed/captured Banka	1
Pinnace 53	ASR launch	captured Banka	1
Pinnace 54	ASR launch	naval gunfire	6
ST257	ASR launch	captured Banka	0
ST258	ASR launch	captured Banka	2
MT941	ASR launch	captured Banka	0
Vaillant	tug	missing	?

16 February:

M/L *Cecelia*	launch	missing	?
Elizabeth	tug	naval gunfire	24
HMM/L *Fanling*	launch	naval gunfire	44
HMM/L *1062*	launch	naval gunfire	38
HMM/L *36*	launch	captured Banka	1
HMS *Pulo Soegi*	auxiliary	naval gunfire	55
SS *Relau*	coaster	captured Banka	0
SS *Rentau*	coaster	captured Banka	0
Pro Patria	Dutch minelayer	bombed & sunk	61

17 February:

HMS *Dymas*	auxiliary	captured Banka	0
HMS *Tapah*	minesweeper	captured Banka	0
HMS *Tanjong Pinang*	auxiliary	naval gunfire	164
HMS *Jarak*	minesweeper	bombed & sunk	?
M/L *Excise*	launch	captured Banka	0
M/L *Hong Fatt*	launch	captured Banka	1
SS *Mary Rose*	coaster	captured Banka	0
M/L *Mary Rose*	launch	captured Banka	0
HMM/L *432*	launch	captured Banka	0

A miscellany of small craft including many sampans and tongkans were also lost. Many fatalities also occurred aboard escaping vessels which were attacked and damaged but succeeded in reaching Sumatra or Java.

Table 8

JNAF claims against the fleeing ships:

13 February:

Ryujo's Air Group (B5Ns): 10,000 ton vessel sunk	10,000 ton vessel burned
	7,000 ton vessel burned
	8,000 ton vessel damaged
	6,000 ton vessel damaged
	800 ton vessel damaged
	700 ton vessel damaged
	small vessel damaged
Genzan, Mihoro and Kanoya Ku:	transport sunk
(G3Ms and G4Ms)	transport damaged

14 February:

Ryujo's Air Group:	torpedo boat tender sunk
	8,000 ton vessel sunk
	1,500 ton special task vessel sunk
	800 ton gunboat sunk
	transport damaged
	minesweeper damaged
Genzan, Mihoro and Kanoya Ku:	2 transports sunk
	minelayer sunk
	4 transports damaged
	minelayer damaged
	2 transports beached
	minelayer beached
F1Ms (operating from Muntok)	submarine sunk
	torpedo boat burned
	transport damaged
	gunboat damaged

15 February:

Ryujo's Air Group:	7,000 ton vessel damaged
	heavy cruiser burned
F1Ms (from Muntok):	gunboat sunk
	transport burned
	2 gunboats damaged

16 February:

Ryujo's Air Group:	200 ton vessel badly damaged
	600 ton vessel attacked & abandoned

Chapter 2

THE FALL OF SUMATRA
Saturday-Monday, 14-16 February

Hurricane IIB, BE332, of 258 Squadron on P.1 airfield, Palembang. This aircraft was later allocated to 605 Squadron and was shot down on 25 February. *(C.T.R. Kelly via A. Thomas)*

Dawn on Saturday 14th found the Palembang area in a high state of tension as word of the approaching invasion fleet began to spread. At P.1 the Hurricane pilots were in good spirits however, following the successes of the previous day; the number of aircraft available had also improved considerably with the arrival of the reinforcements from Java. 232 Squadron had about a dozen fighters on hand and 258 Squadron eight more; of these, 15 had been made serviceable and were ready to take the air.

Early reconnaissance revealed that the Japanese vessels had entered the Banka Strait and, as soon as it was light enough, all 15 Hurricanes were ordered off to escort nine Blenheims of 84 Squadron and six more of 211 Squadron (from P.2), the bomber crews having been briefed to attack an aircraft carrier which was reportedly accompanying the convoy. Meanwhile, shortly before first light, five Hudsons of 8 RAAF Squadron began taking off from P.2, including one flown by Flg Off Bob Richards' attached RAF crew; Richards had difficulty in getting AM952 airborne, clipping the treetops at the end of the runway, sheering off the ends of the propeller blades and knocking off both wingtips! Severe damage was caused to the nose section and fuselage.

Richards immediately ordered the crew to bale out but all declined as the aircraft was only a few feet above the jungle canopy. Instead, Sgt Longworth jettisoned the bombs, which allowed the crippled machine to gain altitude and enabled the pilot to hold it on a level keel. Gradually, as it gained height and the pilot's confidence returned, Richards gently turned the Hudson back towards P.2, only to find the airfield obscured by early morning mist. Unable to attempt a landing there, he headed instead for P.1, where a creditable touchdown was made, as recalled by his very relieved observer, Sgt Longworth:

"A feat of flying — after the initial error — that, in my belief, has never been surpassed. This I must say, because when he stopped his engines, it was to be seen that both wing tips were missing and at least three feet of each airscrew on both engines had been sheered clean off. Not only that, but the pieces missing were in separate large lumps, some of which were in the nose although the rest had found their way through the fuselage, missing both Bobby and I by inches.

"A host of ground crew gathered round the aircraft, all of whom were in the nose although the rest had found their way through the fuselage, missing both Bobby an I by inches.

"A host of ground crew gathered round the aircraft, all of whom were of the opinion that aerodynamically it was impossible for the aircraft to stay in the air as there was no 'bite' on the props to obtain the necessary lift!"

The Hudsons flown by Flt Lt Marshall and Flt Lt Plenty (AE553) proceeded to bomb a cruiser off the north of Banka Island, although no hits were claimed. Meanwhile, Flt Lt Ken Maynard attacked transports near Panjaram Island, only to suffer a failure with the bomb release mechanism; he then carried out a reconnaissance to the south of Muntok. On approaching P.2 he realised that the airfield was under attack so instead flew to Lahat, where he landed safely.

Six Hudsons of 1 RAAF Squadron took off in two waves to attack a Japanese force approaching the Moesi River, estimated as one battleship, three or four cruisers, seven destroyers and between 25 to 30 transports; an aircraft carrier (*Ryujo*) was reported to be about 60 miles behind the convoy. On their way to the target both flights of Hudsons were attacked by fighters over Palembang, but managed to evade these. Nearer the target area they were again attacked by fighters — on this occasion correctly identified as 'Navy 0s' — as in fact air cover for the convoy as it approached Sumatra was indeed provided by A6Ms of the 22nd Air Flotilla operating from Kahang airfield, in southern Malaya. By making use of cloud cover the Hudsons again escaped and reached the convoy, which they attempted to attack, but were then once more beset by the Japanese fighters.

Flt Lt Jim Douglas (A16-85) carried out a diving attack from out of the sun on a transport, then climbed back and carried out another. At this point his aircraft was seen to burst into flames and dive into the sea; there were no survivors, although one member of the crew was seen to bale out, but shortly after his parachute opened he fell into the burning wreckage. Flt Lt John O'Brien (A16-23), who was in the same flight, reported three hits on the transport he attacked, which was seen to fall out of line, listing to starboard and on fire.

When the other flight of Hudsons attacked, Flt Lt Diamond (A16-48) reported two direct hits on the stern of another transport, whilst Flt Lt Williams' crew in A16-54 claimed a further hit and Flt Lt Brydon (A16-17) yet two more direct hits and a near miss, on their respective targets; Brydon's aircraft was badly damaged by machine gunfire and shrapnel, although he managed to get back to P.2. During his attack Diamond's aircraft was pursued by two A6Ms, which fired on the Hudson continuously, putting its starboard engine out of action and shooting away its starboard wheel. By taking the crippled bomber down to 100 feet Diamond succeeded in flying to P.1 on its one good engine, where he carried out a crash-landing.

The loss of the leadership of Flt Lt Jim Douglas would be felt immediately within 1 RAAF Squadron; his commanding officer, Wg Cdr R.H. Davis, unhesitatingly recommended him for a posthumous award of the Victoria Cross:

> "From the outwardly quiet disposition which was his notable feature whilst peace reigned in Malaya, he rapidly displayed fine qualities as a leader from the first night he and his flight went into action at Kota Bharu. He was a lad of considerable courage, capable of clear thinking and above all, a companion to all his officers.
>
> "Without doubt he was an outstanding flight commander and imbued in his flight a similar spirit and high morale. Deeply as all other losses in the squadron were felt, his had a deeper effect. His approach to the attack and determination in his last task, as described by Flt Lt J.T. O'Brien, has caused me to recommend him for the highest award."

Those in high authority deemed not to agree; however the award of the DFC, recommended earlier, was promulgated a few weeks after his death.

The next attack on the convoy was carried out by a further five Hudsons, a mixed formation comprising three aircraft of 62 Squadron and two of 1 RAAF Squadron, which departed P.2 at 1045. They proceeded up the coast to the Bantang Hari River and then out towards the convoy, but soon after sighting this were attacked by a number of A6Ms. The two Australian-crewed Hudsons pressed on and simultaneously dived on separate ships, but then Flt Lt Lockwood's aircraft (A16-21) was seen to be losing height immediately afterwards, with smoke pouring from one engine and two fighters on its tail; it crashed into the sea with the loss of all aboard. Only one aircraft out of this formation returned, Flg Off Gibbes (A16-42) having claimed a direct hit on the transport he attacked.

Similar fates had overtaken the crews of two of the 62 Squadron machines. The A6Ms apparently shot down the Hudsons flown by Plt Offs Richard Johnson and John Robinson (AE592) as they approached the target; both crews perished. The third aircraft, V9233 flown by Plt Off Pat Anderson, was badly damaged and was chased back towards Banka Island, where it ditched in the sea just off the coast; the crew scrambled to safety but became separated, although the observer and one of the gunners later joined forces once ashore.[1]

---

[1] Two days later, escapees from Singapore aboard the motor yacht *White Swan* spotted a lone figure waving a stick amongst the rocks of a small islet, which turned out to be Anderson. Nursing an injured leg, he had been without food or water for 48 hours, and he was soon picked up. Later the same day a sampan from Banka sailed out to meet the yacht, on board which was a member of Anderson's crew, Sgt Eddie Baxter. The other two members of the crew — Sgts Allan Tearnan and Joe Mercer — having survived the ditching, were reportedly murdered by a band of Chinese bandits.

Left: Flt Lt John Lockwood, RAAF, pilot of Hudson A16-21 of 1 RAAF Squadron, which was lost on 14 February, shot down by A6Ms of the 22nd Air Flotilla whilst attempting to attack the Palembang invasion convoy. *(W. Panckridge)*. Right: Sqn Ldr James Thomson, commanding officer of 258 Squadron. *(Sqn Ldr A.H. Milnes)*

At least four of the missing Hudsons had fallen victim to the A6Ms of the 22nd Air Flotilla, whose pilots reported a total of 10 victories between 1235 and 1400, while the fifth aircraft was probably shot down by ships' AA fire. Although the names of the successful pilots are unknown, it is probable that claims were submitted by NAP 2/C Keisaku Yoshimura and NAP 1/C Kozaburo Yasui.

While the Hudson formation was being so savagely mauled, the Hurricanes wasted an invaluable quarter of an hour at the rendezvous before the 211 Squadron Blenheims finally arrived, but not those from 84 Squadron. Unable to delay further, the formation at last set course for its target, the Hurricanes spending 45 uneventful minutes flying through masses of broken cloud. The vessels were sighted and Wg Cdr Bateson (Z7855) led his bombers down to attack, bombing from about 8,000 feet; the returning crews claimed damage to a number of transports. In fact the 989-ton *Inabasan Maru* was sunk, and several others suffered damage from direct hits and subsequent fire.

Meanwhile, Sqn Ldr Passmore's 84 Squadron formation had arrived over P.1 to rendezvous with the Hurricane escort, only to find the sky void of aircraft and the airfield apparently deserted. Sgt Archie Wakefield, flying in Flt Lt Wyllie's aircraft (T2249), recalled:

"P.1 looked deserted, and a red Very light was fired from the ground. The flight then set course for the coast. Soon after leaving P.1, a large number of aircraft flew past in the opposite direction, and soon afterwards I saw paratroops falling on P.1. The Japanese must have taken us as their own aircraft returning from the dropping zone!"

Sgt Allan Ross, airgunner aboard Sgt Sayer's aircraft (Z9723), also witnessed the arrival of the paratroops:

> "As we flew out from P.1, our plane was 'tail-end Charlie', parallel and incoming at about 2,000 feet, large Jap transports passed and I watched in amazement to see the parachutists released over P.1.
>
> "Above the transports were many Jap fighters and not one fighter veered from his obvious task of protecting the drop, thus leaving us completely alone."

Sgt Wakefield continued:

> "We proceeded out to sea, and eventually located a squadron of the Jap navy headed by a battleship. There was no sign of an aircraft carrier, and so the bombs were dropped from about 6,000 feet. No direct hits were seen. On leaving the area, we came upon the aircraft carrier on its own, but there were no bombs left."

Flt Lt Holland however, did carry out an attack on *Ryujo*, and recalled:

> "We found the aircraft carrier in a calm sea under the tropic sun. As we approached, the Japanese warships in support opened fire. We made our bombing run but were disappointed to see all our bombs fall into the sea close by the carrier."

With the bombers on their way home, Sqn Ldr Thomson — the fighter formation leader — ordered all Hurricanes to return to base. As they approached the Palembang area, they entered dense cloud, the two squadrons becoming separated. Several of the aircraft were plagued with faulty radios and communications became extremely difficult. Suddenly, through gaps in the clouds, several pilots spotted groups of Japanese aircraft milling around over the airfield. Calling out warnings, individual pilots — although short of fuel — broke formation and dived to the attack.

What they were seeing was much more than just another bombing attack. 460 paratroops of the 2nd Parachute Regiment had recently moved to Southern Malaya, and at dawn 270 of these had embarked in 34 Ki 56s (licence-built Lockheed 14s) and Ki 57 transport aircraft of the 1st, 2nd and 3rd Chutais of the Parachute Flying Unit. Accompanied by seven more transports of the 12th Transport Chutai, the force had taken off for Palembang, led by Maj Niihara. Taking up station behind a formation of 18 Ki 21 bombers of the 98th Sentai, which were to drop anti-personnel bombs ahead of the paratroop landings, and nine other Ki 21s loaded with supplies, the whole formation was escorted by a strong force of Ki 43s from the 59th and 64th Sentais.

Amongst those on the airfield horrified at the sight of the descending parachutists, were the crew of a Hudson which had just landed. Realising the situation in which they would soon find themselves, the Hudson pilot invited all air and ground crew around his aircraft to climb aboard, as he was about to make a hurried departure for P.2. Included in this party were three members of Flg Off Richards' Hudson crew, who felt obvious remorse at leaving their own skipper behind, as he had left them with their unserviceable Hudson while he reported to Airfield Control.

Earlier, as the force of Hurricanes and Blenheims had been heading out towards the Banka Strait, 226 Group HQ had received a warning from an

Mitsubishi Ki 21 bombers of the 60th Sentai leave their burning target.

Mitsubishi Ki 21 bombers of the 98th Sentai (upper foreground) with Ki 56s (licence-built Lockheed 14s) of the Parachute Flying Unit beyond them, at slightly lower level, arrive over Palembang on 14 February. *(Authors' collection)*

observer post 100 miles north of Palembang, that a large formation of big, low-flying aircraft was approaching. By chance on this morning, Air Commodore Vincent had not gone out to P.1, and at once arranged for the airfield defence officer to be warned to expect a paratroop assault, ordering that rifles and ammunition be issued forthwith. These were scarce, however; before leaving England, most of the RAF ground staff had been issued with rifles and bayonets but, on arrival in the East Indies, these had been taken away and handed over to the Army. As a result about 100 of the men at P.1 remained unarmed — to their considerable peril as it was to transpire. There were no British Army units based in Sumatra other than the crews of the anti-aircraft guns around Palembang and P.1. although some Dutch troops — mainly native levies — were available; two infantry platoons were stationed at each of the main oil refineries at Pladjoe and Soengi Gerong, while three companies were in reserve at P.2, and others were at P.1 and in Palembang town itself.

Shortly after Vincent's warning had been received, the Japanese attack developed, the Ki 21s dropping anti-personnel bombs which caused a number of casualties, while the 64th Sentai's Ki 43s strafed the airfield and buildings; 13 Ki 48 light bombers of the 90th Sentai which had flown to the area independently, then attacked barracks as the paratroopers began to leap from their transports. Some 180 landed in the scrub between the airfield and the town, while another 90, led by Lt Kikuo Nakao, came down to the west of the oil refineries at Pladjoe, on the south bank of the Moesi River, the second major target for their attack.

Palembang town and P.1 airfield were only lightly defended, a few Bofors guns providing the main defence. Wg Cdr Ken Powell, a former 62 Squadron Blenheim pilot and more recently SASO 225 (Bomber) Group, was acting in the capacity of O/C P.1; he happened to be on the perimeter of the airfield when the attack commenced, and went to assist a Bofors gun crew but a shell exploded in the breach of the gun, killing an airman outright and wounding others, including Powell, who suffered injuries to his legs.

By now the Blenheims and Hurricanes were approaching the area, the bombers actually flying through the falling paratroops as they headed for their airfield at P.2. At 226 Group HQ, Grp Capt H.S. Darley broadcast an urgent message to the Hurricane pilots, warning of the landings and ordering them to head instead for P.2. Due to the trouble with their radio receivers, several of the pilots failed to receive the message. It was at this stage that they approached the airfield and first saw the hostile aircraft ahead of them.

Plt Off Bill Lockwood and his No 2, Sgt Ian Fairbairn, observed three formations of 27 bombers and transports, together with 15-20 Ki 43s. Lockwood was unable to contact the rest of the Hurricane formation over the radio, but as he had height advantage, he decided to dive on the leading aircraft. Opening fire, he hit the bomber and possibly holed its fuel tanks, but did not stay to observe results; his victim was possibly Lt Naohiko Sudoh's Ki 21 which was shot down during this operation, although Japanese records suggest it was a victim of AA fire. Lockwood levelled out at low altitude and ran straight into a torrential rainstorm, but managed to find the Moesi River and followed this to Palembang, closely followed by Fairbairn. On coming out of the rain over the airfield, they saw many white objects and suspected that paratroops had landed. As they flew low over the airfield they received a red Very light — a warning not to land — and continued on to P.2.

Although low on fuel, Sgt Gordon Dunn — amongst others — flew around the airfield, strafing the paratroops where he could, having heard the warning that the base was under attack. After using most of his ammunition, Dunn saw several aircraft he thought were Hudsons, dropping bombs at the far end of the runway. He assumed that they were attacking the paratroops, only discovering later that they were, in fact, Japanese bombers.

Some of the pilots — including Flg Off Art Donahue — tried to engage the Ki 43s. The American got his first glimpse of the enemy when his No 2 broke away to give chase:

> "A few seconds later I looked back to see a 'Navy Zero' (*sic*) diving down on me, his big stubby round nose and silver-coloured propeller-spinner identifying him as enemy even at quite a distance. Another was following him. I opened my throttle and swung round hard to face him. I was facing

him before he could get into firing range and I thought it was going to be a head-on show, both of us coming straight at each other, shooting, seeing who would give way first before we collided; but he didn't seem to want that now that he'd lost his chance for surprise.

"Before we were in firing range of each other, he zoomed up away. His partner behind did likewise. They had all the advantage of height and speed, so there was nothing I could do about it, and I lost track of them."

After delivering attacks on various groups of bombers, during which his own aircraft was damaged, Flg Off Macnamara headed back towards Palembang. There he caught sight of, high above, another group of aircraft, which he thought were Hurricanes, and endeavoured to reach them. Before he could gain altitude however, he was 'jumped' by three Ki 43s of the 64th Sentai, the pilots of which reported intercepting a lone Hurricane. The Rhodesian had seen the three fighters well above him, but had assumed that they were making for the other Hurricanes, and had in fact tried to warn the latter that they were about to be attacked.

The Ki 43s came down at great speed, in a 'Prince of Wales' feathers formation, and opened fire, many bullets striking Macnamara's aircraft, which the Japanese pilots claimed to have shot down. The Hurricane tumbled out of the sky, streaming oil and glycol, and Macnamara prepared to bale out; he later wrote:

"Now a very strange thing happened to me. I lost no time in undoing the Sutton harness, pulled off my helmet and was all ready to bale out when some warning came to me — call it what you may — I maintain it was from the Good Lord, for it was so urgent and so life-like that I abandoned the idea of jumping, and glided down, force-landing on the edge of our own aerodrome.[1]

"The warning was in the form of two words — 'don't jump' — loud and clear, and not to be denied. On my glide down I thought plenty. The aircraft might have burst into flames at any moment; my body had the peculiar feeling one gets when warm blood trickles over one's skin — this was due to a goodly burst on the armour plating protecting my back — feeling inside my shirt and trousers I was amazed to find no trace of blood at all! I felt better now and concentrated on getting down safely, and getting down quick!

"As I climbed out and started to make my way across the 'drome, Mick Nash came running over and his first greeting was 'what the hell have you made your way back here for, you fool!'. I was, not unreasonably, annoyed and lost no time in telling him so. He then told me about the bombing and strafing all around the 'drome soon after we had left, and of the dropping of paratroops, who were then busily engaged in closing in on the aerodrome, and how all the pilots had been warned through their radios, while still in the air, to make their way to P.2.

"I then realised that had I jumped out of my aircraft, as was my intention,

---

[1] In the course of the crash-landing 'Ting' Macnamara injured his back, resulting in the protrusion of an intervertebral disc, and eventually spondylitis was diagnosed; he would later undergo surgery but was left severely disabled, and his premature death in his native Rhodesia followed more than three years of hospitalization.

I would have ended up with the paratroops who had, evidently, landed on three sides of the aerodrome. Because of my faulty wireless I had heard nothing of these events. My bullet-ridden tub being out of the question, I scouted around to try and get another aircraft, but there was nothing serviceable."

Flg Off Ting Macnamara of 258 Squadron, who was shot down by 64th Sentai Ki-43s over Palembang on 14 February. *(Sqn Ldr A.H. Milnes)*

Macnamara's damaged Hurricane was only the first of several which landed at P.1, Sgts Lambert and Kelly, both of whom had unserviceable radios, being the next to arrive. Kelly, flying with 258 Squadron's formation, had no suspicion of danger when the Hurricanes flew over a formation of Ki 56 transports at close range, as he took these to be Hudsons. A few minutes later however, he saw an aircraft doing a roll off the top of a loop, and recognized this as hostile. Leaving his place in formation, he flew up alongside Sqn Ldr Thomson and waggled his wings, but the latter waved him back. Dropping behind, Kelly broke away to climb after the intruder, noting that another Hurricane had done the same. He then saw below him three or four aircraft, one a Hurricane but the others Japanese — probably Macnamara and his attackers.

Kelly fired at one without effect, then overshot it. It turned in behind him and a low-level chase "all across southern Sumatra" followed, before he finally managed to shake off his pursuer. He then headed for P.1 to land but, as he approached, spotted a Ki 43 climbing near the airfield:

"The next half-hour or more was a busy one during which I was chased twice over Palembang at treetop and rooftop height by Japanese fighters, shot one down, made attempts to shoot down two others and finally, almost out of petrol, landed at P.1 to discover it queerly deserted."

Just as he switched off his engine, Lambert taxied in and parked next to him; the latter recalled:

"We saw Mick Nash running out to meet us and he gave us the news of the paratroop attack, saying the base was surrounded and telling us of the instructions to land at P.2. Nash put himself at great personal risk to give us this information, as he was completely exposed on the aerodrome to any fire which the paratroopers may have been able to direct towards him.

"A check on fuel indicated virtually empty tanks, but as the lesser of two evils, I taxied out and prepared to take-off for P.2, which was only a short distance away. Kelly did the same. Fortunately we were not attacked by ground fire as we took-off."

Within a few minutes of their departure four more Hurricanes arrived over the airfield and came in to land. These were not from the returning bomber escorts however, but were the survivors of nine replacement aircraft being ferried up from Batavia. These nine aircraft, led by Flt Lt John Hutcheson of 488 Squadron, had set out from Tjililitan airfield at 0700 and, in addition to the six pilots from 232 and 258 Squadrons, there were two further 488 Squadron pilots, Flg Off Noel Sharp and Sgt Jim Meharry. It had been the intention to take-off at 0600, in an attempt to avoid being caught by the regular Japanese raiders, but the departure had been delayed due to transport problems in Batavia.

Once airborne from Tjililitan, Plt Off Jimmy Parker soon discovered that his aircraft had an unserviceable compressor but decided to carry on notwithstanding this. As the flight approached Palembang, these pilots also saw a number of twin-engined aircraft which were initially thought to be Hudsons; however, they soon saw the descending paratroops. The Hurricanes, down to about 15 minutes' fuel, scattered as the escorting Ki 43s converged on them. Plt Off Bill McCulloch's aircraft was hit almost immediately by fire from two of the fighters, the first burst wounding him in the left leg, the second in the right leg and arm and also shooting the tail assembly off his aircraft. As the Hurricane was only a few feet above the jungle, the Australian had no time to bale out, and the aircraft crashed inverted into the trees, shedding a wing.

The fact that his aircraft then fell into a swamp saved McCulloch from further injury. He was able to release himself from the wreck, despite his wounds, then managed to remove the aircraft's compass and, having done so, set out through the dense undergrowth. Failing to make much progress, he returned to the Hurricane, extracted the dinghy, and set out on another course. After many hours of slow and painful travel through the mosquito-infested jungle, he came across a small area of water, and there inflated the dinghy. He soon reached a large river and paddled across, meeting some natives on the other side who took him to their village, where he received some beer and cigarettes, then after about two hours, a Dutch army truck arrived and took him to Palembang. By a strange coincidence, the other McCulloch (258 Squadron's 'Jock') had been shot down in similar circumstances a few days earlier.

Sgt Art Sheerin was also engaged by three Ki 43s, which he managed to evade, but his engine then stopped and he ditched in the Moesi River:

> "According to the manual on ditching, the flaps should have come off on impact. Well they didn't — I did three beautiful take-offs and on the final landing I sank like a stone. After drinking half the river, I surfaced, got into the dinghy and made for the bank."

He met some natives who agreed to take him by small boat to Palembang, although on the way they were intercepted by a Dutch naval patrol boat and he was taken to their nearby Mess, where he found another of the downed Hurricane pilots, Plt Off Campbell; both were then transported to P.2 to rejoin their colleagues. Two other Hurricanes, flown by Hutcheson and Sharp, were also forced to crash-land in the jungle, the former's aircraft coming down in a swamp, where it overturned. Although both pilots suffered shock, neither was injured and, by various means, made their respective ways to safety. The 64th Sentai was undoubtedly involved in the attack on the reinforcement Hurricanes, the unit recording that after the initial success against Macnamara's aircraft, ten

Hurricanes were attacked and two claimed shot down, one by Major Tateo Kato.

Parker, meanwhile, avoided a similar fate by using cloud cover and, as soon as he considered it safe to land, he dived for the ground at high speed, lowered his undercarriage and flaps, and dropped on to the runway. As the Hurricane rolled to a stop — without the benefit of brake power — a Dutch NCO gestured for him to take cover. By this time Plt Off Nash, in his capacity as Duty Pilot, was becoming frantic and, as the last Hurricane rolled in, he jumped into a car and rushed over to warn the pilots. All four aircraft were in need of fuel and it was necessary to arrange for a petrol tanker to come out. The pilots and ground crews felt conspicuous and exposed, expecting the paratroops to burst onto the airfield at any moment, but the aircraft were refuelled safely — in all probability in record time!

As the four pilots prepared to take-off again, they were advised that Flt Lt Ivan Julian was on his way to guide them to P.2. Immediately his aircraft arrived, he circled the airfield and waited for the others to join him; all five aircraft reached P.2 without further event, where Parker indicated to the others that he would land last since he could not steer his aircraft on the ground. He flew an extra circuit as he watched the others land:

> "To my horror, two of them bounced violently as they touched down on the bumpy surface. The under-cart of one failed and it leant over on one wing; the other stood on its nose."

Parker, despite his trepidation, landed safely. He spent most of the remainder of the day, with the aid of two mechanics, removing the compressor from one of the damaged aircraft and fitting it to his own Hurricane.

At P.1 meanwhile, Wg Cdr Maguire had positioned those men who were armed, including the defence sections of 242, 258 and 605 Squadrons. Ground personnel stripped Browning machine guns from unserviceable aircraft and mounted these on mounds of earth, while the Bofors anti-aircraft crews prepared to fire their guns horizontally, over open sights. In all, about 200 men were dispersed in groups, mainly on the road from Palembang which bounded the airfield and continued to Djambi.

After the various Hurricanes had landed, refuelled and been despatched to P.2, a number of Army officers arrived to inspect the positions and give advice. They had their own headquarters about a mile down the road to Palembang, but reported that after firing at the parachutists as they descended, they too had had no further contact with the enemy. For the airfield defenders the waiting seemed to go on for ever; the telephone lines to Palembang had been cut by the Japanese, so there was no contact with the town. Finally, more Army officers appeared and advised the defenders that orders had been given to retire to Palembang. For Maguire it seemed a good opportunity to get his pilots and unarmed personnel out of the trap, and consequently a number of cars and lorries were prepared ready to leave for the town.

Much confused action then ensued. The Japanese had concentrated their forces between Palembang and the airfield, Lt Minoru Okumoto's section having thrown a block across the road about a mile or so from the latter. Subsequent reports indicated that this was cleared at least once, but re-established later. Some vehicles managed to get through but others did not. Certainly much of the main action for the rest of the day centred around this location.

For example, Flg Off Macnamara of 258 Squadron was offered a lift into Palembang with two other officers and a warrant officer; they drove at top speed, the doors of the car slightly open and their revolvers drawn, but managed to get through unscathed. They arrived at 226 Group HQ to find the place deserted and the telephone lines ripped out.

After broadcasting his warning to the Hurricanes not to land at P.1, Grp Capt Darley had joined a party from HQ to drive out to the airfield to assess the situation. Approaching the area, they came under fire from ambush and, as they had only a couple of revolvers between them, retired to organise a properly-armed relief party. On returning to town, Darley was ordered to remain in Palembang to sort out the fighter situation at P.2, where an Operations Room was to be set up anew.

From P.1 meanwhile, Sqn Ldr Brooker of 232 Squadron — together with several other pilots and non-flying personnel — had evacuated by road. The vehicles following theirs were ambushed however, and a petrol bowser over-turned by grenade explosions; one airman, AC1 Hugh Kilpatrick, was trapped under the bowser, whilst AC2 J.L. Duff sustained a broken leg and jaw; he was helped to one side of the road while Flg Off H.L. Wright, 232 Squadron's Engineer Officer, led a party to administer help to the trapped airman. Just then the Japanese attacked and Wright was killed. The trapped airman could not be released and later an orderly crawled up under covering fire and injected him with a double dose of morphine.

Some members of 34 Squadron had been based at Maria School in Palem-bang, and these were hastily preparing to evacuate. On learning of the paratroop landings, Plt Off R.V. Umphleby (observer), Sgt Rod McLeod (pilot), together with one other NCO, set off to see what they could do. About one and a half miles out of town they met more RAF personnel, Umphleby taking charge of the party. Continuing down the road, they came across four wrecked RAF vehicles in which they found two dead airmen, whilst nearby lay two dead Japanese. Leaving this gruesome scene, they ran into a small group of para-troopers who immediately opened fire with machine-guns. Having successfully evaded these, they then encountered another four or five Japanese who had taken over a house on the roadside, which occupied a strategic position. Sporadic fire was exchanged for some time before a group of about 20 soldiers arrived, one armed with a Bren gun.

Umphleby and the Bren gunner worked their way towards the house and opened fire, but were unable to dislodged the paratroopers. Return fire wounded Umphelby in one arm and another airmen in the leg, following which the party withdrew and left the mopping-up to Dutch soldiers who were now arriving.

Meanwhile, when a small party of dirty and bedraggled airmen — survivors of the ambush — appeared at 34 Squadron's billet, two of the unit's Canadian pilots, Flt Lt Don Jackson and Flg Off Don Edmondson, requested permission to see if they could help those trapped. On nearing the occupied house their vehicle was stopped by a Dutch roadblock, so Jackson continued on foot with a party of ten men while Edmondson drove back to Palembang to report the situation to Wg Cdr Ramsay Rae; he was advised that heavily-armed Dutch reinforcements were on their way, and when they arrived they had the situation under control within 20 minutes. As the wounded Umphleby and the Bren gunner rejoined their party, they saw two Japanese soldiers emerge from a

Dutch armoured car, which had been driven into the mass of wrecked vehicles, and both were shot dead as they ran towards the jungle.

In the town Air Commodore Vincent had contacted the local Dutch commander with a view to going to the aid of Maguire and his men on the airfield; a convoy comprising three lorryloads of Dutch troops, together with an RAF van full of food, was hastily organised, Vincent and his driver leading the way in his own commandeered car. Four miles short of P.1 they found the road blocked by the overturned petrol tanker and a lorry, and as they approached this obstruction, they were fired upon from the undergrowth alongside the road. Vincent later wrote:

> "The only one hit was the RAF van driver who swerved across the road and got ditched. The Dutch lorry-loads fired not a shot, and their drivers turned round and drove off leaving us to bring the two from the van, one hit in the arm, and return with ignominy after the supposed escort, leaving the supplies to the Japs. I was disgusted and ashamed."

Meanwhile, a small party from 84 Squadron, including Flt Lt Gill and Sgt Hough — members of the unit's Palembang detachment — had commandeered a lorry, which they loaded with food and water. Accompanied by ten armed airmen, they set off down the road towards P.1 and passed several Dutch pickets before eventually, about six or seven miles along the road, coming to a group of Dutch soldiers with an open truck, on the back of which was mounted a pair of Vickers guns. Ahead of them, about 200 yards up the road and round the bend, was the overturned petrol bowser.

The lorry was parked, and a party of about ten men, including some armed newcomers, were led forward by the 84 Squadron group while those who were unarmed remained with the vehicle. It was learned that a convoy of wounded was trying to get through from P.1, and to help them it was decided to try to set fire to the bowser with incendiary bullets, and thus drive out the concealed Japanese troops. This plan was thwarted when they learned of the injured airman trapped under the bowser. The party was forced to take to the swampy jungle when the Japanese opened fire with machine guns and mortars and, unable to achieve very much, they withdrew. Sqn Ldr Tayler, also of 84 Squadron, later attempted to get another party through to the bowser to rescue the trapped airman, but was turned back by the Dutch.

Jackson's party meanwhile, had reached the bowser, where it was discovered that the trapped airman had died; the area was strewn with the bodies of Japanese, British and Dutch soldiers and airmen. However more Japanese were met further along the road, one of whom was immediately shot dead, although generally the area now appeared free of paratroopers.

Sgt Bill Miller of 84 Squadron, with others, had also proceeded up the road towards the aerodrome, only to be stopped by the Dutch road block. Miller saw a small van which its three airmen occupants were having difficulty starting and offered to help. Inside the vehicle was a badly injured Dutch officer, whom he suggested should be transported to hospital without delay. Accompanied by one airman, Miller drove back to Palembang where he deposited the officer into more capable hands; he recalled:

> "Before I handed him over — he was halfway gone — I took his sword from him. I thought at least I've got a sword and my .38 so I could have a go!"

Some of the newly-arrived reinforcement fighter pilots (from 266 Wing) at P.1 found themselves involved — ill-equipped and untrained as they were — in close-quarter fighting with the paratroopers, as noted by Sgt Frank Hood, RNZAF:

> "Paratroopers! Great panic. Lost all kit. Pete Brown wounded. Lost track
> of Packard and Worts. Both believed killed. Went to P.2."

In fact Sgt N.G. Packard, another New Zealander, was later taken prisoner at Sekajoe, while fellow-countryman Sgt Ewen Worts managed to evade capture and reached P.2 safely. Two Canadians, Sgts Russell Smith and Howard Low were also taken prisoner; both had been placed in charge of parties made up of RAF airmen, AA gunners and Dutch troops, and had put up spirited resistance before being captured.

Another member of the RAF caught up in these traumatic experiences was one of 258 Squadron's drivers, LAC Johnny Johnson. He had been ordered to drive to Palembang from the airfield immediately after the bombing attack, but did not realise that paratroops had landed. About two and a half miles from the airfield, he found his way blocked by a six-wheel Scammel truck and, as he approached, was attacked by about 20 Japanese soldiers, who threw grenades and opened fire. Leaping from his vehicle, Johnson took cover in one of the deep ditches which flanked the road and returned fire with his .38 Webley revolver, claiming later to have hit at least two of his attackers.

When he had emptied his gun, Johnson was captured while attempting to reload. The paratroop commander then relieved him of the revolver and proceeded to shoot him through the thigh with it — presumably to prevent him from being able to escape. The soldiers then apparently decided to kill him, for he was stood against the lorry and several lined up and levelled their pistols at him. At that very moment, however, another vehicle came round the bend in the road and the troops scattered into the ditches, forcing Johnson to go with them.

The latest arrival was full of 258 Squadron personnel and, on reaching the roadblock, was overturned by hand grenades. Those not killed were taken prisoner, joining Johnson in the ditch, where at least four of the wounded were then killed by the soldiers. After that, he lost count of the number of times vehicles were overturned and wrecked, but finally Dutch troops and armed RAF personnel approached the area and began sniping, while a low-flying Hurricane strafed the roadblock. Steadily the Japanese were picked off, while others drifted off in the direction of the airfield.

Johnson's ordeal was not yet over however, for suddenly he felt a violent blow on his back. He had been struck by a burst of machine gun fire aimed by a Dutch soldier, who had mistaken him for a Japanese. At last the battle passed them by. Johnson's companions were able to bind up his wounds and put him on a lorry with about eight other wounded; they were then rushed to Palembang Hospital for treatment.

258 Squadron's Plt Off Nash, the Duty Pilot on Aerodrome Control at P.1, suffered a similar harrowing experience. When Wg Cdr Maguire decided to evacuate all possible personnel, Nash obtained a lift from an army doctor. Their vehicle rounded the bend to find the area in front of the roadblock littered with wrecked cars, so they halted, but before the driver could reverse, a terrific blast blew in the windscreen as a hand grenade was hurled at the car. Nash was

wounded in the neck and, choking on blood and unable to speak, followed the doctor into the ditch, feeling certain he was dying. Japanese troops then inspected the wreckage of the car, but failed to find the two recent occupants, who were well hidden in the ditch, although fearing that they would be discovered at any moment. The searchers did find two men further along the ditch, who had leapt from a car which had been following Nash's, and these unfortunates each received two bullets. A lorry followed and the driver got out. He was heard pleading for his life, followed by a single shot.

Left: Personnel of 84 Squadron prior to their departure for the Far East: Front, left to right: Sgt Bill Miller, Flt Sgt Bill Slee (armourer); Flg Off A.M. Gill. Rear, left to right: Sgt Bill Proctor; Plt Off Ron Millar, RNZAF; Sgt Geoff Bell; Sgt Dave Russell. *(W. Miller)*. Right: Plt Off Micky Nash of 258 Squadron at the Hotel Nederlander in Batavia, his neck wound bandaged, after his escape from Palembang. *(Sqn Ldr A.H. Milnes)*

After about two hours of cowering in the ditch, constantly fearful of being found, Nash and the doctor became aware of renewed action; they soon realised that the paratroopers were being driven back by a force of Dutch soldiers and RAF men from the airfield, who were heading a long column of cars and lorries trying to break through to Palembang. Nash and his companion broke cover and joined this force, which fought its way steadily through to the town, against frequent ambushes and machine gun fire.

The situation was just as confused in Palembang town, where a number of aircrew of 84 Squadron were located. Sqn Ldr Tayler was ordered to take six officers and about 80 armed men to form a bridgehead at the ferry, whilst reconnaissance parties were sent out to locate the parachutists. By mid morning, under the mistaken impression that Japanese forces were moving towards the town and that they would soon be joined by landing forces from the shipping in the Banka Strait, ABDAIR decided that evacuation to P.2 be carried out.

Members of 'A' Flight of the MVAF were amongst those ordered to evacuate by road to Oosthaven, which meant the abandonment of their five Moth aircraft at the airfield, some of which had apparently already been damaged in the fighting. Flt Lt Cooke's 13-strong party left that afternoon and eventually reached the port safely. A small group of 258 Squadron pilots, who had been off-duty in the town, now found themselves isolated from their flying echelon. Two of these, Plt Offs Milnes and Nicholls — the latter having just returned to

Palembang after being missing for seven days following his bale-out — joined forces with some 232 Squadron pilots, commandeered a car, and drove to the railway station, from where they boarded a train to Oosthaven.

The others, including Plt Off Campbell and Sgt Scott, had been joined by Plt Off Jock McCulloch, who had also just arrived back at Palembang. One of the reinforcement pilots, Plt Off R.L. Cicurel, an American, had attached himself to the group, as had Flg Off Tudor Jones, the unit's Engineer Officer; when Flg Off Macnamara arrived back from P.1 and excitedly related what was happening along the road, they decided to round up all the RAF men and arms they could find. Some ancient Italian rifles were discovered at the Dutch Home Guard HQ, together with a few sub-machine guns, and these were issued. However, when permission was sought to take a relief party back to the airfield with arms and ammunition, they were ordered to head for P.2 instead.

After patrolling around the town for a while, unhappy to leave their colleagues to their fate, Macnamara's group decided to ignore the order to evacuate and, commandeering an RAF lorry and its driver, the party of about 18 volunteers set off in this and a car, picking up such information as they could en route from Dutch barricades. They were finally halted about three or four miles short of P.1 by a Dutch officer, who advised that it was not safe to proceed any further by road. British and Dutch troops were moving up each side of the road, and after guarding the barricade for about 45 minutes, it was agreed that the RAF men be allowed to move forward. Dividing into three parties, each led by a Dutch officer — one a colourful character carrying a sabre in one hand and a pistol in the other — they edged their way through the jungle under mortar and machine gun fire. Macnamara later wrote:

> "I am no soldier or woodsman, and pushing through those woods, not knowing whether I would bump into friend or foe, hearing all sorts of noises, etc., was not, to say the least, a very pleasant job. However, finally my turn came to get back and I made my way round to the river below the road block. We had many casualties, but the Japanese had more. One of our squadron warrant officers accounted for 17 of them before receiving a bullet clean through his forehead."

Plt Off Campbell was with Macnamara and his group, and his account was more graphic:

> "Ting (Macnamara) and I ran into some Dutch native troops. They were showing us the way through and there was some gunfire, and we all took cover — we saw these soldiers, looked like Japanese, and Ting, who it turned out was a dead shot, drew a bead on one of them — I drew a bead on the other one, and fortunately missed. Ting didn't. He hit one and it turned out they were Dutch troops.
>
> "But about this time the Japanese did arrive ... about four of five of them. Ting took off in one direction and I took off running away from them. They ran after me and for some reason ... they were going to stick me with a bayonet. They didn't fire their rifles. I had a pistol and was trying to shoot over my shoulder ... Fortunately some native soldiers came along ... and waded in, and just wiped those Japanese out."

Macnamara meanwhile reached the stretch of road leading up to the road-block, which was cluttered with parked, abandoned and overturned vehicles, where he joined others who were working their way along the ditches on the side of the road. However, they were soon pinned down by machine gun fire:

"There were a small number of army types around with rifles and they did all they could. I even saw an RAF lad attempt to fire a Bofors gun from over the cab of a lorry — he was severely wounded by return fire from a machine gun, but a pal of his lost no time in jumping out of the ditch and carrying him back to what safety they could find.

"With some other members of my squadron, we left the ditch and again made for the woods and pushed forward until, with the suddenness of a bolt from the blue, a machine gun rattled out its song of death. That left us with four men and myself. The slightest movement was recorded with a burst of machine gun fire and looking at each other lying deep down in mud, dirt and water, full length, hardly daring to move a limb, we could not help but laugh. We looked so utterly miserable and helpless. We finally wiggled our way to better protection.

"From the position we were in, not more than 20 yards from the spurts of flame from the Japanese machine gun, one of our number crawled forward under the very noses of the Nippon overlords, to drag a wounded comrade back to us, and from there, after many tricky interludes, he was carried safely back to a makeshift Red Cross clearing. I met him afterwards in a hospital in Colombo, where he was making satisfactory progress. After nightfall we finally made our way into the outskirts of Palembang, where we hitch-hiked a ride into the town itself.

"We saw paratroopers hanging in trees, strangled by their own cords, and others who had struck terra firma without their parachutes opening. I like to recall the three who came driving down the road in a Dutch armoured car. We naturally thought that the Dutch had at last broken through to our relief, but after many had revealed themselves from the side of the road, they were greeted with hand grenades. They shot smartly back into hiding and the Japanese, knowing their game was up, and having crashed the armoured car into our stranded vehicles, tried to make a break — a volley of fire from small arms — rifles and revolvers — greeted their exit from the turret.

There now remained on the airfield Wg Cdr Maguire's small party of about 60 RAF men and a few Dutch colonial troops, with very little ammunition left. At one stage, Maguire and 258 Squadron's South African-born Ground Defence Officer, Flg Off Matthys Taute, found themselves in a slit trench, facing a number of Japanese soldiers similarly entrenched. These suddenly climbed out of their cover and started running for the jungle, whereupon three or four were promptly shot by Maguire and Taute, using rifles they had acquired.

Believing that Dutch troops had come to their aid, Maguire and Plt Off O.D. Creegan (232 Squadron's Ground Defence Officer), walked to the main gate of the aerodrome, expecting to meet Dutch soldiers, but instead encountered the remaining 60 or 70 paratroops who had concentrated on the road about half a mile from P.1; Maguire recalled:

"As we reached the top of a slight incline, we saw a Japanese soldier bending over a machine gun. He stood up and saw us at a range of about 50 yards. Although we were both armed, we had Thompson sub-machine guns, and I had no confidence in the ability of these weapons to reach him in time. So, telling Creegan we would have to bluff it out, I laid down my unwieldy weapon and marched briskly up to him.

"He looked very surprised but did nothing. So, sounding as confident as I could, I demanded to see his officer and, to my amazement, he shambled off and produced an officer. This officer had some command of English, and I immediately demanded surrender, saying that I had a large force behind me. He replied that he had a large force and that he would give us safe conduct if we marched out."

Maguire explained that he would have to go and discuss the whole matter with his non-existent senior officer! Their departure was not challenged and they walked back to where they had laid their guns, then briskly back to the airfield where, on arrival, they learned that the remaining unserviceable aircraft and the fuel dump had already been fired. Destroying the fuel dump at the airfield had not been a simple matter — hundreds of 44-gallon drums were stacked together, and the task was left to Flg Off Taute. Having fired his revolver into some of the drums to cause a spillage, a match was struck to ignite a pool of petrol forming in a rain-filled ditch. There was an explosion, and Taute and his assistant were flung across the road, scorched and shocked but not seriously hurt! With fuel dump and abandoned aircraft blazing satisfactorily, Maguire ordered his men to turn their lorries round and prepare to escape in the opposite direction; they beat a hasty retreat up the road towards Djambi.[1]

Two of the unserviceable aircraft which had been set on fire at P.1 were the crash-landed RAAF Hudsons, one of which was A16-48, the machine which Flt Lt Oscar Diamond had belly-landed following the morning shipping strike. Amidst rifle and machine gun fire, he had led his crew towards the damaged 59 Squadron machine (AM952) with the broken propeller tips, which had been abandoned earlier by Flg Off Richards. The engines were started and Diamond attempted to take off, but could not get above 50 mph, so it was deliberately ground looped. After a hurried inspection of a number of dispersed Hurricanes and Buffaloes — all of which proved to be unserviceable — the four Australians took to the jungle and headed for Palembang town, evading a Japanese party en route, who lobbed hand grenades at them; weary, cut and bruised, they eventually reached the town following a ten-hour trek.

At the Pladjoe oil refinery meanwhile, all had not gone well for the defenders, as the Dutch garrison had been taken by surprise and the paratroopers had gained possession of the complex. They were able to beat off counter-attacks until reserves from P.2 and British AA crews were rushed up, and succeeded in driving the Japanese out with heavy losses, but it was then found impossible to carry out the planned demolitions. Although the oil stores and other combustible points were set on fire, no worthwhile permanent damage could be done.

Two hours after the main paratroop landings, a further dozen transports arrived over Palembang, 60 men under Lt Nobutaka Hirose descending to the

[1] After a seven-day trek Maguire's party reached Bencoelen, on the west coast of Sumatra where, by good fortune, a radio station was located. Contacting Java, they were able to arrange for a small coaster to come and pick them up, finally reaching Batavia towards the end of the month. By the time they were evacuated, Maguire's party had been joined by various other escapees and survivors from Singapore and elsewhere, including Flt Lt Denny Sharp who, it will be recalled, had force-landed in Sumatra some two weeks earlier while flying from Singapore. (See Vol. 1, Ch. 9).

west of P.1, while another 30 were dropped to the south of the oil refineries. One Ki 56 transport aircraft force-landed on the west side of the airfield due to engine trouble, whilst another made a planned landing in a swamp south-west of P.1. Aboard this machine was Colonel Sei-ichi Kume, OC the paratroop brigade, and a staff officer of the 16th Army, together with a section equipped with a rapid-fire cannon; this party would rendezvous with the main body next morning.

Assembled at P.2 airfield was almost the whole RAF strength in the East Indies — 35 Blenheims Is and IVs, many of which were unserviceable, 20 Hudsons and 22 Hurricanes. Towards noon 258 Squadron's Flg Off Donahue volunteered to carry out a reconnaissance over the Palembang area; he reported only Allied military and civilian vehicles pouring down the road to P.2, not the Japanese troops that had been feared. He also noted the awesome flames and billowing black smoke from the recently-fired refineries, which were beginning to engulf the town. Having seen Singapore burning only a few days earlier, he remained unimpressed by the scene!

Flt Lt Terence O'Brien of 62 Squadron had been instructed to lead the next section of three Hudsons to attack the convoy, timed for 1230 hours but was ordered instead by Wg Cdr R.N. McKern, the squadron commander, to take the unit's remaining six flyable Hudsons to Java without delay. He was informed that P.2 was about to be evacuated, and that the CO and Sqn Ldr L.W.G. Lilly were to accompany the squadron's ground personnel to Oosthaven, from where they would embark for the sea crossing to Batavia. The six Hudsons thus departed eastwards at 1250 for the two-hour flight, but the crews received a frosty welcome on arrival at Batavia's civil airport, where Flt Lt O'Brien was confronted by an RAF Group Captain who refused to believe that the Japanese had landed in Sumatra! On being ordered to take his aircraft back to P.2 without delay, O'Brien refused, at which point his name and rank were demanded. The Group Captain then departed, uttering threats.

Expecting to be placed under arrest at any moment, O'Brien nonetheless arranged for his six aircraft to be refuelled, on completion of which they flew to Bandoeng, about 100 miles away in the hills, where Air Vice-Marshal Maltby had his headquarters, in order to seek further instructions. Owing to the onset of darkness, the flight was postponed until the morning, the crews being obliged to sleep on the floor of the airport terminal.

Meanwhile, back at P.2, the two Australian Hudson units were also preparing to evacuate on orders received from Group HQ at Palembang, seven Hudson IIs of 1 RAAF Squadron and four Mark IIIs of 8 RAAF Squadron leaving during the afternoon. Amongst the departing Hudsons was Plt Off Oldworth's AE607 of 62 Squadron, which had earlier been left behind; his WOp/AG, Sgt Jim Thomas, later recalled:

> "To leave P.2 my crew had to rebuild our aircraft, which had been crash-landed by others, but we made it flyable (just!) and loaded it up with over 20 volunteers and got them to Bandoeng. We all lost everything, including toothbrushes, as the Japs had overrun our tented area whilst we were bombing their ships."

Following the departure of the Hudsons, further instructions from Group HQ requested that they should be recalled, as it had been learnt that the paratroopers had been dealt with, but by then it was too late. Such was the confusion which prevailed.

At 1450 hours, Sqn Ldr D.K. Banks was ordered to lead four Blenheim Is of 27 Squadron from P.2 on a strike against the invasion forces in the Banka Strait. The aircraft became separated and each carried out two bombing and strafing runs independently, being greeted by intense AA fire; Flt Sgt Sid Stafford's machine (L1258) was shot down into the sea, with the loss of the crew. Wt Off 'Jock' Kennedy reported encountering two convoys of 14 and 24 transports respectively, with a strong naval escort. Sqn Ldr Banks' K7173 also sustained damage, the aircraft coming down in the Moesi River on its way back to P.2, the gunner, Sgt H.A. Oliver, suffering fatal injuries; Banks and the observer managed to scramble to the river bank. Fortuitously for the survivors a small vessel, which was towing five RAF launches from Singapore, was on its way up river and picked them up.

A further strike was ordered, two small formations of Blenheims from 34 and 84 Squadrons setting out from P.2 at 1920 hours. Sgt Ross, who on this occasion was flying as airgunner in Sgt Doug MacKillop's 84 Squadron machine (Z9586), recalled:

> "Flying along the many ships seemed to take ages as pom-poms winked at us and the sky was full of plumes; we were hit in several places but received no injuries. With this over, we headed back to P.2 much relieved, but unfortunately strayed out of our corridor, over the Palembang oil refineries, which were guarded by Ack-Ack groups who, by sending up a warning burst, set us on fire. As we prepared for a wheels-up crash landing on P.2, I read an Aldis-lamp warning which read 'Fire'; no doubt we were trailing smoke. The crew was OK."

With the return of the strike force, the remaining five operational Blenheims of 34 Squadron were ordered to Lahat, about 120 miles to the south-west of P.2. Whilst there was not much advantage operationally in the move, since there were no fuel or bombs stocks there, it did mean that air and ground crews — and their aircraft — would all be based at the same place; additionally and importantly, accommodation would be more satisfactory than that available at P.2. Initially, both 84 and 211 Squadrons were ordered to prepare to follow 34 Squadron to Lahat, but events would overtake them.

With the onset of dusk, the RAF evacuation of Palembang town was well underway. Small groups of men had collected the wounded and as night fell about 120 were evacuated in a fleet of vehicles. However one small group of 84 Squadron aircrew — fortified with a good dose of 'Dutch courage' — had decided to fight a rearguard action should they be called upon to do so, as remembered by Sgt Bill Miller:

> "Having taken the Dutch officer to hospital, I went back to Maria School, where part of 84 Squadron was billeted. Most had evacuated but I met my pilot (Plt Off Macdonald) and Flt Lt 'Dutch' Holland, who had found some whisky and other spirits which gave us a bit more bravado.
>
> "I loaded the van with petrol, ammo and food, and we picked up the odd Tommy-gun and went upstairs in the school with a view to holding on for as long as we could to allow the troops to get away — to be truthful, we got pissed as old lords! We opened up the windows and sat on the windowsills, waiting for the Japs but they didn't come; we were oblivious to the fact that we could have been picked off easily!
>
> "We stayed the night and the following morning drove down to the river."

To get to P.2 it was necessary to cross the Moesi River by ferry, and here at first chaos reigned. The river was a quarter of a mile wide, and there was only one ferry boat in which only four vehicles at a time could be carried.

Pladjoe was still in Allied hands however, and a mixed force was positioned on the road between the town and the airfield at P.1. Indeed, the Dutch commander was quite confident that he could retake the airfield, so much so that Grp Capt Darley was ordered to re-open the Operations Room. However, it was too badly damaged and the idea was dropped. It was accepted therefore that a new Ops Room would have to be established, as planned, at P.2 on the morrow.

Further orders from Group HQ, received during the evening, stated that the squadrons at P.2 were to prepare to destroy unserviceable aircraft. 1 RAAF Squadron had two such aircraft, A16-60 with a crushed fuselage and buckled ailerons, and A16-62 requiring an engine. By nightfall, hard-working ground crew had fitted a new aileron on the former, whilst Flt Sgt Harry Musicka and his crew, with only a bayonet and a few tools taken from a steam-roller, got to work on fitting an old spare engine to the other machine. They were able to report the engine satisfactorily installed by daybreak.

Meanwhile, as darkness approached, the leading Japanese vessels in the Banka Strait anchored off Muntok (Banka Island), opposite the Moesi delta. Two companies of troops went ashore on the island in the face of only token resistance, and secured it; one company remained ashore as garrison. As this was happening, Rear-Admiral Karel Doorman of the NEI Navy led an Allied naval force towards the area from a rendezvous in the Sunda Strait, in an attempt to attack the covering warships by approaching from the north of Banka Island. The force comprised the Dutch cruisers *De Ruyter*, *Java* and *Tromp*, the Australian *Hobart*, the British *Exeter*, with four Dutch and six American destroyers. The weather was not favourable, heavy rain and poor visibility hampering progress. Almost at once, the Dutch destroyer *Van Ghent* struck a reef in the Gaspar Strait and was abandoned; her sister destroyer *Banckert* went to her aid and rescued the survivors.

With the RAF and Dutch units being forced to withdraw from P.1 and other Sumatran airfields, Maj General Lewis Brereton's USAAF HQ received a call to lend support; consequently between 0200 and 0300 three LB-30s of the 19th Bomb Group were despatched from Malang to bomb shipping off Palembang, but bad weather forced all three to return early.

Sunday, 15 February

At dawn, Japanese troops aboard the ships off Muntok began to disembark into landing craft and head up the three main rivers towards Palembang — the Moesi, the Salang and the Telang; the small transport *Otawa Maru* accompanied them, as did the destroyer *Hatsutaka*, eight patrol boats and four sampans. Soon afterwards, Vice-Admiral Jisaburo Ozawa (Commander-in-Chief Palembang Invasion Force) ordered the remaining transports to raise anchor and follow them into the delta for their own protection. The second convoy was ordered to turn back, and the covering force to prepare for a surface battle.

As a result of a severe electrical storm during the night, the telephone line from 225 Group HQ at Palembang to P.2 was disrupted; as this was the only means of communication, Grp Capt McCauley, the Station Commander, and his staff at the airfield, were left to their own resources. At first light a reconnaissance aircraft pin-pointed the position of the multitude of transports and landing barges, many of which were seen in the estuaries of the Moesi and adjacent rivers. McCauley ordered attacks to commence.

First off at 0630 were three Hudsons (two flown by crews from 8 RAAF Squadron, the other by a crew from its sister unit) and three Blenheims of 211 Squadron. Escort was to be provided by half a dozen Hurricanes, but as these became airborne, the pilots encountered heavy fog and were forced to try and land again in the very poor conditions. Flg Off Donahue went down first, and landed safely; he then fired a Very light up through the fog to indicate the whereabouts of the airfield to the others of his flight. One by one, the Hurricanes appeared out of the gloom, but two came to grief on landing, one tipping up onto its nose, while the second, flown by Sgt John Fleming, crashed and overturned. Onlookers rushed to the spot and were able to lift one wingtip sufficiently to allow a lorry to back under it, thereby supporting the machine and allowing the shaken but otherwise unhurt Canadian to be extricated.

The bombers meanwhile, now devoid of escort, proceeded in two separate flights above the fog towards the Moesi delta. Nearing Palembang they encountered a Japanese fighter patrol, so entered the fog bank to escape detection, but on emerging near the coast were spotted by a number of aircraft identified as 'Navy 0s'. Flg Off Gibbes, in the 1 RAAF Squadron machine (A16-42), became separated from his companions and after three further attempts to avoid the fighters, decided to return to P.2 under cover of the fog. The other two Hudson pilots, Flt Lt Ron Widmer and Flg Off Lower, succeeded in evading the fighters and proceeded to attack the assemblage of ships in the Banka Strait; near misses were claimed against a small vessel escorted by two destroyers.

The Blenheim section similarly encountered three Japanese fighters over Palembang although these were successfully evaded; the Blenheims then attacked the landing forces, the crews claiming the sinking of five or six troop-laden barges. All the bombers returned safely under cover of the fog and smoke billowing from the burning oil tanks at Pladjoe.

A second strike force set out, comprising three Hudsons flown by 8 RAAF Squadron crews — which were to attack from 8,000 feet — and three RAF Hudsons flown by crews from the 59 Squadron detachment, which were to bomb from lower level. Sweeping in at 1,000 feet, at least one direct hit was claimed upon a 5,000-ton transport — most probably the *Otawa Maru* — though heavy AA fire prevented the crews observing the result. The Hudsons then attacked barges independently, as recalled by Sgt Les Patrick in Flg Off Siddell's aircraft (AE506):

> "We were to go in at low level — 1,000 feet. We did not go lower as we carried Dutch impact bombs. We split up and attacked separately — diagonally across the river. I remember seeing one of our bombs hit the river bank, bringing down a tree which fell across the vessel; I don't expect it did much damage though. After attacking the ship we made a couple of passes, machine gunning the barges. Sgt Osborne manned the ventral gun — he couldn't miss the troops packed in the barges — Sgt Jones was in the turret, and I had a Vickers K on a side mounting.
>
> "I am sure they were a few soldiers short after we had finished. Had we had 500 lb delayed action bombs they would have been short of a ship or two as well."

On approaching Palembang on the return flight, Flg Off T.D. Boyce's Hudson encountered a number of Japanese fighters near P.1; one of these was claimed shot down by his gunners, whilst the bomber escaped damage. As second pilot aboard one of the 8 RAAF Squadron Hudsons's was Plt Off John Coom, the New Zealander flying his second mission of the day with Flt Lt Colquhoun; of the earlier sortie he recalled:

"We took off in fairly heavy fog and about half way to the coast the fog ended abruptly and we were jumped by 'Zeros.' We smartly returned to the fog and made several unsuccessful attempts to break out to the barges.

"Later on the fog cleared and we took off again. Luckily there were no 'Zeros' and we found the barges which we bombed, and had a great view of the Hurricanes raking them with their eight guns."

Whilst the RAF bombers concentrated on the shipping in the delta area, five B-17s of 19th Bomb Group from Malang, led by Capt Elmer L. Parsel, carried out an attack on other ships north of Palembang. Hits were claimed on an auxiliary vessel, while one crew reported a direct hit on an accompanying cruiser. The appalling weather that had shrouded the invasion fleet now advanced towards Sumatra and Java, and soon both islands were covered with heavy cloud and rainstorms, effectively preventing further attacks by the American bombers.

As pilots streamed into P.2 who had either escaped from P.1 or been off duty in Palembang, the two Hurricane squadrons had many more than there were aircraft for them to fly, and it was agreed that the available fighters should be pooled. At 0900 the fog cleared, and Hurricanes manned by 232 Squadron pilots went off to continue the attack on the landing craft. Plt Off Lockwood:

"I dived from a near-vertical position. As the cone of fire hit the water, I centred it on a sampan and bodies went over the side. I only just pulled out of the dive and recall looking up at the trees on the river bank!"

Plt Off Parker, who had been attached to 258 Squadron since his return from Singapore, now transferred back to his old unit; he later wrote:

"The landing craft were only 20 minutes flying time away from P.2, but there were only two in the middle of the channel that I could see. There were no other aircraft in sight and we came down on the two barges from the south-east, out of the sun. I opened fire at quite a steep angle, a long way off, and saw the pattern of my bullets striking the water near them. As I approached and corrected my aim, the pattern grew more concentrated, and then the de Wilde was bursting all over the first one.

"It seemed that dozens of men dressed in light brown uniforms jumped overside to escape the hundreds of rounds pumping into the barges, but they had no chance. The bullets were still striking the water all round it. Then I was over and up, and the other Hurricanes were following and treating the barge similarly. We went down the river and saw no more landing craft, so turned and came back up to Palembang again, but still nothing moved. I reckoned that we were in any event short of ammunition now, so went back to P.2."

Amongst the strafers was Sgt Sandeman Allen, who recalled:

"The landings were by barge up the river and I seem to remember that we were helped by a number of large alligators which prevented any escape from the barges by swimming!"

It was then the turn of 84 Squadron to take up the attack, nine Blenheims being led to the Moesi estuary by Wg Cdr Jeudwine. Some of the crews attacked *Otawa Maru*, reporting a number of direct hits. The vessel was believed to have been sunk, as sightings of survivors being plucked from the water in the location of this attack were later reported; however this was not the case, for after surviving no less than 39 attacks, the captain of *Otawa Maru* finally decided to turn back. The soldiers seen being rescued from the water were undoubtedly survivors from sunken barges that had also been attacked by the Blenheims; so fierce was small-arms fire from the craft under attack that not one of the bombers escaped being hit, although all returned safely. Sgt Dave Russell, the CO's airgunner in V6093:

"Jeudwine wisely flew along the line of the river-bank, in order that the turret guns could be used at a favourable angle. I only caught glimpses of upturned yellow faces and rifles pointed in our direction as the Jap soldiers stood bolt-upright, disdaining to seek cover as they returned my fire.

"Jeudwine turned back for another run. In the confusing velocity of low-level attack, I could only direct my fire at an indistinguishable mass of khaki that flashed under me and disappeared under the tailplane. I knew that the plane had been holed in several places, but comforted myself in the knowledge that the enemy were in worse discomfort than myself.

"Jeudwine embarked on a third run, slowing the engines to the point of stalling, to give me latitude to direct a continuous stream of tracer into the sea of khaki that filled the sights. Once again the Blenheim screamed over the bristling convoy; the pilot banked steeply beyond the leading barge, then rammed the nose down to make yet another hair-raising low-level sweep of the river."

A further Blenheim strike was launched without delay, Wg Cdr Bateson (Z7855) leading six 211 Squadron aircraft, with an escort of ten Hurricanes provided by 258 Squadron pilots, led by Sqn Ldr Thomson. The Blenheims attacked a 3,500-ton vessel — almost certainly the ill-fated *Otawa Maru* — from low level and a number of direct hits were claimed, reportedly setting the transport on fire. On the return flight, landing barges and other small river craft were also machine gunned. Of the attack, Wg Cdr Bateson noted:

"Low level bombing and machine gun attacks on invasion forces on Moesi and Palembang rivers. Inflicted heavy casualties — aircraft holed."

A number of 84 Squadron Blenheims were still in the area and one of these almost fell victim to another from 211 Squadron, as Sgt Richardson (airgunner aboard Plt Off Coughlan's Z9660) recalled:

"We dived from 4,000 feet and got hits on a large transport but one bomb had hung-up. We were using Dutch bombs which were a bit bigger than ours, so we flew with the bomb doors partially open, which was the cause of the hang-up. When we pulled out of the dive over land, the bomb released and exploded beneath us at very low level, blowing in the camera hatch and holing the aircraft in several places.

Left: Wg Cdr John Jeudwine, commander of 84 Squadron. *(Mrs Erica Hills)*. Right: Flt Lt John Wyllie of 84 Squadron, who was awarded a DFC for his exploits in Sumatra and Java. *(J.V.C. Wyllie)*

"We then flew in line astern up the river, machine-gunning the lines of landing craft packed with Jap troops, and we caused great damage and destruction. We were chuffed that at last we had a chance to get some of our own back, and we got a bit over-enthusiastic as we made repeat strafing runs up the centre of the river, at low level and almost point-blank range.

"I was firing a long burst into these boats when, to my complete astonishment, a Blenheim 'floated' from beneath our aircraft and across my line of fire. I just could not stop firing, it was so sudden. As it drifted across and beneath our path, I could see my bullets making a stitching pattern on the wings, although it was only for a few seconds.

"We understood much later that the Blenheim was flown by Wg Cdr Jeudwine, and I believe that he was not amused and would have liked to have met the WOp/AG behind the guns!"

The Hurricanes, their escort task completed, swept down to strafe numerous small troop-filled craft which were seen moving up the river. During the early sorties there had been considerable, though inaccurate, anti-aircraft fire from the special 'flak-ships', which were covering the barges and sampans, but by now return fire was mainly limited to what the troops themselves could throw up from their vulnerable and open vessels. So far, only a few Hurricanes had been hit and minor damage inflicted. Then however, as the aircraft swept in to attack again, a lucky shot from a 12.7mm anti-aircraft machine gun struck Flg Off Donahue's aircraft:

"I was conscious of having been hit, harder than I have ever been hit in my life — a quick, cruel blow in the calf of my left leg; I had a momentary glimpse through a big rent in my trousers of two holes in the side of my leg,

---

one small and round, the other a gaping sort of thing an inch wide by a couple of inches long, with raw red and blue flesh and muscle laid open, before the blood welled up and started streaming out."

Bleeding profusely and in a near-fainting condition, he managed to get back to P.2 where, under extremely difficult circumstances, he carried out a successful if somewhat bumpy landing:

"I did not mind, though. The feeling of triumph at having made it safely, made the bad landing seem inconsequential! I felt almost boisterous as I taxied up to the watch office. Some of the boys lifted me out... and put a field dressing on my leg. Then I was packed off in an ambulance to the dressing station."

Earlier in the day orders had been given for all operationally unserviceable Hudsons to be flown to Java, and before midday, five RAAF machines departed, including A16-60 and A16-62, the two aircraft which had been repaired overnight; Flt Lt Plenty flew the former machine:

"I flew A16-60 from P.2 to Java loaded with a dozen or so bods. This Hudson had a staved-in top fuselage from bomb damage at Sembawang, and a warped aileron. It ended its days, I believe, at Andir in the KNILM workshops."

During the afternoon further orders were received at P.2 for all remaining aircraft to proceed to Java on completion of allotted tasks. Only three Hudsons now remained. As regards the Blenheims, the respective squadron commanders, Wg Cdrs Jeudwine and Bateson, decided that their commitment precluded despatching aircraft immediately to Java and, by the time all aircraft and crews had completed their tasks and refuelled, it would be impossible to reach Batavia before dusk. Hence, the departure of 84 and 211 Squadrons would be delayed until the morrow. However, odd machines did evacuate; three Blenheim Is of 27 Squadron set out for Batavia during the afternoon and one of these, flown by Wt Off Kennedy, ran into a severe storm. Out of fuel, the pilot was obliged to belly-land some miles short of the airfield. The crew was unhurt and later caught up with the remnants of the squadron at Kalidjati.

Throughout the day evacuation of Palembang continued. In the morning, Grp Capt Darley had collected 30 armed men, setting up guards each side of the river and actually on the ferry boat, their presence persuading the local crew to keep working. Gradually everyone got across and, by evening, the evacuation was all but complete. Darley carried out a last swift tour of the town to make sure all were gone and then, withdrawing the guards, crossed on the last ferry with Air Commodore Vincent, following the others to P.2. The town was left blazing and under a great pall of smoke from the burning refineries. No sooner had P.2 been reached than the order was given to begin evacuating this base, all personnel not involved in operating and maintaining the aircraft being ordered to Oosthaven, 300 miles away on the south-eastern tip of Sumatra, for trans-shipment to Java. With Vincent and Darley was Wg Cdr Barclay:

"I travelled by car, with Air Commodore Vincent and others, from P.1 to Oosthaven via P.2 but, armed as we were, sighted no Jap paratroopers. We reached Oosthaven at 0300 and, at dawn, jettisoned our Buick in the harbour and embarked for Java."

Fortunately for the evacuees, two trains were located in the station close to P.2 and the crews were forced at gunpoint to drive them to Oosthaven, loaded with supplies, wounded and other personnel. Meanwhile, a large convoy of overcrowded vehicles began the long and arduous journey to the port, other personnel making such arrangements as they could for their escape. The route to Oosthaven included many bridges, over small rivers and streams, many of which featured relatively low roof structures; as a result a number of high-sided vehicles and 3.7mm anti-aircraft guns which could not be got under them had to be abandoned. Many of these bridges were demolished after the convoy had passed over them, in order to slow down the Japanese pursuit. RAF personnel at the airfields in Northern Sumatra were ordered to make their way to the west coast, from where they would be evacuated by destroyers.

Meanwhile, back at the airfield, two of 84 Squadron's experienced pilots, Flt Lts Holland (who had successfully escaped from Palembang) and Wyllie, found themselves without aircraft and asked permission to take up two non-operational Blenheim fighters of 27 Squadron. This was refused due to their poor condition, so the two pilots worked with ground crews for three hours on the aircraft and brought them up to a serviceable state, at which point permission was granted for them to be flown. Dispensing with observers for this sortie, Holland and Wyllie took on board their respective gunners, Sgts Bennett and Wakefield, and separately headed northwards; Bob Bennett:

> "Flying low over the river towards the estuary, we saw some small native craft, but no Japs. It must be remembered that the undergrowth overhung the river on both banks, and as our engines could be heard from some distance away, any Japs with some sense would have dived for cover. After flying around for some time, we were forced to return without firing a shot. Pity!"

The fifth strike force comprised another six Blenheims, three each from 84 and 211 Squadrons. They attacked ships which had been lying off Banka Island; these had apparently just moved to the mouth of the Palembang River and were escorted by two destroyers. One direct hit was claimed on the bows of a 8,000-10,000 ton transport, which was reported to have caught fire and developed a heavy list, and was probably the *Tajima Maru*, which suffered some damage. The Blenheims then strafed troops on the deck of this ship from low level, the gunners using their turret guns until all ammunition was exhausted. One of the Blenheims was flown by Sgt Ken Lister:

> "We made one bombing run across the target but no bombs were released, so we turned and came back over the target at 10,000 feet. Once again, the leader did not release his bombs and, therefore, neither did any other aircraft. We were then led quite a way from the target, and the leader then turned us again and started a shallow dive towards the Jap fleet.
>
> "We were still in a tight box of six aircraft; I had my nose under the leader's tail, and my wing men were close beside me, with their noses under the tails of the leading wing men. The dive continued towards the target and eventually the leader dropped his bombs and all the other aircraft also released theirs.
>
> "I nearly had a fit! The release height was only 700 feet, we were still diving at the Jap fleet, with the three leading aircraft firing their one front

gun, and I was in a position from which there was no escape because of the aircraft on either side. The reason for my alarm was simple — the 24 250 lb bombs we had released had instantaneous fuses in both nose and tail pistols, and could cause serious damage to any aircraft above them at heights up to 1,000 feet, and we were about to pass over this exploding pattern of bombs at a height of between 50 and 100 feet!!

"I can only remember being met with a huge wall of spray as we passed over the bomb bursts, and the aircraft being thrown all over the place. When we emerged from the water splash and regained control, the first thing I heard was the broad Devon accent of Ron Pile from the turret, asking: "What the bloody hell's going on? I'm soaked to buggery back here!" The formation was then well and truly split up and we returned individually, flying at low level up the river with our gunners shooting up Japanese landing barges which were moving up the river towards Palembang.

"After landing, an inspection of the aircraft revealed a great deal of damage. Of the many holes, the largest was one about the size of a fist in the starboard inner tank. Some sort of plug was made for this, other emergency repairs were made, and the aircraft was eventually flown to Java by Sqn Ldr Passmore."

Wg Cdr Bateson's aircraft (Z7855) was again hit, this time quite seriously; his gunner, Sgt Bill Baird, noted:

"The raid was punctuated by bullet holes. We strafed the barges and I saw damage being inflicted on our aircraft, and reasoned that the troops were using rifle fire in retaliation."

A third machine, flown by Sgt Bill Cosgrove, also sustained damage, as recalled by his gunner, Sgt Hayes Harding:

"We had just completed a raid on the mouth of the river, and wrote off, I'm sure, many Japs, as the mouth of the river was solidly packed. However, on the second run, I collected a cannon shell in the base of the turret, and it severed the hydraulic line. I collected superficial wounds, shrapnel in the legs about my flying boots (my boots saved me from more serious injury) but, of course, the turret was out of action.

"Bill could not land a plane to save his life — always seemed to drop it from x feet and jolt the teeth out of our heads. When he told me, over the intercom, that we were in for a belly-landing, I remarked: 'Good God, can't you ever land a plane with wheels on? I'd better bale out!'.

"Cosgrove replied: 'Keep quiet you little bugger and cross your fingers!'. In actual fact, he must have run the tail wheel along the ground for at least 200 yards before settling the body down — in fact, the smoothest landing he has ever made — the soft ground did help, however. Actually, he was a good pilot — a bit wild but a good formation flyer — and we had the utmost confidence in him — until we had to land, of course!"

The final bombing sorties were carried out at 1405 hours by two of the remaining Hudson IIIs, on this occasion flown by Flg Off D.C. Stumm of 8 RAAF Squadron (in A16-26) and Flg Off Richards of the 59 Squadron detachment (in AE488). Richards had arrived that morning from P.1 in the company of Sqn Ldr Paul Garrard (59 Squadron detachment CO) — the latter having been in the Control Room when the parachutists landed — and they had taken part in the defence of the airfield, eventually escaping to P.2, where they had arrived armed with Japanese weapons.

As the Hudsons started to take-off however, Richards' aircraft was found to have a defective engine, which failed to give full boost, and was left behind as the other departed. Whilst Richards was making adjustments to the engine, Sqn Ldr Garrard approached to find out the cause of the delay, and then when the engine responded, Garrard decided to go along for the ride.

Sgt Hayes Harding, WOp/AG with 84 Squadron. *(W. Miller)*

The Hudsons independently attacked destroyers and transports, the crews claiming a direct hit on an 8,000-ton transport and two very near misses on a smaller vessel. Sgt Longworth, in Richards' aircraft, was to record:

"Scores of transports apparently at anchor, destroyers and other naval vessels were dotted about the Straits with large numbers of landing craft leaving some of the troop carriers. We were at 6,000 feet by this time. Bobby calmly told me that he would press the (*bomb release*) 'tit' on this occasion, and I told him not to forget that we could not make our usual approach as this time the bombs were instantaneous, not being fitted with delay fuses.

"I must admit that I was rather upset about this decision, as the process of bomb aiming and release kept the tummy butterflies at rest, and this time would be the first occasion I had been a bystander.

"Bobby picked out a big transport which he thought was still laden with troops, there being no landing craft leaving it. He put the nose down to get the ship in his gun sight, and as the flak whizzed around us, the dive got steeper and steeper until I thought we were in a perpendicular Stuka attack! I was watching the height indicator from the corner of my eye as the ship grew larger in the bomb aimer's panel. At 1,000 feet I bawled through the intercom 'let them go!', but Bobby pressed on until at 700 feet I gave up, feeling sure he was going to dive straight in."

Richards released his bombs, which the crew believed exploded on the transport, then dropped the Hudson down to sea level and sped across the Straits just above wave top height. As he flew up the Moesi River, Longworth spotted something suspicious in the shade of the trees and requested Richards to investigate. On doing so, a number of invasion barges were seen tucked tight in their shelter, the Hudson making a couple of passes at low level, all guns blazing, with Sqn Ldr Garrard manning one of the Vickers gas-operated side machine guns.

Eight Hurricanes of 232 Squadron provided cover over the target area, and then four of these strafed the decks of the two destroyers from mast height. However, eight Ki 27s of the 11th Sentai had arrived to operate from P.1, and three attempted to intercept the bombers, but two of these were reported shot down by the Hurricanes, Plt Offs Tom Watson and Reg Bainbridge claiming one apiece; two of the Japanese fighters did indeed sustain damage and both crash-landed on return to base. In return, the three 11th Sentai pilots claimed two 'Buffaloes' shot down out of four they reported engaging! None of the Hurricanes was lost however.

Two F1M floatplanes from the seaplane-tender *Sagara Maru*'s detachment at Muntok patrolled over the ships during the late afternoon, and the crews reported intercepting bombers. Due to the intensity of AA fire from the ships, Wt Off Yukii Makagune, the leading pilot, hesitated in his attack but his companion chased after the Hudson flown by Flg Off Richards. As the F1M approached, Sqn Ldr Garrard gave it a burst of fire from his beam Vickers and, almost immediately, the floatplane was seen to spin down into the sea. Makagune then attacked the Hudson, his fire riddling the fuselage, wounding Garrard in the left arm. Sgt Longworth, now manning the ventral Browning, continued:

> "Unexpectedly Paul Garrard fell on top of me, streaming blood pumping from his arm. I could see the damage to the aircraft as we were hit in various places, and there was a leak down the starboard wing, in spite of self-sealing tanks. There was a big hole where Paul had been standing where an explosive shell had splintered on impact.
>
> "Bobby broke off the engagement and headed for home, while I unfastened a large dressing and foolishly bound it tight over the wound in Paul's arm, thinking the pressure would stop the bleeding. Alas, my poor training in First Aid was Paul's misfortune, for he fainted during my ministrations. I unravelled the bandage as quick as I could to examine where I had gone wrong. I realised my stupidity soon enough as, on closer examination, I found pieces of shrapnel embedded in the arm. The pain of my clumsiness had been too much for him."

Despite the damage to his aircraft, Richards was able to reach P.2 safely, where Sqn Ldr Garrard was taken away by a makeshift ambulance for more skilful treatment to his wound.

The aerial action had been witnessed by those aboard one of the Singapore evacuation vessels, the 1020-ton coaster *Mata Hari*, which had been intercepted in the Banka Strait by a Japanese destroyer. Captives and captors alike watched as the Hudsons attacked the transports, as one captive later recalled:

> "Three (*sic*) of our bombers flew over and bombed a line of anchored Japanese transports but, worse luck, they all missed the target. As the last bomber went by our ship a Jap scout seaplane dived out of the clouds on to its tail. We were holding our breath when there was a burst of firing from the bomber's tail; the Jap plane seemed to stall as if it had hit a brick wall — it dived, recovered, started to climb and then suddenly nose crashed into the sea."

On completion of the sortie the remaining Hudsons departed for Java at about 1500, A16-42 in the hands of Flg Off Gibbes; his passengers included Air Commodore Hunter, AOC 225 Bomber Group, and Flg Off Donahue, the wounded Hurricane pilot. Gibbes flew at low altitude to the south-east of Sumatra to avoid patrolling fighters and landed at Bandoeng at 1705 hours. A little later Flt Lt Ken Smith and his crew, plus three passengers, departed in A16-26.

ABDAIR HQ at Bandoeng had, in the meantime, ordered that as many as possible of the Hudsons which had flown out from P.2 the previous day, should now return to help evacuate the wounded. Hence, about a dozen machines began arriving at P.2 between 1530 and 1600 hours, six of them from 62 Squadron, the others from the Australian units. Surplus gear had been stripped out of them and some even arrived without guns to increase their capacity as transports. Flt Lt O'Brien, leading the 62 Squadron flight, wrote:

> "It was after midday by the time the six of us were away and at Sumatra we were guided in by the huge fires at the oil depot below Palembang...The immense pillar of smoke was visible from a hundred miles away and after we crossed the coast the main column was lost to view in the pall that covered hundreds of square miles to windward of the conflagration.
>
> "From the activity on the airfield at P.2, which included a Hurricane taking off and a Blenheim taxying, it was clear we were still in possession, so we all put down without delay. The Blenheim pilot waved to me and it took a moment to realise it was Stanley Mayhew; he had found a fitter to patch up a Blenheim...and he flew it to Java."

It was left to each pilot as to how many passengers he could take, as the serviceability of each aircraft varied; the Hudsons departed with an average of 12 to 14 passengers, although Flg Off Henry had 21 aboard his aircraft. Unfortunately, when making his landing approach at Batavia, Henry came in too slowly for the excessive load he was carrying, touched down short of the runway, and knocked off his aircraft's undercarriage, although his crew and passengers survived unhurt. Aboard O'Brien's aircraft were all the unit's salvaged tool boxes — vital for the continued maintenance of the aircraft, which thereby reduced the number of passengers he was able to carry to nine. At dusk, the last Hudson to leave fittingly carried Wg Cdr Davis, CO of 1 RAAF Squadron.

Throughout the day, when not providing escort for the bombers, the Hurricanes continuously landed, re-armed, refuelled and returned to make strafing attacks against the troop-carrying barges. The last operation was against a number of aircraft sighted on the beach on the south-west of Banka Island. Flt Lt Julian led his flight down to strafe what were believed, at the time, to be A6Ms but were most probably F1Ms from the seaplane tenders; two were claimed destroyed, one by Julian.

The number of casualties suffered by Colonel Tanaka's troops during the series of strafing attacks has never been accurately ascertained, but is believed to have run into hundreds. Certainly the programme for the invasion was seriously upset and by mid afternoon all movement on the rivers up to Palembang had ceased. Ironically, it was at this point that the Hurricanes were ordered to withdraw to Java, all flyable aircraft departing without delay, manned in the main by 232 Squadron pilots.

There were not sufficient aircraft for all pilots but, as the majority of 258 Squadron's pilots were still in or around Palembang town, only three of the unit's NCO pilots were left at P.2 to make their own way to Java, together with a number of the replacement pilots who had arrived earlier at the airfield, including Sgt John Vibert, a New Zealander. He had walked to P.2 from Palembang, where he had presented himself to Sqn Ldr Thomson and asked to join 258 Squadron, his request being granted. However later in the day when the order was announced to evacuate P.2, he started walking again and subsequently boarded a train heading for Oosthaven, where he embarked for Java and re-joined the squadron there.

The three stranded 258 Squadron pilots, Sgts Terry Kelly, Bertie Lambert and Art Sheerin, returned to the airfield, where several unserviceable Hurricanes remained. One of these was Z5481, which Kelly had flown during the past two days, so he decided to start the engine. It made a terrible grinding noise while taxying, and pulled savagely to port when he began his take-off run but, by giving the engine full boost, he obtained sufficient power to get into the air, where the aircraft flew perfectly.

Lambert also found a flyable Hurricane and took-off, but Sheerin experienced greater difficulty. Having not found a suitable machine, he was then approached to fly a Blenheim full of ground personnel, who were awaiting a pilot. Initially agreeing to give this a try, he then spotted a Hurricane concealed in the undergrowth. On inspection, he noticed it was minus its tailwheel but, notwithstanding this, he jumped in, started up and taxied out to the runway. Just then a Flight Lieutenant clambered onto the wing and indicated that he had personally hidden the aircraft and that he intended to fly it to Java. Unperturbed, Sheerin increased speed — which dislodged the officer — took off and joined up with the other two, all eventually landing at Kemajoran without mishap.

232 Squadron had also 'abandoned' two of its pilots; Sgts Dunn and Kynman had been ordered to stay behind long enough to destroy any Hurricanes that could not be made serviceable, but Grp Capt McCauley ordered them aboard the last train to leave, assuring them that he would see that any unserviceable aircraft were burned.

Whilst air operations had continued unabated from P.2 airfield until mid-afternoon, many dozens of men were making their way southwards from Palembang town. Protection from air attack was afforded by just one lone Blenheim, as noted by Sgt George Dewey, an Australian of 34 Squadron:

> "On the afternoon of the 15th we flew backwards and forwards over the road
> from Palembang to Oosthaven to protect ground parties from fighter attack!
> Landed at Lahat."

The adventures which befell 84 Squadron's personnel were typical of the confusion which reigned. Sqn Ldr Tayler and the unit's other remaining officers, together with Flt Lt Jackson of 34 Squadron, had agreed to carry out earlier instructions to move surplus aircrews to Lahat, but to go by way of P.2 in case these orders should have been modified. With the arrival of dawn, the Ford three-tonner which had been used the previous day was taken by Flt Lt Gill to be refuelled, but this proved to be a lengthy operation due to lack of fuel at the various pumps visited. When he finally returned at 0800 he found that Plt Off Macdonald had located a small civilian van, and the two vehicles set off with 17 aircrew members and one fitter, plus crates of ammunition and their personal kit.

On arrival at the ferry much congestion was encountered, the Dutch claiming priority for their troop-laden vehicles, which were on their way to challenge the Japanese invaders progressing up the river. It was not until just after midday that 84 Squadron's vehicles succeeded in getting across the river, where Sgt Hough had acquired another van in which he transported a number of wounded to P.2. Macdonald's van was therefore driven directly to Lahat, whilst the three-tonner picked up a number of 226 Fighter Group officers and a wounded Fleet Air Arm officer, while on the way to P.2. The airfield was finally reached at about 1500, where the arrivals learned that they were to depart immediately for Oosthaven, in preparation for evacuation to Java.

Driving the heavily-overloaded three-tonner throughout the night, the party encountered a decrepit local bus full of small-arms ammunition. This was being driven by one of 84 Squadron's drivers who had just arrived at Oosthaven aboard the transport vessel *Yoma*, along with other members (including spare aircrew) of 84 and 211 Squadrons' Sea Parties from the Middle East; the ammunition-loaded bus was destined for P.2, but the driver was advised to return whence he came, which he wisely did. On arrival at Oosthaven, Sqn Ldr Tayler reported to a Group Captain at the docks, who ordered him to join the party of armed airmen ashore, while the remainder of the lorry party were ordered to embark aboard the *Yoma* without delay.

Tayler now found himself in charge of about 200 armed airmen, who were ordered to hold Natar, a junction of road, rail and stream about 20 miles north of Oosthaven. On the following day however, they were ordered to embark aboard a small, fast ammunition vessel departing for Batavia.

Another group of airmen left stranded in Palembang town was the 258 Squadron detachment under Flg Off Macnamara. Having returned from their skirmishes with the Japanese paratroopers on the road to P.1, they found that Sgt Scott and his party were missing. Unbeknown to his colleagues, Scott and survivors of his group had been cut off in the fighting, so they had headed for the railway station, eventually reaching Oosthaven by train. Although the ship they boarded called in at a Javanese port, the captain refused to allow Scott ashore to rejoin his squadron, and he was carried on to Ceylon.

Shortly after midday, Flg Off Tudor Jones and AC1 Peter Lamont saw an abandoned Dutch motorboat drifting down the river with its engines running. They were able to leap aboard as it came within reach; one engine had seized but Lamont succeeded in getting it working. Meanwhile Tudor Jones had rounded up his four companions — Macnamara, Campbell, McCulloch and Cicurel — and with Lamont at the wheel, the craft headed for the railway station, about a mile upstream. On arrival they discovered that the last train had departed; they considered heading out to sea and around the coast to Java, but were advised to avoid the Moesi delta because of the amount of Japanese traffic on it. Armed to the teeth, they headed upstream instead and after checking that P.2 had also fallen into Japanese hands, made Matapoera their target, where they hoped to pick up a train.

By the following midday they had reached a village where a friendly local chief advised them that further navigation upstream was not possible. He exchanged a lorry and driver for their boat, enabling them to set off by road for their destination. Before long however, a demolished bridge halted them and, though able to get across the river in native canoes, the lorry had to be left behind. A gruelling 20 mile walk now began, during which the party split into two groups, Tudor Jones and Campbell forging ahead. They reached Matapoera and were at once offered lifts in a number of cars that were just leaving; realising that there was no room for the others, they decided to press on, rather than ask the drivers to wait.

Macnamara and the rest of the party arrived, having completed the walk in ten hours, but were totally exhausted. Any hopes of a train were quickly dashed — the last one had gone some time before, and the town had been all but abandoned. Among many wrecked vehicles they discovered a serviceable car but, as they strove to get fuel for it, a truck carrying some Dutch and British sailors arrived, survivors of a minesweeper bombed at Pladjoe. These had arrived purely by chance, having become lost. They were happy to take aboard the British party, who were able to direct them onto the correct road for Oosthaven, along which they drove throughout the night. Following a stop for breakfast in a still-inhabited town, they reached the port on the morning of the 17th, as demolitions were still taking place. A ferry steamer was just about to leave and, getting aboard this moments before it sailed, the RAF men were reunited with the rest of their party, who had arrived some hours earlier. Ting Macnamara was recommended for the award of the Military Cross for his performance over these two days, though the award was apparently never approved at higher level.

The losses inflicted on the invading forces by the Hurricanes and the bombers during the day could only delay the inevitable and, as soon as darkness fell, the landing craft were able to proceed to Palembang. Colonel Tanaka's surviving troops made contact with the paratroop survivors that night — nearly 36 hours behind schedule. A further 96 paratroops, led by Lt Ryo Morisawa, were dropped over P.1 at about midday. Of the 360 dropped on the first day, almost 25% had become casualties, of whom 37 were killed, a relatively small price to pay for the gains achieved. It was already clear to General Wavell that he could not hope to hold Sumatra.

With the departure of the Hudsons and Hurricanes from P.2, by the evening there remained about 20 Blenheims belonging to 84 and 211 Squadrons. Wg Cdr Bateson wrote:

> "Since most of 211 and 84 Squadron Blenheims were unserviceable, and it was obvious that insufficient road transport was available to take aircrews and groundcrews to Batavia, I decided with OC 84 to remain overnight and try to get sufficient aircraft serviceable to get us all out — that meant putting up to seven people in a Blenheim. My hope was that the Japs would concentrate on looting Palembang and the airfield before coming on to P.2."

The Blenheims were moved to the far end of the airfield, where tents were pitched for the night. Sgt Archie Wakefield:

> "By this time I was feeling hungry, and so wandered off back to the admin buildings at the start of the runway. There I found a grocery store which had been abandoned. There were tins of all sorts — sausages, fruits, etc, and also a delivery bicycle with a front carrier. I piled this with tins, and rode back to the far end of the field, where we had a real feast. Others used the bike to get more supplies, and we sat there in the dark, eating and drinking, whilst the CO played his guitar and sang!"

Another airgunner, Sgt Eric Oliver, achieved even greater success and popularity when he returned to the assembled group with his 'find':

"We were pretty bored with ourselves and we believed there must be some booze at the old canteen. I looked around and found a tractor, and chugged all the way down to the buildings at the other end of the field — they were huts, not barrack rooms. I looked around the buildings — like a deserted Wild West town — windows flapping, doors banging; the people had grabbed all their essentials and had taken off; kit bags, photographs and belongings everywhere, but what was the object of picking them up? We didn't have space (in the aircraft) to carry our own belongings.

Sgt Eric Oliver, WOp/AG with 84 Squadron (*E. Oliver*)

"I went into the bar — it was empty but nothing was locked up. I sampled this and that, and wondered how to carry some back to the boys. By then I was getting a bit drunk! I looked around and found an old round bath — a zinc tub — and then some rope. I tried to fasten it onto the back of the tractor, but it wouldn't work, what with the weight and the tub being ungainly. So, I dragged it like a sledge across the grass with the tractor.

"By the time I got back to the boys there was more broken glass than booze! That's all I remember of the final night at P.2."

Whilst the day's main action centred in and around the Banka Strait, the Japanese covering force of warships had prepared to engage the approaching Allied fleet. Shortly before 0700, a patrol of A5Ms from *Ryujo* attempted to intercept a shadowing Dutch flying-boat, but failed to make contact. An hour later, the crew of a reconnaissance floatplane from the cruiser *Chokai* reported sighting the Allied fleet and, at 0805, seven B5N single-engined light bombers took-off from *Ryujo* to attack the warships. After a flight of almost two and a half hours, the formation came upon *Exeter* and carried out an attack, during which the crews believed some damage had been inflicted; the blast from a near miss seriously damaged Pty Off(A) Bill Crozer's embarked Walrus amphibian (R6587). The attack was repeated an hour later by six more B5Ns, but without effect on this occasion.

Captain Oliver Gordon, *Exeter*'s commander, later wrote:

"Each wave of bombers as it came towards its target received a hot reception from the Allied ships and then, as the bombs dropped, the target ships would make independent and rapid alterations of course; seconds later, the sea would be alive with great soaring sheets of water."

In between the two B5N attacks, a force of 23 G3Ms of the Genzan Ku from Kuching carried out a high-level attack on the force, without result apart from AA shrapnel damage to eight of the attackers. Although by midday the fleet had closed to within 80 miles of the Japanese force, this had now retired northwards, whilst the Allied force found itself within range of further attack by Japanese land-based bombers. Admiral Doorman decided that it was unwise to go on and ordered the fleet to return to Tanjong Priok. As they withdrew eastwards, another high-level attack was carried out by 27 G3Ms of the Mihoro Ku, flying out of Kuantan. Again the fleet escaped damage and the fierce AA resistance caused damage to almost half the raiders, although all returned safely.

HMS *Exeter* under attack off the Sumatran coast on 15 February; her Walrus (R6587) can be seen perched on the catapult. *(Authors' collection)*

At 1430 a further seven B5Ns launched an attack, but again without success; this was followed two hours later by yet another such raid, this time by six aircraft; two near misses were claimed on a cruiser but two of the bombers sustained AA damage. The final assault came shortly before dark, when 17 G4Ms of the Kanoya Ku — following a five hour flight from Thu Dau Moi airfield (Saigon) — at last spotted the fleet. An attack was carried out but no hits were gained, although almost all the bombers suffered shrapnel damage, and one crashed when attempting to land at Ledo, Borneo, whilst another was severely damaged on landing at Kahang.

Despite a total of 93 bomber sorties flown against the Allied warships from 1000 until dusk, negligible damage had been inflicted, only two destroyers — the American pair *Bulmer* and *Barker* — reporting light damage from near misses, while *Exeter* suffered nothing more serious than splinter holes. The B5Ns from *Ryujo*, although able to carry torpedoes, were not used in this capacity owing to lack of crew training; additionally it was discovered that the torpedoes on board the carrier had been poorly maintained, while it had not proved possible to arm the land-based G3Ms and G4Ms with such weapons due to the poor state of the airfields in use.

Monday, 16 February

At first light the Blenheims — including odd machines which had been abandoned by 27 and 34 Squadrons — started to slip away from P.2, each machine carrying ground personnel as well as crew. Plt Off Coughlan's Z9660 carried five passengers in addition to the crew, including the injured Sgt Crowe. Few of them could be called serviceable, but all had been patched up to reduce the more obvious leaks of oil and hydraulic fluid, gun-cleaning wadding having been employed to good effect. Amongst those watching the aircraft climb away was Wg Cdr Bateson:

> "I remember it was a beautiful morning and as each aircraft lumbered into the air, it became more beautiful. That left the OC 84 and myself to go. We had delayed starting fires to avoid detection but now destroyed everything we could. Then OC 84 took off, closely followed by my own battered Blenheim."

One of the Blenheims was lost on the flight to Java. This particular machine had previously suffered problems with its starboard engine, however all concerned agreed to give it a try. Following a seemingly smooth take-off by Sgt Noel Geappen, RAAF, trouble again occurred with this engine after about an hour, and the pilot shouted to his passengers that he would have to try to put the aircraft down.

The Blenheim was flying over thickly wooded mountainous jungle, south-east of Lahat, but after some while the observer drew the pilot's attention to the silver thread of a river in a valley. As the aircraft dived down the crew could see that the river opened out into a reasonably wide lake; all aboard braced themselves for a crash-landing on the water but the Blenheim broke up on impact and sank. Of the eight persons on board only Cpl R.F. Shaw survived:

> "I remember seeing the water rushing by but at the moment of impact I must have blacked out, for when I came to I found myself flying through the air. I must have blacked out again as I hit the water for the next thing I remember was struggling to the surface. As I reached the air, I gasped for breath and looked around, treading water. Apart from the surface of the water being disturbed, there was nothing else to see. The aircraft and its occupants had disappeared completely.
>
> "By the pain I was suffering I knew I was severely injured (broken ribs and a punctured lung amongst other injuries), but hadn't time to really think about it. I then saw papers and charts waving in the water like fish, as they floated to the surface, and then a petrol tank bobbed up. It took me great effort and time to reach the tank and drag my body half onto it; the pain in my chest was crucifying me.
>
> "After a time I took notice of what shore I could see, but it was covered in trees and too far away for me to reach. How long I was on the tank before I first saw signs of other humans, I don't know, but eventually a canoe approached with two men inside it, and they were joined by other canoes. However, they paddled in a circle around me, simply watching for what seemed quite a long period. At last somebody made up their mind, for a canoe came in close but instead of lifting me into the boat, they attached a rope to the tank and towed us to the shore."[1]

Ron Shaw was carried ashore and put down beside a tree; after about an hour, a well-dressed, English-speaking, Sumatran arrived and instructed the others to carry the injured airman along a jungle path to a waiting car; he was driven to

---

[1] As related to Chad Middleton of 84 Squadron.

a Dutch bungalow, from where he was taken by ambulance to Oosthaven, and thence to Java by ship.[1]

A second Blenheim was almost lost during the evacuation, as recalled by Sgt Ross aboard Sgt Sayer's aircraft:

> "We took off at first light and over Sunda Strait ran into a violent storm with shocking turbulence, and flak. Our plane got out of control, with apparatus and loose equipment flying around my turret; miraculously George regained control and we came out of the storm to be about 150 feet over three or four naval ships. We hit cloud again and never did know of their identity or nationality."

At Lahat 34 Squadron was forced to destroy one unserviceable Blenheim, but the remaining four were ordered to Batavia. None of these aircraft could be considered serviceable; the CO's machine was devoid of its sliding roof and the undercarriage had to be operated by hand; a second was minus the front perspex panels in the bomb aimer's position, whilst the only working instruments were the RPM and oil gauges; another aircraft was without functioning flaps. One of the Blenheims had just got airborne when its starboard engine cut, forcing Sgt D.B. Williams to return immediately to Lahat, where a creditable landing was made. Finding the airfield apparently deserted, and unable to carry out the necessary repairs themselves, Williams and his crew set fire to the Blenheim, then found a truck and drove to Oosthaven.

Another aircraft to escape from Lahat was the MVAF's Miles Falcon ('32'), which had arrived from Djambi the previous evening in the hands of Plt Off K.G. Hamnett and Sgt H.F. Frederiksen. Two further aircraft of 2 Detached Flight were due to arrive from Pakan Baroe, but events prevented this. Instead, Flg Off J.D. Mead in Tiger Moth '43' of 1 Detached Flight, accompanied by another ('28'), flew to Padang, whilst a third ('34' flown by Sgt Tom Graham) attempted to follow, only for it to force-land in a paddy-field en route. The two aircraft which succeeded in reaching Padang were eventually destroyed there by the RAF, whilst the personnel of 2 Detached Flight under Flt Lt Nixon reached Padang by road and train, where they were picked up by a cruiser and evacuated to Java.

Whilst the Blenheims from Lahat droned eastwards towards Java, Flg Off Gibbes of 1 RAAF Squadron had been ordered to fly back to Sumatra — first to Lahat and then to Djambi — with evacuation orders for the respective airfield commanders. The Hudson was forced down to 1,000 feet by storms, arriving at Lahat just after first light, where he was informed by Wg Cdr Noble that Djambi had already fallen to the Japanese. With the Hudson's tanks topped up from cans, and Noble embarked, Gibbes set out for the return flight to Bandoeng. On nearing the coast of Java, both engines cut out due to water in the fuel; Gibbes prepared to make a belly landing, but first switched over to a tank which had not been topped up at Lahat, whereupon the engines restarted. An emergency landing was made at Tjililitan airfield, where the problem was rectified.

With the flying echelons of the RAF now effectively out of Sumatra, Palembang would become a prime target for Allied air attack as the Japanese moved in.

---

[1] Ron Shaw recovered from his injuries but was taken prisoner when Java fell; sadly, he was killed when the Atomic bomb was dropped on Nagasaki on 9th August 1945, the only British airman to loose his life in the attack.

Chapter 3

THE BATTLE FOR BATAAN AND CORREGIDOR
1 January — 12 May

By the beginning of the New Year, US and Philippine forces on Luzon had been pushed back to the Bataan Peninsula (see Volume One, Chapter 5), where they began to consolidate their positions for the final defence. Here the remaining aircraft were also established — which included 18 original and two rebuilt P-40s, plus two P-35As, which had been flown to Pilar Field on north-eastern Bataan on 29 December. Groundcrews of the 17th Pursuit Squadron had been hard at work converting rice paddies into landing strips for some days. Cabcaben Field had been established on the south-east coast of the peninsula, and Bataan Field about three miles north of this. On 2 January five P-35As and the sole surviving A-27 took off to fly to Bataan Field, but on arrival were met by AA fire. 2/Lt Oscar D. Wyatt Jr's aircraft was heavily damaged and he turned for Pilar, but crashed and was killed. 2/Lt Robert A. Krantz's P-35A was also hit and he too headed back to Pilar; on landing he overshot the runway and the aircraft was written off. The three remaining 0-49s were flown to Corregidor joined by the A-27, where two of the observation aircraft tipped up on their noses on landing, effectively rendering them unserviceable.

There was little chance of reinforcement. The American bomber force had retreated to Australia and the future looked bleak, as the seemingly invincible invaders continued their push southwards. With so few aircraft remaining, large numbers of USAAF members, both air and groundcrew, now found themselves classified as infantry. Such training in this role as could be given was provided by those with any relevant experience, while a wide variety of weapons were accumulated, including Lewis guns, Browning automatic rifles, Navy Marling machine guns, and some British Bren carriers, taken from a vessel which had been on its way to Hong Kong when the colony fell. Several .50-inch Brownings from aircraft were also obtained, but these tended to overheat after a few rounds had been fired, as they were designed to be fired with an aircraft slipstream to cool them.

Food was to be in short supply from the start and, within a week, all commands on Bataan had been placed on half rations. The southern half of the peninsula was extremely malarial and it was not long before the supply of quinine ran out. Over 80% of US and Filipino troops had contracted malaria by the end of the campaign; dysentry also became common.

———

Wreckage of two Seversky P-35As found on Nichols Field by the Japanese. *(Clark AFB Museum)*

As the New Year heralded the epic defence of the peninsula, JAAF light bombers were over the area daily, claiming many vehicles destroyed or damaged during the opening days of the month. Navy bombers joined in this assault on 2 January, but then resumed attacks on Corregidor, raiding this target for the next four days in some strength. Mariveles was also attacked on the 4th and 5th by bombers of the 1st Ku; in the meantime, Japanese troops had entered Manila on the 2nd and taken over the Cavite Navy Yard, with all the spoils of war therein.

The 74th Independent Chutai moved to Cabanatuan airfield on the 3rd but, en route to its new base, the unit's Ki 36s were attacked by a pair of Pilar-based P-40s, which had just been strafing this airfield. The commanding officer, Capt Sadao Hori, was shot down and killed by 2/Lt Earl R. Stone Jr of the 17th Pursuit Squadron. Hori was posthumously awarded an individual citation.

In an effort to raise American morale, a major interception by P-40s was planned. After attacking a Japanese bomber formation, the fighters would head for Del Monte. Lt William E. Dyess was to lead the mission, with the other 17 pilots drawn from all four squadrons of the 24th Fighter Group. At 1100 on the 4th therefore, nine P-40s took off from Pilar, led by Lt F.C. Roberts, and flew to Del Carmen to rendezvous with the other nine. When these did not appear, they returned to Pilar, refuelled and set off for Del Monte but ran into bad weather en route, only four reaching their destination. Lt David L. Obert and 2/Lt Walter Wilcox landed independently at Cebu, where they refuelled and then headed for Mindanao, but Wilcox crashed on Bohol Island and was killed. Meanwhile, Lt Vogel had come down in a pineapple field whilst 2/Lt J.P. Cole crash-landed on Negros Island; badly injured, he was eventually moved to Del Monte by boat. On arrival at Del Monte, Roberts and the survivors of his flight discovered that the operation had been cancelled.

Later in the day 1/Lt Robert Wray took off from Orani Field at the top of the Bataan peninsula, which was now perilously close to the front lines, to pursue a reconnaissance aircraft north of Zambales. Four fighters attacked him, but he turned into these and one disappeared over a hill, trailing smoke. The others pursued him, but one appeared to crash into trees whilst following him at low level. No further sorties were undertaken from Orani thereafter.

Maj General William F. Sharp, officer commanding on Mindanao, intimated that he suspected the pilots had deliberately escaped from Bataan without orders, but allowed them to stay at Del Monte where, for two weeks, the four serviceable P-40s undertook a number of reconnaissances, before being ordered back to Bataan.

In the meantime operations had continued. The Tainan Ku A6Ms at Legaspi resumed their series of strafing attacks, four led by Lt Masuro Seto strafing four floatplanes in Mariveles Bay on the 5th, where one floatplane was claimed burned and the other three plus a small flyingboat were believed either destroyed or damaged; they had found Pat Wing 10's Utility Squadron, which was destroyed, two Curtiss SOC Seagulls, two Vought OS2U Kingfishers, and a Grumman J2F Duck amphibian all being sunk. The leading section of A6Ms then engaged two P-40s south of Limay, NAP 3/C Saburo Nozawa claiming one of these shot down. It would appear that his victim was 2/Lt Percy Ramsey, who had taken off from Bataan Field with another pilot on a reconnaissance sortie, but was at once attacked and shot down, baling out. On receipt of this report, three more A6Ms were sent off during the afternoon to reconnoitre Limay airfield, but the pilots could not see anything on the ground. NAP 3/C Shizuo Ishii, the third man in this formation, then found a lone P-40 and gave chase, forcing this to crash into the ground. The leader's A6M had been hit however, and NAP 2/C Kazuo Yokokawa was obliged to force-land at Nichols Field, which was no longer in US hands. NAP 2/C Yoshisuke Arita landed alongside to ensure that Yokokawa was alright, then took off and returned to base with Ishii. After making repairs, Yokokawa was able to follow next day.

Japanese troops examine a wrecked B-17D at Clark Field. *(E. Mikesh)*

On 6th two pairs of P-40s took off from Pilar on a reconnaissance. The first pair flew up the Lingayen Gulf, but on return 2/Lt Stephen H. Crosby was attacked as he went in to land. His attacker was driven off by another P-40, but his aircraft was then hit by AA, although he subsequently got down safely. His saviour had been 2/Lt Joseph L. McClellan, who had seen a Ki 30 on his tail, which he attacked and claimed as a probable.

The second pair, 2/Lts Elmer 'Bud' Powell Jr, and William M. Rowe, encountered six Ki 48s over Manila Bay. Powell attacked the second 'vic' of three, but was hit in the eye by return fire, and baled out.

Two days later on 8th three P-40s set off on a reconnaissance and strafe, but on return saw three Ki 30s strafing Pilar airfield, but were unable to shoot any down. However, Pilar was now abandoned, nine P-40s, two P-35As and the A-27 concentrating at Bataan Field, where they were ordered to undertake reconnaissance sorties only.

The Japanese Army was now preparing to launch an offensive down both sides of the Bataan Peninsula on the 9th, but with so few important targets remaining, there was no longer the need for the whole of the 5th Flying Division to remain in support. Activity for most of the division had ended abruptly on the 7th, while next day the 10th Independent Hikotai was re-organised and strengthened to remain as the Army's air support, under the command of Colonel Komotaro Hoshi. At this point the division was based as follows:

5th Flying Division Headquarters: Vigan

4th Flying Battalion

8th Sentai, Tuguegarao:	30 Ki 48s (14 serviceable)
Vigan:	7 Ki 15s and Ki 46s
14th Sentai, Tuguegarao: (part)	⎱ 25 Ki 21s (18 serviceable)
Formosa: (part)	⎰
16th Sentai, Vigan:	36 Ki 30s (30 serviceable)
24th Sentai, Nagirian:	⎱
50th Sentai, Vigan:	⎰ 73 Ki 27s (50 serviceable)
Clark Field: (3rd Chutai)	

10th Independent Hikotai:

52nd Ind Chutai, Del Carmen:	9 Ki 51s
74th Ind Chutai, Cabanatuan:	8 Ki 36s (6 serviceable)
76th Ind Chutai, Tuguegarao:	7 Ki 15s
Bandai: (detachment)	2 Ki 46s
11th Transport Chutai, Tuguegarao:	9 transports (7 serviceable)

The 10th Hikotai had been strengthened by the arrival of the 16th Sentai, which moved to Clark Field on the 11th for these duties, and the 3rd Chutai of the 50th Sentai, which was already at this latter base. The remainder of the 4th Flying Battalion began leaving for Indo-China and Thailand, from where most of its units would join in the operations over Burma (see relevant chapters). During its activities over the Philippines since 6 December, the division had lost 42 aircraft; amongst the aircrews 45 had been killed, 40 wounded and six were missing. Aircraft losses had been as follows:

8th Sentai	8 Ki 48s and one Ki 46
14th Sentai	3 Ki 21s

16th Sentai	1 Ki 30
24th Sentai	4 Ki 27s
50th Sentai	12 Ki 27s
52nd Ind Chutai	5 Ki 51s
74th Ind Chutai	4 Ki 36s

During mid January the Japanese advance made some progress, forcing the defenders to retreat to their final defence line, anchored between Orion and Bagac. Navy bombers again raided Corregidor and Mariveles during this period. At this time a number of engagements occurred and were recorded by both the Japanese and Americans, but on different dates. Due to the confusion and lack of precise records at Bataan, it is likely that the Japanese dates were the more accurate. Therefore, whilst it is difficult to equate the various actions with each other, with any degree of precision, it is believed that they do so relate.

On 11 January Maj Reginald Vance, Gen MacArthur's air officer set out to fly Maj Gerald Wilkinson, the British liaison officer, to Del Monte in the A-27. Oil pressure dropped as they took off and the aircraft crashed. Both men survived unhurt, but the A-27 was destroyed. On this same date the two remaining P-35As were flown out to Del Monte. Reportedly on this date a specially stripped P-40E at Del Monte was taken on a reconnaissance by 2/Lt Gordon S. Benson. In the Davao area he encountered three Zeros, which damaged his aircraft. Escaping their attack, he crash-landed in the water off-shore, and 'planed' onto the beach, where his attackers then strafed the aircraft.

On the 17th, Ki 27s of the 50th Sentai's 3rd Chutai attacked Limay airfield, claiming three aircraft burned on the ground. A week later, reportedly on the 24th, Ki 30s from the 2nd Chutai, 16th Sentai, which attacked Pilar Field were engaged by P-40s and lost two of their number. Two days later, on the 26th, this Sentai's aircraft were again reportedly engaged by a pair of P-40s, claiming one shot down for the loss of one more Ki 30. Lt Noboru Mune of the 50th Sentai also claimed a P-40 during the month, but the exact date is not known. Next day the unit was out again, this time attacking Limay airfield where one aircraft was claimed burned and one damaged on the ground.

Because of the constant air attack on front line troops, the Bataan-based P-40s were ordered to undertake some patrols on 17th. Several attacks were made on reconnaissance aircraft without effect, but then at 1025 two P-40 pilots spotted an observation aircraft east of Cabcaban, which Lt Marshall J. Anderson claimed to have shot down into Manila Bay in full view of the ground troops. Nine bombers were then seen, but these withdrew, but two more observation machines were then seen at the north end of the peninsula, and one of these was claimed by 2/Lt Jack W. Hall. Both were to be awarded DSCs for this flight.

Next day two P-40s were off again, 2/Lt William M. Rowe attacking two Ki 30s, both of which fell smoking into cloud. He followed and encountered a Ki 27, which he also hit and which went down smoking. As these engagements took place over the Japanese lines, no confirmations were forthcoming. Two more fighters went off over Subic Bay in the afternoon, where south of Silanguin Island a large vessel was seen with a catapult aircraft circling. Wilson Glover and 2/Lt John H. Posten attacked and it went down, smoking heavily. They then chanced a two-seater observation aircraft which evaded them.

As Bataan was now down to five P-40Es and two P-40Bs, four of the six at Del Monte were ordered to transfer there. Four of those already there were in the air to cover the arrival of the new aircraft, when eight Japanese aircraft were seen. Marshall Anderson and 2/Lt Lloyd Stinson engaged fighters, ground observers later reporting that two of these had crashed. Stinson thought he had got both, but one was credited to Anderson, who was shot down and baled out, but was killed on his parachute. He may have been Lt Mune's victim; Stinson's P-40 was also slightly damaged.

Nipa hut used as a headquarters on Bataan — typical of the primitive conditions under which the US forces were obliged to live. *(S. Grashio)*

Four P-40s took off in pairs on 26th, 2/Lts Posten and Stone seeing and attacking a trio of Ki 30s, one of which they shot down in flames between them. They claimed damage to the other two, but next day I Corps reported that both these had crashed into their lines. As no claims are recorded for them, it seems probable that this engagement may embrace both those reported by the 16th Sentai for 24th and 26th.

That evening three pilots took off with loads of 30lb fragmentation bombs, but the third crashed, the bombs exploding; despite this, a shaken 2/Lt Roberts survived. Although General Harold H. George, commanding what remained of the USAAF in the Philippines, husbanded his remaining fighters carefully, he did allow one attack to be launched on Nichols and Neilson Fields, which was undertaken by six aircraft later that night with reported success. However, by the end of January availability of fighter aircraft on Bataan had fallen to seven P-40s, only four of which were serviceable. Claims by Japanese crews for aircraft destroyed on the ground must have related to wrecks or dummies however, for the Americans had become adept at effective camouflage by then, and no such losses were suffered during the month. Towards the end of the month, a B-24 flew into Del Monte at night in order to pick up 25 much-needed ground crew sergeants. Major Gerald Wilkinson, the British liaison officer, was also ordered to leave aboard the departing bomber. To accomplish this flight from Australia, Lt Theo Boselli, the B-24's pilot, had avoided patrolling Japanese aircraft — by changing course four times — and relied on the stars to guide him to the unlit airstrip.

It was about this time that US President Franklin D. Roosevelt sent a message to the people and defenders of the Philippines:

> "The world will long remember what you, the people of the Philippines, are doing, and what you have been doing since this war began. I renew my solemn pledge to you that your freedom will be redeemed and your independence established and protected.
>
> "The entire resources in men and materials of the United States have been mobilized behind the pledge. Stand firm, people of the Philippines, your day is coming."

In an effort to shorten the campaign, the Japanese sought to land elements of the 2nd Battalion of the 20th Infantry Regiment five miles behind the US lines, in the sort of infiltration attacks that had proved so successful in Malaya. During the night of the 22nd/23rd therefore, 1,000 men set out in barges, but these became disorientated in stormy tides and, when attacked by a US motor-torpedo boat, two of the barges were sunk. Split into two groups, the Japanese failed to reach their original destination, about 60% of the remaining infantry-men coming ashore at Quinauan Point, several miles south of the target area. The remainder landed at Longoskawayan Point near Mariveles, were they were ineffectively attacked by an untrained unit of US sailors, leavened with a few Marines. At Quinauan Point elements of several air force units (mostly 34th Pursuit Squadron) were bewildered by this first taste of ground combat, and awaited reinforcements. The Japanese, at first thought to be only a few stragglers, proved very difficult to dislodge and only after hard fighting by Philippine Scouts from the 45th and 57th US Infantry Regiments, were they finally eliminated after about two weeks.

Indeed, the Japanese sent 300 reinforcements to Quinauan Point, but these too got lost and landed a mile north at Aglaloma Point, where they were opposed by 17th Pursuit Squadron troops. On the night of 1/2 February the rest of the 20th Regiment's 1st Battalion attempted to land, but were spotted and strafed by the four remaining P-40s, which also dropped 100 lb bombs. About half the force was killed by these, by torpedo boats or artillery. Although some 400 got ashore they were eventually wiped out after a long, hard fight.

General George then received information that San Jose airfield had been taken. This was an important midway point between Bataan and Del Monte, so Lt Obert was sent off on 3 February, with two others, to investigate. They found the field still in friendly hands, landed and loaded their P-40s with 100 lb sacks of sugar for Bataan. 2/Lts Jack Hall and Ed Woolery, who were still carrying bombs, were ordered to release these on the Japanese lines during the return flight — Obert having inadvertently released his bombs on San Jose! While attacking positions in Manila Bay, Hall and Woolery apparently collided and were both killed.

In order to neutralize the big guns on Corregidor, the Japanese had emplaced some high-angle howitzers near Cavite. These could not be spotted by observers, as they were located behind high ground, so a PT-13 trainer was equipped to photograph them, flown by Capt Jesus Villamor, former commander of the now defunct Philippine 6th Pursuit Squadron. Escorted by five P-40s led by Lt Obert, Villamor climbed to 10,000 feet on the morning of the 9th and managed to get the required photographs before six Ki 27s of the 50th Sentai attacked as the formation returned to its own airfield. Although the P-40s went for the interceptors, one kept after Villamor, who threw the little aircraft into a dive, despite warnings that this might cause the wings to fold up, then fled for the airfield, pursued right to his landing by the persistent fighter. He received a DSC for the mission and was also presented by General George with a scarce bottle of Scotch whisky.

Cpl Satoshi Anabuki claimed his first three victories over the Philippines with the 50th Sentai. He was later to see service in Burma, surviving as the Japanese Army's top-scorer of the Pacific War, credited with at least 51 victories.

had been fighting the other Japanese fighters, but 2/Lt Earl Stone, who had been credited with three victories, failed to return, and 2/Lt Posten's aircraft was shot-up. Cpl Satoshi Anabuki (who was to become the highest-scoring JAAF pilot of the war) claimed two victories during this action. No claims were

A group of ground crew on Bataan with a P-40E, beneath a camouflage net. (*T. Hatzer via C. Marvel*)

made by the US pilots, but HQ subsequently credited them with all six Ki 27s shot down! It was believed that Stone had chased one into cloud which masked Mount Bataan, both aircraft apparently crashing into the upper slope of the mountain. Two more were credited to 2/Lt Ben Brown, one to Posten, and apparently one each to Lt Obert, the flight leader, and 2/Lt Stinson. One Ki 27 was seen to force-land at Pilar, where it was shot at and set on fire by US artillery.

At the end of February the Bataan flying detachment was commanded by newly-promoted Capt Dyess who took over from Ben Brown; there were six operational P-40s divided into two flights, one under the control of Dyess, the other led by Lt Joseph H. Moore (former commander of the 20th Pursuit Squadron). On 25 February Lt Bill Rowe took off to cover the landing of another P-40, but was then despatched after an enemy aircraft. A Ki 27 then attacked him, but he managed to escape with two bullet holes in one wing. The detachment undertook its last major action when Dyess learned — on 2 March — of the arrival of several Japanese ships in Subic Bay, north-west of Bataan. These were obviously bringing in supplies for a renewed offensive, therefore an attack was planned.

Capt William E. Dyess, commanding officer of the flying detachment on Bataan. He is seen on his return from a bombing sortie over Subic Bay on March 4, for which he subsequently received a DSC. With nine others he later escaped from a Japanese prison camp, only to die in a flying accident back in the United States. *(S. Grashio)*

T/Sgt Jack O'Day, a technical NCO, had devised a shackle to enable a 500 lb bomb to be carried beneath Dyess' P-40. Consequently, two days later, five flyable P-40s were bombed-up, 2/Lt Posten attacking first with six 30 lb fragmentation bombs, without observed result. At 1230 Dyess took-off with a 500 pounder, covered by Lt Donald M. Crosland. Climbing to 10,000 feet, he observed a large transport being unloaded, then diving to 2,000 feet he bombed and strafed this, also machine-gunning two smaller vessels. Two more sorties were carried out but 2/Lt Erwin B. Crelin failed to return from the first of these, believed shot down by AA fire, while 2/Lt John P. Burns crash-landed a P-40B on return from the second. Undaunted by these losses, Dyess made two further attacks, his bomb hitting the large transport during the second of these sorties.

2/Lt Brown later commented:

> "Although I was Dyess' relief pilot, he still made four shuttle hops, refusing to let me fly in his place. At the end of the day Dyess had sunk one tanker, beached another tanker, sank four launches and strafed troops and harbour installations."

Late in the afternoon two more P-40Es repeated the attack, 2/Lts Lloyd Stinson and Jim Fossey claiming one small cargo vessel sunk by machine-gun fire. On returning to Mariveles the American pilots encountered a vicious tail wind, causing both to crash-land; both fighters were deemed irreparable, although one would subsequently be rebuilt by cannibalizing the others. For the time being, only Dyess's aircraft, "Kibosh", remained available.

In addition to the P-40s there existed a motley collection of light aircraft — mostly ex-civilian, including the remaining Beechcraft 18s, a Waco biplane and a Beechcraft Staggerwing — known as 'The Bamboo Fleet' — which maintained a service between Bataan, Cebu and Mindanao, evacuating critical personnel and flying in urgent supplies. The Waco was flown on a number of missions by Capt Richard W. Fellows, who had been OC the Philippines Air Depot, transporting otherwise stranded fighter pilots from one location to another.

Early March brought some changes within the 10th Hikotai, while on the 7th, during a raid over Limay, Colonel Yanase, commander of the 16th Sentai, was badly wounded by AA fire, his place being taken by Lt Colonel Shojiro Kawamorita. Location and strength of units were now:

16th Sentai	Nichols	32 Ki 30s
76th Ind Chutai	Nichols	9 Ki 15s
52nd Ind Chutai	Nielson	10 Ki 36s and Ki 51s
74th Ind Chutai	Zablan	8 Ki 36s and Ki 51s
3rd Chutai, 50th Sentai	Zablan	10 Ki 27s for the defence of Manila

With the continued stubborn resistance of the US Forces, General Masaharu Homma[1], the Japanese commander of the 14th Army in the Philippines, was obliged reluctantly to request reinforcements, as he now had only 3,000 men, one unit of his 48th Division having been removed for service in the Netherlands East Indies.

The night of 11th/12th March saw the departure of General Douglas MacArthur (GOC Philippines) and his family, recalled on the orders of President Roosevelt; he took with him General George. Overall command of the US and Filipino forces now passed to General John Wainwright, with Maj General Edward King taking command of the Bataan garrison. MacArthur's party left Corregidor aboard four Navy patrol boats for Mindanao, from where they would be flown to Australia in four B-17s due to arrive there that day. In the event, one crashed into the sea off the Australian coast and two were forced to turn back with engine problems. In consequence, on the party's eventual arrival at Del Monte on the morning of the 13th, MacArthur, spying the old war-weary B-17 which was to take them out, apparently "flatly refused to ride in a brokendown crate piloted by an inexperienced boy", following this outburst to Maj General Sharp with a rather melodramatic radio cable to General George H. Brett (C-in-C USAAF, Asia) in Australia:

---

[1] General Homma, as a young officer, had spent eight years attached to the British Army and had seen service with the BEF in France in 1918.

"The best three planes in the United States or Hawaii should be made available with completely adequate experienced crews. To attempt such a desperate and important trip with inadequate equipment would amount to consigning the whole party to death and I could not accept such a responsibility."

On receipt of this message, Brett contacted Vice-Admiral Fairfax Leary, commander of US forces in Australia and New Zealand, who agreed to meet MacArthur's demands, ordering that three new B-17s be despatched post haste. These arrived at Del Monte on the night of the 16th, although the aircraft allocated to MacArthur's party developed engine trouble when the machine was readied for the return flight, forcing a transfer to a second aircraft. The flight to Australia proved uneventful; on arrival MacArthur sent a brief message to those left behind:

"I came through, and I shall return."

This widely publicized remark did not go down well with the majority of those Americans left behind, many of whom felt that MacArthur had abandoned them to an inevitable fate. However, to the average Filipino, MacArthur remained a god-like figure and his "I shall return" was considered to be an almost personal guarantee that they would not be forgotten nor foresaken.

A reconnaissance was flown over Nichols, Nielsen, Zablan and Del Carmen airfields on 14th by Lt Bill Rowe in a P-40B repaired with a P-40E wing and other parts, which was referred to as a 'P-40 Something'. This reconnaissance was repeated next day by Lt Leo B. Godden.

Meanwhile, efforts to get supplies to Corregidor and Bataan by submarine and surface craft through the Japanese naval blockade, had failed. One such vessel that paid the penalty for tempting fate, was the little inter-island steamer *Legaspi*; its master had agreed to ferry foodstuffs from Mindanao to Corregidor under cover of darkness but, having made two successful runs, it was intercepted and sunk whilst attempting a third. To date, about 1,000 tons of foodstuffs had arrived in this fashion, sufficient only to feed Bataan's 80,000 troops and 26,000 civilians for four days. Most of the local native water buffalo had already been slaughtered to supplement the meagre rations, and the US Army's remaining 250 cavalry horses and 48 pack mules were destined for the cooking pot, including General Wainwright's own prized jumper.

At this stage, heavy aerial reinforcement was brought in by the Japanese to assist in the reduction of the troublesome garrisons. Between the 14th and 16th the G4M bombers of the Takao Ku flew to Clark, joined on the latter day by the 60th Sentai from Saigon and the 62nd from Phnom Penh, both recently re-equipped with the latest Ki 21-II bombers, following their earlier involvement over Burma. The 60th brought in 35 of these aircraft and the 62nd a further 25. The seaplane tender *Sanuki Maru*, equipped with half a dozen F1M float-planes, also arrived to assist with the blockade of Manila.

The new assault opened on the 24th, when 26 Ki 21s of the 60th Sentai raided Corregidor, followed by 19 more such bombers from the 62nd Sentai. A reconnaissance aircraft from the 76th Chutai flown by Maj Katsushige Takada, the commanding officer, accompanied them. On board this aircraft to observe results, was Colonel Hoshi, the Hikotai Commander. One 60th Sentai chutai bombed Limay, whilst the 16th Sentai made 54 sorties over the Bataan frontline in two waves, dropping 323 50kg bombs. Three more 60th Sentai Ki 21s returned to Corregidor in the evening, 18 Takao Ku G4Ms also attacking the same target. Next day brought 57 Ki 30 sorties and 41 by Ki 21s against Cabcaben, Corregidor and the frontline. One Ki 21 flown by Lt Yasushi Touyama was hit by AA and force-landed at Clark, with a large hole in the fuselage and one member of the crew dead. Attacks of this intensity continued daily, divided between Corregidor and targets on Bataan. One 62nd Sentai Ki 21 was shot down over Corregidor by AA on the 30th.

60th Sentai Mitsubishi Ki 21 bombers over Corregidor in March. *(M. Takahashi)*

In the meantime, three more B-17s had been sent to Del Monte, arriving on the night of 26th/27th, to evacuate the terminally ill President Manuel Quezon, his family and his aides; the presidential party reached Mindanao following an arduous journey by submarine, steamer and patrol boat. On his safe arrival in Australia, President Quezon sent a message to the Filipino people and the Philippine Army:

> "At the request of General MacArthur, I have left the Philippines and joined him at his headquarters in Australia. On previous occasions suggestions have been made to me that I leave the Philippines, but I refused to do so, determined as I was to carry on with affairs of Government in Philippine territory.
>
> "Upon the appointment of General MacArthur to command the Allied Forces in this part of the world, he invited me to join him on the grounds that we would continue as we have done in the past, to co-operate better if we were together than if we were separated and with the difficulties in the the means of communication.
>
> "Having no other objective in mind than to free the Philippines, I did not hesitate to accept the suggestion of General MacArthur despite the hazards that the trip involved. And so I am here where I expect to be able to be of assistance in the reconquest of every foot of territory of our beloved country.
>
> "It is my hope that the results of the appointment of General MacArthur to the High Command and my having followed his advice to join him will

soon be felt in the Philippines. I call upon every Filipino to keep his courage and fortitude, and to have faith in the ultimate victory of our cause."

April was to herald the opening of the major ground offensive, the push beginning on the 3rd, supported by 59 sorties by the 16th Sentai, 54 by the 60th Sentai and 34 by the 62nd, similar levels of support being provided over five days. There was still some isolated resistance, AA gunners inflicting damage on a dozen of the attackers on the 7th, four being bady damaged.

The ground offensive, spearheaded by the newly arrived 4th Division and supported by a large artillery bombardment, quickly broke through the weakened and disspirited American and Filipino lines. On the 6th Lt Obert and 2/Lt Posten were flown to Del Monte by Capt Fellows in the Waco to collect two newly-erected P-40s, the only reinforcements to be received throughout the campaign (see below). Two days later Lt Sam Grashio flew a reconnaissance, and later the same aircraft was used by Lt I.B. Donalson to bomb the Japanese lines as he flew it out to Cebu, where he crashed on landing.

Lt Raymond M. Gehrig, together with Capt John Randolph and passenger, escaped from Bataan in two PT-13 trainers, and landed initially at Kindley Field on Corregidor, from where they departed for Mindanao. On arriving at Del Monte they were confronted by a senior officer who suggested that they had left Corregidor without permission, despite protests to the contrary. Retracing their course back to Corregidor, they succeeded in convincing their superiors that they had departed Bataan on orders, and again set out southwards. This time they were obliged to land on Panay Island, where they abandoned their machines and continued their journey by boat, but reached only as far as neighbouring Negros Island.

On learning of the plight of his colleagues, Lt John L. Brownewell received permission to fly one of the remaining P-35s from Del Monte to the small airstrip on Negros, where he soon located the two pilots. Squeezing one in the cockpit and the other in the luggage compartment, Brownewell flew them back to Del Monte, an action for which he was awarded a DFC.

When darkness fell on the 18th it was clear that the end for the Bataan garrison was nigh. Ammunition and other dumps were blown up, including the British ammunition vessel *Yu Sang*, which had been taken over by the US Navy. The surviving aircraft and pilots were ordered out. Lt Moore took the remaining P-40, while Capt O.L. Lunde flew out a battered P-35A with another pilot in the baggage compartment. Capt Dyess then sent off the other P-35A with 2/Lt Ben Brown and Lt Henry G. Thorne (former commander of the 3rd Pursuit Squadron) in the cockpit, plus a third pilot in the baggage compartment. Despite the additional weight, this aircraft managed to carry a few fragmentation bombs which were released on the Japanese lines!

Pilots and aircraft of 'The Bamboo Fleet' were still undertaking highly dangerous supply and courier missions. An addition to the fleet was a Grumman J2F Duck utility amphibian, which had been hastily repaired by members of the 20th Pursuit Squadron at Cabcaban Field, on the western tip of Bataan. One of those involved was Lt Roland S. Barnick, who later wrote:

"One of its motors had a hole burned through between the cylinder wall and the piston, thus rendering the ship useless. After some investigation we discovered that there was another J2F which had been sunk in the Bay at the outbreak of the war."

Undoubtedly, this was one of the aircraft which had been shot-up in Mariveles Bay by the Tainan Ku A6Ms on the 5 January. Barnick continued:

> "With the co-operation of the Navy we pulled off one of the barnacle-covered cylinders and, much to our surprise, found that it was in fair condition, considering the fact that it had been submerged for approximately three months!
>
> "We worked in shifts for two days and two nights in an attempt to repair our Duck. We made the replacement and final adjustments by flashlight. On first attempt the engine fired and kept on running. There was little time for testing the ship.
>
> "There were several factors which made the take-off and flight rather a precarious one. The airplane with five passengers and pilot was greatly overloaded. Second, on take-off I discovered that the propeller would not change pitch. Third, I'd never flown a Duck before. Fourth, it was as dark as the inside of a cow, and all there was in the cockpit for night flying was the bank-and turn indicator and an inaccurate magnetic compass."

Nonetheless, Barnick succeeded in getting clear of Cabcaben Field with inches to spare, having bounced the aircraft along the airstrip to increase lift! The overloaded amphibian struggled to about 70 feet but would go no higher, until all excess baggage was jettisoned, including parachutes. Eventually a secret airstrip near Cebu was located, where the Duck landed to refuel, following which it continued on its way to Iloilo. Next day Barnick flew the aircraft to Mindanao and was followed, to the same destination, by another aircraft of 'The Bamboo Fleet', the Waco biplane in the hands of Capt Bradford.

After being used by Lt Moore to fly in a load of confectionery from the southern island, the J2F was christened the 'Candy Clipper'. Shortly after, during one of these clandestine supply flights, and with three men aboard, the Waco was shot down between Cebu and Del Monte by two Japanese Navy patrol aircraft. Sometime earlier, another of the blockade runners had been shot down, when the Beech Staggerwing cabin biplane fell foul of patrolling fighters. Dates of these two losses have not been ascertained.

With Bataan conquered, the Japanese again reduced their strength in the Philippines, the 62nd Sentai leaving Clark for Nanking on the 26th, to operate over China. Meanwhile, the Ki 27s of the 84th Independent Chutai arrived at Zablan from Hanoi, to relieve the 3rd Chutai of the 50th Sentai, which left to join the parent unit in Burma.

The bombers now moved their attention to the island fortress of Corregidor, headquarters of the US Command, from where General Wainwright issued a message of defiance to his men:

> "Corregidor can and will be held. There can be no question of surrendering this mighty fortress to the enemy. It will be defended with all the resources at our command.
>
> "I call upon every person on this fortress to consider himself from this time onward as a member of a team which is resolved to meet the enemy's challenge each hour of every night and day.
>
> "All men who have served here before will remain at posts, while those who have come from Bataan will be assigned to appropriate tasks and battle stations. It is essential above all that the men who have joined us from the

mainland promptly rid themselves of any defeatist attitude which they may have, and consider themselves to be part of this fighting unit.

"Bataan has fallen — but Corregidor will carry on! On this mighty fortress — a pearl of great price on which the enemy has set his covetous eyes — the spirit of Bataan will continue to live!"

Stirring but hollow words. Wainwright knew that Corregidor could not hold out for long, also that the prospect of help or reinforcement did not exist. It was just a matter of time.

The 29th saw 33 sorties by Ki 30s against the AA positions and heavy bombing by the 60th Sentai Ki 21s, which made 50 sorties. The start of the new month brought with it intensification of the bombardment of Corregidor. From the second day of May, aircraft of the 52nd Independent Chutai began spotting for the artillery, now located at and firing from the southern tip of Bataan. Landings on the island received air cover on the 5th; the last air attacks were made next day and, by midnight on the 6th/7th, the fortress had surrendered. General Wainwright, his staff and 13,000 American and Filipino troops went into captivity, less than half of whom would survive their ordeal.

On the southern island of Mindanao resistance was continuing however. By mid March only one P-40 and two P-35As remained serviceable, but a blockade runner, SS *Anhui*, had run aground off Cebu on 9th, three new P-40Es in crates being off loaded onto barges and sailed to Mindanao. Here they were erected by the Provisional Mobile Depot Unit. Two were collected by pilots from Bataan, but returned after the fall of the peninsula. Work continued to make aircraft serviceable, and by early April at Del Monte there were five P-40s and a P-35A protecting the airfield, which was being repaired, mainly as a 'way' station for the evacuation of key personnel to Australia. The day after Bataan fell, the Japanese invaded Cebu, and the aircraft there — a Bellanca biplane, once belonging to the Philippine Air Taxi Service, two P-40s and a P-35, all with refugees from Bataan — were able to escape before the airfield fell. During the morning Lt Dave Obert dive-bombed the invasion shipping in Bugo Bay with a 100lb bomb. Later in the day he flew over Cebu City to confirm that it was indeed under Japanese control, and in flames. The invading force, the Kawaguchi Detachment of 4,800 men, took the city in less than a day. By the 16th all important positions had been overrun and, by the 20th, Panay, including Iloilo and San Jose, were in Japanese hands.

Whilst flying a reconnaissance from Del Monte in one of the P-40s during the afternoon of the 10th, Lt Walter B. Putnam made two unauthorised strafing attacks on the invasion shipping, during which his aircraft was hit many times. On a second sortie he spotted a Japanese floatplane 15 miles south-west of Cebu, which he engaged and claimed shot down. In fact NA 1/C Saburo Takayasu's F1M from *Sanuki Maru* (which had arrived off Cebu to assist with operations in the area) suffered just three hits, while the Japanese crew believed they had shot down the P-40! It seems that he also claimed a second floatplane shot down, and believed that he had sunk two transports, a motor launch and several barges!

Next day, word was received at Del Monte that a force of bombers was on its way from Australia. It was decided that Davao airfield was to be attacked by the remaining P-40s, in an effort to neutralize the threat posed by any Japanese aircraft which might have arrived there, and which would therefore be capable of intercepting the incoming bombers. Lt Obert, with 2/Lts Brown and Posten, carried out the low-level attack on 12th, finding only three aircraft present, which they strafed and left smoking. Late that afternoon, three B-17s of the 19th Bomb Group and ten North American B-25s of the 3rd Attack Group arrived under the command of Brig-General Ralph Royce, who flew in Capt Frank V. Bostrom's B-17. It was decided that the B-17s would operate from Del Monte, one flight of B-25s under Colonel John H. Davies from a nearby satellite strip, and the other flight, under Capt Herman F. Lowery, from Valencia strip, 40 miles to the south.

At dawn on the 12th, one B-17 and both flights of B-25s rendezvoused near Del Monte, the crews briefed to carry out an attack on shipping reported assembled in the harbour at Cebu. Apparently taking the defences by surprise, a number of ships were claimed hit and set on fire, as were dock installations. Meanwhile, Capt Bostrom carried out a sea reconnaissance, searching for concentrations of Japanese shipping; none were found, so he flew to Nichols Field instead and released his bombs there.

Four F1M floatplanes from *Sanuki Maru* were despatched for an early morning bombing raid against Del Monte, but these found 1/Lt Harold F. Cocanaugher over the airfield in the last P-35A, seeking to provide cover. He engaged two of the intruders without effect. Meanwhile Lt Brownewell took off in a P-40E and Lt Gus Williams in a P-40B to intercept, Brownewell shooting down one F1M; NAP 1/C Tsutomu Hiromura and his observer were killed when their aircraft crashed three miles south of Marco. The remaining three F1Ms however arrived over Del Monte unhindered and released their bombs with accuracy, destroying one of two recently-returned B-17s; shrapnel, debris and blast damaged the other two, including one which had just become unserviceable. Williams however, almost crashed when his battered aircraft fell out of control. Brownewell then flew on to Davao, where he strafed four aircraft. Meanwhile, the B-25s had returned to their respective airstrips and had thus avoided attack. By 1330 they had been refuelled and rearmed and set out to seek an aircraft carrier — presumably *Ryujo* — which had been reported in the area, but this was not found. The bombers therefore headed for an alternative target and carried out a repeat attack on the harbour at Cebu, where further damage was inflicted before all aircraft returned safely to Mindanao.

That afternoon Lt John Burns crashed one of the P-40Es while taking off, and was killed in the fire which followed. Several days later flying the P-40B in which Williams had experienced trouble, 2/Lt Lawrence E. McDaniel was killed when it again went out of control as he approached to land. On another mission, Lt Varian K. White was attacked by two fighters but managed to escape.

The B-25s were off again at 0600 on the morning of the 14th, one flight again attacking Cebu, the other visiting Davao. Further damage was claimed, with only little resistance from AA defences. Yet a further raid on Davao was carried out, the dock area receiving much attention; at least one ship was believed to have been sunk and several others damaged, whilst large fires were seen throughout the dock installations. A "terrific explosion" was reported and was assumed to have been the result of a direct hit on an ammunition dump.

While the B-25s were away, the two patched-up B-17s loaded with evacuees, managed to get away from Del Monte, just as another Japanese raid approached, bombs falling as the American aircraft cleared the boundary fence. Despite their condition, both B-17s reached Australia safely, where the undercarriage of one collapsed on landing, although no one was hurt. Shortly before midnight the B-25s, also loaded with men, departed for Australia, where all arrived without mishap. Of the bomber force's brief stay in the Philippines, the official report stated:

> "The four-day mission was completed without the loss of a single man and with the loss of only one B-17 on the ground. The ten B-25s and two B-17s had sunk or badly damaged four enemy transports — one large, two medium and one small — and scored direct hits on two others, and near misses on eight others; in addition they had succeeded in badly damaging the warehouses and docks at Davao and Cebu, and in damaging Nichols Field and buildings in the city of Davao."

On his return to Australia, Brig-General Royce commented to the news media:

> "Our raids threw the Japanese into a terrific panic. Imagine their bewilderment at the sudden appearance of a big bunch of bombers, which let loose everything they had on them. They did not know where the bombers came from."

There was subsequently some understandable bitterness, when it was discovered that all the bomber personnel had been decorated for their part in this operation, although there were no decorations for the fighter pilots. What made the situation even worse, was that the bombers were credited with destroying the three Japanese aircraft at Davao!

Evacuation began on 23 April when an LB-30 flew in to take out specified Air Force personnel. On the night of the 25th/25th a lone B-17 arrived at Del Monte from Australia, its task to evacuate 27 selected personnel; amongst the passengers was Colonel Carlos Romulo, MacArthur's Aide-de-camp, who had been ill in hospital and was, only now, able to undertake such a flight. Romulo had been one of the last to escape from Bataan, having been a passenger in the salvaged Duck amphibian. Meanwhile, Capt Bill Bradford, another veteran of 'The Bamboo Fleet', made one more sortie to Corregidor in the Bellanca but crashed on take-off in the darkness on the trip back. On the 29th, Lt Boselli and his LB-30 arrived from Australia on the ultimate evacuation flight to pick up the remaining pilots at Del Monte, Lts Obert and Brownewell being flown out with 35 others packed tightly into the aircraft, which "called for some careful figuring and stowing away." However, several other pilots did not get away. That evening Capt Ramon Zosa of the PAF bombed vessels in Parang harbour in the P-35A, carrying two 100lb bombs.

The morning of the 29th saw the Kawaguchi Detachment come ashore at Parang in western Mindanao, and begin to push north-eastwards. Of more immediate threat to Del Monte, the Kawamura Detachment landed at Mocajalar Bay, only 15 miles away, pushing steadily southwards in the face of sustained resistance, but enjoying considerable air support. On 2 May Zosa was off in the P-35A again, once more armed with two 100lb bombs, but this time accompanied by two P-40Es, each carrying a 500 pounder, to attack the invasion force. Taking off in the dark, Lt Glover crashed. The remaining pair bombed without effect, and then strafed. Zosa and Lt Crosland were off again at dawn on 3rd, strafing only this time, before heading to Maramag where one more repaired P-40 was available. Zosa flew the P-35A to a small strip, where it was hidden. The last operational sortie by the 24th Fighter Group was undertaken by Lt Crosland on the 6th, when he bombed and strafed a large transport vessel off the north coast of Mindanao. Del Monte fell two days later, remaining USAAF personnel retreating on Malaybalay, where they surrendered on the 12th with the rest of Maj General Sharp's command on Mindanao. The pilots of the two surviving P-40s had been planning to fly them out when surrender was ordered, the aircraft falling into Japanese hands. They were later flown by US pilots under escort to Malaybalay Field, and then on to Davao. They were accompanied by a PT-13 flown by Lt John Volkenaar and three Japanese aircraft. This was to be the last flight over the Philippines by American-flown aircraft until 1944. By the time of the surrender, pilots of the 24th Fighter Group had been officially credited with shooting down at least 45 Japanese aircraft, together with a further 30 destroyed on the ground.

Four members of the 17th Pursuit Squadron in Australia after evacuating from the Philippines. These include Lt John Brownewell (far left) and Lt Boyd D. Wagner (second from right). *(J. Brownewell)*

When Maj General King surrendered Bataan, over 76,000 men including 12,000 Americans went into captivity — the greatest capitulation in US military history. This was followed by the subsequent surrender of Corregidor with its 13,000 strong garrison, both events occurring closely after the fall of Singapore and its 130,000-man garrison, and the capitulation of the Netherlands East Indies, with the Dutch armed forces (a further 42,000 men) — the resultant shock to the Allied High Command was immeasurable. The all-conquering Japanese seemed unstoppable.

However, even with the tremendous successes achieved in such a short period of time against two of the mightiest military powers, the Japanese were far from magnanimous in victory. In spite of an assurance to the defeated Maj General King that "the Imperial Japanese Army are not barbarians", and that his men would not be ill-treated, the prisoners from Bataan were marched, in intense heat, to San Fernando, Pampanga, a distance of about 75 miles. Many were sick and wounded but all were forced to march with the others. Those who fell by the wayside were shot or bayoneted. The journey lasted nine days, the guard being relieved every three miles or so by fresh troops, who accompanied the column in captured US trucks.

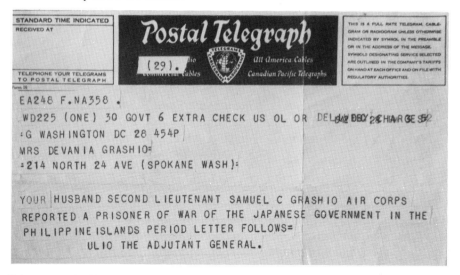

Telegram received by Lt Sam Grashio's wife in December 1942. Grashio was one of the nine pilots who escaped from a Japanese POW camp in April 1943, and managed to return to the United States. *(S. Grashio)*

For the first five days the prisoners received neither food — except what brave Filipinos were able to throw to them — nor water, except what could be obtained from roadside ditches or buffalo wallows. On the sixth day the prisoners each received one cupful of rice. On the ninth day — having covered 55 miles — the survivors were told that they would have to walk no further, as they were to be transported by rail the rest of the way to their destination, Camp O'Donnell. Relief was short-lived however, when they were herded into small railway coaches — 100 men to each coach. Of the appalling conditions, a subsequent official account revealed:

> "So overcrowded were they, that there were many who — during the whole trip — never touched the floor. Hundreds fainted from lack of air, and many died of suffocation."

It is not known exactly how many died on the march although evidence would suggest at least 8,000 Americans and Filipinos perished.

Chapter 4

JAVA — THE TARGET
1-15 February

At the end of January the remaining Dutch fighters in Sumatra were withdrawn to Java, leaving the defence of the former island wholly in the hands of the RAF. With Borneo now occupied by the Japanese, the ML had become entirely based in Java, the main strength comprising about 65 fighters and some 45 Glenn Martin bombers.

Kapt Andrias van Rest, commanding officer of 1-VlG-V, was Sumatran-born. He later became a US citizen. *(Authors' collection)*. Right: Lt Pieter Tideman, commander of 3-VlG-V *(P.G. Tideman)*

In the west, disposed mainly for the defence of Tanjong Priok, Bandoeng and Buitenzorg, were:

1-VlG-V   15 Brewster 339s at Andir under Kapt A.A.M. van Rest

2-VlG-V	8 Brewster 339s at Tjisaoek under Kapt JP. van Helsdingen
3-VlG-IV	11 Brewster 339s at Tjililitan under Lt A.J. de Vries

3-VlG-V had been absorbed by 1-VlG-V on 1 February, with the last of the 15 aircraft arriving at Andir on 4 February from Samarinda II, while 3-VlG-IV had recently been formed from newly-qualified pilots. Two of the latter unit's aircraft and one pilot had already been lost in training accidents, shortly after 3-VlG-V had lost two of its pilots in bad weather accidents.

The reconnaissance unit, Verkenningsafdeling 1 (abbreviated to VkA-1) with 12 CW-22s and one Fokker CX at Tjikembar under Lt J.W. Verhoeven, was directly under the command of the ML, as was Lt A.L. Cox's VkA-4. This unit was based at Djokjakarta with a dozen Lockheed 212s. The FK-51 equipped VkA-3 was controlled by the Army and had four aircraft based at Tjililitan, four at Malang and four at Magelang, under the overall command of Lt D. Berlijn. Two further FK-51s (K101 and K103) were on loan to the USAAF as courier aircraft. Djokjakarta was also the home for VkA-2's 11 CW-22s and two Fokker CXs, which Lt W.A. Meelhuisen commanded.

The position of the bombers appeared quite healthy – on paper. In the west, the Glenn Martins were divided as follows:

1-VlG-I	8 aircraft at Andir under Kapt R. de Senerpont Domis.
2-VlG-III	6 aircraft at Tjililitan under Kapt W.F. Boot; the unit had amalgamated with 1-VlG-III on 1 February and moved to Tjisaoek three days later.
3-VlG-III	8 aircraft at Semplak under Lt A.B. Wolff; the unit moved to Andir on 11 February.

Also available were the two Albacores and five Vildebeests of 36 Squadron,

Left: Kapt Max van der Poel, leader of the Curtiss-Hawk equipped 1-VlG-IV at Madioen. *(Authors' collection)*. Right: Lt R.A.D. Anemaet briefs his CW-21B pilots at Perak. *(R.A.D. Anemaet)*

and eight Vildebeests of 100 Squadron, which had arrived at Kemajoran, near Batavia, on 31 January, still smarting from their losses over Endau less than a week before. The Catalinas of 205 Squadron had also moved to Batavia where, with the remaining USN PBYs, they came under the overall control of the Dutch.

Coupled with the Blenheims and Hudsons in Sumatra, this was the nearest to a concentration of striking forces that the Allies were to achieve before the fall of the Indies however. It was theoretical, as the various units seldom operated in unison, and were never concentrated on one target.

In the east of the island, disposed for the defence of the main Naval Base at Sourabaya, were:

1-VlG-IV   8 Curtiss Hawks at Madioen under Kapt M.W. van der Poel
2-VlG-IV   13 CW-21Bs at Perak under Lt R.A.D. Anemaet

These fighter units were reinforced by the recently-arrived 17th Pursuit Squadron (Provisional) of the USAAF with 12 P-40Es, which now moved to its permanent base, Blimbing. This was a grass strip near Djombang, on the Sourabaya-Madioen-Soerakarta railway, which was at that time unknown to the Japanese.

There was one afdeling — 1-VlG-II — of Glenn Martins at Maospati, under the overall command of Lt H.J. Otten. This unit was about to move to Pasirian, but immediately transferred from there to Malang, due to muddy conditions at the former airfield. The US contingent had been reinforced by 13 more B-17Es and four LB-30s. This reinforcement allowed the remaining B-17Ds to be flown to Australia for overhaul. While the 19th Bomb Group remained at Malang, the 7th now moved to Djokjakarta.

1-VlG-IV seen at full strength, with 13 Curtiss H-75A-7 Hawks at Madioen. The pilots are being briefed by Kapt van der Poel. *(Air-Britain archives via Charles W. Cain)*

Against this motley force, the Imperial Japanese Navy was completing the move of the greater parts of the 21st and 23rd Air Flotillas to southern Borneo and to Menado and Kendari in the Celebes, from where they were in range of eastern Java.

Curtiss-Wright CW-21B Interceptors of 2-VIG-IV *(Authors' collection)*

Sunday, 1 February

Early in the morning three reconnaissance C5Ms of the Tainan Ku left Balik-papan en route for Sourabaya, arriving over the main American airfield at Malang just before midday, to observe the concentration of aircraft. Two of the C5Ms returned during the afternoon, but that flown by NAP 2/C Masami Nishido, with Wt Off Wataru Furukawa as observer, was never seen again.

Further north, near the Anambas Islands, an F1M floatplane from the tender *Sagara Maru* encountered two flyingboats, which NAP 1/C H. Ichikawa at once attacked. After a combat lasting 25 minutes, during which he made three

A Tainan Kokutai C5M reconnaissance aircraft. *(Hisamitsu Yamazaki)*

attacking passes, in which his rear gunner also participated, all ammunition was exhausted. One of the 'boats was seen leaving a substantial trail of leaking oil, and Ichikawa claimed its probable destruction.

During the late evening, three LB-30s from Malang raided shipping off Balikpapan, Lt Dougherty claiming a ship sunk; the other crews reported a fuel or ammunition dump hit when large fires were started. Eight B-17Es attempted to repeat the attack next day, bombing shipping sighted 10 miles off Balikpapan; again one transport vessel was claimed sunk, and another damaged.

Monday, 2 February

Furnished with the information gleaned by the reconnaissance crews, 17 A6Ms and a single C5M of the Tainan Ku left their airfield at Balikpapan at 0900, led by Lt Masao Asai, to make an attack on Maospati airfield, near Sourabaya. Arriving over the Javanese coast at 1205, the A6M pilots spotted a lone twin-engined aircraft in flight. Aircraft from the unit's 3rd Chutai were leading the formation, NAP 2/C Yoshisuke Arita and NA 1/C Yoshio Motoyoshi, who formed the 2nd shotai, breaking away to shoot this down. Their victim was an old USAAF B-18 bomber — 36-338 flown by Maj Joseph A. Burch — one of the survivors of the Philippines fighting, which had been pressed into service on the Java-Australia shuttle service as a transport; it fell south of Dedjong Ponkau, near Sedajce. The loss of this particular aircraft was of some considerable importance, since it was carrying Colonel William H. Murphy, an American radar expert, and his staff of three, as well as Maj Straubel, new commanding officer of the 7th Bomb Group, on his way to take over his command. Straubel was thrown clear, as was the co-pilot, 2/Lt Russell M. Smith; however, in valiant but vain efforts to extricate the others, both suffered fatal burns from which they died next morning in hospital.

Some 25 minutes later, at 1300, the six A6Ms of the 6th Chutai swept down on Maospati in pairs, strafing the airfield thoroughly and claiming two small aircraft destroyed in flames, with two more damaged. Six more fighters of the 4th Chutai, also flying in pairs, were providing cover to this assault and these reported engaging a number of Buffaloes, one of which was claimed shot down by Lt Jun-ichi Sasai, the chutai leader, his wingman NAP 2/C Susumu Ishihara, and NA 1/C Shizuyoshi Nishiyama, the No 2 man of the 2nd Shotai. The A6Ms then withdrew, landing back at Balikpapan in mid-afternoon.

Tuesday, 3 February

The Japanese fighter incursion over eastern Java on the 2nd was but a forerunner of events to come. From bases in Borneo and Celebes an armada of Japanese naval aircraft began roaring into the air on this Tuesday morning, 26 G3Ms of Takao Ku, led by Lt Cdr Taro Nonaka, and 27 of Kanoya Ku, led by Lt Cdr Toshiie Irisa, setting course for Sourabaya and Madioen respectively, while 19 other G3Ms of the 1st Ku headed for Malang, Lt Cdr Takeo Ozaki at their head. To support them, the fighters also took to the air in force. First off at 0915 were 17 A6Ms and a C5M of the Tainan Ku, led by Lt Hideki Shingo, which headed for Malang. They were followed a few minutes later by 27 A6Ms and two C5Ms of 3rd Ku, led by Lt Tamotsu Yokoyama, which were to cover the attacks on Sourabaya and Madioen. Link-up with the bombers left something to be desired; as a result the Takao formation that headed for the Sourabaya Naval Base did so without escort.

A6M Zero-Zen fighters of the 3rd Kokutai, long-range tanks beneath the fuselages, set off for the flight to Java. *(Authors' collection)*

At the warning of the approaching raids, the Dutch fighters in eastern Java were ordered off, seven Hawks from 1-VlG-IV and a dozen CW-21Bs from 2-VlG-IV getting into the air, joined later by six P-40s of the 17th Pursuit Squadron. To spread the patrol area, the CW-21Bs were ordered to split up into three sections.

Almost at once, the Hawks spotted a number of unescorted bombers (the Takao Ku formation) and gave chase, catching them just as they began entering a bank of cloud. At this point Sgt Mulder found his engine racing roughly and had to turn back to base. As he approached Maospati the engine stopped, but

As the raiders approach, CW-21Bs of 2-VlG-IV scramble in unit strength. *(Authors' collection)*

Eight Curtiss Hawks of 1-VlG-IV over Java in formation similar to that taken up on 3 February, before intercepting JNAF raiders. *(Authors' collection)*

as he turned into his final approach for an emergency landing, the Hawk was attacked and set on fire by an A6M. Keeping the burning fighter under control, he was able to carry out a landing, leaping from the still-moving machine to take cover in a bomb crater.

Shortly afterward, Sgt A. Kok suffered similar technical problems and, as he came into land, was also attacked and his aircraft burst into flame. As with Mulder, he managed to get down, braked violently and was also able to scramble out into a crater. He reported having seen another Hawk going down in flames, and it was thought this must have been the aircraft of Kapt Max van der Poel. The latter baled out but landed in a swollen river and was drowned; he was believed to have shot down one of the A6Ms before his demise.

On the ground, at Maospati, Cpl Ken Perry of the 17th Pursuit Squadron witnessed the one-sided air battle:

> "We had been expecting a raid. At about 10 o'clock the sirens again began their death song and the seven Dutch planes again took to the air. Suddenly the Dutch fighter planes attacked the Zeros and dogfights were numerous. We cheered a Dutchman who was diving on a Jap. But it was the gallant Dutchman who burst into flames and went down. Only a couple of us had seen a second Zero dive down from above.
>
> "We saw a Dutch plane coming in for a crash landing on the runway. Three Zeros were following him down in formation, firing all they had. The Dutchman burst into flames before he hit. We took off our hats. One of the Japs circled our pillbox not 100 feet above us. We could have hit him with a .45 pistol but there wasn't any gun to be had."

By this time one of the bombers had been claimed possibly shot down by Sgt Maj P. Boonstoppel, and several others appeared to have been damaged, one of which was seen flying with one engine out of action. The bombers were pursued towards Madoera but the A6Ms then struck in defence of their charges; Ens Count F.J. van der Does de la Bije was shot down and killed over Madoera, while Ens H.G.G. Droge, who was also shot down, managed to bale out. Only two pilots were able to land back at Maospati.

Meanwhile the approaching A6Ms of the 3rd Ku had spotted some of the CW-21Bs and attacked them en masse. Against such overwhelming opposition the Curtiss fighters also fared badly. 2/Lt J. Kingma's section was engaged from behind by an estimated 16 A6Ms and, as he turned his aircraft to meet the threat, his two companions — Ens J. Hogenes and Sgt F. van Balen — were both shot down in flames and killed. Kingma engaged his attackers and believed he had shot down two, before he fell to another; he baled out badly burned. Sgt H.M. Haye, the survivor of this section, also claimed an A6M shot down, although his own aircraft was then shot-up from behind; he prepared to bale out but found that his aircraft was still flyable and made a creditable landing at Ngoro.

Lt W.A. Bedet was leading a section of three CW-21Bs when attacked, his aircraft (CW-354) taking a cannon-shell hit on its windscreen; fragments wounded Bedet in the chest and one arm although he was able to land at Perak, but after so doing, he collapsed and was dragged to safety. Sgt F. Beerling's aircraft also sustained damage, the pilot making an emergency landing at Ngoro, while Sgt J. Brouwer was obliged to force-land his damaged machine at Kamal and suffered severe concussion as a result. The fourth pilot of this section had been delayed in taking off and, when Ens D. Dekker did get airborne, he attempted to join up with a section of fighters which he believed to be the CW-21Bs; in fact they were A6Ms! On realising this, he fired at one at point-blank range before being attacked by others; with his engine damaged he managed to crash-land on a beach on the south coast of Madoera.

Lt Anemaet's section had been in the process of going in to land at Perak to refuel when they were hit by the A6Ms. He recalled:

> "My own flight never made visual contact with the enemy until the last moment, when we were preparing to land at Perak for refuelling. We did not know that the enemy bombers had bombed the airfield in the meantime so, when I landed, my plane ran into a bomb crater."

The A6Ms shot down Sgt R.Ch. Halberstadt's aircraft as he approached to land, the pilot losing his life, although the other two CW-21Bs, piloted by Ens A.W. Hamming and Sgt N. Dejalle, managed to get down safely.

A Ryan STM floatplane, with a student at the controls, was on its final approach to alight in a bay at Sourabaya harbour as the raiders attacked, exploding bombs causing water geysers to erupt in the trainer's path. On realising what was happening, the instructor, Lt Ernest Lee (one of a dozen US Navy instructors attached to the Dutch Naval Flight School at Sourabaya), immediately attempted to regain control but the aircraft plunged into the water and sank. Both Lee and the student survived the ditching and waded ashore, only to be fired upon by Dutch troops who believed them to be Japanese! Neither was hurt however.

The victorious pilots of the 3rd Ku, having strafed the flyingboat base, claimed four flyingboats shot down, a dozen more and one floatplane burned on the water, and five more badly damaged. Between them, two shotais also claimed to have badly damaged a single B-17 on the ground at Madoera. Dutch losses of naval aircraft were indeed severe; three Do 24s (X-6 of GVT-1, X-30 and X-37 of GVT-5) were all destroyed, as were three Dornier Wals, three Fokker

Ryan STM floatplane in Dutch Naval service. *(Authors' collection)*

Wt Off Sadaaki Akamatsu, long-serving fighter pilot in the 3rd Kokutai, already had 11 victories claimed over China when the Pacific War broke out. He was to serve throughout the war, becoming one of the IJNAF's top-scorers.

C-XI floatplanes (W-4, W-10 and W-14), two Fokker T-IVs and the Ryan STM floatplane. Of the Wals, D-43 was shot down while on a training flight, while D-41 was damaged in the air. Catalina Y-61 of GVT-3 was also shot down over the Madoera Strait, and one PBY of PatWing 10 was damaged in Sourabaya harbour.

As the 3rd Ku engaged in battle over Sourabaya, the small formation of Tainan Ku A6Ms arrived over Malang, where they caught a number of 7th Bomb Group B-17s on the ground at Singosari airfield, bombed-up and ready for take-off. Four of the bombers — two B-17Ds and two B-17Es (one of which was 41-2427, the other possibly 41-2460) — caught fire and two of them exploded into flames when their bomb loads went up; one of the others was only partly burnt but the following day suddenly burst into flames and was gutted.

Ten miles to the south of the airfield, the last B-17C still on operations (40-2062) was caught, while on a test flight, and was shot down by NAP 2/C Yoshiri Hidaka of the 2nd Chutai; Lt Ray L. Cox and his crew, which included two volunteer gunners from the 131st Field Artillery, were killed when the bomber crashed into mountains. Hidaka's wingman, NAP 3/C Saburo Nozawa, spotted a twin-engined flyingboat and shot this down as well, which was almost certainly Y-40 of GVT-5, reported lost to Japanese fighters on this date. Their duty done, the Tainan pilots then headed for home. As a result of the strafe, the kokutai was subsequently to claim five four-engined bombers, one twin-engine and one small aircraft destroyed on the ground at Malang.

B-17E (probably 41-2460) burning after Japanese raid on Malang on 3 February. *(Authors' collection)*

The six P-40s of the 17th Pursuit Squadron's standby flight had been late receiving the order to scramble, and were without their commanding officer, Maj Charles A. Sprague, who was away at ABDA Headquarters on the matter of the unit's incomplete equipment. As the P-40s clawed into the sky they could see the bombers approaching in formations of nine aircraft each, in line astern at 21,000 feet. The fighters were still 4,000 feet below as 17 of the bombers released their loads, which crashed into the stricken naval base, before they turned for home.

The Americans gave chase, two of them finally catching the rear formation of G3Ms 85 miles out to sea, near Bawean Island. Lt William J. Hennon attacked the rear aircraft of one line, sending it smoking into the sea. No interference was experienced from escorting fighters during the pursuit, since these were still involved in their fight with the Dutch Hawks and CW-21Bs at this time.

Following this engagement, two other P-40 pilots spotted the A6Ms of the Tainan Ku on their way out from Malang and flying at about 8,000 feet. Lts Walter L. Coss and James M. Rowland dived to attack, the former shooting down the No 2 aircraft of the first Chutai. The A6M, flown by NA 1/C Kyoji

2/Lt William J. Hennon, seen here with a couple of P-40s, claimed five victories over Java with the 17th Pursuit Squadron (Provisional). He later added two more over Australia. *(Bill Wolf)*

Kobayashi, was seen to fall in flames, and the pilot was killed. The Americans were then 'jumped' from above by other A6Ms and Rowland was shot down, his P-40 falling out of control to crash. Coss then claimed a second fighter shot down, identified as a 'Seversky-type', before he evaded others and returned to base. There seems little doubt that Rowland was a victim of 3rd Ku fighters, which made several claims for P-40s, whilst the Tainan pilots were unable to engage their attackers.

A few miles south of Madoera Island was anchored a prize the Japanese bombers missed, owing to heavy cloud cover — an assemblage of warships including the cruisers *Houston* and *Marblehead*, *De Ruyter* and *Tromp*, with three Dutch and ten American destroyers. These had gathered at the behest of Rear- Admiral William R. Purnell, USN (Chief of Staff, US Asiatic Fleet) who had arrived by PBY. When news of the approaching Japanese force was received, *Houston*'s four SOC-3 scout aircraft were ordered to depart — as they posed a serious fire hazard should there be an attack — these taking off from the sea with some difficulty. As the raid receded, the pilots of the scout planes were shocked to see a Japanese aircraft dive past them, making for a PBY which was coming in to land, piloted by Ens Leroy Deede, who was arriving to collect Rear-Admiral Purnell. There was a brief exchange of fire between the PBY's gunners and their attacker, following which the latter "burst into a sheet of yellow flame" and dived into the sea. This was NAP 1/C Minoru Morita's C5M of the 3rd Ku, in which he and his observer, Lt Tetsutaro Suzuki, were killed. Part of the wreckage of the reconnaissance machine was brought ashore later.

Something over an hour and a half later, the Tainan Ku formation chanced upon nine B-17s returning to Java, after the third attack in as many days on

Balikpapan. The two A6Ms of the 2nd Chutai broke away to pursue and attack, but reported being unable to shoot any down. Their fire was more effective than they thought, as Lt T.B. Swanson's aircraft (41-2469) caught fire following the attack and he ordered the crew to bale-out; five did, but the others remained with the aircraft which crash-landed on Arendis Island, off the south-east coast of Borneo. A PBY later rescued the crew, one of whom had an injured leg. Another B-17 returned from the mission with two wounded on board; a third had died, apparently from lack of oxygen.

Allied losses during this raid amounted to 16 fighters shot down or crash-landed due to combat, three flyingboats and two B-17s shot down. At least ten more — possibly as many as 13 — flyingboats and floatplanes were destroyed at anchor, while losses to aircraft on the ground amounted to at least four B-17s. Apart from Perak airfield at Sourabaya and the Naval Base, and Singosari airfield at Malang, the airfield at Madioen had also been heavily bombed. During the raid 33 people had been killed and 141 more injured as a result of the bombing.

The claims of the Tainan Ku during its more limited actions had been close to exactitude, but not surprisingly in the whirling dogfight over Sourabaya Bay, the 3rd Ku had considerably overestimated the damage it had inflicted, many pilots obviously double and treble claiming on the same aircraft. Apart from the single loss of the Tainan A6M, the 3rd lost three of its fighters flown by NA 2/C Hatsumasa Yamaya, NA 3/C Sho-ichi Shoji and NA 3/C Masaru Morita.

NA 1/C Masao Masuyama, one of the successful 3rd Kokutai pilots on 3 February about to climb into the cockpit of his A6M. *(Authors' collection)*

At the end of the day the 3rd Ku's claims totalled 33 fighters shot down and five probables, against 16 actual losses. They also claimed four flyingboats against two and one damaged, claiming 13 more on the water, with five damaged. As nearly as can accurately be ascertained, their claims were as follows: 15 Curtiss-Wrights, two P-36s, three P-40s, nine Buffaloes and four aircraft identified as 'Hurricanes' shot down, and one P-36 and one P-40 probably destroyed (see Table 9).

Efforts to reinforce the East Indies continued however. During the day, two more pilots plus a number of ground crew personnel reached the 17th Pursuit Squadron although, at Headquarters, Maj Sprague was informed that little else was likely to be forthcoming.

In Western Java a number of transports from the latest convoys reached Batavia, including *Warwick Castle*, *Empress of Australia* and *City of Canterbury*, bringing with them a new batch of Hurricane pilots (see Chapter 1). The 4,681-ton aircraft transport HMT *Athene* also arrived at this time, aboard which were 39 crated Hurricanes. Amongst technical personnel arriving at this time to assist with the assembling of these aircraft was LAC Pat Cowle of 242 Squadron, who recalled:

> "I was a Fitter II and helped assemble the Hurricanes which were towed from Batavia docks to the civil airport. These planes were equipped for desert warfare with large air intakes and long range tanks. The tanks were removed, mainplanes assembled, plugs fitted and engine oil primed, and the aircraft ground tested."

Wednesday, 4 February

On their return to base following the previous day's attacks, Japanese crews of the 23rd Air Flotilla had reported seeing the Allied cruisers off Madoera Island. This was part of Admiral Karel Doorman's Combined Striking Force underway to try and forestall Japanese landings at Makassar in southern Celebes, by raiding a concentration of transport vessels at Balikpapan. Consequent upon this report, 27 G4Ms of the Kanoya Ku and nine of the Takao Ku, together with two dozen G3Ms of the 1st Ku, accompanied by seven C5Ms, were sent out early in the morning to attack the ships at sea.

At 0954 nine bombers were seen preparing to make an attack, the two American cruisers being targeted. The first two bombing runs were evaded but on the third *Marblehead* was narrowly near-missed by a stick of bombs; *Houston*'s gunners hit one of the G4Ms, flown by NAP 3/C Yasuo Hirata of the Takao Ku, which then circled slowly down and finally crashed into the sea, near *Marblehead*.

On the approach of the bombers, *Houston* had attempted to launch her SOC-3 scout floatplanes, but only that flown by Lt Tom Payne had got clear before the guns opened fire. A second floatplane, with the crew strapped in, had suffered an engine malfunction and, as Ens Walter Winslow later wrote:

> "Jack (*Lt Jack Lamade, the pilot*) was having one hell of a time. Concussion from one of the guns positioned just behind Jack's plane instantly ripped away most of the fabric from its tail section. He (and his gunner) sat there helpless as the bombers moved closer.
> "After the first attack Jack (and his gunner) scrambled out of the plane, pretty shaken. It had been nerve-racking sitting in the cockpit while friends

Table 9

3rd Kokutai claims — 3 February

Lead Chutai

1st shotai

Lt Tamotsu Yokoyama
NAP 2/C Kaneyoshi Muto
NAP 3/C Yasunobu Nabara

} one P-36 destroyed
one B-17 shared badly damaged on
the ground at Madoera

2nd shotai

Lt Sada-o Yamaguchi
NAP 1/C Yoshiaku Hatakeyama
NAP 3/C Masaru Morita (MiA)

} one Curtiss fighter and one
P-40 shot down (one of these
a probable)

3rd shotai

Wt Off Sada-aki Akamatsu
NAP 1/C Shigeru Yano
NAP 3/C Shigeru Nomura

} five Curtiss fighters and two
flyingboats shot down, one P-36
probable

1st Chutai

1st shotai

Lt Takeo Kurosawa
NAP 1/C Yoshihisa Tokuji
NA 1/C Toru Oda

} three Curtiss fighters, one P-36
shot down; three flyingboats
burned on the water

2nd shotai

Ens Tsuneo Nakahara
NAP 1/C Motabuki Hide
NAP 3/C Isaburo Yahata

} one flyingboat shot down, four
burned; one flyingboat badly
damaged; one B-17 shared badly damaged

3rd shotai

NAP 1/C Shigeo Sugio
NAP 2/C Hatsumasa Yamaya (MiA)
NA 1/C Masao Masuyama

} seven Buffaloes, one Curtiss,
one flyingboat shot down

2nd Chutai

1st shotai

Lt Takaichi Hasuo
NAP 2/C Bunkichi Nakajima
NAP 3/C Sho-ichi Shoji (MiA)

} three P-40s shot down, two
flyingboats burned on water,
two flyingboats badly damaged

2nd shotai

Wt Off Kazuo Kubo
NAP 2/C Katsujiro Nakano
NA 1/C Suehiro Yakamoto

} four flyingboats burned
on water

3rd shotai

NAP 1/C Masayuki Nakase
NAP 3/C Shigeo Okazaki
NA 1/C Seiji Tojiri

} four Hurricanes, two Buffaloes and one
Curtiss shot down; one flyingboat
burned and one badly damaged on water

blew the plane to bits with concussion and the enemy dropped bombs around them.

"Jack's damaged plane was quickly stripped and, because it was a fire hazard, pushed over the side. Even with a dead engine and pilotless, the little seaplane looked as though she might make a perfect landing, but just at the last moment the nose of her pontoon dug into a wave, and she cartwheeled, sinking almost immediately."

A further seven G3Ms of the 1st Ku approached at 1027 and attacked *Marblehead*, one bomb penetrating her deck and exploding below; a second hit aft and a third near-missed, damaging her bow plates. 15 of her crew were killed and a further 34 seriously wounded. However, she remained afloat and with an escort provided by *De Ruyter* — which had also suffered minor damage from near misses — and the destroyers, managed to reach Tjilatjap. Meanwhile, *Houston* had come under further attack, her gunners believing they had hit two of the attackers which were "definitely forced out of the formation and vanished slowly over the horizon." One was undoubtedly Lt Cdr Takeo Ozaki's aircraft which, nonetheless, continued to fly on one engine, eventually landing at Kendari after a five hour flight.

Houston had not escaped damage herself on this occasion however, one bomb having exploded on her main deck. Many men were badly burned and some had severe shrapnel wounds in arms and legs. *Houston* suffered 48 killed and a further 50 seriously wounded, but the cruiser was not severely damaged. Fires were soon under control and she was able to reach Tjilatjap, where her dead and wounded were removed.

After debriefing the returning bomber crews, Vice-Admiral Tada, commander of the 21st Air Flotilla, judged that they had sunk a 'Java-type' cruiser, badly damaged a 'De Ruyter-type' and damaged two more to a lesser extent. Just the one G4M had failed to return.

Another American fighter unit, the 20th Pursuit Squadron (Provisional), had been formed in Australia and now despatched to Java 13 more P-40Es, flown mainly by pilots of the recently arrived 35th Pursuit Group. During the day, these were led by an LB-30 to Timor Island, on the first leg of the journey to the besieged island.

Thursday, 5 February

This was to prove another bad day for the forces attempting to defend Java. Again it was to be the 23rd Air Flotilla A6Ms which were to play a major part in their discomfiture. The 3rd Ku was once more to be particularly busy, beginning at 0720 when single aircraft were despatched to patrol over Ambon Island, to where the bombers of the Takao and 1st Kokutais of the 21st Air Flotilla were to transfer during the day. Whilst engaged on such a patrol, NAP 2/C Kunimori Nakakariya intercepted and shot down a Catalina flyingboat of PatWing 10, in which Ens Carl Hendricks and his crew perished.

At 0820, 27 A6Ms and a C5M of the Tainan Ku took off for Sourabaya, while at 0835 ten A6Ms and a C5M from the 3rd Ku set out for Denpassar on Bali Island. Finally at 0915 another 11 A6Ms and a C5M of the 3rd followed the Tainan formation towards Java. On Java, as the Tainan A6Ms approached, the Allied fighters were scrambled once more, though in much smaller numbers then two days earlier. Lt Anemaet led off the four remaining CW-21Bs, while

Ens S.F. Beukman and Sgt R.M.H. Hermens took off in the last two Hawks. Seven P-40Es were also scrambled but on this occasion failed to see any action.

As the Tainan aircraft approached their target, the C5M turned back. Thereafter the 1st Chutai and the 4th shotai of the 3rd Chutai each reported meeting four fighters, while the 2nd Chutai met one. These were reported as Curtiss-Wrights and Buffaloes, and three of the former were claimed shot down, plus one probable: one was shared by Lt Hideki Shingo, NAP 1/C Kuniyoshi Tanaka and NAP 3/C Toshiaki Honda of the 1st Chutai; a second shared by NAP 1/C Saburo Sakai, NAP 2/C Kazuo Yokokawa and NAP 2/C Tsunehiro Yamagami, also of the 1st Chutai, while Sakai also claimed the probable; the third was shared by NAP 1/C Yoshimichi Saeki and NAP 3/C Shizuo Ishii of the 2nd Chutai. It would seem that those engaged were with the four CW-21Bs of 2-VlG-IV. These were attacked by surprise, by a reported 26 fighters, as Lt Anemaet recalled:

> "We had no opportunity to dog-fight. I managed to half-loop, half-roll into
> a formation and shot down their leader."

Two CW-21Bs were badly hit, Ens L.A.M. van der Vossen force-landing unhurt on the south coast of the island.

The 2nd Chutai also engaged six B-17s, which were just setting out to raid Balikpapan, its eight A6Ms attacking head-on and reporting that two of the bombers streamed black smoke. In fact Lt Edwin S. Green's 41-2483 was damaged in the attack; the mission was then called off and the bombers returned to base. The abandonment of the sortie was due mainly to the fact that two of the bombers reported that their top turrets failed to function during the attack, although other gunners claimed one of the attackers shot down, and a second as damaged.

The 1st and 2nd Chutais then strafed the Morokrembangen flyingboat base at Sourabaya — target of the 3rd Ku's attack two days earlier — one flyingboat being claimed in flames by Lt Shingo's shotai and one damaged by NAP 2/C Hidaka and NAP 3/C Nozawa of the 2nd Chutai.

About half an hour later, the second of the 3rd Ku's formations to leave Celebes also arrived over the Sourabaya area, where at midday a lone fighter identified as a P-36 was seen by the top cover and shot down by the 2nd shotai of the 1st Chutai. Somewhat later, another P-36 was claimed over Madoera Island by the same shotai, both being credited to NAP 1/C Masayuki Nakase and NA 1/C Tamekichi Ohtsuki, who made up this section. Both Hawks were indeed lost; Ens Beukman's aircraft (C-337) was reported shot down by fighters and crashed into the ground, the pilot being killed, while Sgt Hermens' C-332 was hit hard, all its electrical circuits being put out of action. The fighter was totally destroyed in a crash-landing, although the pilot survived unhurt.

Meantime the kokutai's 2nd Chutai had discovered two flyingboats moored off the east coast of the island, each at a different position, which they strafed and destroyed. Finally, as the formation headed for home, a Dutch Catalina — Y-72 of GVT-5 — was seen in the air and was shot down by Nakase and Ohtsuki, assisted by NAP 1/C Motabuki Hide and NAP 3/C Yasunobu Nabara, who were escorting the reconnaissance C5M.

The top cover of the Tainan formation had also intercepted a flyingboat during the mission — which may have been the same aircraft as that engaged by the 3rd Ku pilots — and this was claimed shot down by NAP 1/C Keishu

Kamihira of the 4th Chutai. However, one of the Dutch Naval Flying School's Ryan STM floatplanes also fell victim to the A6Ms, the US instructor pilot of which was again Lt Lee, who had survived a ditching at the hands of the Japanese two days earlier. On this occasion the Ryan was intercepted by a lone A6M when flying at 7,000 feet, 20 miles north of Sourabaya. Pursuing the rapidly descending trainer to sea level as it attempted to get away, the Japanese pilot was forced to make three passes at the slow-flying, jinking, trainer before he was able to inflict any damage; bullets ripped into its rear fuselage, floats and also smashed the windscreen, as both Lee and his pupil ducked their heads. A second A6M joined the attack, gaining strikes on the floatplane's wings, while the other circled above. Each made a final pass before they withdrew and climbed away. Although the Ryan had survived the 25 minute engagement, it was so badly damaged that it sank as it touched down in a rice paddy.

NAP 1/C Keishu Kamihira of the Tainan Kokutai, who claimed a flyingboat shot down on the 5 February attack on Eastern Java. *(Authors' collection)*

Following this action at least one Ryan was modified locally by the installation of a .30-inch machine gun under its cowl, synchronized to fire through the propeller arc, but whether the gun was fired in anger is unknown. One source suggests that on another occasion when a Ryan was engaged by Japanese fighters, the Dutch pilot either deliberately rammed, or collided with, one of his assailants. Confirmation of this alleged incident has not been forthcoming however.

The Japanese pilots underestimated their success during these attacks; three Do 24s (X-22 and X-31 of GVT-6, and X-33 of GVT-7), two Dutch Catalinas

Nose of a Ryan STM showing the modification made to incorporate a single .30-in Browning machine gun above the engine. *(Authors' collection)*

(Y-43 and Y-50 of GVT-3) and one US PBY were destroyed at their moorings and another PBY demolished in its hangar, when two 500 lb bombs exploded from the heat of the fire. The 3rd Ku recorded that three of its A6Ms suffered damage during these actions.

With the arrival of daylight, 12 of the 13 reinforcement P-40Es from Australia which had arrived at Timor's Koepang airfield, had flown on to Bali, where they landed to refuel at Denpassar airfield, before making the final 'hop' to Sourabaya. Seven were refuelled swiftly and took off again to cover the others, as they were likewise dealt with. No sooner were they in the air than Japanese aircraft were spotted overhead — ten A6Ms from the 3rd Ku and 31 bombers — 23 of the Kanoya Ku and eight from the Takao Ku. Three more P-40s were hastily scrambled, and all were soon engaged in a desperate battle for survival.

The 3rd shotai from the Japanese formation came in low in an attempt to strafe, but found themselves engage by three pairs of P-40s. NAP 1/C Yoshihisa Tokuji, NAP 3/C Masakichi Sonoyama and NA 1/C Toru Oda jointly claimed four shot down and two probables. The 2nd shotai dived to their assistance, Wt Off Sadaaki Akamatsu, NAP 1/C Shigeru Yano and NA 1/C Suehiro Yakamoto claiming four more of the American fighters — though these were probably in fact the same aircraft engaged by the other pilots. The 1st shotai remained above to give cover while Lt Takaichi Hasuo, NAP 1/C Bunkichi Nakajima and NA 1/C Seiji Tojiri claimed a single P-40 between them, to bring the total claims to nine destroyed and two probables.

Early in the fight Lt Larry D. Landry was shot down and killed, his aircraft crashing into the sea, while Lts William L. Turner and Cornelius L. Reagan were both hit and crash-landed, Turner having claimed one of the attackers shot down first, as did Lt Gene L. Bound before he was obliged to bale out of his own stricken aircraft. Lt Paul B. Gambonini had scrambled as the attack came in, and before his aircraft had been fully refuelled. He landed his damaged P-40 in the midst of the bombing which had by then got underway and although he escaped injury, his aircraft and one of the others which had not got off the ground, were destroyed. Meanwhile, Lt Dwight S. Muckley was attacked as his aircraft reached 8,000 feet, probably by the 3rd Ku's top cover. With wings, propeller, radio and the tyres of his main landing gear badly shot-up, he dived to 3,000 feet, subsequently landing at Perak, in a near-hysterical condition. Capt William H. Lane claimed one victory, escaped serious damage and also reached Java, landing at Perak with Lt Jesse R. Hague, who made the flight unscathed.

A successful 3rd Kokutai A6M pilot, NAP 2/C Bunkichi Nakajima. *(Authors' collection)*

When the fighting was over, claims were put in for a total of four aircraft shot down, including one credited to the deceased pilot, Lt Landry, although the final assessment was two confirmed and two probables. Five P-40s had been totally destroyed but three had reached Java; two more were destroyed at Denpassar by bombs, and three others damaged. These trickled in over the next three days, as and when they could be made airworthy. Crippled as a unit in its own right, this remaining section of the 20th was incorporated into the 17th Pursuit Squadron.

Friday, 6 February

However the rest of the 20th Pursuit Squadron — a further ten P-40Es — were on the way. The fighters had taken off from Darwin during the day for Timor, led by a Beechcraft 18. Between Waingapoe and Timor a twin-engined aircraft attempted to attack the Beechcraft; the American pilots identified this as a 'Messerschmitt 110' but it was in fact a G3M of the 1st Ku — one of three out searching for the Allied fleet. Three of the P-40s, flown by Lts Robert C. McWherter, Andrew J. Reynolds and Hubert J. Egenes, went to the rescue, shooting down Wt Off Seiai Iwamoto's aircraft into the Savu Sea. As a result of these exertions Egenes and McWherter then ran out of fuel and crash-landed on Timor, only Reynolds managing to land with the other seven at Koepang airfield. This base, and that at Medan, were both subjected to air raids during the day, but these missed the arrival of the P-40s, which were able to fly on to Java next day.

2/Lt Andrew J. Reynolds of the 20th, and later, 17th Pursuit Squadrons (Provisional), would claim three Zeros shot down during February. In summer 1942 he would become, for a time, the top-scoring USAAF pilot in the South-West Pacific Theatre. *(Bill Wolf)*

On Java a further P-40 was lost when Capt Willard Reed, a Marine Corps pilot on loan to the Dutch to instruct their pilots in flying Catalinas, was killed whilst air testing one of the fighters; the experienced Reed had attached himself to the 17th Pursuit Squadron on the outbreak of action over the island. The engine of this P-40 cut as he came in to land, and he crashed into a flooded paddy field, the aircraft turning onto its back. During the crash Reed's arm was broken and, consequently, he was unable to free himself and so drowned.

The flooded paddies could have their uses however. Following the recent heavy losses of flyingboats, GVT-17 moved inland to operate from such a field at Teloengagoeng, near Kediri, from where it was to carry out mining sorties. Dutch naval aircraft were out again, bombing Japanese shipping near Tandjoeng Datoek in southern Borneo, where new landings were taking place. Samarinda airfield was now occupied as a result of these landings, providing yet another base within range of Java.

Saturday, 7 February

The reaction to the raids on Tandjoeng Datoek was swift in coming. Nine Tainan Ku A6Ms strafed the Sourabaya flyingboat base in the early afternoon, claiming two aircraft shot-up on the water. On Timor GVT-7 at its auxiliary base at Rotti, suffered a bombing attack at a most inopportune moment. Do 24 X-35 had been pulled up on the beach for repairs, whilst X-13 had just landed. Both these aircraft, together with X-32, which was moored inshore, were destroyed. On this very date GVT-6 arrived at Koepang with two Do 24s to relieve GVT-7 but when the crews of the latter unit arrived from Rotti by ship, they took over these aircraft, all the personnel of both units flying back to Sourabaya. Here GVT-7 was later reformed with X-1, X-20, X-24 and X-36.

Meanwhile, the two Buffaloes flown by 4 PRU pilots (Sqn Ldr C.R.G. Lewis and Flt Lt Don Pearson), which had arrived at Palembang from Singapore en route for Java on this date (see Volume One, Chapter 9), were refuelled hastily and continued their journey to Batavia, where bad weather was encountered, as recounted by Pearson:

> "While refuelling was taking place (at Palembang) the CO asked me if I would care to spend the night and try to find the advance party, especially as the weather forecast for Batavia was bad. However, since I had noticed two or three senior GD officers waiting in the control building for a flight to Batavia, I said that our aircraft might have disappeared by morning if we stayed overnight.
>
> "So we continued on our journey despite a very shaky formation take-off. About 50 miles from Batavia we ran into very heavy monsoon rain as forecast. However, it was not too difficult to follow the coastline to Batavia. Due to the poor visibility and to the fact that I could not trust the brakes I decided to land well behind the CO.
>
> "I lost sight of the lead aircraft on the approach. On my right was a burnt-out B-17, a wrecked Blenheim on my left and, at the end of the runway, another aircraft on its back with the wheels still turning and a very large man dressed in tropical whites running towards the wreck. The CO had overshot, run into soft mud and turned over."

Sqn Ldr Lewis was extricated from the overturned Buffalo and taken to hospital, where his injuries required 25 stitches.

From the 17th Pursuit Squadron Lts Walter Coss and Jack D. Dale left for Australia to lead back further formations of reinforcement P-40Es. With the continuing trickle of additional fighters, the unit now had 22 pilots, so a second airfield was prepared at Ngoro, situated about ten miles from Blimbing. This would allow better dispersal of aircraft, and also a greater speed of turn-around during operations.

Sunday, 8 February

Nine B-17Es of the 7th Bomb Group took off during the morning, crews briefed to bomb Kendari in the Celebes, where the major force of Japanese Navy medium bombers were based. The formation was led by the experienced Capt J.L. Dufrane, and set course across the Java Sea. Shortly after setting out, one bomber suffered technical trouble and was forced to return but, when halfway to the target, the remainder of the bombers came under attack from an estimated nine to a dozen fighters, which made the best-executed assault yet encountered by a B-17 formation.

The aircraft were again from the Tainan Ku, which had despatched nine A6Ms and a C5M from Balikpapan to strafe Denpassar airfield on Bali. The C5M was forced back early, but after two hours flying it had become obvious that bad weather was going to make the mission impossible, so at 1030, when south of Kansgean Island, the fighters had turned instead towards Sourabaya. Ten minutes later, by chance, they came upon the B-17s and at once made a head-on attack. The results were spectacular; Dufrane's bomber (41-2456) immediately fell in flames, only one member of the crew being seen to bale out. Capt Donald R. Strother took over the lead, but his bomber (41-2471) was also hit, first one engine, then a second being put out of action. Another frontal attack caused Lt William J. Prichard's B-17 (41-2492) to begin burning, and an instant later it blew up.

Lt Paul M. Lindsey's 41-2483 had its tail section so badly shot-up that it took the combined strength of the pilot and another crewman to hold it on an even keel. However, when turbulence was encountered it went into a spin, causing three of the crew to bale-out. Lindsey not only succeeded in regaining control of his aircraft, but without a co-pilot, navigator or map, somehow found his way home in the adverse weather conditions, landing safely at Malang with a wounded man on board.

With two other aircraft also badly damaged, the formation turned back, using cloud to evade further attacks. Apart from Lindsey's aircraft, two others reached Malang, where Capt Joseph J. Preston landed his fire-damaged machine safely, while Capt Strother put his bomber down at Djokjakarta and Lt Swanson his similarly damaged 40-2458 at Pasirian. The gunners fought back furiously, optimistically claiming five of their attackers shot down; in fact two were hit, but both managed to return to base.

Japanese claims were for two B-17s destroyed and three probables, all of the latter pouring black smoke. The successes were credited jointly to all nine pilots: Lt Shingo, NAP 1/C Tanaka and NAP 3/C Honda; NAP 1/C Saburo Sakai, NAP Yamagami and NAP 3/C Takashi Yokoyama; NAP 1/C Saeki, NAP 3/C Nozawa and NAP 3/C Ishii. Immediately after the combat the A6Ms turned for home, their ammunition exhausted.

During mid-morning, a pair of A6Ms from the 3rd Ku detachment on Ambon took off for a strafing attack on Dobo and Kapalauan Aru, where NAP 1/C Yoshihiko Takenaka and NAP 3/C Nobutoshi Furukawa strafed and left burning a flyingboat. This was probably a Grumman G-21a Goose amphibian (PK-AKB) of the Netherlands New Guinea Petroleum Company, which had earlier been rendered irreparable at Dobo. Two other pilots, Lt Toshitada Kawazoe and NAP 3/C Tadahiro Sakai, left an hour and a half later, flying to Saunlaki, where they also reported strafing and burning a flyingboat, at almost exactly the same time as the other pair made their attack. Meanwhile the 17th Pursuit Squadron, which was involved in an indecisive high-altitude battle over Sourabaya during the day, lost another P-40E and pilot when Lt Philip T. Metsker, flying to Koepang, Timor, lost his way and crashed.

Monday, 9 February

A Japanese convoy of six transports, one cruiser, two destroyers and three auxiliaries sailed from Kendari to Makassar in south-western Celebes where, by nightfall, the Dutch garrison was overcome, the whole island then coming under Japanese domination. A Beech Staggerwing (PK-SAM), belonging to the Christian and Missionary Alliance, was destroyed by the NEI army at the airstrip at Makassar, to deny it to the invaders, effectively trapping the Rev Fred Jackson on the island; he was subsequently captured and killed. Later during the day the US submarine *S-37* attacked the landing force, sinking the destroyer *Natsushio*.

The 3rd Ku provided patrols over the ships, the first pair flying low over the area mid morning and strafing a Dutch armoured car. Ground fire struck the leading A6M, flown by NAP 1/C Masayuki Nakase, and he crashed to his death. Nakase was at this time one of the Navy's top fighter pilots. He had been one of the first to fly A6Ms in China during 1941, where he had claimed five victories during his first combat there. He was considered to have a personal score of 18 victories at the time of his death.

Before this loss had occurred however, a further pair of A6Ms left Ambon, strafing a wireless station at Saunlaki and then carrying out a low reconnaissance over the airfield there. Ground fire struck the No 2 aircraft; although NAP 3/C Yoshiro Hashiguchi suffered a wound in the right thigh, he managed to fly back to Ambon and land safely.

Another Dutch flyingboat was lost during the day, when Catalina Y-38 of GVT-17, on a shipping patrol, had to make an emergency landing at Wester-vaarwater, near Sourabaya. The 'boat was taken in tow but was severely damaged by its tug, and subsequently sank.

On Java, the 17th Pursuit Squadron was scrambled during the morning, four flights of P-40s being directed by Dutch radio onto 18 bombers flying in two flights of nine. While five P-40s attacked, the rest scattered over a wide area for maximum coverage, reaching 24,000 feet. Four of the attacking pilots made one pass each, but the fifth, Lt McWherter, attacked one 'Type 96' bomber at which he fired four times; this was seen to pour smoke, but carried on flying. The Dutch later reported seeing one go into the sea north-east of Sourabaya, and this was subsequently credited to McWherter. The unit involved has not been identified from Japanese records.

From Australia more reinforcements now set out — on this occasion P-40Es of the 3rd Pursuit Squadron and Douglas A-24 Dauntless dive-bombers of the 91st Bomb Squadron. Seven of the 3rd's P-40s had already been lost in accidents while flying up from Brisbane to Darwin. Nine of the survivors then took off for Timor in company with three A-24s, led by an LB-30. One P-40 had to turn back, but the rest arrived to find Timor covered in thick rainclouds. Unable to find the airfield at Koepang, all eight fighters crashed while attempting to make force-landings. The A-24s were more successful in finding their destination, but were mistaken for Japanese aircraft as they approached and all were badly damaged by the AA defences!

During the day Western Java suffered its first air attack, a bombing and strafing raid being made on the Batavia area by 27 bombers of the 22nd Air Flotilla, covered by 13 A6Ms and accompanied by a single C5M to observe results. Tjililitan airfield and Kemajoran civil airport were hit. At the former the alarm was given late and only four Brewsters of 3-VlG-IV attempted to scramble and were immediately attacked by the escorting fighters. The Brewster of Sgt H. Huys was hit and set on fire just as it was gaining speed for take-off, but miraculously the pilot escaped without injury. His colleague, Sgt J. Berk, was not so fortunate and was killed when his aircraft was shot down, while Ens C.H. Weijnschenk, the section leader, crash-landed his burning machine in a paddy field. Meanwhile Lt J.A. Butner, a former bomber pilot of 1-VlG-I, who was still under training as a fighter pilot with 3-VlG-IV took-off on his own. However, he immediately came under attack although he was able to land his badly damaged aircraft at Kemajoran. Only Sgt F.J. de Wilde returned safely to Tjililitan. B-3120 was amongst those Brewsters lost in this action.

Two Glenn Martins of 2-VlG-III, both old WH-2 models, were caught in the air about to land, and M-538 was promptly shot down, crashing near Bakasi with the loss of Sgt Maj L.M. Galistan and his crew. The other, M-537, was returning from a reconnaissance mission which had taken it to Christmas island, when it was shot down, but it crash-landed near Tangerang, all members of 2/Lt G. Hagers' crew surviving.

The crew of Glenn Martin WH-2 (M-538) of 2-VlG-III prepare for a mission. This aircraft was shot down on 9 February. *(Authors' collection)*

Meanwhile, two FK-51 biplanes of VkA-3 were set on fire on the ground, a third — which had just taken off — narrowly escaped being shot down as the pilot skilfully manoeuvred at low speed; four more Brewsters of 3-VlG-IV were also destroyed on the ground. Following this attack the two surviving Brewsters were flown to Tjisaoek to join Kapt van Helsdingen's 2-VlG-V.

Amongst the aircraft casualties at the airport was one of KNILM's DC-5 airliners, PK-ADA; another of the airline's machines, a Fokker F-VIIB (PK-AFG) was also destroyed, while a Lockheed 14 (PK-AFP) was damaged. A privately-owned Bellanca 14 (PK-KRS) was also destroyed during this attack as were four RAAF Buffaloes, which had been evacuated from Singapore, three others suffering damage.

Fokker F.VIIB3/m, PK-AFG, destroyed during an air raid on Kemajoran civil airport, Batavia, on 9 February. *(Authors' collection)*

It was reported that a number of newly-erected RAF Hurricanes were also damaged during the attack on Kemajoran, although it would seem that the damage on this occasion was exaggerated, as recalled by LAC Cowle of 242 Squadron:

> "The airfield was strafed by Jap fighters and many planes were destroyed although only one round passed through a hangar full of Hurricanes being assembled. This round passed through an engine; we removed the airscrew from this machine to fit to another which had had its prop badly damaged when being towed from the docks."

On a lighter note, he added:

> "We had an old gramophone in our maintenance flight with about three records, one of which — 'Somebody Loves Me' — was often playing while I ground myself into the dust as flat as possible when the Japs came over.
> "On one occasion a Canadian flight sergeant and I were running in a real panic off the airfield when the siren went. We came to a deep, broad, slimy brook — he chanced it and jumped — and fell in the filthy mess. I hesitated — and just then the all-clear went."

Tuesday–Thursday, 10-12 February

Increasingly bad weather now reduced the number of raids on Java for some days, but in Borneo forces landed at Bandjermasin in the south, their invasion being timed to coincide with an overland advance from Balikpapan. The last Dutch personnel were evacuated, leaving the whole of Borneo in Japanese hands. Flying back from there with some of the evacuees on the 11th, Do 24 X-29 of GVT-6 had to make an emergency landing on the sea and was lost with all hands.

A further flight of 3rd Pursuit Squadron P-40Es, led by Capt Grant Mahony, departed Darwin during the morning of the 10th, all nine landing at Pasirian next day. However one crash-landed and another tipped onto its nose, both aircraft becoming unserviceable. After refuelling, the other seven flew on to Ngoro after refuelling, thus bringing the 17th Pursuit Squadron, into which they too were now amalgamated, up to a strength of 30 fighters (of which 24 were serviceable); five had been written off for spares, while the two damaged aircraft at Pasirian awaited repair. Among the new pilots arriving were several more veterans of the Philippines and an ex-China hand, who had also been an instructor at the University of Tokyo! Pilot strength now stood at 47, including two transport pilots and two Dutch liaison officers.

Only one of the three A-24s which had reached Timor was fit to fly on to Java on the 10th, the other two returning to Darwin for repairs. However 11 more of these dive-bombers left Australia next day. One crashed at Soemba en route, but ten reached Modjokarto on the 12th, where work began at top speed to ready as many as possible for operations. More P-40s were now available in Australia, but the newly-formed 13th Pursuit Squadron (Provisional), and the remnants of the 3rd which had not yet reached Java, were now ordered to Perth to go aboard the seaplane tender *Langley* for shipment to the war zone.

Capt Grant Mahony, who served with distinction in the Philippines and in Java, where he flew with the 3rd Pursuit Squadron, and with the 17th Pursuit Squadron (Provisional). *(Bill Wolf)*

The Dutch also received some aircraft reinforcements during this period when Lt Anemaet was ordered to take the remaining six CW-21Bs (including two repaired machines) of 2-VlG-IV to Andir, where he handed over command of the CW-21B Flight to Lt W. Boxman. At Andir a dozen RAF Hurricanes were now made available to the Dutch, Anemaet reforming 2-VlG-IV with these; four pilots from his own afdeling joined him and seven pilots were posted in from 1-VlG-IV [1] while Lt J.B.H. Brunier arrived from 3-VlG-V. Jan Brunier

---

[1] These pilots were: 2/Lt A.J. Marinus, Sgt Maj P. Boonstoppel and F.J. de Wilde, Sgts A. Kok, H.J. Mulder, J.C. Jacobs and R.M.H. Hermens from 1-VlG-IV; Ens L.A.M. van der Vossen and A.W. Hamming, Sgts N. Dejalle and F. Beerling from 2-VlG-IV.

had served with the RAF in England in 1941, when he had flown Spitfires with 92 and 611 Squadrons and had been credited with two victories, for which he had received the Dutch Vliegerkruz.

The Hurricanes were assembled and tested and, after a short briefing, the pilots flew them to Kalidjati to undertake a period of training. At this stage the aircraft were not equipped with radios, and the Dutch pilots had no suitable oxygen masks. Therefore, when flying above 15,000 feet, they simply placed the end of the supply tube in their mouths and breathed in the oxygen, in this far from satisfactory manner.

Limited raids continued on the 10th and 11th in eastern Java despite the weather, Sourabaya and Malang being bombed on the former date and again the next day. On the latter occasion Lts Jesse Hague and George E. Kiser of the 17th Pursuit Squadron were scrambled and attacked bombers raiding the Malang fortress, two of which they claimed shot down.

Three LB-30s attacked ships in the Makassar Straits on the 10th, 2/Lt F.A. Norwood and Lt V.J. Poncik each claiming a direct hit on a "converted aircraft carrier" which then "exploded and was left burning". This was obviously the seaplane tender *Chitose*, which was damaged by air attack south of Celebes on this date. Next day, seven B-17Es of the 19th Bomb Group, together with four more from the 7th Bomb Group, raided shipping off Makassar and claimed a transport possibly sunk, although results were uncertain due to poor visibility and darkness.

Java was about to receive further — and unexpected — reinforcements, for (as already recorded in the preceding chapters) the Japanese were on the point of launching an air and seaborne invasion of southern Sumatra, which would swiftly drive out the RAF. With Singapore on the point of capitulation, Borneo, Celebes and Ambon gone, and the Americans in the Philippines holding out only on Bataan and Corregidor Island, Java was about to become the last beleagued bastion of the Allies in the Indies.

Elsewhere in the southern part of the battle area, other operations had continued from early in the month. At Port Moresby (New Guinea) were elements of three RAAF units. An as yet un-numbered 'scratch' squadron with seven Hudsons (referred to here as the Port Moresby Hudson Flight), under the command of Wg Cdr J.M. Lerew, former CO of the now-defunct 24 RAAF Squadron, joined six Catalinas of 11 and 20 RAAF Squadrons which had arrived earlier. RAAF-manned P-40Es were expected from the mainland in the near future.

Tuesday, 3 February

Port Moresby suffered its first air raid in the early hours, six bombers attacking from 8,000 feet. When darkness descended, five of the Catalinas set out to bomb Rabaul, where nine fighters of the 4th Ku (24th Air Flotilla) were already ensconced. As the Catalinas approached, night flying fighters were encountered and these attacked two of the flyingboats. One managed to evade but the other — A24-5 flown by Flt Lt G.E. Hemsworth — was badly damaged, although one of the gunners, Sgt Douglas Dick, on his first operational sortie, claimed one of the attackers shot down in return; he was granted a probable. The Catalina's port engine and fuel tank were hit during the attack; Hemsworth feathered the damaged engine and ordered the bombs and all other removable equipment to be jettisoned to reduce weight, after which the flyingboat staggered back to Port

Later to become Japan's premier fighter pilot of the war, Hiroyoshi Nishizawa claimed his first victory against an RAF aircraft over New Britain on 3 February 1942, in an obsolescent Mitsubishi A5M fighter of the 4th Kokutai.

Moresby on one engine following 140 hours in the air. It seems that the Catalina was attacked by Lt Hiroyoshi Nishizawa, later to become the JNAF's top-scoring fighter pilot.

Friday, 6 February

Flt Lt D.W.I. Campbell's Hudson (from Port Moresby) was intercepted while reconnoiting over Rabaul during the morning, when the aircraft was riddled by gunfire which severely wounded the pilot in the left wrist and hand, his co-pilot suffering equally severe wounds to an arm and leg, while the gunner was hit in his left leg. Despite his wounds, Campbell managed to fly the 500 miles back to Port Moresby, helped by the one uninjured member of the crew, Sgt G. Thompson, who administered first aid, and assisted the pilot in flying the crippled aircraft.

The Japanese tentacles continued to extend and, on the 8th, troops disembarked from two transports and a destroyer to seize Gasmata, in southern New Britain. The following night five Hudsons, led by Wg Cdr Lerew, and three Catalinas from Port Moresby attacked without apparent results.

Wednesday-Saturday, 11-14 February

Wg Cdr Lerew again led three Port Moresby Hudsons to attack Gasmata by day, undertaking a mast-height attack on the shipping there, claiming two transports set on fire. As the bombers climbed away, they were attacked by five 4th Ku fighters, NAP 1/C Satoshi Yoshino (in an old A5M) manoeuvring onto the tail of Lerew's aircraft (A16-126), gaining hits on its engines; flames were seen spewing into the slipstream and Lerew ordered his crew to bale out, following them shortly afterwards.

He landed in treetops about two miles behind Japanese lines; however, his crew perished. Yoshino meantime engaged and shot down A16-91, flown by Flg Off G.I. Gibson; Sqn Ldr Bill Pedrina's crew reported that Gibson's aircraft crashed into a hillside, his gunners believing that two of the attackers had also been shot down, one of which allegedly fell in flames.

Three days later Yoshino claimed a further victory, but the identity of this has not been established, although it may have been the Hudson (from Port Moresby) flown by Flt Lt W.L. Milne which, nonetheless, returned safely following an attack by a Japanese fighter. This aircraft had carried out a reconnaissance of Simpson Harbour, Rabaul, where the crew reported sighting an aircraft carrier, five other warships, 11 transports, and nine flyingboats on the water; they also identified three seaplanes on the slipway and six bombers and eight fighters on the airfield. Not for some days would there be any further action over the area.

Chapter 5

DISASTER AT DARWIN;
LUCK OF THE *LEXINGTON*

With Sumatra finally in their hands, the Japanese now made their next moves, aimed at the virtual isolation of Java. These included the invasion of Bali island, a series of heavy air attacks on major targets throughout Java itself, and occupation of Timor.

Timor was the vital link in the 'stepping stones' air reinforcements route from Australia, therefore its loss would mean that no more short-range aircraft could be delivered to the East Indies by air. That this critically important island was likely to suffer an early invasion, now that Ambon and Celebes were in Japanese hands, was obvious to the Allies and efforts were put in hand to counter this threat. On 15 February therefore, three US Army transports − *Meigs*, *Mauna Loa* and *Port Mar*, together with the Australian coaster *Tulagi* − carrying 1,800 Australian and US troops and equipment, set sail from Port Darwin to reinforce the defences on Timor. The convoy was escorted by the US cruiser *Houston*, an American destroyer (*Peary*) and two RAN sloops (*Swan* and *Warrego*).

Hardly was the convoy underway, than it was spotted by one of the wide-ranging H6K flyingboats of the Toko Ku, which proceeded to shadow the vessels and report on their position. A desperate call by *Houston*'s' Capt Albert Rooks to Darwin for fighter protection, brought a lone P-40E to their aid. Flown by Lt Robert J. Buel of the 21st Pursuit Squadron, the fighter was one of only two available.

Initially Buel was unable to locate the flyingboat despite *Houston* firing her guns in the intruder's direction, but he then spotted it and his progress through the sky was followed by many anxious upturned faces aboard the vessels of the convoy. The P-40 was seen to pursue the flyingboat, as recalled by Ens Walter Winslow, an SOC-3 'scout' pilot aboard the cruiser:

> "Both planes soon disappeared from sight, but soon afterwards a brilliant flash of fire and considerable black smoke were observed on the horizon. We prayed that the P-40 had been the victor."

The crew of the H6K apparently identified the interceptor as a 'Spitfire' as it closed in, bullets ripping into the fuselage of the flyingboat forward of the fuel tanks, killing the W/T operator and causing a fire to break out. However, Buel's aircraft was also badly hit, diving into the sea in flames. The crippled flyingboat, with the fire spreading rapidly, was ditched skilfully, enabling the survivors to escape; they eventually reached Melville Island, where they were taken prisoner.

With the threat of Allied reinforcements possibly landing on Timor, the Japanese High Command designated the convoy a priority target. At 1100 on 16 February, Japanese bombers were sighted off *Houston*'s starboard bow, and her two SOC-3s were ordered off, the crews briefed to fly to Broome. Lt Jack Lamade was catapulted just prior to the attack, and reached Broome safely but, as Ens Winslow waited to be launched, the cruiser's big guns opened fire, the concussion shredding the fabric covering the tailplane and rear fuselage of his aircraft!

The attack was carried out by a total of 35 G4Ms and ten H6Ks from the 1st and Toko Kokutais, which approached in waves and with determination, but skilful manoeuvring and constant fire from the escorting warships — particularly from *Houston* — ensured that no direct bomb hits were suffered, although the Japanese crews thought they had gained two such on one transport and four near misses on two others. Nonetheless, all four transports sprung leaks as a result of near misses, which also caused three casualties — one fatal — aboard *Mauna Loa*. Although a dozen of the attacking aircraft sustained shrapnel damage, the assault on the convoy had the desired effect, for the ships were all forced to turn back towards Darwin, leaving Timor with no real defences.

Following the attacks on Rabaul and New Guinea in late January (see Volume One, Chapter 6), the four Japanese carriers of the 1st Carrier Fleet — *Akagi*, *Kaga*, *Shokaku* and *Zuikaku* — had returned to Truk at the end of the month. An attack on the Marshall Islands — the first US Navy carrier strike of the war — carried out by aircraft from the USS *Enterprise*, had sent them racing northwards in an abortive attempt to intercept. *Shokaku* and *Zuikaku* then headed for Japan to counter any possible strike on the home islands, while *Akagi* and *Kaga* steamed back southwards to Palau to join *Hiryu* and *Soryu*, fresh from their support of the Ambon landings (see Volume One, Chapter 6).

On 15 February all four carriers, with their cohorts of cruisers and destroyers, departed Palau under Vice-Admiral Choichi Nagumo's command, arriving in the area of the Ceram Islands three days later. The fleet waited near Amboina for the moment to launch a strike against Darwin at dawn on the 19th.

Darwin was overflowing with Allied ships and aircraft. As the main supply base from which reinforcements and equipment could be delivered to the East Indies and to the forces still resisting in the Philippines, its importance was obvious. For the Japanese it posed the greatest threat they faced at this time, not only to their proposed invasion of Timor but also to their important base at Rabaul. Regular aerial reconnaissance of the port and its surrounds was undertaken, while an attack by the full weight of the 1st Carrier Division was planned. This was to be launched by land-based bombers of the 21st and 23rd Air Flotillas.

One obvious target for attack was the small and old aircraft carrier USS *Langley*, which was at Darwin at this time. The United States' first operational carrier, *Langley* had ended her days as a first-line warship and was being used for ferrying of vital aircraft. For the time being she was to escape however, sailing for Fremantle on the 17th. Her orders were to pick up 27 new P-40s and their pilots, and deliver them to Burma, via the port of Colombo, Ceylon. However, as she was to pass close to the southern coast of Java en route to Ceylon, her captain was advised that he might be instructed to divert the fighters there if events deemed such action necessary.

On Timor meantime, the non-arrival of the Allied reinforcements, coupled with increased Japanese aerial reconnaissance activity, had convinced the authorities that an invasion was imminent. On the 18th therefore, all RAAF staff except for maintenance parties, were ordered to prepare for evacuation and, next day, six Hudsons flew in from Darwin to carry them out.

Dawn on the 19th found 47 vessels at anchor in Port Darwin harbour, although only 11 of these were merchant ships, including the four returned transports of the aborted Timor convoy; there were two tankers and a hospital ship and, of the others, 32 were RAN craft, mainly auxiliary and boom defence vessels, although the total included two sloops, five corvettes and a base repair vessel. Also present were the US destroyer *Peary* and the small seaplane tender *William B. Preston*, the latter a converted destroyer which had escaped from the Philippines. There were also a number of flyingboats in the harbour, both military and civil.

At RAAF Darwin airfield were nine Hudsons of 2 and 13 RAAF Squadrons, including the six machines which had just returned from Koepang with evacuees; in addition, en USAAF P-40Es of the new 33rd Pursuit Squadron had just arrived; there was also the sole remaining P-40 of the 3rd Pursuit Squadron. This aircraft and its pilot, Lt Robert G. Oestreicher, now joined the 33rd Squadron, which was about to begin the flight up to Java. Also on the airfield was a single LB-30, the personal aircraft of Maj General Patrick J. Hurley, USAAF, who had just arrived on a visit. Darwin Civil Field was the temporary home of five unserviceable Wirraways of 12 RAAF Squadron, while nine more of these aircraft were at nearby Batchelor airfield. At Daly Waters were eight more Hudsons; a variety of civil light liaison aircraft were spread between these three bases.

First off from the carriers that fateful morning were the B5N bombers − 18 from *Akagi* leading the way, headed by the strike force commander, Cdr Mitsuo Fuchida. Then came 18 more from *Soryu* led by Lt Heijiro Abe, 18 from *Hiryu* led by Lt Cdr Tadashi Kusumi, and 27 from *Kaga* led by Lt Cdr Takashi Hashiguchi. Close behind the bombers came the fighter escort, which comprised 18 A6Ms − nine from *Soryu* led by Lt Iyozo Fujita and nine from *Hiryu* led by Lt Sumio Nono. The initial launching was to head for Melville Island, some 90 minutes flight away, where it would rendezvous with the faster dive-bombers, which would follow with their own escort.

Half an hour after the first B5Ns had taken off, the D3A dive-bombers began to follow − 17 from *Hiryu* led by Lt Michio Kobayashi, and 18 each from *Akagi* (Lt Takehiko Chihaya), *Soryu* (Lt Cdr Takashige Egusa) and *Kaga* (Lt Shoichi Ogawa). Escort was provided by nine A6Ms from *Kaga* (Lt Yasushi Nikaido) and nine from *Akagi* (Lt Cdr Shigeru Itaya). Other fighters from *Soryu* were launched three at a time during the morning to fly defensive combat air patrols. Meanwhile from Celebes and Ambon 54 G4Ms, drawn equally from the Kanoya and 1st Kokutais − led respectively by Lt Cdr Toshiie Irisa and Lt Cdr Takeo Ozaki − set course for the same target.

At 0915 ten P-40Es took off from RAAF Darwin and formated on a lone B-17 circling above, which was to lead them to Timor's Koepang airfield on the first leg of their journey to Java. No sooner were they underway however, when bad weather ahead was reported and they were ordered to return to base. Darwin was now in a state of high tension due to the recent sightings of hostile aircraft on reconnaissance so, as a precaution, Control ordered half of the returning fighters to patrol overhead while the others landed and refuelled. Despite this however, when a signal from a coastwatcher on the northern tip of Melville Island was received at RAAF HQ, reporting a "large number of aircraft", it was interpreted as possibly referring to the P-40 formation, even though Melville Island was north of the proposed route!

A second radio message was received at RAAF HQ at 0937 — from Father John McGrath of the Catholic Mission on Bathurst Island — which mentioned "an unusually large air formation bearing down on us from the north-west", but was still not acted upon. As a consequence of this indecision no advance warning was given at Darwin of the impending attack, a warning that might have saved many lives.

Meantime, as the Japanese dive-bomber formation approached the rendez-vous area, a flyingboat was spotted north-west of Bathurst Island, circling above the US supply vessel *Florence D*; one of the escorting fighters, flown by NAP 1/C Yoshikazu Nagahama of the *Kaga* formation, broke away to attack the PBY, Lt Thomas H. Moorer's 22-P-18 of VP-22. The flyingboat's port engine and fuel tank were hit, Moorer managing to ditch the blazing aircraft despite it bouncing three times before it came to a halt. All the crew, including the wounded second pilot, scrambled into the liferaft and were soon picked up by the ship they had been protecting.

By the time Nagahama had completed his attack on the PBY, he had lost the remainder of his formation and proceeded alone, missing the rendezvous. As a result, he was the first of the attacking force to reach the Darwin area, where below he saw the five patrolling P-40s. Throwing caution to the wind, he dived to attack. The American pilots had received no warning that hostile aircraft were in the vicinity but Lt Oestreicher, who was leading the patrol, suddenly spotted Nagahama's A6M diving on them. Not realising this was a lone aircraft, Oestreicher jettisoned his belly tank and threw his aircraft into a dive. Obviously in something of a panic, the others attempted to follow but Nagahama was already upon them, shooting down Lts Jack R. Peres[1] and Elton S. Perry almost straight away, both P-40s plunging into the sea. Nagahama then closed in on Lt Max R. Wiecks' aircraft and shot this down also, the pilot managing to bale out, following his aircraft into the water. After many hours in the sea Wiecks reached land, and was later rescued. Meanwhile, Lt William R. Walker's P-40 also came under attack, the pilot suffering a wound to his left shoulder. Despite the injury, Walker succeeded in crash-landing his damaged aircraft back at base.

As the main formation approached, Lt Oestreicher alone attacked the bombers, one of which he claimed to have shot down in flames, reporting that a second was left trailing smoke, before making good his escape in cloud; although his aircraft had been hit by return fire he was able to land without mishap. *Soryu*'s B5Ns reported being attacked by fighters and had four aircraft hit, while a few minutes later the D3As from this same carrier also reported fighter interception, one dive-bomber being hit six times while another from this formation failed to return; the crew of the D3A was later rescued by a Japanese destroyer.

The main force of A6Ms then arrived over Darwin, strafing harbour traffic as they swept in at low level, catching the auxiliary minesweeper *Gunbar* as it

---

[1] The body of Lt Jack Peres was found the following September, when aborigines came across his burnt-out P-40 in the sea about 20 miles down the coast from Darwin. That it took so long to find him is an indication of the inhospitable and barren desert on the edge of which Darwin is situated.

was passing through the boom gate; the craft was damaged and suffered a number of casualties. The B5Ns followed; approaching from the south-east, they bombed the harbour and town from 14,000 feet, concentrating on shipping at anchor, the railway quay, and government offices. Within the first few minutes bombs fell on the wharf, where oil fuel was ignited and buildings demolished. Amongst the first ships to be hit was the 5,952-ton *Neptuna*, whose cargo included 200 tons of depth charges. Struck by two bombs, the freighter was soon ablaze, and exploded, with the loss of 45 of her crew: red hot fragments of the vessel showered the harbour.

The tanker *British Motorist* also suffered two direct hits, and was left sinking, her master amongst those killed, whilst an Australian cargo ship, *Zealandia*, was set ablaze, becoming a total loss. Two of the US supply ships were targeted, *Meigs* being devastated by an estimated 20 direct hits and one torpedo (sic), whilst *Mauna Loa* slowly sank by the stern. Another American vessel, the 3,289-ton freighter *Admiral Halstead*, carrying 14,000 drums of high octane aviation fuel, was damaged by a near-miss, as was the hospital ship, *Manunda*, which then suffered a direct hit; although there were 16 fatalities as well as many injured aboard, she continued to operate in her specified role. The lugger *Malvie* and the small coaster *Kelat* were also sunk, as was the destroyer *Peary*, with great loss of life; an eyewitness later recalled:

> "I saw a big bomb hit the *Peary* amidships. There was a terrific explosion and the ship sank in five minutes or less, her captain, Lt Cdr John Bermingham, and many of her crew with her."

Another bomb hit the seaplane tender *William B. Preston* just forward of the after deckhouse on the port side; she caught fire but her gunners fought back tenaciously, manning recently-installed .50-inch machine guns taken from wrecked PBYs. As one of her crew proudly commented:

> "The tender proved too hot a target for the Jap strafers!"

With her afterdeck blazing furiously and black smoke billowing from her funnels, she was guided out to sea by Lt L.O. Woods − her acting skipper − away from the immediate danger of exploding ships. All told, eight vessels were left blazing or sinking, while two other merchantmen − *Barossa* and *Port Mar* − together with the coaster *Tulagi* − were all beached, although later salvaged.

Four of *Hiryu*'s B5Ns were hit, while a further seven from *Kaga* were damaged. Immediately after the level bombers had completed their bomb run, the dive bombers and escorting fighters dived down to make their attacks. The D3As from *Akagi*, *Soryu* and *Hiryu*, joined by the 2nd Chutai of the *Kaga* force, attacked the shipping while *Kaga*'s 1st Chutai attacked the main Darwin air-fields, engaging some Allied aircraft there without result, then strafed others on the ground. During this particular attack one of *Kaga*'s D3As was shot down, with the loss of NAP 1/C Musashi Uchikado and Wt Off Katsuyoshi Tsuru, and six others damaged. The downed aircraft was most probably shot down by Hotchkiss machine gunners of 19th Machine Gun Regiment, located at Winnellie Camp, six miles south-east of the town. They reported that it trailed smoke after being hit, following which it crashed in flames half a mile away; when the raid was over, the successful gunners were taken to see the wreck and many souvenirs were obtained.

On the approach of the raiders, the five P-40s on the ground at the RAAF base attempted to take off, led by the commanding officer, Major Floyd S. Pell. The A6Ms were on them like a flash, those from *Hiryu, Akagi* and *Kaga* all attacking. Pell baled out at 70 feet but his parachute barely had time to open before he hit the ground. Observers saw him, obviously badly injured, trying to crawl away when A6Ms came down and strafed him; he was killed — probably the victim of *Hiryu*'s fighters. Meanwhile, Lt Charles W. Hughes had failed to get airborne and was strafed and killed in his cockpit. As Lt Robert F. McMahon got into the air, he encountered three A6Ms and managed to get behind them; he missed the first but believed he gained strikes on the second. His under-carriage then dropped down which restricted manoeuvrability, consequently the P-40 was soon under attack and shot full of holes, while the pilot was slightly wounded in one leg. AA fire from the harbour area forced the A6Ms to break away and as McMahon nursed his burning aircraft towards the airfield, he spotted a dive-bomber; opening fire on this, he saw the rear gunner slump over his gun but with his faltering engine spewing flames, he baled out at 700 feet, landing safely.

The last two P-40s to get airborne were flown by Lts Burt Rice and John G. Glover, the former's aircraft immediately coming under attack. It fell into a spin and Rice baled out, hitting his head as he did so, causing him to land in a semi-conscious state. Glover fired at the A6M which had been chasing Rice and "saw it going down." He then tried to protect Rice on his parachute by orbiting, but was then hit. With his aircraft barely controllable, he headed for the airfield, crash-landing on the boundary; the P-40 cartwheeled several times, Glover emerging with serious facial injuries. Helpers rushed to his aid and he was soon on his way to hospital.

Hiryu's pilots reported shooting down one P-40 just as it was taking off — obviously Pell — and strafing the descending pilot when he baled out. *Kaga*'s A6Ms all attacked two P-40s, one being claimed shot down and one probable. Two more were then seen and these were also shot down. *Akagi*'s pilots were also involved, claiming four P-40s shot down, all shared with aircraft of the other units. Total claims appear therefore to have been for four P-40s confimed and one probable over the airfield. Again the claims were extremely accurate. One of *Hiryu*'s fighters (flown by NA 1/C Hajime Toyoshima, third man of the 1st Shotai) failed to return — probably the victim of Glover — and was seen to crash-land on Melville Island.

It was at this moment that *Kaga*'s dive-bombers attacked the airfield, before departing soon after 1030. Meanwhile the A6Ms went down to strafe and *Akagi*'s fighters claimed four aircraft in flames and four damaged, *Kaga*'s one destroyed, while *Hiryu*'s claimed three large and two small aircraft in flames, one large and two small badly damaged. On the airfield the deputy Station Commander, Sqn Ldr A.D. Swan, aided by Wt Off H.W. Chapman, manned a Lewis gun, while Wg Cdr A.R. Tindal, who was the Armament Officer of Northern Area HQ, fired at the strafers with a Vickers gun mounted on top of a trench, until he was fatally wounded. One bomb fell on a trench in which sheltered four members of the transport section, all of whom were killed.

Hiryu's fighters also strafed an airfield referred to as being at Cape Gunpeal, claiming a large transport aircraft badly damaged. This was probably the airfield on Bathurst Island, where a USAAF Beechcraft liaison biplane was destroyed on the ground by six strafing A6Ms. The *Hiryu* aircraft were not yet finished however, going on to strafe two flyingboats at their moorings, which they claimed destroyed in flames. These were also attacked by the lone Nagahama, who claimed one on fire, while another was claimed by strafing D3As from the *Soryu* contingent. Three USN PBYs of PatWing 10 were indeed lost in these circumstances.

On the way back to the carriers *Akagi*'s A6Ms strafed a cargo vessel, while those from *Soryu*, which had seen no action so far, attacked a warship identified as a cruiser. Apart from the one fighter lost, a dozen more were damaged – seven from *Hiryu*, three from *Akagi* and two from *Kaga*, but all returned to their respective carriers safely.

As the raid abated, Qantas pilots Capts W.H. Crowther and H.B. Hussey decided to get their slightly damaged Empire flyingboat *Camilla* into the air, reaching Groote Eglandt safely; she had apparently escaped detection during the raid due to smoke from the burning *Neptuna* concealing her. Eight minutes after the flyingboat's departure, the freighter blew up. At 1040 the 'All Clear' sounded. Darwin was left in utter confusion. The emergency services failed, servicemen and civilians lay dead and dying everywhere; ships, aircraft, buildings and dumps blazed, sending clouds of black smoke and dust writhing skywards to create a terrible scene of death and destruction. Panic was rife and rumours of imminent invasion led many civilians to flee the town.

It was not yet over however, for at 1158 the medium bombers from Kendari and Ambon approached in two formations, accurately bombing the RAAF airfield again. When the bombers were first sighted, some wondered whether a paratroop attack was underway. The pattern-bombing attack which followed quickly replaced the defenders' fears with a deadly reality of a different kind. The RAAF station was devastated – the hospital, two hangars, messes, equipment stores, recreation huts, four dormitories and other buildings – were all wrecked, although only six airmen were killed. Amongst the aircraft

Damage to the main hangar at RAAF Darwin. *(RAAF)*

destroyed on the ground in this attack were the last two P-40s — Oestreicher's damaged machine and the one that had been crash-landed by Lt Walker. There was much panic amongst the survivors and many servicemen fled into the bush. Most had strayed only a few miles but four days later 278 men were still missing!

Amongst the patients in Darwin Hospital was Capt Aubrey Koch, the wounded Qantas pilot who had been shot down near Koepang almost three weeks earlier (see Volume One, Chapter 6); he later wrote:

> "There was practically no warning. I heard the sirens and the roar of Japanese planes almost simultaneously. I got out of bed and crawled underneath it. I had been there no time when the first bombs fell. Three of them landed very close.
>
> "After the first wave of bombers had passed I decided to make for the beach, about 200 yards away. I could only just walk. A doctor and nurse assisted me to a clump of bushes. Some of the Jap machines were diving low and machine-gunning buildings. I could hear the crunch of bombs in other parts of the town. As I lay in the bushes I saw a Wirraway (*he obviously mis-identified a P-40 as no Wirraways were airborne*) being chased by a Japanese fighter, and I believe our plane was shot down."

A stick of bombs fell on the Qantas hangar at the civil aerodrome, but fortunately none of the company's aircraft were inside. Two members of Qantas staff suffered minor injuries during the raid.

Damage to the Qantas hangar at Darwin. *(Qantas)*

When stock could be taken, the results of the raids were seen to be severe indeed. The carrier bombers had sunk the American destroyer *Peary*, the corvettes, an American troop transport, one tanker and five merchant ships. The seaplane tender *William B. Preston* was afloat but wrecked, while three more merchant vessels had been beached and another two had suffered less severe damaged. Amongst the aircraft, all 11 P-40s were a total loss, as were six Hudsons (A16-6, Al6-57, A16-72, A16-78, A16-135 and A16-141) together with Maj General Hurley's LB-30, three USAAF Beechcraft and three of Patwing 10's PBY flyingboats; one more Hudson and a Wirraway were damaged. 243 persons had been killed and 330 injured − 200 seriously, 19 of whom later succumbed to their injuries − an appalling indication of the lack of warning and of proper air-raid precautions. Amongst those killed were 172 seamen, 35 civilians, seven RAAF and seven USAAF personnel, and the crews of two anti-aircraft guns.

On this occasion claims made by the Japanese were very close to actual results. *Akagi* bombers were credited with two cargo vessels in flames, two damaged and a destroyer damaged; *Kaga*'s crews claimed two 5,000-ton vessels sunk and many ground targets hit, while *Soryu*'s crews claimed one destroyer sunk, one more on fire, one cargo vessel and one tanker on fire, and an oil tank ashore burned; *Hiryu* bombers were credited with three ships of 1,000 tons sunk − one of them a tanker − and one of 7,000 tons and a cruiser, as damaged. In the air, one flyingboat and seven P-40s were claimed shot down, with two more fighters credited as probably destroyed. Claims for aircraft destroyed on the ground totalled 14 destroyed and eight damaged, plus four flyingboats on the water.

For the defenders, apart from the two aircraft credited as shot down by the US fighters (one of which was apparently not confirmed), two more claims were submitted by the anti-aircraft gunners − the D3A as recorded, and a second by a heavy AA gun battery located at Darwin Oval. This was reported to have fallen into the harbour following a direct hit whilst attacking the tanker *British Motorist*. Actual JNAF losses were two D3As and one A6M over Darwin, plus one B5N lost on return; 34 more aircraft had been hit and damaged to some extent, though generally such damage was only slight. For the time being however, Darwin had virtually ceased to operate as a port.

As the raiders turned back towards their carriers, Cdr Fuchida radioed Vice-Admiral Nagumo to tell him of their successes, and of the force-landing on Melville Island of Toyoshima's A6M. A floatplane was promptly despatched to search for the downed pilot and landed on the beach; no sign of the pilot could be found however. Toyoshima was later captured by aborigines and handed over the the authorities at Darwin.[1]

During the return flight to the carriers, D3A crews from *Kaga* reported seeing a vessel reported as a 'camouflaged cruiser'. Consequently, a couple of hours or so after all aircraft had landed back aboard, nine D3As each from *Soryu* and *Hiryu* were launched on an armed search, led by Lts Masai Ikeda and Michiji Yamashita. About 90 minutes later this 'mystery' vessel − which was in fact the 3,200-ton US supply vessel *Don Isidro* − was spotted in the area of Cape Fourcroy (south-west coast of Bathurst Island). *Soryu*'s aircraft attacked, the vessel sustaining five direct hits, while one D3A was hit by return fire. The crippled ship drifted towards Bathurst Island, where 84 survivors eventually got ashore after being in the water for 10 hours. By the time HMAS *Waterhen* arrived to rescue them, 11 had died and two more passed away before the destroyer reached Darwin, having been bombed − and missed − en route by one of the omnipresent, far-ranging H6K flyingboats.

---

[1] For reasons known only to himself, Hajime Toyoshima apparently informed his captors that his name was Tadao Minami. He was subsequently one of the ringleaders of the Cowra POW camp breakout which occurred on 5 August 1944, when 231 Japanese prisoners and four Australian soldiers were killed; amongst the former was Toyoshima.

Meanwhile *Florence D* — heading for Darwin with the rescued PBY crew aboard — had been sighted by the D3As from *Hiryu* and the old freighter suffered two direct hits. Lt Moorer, the PBY pilot, ordered his men to abandon ship when the crew went overboard, but one airman failed to escape before the vessel sank. Two lifeboats picked up the survivors; Moorer assumed command as the ship's master had been severely wounded. It was two days before the survivors were spotted by a searching RAAF aircraft and they were rescued the following morning by a RAN subchaser, HMAS *Warrnambool*.

With the threat at Darwin neutralised, the Japanese now launched their invasion of Timor. The invasion force was once more a substantial one, carried from Ceram in nine transports. Direct escort included a light carrier and ten destroyers, whilst a covering force of two cruisers, four destroyers and an auxiliary were also in support.

At 0500 ships of the naval escort began shelling at Dili and Koepang, the RAAF rear parties at once fleeing across country to the other side of the island. One party of six officers and 23 airmen, under the command of Flt Lt B. Rofe, remained at Penfoei airfield, to destroy what they could and to deny it to the invaders. Before their task was completed, Japanese transports and warships appeared shortly before nightfall, and landing parties came ashore. Next morning the airfield was shelled but by then Rofe had decided — having failed to make contact with Darwin by radio — to split his group into two separate parties, each equipped with a portable transmitter. One party, led by Flg Off F.G. Birchall, was to head for Babaoe, whilst Rofe's party was to make for Tjamplong.

Within minutes of starting out however, Japanese aircraft appeared overhead and commenced dropping paratroopers. Their arrival was part of the Japanese plan to speed up the landings, bombers from the 21st Air Flotilla dropping 308 men of the Yokosuka 3rd Special Naval Landing Force on Koepang airfield during the morning. Due to the lack of any opposition to the seaborne landings however, these troops reached their objective in advance of the paratroops. Next day a further 323 troops would be parachuted in and the island swiftly secured, allowing aircraft of the 21st Air Flotilla to move in to the airfields, where they would be joined by fighters of the 3rd Ku.

Meanwhile, the two parties of RAAF evaders had reformed and, taking stock of the new situation, headed instead for the northern hills, with the intention then of making for the coast, where they hoped rescue would occur by flying-boat. Contact was finally made with Darwin and a flyingboat was promised for the night of 4 March, which would alight near Kapsali. That gave them 12 days to make their way across the island and, following much hardship and adventure, the exhausted party arrived at the rendezvous on time. They waited all night on the beach but the flyingboat did not arrive — unbeknown to them, it had been damaged during a raid on Broome the previous day (see Chapter 8). Further contact with Darwin was made, the dire situation was explained, and a promise was received of an air supply drop until a flyingboat could be made available.

Thus on 7 March a supply aircraft was despatched from Darwin but was unable to find the dropping area; a second aircraft was sent six days later, but all that could be found by Rofe's party were empty parachutes. By this time the majority were sick with fever and tropical ulcers; several were unable to walk and, within the next four weeks, one officer and three men died. At last, on 17

April, the US submarine *Sea Raven* surfaced off Cape Koeroes. Half the RAAF party, which had been joined by four Australian soldiers and two survivors of a shot down Hudson, were taken off that night; the remainder the following night.

The Luck of the *Lexington*

Even as the assault on Darwin was occurring, one of the precious US Fleet carriers, USS *Lexington*, together with her escort of four heavy cruisers and nine destroyers (Task Force II), was heading up from the south to launch its own air group's first strike of the war, against the new Japanese naval base at Rabaul. The carrier was still 200 miles short of its objective at dawn on 20 February, as SBD Dauntless scout-bombers of Scouting Squadron VS-2 were launched to search ahead for signs of hostile shipping.

At 1030 however, the American warships were located by an H6K flyingboat of the Yokohama Ku, flown by Lt Noboru Sakai, which was itself 'spotted' on the radar screens of the carrier. Four Grumman F4F Wildcats of Fighting Squadron VF-3 were scrambled immediately, climbing through scattered rain clouds in search of the intruder. The big four-engined aircraft was seen through a gap in the cloud by Lt Cdr John S. Thach (in F-1). At once he and his wingman, Ens Edward R. Sellstrom (in F-2), dived after it. As they closed on the flyingboat, return fire began to be directed at them. Thach opened fire, hitting the fuel tanks, which spewed out a spray of petrol; ignited by his tracers, great sheets of flame spread behind the doomed aircraft and it went spinning into the sea.

No sooner had Thach and Sellstrom returned to the carrier when a second 'hostile' appeared on the radar screen — which was in fact another H6K, flown by Wt Off Kiyoshi Hayashi, having departed Rabaul at 0800 with orders to follow-up on the sighting made by Sakai. To meet this latest threat, another section of Wildcats — flown by Lt Onia B. Stanley Jr (in F-7) and Ens Leon W. Haynes — were vectored onto the flyingboat which they shot down; the crew perished when their aircraft plunged into the sea in flames and blew up.

Since the Japanese forces on New Britain had been warned of the carrier's approach, by the report sent by one of the H6K crews before they were shot down, Capt Frederick C. Sherman, commander of *Lexington*, made preparations for the attack on his ship, which he knew must follow. Relays of scouting aircraft flew well ahead of the carrier and her escort, to provide an early report of any approaching hostile force, while fighters flew combat air patrols in the immediate vicinity of the task force.

A detachment of the newer G4Ms, which had just begun to supplement the G3Ms in the 22nd Air Flotilla's Genzan Kokutai, had recently arrived at Rabaul (between 14-17 February), where they formed part of the new 4th Ku, a composite unit including the A6Ms which had been in action against the RAAF aircraft from Port Moresby earlier in the month (see Chapter 5). When news of the American carrier's approach was received at Rabaul, an immediate strike was prepared and launched. Before the bombers departed, a further H6K headed out in the hands of Ens Motohiro Makino, to regain contact with the US vessels. 18 bombers were readied initially, each armed with a pair of 250kg bombs, since no torpedoes were yet available at Vunakanau airfield. One aircraft proved to be unserviceable however, but the remainder took off in two formations at 1420, under the overall command of Lt Cdr Takuzo Ito, who flew as an observer in the lead aircraft of the 1st Chutai, accompanied by Lt Yogono Seto; their pilot was Wt Off Chuzo Watanabe.

Ito's 1st Chutai comprised eight aircraft, in two threes and a pair; the 2nd Chutai, led by Lt Masayoshi Nakagawa, comprised nine bombers in three vics, each of three aircraft. Because of heavy cloud, Ito ordered that the two sections should separate in order to allow a greater area of search to be covered. The bombers passed Cape St George, the southern tip of New Ireland, soon after take-off, but it was afternoon before they reached the area in which the American warships were located.

Shortly after noon, Vice-Admiral Wilson Brown, the task force commander, had decided to call off the strike since the element of surprise had gone, but at the prompting of Capt Sherman he agreed to hold course for the time being, as a feint to draw off Japanese forces from the East Indies.

As afternoon drew on, six Wildcats of VF-3's second division, led by Lt Cdr Donald A. Lovelace, patrolled overhead, while on deck Lt Noel A. Gayler's third division prepared to take-off to relieve them. A further four Wildcats were refuelled, but at a lower state of readiness. Just after 1600 the fighter controller sought permission to launch Gayler's section early, and this was given. Just as it was being readied on deck, the first signs of the incoming enemy formation were seen on the radar, 75 miles out. By 1625 they were only 47 miles away and it was clear that a serious attack was coming in. Meanwhile, Gayler's section had been scrambled and was vectored towards them, climbing hard without waiting to form up.

At the same time Lovelace — who had led his flight of six aircraft in for an early landing, on seeing the third division go off — was warned not to come aboard, as efforts were underway to get the other four Wildcats and 11 SBDs of VS-2, all of which were fully fuelled, off the deck, before an attack developed. At about 1635 Gayler's pilots sighted the first part of the incoming force — the nine G4Ms of Lt Nakagawa's 2nd Chutai, which had made the initial sighting of the task force. The formation flown by the chutai may be seen in Table 10.

Lt Gayler (in F-1) and Ens Dale W. Peterson (in F-5) made the first attack, diving from 13,000 feet and sending down one bomber in flames, before climbing for a second attack. Immediately behind them came Lts Rolla S. Lemmon and Howard F. Clark, who made a similar attack, sending down a second bomber. The leader of the third pair, Ens Willard E. Eder, had found that his wingman, Ens John Wilson, was suffering a rough-running engine and was dropping back. After waiting unavailingly for him to catch up, Eder attacked alone from behind and below, firing at one of the rear G4Ms. As he did so, three of his four guns stopped and, at that moment, Gayler apparently attacked the same aircraft from above, on his second pass, and it too went down. This initial attack lasted just two minutes; shipboard observers had seen nine bombers ten miles out, reporting that three were seen to fall, whilst crew aboard the destroyer *Phelps* reported only six bombers breaking cloud and heading for the ships.

Two minutes later, at 1643, the four remaining Wildcats aboard *Lexington* began taking-off, piloted by Lt Cdr Thach, Ens Sellstrom, Lt Edward H. O'Hare and Lt Marion W. Dufilho, the first SBDs then beginning to follow them. At that moment Ens Peterson, Gayler's wingman, launched his second pass on the bombers and sent another out of formation. This seems to have been Nakagawa's lead aircraft and, as the remainder of the formation entered the

TABLE 10

4th Kokutai Bomber Formation

1st Chutai

1st shotai

Lt Cdr Takuzo Ito*

NAP 1/C Susumu Uchiyama*   NAP 1/C Kosuka Ono

2nd shotai

Lt Akira Mitani

NAP 1/C Koji Maeda   NAP 2/C Ryosuke Kogiku

3rd shotai

NAP 1/C Bin Mori   NAP 2/C Tokiharu Baba

2nd Chutai

1st shotai

Lt Masayoshi Nakagawa

NAP 2/C Akira Morita*   NAP 2/C Takaji Fujimoto

2nd shotai

Wt Off Masao Kawasaki*

NAP 1/C Noburo Fusetari*   NAP 1/C Takegoro Ogawa*

3rd shotai

Ens Shin Ono

NAP 2/C Goichi Ishizaki*   NAP 1/C Hiromichi Tatewaki*

* denotes aircraft captains who were not pilots, since airmen of more senior rank were included in the crews as observers, and enjoyed overall command.

task force's AA barrage, the loss of the leader appeared to confuse them. They were seen to hesitate before re-grouping, then the formation swung to the starboard flank, flying parallel to the carrier, before beginning their bombing approach from astern. Lt Lemmon attacked and shot down another.

By now second division Wildcats, although low on fuel, had been able to join the attack, at which point however, a stricken bomber − believed to be that flown by Nakagawa − attempted to dive into the carrier. Under fire from the AA, this aircraft crashed into the sea. Meanwhile another bomber, forced out of the formation by second division pilots, crashed into the sea in flames, just before the remaining three released their bombs and headed away. The three survivors were pursued, but now achieved their first success, when their return fire struck Lt Howard L. Johnson's aircraft (F-11), forcing him to bale out, wounded in the legs by 20mm shell fragments; he was picked up by the destroyer *Patterson*.

At this stage Thach and Sellstrom were able to join the pursuit, but the controller ordered O'Hare and Dufilho to remain over the carrier. Thach (now flying F-13) attacked one bomber then, looking over his shoulder, spotted a second approaching directly from astern. As he tried to warn Ens Wilson, who was nearby, a 20mm shell hit the latter's cockpit, apparently killing the pilot where-upon the Wildcat (F-9) dived straight into the sea. Thach at once turned his attention to the bomber which had shot down Wilson, his fire riddling its fuselage. Making a second attack, he concentrated on one engine, whereupon it blew up and the wing fell off. During this attack, a second division pilot also attacked one of the two bombers fired on by Thach and claimed a share in its destruction.

By then however, the five remaining second division Wildcats were desper-ately low on fuel and circled the carrier waiting to land, as the deck party got away the remainder of the SBDs and parked TBD Devastator torpedo-bombers further up the deck, to make room. Following their rapid take-off, one of the SBDs, flown by Lt Edward H. Allen, caught up with an obviously stricken Japanese bomber, the pilot of which had succeeded in regaining control before it hit the sea. Allen fired at this and it went into the water at once. A second damaged bomber was then seen and Allen flew up alongside, allowing his gunner, ARM 1/C Bruce Rountree, to rake the fuselage with his rear guns, and the G4M burst into flames: the pair were awarded a share in its destruction.

Only one aircraft of the ill-fated 2nd Chutai remained in the air, two of the third division pilots continuing to pursue this. Thach raced after them, to bring them back before they got out of range of the carrier, so they had to let the badly shot-up bomber go. It was not to escape however, for 80 miles west of the fleet it was encountered by Lt Walter F. Henry of VS-2, returning in his SBD from a search and, turning onto its tail, from which no return fire was experienced, he shot it down. He then spotted another G4M floating in the water and strafed this until it blew up and sank. All nine bombers of the 2nd Chutai had thus fallen victim to the defences.

At the very moment when all but two of the defending fighters were either chasing the 2nd Chutai's survivors, or circling the carrier, low on fuel, Ito's 1st Chutai sighted the task force. They had appeared on the radar at 1649 − and again seven minutes later − the Japanese crews making their own first sighting on the hour and coming into visual range of the fleet two minutes later.

O'Hare and Dufilho were ordered to intercept, making contact at 1705, and incorrectly identifying the formation as nine, rather than eight, in strength. The bombers began diving from 15,000 to 11,000 feet to attack and were moving fast, but the Wildcats had the benefit of greater altitude. O'Hare (in F-15) carried out a pass from the starboard flank, picking on NAP 2/C Baba's aircraft. One of the best marksmen in the squadron, O'Hare's fire struck the starboard engine and wing root, the G4M slowing and falling away to crash. He then turned to attention to NAP 1/C Mori's aircraft, again hitting the starboard engine and also the port wing tank. However, the damage was not fatal and Mori was able to dive away to lower altitude, while O'Hare climbed up ready for a second pass, believing that he had shot down both aircraft.

When Dufilho attacked, it was to find that his guns would not fire − they had jammed due to shifting ammunition belts and he was able to take no further part in the action. O'Hare meanwhile, began an attack from the port flank, setting NAP 1/C Maeda's aircraft on fire and, as this too fell back, he went after NAP 1/C Uchiyama's aircraft on the port side of the lead vic, which dived away to crash with its port wing in flames. All return fire from the remaining bombers was now directed at O'Hare's Wildcat but, with the benefit of the speed gained in the attack dive, it was not hit. Apparently the fire extinguishers in Maeda's damaged aircraft had been effective and, with the flames dowsed, he pulled his aircraft back into formation in time for the bombing run.

Lt Edward H. 'Butch' O'Hare of the *Lexington*'s Fighting Squadron VF-3, who was credited with shooting down five attacking G4M bombers of the Genzan Ku on 20 February. He was awarded the Medal of Honor for this feat. *(Authors' collection)*

Beginning his third run, again from the port flank, O'Hare could see five bombers still in formation (those captained by Ito, Ono, Mitani, Kogiku and Maeda) and took this to mean he had shot down four. He now attacked the lead aircraft, just as bombs were released, and hit its port engine. As the other four G4Ms released their bombs, Ito's pilot, Watanabe, attempted to crash into the *Lexington*, just as Nakagawa had done. He too was unsuccessful, the bomber going into the water alongside the carrier at 1712. Meanwhile, Sherman's skilful manoeuvring of his unwieldy ship avoided the bombing and none of the missiles exploded closer than 3,000 yards.

O'Hare continued to pursue the four remaining bombers, but his ammunition was virtually exhausted so he turned back to land, reporting that he had shot down five of the raiders. In fact, he had brought down three and badly damaged two more — his determination and marksmanship had probably saved the carrier from severe damage. Throughout the engagement his Wildcat had been hit by only one 7.7mm machine gun bullet from the bombers, and by a few pieces of 'friendly' AA shrapnel.

Despite the bombing attacks, the five second division Wildcats had all got aboard safely, while the remainder of the aircraft in the air gave chase to the fleeing G4Ms. Eight miles out, Ens Sellstrom intercepted the four bombers still in formation and shot down Mitani's aircraft; survivors later reported that they believed this pilot had also crashed onto a US ship. 40 miles out, Gayler met another bomber and claimed it shot down, while Allen and Rountree of VS-2 saw three in formation, 30 miles out, and began a long stern chase in their SBD, shooting-up one without apparent results; this was possibly Ono's aircraft, which returned badly damaged and with three of the crew dead, force-landing on the tiny island of Nugara, near New Ireland. Only Maeda and Kogiku landed back at Vunakanau, their aircraft riddled with bullets and shell splinters. Mori, remaining at low altitude, struggled to keep his aircraft flying and eventually ditched in Simpson Harbour (Rabaul) at 2010.

The 4th Ku had thus lost 15 of the 17 bombers deployed, 13 of them over the target area, while the two survivors were badly damaged; 88 aircrew had lost their lives. To the Japanese the sacrifice did not appear to be in vain however, for the survivors reported that the attack had sunk a cruiser and a destroyer, while Lt Cdr Ito's 'taiotari' dive on the carrier was believed to have left it badly damaged and on fire. Eight intercepting fighters were also claimed to have been shot down.

In addition to the two H6Ks lost in the morning, that flown by Ens Makino, which had set out at 1400, also failed to return, its loss not having been accounted for. Sometime later an E13A floatplane from *Kiyokawa Maru* was launched from Rabaul, the crew spotting the ships at 1815 and continuing to shadow. This however, also failed to return, the 19th loss of the operation for the air forces on Rabaul; again its loss has not been accounted for.

VF-3 had claimed 15 bombers and two flyingboats destroyed during the day, Lt Henry of VS-2 being credited with a 16th bomber — claims remarkably close to the actual losses on this occasion. Lt 'Butch' O'Hare, who it was reckoned had expended only about 60 rounds of .50-inch ammunition on each of the bombers he had attacked, was initially credited with six victories, subsequently reduced to five. He was to be awarded the Medal of Honor — the first to go to a fighter pilot in World War II — and was promoted to Lt Cdr. The award of a Navy Cross was made to Lt Cdr Thach and six other pilots, whilst eight more received DFCs.

Final credits for the day were assessed by VF-3 as follows:

Lt Edward H. O'Hare	five bombers
Lt Cdr John S. Thach	one flyingboat shared; one bomber; one bomber shared
Lt Noel A.M. Gayler	one bomber; two bombers shared
Lt Rolla S. Lemmon	one bomber; one bomber shared
Ens Dale W. Peterson	one bomber; one bomber shared
Ens Edward R. Sellstrom	one flyingboat shared; one bomber
Ens Richard M. Rowell	two bombers shared
Lt Cdr Donald A. Lovelace	one bomber shared
Lt Albert O. Vorse Jr	one bomber shared
Lt Howard F. Clark	one bomber shared
Lt Robert J. Morgan	one bomber shared
Lt Onia B. Stanley Jr	one flyingboat shared
Ens Willard E. Eder	one bomber shared
Ens John H. Laclay	one bomber shared
Ens Leon W. Haynes	one flyingboat shared

No loss or damage had actually been suffered by the ships of Task Force II. The total cost had been two Wildcats and one pilot, with seven more suffering slight damage. Despite this outstanding defensive success however, the discovery of the carrier made it too dangerous to remain in the area, with the Japanese 1st Carrier Division not far away. Vice-Admiral Brown was therefore obliged to order a withdrawal and *Lexington* turned away, the strike against Rabaul cancelled.

Following these actions, to bring the striking forces at Rabaul back up to strength, the Japanese detailed the G3M-equipped 1st Kokutai from the 21st Air Flotilla and despatched it to join the 4th Ku there. These bombers could be spared since the aircraft of the Kanoya Ku − now based on Timor − provided sufficient striking power at this base, for the imminent operations over Java.

Chapter 6

JAVA ON THE ANVIL
16-28 February

The necessity for the Japanese forces to establish themselves on the new airfields in Sumatra ensured that the Allies were able to enjoy a few days of relative quiet in Western Java, where strenuous efforts were expended to form the scattered remnants of the RAF's squadrons into some semblance of an air force. Even as the survivors of the Palembang debacle started arriving on the island, the residue of 488 Squadron had managed to get three Hurricanes fully operational and at readiness at Tjililitan; by the 16th the number had risen to five. 15 more Hurricanes had flown in from P.2 during the 15th, but most were unserviceable on arrival. The decision was now taken to reduce drastically the number of units which were to remain operational, and the first move was the disbandment of 226 Group.

With Air Vice-Marshal Pulford and a number of his senior officers missing, overall command of the RAF on Java passed to Air Vice-Marshal Maltby. All squadrons now came under the direction of WESTGROUP, which Maltby continued to command with headquarters at Soekaboemi, whilst Air Commodore Vincent took over the Fighter Control HQ. For the time being ABDAIR remained responsible for the control of the actual operations flown. Maltby was to have the benefit of just two radar units, both salvaged from Singapore and Malaya; these were sited at Batavia and Wg Cdr Gerald Bell, former OC Kallang, arrived to take command:

> "We managed to deploy such radar equipment as we had been able to bring away from Malaya and linked that into a makeshift Operations Room from which we controlled, as best we could, such fighter aircraft as had managed to reach the two airfields in the Batavia area."

For fighter defence, two squadrons were to be reformed, while 232, 258 and 488 Squadrons were effectively disbanded. Initially the ground party of 242 Squadron, which was still in Java with no air component, was to have the aircrews of 232 Squadron transferred to it en masse. Although a dozen of the 39 Hurricanes delivered on 4 February had been handed to the Dutch and 17 more had been sent up to Sumatra, a total of 25 of these fighters were still available (including the survivors of earlier deliveries), and of these 18 were operational. These were now concentrated at Tjililitan in the new 242 Squadron under Sqn Ldr Brooker, with the flights commanded by Flt Lt Ivan Julian and Act/Flt Lt Jimmy Parker.

The second unit to reform was 605 Squadron — again the ground party being available and fresh, although having no aircrew. Newly-promoted Sqn Ldr Ricky Wright was posted from 232 Squadron as commanding officer, bringing with him Act/Flt Lt Joe Hutton as his deputy, the other pilots being drawn equally from 258 and 488 Squadrons plus a smattering of new arrivals (see Table 11). Sqn Ldr Thomson called a meeting of 258 Squadron pilots to decide who would remain, Flg Off Dobbyn having been nominated to command the flight. Volunteers were called for but only Plt Off Campbell and newly-arrived Sgt Vibert stepped forward. Cards were drawn to decide who would remain with them, Sgts Kelly, Lambert and Healy drawing the low cards which determined their fate.

Table 11

Pilots — Reformed 605 Squadron
Sqn Ldr E.W. Wright, DFM
Flt Lt J.C. Hutton (Deputy CO)

'A' Flight	**'B' Flight**
Flt Lt F.W.J. Oakden, RNZAF	Flg Off H.A. Dobbyn, RNZAF
Flg Off N.C. Sharp, RNZAF	Plt Off J.A. Campbell
Plt Off H.S. Pettit, RNZAF	Plt Off G.D. Binsted*
Plt Off G.P. White, RNZAF	Plt Off R.L. Cicurel*
Plt Off W.J. Greenhalgh, RNZAF	Sgt C.T.R. Kelly
Sgt E.E.G. Kuhn, RNZAF	Sgt P.M.T. Healy
Sgt W.J.N. MacIntosh, RNZAF	Sgt A. Lambert
Sgt H.J. Meharry, RNZAF	Sgt J.G. Vibert, RNZAF
Sgt K. Collins, RAAF*	Sgt C.E. Sharp, RNZAF
Sgt A.D. Jack*	Sgt F.N. Hood, RNZAF*

*Those indicated thus were new arrivals and, apart from Sgt Vibert, it is unlikely that they actually flew on operations, due mainly to the lack of Hurricanes; it was intended to re-equip the squadron with P-40s.

Although the two squadrons had sufficient Hurricanes for only one unit, it was hoped to re-equip 605 Squadron with American P-40Es when supplies arrived from Australia — as had originally been planned for the now-defunct and disbanded 243 Squadron.

With the disbandment of 232, 258 and 488 Squadrons, the personnel no longer required left for shipment out of the fighting zone. Those 488 Squadron pilots not attached to 605 Squadron, together with the remains of 243 and 453 Squadrons, with the crews of 8 RAAF Squadron, departed Tjilatjap (the largest port on the south coast) aboard *Deucalion* and *Orcades* for Fremantle (Australia) on the 22nd, leaving in a violent tropical storm. Those 258 Squadron pilots not posted to 605 Squadron, the wounded pilots of 232 Squadron and the ground crews of 232 and 488 Squadrons departed Tjilatjap on the night of 26/27 February on *Kota Gede*. Also aboard this vessel were surplus aircrew and ground personnel from all bomber squadrons, together with those from miscellaneous units.

The bombers were also re-organised. The remaining nine serviceable

A group of 258 Squadron pilots. Left to right: Sgt Bertie Lambert, Flg Off Harry Dobbyn, Sgt Terence Kelly, unknown, Sgt Art Sheerin, Plt Off Art Brown, Sgt Pip Healy. *(Sqn Ldr A.H. Milnes)*

Vildebeests and one Albacore of 36/100 Squadron were fully operational at Tjilkampek, but could carry only bombs as no torpedo facilities were available in Java. The composite unit was now re-numbered 36 Squadron under the command of Sqn Ldr John Wilkins.

The surviving Blenheims and crews were assembled at Kalidjati, under the overall control of Grp Capt Whistondale; few of the 29 aircraft were in operational condition. There were 22 Mark IVs — ten on the strength of 84 Squadron, eight of 211 Squadron and four of 34 Squadron (all of which were unserviceable) — plus seven short-nose Mark Is, including two fighter versions, assembled under 27 Squadron's banner. As this latter unit and 34 Squadron now effectively ceased to exist, a number of their aircrews were ordered to evacuate. In all, 20 complete crews from all four squadrons were retained to operate the Blenheims, under Wg Cdr Jeudwine of 84 Squadron and Wg Cdr Bateson of 211 Squadron. The crews were billeted at Soebang village (a dozen miles from the airfield) and messed with the Dutch, as recalled by 84 Squadron's Sgt Eric Oliver:

> "Catering facilities were a little primitive. I recall lining up with a pile of plates; there was a big tub of bubble and squeak (mashed potatoes and green-leaf vegetables); we were supposed to dip our plate into the mashed mess and pull out a dollop!"

Bomb-loading and refuelling facilities were lacking here, as they had been at P.2: 211 Squadron's Sgt Jock Richardson:

> "In Sumatra and Java we bombed-up manually and belted ammunition for the guns. Oh, memories of 'Ginger' Coughlan (*his pilot*) straining with a 250

pounder on his back and 'Kiwi' Cummins (*his navigator*) hooking it on the rack, whilst I steadied the bomb!"

The Hudsons were concentrated at Semplak (where Grp Capt H.M.K. Brown — former CO at Seletar — was RAF commander) and were in a similar unhappy situation, with 1 RAAF Squadron totalling 14 Mark IIs, of which only three were serviceable, while 8 RAAF Squadron and 62 Squadron shared a dozen Mark IIIs, of which barely half were serviceable. It came as a shock to the aircrews when they discovered that the airfield was practically defenceless, as recalled by Flt Lt Terence O'Brien:

"I suddenly realised what was odd about all the gun-sites in the field; there was no activity around them, no men, no trucks, and no movement of the guns themselves."

Making his way over to the nearest 'gun', his suspicion was confirmed:

"Sure enough it was a wooden gun, an elaborate structure with a trailer and lorry wheels but with less offensive power than a toy water pistol. Presently I learned that all the guns about the field were wooden dummies. As were the four tanks. The airfield was utterly defenceless. Suddenly all those aircraft lined up along the edge of the strip, for here there was no jungle for sheltered alcoves, looked terribly vulnerable."

The four remaining Catalinas — aircraft FV-N,-U,-V, and -W — of 205 Squadron were at Tanjong Priok (Batavia), from where a handful of Dutch Catalinas of GVT-2, GVT-3, GVT-16 and GVT-18 were operating. However, orders were issued for 205 Squadron to transfer to Tjilatjap, on the south coast. All told, seven light aircraft of the MVAF had by now reached Batavia — three Tiger Moths, two Cadets, the Falcon and the Witney-Straight — and were reformed into a single Flight under Flt Lt Dane, although Sqn Ldr H.W. Chattaway had assumed overall command of the MVAF following the unauthorized departure of Grp Capt Nunn (see Chapter 1). Initially it was hoped that the unit would re-equip with the Wirraways of W Flight, but these were not forthcoming. It was then rumoured that the MVAF Flight would receive a dozen new Tiger Moths courtesy of the now defunct Dutch Volunteer Flying Club, but it transpired that these were being disassembled and packed ready for shipment (aboard the Dutch freighter *Tjinegara*) to Australia, as were the 34 surviving Dutch Naval Air Service Ryan STM trainers.

In view of the shortage of suitable aircraft, Air Vice-Marshal Maltby decided to release the majority of MVAF air and ground personnel, retaining sufficient only to man the one Flight, together with 15 ground staff. Sqn Ldr Chattaway elected to remain in command and Flt Lt Henry Dane volunteered to stay with his Flight, whilst Flg Off M.G. Harvey was put in charge of ground personnel.

While the RAF was re-organising in this way, the defence of Western Java continued to be in the hands of the Dutch, nearly all the remaining strength of their air force being established there, including all the three Brewster afdelings, all but one of the Glenn Martin units, one of the two CW-22 Falcon afdelings (VkA-1), and 2-VlG-IV. This latter unit, with its new Hurricanes (and six CW-21Bs) painted with the orange triangle markings, moved from Andir to Kalidjati on the 16th, for the defence of Bandoeng but, two days later lost one of its aircraft which crashed while on a training sortie.

Top: Tiger Moths of the Dutch Volunteer Flying Club, which were despatched to Australia for safety. *(Authors' collection)*. Above: Ryan STM trainers of the Dutch Navy: surviving aircraft were despatched to Australia. *(Authors' collection)*

Following the move of the Dutch units to the west, Eastern Java was left almost entirely in the hands of the USAAF, apart from the Dutch Navy's flying-boats and a single afdeling of CW-22s at Djokjakarta (VkA-2). On the 17th, the 91st Bomb Squadron (Light) moved its seven serviceable A-24s from Modjokerto to Malang, the main base of the heavy bomber units. Air defence there now rested entirely on the still-strong 17th Pursuit Squadron (Provisional) and, during the 16th, Maj W.P. Fisher, former commander of the 19th Bomb Group, was posted to Dutch Fighter Control in Sourabaya to co-ordinate this unit's activities. Further reinforcements were on the way, as the next day the carrier *Langley* sailed from Darwin to Fremantle in order to pick up the 37 P-40Es comprising the air strength of the 13th Pursuit Squadron, plus the residue of the 33rd Pursuit Squadron. Although the ship was under orders to head for Colombo, Ceylon, it was to pass close to Java so that the aircraft might be diverted there if necessary.

A Douglas A-24 Dauntless dive-bomber of the ill-fated 91st Bomb Squadron (Light). *(Richard Slater)*

Monday, 16 February

As the last RAF aircraft withdrew from Sumatra, other Allied bombers from Java continued to attack the Japanese invasion force. First off at 0830, were six B-17Es from Malang, but these encountered severe weather and returned to base. An hour and a half later a further attempt was made by seven B-17Es, led by Capt R.E. Northcut, one of which returned with engine trouble. In an attempt to beat the weather, the others flew the whole way at under 4,000 feet, taking five hours to reach the Banka Strait. Bombing from 2,000 feet, the crews could clearly see men in the barges and on the decks of two large transports. They were flying so low that several of the bombers were damaged by fragments of their own bombs, as well as by machine gun fire, but no one was wounded aboard the six aircraft, which all returned safely, the crews claiming to have sunk both transports and two barges.

Five Glenn Martins of 3-VlG-III were prepared for an attack against shipping on the Moesi River, in addition to bombing P.1 airfield, but one aircraft failed to take-off. The remaining four became separated en route and attacked individually. One crew member reported:

> "My aircraft arrived over Palembang all by itself and was immediately attacked by a floatplane, while all the ships in the Moesi opened up on us. We released four bombs but the fifth hung-up. I went into the bomb-bay and started to dance on the bomb, bracing myself against the sides of the plane, and kicked it loose. I could follow the bomb all the way down. It made a direct hit on a ship — pure coincidence in my opinion."

The other Dutch bombers similarly encountered defending fighters and claimed three of the attackers shot down, but Sgt J. Bakker's aircraft (M-578) failed to return; a second crashed in southern Sumatra during an emergency landing, when two of the crew were killed. The attackers included F1M floatplanes of the *Kamikawa Maru* detachment, two of which reported intercepting three or four twin-engined bombers over the shipping during the afternoon. Lt Minematsu made six attacks, claiming one bomber probably shot down, but his own aircraft was hit many times and he was forced to alight on the sea, some 40 miles west of Muntok; the destroyer *Hatsuyuki* rescued the crew, the wrecked aircraft being set alight and sinking later. The other floatplane also made several attacks, but with no observed success. Lt Toshiru Kubotani of the 1st Sentai, who had led his flight of Ki 27s to shoot down the 205 Squadron Catalina on the day before war broke out, was killed during the day; it is not known whether he was engaged in intercepting the Glenn Martins or if he was lost in a flying accident.

Another attack on the Japanese invaders, but of a different nature, was now in the offing. On the previous day (15th), Maj Sprague, commander of the 17th Pursuit Squadron, had been ordered to Allied HQ in Bandoeng for a briefing on a planned fighter-bomber raid on shipping and landing craft in the Moesi delta area. At the same time, the rest of the squadron flew off eight P-40Es to Maospati airfield, west of Madioen, where they were fitted to carry four 20kg bombs apiece; from there the pilots took their aircraft on to Batavia that evening, where they discovered a lack of accommodation. Fortunately, friendly war correspondents were able to find beds for them at the 'full-up' Hotel des Indes. An Operations Room was established at Lembang, but one P-40E crashed while landing and was damaged. Next day (16th) a heavy mist was reported over the Palembang area, so the fighters remained on the ground although the bombers went out.

Tuesday, 17 February

An RAAF Hudson carried out an early morning reconnaissance of Medan and P.2, this aircraft being followed to Sumatra by six Glenn Martins, the crews of which claimed a hit on a Japanese troop ship on the Moesi River, whilst the air gunners reported shooting down two Japanese fighters which attacked their aircraft; one Glenn Martin failed to return, having been shot down about 80 miles north-west of Oosthaven.

By now the second Japanese convoy of troop transports had finally steamed up the Moesi, anchoring at Palembang, where disembarkation had taken place. The attacks on the landing parties from the first convoy had proved most effective, and had shaken the Japanese somewhat, whilst the resistance to the paratroopers, and the losses inflicted on them, had slowed down their programme substantially. However, the precipitate withdrawal from Oosthaven and elsewhere, had resulted in much useful material being left behind and when the last Allied ships left Oosthaven on the 17th, it was already becoming embarrassingly apparent that the Japanese were not actually on the heels of the fleeing evacuees.

At 0730, Maj Sprague led off eight bomb-carrying P-40Es to attack shipping in the area of the Moesi delta. Over the target they encountered an equal number of patrolling Ki 27s from the 11th Sentai detachment, six of these attacking the American fighters. At once Sprague released his bombs, followed by Capt Coss, and Lts Gerry McCallum and Joe Kruzel, as the fighters closed. Sprague reported shooting down one Ki 27 almost immediately, which fell away smoking towards the jungle; two others were claimed by McCallum and Kruzel.

Meanwhile, Lt Egenes cooly made a bombing run, followed by Capt Mahony and his flight. Having released their bombs in a dive, on ships and among barges alongside the river bank, they climbed to join the others. Egenes reported shooting down a 'Zero' (sic). Lt Kiser attacked three 'Type 97s' while still carrying his bombs, claiming that he had "shot one to pieces" before completing a bombing and strafing run. Meanwhile, Mahony claimed two others as probably destroyed and the jubilant Americans returned to base without loss. They appear to have all fired at the same aircraft however, for the 11th Sentai lost only one Ki 27, from which the pilot baled out safely; the Japanese pilots claimed three of the P-40Es shot down. Next morning the P-40Es were flown back across Java to their base at Ngoro.

1/Lt George E. Kiser, one of the 17th Pursuit Squadron (Provisional)'s leading pilots, subsequently gained further success over Australia and New Guinea. *(Bill Wolf)*

An LB-30 arrived at Malang during the late afternoon, bringing Air Marshal Peirse, Maj General Brereton, Lt Colonel Eugene Eubank and Brig General Patrick J. Hurley on an inspection visit, during which medals were to be presented. The LB-30 carrying the party, flown by Lt C.B. Kelsay, had appeared out of a heavy cloud over the airfield, straightened out, then hit the ground and was completely hidden with the splash of mud and water. However, no one aboard was hurt. Brereton awarded 74 medals to the assembled Bomber Command personnel at Singosari. Of the situation at Malang, he later wrote:

> "Combat replacement crews did not exist. Reinforcing aircraft contained only skeleton navigating crews. Fatigue and combat weariness had worn men to their last ounce of resistance. Pilots returned from attacks crying with rage and frustration when a crew member was killed or when weather or

mechanical failure prevented successful completion of the mission. A flight commander, a fine leader, committed suicide. Boys were on the verge of mental and physical collapse."

Brereton, in company with Peirse, departed Malang early next morning for the two hour drive to Blimbing, where the collection of P-40Es were based which now represented the 17th Pursuit Squadron.

The JNAF continued its relentless harassment of Java-bound shipping, G3Ms of the Genzan Ku sinking the Dutch merchantman *Sloet van Beele* in the Gaspar Strait (between Banka and Billiton islands) at 1615, survivors taking to lifeboats. Some 40 minutes later, B5Ns from *Ryujo* bombed the stranded Dutch destroyer *Van Ghent* (see Chapter 2), and promptly despatched her. By chance, Catalina Y-45 of GVT-18 happened upon the survivors of the freighter, the pilot gallantly putting his flyingboat down nearby. By the time all had been gathered aboard and crammed into every available nook and cranny, a total of 79 grateful seamen and five crew prayed that the aircraft would be able to get airborne. It eventually did and returned safely to Tanjong Priok.

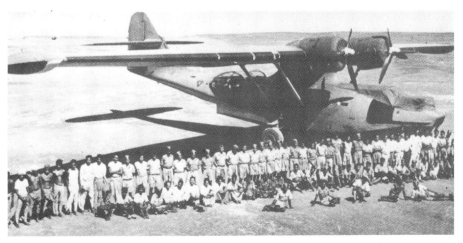

On 17 February, the crew of Catalina Y-45 of GVT-18 — rescued 79 survivors of a sunken Dutch vessel. Assembled here are an appropriate number of men to recreate an impression of the aircraft's achievement. *(Authors' collection)*

Wednesday, 18 February – Western Java

Early in the morning three Hudsons were despatched to raid Pladjoe oil refinery, but the operation was not a success due to bad weather; Flt Lt Herb Plenty of 8 RAAF Squadron (in AE553) at least reached the target area undetected, using the heavy cloud to his advantage and thus avoided any fighters which might have attempted an interception. Another crew was briefed to carry out a reconnaissance of the Palembang-Oosthaven road en route, while Flg Off Siddell of the 59 Squadron detachment (in AE506) had been detailed to carry out a reconnaissance of P.1 and P.2, plus the oil refinery. On approaching P.2, Siddell took his aircraft down to treetop height but, as the airfield appeared void of aircraft, bombs were not dropped. Fighters could be seen over P.1 and, avoiding these, Siddell headed for the northern coastline of Sumatra as he sped for home. A lookout for shipping was maintained, but no targets were sighted.

Due to the adverse weather conditions prevailing over Sumatra, a B-17 operation against the same targets was cancelled. A further Hudson, V9121 flown by Flg Off Terence O'Brien of 62 Squadron, was ordered to carry out a reconnaissance over the Java Sea, but again bad weather interfered and nothing of importance was sighted. The reconnaissance of the Oosthaven-Palembang road by the Hudson crew, showed no immediate occupation of Oosthaven port to be likely and, consequently, it was decided to attempt a salvage operation. Grp Capt G.E. Nicholetts led 50 RAF volunteers drawn from 605 Squadron aboard the Australian corvette *Ballarat*, which departed at once for Oosthaven. On arrival, they found the port deserted, and were able to spend 12 hours loading valuable RAF equipment and Bofors ammunition, whilst doing as much damage as possible to what remained. Not until they were well away did the first Japanese troops enter the town.

In other ways the Japanese were quicker off the mark however, beginning to fly in more of their air units to the newly-acquired airfield at P.1. During the morning 16 more Ki 27s from the 11th Sentai, 20 Ki 43s from the 64th Sentai, and a part of the 27th Sentai, flew into the airfield, the rest of the 3rd Flying Battalion arriving that afternoon. Soon, all available Ki 43s of both the 59th and 64th Sentais were established at P.1, from where they could operate over Western Java with ease. Within two days, Japanese forces secured Tandjung-karang, then the 12th Flying Battalion Ki 27s were moved to this location. Meanwhile, three C5Ms and 15 A6Ms of the 22nd Air Flotilla Fighter Group moved to Muntok from Borneo. Thus, the arrival of the Army Air Force in Sumatra allowed the land-based elements of the Navy's 21st and 23rd Air Flotillas to concentrate their attacks on Eastern Java, together with the other islands in the chain towards Australia.

It was, by this time, abundantly clear to the Allies that the panicky withdrawal from Palembang had been unnecessarily hasty. Although withdrawal in the face of the stronger forces available to the Japanese would undoubtedly have become inevitable, P.2 airfield had not even been discovered at that stage. A resolute fighting defence of the town and harbour, followed by a slow withdrawal towards Oosthaven, would have allowed the still-substantial numbers of aircraft at the jungle airfield to have created more havoc with the landings; possibly even, to have rendered the arrival of the second convoy as costly as the first. Instead, panic and confusion had again reigned supreme. The aircrews felt aggrieved, certain that they could have kept up their attacks for much longer; they considered themselves badly let down yet again. Palembang was yet one more in a line of major and minor disasters however, for worse was very soon to come.

Eastern Java

While all remained quiet in the west, in the east Japanese Naval aircraft returned to attack once more. Tainan Ku A6Ms were now established at Bandjermasin/Martapura airfield on the south-eastern tip of Borneo, and at Makassar/Maros in southern Celebes. During the morning 15 A6Ms and one C5M set out to strafe Maospati airfield in eastern Central Java, while half an hour later eight more of the fighters set course for Sourabaya as escort for 21 G4M bombers of the Takao Ku from Kendari.

One formation of nine bombers missed the rendezvous with the escort and proceeded towards Sourabaya alone. They were intercepted by a dozen P-40Es from the 17th Squadron, which had received sufficient warning to position themselves well. Nearly every pilot made several undisturbed passes at the bombers, the first attack being led by Lt Nathaniel Blanton, who hit the lead bomber, which began to smoke. The formation then started to break up and after further attacks four bombers were believed to have gone down. The Dutch subsequently reported that all nine had been seen to fall, although US records indicate that six bombers were credited to the unit: Capt Mahony claimed one and a probable, while Lts Blanton, Marion Fuchs, Ed Gilmore, Ben Irvin and Roger Williams were credited with one apiece.

Nine more bombers were then seen, this time with fighter escort, and Lt Morris C. Caldwell attacked these bombers which were in stepped-down formation, claiming that he set the top and bottom bombers on fire and that they crashed into the sea. His P-40E was hit by return fire and, after an attempt to return, he managed to bale out, but wrenched his back in so doing. These claims do not appear to have been confirmed. Other P-40s engaged the escorting fighters, three of them being claimed by Blanton, Reynolds and Frank Adkins.

Actual Japanese losses totalled four bombers: in Lt Yoshinobu Kusuhata's chutai the rear aircraft, flown by NAP 1/C Kinichi Shimada was shot down by P-40s, while Ens Hisao Yamada, the second element leader in Lt Koushirou Yakomizo's chutai was also lost to the fighters. NAP 2/C Kiyonori Shimono's G4M was reported hit by an AA shell just after bombing and went down at once. Nine more bombers were hit and damaged, one ditching during the return flight, the others returning with four crewmen dead.

The Tainan Ku reported that its eight escorting A6Ms engaged 20 P-40s and claims for six destroyed and three probables were submitted. Possibly on this occasion, these over-optimistic claims reflected the pilots' disquiet at their failure to protect the leading bomber formation. The A6Ms were flying in pairs and individual claims, within the formation, were as follows: Lt Masao Asai one, NAP 2/C Yoshie Shinohara two and one probable, NAP 2/C Yoshisuke Arita one and one probable, Lt Junichi Sasai one, NAP 2/C Susumu Ishihara one, NA 1/C Yoshio Motoyoshi one probable.

Despite the interception, some bombers got through to attack Sourabaya harbour, where the old non-operational cruiser *Soerabaja*, a submarine and some small vessels were sunk. Claims were submitted by the bomber crews for direct hits on two light cruisers and two destroyers. Meanwhile the larger Tainan Ku formation had strafed Maospati airfield, where the 1st and 3rd shotais of the 1st Chutai claimed two Brewsters destroyed on the ground. The 2nd shotai (NAP 1/C Saburo Sakai, NAP 2/C Hideo Izumi and NAP 3/C Takashi Yokoyama) engaged a Fokker C-XIW floatplane, 'W-12' from the cruiser *De Ruyter* — and a transport aircraft in the air, Sakai shooting down the former in flames over Maospati; he noted simply of his victory:

> "En route to Malang we encountered a Dutch floatplane and I broke for-
> mation long enough to send him crashing into the ocean."

The 2nd Chutai saw nothing during this operation and returned with their guns unfired. The AA defences claimed four aircraft shot down during this attack, but no losses were actually suffered.

The reason for the attacks was soon evident. That night two transport vessels, escorted by the cruiser *Nagara* and seven destroyers of the 2nd Destroyer Flotilla, landed troops of the Japanese 48th Division from Makassar (Celebes), on the south side of Bali island. No resistance was encountered and the airfield at Denpassar was swiftly secured.

Thursday, 19 February – Western Java

In the west, Java suffered its first attacks, by the newly-arrived JAAF units at Palembang. The first such raid was made on Buitenzorg, 19 Ki 43s of the 59th and 64th Sentais, led by Maj Tateo Kato, escorting five Ki 48s of the 90th Sentai over the area soon after 0930.

On 19 February, Sgt N.G. de Groot of 3-VlG-IV was shot down and killed near Semplak while flying B-3119; one of the other two aircraft depicted, B-3122, was also lost this day, Sgt L. van Daalan of 3-VlG-V baling out. *(Authors' collection)*

Eight Brewsters of 1 and 2-VlG-V were scrambled over Semplak, reporting meeting 35 Japanese aircraft and claimed two fighters, identified as 'Zeros' shot down. Sgts Scheffer and Hart each fought a Ki 43, but both were shot down and baled out, while Ens Kuijper and Sgt de Groot were also brought down (the latter flying B-3119), losing their lives. Lt August Deibel fired twice at one fighter but, after a ten minute dogfight, he was wounded by shell splinters (believed to have been from a 20mm cannon), and force-landed on the airfield. On this occasion, the Japanese pilots identified their opponents as nine Curtiss Hawks and claimed seven "easily" shot down.

The bombers raided Semplak airfield, where the crews claimed the destruction of four of 16 large aircraft seen; in fact they knocked out four Hudsons, either

Left: Lt August Deibel of 1-VlG-V, one of the most successful of the Dutch pilots, who was credited with three victories. *(Authors' collection)*. Right: Sgt Jan Scheffer of 1-VlG-V, who was later to die as a POW. *(Authors' collection)*

burnt out or riddled by shrapnel and machine-gun bullets; other casualties included an ML Lodestar and two KNILM Sikorskys — an S-43W (PK-AFU) and an S-43B (PK-AFX), the latter struck by burning debris from an exploding Hudson. A Grumman G-21a (PK-AFR) of KNILM was also destroyed, as was another of the airline's machines, an elderly Fokker F-XII (PK-AFI), and a Ryan STM trainer.

Fokker F.XII PK-AFI was destroyed during an air raid on Kemajoran civil airport, Batavia, on 19 February *(Authors' collection)*

One of the Hudsons rendered unserviceable was that flown by Flg Off Siddell, which had just returned from a reconnaissance sortie; Siddell's gunner, Sgt Les Patrick, recalled:

"We had been on a recce to Palembang and Banka Island and had landed, and were parking the aircraft. We were all out of the aircraft when the 'Zeros' came over and the only thing to do was get under cover as quickly as possible. I covered 100 yards in what seemed like five seconds and leaped over a 10-feet high fence and across a stream! No one in the crew was injured but our aircraft was riddled and I think one or two other aircraft were also hit."

Another witness to the raid, Plt Off John Coom, remembered:

"On the first dive bombing of Semplak, the Japanese hit a lovely wooden hangar and ruined a Sikorsky amphibian, a Ryan trainer and a Hudson. One delayed action bomb found an underground petrol storage tank, and burned like a blow lamp."

As a result of this latest devastating attack, KNILM officials issued instructions for the airline's remaining aircraft to withdraw to Australia forthwith, and that night saw the departure of eight machines, mainly Lockheed 14s, DC-3s and DC-5s, six more following as soon as they could be made ready for the long flight. The Dutch army ordered that any unairworthy machines should be destroyed, to prevent them falling into Japanese hands, and amongst those put to the torch were two of the old Fokkers — PK-AFD and AFH — a DH89A (PK-AKV) and a DC-2 (PK-AFJ). It was agreed that the machines flown to Australia would commence a shuttle service to Java, bringing in urgent supplies and taking out refugees.

From Tjililitan a patrol of Hurricanes from 242 Squadron had just departed, newly-arrived Sgt John Isdale the last to leave, when four A6Ms dived on the airfield, the pilots apparently having not seen each other. The Japanese fighters made one pass, during which one of 242 Squadron's ground crew suffered a minor wound, before they flew away to seek better targets.

Meanwhile, following the raid on Semplak, Flg Off Bernie Hughes took off in Hudson A16-44 to join a mixed force of seven Blenheims for a bombing raid on P.1 but failed to rendezvous, so returned. The Blenheims set off — three crewed by 84 Squadron personnel and one by a 34 Squadron crew, led by Flt Lt Holland; the other section was from 211 Squadron, with Wg Cdr Bateson at their head but, before the Sumatran coast was reached, Sgt George Dewey was obliged to return when his aircraft developed electrical problems (although, after rectification of the fault, he followed the others), the remaining six continuing to the target area in two separate flights. Holland's gunner in V6092, Sgt Bob Bennett, wrote:

"The morning was fine, with some broken white cloud which was to increase on nearing the target. Formation flying was, therefore, abandoned and we split up to carry out individual attacks, using the cloud cover to our best advantage. We continued to fly through patchy cloud, enabling intermittent glimpses of sea beneath us, and later land after crossing the coast of Sumatra.

"This cloud cover was in our favour as it restricted the deployment of enemy fighters in the vicinity and gave us some protection from ground batteries. A lone Blenheim was a prime target for a fighter as there was no protection for an underneath attack, apart from a single Vickers gun firing backwards, situated under the navigator's seat, and there were blind spots under the tail planes. The only chance we had was to get down to nought feet provided there was time, and then use the twin Brownings in the gun turret.

"Eventually Doug Argent (the navigator) announced that we were

Left: Sgt Bob Bennett of 84 Squadron, who claimed a Japanese fighter shot down on 19 February. *(R.C.H. Bennett)*. Right: Sgt Allan 'Jock' Richardson of 211 Squadron, who also claimed a Japanese fighter during a running fight on 19 February. *(Flt Lt A.R. Richardson)*

approaching P.1, and (*Flt Lt Holland*) started to look around for a hole in the cloud to come in near the target. So far, so good — no fighters and no ack-ack either, which was strange, as the Japs usually blasted away at anything that moved or could be heard. Doug was spot on course and the aerodrome appeared ahead. Rows of aircraft were lined each side of the runway, wing tip to wing tip. We levelled out, took one side and dropped the stick of bombs amongst them — couldn't miss!

"Still no ack-ack, just the usual noise of our engines. This meant only one thing — there must be fighters up, looking for us in the gaps between the clouds. Next item on the programme was to get the hell out of it, back into some cloud cover if possible and make for home. We turned on course for base, hoping that the cloud cover would hold for a while longer, all the time keeping a lookout for fighters, which must be somewhere near."

A second Blenheim penetrated the low cloud and released its bombs over the airfield, where one Ki 27 was destroyed on the ground and two others damaged, while 1,200 gallons of petrol were burned. A third Blenheim, piloted by Sgt George Sayer, dropped its bombs on a ship tied up in Palembang River, the crew having been unable to locate the airfield due to the heavy ground mist. As the raiders withdrew, they were attacked by two "fighters with spats" — both which were claimed shot down — one by Sgt 'Sandy' Ross, Sayer's gunner, who recalled:

"Heard gunfire and then saw the belly of a Jap fighter as he made away from our tail — too sudden for me to get a shot. How could he have missed us?

"A few minutes later, heading east for Java — I estimate it would have been about 12 miles east of Palembang — suddenly appeared diving from astern, two fixed-undercart planes; their initial closing speed slackened and they were near enough for me to pick off the left one; pieces of the cowling broke off and were plainly visible; the pilot's head was low and forward as the plane made a steep twisting descent.

"Soon after, the other Jap plane could be seen losing ground to us. Initially I had reported to George the presence of the two aircraft and suggested — or rather pleaded — that he go for cloud cover, if any. He replied: "No cloud cover, only ground mist with a few tips of mountains showing!" He dived for this, throttles through the gate, and after only a few seconds in the mist we came out and nothing else was in sight."

The other fighter was claimed by Sgt Bennett, in Flt Lt Holland's aircraft; the Blenheim was badly shot up during the exchange, as recalled by Bennett:

"There was a sound like a sharp fall of hailstones on a tin roof — the whole plane shuddered, but kept on going. From past experience we knew it was not ack-ack fire this time, and I made some stupid remark like, 'There must be something behind us, Dutch.'

'Je-ee-ze', came the reply over the intercom. It was enough, both Dutch and Doug knew the score, and while they concerned themselves with looking for some cloud cover, I tried to see where the fighter was. He must have been in the blind spot under the tail, otherwise I would have spotted him coming in to attack, and maybe he was now coming in for a further go.

"Dutch banked to port a few degrees and there he was, perched on top of a patch of cloud about 200 yards astern, slightly below us. Great! Perfect target! Quick aim , and both Brownings chattered away. I saw pieces fly off the fighter and he fell into the cloud and disappeared, leaving a trail of black smoke behind him. I told Dutch what had happened and that I was fairly sure I had got him.

"So far, so good, but there could be others about, and we also had to assess the damage caused by the attack. Luckily no one was hit, but oil was beginning to spread all over the starboard wing and, although the engines sounded rough they were still going, and we were still airborne! Fortunately, the hydraulics to the turret were still sound, otherwise we would have been defenceless.

"We still had about three-quarters of an hour flying time to make base, and it was vital for us to get back to Java before the engines packed up, or we would have to come down in the sea. The idea of three men in an inflatable dinghy did not appeal to us, even supposing the damn thing was still seaworthy. The idea was to keep flying as long as possible, and if that could be achieved, we stood a good chance of making it.

"Our luck held, and we were able to make Kalidjati before the engines failed. Fortunately, the landing gear still worked, and Dutch made a good landing. Another mission completed and we were all in one piece!"

Meanwhile the 211 Squadron trio, having attacked the target, broke formation and returned independently. Plt Off Coughlan's aircraft (Z9960) was immediately pursued by seven fighters and a running fight continued for 40 minutes before the Blenheim escaped. During this action Sgt Jock Richardson, the air gunner, claimed one of the attackers shot down and probably a second which had apparently tried to ram the bomber! He recalled:

"We were jumped by seven plus Jap fighters, some of them Army 97s (*Ki 27s*), and they came down from height from the sun, in line astern. My last glance at the scene below before this, was to see Jap Naval ships anchored in the river in the centre of Palembang.

The fighters kept up continuous attacks from astern and quarters, sometimes two at once. 'Ginger' Coughlan was an absolute 'ace' with a Blenheim, and could make it do almost anything. There is no doubt that his fantastic flying was the major reason for our survival, as we did steep turns in clouds, stall turned, dived, climbed and dodged determined attacks as I shouted continuous evasive instructions from the rear turret.

"One fighter overshot his attack as he followed us out of a cloud, and I raked him point-blank from engine to tail. Almost immediately white smoke started pouring out from the engine, then later black, oily smoke, as it turned over and dived vertically into the ground from a height of about 2,000 feet.

"The remaining fighters continued attacking and I got some more hits, especially on one which literally formated with us, obviously out of ammo, but we could not confirm it as destroyed.

"The running fight had been going on for quite a time and, as we were heading south for Java as much as we could, the fighters gradually broke off. However, one fighter had climbed well above us and some instinct had made me look up vertically; coming straight down at us in a vertical dive was the lone fighter. I screamed at 'Ginger': 'Left, left, for Christ's sake,' and the slipstream of the Jap shook us as he dived past, missing our Blenheim by feet.

"I could see every detail in that moment as he flashed by: the goggled Jap face staring at us, the prop, engine nacelle, fuselage panels, cockpit hood etc. He did not appear again and, as we were fairly low by that time, he may have hit the ground.

"We were in the clear at last in a beautiful blue sky with puffy white clouds, and below, the dark green of the jungle, broken only by the shimmering reflections of the sun on the swamp waters in between. It was hard to believe that, only a few minutes previously, death had been a very great possibility."

On its return to Kalidjati Z9960 was found to have a cracked mainspar — a legacy from the bomb explosion over Palembang four days earlier — and was considered no longer airworthy; the Blenheim was later burnt to deny it to the Japanese.

Identification of the fighters involved has been difficult to establish. Ki 27s from both 1st and 11th Sentais were currently based at Palembang and presumably aircraft from one — if not both — of these units participated in the engagements. However, Japanese Navy records state that three 'bombers' — believed to have been D3As — patrolled the Sunda Strait during the day and that two were attacked by 'fighters', one of which was claimed shot down, and another probably so.

Six Glenn Martins later raided the Pladjoe oil refinery, followed by a single Dutch bomber attacking the same target during the evening, after which four large oil tanks were reported burning. Three other Glenn Martins carried out a raid on P.1, bombing independently due to bad weather; all returned safely, as did another trio which attacked shipping on the Moesi River.

In the afternoon, at about 1640, a larger force of 28 Ki 43s from the 59th and

64th Sentais, together with nine Ki 48s, returned, this time to raid Bandoeng, where a dozen Brewsters from Lt Pieter Tideman's 3-VlG-V (now operating again as an independent unit) were up to engage the force, which they reported as a dozen bombers and 36 fighters. This time the Japanese — although engaging similar aircraft to those met during the morning — identified the Dutch fighters as 20 P-43s, once again claiming seven shot down, plus three probables. Tideman recalled:

> "We could not reach the bombers properly — we did not shoot down any but got tangled up in huge dogfights with the 'Zeros' (*sic*). One of my best officers — Lt Tukker — was shot down and killed. A very good NCO — Sgt van Daalan (flying B-3122) — was shot down but saved himself by parachute; got severely burned on face and arms though. Another NCO — Sgt Adam — was so fanatic that he did not want to sidestep a head-on Jap. He collided, bringing down the Jap; lost his own wing partially and jumped to safety with his parachute. Also, Lt de Haas, an airline pilot (who was enlisted in my squadron as were two other airline pilots, Lts Simons and Andre de la Porte), saved himself by jumping after his machine guns jammed.

> "As for myself, I can only say that I had several severe dogfights. Although I must have hit quite a few Navy 0s, I did not see one of them go down to the deck because the Japs operated in groups of three: one taking up the fight, the second staying close behind him and the third taking a position higher on his tail. So, as soon as I got No 1 in my gunsight and opened up with my machine-guns, after a burst or two, I saw No 2 or No 3 coming in on me. So as not to get shot down myself, I had to turn my attention to the one behind.

> "During the action I was hit badly several times (not personally) but was able to land normally. I remember the first hit I received came from a cannon shell hitting my right wing, where I could see a huge hole. I was shocked to death at first — later I got used to the sound of hitting bullets!"

The light bombers attacked the airfield, claiming five large aircraft burned. In fact a B-17 (41-2493), a Hudson and some small trainers were destroyed, including a Bu 131 (RJ-002), an impressed NEI Army Air Force Waco biplane — WT-927 ex PK-SAK — and a number of Ryan STMs; one further B-17 was severely damaged. It may have been during this raid that six Dutch fighters under repair at Andir — three Hawk 75As, two CW-21Bs and one Brewster — were destroyed by bombs.

As the formation headed back for Palembang, two B-17s were seen in the Buitenzorg area and the Ki 43s swarmed all over these. They were claimed probably destroyed when many parachutes were seen to blossom forth from both, although neither bomber was observed to crash; in fact 41-2503 was lost. Return fire struck the 64th Sentai Ki 43 flown by Sgt Maj Akeshi Yokoi and he was obliged to crash-land in the sea near an island during the return flight, subsequently being rescued by a Navy floatplane.

64th Sentai pilots were credited with four victories as a result of the two raids, including two by Capt Katsumi Anma and one each by Yokoi and Sgt Yoshito Yasuda, while 59th Sentai claimed the rest, Wt Off Takeomi Hayashi being credited with one of the B-17s.

Late-model Dutch Brewster B-349, B-3119. This aircraft was shot down on 19 February. *(Authors' collection)*

Eastern Java

With the onset of daylight, American bombers were sent out to attack the Bali invasion force — thought to comprise four transports, two cruisers and five to six destroyers — while pairs of A6Ms were despatched by the Tainan Ku to patrol above the ships. The first three B-17s, off at 0500, escaped interception, two of them bombing without effect. Only Lt P.L. Mathewson (40-2484) reported gaining any success, believing he had scored a direct hit on a cruiser. Four more bombers were forced to turn back just after 0605 when intercepted by two A6Ms flown by Lt Kiyoharu Shibuya and NAP 2/C Kunimatsu Nishiura, but these pilots failed to achieve any decisive results; in return, the gunners claimed one of their attackers shot down, although neither was lost.

Three LB-30s followed at 0645, but these too were attacked by Shibuya and Nishiura; the Americans reported the Japanese fighters as nine strong, and claimed two shot down. All three bombers sustained damage during the attacks. Two more B-17 formations followed at 0800 but, although intercepted by the same pair of A6Ms, neither was hit. Two of the bombers, attacking in unison, claimed a near miss, whilst another straddled a destroyer with bombs. During these various interceptions one of the A6Ms suffered serious damage and the other was hit twice.

Somewhat later, two A-24s of the 91st Bomb Squadron — flown by Capt Harry Galusha and Lt Julius B. Summers — took off from Malang, avoided the patrolling A6Ms and attacked the ships, damaging the transport *Sugami Maru*, which was struck by one bomb; despite the explosion, which destroyed one engine, the transport was able to get under way and with a destroyer escort returned to Makassar. The A-24 crews believed they had also sunk a cruiser although in fact none of the warships were damaged; Galusha and Summers were each later awarded a Silver Star for their actions.

Soon after the A-24s had departed Malang, an air raid approached. This comprised 18 bombers from the 23rd Air Flotilla escorted by 23 Tainan Ku A6Ms. Due to adverse weather conditions, the bombers diverted from their priority target of Sourabaya and raided Bawean Island instead. The fighters therefore left the bombers just before 1300 and headed on to the port where, soon after arrival, they reported engaging over 30 — possibly as many as 50 — P-36s and P-40s.

The Americans reported meeting only eight A6Ms but, as they were engaged by both the 1st and 2nd Chutai, it is assumed that they initially engaged only one (possibly the latter), the other then joining in. For the defenders it was a disastrous combat: Capts Mahony and Lane were shot down, as were Lts Hague, Kruzel, Gilmore, Blanton and Quanah P. Fields; the latter, a Cherokee Indian known as 'Chief', baled out but was shot on his parachute and killed, with a bullet through the head; Ed Gilmore, a Philippines veteran, was badly burned, but his life was saved by Dutch doctors, while Blanton came down unhurt on a beach by the Straits of Madoera. Five claims were submitted for A6Ms shot down, one each by Mahony, Kruzel, Lane, Hague and Reynolds.

Lt Joseph J. Kruzel of the 17th Pursuit Squadron (Provisional) in front of his dragon-emblazoned P-40E at Ngoro airfield, flanked by his crew chief and armourer. *(Richard Slater)*

The Tainan pilots claimed 14 destroyed and three probables; each of the chutais involved claimed seven — a classic case of double-claiming during a confused combat. They suffered one loss, Lt Masao Asai, leader of the 2nd Chutai, who failed to return. Apart from three claims by NAP 1/C Saburo Sakai of the 1st Chutai, it is not known whom the claimants were although the following pilots also participated in the action:

1st Chutai:	**2nd Chutai:**
Lt Hideki Shingo	Lt Masao Asai
NAP 2/C Tsunehiro Yamagami	NAP 2/C Yoshie Shinohara
NAP 3/C Saburo Nozawa	NAP 3/C Takeo Kume
NAP 3/C Kazuo Yokoyama	Wt Off Gitaro Miyazaki
NAP 1/C Kuniyoshi Tanaka	NAP 3/C Kosaku Minato
NAP 3/C Toshiaki Honda	NAP 3/C Sadao Uehara
NAP 2/C Yoshisuke Arita	NA 1/C Yoshio Motoyoshi

In a single day, Java had lost 15 more of its meagre force of fighters, with a further two badly damaged — this on the same day as the disastrous Darwin raid (see chapter 5).

With the Japanese now possessing airfields in Southern Sumatra, Bali, Borneo and Celebes, Java was surrounded and could no longer be safely reinforced by air. Wavell therefore advised the Chiefs-of-Staff that in his opinion Java's air defences could not survive another fortnight — an estimate he was to halve two days later! Nonetheless, efforts continued to provide an efficient fighter Operations Room in Batavia — to control the defence of West Java — and one was operating within a week.

With darkness on the night of the 19th, two Allied naval forces sailed to contest the Bali landings. These comprised in one case the cruisers *De Ruyter* and *Java*, two US and two Dutch destroyers, and in the other the cruiser *Tromp* and four US destroyers. They engaged the Japanese covering force, claiming one destroyer damaged and one transport sunk, but in return *Tromp* was badly damaged and one Dutch destroyer — *Piet Hein* — was sunk.

Friday, 20 February – Western Java

At dawn, a number of Hurricanes of 242 Squadron scrambled from Tjililitan and climbed to 20,000 feet, but one suffered a glycol leak, Sgt Newlands returning to base early. Despite a ground loop following a cross-wing landing, his aircraft was not damaged. Meanwhile the rest of the unit had engaged Japanese aircraft over Bantam Bay, Flt Lt Julian claiming one fighter (a Ki 27) shot down, while a second was claimed jointly by Plt Off Watson and Sgt King. Sgt Kynman overshot on landing and his Hurricane was damaged (earning him seven days as Duty Pilot as a punishment!). Two Dutch Brewsters flew into Tjililitan early in the morning, parking near the RAF Hurricanes, and were serviced by a number of Dutch groundcrew personnel who had also arrived at the airfield. Shortly after their arrival, a Japanese fighter attack on the airfield occurred, as LAC James Home of 242 Squadron noted:

> "Our latest casualty was a wounded Bill Hocken whose leg was hit by either shrapnel or cannon shell, and he was followed by a shocked petrol bowser driver who got one through his cab window. At least the time spent on the drome was a reminder of home during the Battle of Britain days."

Later, six more Hurricanes were scrambled over Batavia harbour, where a lone floatplane was sighted at 9,000 feet by Sgts Ron Dovell and Tom Young, the latter firing at extreme range; he recalled:

> "Almost immediately smoke poured from it and he (the Japanese pilot) turned his aircraft towards me and passed so close I could plainly see the pilot. I felt he was anxious to take me with him."

He was credited with its destruction. It is uncertain whether the crew of the floatplane managed to report on shipping movements at Tanjong Priok before they were attacked, although Japanese aerial reconnaissance during the morning did note five cruisers, eight destroyers, more than 50 merchant ships, ten flyingboats and three floatplanes in harbour.

Three Blenheims were despatched from Kalidjati to raid shipping at Palembang, while two Hudsons from 1 RAAF (A16-44 flown by Flt Lt J.G. Emerton and A16-28 captained by Flg Off J.M. Sutherland) and two more from 62 Squadron departed Semplak early to attack shipping in the Banka Strait. Nearing the target area the Hudsons became separated and fighters attacked, allowing only one crew the opportunity to release their bombs on shipping in the Moesi River, where four direct hits were claimed on transports. Despite the interception, all returned safely. A Japanese report suggested that one aircraft bombed the Pladjoe oil refinery.

The complexity of the RAF component was being rationalised further, 34 Squadron at Kalidjati handing its remaining Blenheims and crews over to 84 Squadron during the day, while at Semplak 8 RAAF Squadron and 62 Squadron were now disbanded and the Hudsons passed to 1 RAAF. This unit was to be established with 30 crews, the extra being drawn from the disbanded units, including four from 62 Squadron. The surplus aircrew however were ordered to Darwin together with 453 Squadron, leaving on the 22nd. The Dutch were also pursuing a policy of evacuating aircraft no longer of use in the East Indies and thus six of the older Dutch flyingboats (Catalina Y-49 and Do 24s X-5, X-7, X-8, X-9 and X-10) departed for Australia, where they were to be used for training purposes.

Eastern Java

Meanwhile early in the morning, seven A-24s of the 91st Bomb Squadron moved from their base at Sourabaya to Malang to bomb-up, then to rendezvous over Singosari with 16 P-40s from the 17th Pursuit Squadron, before heading for Bali to attack shipping in the Lombok Strait. Arriving overhead at 12,000 feet, the crews saw six vessels unloading barges near the island of Nusa Besar, so dived to attack. Maj E.N. Backus (40-786) claimed three hits on a cruiser, while three other pilots claimed two hits each, Lt Richard B. Launder (40-804) claiming to have blown the bows off one such warship. An oil lead then burst in his aircraft — probably due to an AA hit — and he came down in the sea just off the coast, he and his gunner, Sgt I.A. Lnenicke, getting ashore on Bali where they were aided by a local Balinese chief, who organised a boat to take them back to Java. A second A-24 (40-796) was seen to crash into the sea at the end of its dive — probably a victim of AA fire; 2/Lt D.B. Tubb and his gunner were both killed. Several sections of 3rd Ku A6Ms from Makassar were on patrol over the area, four having taken off at 0715, followed by three more an hour later. At 0945 NA 1/C Tanekichi Ohtsuki left the second trio in order to reconnoitre over a cruiser and a destroyer, but failed to return, his two compatriots seeing nothing. However at 0955 the second shotai of the first patrol spotted the last three A-24s just as they went into their dive, also spotting the escort, reported as 20 plus fighters. NAP 1/C Yoshihisa Tokuji and NAP 1/C Masao Masuyama at once attacked the latter with the advantage of surprise, and claimed five shot down between them. The first shotai from this patrol split up, NAP 3/C Isaburo Yahata climbing high to try and find the bombers, but seeing nothing while, at

A pair of Curtiss P-40Es of the 17th Pursuit Squadron (Provisional) in Java in February 1942. The aircraft in the foreground is believed to be that flown by Lt Joseph J. Kruzel, one of the more successful American fighter pilots of the campaign. *(via P. Boer)*

1015, Ens Tsuneo Nakahara spotted two fighters strafing and claimed one of these shot down.

Maj Charles Sprague, the 17th's commander, and Lt Wilfred H. Galliere were both shot down and killed, while Lt Thomas I. Hayes just made it back, crash-landing at Ngoro, his aircraft practically shot to pieces. Lt Robert S. Johnson had undertaken the flight on his main fuel tank, instead of first using the new drop tank which the aircraft was carrying, and after jettisoning the latter when the combat started, he quickly ran out of fuel, landing on a beach in south Java; he was picked up at once by a boat from the US Asiatic Fleet schooner *Lanakai*. Lt William C. Stauter reportedly also ran out of fuel and crash-landed on a beach, returning safely on a bicycle 'borrowed' from a Javanese. During the combat two A6Ms and a single-engined bomber were claimed shot down (the fighters by Lts Jack Dale and Joe Kruzel, the bomber credited to Lt Bill Hennon) while one more A6M, which was seen on the ground at Denpassar, was claimed probably destroyed by Capt Mahony. The loss of Maj Sprague was a severe blow. The commander of a patrolling US submarine, *Seawolf*, reported seeing a parachute coming down over Nusa Besar, which was probably that of Sprague. A Japanese radio report was later intercepted which suggested that an American air force major had been captured on Bali. Whatever his immediate fate, Sprague did not survive.

Three B-17s from Madioen and seven more from Malang subsequently bombed the ships off Denpassar. These were intercepted, two bombers sustaining damage whilst gunners claimed three of the attacking fighters shot down. Four hours later the crew of a lone B-17 flown by Capt Felix M. Hardison, reported bombing and sinking a transport off Madioen.

Following these attacks, nine Tainan Ku A6Ms — which had at once moved forward to Bali — were ordered off to strafe Malang airfield, while 13 aircraft of the 3rd Ku were despatched to Sourabaya. Although the latter pilots saw no aircraft on the ground, the former found the B-17s undispersed and in the process of being refuelled, service personnel swarming all over them. Believing the fighters to be the missing remnants of the returning P-40s, the men did not at once run for cover as the A6Ms swept in, guns blazing. Five of the seven bombers were hit, three exploding in balls of fire while the other two were badly damaged. Surprisingly, despite the devastation caused, only nine men were injured during the attack. The Japanese claimed four B-17s burned, plus another and one twin-engined aircraft damaged.

To the north on this date, 450 Japanese paratroops landed at Koepang and Dili (Timor), their arrival coinciding with seaborne landings. In support of the operation, 17 G3Ms of the 1st Ku bombed Koepang, losing Lt Norio Fukuoka and his crew to AA fire. Fierce resistance was initially encountered on the ground before Koepang fell and the airfield was occupied. Of the main Dutch islands, only Java now remained in Allied hands.

Saturday, 21 February – Western Java

At 0900 two Hudsons of 1 RAAF Squadron, A16-44 flown by Flt Lt J.G. White and A16-28 in the hands of Flt Lt Ken Smith, departed Semplak to carry out attacks on P.1 whilst also reconnoitring the Moesi River. The airfield was bombed but on approaching the Moesi they were attacked by fighters — a running engagement ensued until clouds were reached, neither aircraft suffering any damage.

Not so fortunate was another Hudson — AE493 flown by Plt Off P.M. Bonn of 62 Squadron — which was despatched to carry out a lone strike against shipping reported (by a Hurricane pilot) south-east of Singapore. The Hudson was also intercepted by fighters and severely damaged, although Bonn succeeded in reaching Java before misfortune overtook the crew; AE493 crashed ten miles north-west of Buitenzorg and Bonn was seriously injured, dying later that day in the Military Hospital at Batavia; his observer, Flt Sgt W.F.F. Perkins, died two days later. Six Glenn Martins were also despatched to raid Pladjoe but were intercepted 100 miles north-north-west of Oosthaven en route. The aircraft flown by Ens Thijs Postma was shot down, probably by an F1M floatplane; Postma was the only member of the crew able to bale out and survive, despite being shot at by an F1M as he floated down.

An hour before midday, a mixed flight of five Blenheims, drawn from 84 and 211 Squadrons led by Wg Cdr Bateson, set off from Kalidjati to continue the series of mini attacks on shipping in the Moesi River and to bomb oil tanks at Pladjoe. The formation ran into a severe storm and Sgt John Burrage's aircraft was lost, the all-Australian crew perishing. Flt Lt Wyllie, leading one section, recalled:

> "I took three aircraft into a line squall. These weather fronts can stretch for miles and there is no flying around them, under them, or over them. Only two aircraft came out the other side. The one I lost was a very young Australian, too inexperienced to fly on instruments alone through the massive turbulence these storms have in their immense rumbling bellies.
>
> "I was lucky when the other equally inexperienced Australian joined me on the other side. We left great clouds of oil smoke over the tank farm."

The other section attacked shipping independently; a near miss was reported on one vessel and a launch was claimed sunk. None of the Blenheims were intercepted and the remaining aircraft all returned safely, without further incident.

Learning that the weather around Batavia was likely to be bad, Maj Kato led the Ki 43s of the 59th and 64th Sentais, together with the 90th Sentai's light bombers, towards Kalidjati. On approaching the target area, he left the 59th and 90th Sentais to head for the airfield, leading the 64th towards cloud-covered

Bandoeng instead. Arriving there soon after midday, at about 20,000 feet, they spotted seven fighters identified as P-43s, which attacked from above but were evaded. Four were then seen below and were 'bounced', Kato and his wingman, Lt Hinoki, claiming one probably shot down, although one of the unit's Ki 43s failed to return. It seems very likely that their opponents were once more Brewsters from 3-VlG-V and their commander, Lt Tideman, recalled:

"Another attack came with 21 'Zeros' (*sic*). We had nine Brewsters against them that day. Obviously their target was to strafe the airport at Andir. Again we managed to keep them busy in dogfights preventing them doing the strafing. This time I saw a 'Zero', which I had a good aim at, diving down steeply with smoke trailing behind. Again, I did not see the crash. After the action the Japanese retreated and I was able to form a patrol of three with Lts Simons and Benjamins. Cruising over the hills north of Bandoeng — between clouds — we waited for the all clear signal to come from our ground station.

"Flying in formation I was suddenly badly hit from behind and below. My Brewster was afire. However, as I was about to jump, the fire stopped and I was able to land normally. Afterwards, discussing how a thing like this ever could happen to us, Lt Simons told me, almost crying, that all of a sudden he had seen the Jap climbing up from below behind my tail. Grasping his mike to warn me, the thing had slipped out of his hand and he saw the Jap — almost abreast — opening up on me at close quarters. Certainly I was lucky that time and my armour plate behind my seat took the beating, as we later discovered."

Meanwhile the bombers completed their attack on Kalidjati, bombing a reported 23 large aircraft on the ground (while the Blenheims were still away on their raid), claiming six destroyed. Apparently five Glenn Martins were destroyed during attacks on this airfield, including M-540, M-549, M-560 and M-580, together with a Lodestar transport. Total Dutch claims by AA and fighters amounted to four shot down — including one by Lt H.H.J. Simons — and five damaged, but the only loss appears to have been the single Ki 43 to the Brewsters — probably Tideman's victim.

The RAF Hurricanes at Tjililitan were not engaged, most of the day being spent dispersing the aircraft into 'hideouts' in the surrounding jungle. Around this time Flt Lt Parker and Plt Off Fitzherbert were sent off to try and catch a reconnaissance aircraft. Jimmy Parker recalled:

"We had been warned of no other aircraft in the area but I saw half a dozen specks a very long way off in the distance against some white cloud. It took me about a quarter of an hour of cruising and climbing to get into the right position against the sun and then the pair of us hurtled down against them, only to find they were Dutch Buffaloes. I was very pleased they had not seen us but they joined up with us and we climbed back to 25,000 feet.

"Soon afterwards I saw the recce aircraft a long way below us, almost vertically. I dived steeply down and throttled back in order not to overshoot and we were all strung out in a line at the same height as the Jap preparatory to overtaking and firing in turn, when he suddenly increased speed enormously and we were unable to get within 600 yards of him. He just accelerated off to the north and we had no hope of catching him. He had a

Dutch pilots of 1-VIG-V. In the left foreground (with cigarette) is Lt G.J. de Haas, who was shot down on 19 February. At right, at the end of the table, is his fellow flight commander, Lt H.H.J. Simons. *(Authors' collection)*

very fast aeroplane (twin-engined) and the pilot had clearly worked out our tactic and flown slowly until we had lost our height and speed."

Their opponent was undoubtedly one of the speedy reconnaissance Ki 46s, probably from the 81st Independent Sentai operating out of P.2.

Tjilatjap — where three Catalinas of 205 Squadron had arrived earlier in the day from Tanjong Priok — saw the arrival of the American cruiser *Houston* during the late afternoon. As she prepared to enter harbour, she was approached at low level by Catalina FV-V flown by Flt Lt J.C. Lowe. Dutch AA gunners defending the port thought the flyingboat was a Japanese raider and opened fire, blowing a hole in the aircraft's port wing! In order to make a safe emergency landing, Lowe ordered the depth charges to be jettisoned, the explosion of which almost wrecked the flyingboat which was, in fact, damaged beyond repair. Meanwhile, Capt Rooks of the *Houston*, observing the dropping of the depth charges, assumed a Japanese submarine was in the area and turned back out to sea, returning half an hour later when the commotion had receded. *Houston* had come in to refuel, an operation which proceeded throughout the night, the cruiser departing again at 0730.

Eastern Java

In the east the JNAF was also again active, and further combats followed. Early in the day seven Tainan Ku A6Ms were scrambled from Bali after an LB-30 — one of two which attacked shipping off the island — but were unable to catch it. Four hours later six B-17s repeated the attack, one sustaining damage from AA fire. About the same time seven more A6Ms set off to attack Maospati and Malang airfields; three small aircraft were claimed destroyed on the ground at the former location. A larger raid was mounted at 0930, six Tainan Ku A6Ms and six from the 3rd Ku — all operating from Bali — taking off to escort 21 Takao Ku bombers to attack shipping at Sourabaya. 16 P-40s were scrambled by the 17th Squadron to intercept the bombers which were at 20,000 feet, but the A6Ms swept down onto them and broke up the attack, Lt Thomas Hayes being shot down and killed at once. Lt Wally Hoskyn was reportedly seen attacking one A6M as another closed on his tail; he was then believed to have shot down at least one, and possibly two, fighters before he was shot down and killed. Another A6M was claimed by Lt Frank Adkins, and two more by Capt Mahony and Lt Dale. As a result of the combat, Hoskyn was posthumously awarded a Silver Star. The squadron noted that both he and Maj Sprague had just had names painted on their P-40s before they were killed, and the practice was thereupon dropped.

The two Japanese escorting units seem to have attacked jointly, and double-claimed. The three pilots of the 3rd Ku's 1st shotai of the 1st Chutai (Lt Takeo Kurosawa, NAP 1/C Isaburo Yahata and NA 1/C Toru Oda) reported seeing at least ten P-40s, and claimed three shot down. Lt Junichi Sasai and his two wingmen from the Tainan Ku also dived on ten P-40s, Sasai claiming one and NAP 1/C Keishu Kamihira two. A seventh P-40 was claimed shot down by gunners of the Takao Ku, whose bombadiers claimed damage to a cruiser and a merchant vessel during the raid. One G4M was hit during the fight and force-landed, but the fighter units suffered no losses. During the return flight, the 3rd Ku's 2nd Chutai, led by Ens Tsueno Nakahara, flew to Malang airfield were they carried out a strafe and claimed one B-17 in flames, two medium and one small aircraft badly damaged.

Sunday, 22 February – Western Java

Three crews of 211 Squadron were briefed to attack a trio of Japanese sub-marines which were reported to be active in the Sunda Strait area, but as Plt Off Coughlan's aircraft (R3733, an 84 Squadron machine) began to climb away from Kalidjati, its starboard engine spluttered and cut, obliging the pilot to land. The remaining two Blenheims carried out a fruitless search for the submarines and returned without incident.

Meanwhile, three Hudsons set out from Semplak at 1000, A16-28 flown by Flt Lt John O'Brien, A16-44 with Flg Off Gibbes at the controls and AE506 captained by Plt Off Fitzgerald, their tasks to obtain photographs of Oosthaven, P.1, P.2 and the oil refinery, and to bomb shipping on the Moesi. The two RAAF aircraft were attacked by fighters although both evaded and escaped damage, while Fitzgerald, flying independently, reached the target area undetected and claimed two direct hits and one near miss on a 10,000 ton ship in the Banka Strait, which was apparently left burning fiercely.

While the Hudsons were away, defenceless Semplak was attacked by an estimated 20 A6Ms — half of which strafed at almost ground level, whilst others acted as cover at about 3,000 feet. After about ten minutes the two formations changed over and the strafing continued unchallenged — six Hudsons (AE529, AE537, A16-35, A16-42, A16-54 and A16-81) and a Dutch Lodestar (LT9-21) were burnt out and three other Hudsons (AE583, V9121 and A16-56) were severely damaged; Flt Lt Terence O'Brien wrote:

"With no thudding of AA fire to disturb the sound of the approaching aircraft we could tell they were not bombers, and a cautious glance above the rim of the trench was enough to confirm it. They were Zero fighters, just about to break formation so as to attack in line astern, one group staying above as cover.

"I think there were nine machines in the first group but it was difficult to tell because each one made more than one steady gun-chattering run down the strip . . . so low I could see a pilot clearly in helmet and goggles sitting upright in the cockpit. Had we had just a single machine gun, even a repeater rifle, they must have suffered. Even our revolvers had been handed-in to be checked that morning!

"It was the end. I could have wept at the sight of V9121 (*O'Brien's aircraft*); it had not burned but it would never fly again. It was riddled with cannon shell and bullets to such an extent that large chunks of fuselage and wings had ripped away. Cockpit and turret were smashed."

Sgt Jim MacIntosh, a member of the New Zealand Flight of 605 Squadron. *(W.J. MacIntosh)*

With no aircraft remaining, the 62 Squadron detachment were ordered to make for Tjilatjap, from where they would be evacuated on the *Kota Gede* on the night of 27th/28th.

During the morning 605 Squadron's 'A' Flight undertook the unit's first patrol, the New Zealanders spotting six bombers and 16 escorting fighters north-west of Java — possibly the force which had raided Semplak — but losing them in cloud. Sgt Jim MacIntosh, flying BE332, noted:

> "Sharp, Pettit, White, Kuhn and self, led by Oakden, mixed with six Jap bombers escorted by 16 'Zero' fighters in patchy cloud. Nothing decisive."

A second patrol was flown later by the same six pilots, when they reported seeing AA bursts over Batavia but failed to sight any raiders. Following the day's raids in the west, the remaining six Hudsons of 1 RAAF Squadron moved from Semplak to Kalidjati, 60 miles to the east, which was now better-defended, a battery of eight Bofors guns having just arrived there.

JNAF bombers continued to hunt Allied ships heading for Java, two small armed traders — *Larut* and *Raub* — being bombed off the eastern coast of Sumatra during the day, both sinking, as did two larger steamers (*Hanne* and *Bintang*) following aerial attack. It was on this day that a convoy of six ships left Fremantle (Australia) including the old aircraft carrier USS *Langley* with 32 assembled P-40Es lashed to her deck, and the British freighter *Sea Witch* with a further 27 P-40Es in crates; three of the other vessels carried ten more crated fighters between them, and were ordered to head for Burma, while *Langley* and *Sea Witch* were now instructed to make for Java. As they left harbour they separated, each vessel making its own way.

The 17th Pursuit Squadron now had too many pilots, following recent losses of aircraft; on the 23rd therefore, Maj Fisher ordered 20 officers and 20 men to Tjilatjap to meet the incoming vessels and bring back more aircraft. 16 more men followed next day, but at the last moment the order was cancelled and all 56 were ordered instead to leave Java at the first opportunity.

Eastern Java

Early in the morning (22nd), six Tainan and three 3rd Ku A6Ms from Bali strafed Djokjakarta. The Tainan aircraft went in first, claiming a B-24 and two twin-engined aircraft in flames, plus nine other aircraft destroyed or damaged; the 3rd Ku shotai then followed to claim two large and one medium-sized air-craft destroyed and eight damaged. Amongst the aircraft assembled on the ground there was an LB-30 — parked outside the hangar — where it was destroyed, as were four CW-22s and the airfield's only fire-engine. Two or three Glenn Martins also sustained damage during the attack, as did a Brewster. The Tainan fighters then swept northwards to Semarang, where they strafed a P-40 before returning to base. AA defences claimed three Japanese aircraft shot down, but none were even damaged.

Two B-17s raided Denpassar (Bali) during the morning, claiming some Japanese aircraft destroyed on the ground, although no losses were recorded. Four Tainan A6Ms were scrambled, but failed to intercept. While in the air however, NAP 1/C Toyo-o Sakai passed near Pasirian in pursuit of the bombers, and spotted six B-17s and two Glenn Martins on the ground there. Diving down, he carried out a strafing run, claiming one B-17 in flames and reported that he believed that his fire had destroyed the other seven bombers! During the afternoon the unit despatched six more A6Ms to attack this airfield (Sakai included), and the pilots of these claimed four B-17s, a P-40 and two twin-engined aircraft destroyed. The A6Ms then flew on to Malang, but nothing was reported here. During the two attacks actual US losses amounted to two B-17Ds (40-3062 and 40-3066) totally destroyed and two others damaged beyond repair, whilst an unserviceable P-40 was further damaged, to be subsequently written off; the Dutch suffered damage to two or three Glenn Martins.

Monday, 23 February

Three Blenheims, crewed by 84 Squadron personnel and led by Wg Cdr Jeudwine, set out to bomb P.1, where about 40 aircraft were reported dispersed on the airfield, several of which were claimed destroyed and damaged by bombs. On the return flight, what were believed to be three Japanese submarines[1] were seen on the surface, north of Western Java, and one of these was attacked by Flg Off Fihelly's aircraft, although it had by then submerged, as recalled by his gunner, Sgt Oliver:

> "We thought we saw something. We let our bombs go at something — it was just a dark shape in the water."

Six airworthy Hudsons were flown over from Semplak to Kalidjati, from where they were to carry out an attack on shipping at Banka. Departing at 1100, Flg Off Gibbes' aircraft (A16-28) was attacked by two fighters, described as 'Navy 0s', but reached the sanctuary of cloud and escaped damage; the other aircraft, AE506 flown by Flg Off Lower, was also attacked by fighters which came up from Muntok airfield, but he also evaded and escaped.

Nine Tainan Ku A6Ms escorted bombers over Malang during the morning, being engaged by 17th Squadron P-40s, which had scrambled to 22,000 feet to intercept. The first two flights of American fighters attacked three bombers and three fighters, but were driven off by the other escorts without seeing the results of their attack, although hits were believed to have been obtained on all of them; Lt Ray Thompson then claimed one A6M over Malang, while Lt Bill Turner claimed a bomber over Sourabaya. The Americans reported that 15 more escorts then appeared and drove off four P-40s just as they were attacking the bombers, though their leader, Lt Blanton, was able to claim a second bomber shot down, whilst Lt Jim Morehead claimed two more and Lt Kiser another. The Tainan Ku's 1st shotai (Lt Shingo, NAP 1/C Tanaka and NAP 3/C Honda) and 2nd shotai (Lt Shibuya, NAP 1/C Otojiro Sakaguchi and NAP 3/C Kiyotaka Fukuyama) each claimed one P-40 shot down, while the 3rd shotai (Wt Off Miyazaki, NAP 2/C Ishihara and NA 1/C Motoyoshi) claimed a probable. On this occasion it appears that neither side actually suffered any losses.

Whilst the raid on Malang was underway one of the Dutch flyingboats, Do 24 X-21 of GVT-6, undertook a reconnaissance to Bali, but was shot down by NA 1/C Shizuyoshi Nishiyama of the Tainan Ku, who had been scrambled to intercept. Meanwhile, other Dutch aircraft laid magnetic mines in the Banka Strait and the Moesi River, while three Glenn Martins bombed P.1, the crews reporting that they had left three Japanese aircraft burning on the ground there. Later, two B-17s carried out a further attack on Denpassar airfield, where Capt

---

[1] A handwritten annotation to the official report suggested that the three "Japanese submarines" attacked were probably "sea mammals!"

2/Lt James B. Morehead of the 17th Pursuit Squadron (Provisional), who claimed two bombers shot down on 23 February 1942. *(Bill Wolf)*

Preston (41-3062) and Lt Robert C. Lewis (41-3061) reported seeing a line of Japanese bombers, believing that six of these were possibly destroyed, as a result of their bombing.

The Japanese Navy moved 15 A6Ms and three C5Ms of the 22nd Air Flotilla from Kuching to Muntok, while nine more A6Ms and two C5Ms of 3rd Ku accompanied seven Toko Ku flyingboats to Koepang, Timor.

Far to the south, four B-17s of the 7th Bomb Group took off from Port Moresby, New Guinea, to attack shipping at Rabaul; they achieved no observable results and were intercepted by fighters of the 4th Ku, Wt Off Mototsuna Yoshida claiming one bomber shot down over the port; no loss actually appears to have been suffered. Next day the Japanese reciprocated, ten bombers raiding Port Moresby airfield where an RAAF Hudson and one civil aircraft were destroyed.

The Dutch now overpainted the orange triangle markings of their aircraft with a red, white and blue square to avoid any possible confusion with the red Hinomaru on Japanese aircraft. Another of their flyingboats was lost when Catalina Y-47 (of GVT-18) crashed during a night landing at Tanjong Priok; five members of the crew were killed.

Tuesday, 24 February – Western Java

The 24th was indeed a confused day during which much occurred in the air. During the morning a big JAAF raid was launched over Western Java, 14 Ki 43s of the 59th and 13 of the 64th Sentais sweeping over the area. The Japanese fighters reported meeting seven Hurricanes and two 'P-43s', and claimed five of these shot down. Hurricanes flown by pilots of 242 and 605

Squadrons had scrambled and climbed to 20,000 feet where they spotted two Japanese aircraft over Batavia; one of these — a fighter — was claimed shot down by Plt Off 'Red' Campbell of 605 Squadron.

Dutch Hurricanes of 2-VlG-IV were also up over Kalidjati. Sgt Jacobs crash-landed after his aircraft was hit while Ens Hamming crashed into a bomb crater as he attempted to land, his aircraft subsequently being destroyed by strafing fighters. The four serviceable CW-21Bs of 2-VlG-IV were also in the air, attempting to defend Bandoeng, where Ens D. Dekker was shot down and killed, while Sgt H.M. Haye force-landed, his aircraft being damaged beyond repair; Lt W. Boxman was also shot down, reportedly by Dutch AA, but baled out. Only Sgt O.B. Roumimper landed safely, coming down on a highway near Bandoeng.

Meanwhile, at about 1030, 16 Ki-21s of the 75th Sentai attacked Kalidjati, whilst 17 of the 90th Sentai bombed Bandoeng, where three large and three medium-sized aircraft were claimed destroyed. In fact, one CW-21B (CW-363) was destroyed on the ground and three B-17Es were strafed and burned; a 1-VlG-I Glenn Martin (M-545) was also severely damaged by bomb blast.

The Japanese crews claimed seven large and three small aircraft destroyed at Kalidjati, with a further nine and five respectively damaged. Two Hudsons, A16-28 and A16-82, were in fact written off, as were two unserviceable Blenheim IFs of the disbanded 27 Squadron, and two Glenn Martins; a hangar was also set on fire. As the raid came in, six crews of 84 Squadron had been awaiting the order to take off on a further mission to P.1; Sgt Hayes Harding:

> "We were sat on the cement patio, I saw these planes appear over the horizon, and made a dash for the slit-trenches — they gave us quite a pasting; however, nothing dropped near me. I cannot recall casualties.
>
> "We had been briefed for an op and were told that there was a standing patrol over the target of nine Navy 0s, so we were told to get in and drop to ground level after the run, and scatter to get home. This was the only raid that I can honestly say I was scared to go on — I felt sure 'this is it.'
>
> "As we were on our way out to our aircraft by lorry, a second wave of aircraft came across — we jumped out of the lorry and dropped flat on the ground. I saw someone disappear into a crater from the previous raid and followed suit smartly — with my head buried about two feet underground, fingers in ears, mouth open (previous instructions) — and scared to hell!

Sgt Dave Russell similarly recalled:

> "We climbed aboard the open truck and were bumping toward the aircraft dispersal points, when a flight of Japanese bombers, flying at nought feet, suddenly screamed into view over the field. The dispersal-truck was like a sitting duck. The abruptness of the attack took everyone by surprise and threw us into disorder.
>
> "A chorus of hysterical shouts giving conflicting advice to the driver worsened the situation. Some howled for the driver to stop, others to accelerate. The driver put his foot to the boards and the truck shot drunkenly forward, then he changed his mind about making for the trees, suddenly braked violently and screeched to a stop.
>
> "Bodies shot in all directions, seeking what cover they could find in the bomb craters pitting the surface of the drome. The air was torn by

explosions. The bombers vanished as abruptly as they had appeared, leaving a couple of Blenheims and a hangar in flames; other aircraft were badly damaged. Much shaken, we emerged from the bomb craters and climbed back aboard the truck."

Of the six Blenheims, two had been destroyed and another riddled with splinters, while Plt Off G. Maurice (Plt Off Macdonald's observer) had been wounded in one arm by shrapnel. Sgt Harding continued:

"Raid finished — back to the lorry and out to our dispersal points. On arrival found a sizable hole in our port wing, which the sergeant fitter said was of no consequence. After Cosgrove had tested the ailerons, etc — I loaded up the guns in the turret. We taxied out for take-off and off we went. I did not want to go on that raid!"

Sqn Ldr Passmore led off the three airworthy Blenheims on their mission to P.1, the other two flown by the Australian pair, Flg Off Fihelly and Sgt Cosgrove. Fihelly's gunner, Sgt Eric Oliver, had good reason to remember this mission:

"We took off and when we got over the sea we tested our guns — Harding's guns were not working so Cosgrove waggled his wings and turned back.

"As we approached Palembang there was smoke still coming from the oil refinery. I was thinking I'd better watch the sun — mustn't be jumped. But lo and behold, they came up from below — six Army 97s, with fixed undercarriages.

"The first thing I knew was the crackle of gunfire and I looked down and saw Passmore's aircraft — his gunner, Streatfield, was blasting away at three fighters. I yelled into the intercom. We split up but Tommy (Flt Sgt Gomm, the bomb-aimer/navigator) was shouting 'left! left!' as he lined up to drop the bombs on the oil refinery.

"I was firing in short bursts. Eventually I heard Tommy shout 'bombs away' and we turned away. What did us was that we were banking sideways, giving the fighters a real good shot at us. I yelled into the microphone but Fihelly took no notice (Tommy told me later that he was determindly heading for a nearby cloud).

"Bullets were actually hitting my turret. My instincts were to duck behind the armour plate, but we would have been blasted out of the sky (I saw my bullets hitting the fighter on our tail, and had we got back I would have claimed one probably destroyed). Streams of bullets were going over our starboard engine and one must have cut an oil pipe.

The Ki 27s were from the 11th Sentai, Sgt Maj Yutaka Aoyagi reporting the shooting down of one Blenheim for his 11th victory, having been credited with 10 Russian aircraft during the fighting in Mongolia. Oliver continued:

"We eventually got into cloud and when we came out again, we had got away from the fighters, but were streaming oil from the starboard engine. All of a sudden there was an almighty lurch and the prop came off!"

As Fihelly had previously crash-landed a Blenheim in the Middle East, he elected to try again rather than risk the crew baling out and becoming separated in hostile terrain. He was able to control the Blenheim sufficiently on its one good engine, coming down low over the coast and carried out a skilful ditching about half a mile off-shore, the aircraft skidding into a mud bank. The crew were able to obtain a small boat from local inhabitants and began the long and difficult journey south to Java.

Earlier on the 24th, Glenn Martins had raided the Pladjoe oil refinery, Japanese records indicating that three attacked first, during the early hours, and then two more, the latter destroying one Ki 27 fighter on the ground, badly damaging one more and slightly damaging another two. Patrolling Ki 43s from the 59th Sentai claimed one shot down, and indeed Sgt F.H. van Onselen and his crew failed to return.

During the afternoon 13 Ki 43s of the 59th and 17 bombers of the 90th Sentai returned to Java, this time to attack Tjililitan. On this occasion ten intercepting Hurricanes were reported and two claimed shot down, while one large and three small aircraft were claimed on the ground. Seven Hurricanes were on readiness at Tjililitan in the afternoon, four 242 Squadron machines and three from 605 Squadron's 'B' Flight; a further six 'A' Flight aircraft were on standby; Sgt Lambert of 'B' Flight recalled:

> "They were well dispersed and there was an agreed signal to be given if we were to scramble. After a most uncomfortable wait in a very high atmospheric temperature of early afternoon, we took off. Due possibly to the wide dispersal prior to take off and individual take offs, there was some little confusion in forming up into formation which, I believe, was to be led by Sqn Ldr Wright.
>
> "A short time after take off, and whilst still at fairly low altitude, an aircraft came up on my port side, as if looking for a section leader, and then turned underneath my aircraft with the intention of coming into the No 2 position on my starboard side. Unfortunately, the manoeuvre resulted in the other aircraft coming up underneath my starboard mainplane and its propeller cut off the outer half of the wing.
>
> "It was immediately obvious that my aircraft would be uncontrollable and I prepared to bale out. Whilst unfastening my oxygen and R/T connections — having unfastened the seat straps — the aircraft flipped onto its back and I was shot out — the altitude being low — 1-2,000 feet. I pulled the cord immediately and the chute opened at, I would think, 1,000 feet. As I looked down to see where I would land. I saw my aircraft, in an inverted spin, hit the ground.
>
> "I landed in a paddy field close to a native village, fortunately on a dry path. I wandered into the village and after unsuccessful attempts to communicate, I managed to get a youth to understand that I wanted to get to Batavia. After collecting my chute, which two more youths insisted on carrying, we set off along a path through trees.
>
> "I recall that on looking round after walking a short way we were leading a procession of what must have been a large percentage of the villagers. We eventually met a native policeman and a Dutch police officer, who had seen the crash and were looking for the pilots. After taking me to their mess, I was given a lift back to base. The other pilot, I learned on my return, had force-landed with the airscrew reduced to stubs as a result of the collision. He too, was uninjured."

The remaining pilots reported intercepting unescorted bombers meanwhile, as these were attacking Tjililitan, and three were believed to have been shot down, one each by Flt Lt Hutton and Sgt King, the other shared by Plt Off Watson and 2/Lt Anderson. Actual losses inflicted on the raiders are not known.

It would seem that the escorting fighters of the 59th Sentai had become entangled with the Hurricanes of 605 Squadron's 'A' Flight, which had also been scrambled as the raiders, estimated at 40 plus, approached Kalidjati. At 14,000 feet 'A' Flight become involved with many fighters, and Sgt MacIntosh (flying BE332) reported:

> "General mix up. Sharp and Kuhn claim one each, self fired long burst into Jap fighter but could not follow it due to pressure from many others. With the heavy odds against us, we find it almost impossible to follow up any attack."

Seated in the cockpit of his Hurricane, 'Miss Carronvale', is Sgt Jim MacIntosh of 605 Squadron. *(W.J. MacIntosh)*

Following his success, Flg Off Sharp was attacked and his aircraft (possibly BG876) damaged, forcing him to bale out; he came down in a canal where he was nearly drowned under the weight of his parachute, before two Javanese pulled him out. On recovery, he managed to reach Tjililitan after a trek lasting three days. Plt Off Pettit's aircraft also came under attack:

> "My aircraft was damaged by a 'Zero' (*sic*) which attacked me from the rear. It was superficially damaged and I was grateful for my armour plating. I was followed down by three fighters but managed to elude them and, having done this, the sky seemed empty with the exception of one aircraft which I chased for some miles, only to find it was another Hurricane."

At about the same time, 13 more Ki 43s of the 64th Sentai and five 75th Sentai bombers attacked Batavia, where the Japanese fighter pilots claimed two four-engined flyingboats shot down. These were by no means the only claims made for flyingboats during the day however. A6Ms from the 22nd Air Flotilla, which had moved to Muntok on the 23rd, reported finding two Dornier flyingboats in the area and shooting down one. Dutch Naval aircraft were out to bomb the Japanese convoy near Muntok during the day, and two Do 24s of GVT-8 were shot down by fighters, whilst returning from such a mission. The crew of X-17 was lost, but that of X-18 managed to swim ashore and returned later.

Eastern Java

At much the same time two Tainan Ku A6Ms patrolling over a convoy anchored off Makassar (Celebes) also reported attacking a flyingboat, which was shot down by Lt Katsutoshi Kawamata, although his wingman, NAP 3/C Makoto Ueda, failed to return. It seems fairly certain that this was PBY '42' of PatWing 10, flown by Lt John Robertson, which radioed to report sighting the convoy. Ordered to attack the ships, the aircraft went in and achieved a near miss, but the crew then reported:

"Am being attacked by aircraft north. Many planes in fleet."

The Catalina failed to return.

Various floatplanes from *Sanyo Maru* and *Sanuki Maru* were operating over the general area from the Anambas to Sourabaya, one of these from the latter vessel, flown by NA 1/C Saburo Takayasu, encountering a twin-engined flying-boat reportedly 345 miles off Kota Baru (Laut Island, south-east of Borneo) during the afternoon, and claimed it shot down in collaboration with two fighters, his own aircraft receiving five hits from return fire.

Thus four or five flyingboats were claimed in total. It is clear that the 22nd Air Flotilla A6Ms attacked the Do 24s and, from the area reported, these were probably also engaged by the Ki 43s. Whether Takayasu's floatplane was engaged with the Dorniers or the PBY is uncertain, though the latter seems considerably more likely. By this date PatWing 10 was down to its last three serviceable Catalinas in Java.

Other Allied bombers were out during the day, seven B-17Es being des-patched to attack the assemblage of shipping at the mouth of the Makassar River — reported earlier by the doomed PBY crew — and claimed two transports probably sunk.

Nine Takao Ku G4Ms attacked Malang airfield during the morning, claiming two twin-engined bombers damaged, while 24 other bombers attacked Sourabaya harbour in two waves, claiming a merchant vessel sunk and three other ships damaged. In fact the Dutch freighter *Kota Radja*, laden with rubber, was hit; blazing furiously, she went aground on the Queen Olga Rock, dis-charging thick, black, acrid smoke for several days before she burnt herself out.

Nine A6Ms — six from the 3rd Ku and three from the Tainan Ku — provided escort, engaging intercepting P-40s without result. A dozen of the latter had taken off to intercept what was recorded as the biggest raid yet on Sourabaya by a reported 54 bombers and 36 fighters. Some P-40s were badly shot-up during the engagement, but two bombers were claimed shot down, one by Lt George Kiser (for his fifth victory, two of which had been claimed in the Philippines) and the other by Lt Robert B. Dockstader; a report of the action read:

"The Americans met them this time at 21,000 feet with four flights of fighters. Kiser caused one big bomber to bend its flight over until it went searing into the ground — in flames. Dockstader shot-up another badly and the sharp eyes of the Dutch air control saw it fall into the sea."

The day saw further moves and changes. Aircraft of 22nd Air Flotilla now began moving to P.2 from their bases in Borneo, 27 bombers and a transport of the Genzan Ku and six from the Kanoya Ku flying in during the day. Japanese AA opened up and one of the Genzan bombers was hit, being obliged to carry out a force-landing.

On the Allied side, Maj General Brereton left Java for Ceylon in an LB-30, taking with him Capt Mahony from the 17th Pursuit Squadron; Lt Gerry McCallum, the unit's engineering officer, was promoted to command in his stead. Brereton had asked Wavell to release him from his duties as Deputy Air Commander, ABDA, as he wished to give his full attention to the USAAF forces under his command; he wrote:

> "I felt it necessary to request General Wavell to relieve me of my duties. The morale of my own air force was low and my presence was required with it. I was criticized by General Wavell and General Brett for what appeared to them to be a somewhat unwarranted and pessimistic attitude.
>
> "I was also having some honest differences with Peirse (Air Marshal Sir Richard Peirse, Commander of the Allied Air Forces in ABDA) concerning the employment of American bombers. It was evident that Peirse was being subjected to the strongest pressure to employ them piecemeal and concentrate them on the Malay Peninsula, whereas in my judgement the whole bomber effort had to be directed against the Japs in the Macassar Straits. In view of our differences, I did not want to embarrass Peirse by continuing to act as his deputy."

Command of the USAAF in Java was passed to Lt Colonel Eubank, Brereton leaving him clear instructions:

(1) To operate the American air units in Java as long as an effective operational force existed. The decision for the termination of operations was to be made by Eubank, and Dutch Headquarters notified.
(2) To evacuate personnel not needed for the tactical operations of equipment available to Australia.
(3) As aircraft became unsuitable for tactical operations, to remove personnel so released from the combat zone.
(4) To include in each evacuation a proportionate share of personnel with combat experience. These to be used for reconstituting units.

Meanwhile, in Java, WESTGROUP now moved from Soekaboemi to Bandoeng, taking over ABDAIR's former Headquarters. This command now took operational control of ABDAIR's squadrons under the new title: BRITAIR. Conveniently, the staff of the Dutch AOC in Java, Maj General L.H. van Oyen, was located in the same building, greatly simplifying liaison. Next day Wavell would close his HQ, the ABDA command passing to the Dutch and with it the control of all remaining British forces, which would now receive their orders from the Dutch Naval and Army Commanders. However, although ordered to leave by Wavell, Air Vice-Marshal Maltby elected to remain in charge of the RAF units, as he considered that the officer selected for this dubious honour, Air Commodore Staton, was insufficiently experienced for such a duty. Therefore Maltby remained, although the staff of ABDACOM and ABDAIR departed with Wavell by air during the following night, the party including Air Marshal Peirse. The subsequent flight to India almost ended in disaster when a fire broke out aboard the LB-30, which was however speedily dealt with by the crew without even waking the sleeping VIPs!

Wednesday, 25 February – Western Java

The day started badly with the non-arrival of an expected Dutch airliner from Australia. A KNILM DC-3, having completed the 900 mile flight from Broome, failed to arrive at Semplak with urgent supplies. Unfortunately the crew of PK-AFZ had become lost in bad weather as they approached Java and, instead, flew on to Sumatra. Running out of fuel, the airliner force-landed near Djambi.

Four Glenn Martins were despatched to bomb Pladjoe, but turned back when attacked by six fighters — a patrol of 11th Sentai Ki 27s, again led by Sgt Maj Aoyagi — although the aircraft flown by Ens Th. Magnee of 2-VlG-III was shot down from a height of about 3,000 feet, crashing south-west of Tanjungkarang. Five Blenheims set out from Kalidjati to attack P.2 airfield but ran into bad weather and returned.

22nd Air Flotilla launched its first major attack on Western Java during the morning, 27 Genzan Ku G3Ms being escorted to Batavia by 13 A6Ms and a C5M from the attached fighter unit. Two dozen 59th Sentai Ki 43s and 32 light bombers from the JAAF's 3rd Flying Battalion also appeared over the area in two waves to attack Semplak. 242 and 605 Squadrons each scrambled Hurricanes from Tjililitan, five aircraft of 605 Squadron's 'B' Flight engaging the Navy fighters. With the advantage of early warning, Flt Lt Harry Dobbyn had briefed his pilots to climb to 33,000 feet. The Flight's pilots had devised tactics to combat the manoeuvrability of the opposing Japanese fighters by climbing to maximum height, diving to attack and then continuing in the dive, either to head for home or up to regain altitude — in effect similar tactics to those employed with success by the AVG in Burma.

On reaching altitude, the Hurricane pilots saw below them two separate circles of Japanese fighters, each about 15 strong — one above the other — so they peeled off to attack; Sgt Kelly reported:

> "The three Sergeants did the planned attack, Campbell did not. What Dobbyn did, we did not see."

Tactics adopted made it impossible to make claims accurately, but Kelly was sure that he had damaged one fighter. Only three of the 605 Squadron flight returned to Tjililitan, Dobbyn and Campbell both failing to appear. It transpired that each had disregarded the planned tactics and become engaged in dog-fighting — the leader being shot down and killed. Dobbyn's wrecked Hurricane (possibly BG821) and body were later found in a swamp in the Krawang area, 30 miles north-east of Batavia. Campbell reported:

> "A 'Zero' took on the Hurricane ahead of me (*probably Dobbyn's aircraft*), and I went after that one. This guy was kind of dumb. He'd do things like half rolls and a couple of slow rolls in front of me. Finally I nailed him. He went up in a steep climb. The wing came away and I watched him go spinning down."

This was almost certainly NAP 1/C Suehara Ide, who failed to return and was later reported to have been killed. Campbell was then attacked by another fighter and his aircraft, BE332, received severe damage and went into a dive, half the wing breaking away. He continued:

"In my flying I never closed the cockpit canopy completely. I had a thing about it — about trying to get out and finding myself locked in. And now the track was damaged, so I couldn't get it open or shut. I couldn't believe this was happening to me. It was more like something remote, away from me. I was scared at first, then angry with myself. I could see the ground coming up. I told myself that when I hit the ground it probably wouldn't hurt because it would be over so fast. I stood up on the seat, braced my back against the canopy and gave a big shove. Out I shot, high above Java. It was almost as though the canopy had exploded."

Sgt Lambert remembered Campbell's head-first free fall:

"He fell for some thousands of feet and as he fell his revolver became dislodged from its holster and he watched it for some time falling in front of him until he eventually pulled the cord."

Shot down on 25 February after four victories with 258 and 605 Squadrons, Plt Off John 'Red' Campbell, a US citizen, would spend the rest of the war as a POW. *(Sqn Ldr A.H. Milnes)*

As Campbell drifted down an aircraft came towards him and he feared he was about to be machine-gunned. However, it was a Hurricane and it spun down like a falling leaf — either his own aircraft or more probably Harry Dobbyn's. He landed in a paddy field, suffering a badly twisted leg, shrapnel wounds and deep cuts from contact with the canopy; he also feared a broken back since his left arm was partially paralysed. Searching natives found him in the jungle and eventually he was taken to a Dutch officer in a river patrol craft. This same officer had found Dobbyn's remains. Campbell was returned to Tjililitan, arriving at 0300 on the following day. He would not fly again.

The A6M pilots reported meeting eight Spitfires (!) and claimed four shot down; apart from the loss of NAP 1/C Ide, the reconnaissance C5M also failed to return — probably shot down by Sgt Sandeman Allen of 242 Squadron (flying BE202), who recalled of his fifth victory:

"I do not remember the detail but I was separated from the section and I was caught by some 'Zeros'. I was claiming damage only to one but Sqn Ldr Wright was in the area, and he confirmed the destruction because the plane nearly hit him as it went down."

242 Squadron's successful Sgt James Sandeman Allen, whose victory on 25 February was his fifth. (J.A. Sandeman Allen)

The Japanese also claimed two small aircraft destroyed on the ground at Semplak where, in fact, one Hudson under repair was further damaged, but no less than 11 of the Genzan G3Ms were hit by AA fire. The 59th Sentai pilots also reported meeting eight interceptors and claimed four shot down, while the JAAF bomber crews claimed the destruction of seven aircraft on the ground; all these raiders returned safely.

The situation with regard to the Hudson force was far from encouraging at this stage: two aircraft were undergoing repairs at Semplak (including AE553); two others were undergoing major inspections at Bandoeng (including AE485) whilst two more were receiving major repairs (also at Bandoeng); yet another two were undergoing minor repairs at Kalidjati and one unserviceable aircraft was at Kemajoran (AE488); however, this latter machine would fly to Kalidjati next day.

The Japanese Army Air Force — quite properly — was jubilant with the successes gained during the past week, announcing that the 3rd Flying Battalion assessed its results during the period 19-25 February as:

33 enemy aircraft shot down
53 enemy aircraft destroyed on the ground
150 enemy aircraft damaged on the ground

The claims were achieved in 345 sorties, including 203 by fighters, for the loss of three aircraft. Additionally, Vice-Admiral Nishizo Tsukahara (Commander-in-Chief 11th Air Fleet) reported that Japanese Navy fighters had shot down 32 aircraft since 18 February, plus 11 probables, and burned 48 aircraft on the ground in Eastern Java.

Eastern Java

In the east two 3rd Ku A6Ms flown by NAP 1/C Shigeo Sugio and NAP 3/C Masakichi Sonoyama were off early in the morning to escort a Tainan Ku C5M from Bali on a reconnaissance over Sourabaya. In the target area the reconnaissance crew spotted a Catalina flyingboat at about 150 feet and signalled the fighters to attack. They made two side passes at it and succeeded in shooting down aircraft '44', one of PatWing 10's few remaining PBYs; the crew perished.

Just before this pair landed, nine Tainan Ku A6Ms were off to escort 22 Takao Ku G4Ms over Sourabaya, where they reported engaging 13 P-40s; these were in fact a dozen 17th Pursuit Squadron aircraft led by their new CO, Capt McCallum, to intercept a reported 54 bombers and 36 fighters. As eight P-40s went for the bombers, six of the A6Ms dived on them and were, in turn, attacked by the four remaining P-40s. Lt Ben Irvin, about to engage the bombers, saw the Japanese fighters following, dropped back and claimed one shot down, but McCallum was also hit; he baled out but was attacked on his parachute and shot through the head and heart. Of the flight of P-40s which attacked the A6Ms, Lts Hennon and Reynolds each claimed one shot down. No Japanese fighters were actually lost during this fight, but four were reported to have been hit and damaged. In return the Tainan pilots between them claimed four P-40s shot down and four probables, which were credited to Lt Sasai's shotai (NAP 2/C Ishihara and NA 1/C Nishiyama) and that led by Wt Off Watari Handa (NAP 3/C Muneichi Ohshoya and NA 1/C Haruo Kasai).

The Allied Command were well aware that invasion was imminent — it was only a question of where and when. The Dutch fully expected landings in both east and west Java, but considered an invasion of central Java less possible. Only token forces were left in the hinterland therefore, the available defences continuing to be concentrated at the extremities. This assessment of Japanese intentions was quite accurate and Japanese preparations were indeed already complete and well underway, under the overall command of Vice-Admiral Takahashi. Two major invasion convoys had been assembled, and these were now fast approaching, together with their covering forces.

The Western Invasion Force had sailed from Indo-China's Camrahn Bay on 18 February, carrying the Headquarters of the 16th Army, the 2nd Division and the 230th Infantry Regiment from the 38th Division, in 56 transport vessels. Covered initially by the 5th Destroyer Flotilla, it was joined on the 26th by the 7th Cruiser Squadron, the light aircraft carrier *Ryujo*, and the 3rd Destroyer Flotilla, all under the command of Rear-Admiral Takeo Kurita.

The Eastern Invasion Force had set sail on the 19th from Jolo Island, its 41 transports loaded with the 48th Division, which had recently seen action in the Philippines. Escorted by Rear-Admiral Nishimura's force comprising the light cruiser *Naka* and six destroyers, the convoy called first at Balikpapan in eastern Borneo to embark the greater part of the 56th Regimental Group. The vessels set sail again on the 23rd.

Meanwhile, Vice-Admiral Takeo Takagi's force of two heavy cruisers — *Nachi* and *Haguro* — and the 2nd Destroyer Flotilla had stationed itself at the southern end of the Strait of Makassar, to cover the approach of the Eastern Force and it was over these ships that much of the recent Allied air effort had

Japanese cruisers on the flank of one of the invasion forces. That in the foreground is about to launch an E8N reconnaissance floatplane from its catapult. *(Authors' collection)*

been expended. As early as the 20th, Allied reconnaissance had spotted the Eastern Force convoy leaving Jolo, and had also reported the beginnings of a build-up of vessels at Muntok on Banka Island, where the Western Force was soon to arrive. The Eastern Force was spotted again on the 24th, soon after it had left Balikpapan and, at its rate of progress, arrival off Java by the 27th was estimated. Takagi's covering force struck first, his destroyers landing a small party of troops on the 25th on Bawean Island, only 85 miles north of Sourabaya, where a radio station was established.

Following the attacks on Darwin on 19 February (see Chapter 5), Vice-Admiral Nagumo's 1st Carrier Fleet had sailed to Kendari (Celebes), where its two battleships, four carriers, two heavy cruisers and destroyer flotilla were joined by two more battleships, three heavy cruisers and three destroyers under the command of Vice-Admiral Nobutake Kondo. On the 25th this formidable fleet sailed for the Indian Ocean, to cut off the Allied escape route from Java. The trap was set and closing fast.

Clearly the time was now due when the remaining strength of the Allied navies would have to sortie, if any delay or interruption to the Japanese plans was to be achieved. During the 25th Vice-Admiral Helfrich ordered all available warships in the west to join Rear-Admiral Doorman's Eastern Striking Force at Sourabaya. Thus, *Exeter, Perth* and three British destroyers at once sailed from Batavia, leaving behind the other Australian cruiser — *Hobart* — and two destroyers which were not fully refuelled due to the loss of an oiler during one of the recent air attacks.

Thursday, 26 February – Western Java

Three Blenheims of 84 Squadron were despatched to bomb shipping at Muntok, where it was believed a direct hit was gained on a transport, although no explosion was seen. On the return flight Sgt Cosgrove and his crew spotted the Japanese invasion fleet heading for Java. The Dutch despatched four Glenn Martins of I-VlG-III in the same direction, one of which bombed Pladjoe; the other three were intercepted over Banka by Ki 43s and 2/Lt R.C. Schäftlein was shot down for the second time in under six weeks; he and his crew were lost. One of the attackers was claimed shot down by the Dutch airgunners but no Japanese losses are known.

At P.2 airfield, 25 G4M bombers of the Kanoya Ku now arrived, as did five A5Ms for airfield defence duties, while 29 bombers of the Genzan Ku returned to Indo-China. Meanwhile, at Kahang airfield in Johore, ten bombers of the Mihoro Ku flew in from Indo-China. These were soon operational, being despatched at 0855 to search for warships reported in the Java Sea by four Takao Ku G4Ms, which had located three light cruisers, three destroyers and two torpedo-boats. The Mihoro Ku bombers returned to Kahang at 1800, having sighted nothing. To the south of Java five further G4Ms from the Takao Ku patrolled the Indian Ocean, where they located the carrier *Langley* on its way to Tjilatjap, accompanied by a submarine.

With confirmation that a probable invasion force had been spotted approaching from the west, when darkness fell the Australian cruiser *Hobart* and her two consorts were ordered to sortie from Batavia and attack this shipping, in the Muntok area. Nothing was found however, so the ships returned to port.

From Tjilatjap that night departed five merchantmen, each packed with evacuees, their masters briefed to make for Australia. One of these was the

9,500-ton *Kota Gede*, aboard which were no fewer than 2110 officers and men of the RAF, 42 Army personnel and three civilians, including Flt Lt O'Brien of 62 Squadron, who noted:

> "The vast majority of the men went down into the holds. There were five of these. These were open during the daylight but shut up at night when the men enjoyed warmth and shelter from rainstorms, which we on deck did not have. There were four lifeboats and no extra lifebelts, so that in the event of the ship sinking only a fraction of us could have hoped to survive."

Aboard this vessel were Sgts Richardson and Crowe of 211 Squadron. They had been ordered to leave Soebang but the vehicle carrying them had broken down so they commandeered a car from its Chinese owner and eventually reached a railway station, where they boarded a troop train; Richardson:

> "It was full of mainly Army and RAF being taken to Tjilatjap to evacuate, so we joined the train. In Tjilatjap we were told to get on the second ship out from the quay, but after celebrating with a few beers, we only managed to get to the first ship and, being fairly exhausted, fell asleep.
> "During our brief celebrations we bought large bags of shag tobacco and rolling papers, as we could not buy cigarettes, and it turned out to be a lucky buy. Cigarettes were very short on ship and we changed some for water or any little food that was available. There was room only to sit down — to lie down was a luxury — so for 20 cigarettes I bought a place on the gratings of the catwalk in the engine room, where even the intense heat could not spoil the absolute heaven of just lying down flat!"

Although all the evacuating vessels were under War Department control, *Kota Gede*'s master, Capt Frederik Goos, disobeyed orders and steamed for Ceylon instead of Australia. On arrival at Colombo he expected to face a Court Martial but, instead, was decorated subsequently for saving 2,000 lives as all the other ships that left for Australia were torpedoed or sunk. This was not strictly true but, as will be seen, many fleeing vessels would fall to JNAF bombers, warships and submarines.

Another of the small convoy to reach safety was the old Dutch freighter *Abberkirk*, on board which was Sgt Charles MacDonald, the wounded navigator of 100 Squadron, who had arrived at Tjilatjap from Sumatra aboard the cruiser *Danea*. He had spent a week in Java, moving from place to place in a state of growing confusion until he finally obtained a place aboard the ship.

Eastern Java

In the east the 26th proved to be a somewhat quieter day, as the defenders prepared for the onslaught, and only two serious air raids were recorded, the biggest when 26 bombers and eight escorting A6Ms attacked Sourabaya Navy Yard. The 17th Pursuit Squadron scrambled nine aircraft, but these were driven off by the A6Ms. Lt Hennon followed the formation alone and, when attacked by two of the escorts, claimed one shot down into a rice paddy, returning safely. This was Bill Hennon's fourth and the unit's 47th — and last — victory claim in the East Indies.

During the late morning the Eastern Invasion Force was again found in the Makassar Strait — by Do 24 X-28 of GVT-6 — and was shadowed for several hours. The Dornier carried out an attack on the destroyer *Amatsukaze*, releasing only one bomb which fell about 500 yards ahead of its intended target. Following this attack, fighter cover was called for; two A6Ms from Balikpapan arrived soon after midday. Before they did so, two B-17s dropped out of cloud and carried out an attack from about 13,000 feet, dropping six bombs, two of which fell some 500 yards short of the destroyer *Hatsukaze*. The escorting cruiser *Jintsu* and several destroyers threw up a protective barrage, although neither bomber was damaged.

To strengthen the defence in the east, the Dutch now ordered most of their remaining fighters to move there; therefore the six Hurricanes of 2-VlG-IV and six Brewsters from Andir flew to Blimbing airfield, Ngoro, during the afternoon. In the light of recent combat, it had been decided that the little FK-51 biplanes were not likely to be of real use in the reconnaissance role and these were ordered to Andir to be put in store, their duties being taken over by the two CW-22 afdelings.

Friday, 27 February – Western Java
In the west the Blenheims were still concerned with attempting to nullify the threat from Sumatra. Two Blenheims were despatched to carry out attacks in the Palembang area, where one bombed shipping in the river — without observed results — whilst Flt Lt Wyllie attacked P.2. Up to 30 G4M bombers of the Kanoya Ku were seen, these being bombed and strafed.

The units at Palembang returned to the attack during the day, raiding Tanjong Priok during the morning and Buitenzorg in the afternoon, where three Dutch aircraft were destroyed on the ground. RAF Hurricanes of the 242 and 605 Squadrons were scrambled to intercept the morning raid; Plt Off Bill Lockwood recalled:

> "I was flying weaving positions in a V formation, climbing continually into the sun. We climbed to a height of approximately 25,000 feet at which time I lost formation in the sun. I levelled out and was puzzled as to where they had gone without trace. As I looked around, above and below for my buddies, I noticed a nice, neat formation of 'Zeros' flying about 2,000 to 3,000 feet below to port and in the opposite direction.
>
> "As I sighted them, they also spotted me and went into a defensive circle to the left. I was also making a left circle above them and was in a quandry as to how to make an attack. The 'Zeros' were standing on their tails momentarily to fire at me, dropping off as they stalled. I maintained height above them and decided to reverse my circle and drop down for a head-on attack as they came around in the opposite direction. This did not prove very effective as I only had time to meet one or two without scoring many hits or being hit. I became surrounded and decided to use the Hurricane's advantage of superior diving speed and returned to base."

The other Hurricanes had made contact with a number of fighters and Flt Lt Hutton possibly claimed one shot down, while Sgt Lambert recalled:

> "One which I attacked must surely have been damaged but there was no indication of this. The engagement quickly broke up and we returned to base individually."

Four of 242 Squadron's aircraft were off again after the Buitenzorg raid, led by Flt Lt Parker. As they commenced the climb two of the Hurricanes broke away and returned to Tjililitan. With Sgt Dunn for company, Parker continued up to about 20,000 feet. Below them at about 17,000 feet they caught sight of a group of distant aircraft against the pale blue of the horizon. Manoeuvring up sun, they counted between 12 and 15 fighters, straggling along and apparently not having seen the two Hurricanes. As they dived onto the group, three of the Japanese aircraft started to dive and turn to port, whilst the others pulled round to starboard and up in a slow climbing turn. Parker kept after the first three and brought his sights to bear on the leader. He later wrote:

> "I only needed a little deflection at our angle of approach and I'd have him. To my surprise when I pressed the tit I heard only a couple of rounds from one of my guns and the rest were silent. I didn't know what had stopped them and nearly broke my thumb pressing on the button, but there were no results in the half-dozen seconds it took to overhaul the Zero. I dived within a few feet of him and saw his helmeted head peering coolly around as I passed his tail and then went into a long dive away. That was a very well-disciplined pilot to have remained as a target for so long in order that his friends could come round and take us, particularly when they would anyway have been too late to save him if my guns had fired!".

Sgt Dunn, following his leader in the dive, hesitated before firing, having observed Parker not firing, fearing that he may have misidentified the Japanese fighters for Dutch Brewsters:

> "I continued my attack as a practice and I was close enough to see the 'Flaming Arsehole', as we called the Nip roundel; I knocked chucks off one 'Zero' and continued to dive on by."

Parker continued:

> "I taxied the Hurricane straight down into the ulu in a furious rage, instead of leaving it by the Flight Office to be refuelled and re-armed, and stamped back up to the dispersal hut to sound off about the inefficiency of the armourers. To my surprise, Air Commodore Vincent was there with Sqn Ldr Brooker, and he tore me off a hell of a strip for not having checked my guns and everything about the Hurricane before I'd taken off.
>
> "Brooker looked very sympathetic and the other pilots were almost mutinous because we all relied on our ground crews, but we all stood and listened to his tirade. Evidentally he must have heard that we were not too confident of the Hurricanes because he swore they were a match for the 'Zeros', and to prove it he took one up and threw it about the sky. We were not impressed and had no enthusiasm ourselves for aerobatics, even if the raid was over, and then we had another talk from him."

As if to emphasise the point, Vincent then calmly stated that he was going on readiness and took his place in one of 605 Squadron's aircraft. He declared he would fly No 2 to the section leader — Sgt Bertie Lambert. As it happened there was no scramble during the period of the standby, so he did not actually fly, but he obviously had every intention of doing so. Indeed, he had frequently done so during the Battle of Britain — despite his age and seniority — when he had been credited with at least two German aircraft shot down, to add to his Great War victories.

To the north of Java, as the Western Invasion Force approached, protecting

Air Commodore Stanley Vincent, World War I and Battle of Britain fighter pilot, who took over the Fighter Central Headquarters on Java in February. *(AVM S.F. Vincent)*

Ki 27s of 12th Flying Battalion intercepted a Dutch Catalina of GVT-2, which they promptly shot down. Lt Wilhelm Dittmar and his crew of Y-63 survived and took to their dinghy, eventually reaching Java.

Glenn Martins and Hudsons continued to fly sea reconnaissances searching for signs of an invasion force but, even when probable sightings were made, Air HQ did not necessarily accept the inevitability of the situation. One such encounter with the force was experienced by Flg Off Siddell's Hudson crew in AE506; Sgt Patrick recalled:

> "We were on a recce and encountered heavy cloud then a severe electrical storm; the instruments oscillated and the aircraft became lost. Harry (Siddell) decided to fly below cloud base to establish our position; on emerging we found ourselves almost over a large Japanese convoy heading towards Java."

Escorting warships opened fire and the Hudson suffered slight damage before escaping in cloud. On landing, the report of the sighting of what proved to be the invasion convoy, was not fully accepted, much to the chagrin of the Hudson crew.

Eastern Java

An all-night search for the Eastern Invasion Force by Rear-Admiral Doorman's fleet proved fruitless, but the crew of a Japanese reconnaissance floatplane soon located — and reported at 0935 — one heavy cruiser, one light cruiser and two destroyers, 35 miles from Batavia. Other floatplanes also shadowed the Allied fleet, and continuously reported its progress. Capt Oliver Gordon (HMS *Exeter*) recalled:

> "We picked up single aircraft on our radar (shortly after dawn); then we sighted them as they flew high on reconnaissance; and during the morning we had minor bombing attacks, mostly by single aircraft, with none of our ships suffering any damage."

One of the attacking bombers was in fact a B-17 — one of four which had set out from Malang, the other three returning early with engine problems — Lt Mathewson, pilot of 41-2507, later realizing his error; fortunately the accuracy of his bomb aimer was found wanting, and no damage resulted from the attack. In the event, the invasion force was not sighted by the Allied fleet and, at 1030, when some 60 miles to the west of Sourabaya, Doorman ordered a return to harbour.

Meanwhile, Tainan Ku A6Ms from Borneo patrolled over the Eastern Invasion Force throughout the morning, and during one such patrol around midday NAP 2/C Tsunehiro Yamagami and NAP 3/C Shizuo Ishii reported sighting two B-17s — aircraft from Madioen flown by Capt Hardison and Lt Bernice M. Barr — which carried out inaccurate bombing attacks on the transports, through gaps in the clouds. The bombers were not intercepted by the A6Ms but, ten minutes later, Ishii claimed a flyingboat shot down. He may have attacked the sole remaining PBY of PatWing 10, which spotted the Eastern Force convoy during the morning and ran a gauntlet of fire before returning safely to Sourabaya. A patrol of three A6Ms which took-off at 1400, failed to return because of foul weather; however, all three force-landed and the pilots later returned to their unit.

At 1437 eight Kanoya Ku bombers attacked the returning Allied fleet and claimed two direct hits on the first ship they sighted — the British destroyer *Jupiter* — although the bombs actually fell harmlessly into the sea. The leading destroyers of Doorman's force had just entered harbour, when the Admiral received reports of a sighting of the Japanese warships 90 miles to the north (possibly the report submitted by Flg Off Siddell), and signalled by flag to the other cruisers:

> "Am proceeding to intercept enemy units. Follow me."

The whole force commenced a turn about, completing the manoeuvre in about a quarter of an hour.

Following the attacks on the fleet, five of the Brewsters newly-arrived at Blimbing went out, at 1600, to cover Doorman's force for two hours, although one of these failed to return. It was assumed that the aircraft had suffered engine failure, the pilot being reported missing.

Two Japanese heavy cruisers — *Nachi* and *Haguro* — were sighted initially by Doorman's force as it raced northwards, these opening fire from long range. As the gap closed, two more cruisers — *Naka* and *Jintsu* — and at least a dozen destroyers were seen and battle commenced in earnest. *Exeter* and *Houston* at once replied, observers reporting hits on their respective targets. At this time, shortly after 1630, three A-24 dive bombers, led by Capt Galusha in 40-15757, arrived on the scene, the crews having been briefed to attack the transports. Ten P-40s from the 17th Pursuit Squadron provided escort, in two flights led by Lts Kiser and Dale. A burning Japanese cruiser was sighted — presumably a victim of either *Exeter* or *Houston* — and was photographed by one of the P-40 pilots, Lt Lester J. Johnsen, using a small hand-held camera.

Although ordered to attack the transports, Capt Galusha initially searched for an aircraft carrier, carrying out his orders only after failing to find one! As a result of their attack on the convoy, Galusha and his two companions, Lt Summers and 2/Lt James A. Ferguson, apparently claimed three transports sunk, although accompanying P-40 pilots confirmed the sinking of one only, estimated to be of about 14,000 tons.

When the Japanese destroyers made an attack at 1705, *Perth* reported sinking one and damaging another, although this failed to prevent a determined assault, the destroyers firing some 60 torpedoes at the Allied force. By this time however, *Java* had been struck by a 6-inch shell, *Houston* by two 8-inch shells and *Exeter* by another, which exploded in her No 1 boiler room, killing 14 of her crew. Although losing speed, Capt Gordon was able to turn the damaged *Exeter* hard to port to avoid a torpedo. Observing this manoeuvre, *Houston* followed suit, causing *Perth* and *Java* also to swing hard to port. Realising that his fleet was moving away, Doorman ordered *De Ruyter* to follow, the escorting destroyers dispersing in all directions in confusion.

At this stage, the Dutch destroyer *Kortenaer* was ripped in two as a torpedo hit her amidships; she exploded and sank, although over 200 of her crew were later rescued from the sea by HMS *Encounter*. Japanese floatplanes were still circling the Allied ships, keeping out of gun range, reporting every move. Doorman frantically tried to rally his force, flying a "Follow me" pennant, and headed towards the crippled *Exeter*. Eventually *Houston* and the others followed, while the destroyers commenced making smoke to protect *Exeter*'s plight from prying eyes.

As the Japanese warships closed in on *Exeter*, her three escorting destroyers — *Electra*, *Jupiter* and *Encounter* — "charged through the smoke to intercept this numerically superior force." Almost immediately *Electra* was mortally hit, sinking soon after (54 survivors were later picked up by the US submarine *S-38* and taken to Sourabaya). Her crew believed that she had inflicted damage on a cruiser and a destroyer before her demise. The Japanese destroyers then withdrew when they realised that they were within range of the cruisers' guns. As the two surviving RN destroyers retired, *Jupiter* encountered what her crew believed was a submarine on the surface, firing a torpedo at this from close range. Watchers aboard *Houston* reported that "two large chunks of metal flew high into the air to tumble end over end back into the sea." A large oil slick then bubbled to the surface along with much debris.

By now *Exeter* had managed to raise her speed to 15 knots, at which she was ordered to return to Sourabaya, escorted by one of the Dutch destroyers. Meanwhile, Doorman reformed the survivors of his group and, as they emerged from the smoke screen, Japanese cruisers were again sighted. Gunfire was exchanged, Doorman meantime ordering the four old American destroyers — *John D. Edwards, Alden, Paul Jones* and *John D. Ford* — to carry out a torpedo attack; the missiles were released from about 10,000 yards without apparent effect, while *Houston* reported gaining a hit on one of the cruisers when flames and smoke were seen emitting from its aft.

With the rapid onset of darkness only sporadic engagements were reported; Doorman still desperately sought the invasion force and headed northwards again. At 1830 he signalled Vice-Admiral Helfrich at Lembang:

"Enemy retreating west. Where is convoy?"

Helfrich was not able to supply any new information as to the convoy's exact location, nor was he aware at this stage that American aircraft had located and attacked the assemblage of transport vessels. He later commented dejectedly that there was a scandalous lack of co-ordination.

The fleet's movements were constantly under observation by reconnaissance and spotter aircraft. Capt Hector Waller of *Perth* wrote:

"At 2150 another aircraft flare appeared overhead and shortly afterwards a line of about six brilliant calcium flares in the water straddled our line at right angles. This happened every time we steered a new course and it was soon obvious that our every move in the moonlight was being reported."

The losses continued however when *Jupiter* ran into a Dutch minefield off Tuban Bay and sank with the loss of about one third of her crew. Then, at about midnight, the heavy cruisers *Nachi* and *Haguro*, which had been trailing the fleet, released 32 torpedoes with great success. *Java* and *De Ruyter* were both mortally struck, sinking with considerable loss of life, including that of Rear-Admiral Doorman. Recalled Ens Winslow aboard *Houston*:

"During the few precious moments he had left on earth, the indomitable Admiral Doorman directed the *Houston* and *Perth* not to stand by for survivors, but to retire to Batavia."

In return for the loss of two cruisers and three destroyers sunk, plus two more cruisers damaged, Allied claims for at least one destroyer and two submarines sunk and two cruisers damaged were submitted. However, the Japanese admitted only that the destroyer *Asagumo* had been badly damaged. The engagement had caused the Japanese transports to withdraw northwards, but the effect had been only to delay the invasion by 24 hours.

Many miles to the south of Java another drama at sea was about to unfold. On its way from Fremantle, was convoy MS-5. It had originally been intended that the carrier *Langley*, loaded with the assembled P-40s, and the freighter *Sea Witch*, carrying a further 27 crated fighters, would peel away from the convoy near the Cocos Islands and make a dash for Tjilatjap, escorted by the US light cruiser *Phoenix*. However, so desperate was Vice-Admiral Helfrich for fighters that he sent a signal instructing *Langley* to break away earlier and head directly for Tjilatjap, from where two non-operational US destroyers — *Edsall* and *Whipple* — would steam to meet her. However, first to arrive were two Dutch Catalinas, which signalled that they and a minesweeper were to provide escort instead. Rather than reduce speed to that of the minesweeper, *Langley*'s captain, Cdr R.P. McConnell, decided to press on towards harbour at full speed, and it was not until after dark that he received a signal from Java confirming the Catalinas and minesweeper as his escort. At this McConnell ordered reverse course to try and locate the minesweeper, wasting valuable time! It was well past 0700 before the Catalinas were again sighted, circling above the two US destroyers rather than the minesweeper!

The three American vessels then headed for Tjilatjap at full speed but they had already been spotted by a reconnaissance aircraft of the 23rd Air Flotilla from Bali. The 'snooper' had also been sighted by the speeding ships, McConnell radioing Java for air cover, unaware of the lack of available fighters. Then, at 1140, more aircraft were seen, two chutais of G4Ms from the Takao Ku — which had departed Krendi on a routine patrol — manoeuvring to attack. *Langley* evaded the first bombing run but the other chutai, led by Lt Jiro Adachi, gained five direct hits with 250kg and 60kg bombs. At the same time six escorting A6Ms of the 3rd Ku (led by Lt Tamotsu Yokoyama) and nine from the Tainan Ku (led by Lt Yukio Maki), strafed the carrier's decks, claiming to have set fire to several of the aircraft thereon.

Langley was devastated. Many of the P-40s lashed to her deck burst into flames; the bridge steering was shattered; the water mains burst and fires broke out all over the ship; she took in water and developed a 10° list to port, although casualties were surprisingly few. Burning aircraft were hastily pushed over the side but to no avail. Unable to quell the flames, McConnell ordered abandon ship, all but 16 of her crew and passengers being rescued by the two destroyers. Of the 33 pilots of the 3rd and 13th Pursuit Squadrons aboard, all survived the attack although two suffered injuries. Having picked up the survivors, *Whipple* then proceded to sink the wreck with torpedoes and gunfire.

Qantas Empire 'C' flyingboat G-AETZ 'Corio', which was shot down by Japanese fighters on 27 February. *(Authors' collection)*

On the way back from the attack on *Langley*, the A6Ms encountered two flyingboats — one four-engined and one twin-engined — which were attacked by all, the former being claimed shot down and the latter probably so. The four-engined aircraft was Qantas Airways Empire 'C' 'boat G-AETZ 'Circe', which was shot down between Java and Broome, with the loss of Captain W.B. Purton, his crew and passengers. This aircraft was one of three such, which had been maintaining a regular shuttle service. The other victim was probably the Dutch Catalina Y-65 of GVT-5, which had to be written off due to damage suffered during an airfight. One A6M was lost during the action, NAP 1/C Toyo-o Sakai failing to return.

Captain W.B. Purdon, pilot of G-AETZ 'Corio', lost with his aircraft, crew and passengers on 27 February. *(Authors' collection)*

Saturday, 28 February – Eastern and Southern Java

Early in the morning the alerts were sounding again, and at 0900 a dozen P-40s and four Brewsters were off from the Ngoro airfields but nothing was seen. Sourabaya was not to escape for long however, for during the afternoon — shortly after 1400 — the bombers appeared overhead to attack the port, escorted by a dozen Tainan Ku A6Ms. Again P-40s and Brewsters were scrambled but the American fighters, their engines worn out from long and constant use, could not reach the bombers and returned to base. The A6Ms attempted to bounce the Dutch fighters which dived away, the pilot of one Brewster baling out. Allied reports indicated that he had suffered engine failure although the Japanese pilots reported attacking four Brewsters, claiming one shot down by NAP 1/C Saburo

Sakai, and one probable by NAP 3/C Saburo Nozawa, the former reporting of this, his 13th victory:

> "I cut easily inside the Buffalo's turn, heeling over in a vertical bank and coming out of the turn 200 yards from the enemy plane...I jabbed impatiently on the button. Several bullets hit the Buffalo's engine and smoke burst back from the plane. The Brewster went into a series of repeated slow rolls until it disappeared into the cloud."

One of the most successful Japanese pilots of the war was the Tainan Kokutai's NAP 1/C Saburo Sakai, who claimed a Brewster shot down over Java on 28 February. *(Authors' collection)*

It seems probable that Sakai's victim was Ens C.A. Vonck of 1-VlG-V, who was reported to have been shot down by A6Ms over Sourabaya about this time.

At 0640 three B-17s had set off from Madioen to attack the Eastern Invasion Force but Capt Preston's aircraft was obliged to return early due to faulty guns. The remaining pair reached the convoy, where Lt D.H. Skiles (41-2417) and Lt Evans (41-2464) claimed one transport sunk and another damaged. By the early afternoon the convoy was about ten miles off Java. Elsewhere, Tainan Ku fighters patrolled over Bali during the day, one pair attacking a B-17 in the early evening, but failed to shoot it down.

The biplane torpedo-bombers of 36 Squadron were again called into action, Sqn Ldr Wilkins leading eight Vildebeests and one Albacore on the 300 mile flight from Tjikampek to Madioen, from where they were to support the Americans in attacking the Eastern Invasion Force. Following arrival, while the biplanes were being refuelled, the crews attended a briefing in the corner of a hangar where two B-17s were being serviced. Flg Off Gotto recorded:

> "In one corner the Yanks had set up an iced-drinks bar where they sold 'paps' of many weird and wonderful hues. Despite holes caused by enemy fighter

attacks in the hangar roof and doors, the lights were full on. In our corner, sucking orange 'paps', we gathered round Wilkins, to be briefed. On our roadmaps, the only ones we had, he showed us that in the bay, due north, was a large Jap convoy of transports. We were to go and attack, return, refuel and attack again, then return that same night to Tjikampek."

They were to attack in two flights of three Vildebeests, with the Albacore to go on its own, each section to start from a different point on the coast, then fly out to sea on parallel tracks. At 1900 aircraft started to take off but those piloted by Gotto and Flg Off Reg Lamb became stuck in the mud just off the runway, and one other failed to start. About 200 coolies appeared and bodily lifted both machines, complete with bombs, back onto the concrete runway. All three managed to get off at the second attempt.

After a long search, two sub flights and the Albacore (the latter flown by Plt Off Doug Cummins) encountered the Japanese force, about five miles north of Rembang and Sqn Ldr Wilkins led an attack, all pilots dropping their bombs from low altitude and most claiming direct hits on transports. Flt Lt Allanson reported:

"I obtained a direct hit amidships with a salvo of six bombs on a ship of about 3,000 tons, which broke in half and sank (reported by my observer, Plt Off Glowrey, and Sgt Hornabrook, WOp/AG). I think I used the remaining two bombs against a destroyer but in view of the small size (of the bombs — 50 lb) no very serious damaged was likely to have been caused."

Flg Off Gotto, with his Australian crew of Sgts Toohey and Barnes, observed a Japanese cruiser heading north:

"I was at about 2,000 feet and dived from the cruiser's starboard bow across to the port quarter. However I didn't allow enough for the speed of the ship. I realised this just before dropping so I only released the first two bombs, intending to have another dive. The bombs dropped about 50 feet astern of this ship and would have done no damage. The AA opened up but no searchlight. As I pulled out of the dive we saw, much closer to the shore, 30 transports lying at anchor and I was mighty pleased I had two bombs left.

"The ships were roughly in three lines paralled to the coast, the nearer being about half a mile off shore. The most westerly one in the rear rank was, as far as I could see, a bit bigger than its neighbours so I selected it as my target. There was still a little AA from the cruiser but we were now out of range. I took my time and dived from 1,500 feet to about 700 feet and released my two bombs together. I felt the blast of the explosion hit the aircraft and immediately afterwards Barnes shouted, in a very excited voice 'direct hit amidship!' I did a climbing turn and could see a bright red glow in the centre of the ship."

On the return flight Gotto was unable to find Madioen airfield in the dark and was forced to come down in a paddy field near Kendiri, some 60 miles from base. The Vildebeest, K6380, flipped over onto its back but none of the crew were hurt.

On returning to Madioen the squadron was ordered to carry out one more sortie, the target being changed from transports to landing craft. One of the American spectators — a B-17 pilot — commented in obvious admiration:

"They flew across the convoy at 500 feet, returned, landed, looked at the hundreds of holes in their wings, laughed like hell, got another drink of whisky, and went back."

As the Vildebeests headed for the beaches K6377, flown by Sqn Ldr Wilkins, was hit on arriving over the coast — it was believed possibly by a night fighter — and was forced to crash land, only the badly injured gunner, Sgt Brooker, surviving with a smashed knee-cap. A further aircraft, piloted by Flg Off Reg Lamb, was hit by AA and ditched about half a mile offshore, between Semerang and Pekalongan. The crew managed to get ashore and eventually reached Bandoeng. Flt Lt Allanson continued:

"I attacked a large transport of about 10,000 tons with a salvo of all eight bombs. My observer shouted that we had got another hit and I circled to observe the results. There was no evidence that the ship was sinking rapidly nor was there any fire. On questioning my observer after landing, I came to the conclusion that the salvo must have resulted in a very near miss. No doubt the decks were crowded with troops and heavy casualties must certainly have been caused."

Flt Lt Hutcheson, who also flew two sorties, later wrote:

"Again the attack was well pressed home at low altitude, but many pilots complained that their bombing was becoming inaccurate owing to excessive fatigue. In view of the mistakes I made, I feel that in justice to myself and my officers, I should describe the state of extreme exhaustion of all the pilots. During the night we had flown 14-15 hours in open cockpit aircraft, and in the previous 48 hours had not had more than four or five hours sleep. On the return journey from Madioen I nearly crashed on several occasions through falling asleep in the air."

Plt Off Tom Lamb had been unable to locate the ships on his first sortie, and after about two hours returned to Madioen to seek more information; he recalled:

"So off we went again and, this time, had success. I attacked a large transport with my four 110kg bombs. One bomb was a direct hit on the stern and the other three dropped close along the port side, There was some flak, presumably from protecting ships, but it was not intense."

When photographic evidence of damage inflicted had been assessed by Combined HQ at Bandoeng, the squadron was credited with the sinking of no fewer than nine vessels. Meanwhile, the missing crew — Gotto, Barnes and Toohey — were on their way back to Madioen by car but, when they arrived, they discovered that their squadron had returned to Tjikampek. On approaching the base commander, Gotto was informed that the Americans were preparing to evacuate the airfield and was offered the choice of an A-24 or a Dutch Brewster in which he could return to Tjikampek, both of which were about to be demolished. Although concerned about his ability to fly the dive-bomber, he accepted the offer and, having made arrangements for his crew to drive a lorry loaded with ammunition, food and beer to Tjikampek, managed to get airborne shortly before midnight. Flying along the coast he came under heavy AA fire and saw about 30-40 ships:

"I felt the lack of a parachute and straps very acutely. The machine was hit but continued to fly and somehow or other I found myself inland, out of range of their guns."

Eventually — after a flight lasting about three hours — Tjikampek was reached, but on approach Gotto was worried that he might be fired upon by the airfield defences and, if he survived that, that he might crash on landing or crash into a demolition hole. However, he made a safe landing, avoiding burnt wrecks of a Vildebeest, an Albacore and a Hurricane. Finding that the airfield had been evacuated, he made for the nearby town, hoping to get a lift but nothing came his way. Returning dejectedly to the airfield, he decided to have a go at flying the A-24 to another location, co-opting three local roadsweepers to help start the aircraft:

"We were just getting underway when over the treetops, at about 500 feet, came a biplane. At first I thought it was probably a Vildebeest but suddenly I noticed it was a floatplane. I covered the 50 yards to the trees in record time."

The two small bombs dropped failed to cause any serious damage but when the floatplane returned for a strafing run, one bullet pierced the A-24's engine cowling; oil ran out of the air intake, putting an end to any hope of Gotto getting away by that means. Nonetheless, he did eventually reach Bandoeng, having gained lifts in a car and a lorry, where he rejoined the squadron.

During the night the pitifully weak attacks on the convoy continued, six B-17s and one LB-30 bombing from 10,000 feet. Three hits were claimed on two transports by Capt C.A. Bevan's B-17 crew of 41-2489, while Capt H.C. Smelser's crew of 41-2449 believed that they had sunk four transports and possibly two others! A 10,000 ton transport packed with troops was claimed destroyed following Capt Hardison's attack; the LB-30 brought its bombs back, the pilot having been unable to locate the target area. The Japanese reported that, at 2120, the cruiser *Yura* and some destroyers were bombed by two aircraft, although they suffered no damage. Before reaching Kragan, the convoy was reportedly bombed by aircraft described by the Japanese as dive-bombers — presumably the Vildebeests. The transport *Tokushima Maru* was damaged by near misses and was stranded, while the *Johore Maru* was damaged by a direct hit, with 150 dead and wounded, but was able to proceed to reach Kragan. Apparently the cruiser *Kinu* was also damaged during these attacks.

Western Java

Even at this late stage, three Blenheims were despatched from Kalidjati at 1030 to carry out what was to be the last raid on Palembang. One of the bombers was piloted by Sgt Dewey:

"I did two trips with Dutch bombs which had square tails and as a result kept the bomb doors partially open. Also, the aircraft I flew had no .303 ammunition — so we belted up some American .30 rounds and put them aboard. We tried a short burst and could practically see them falling out of the badly-worn barrels of the turret guns! When we had to use the guns at Palembang, both became u/s and jammed and the combined efforts of Sgts Frye and Hare were unavailing."

On the outward flight Dewey's crew spotted the invasion fleet heading south. Returning from the raid at about 1400, Dewey again sighted the Japanese force, now much further south. On reporting the sighting, very little notice was apparently taken amid the confusion prevailing.

Air Vice-Marshal Maltby now ordered Air Commodore Vincent to hand over command of the fighters to Wg Cdr Maguire — who had only arrived the previous day by sea from Palembang with other evacuated RAF personnel — and depart at once with his seven HQ staff for Tjilatjap. Before leaving, Vincent went to see his "gallant fighter boys" to say goodbye to them and write letters to those he was unable to visit. He and Maguire arrived at Tjililitan early in the morning, where they were introduced to some of the pilots. Vincent recorded:

> "To say how I was seemingly deserting them at their very worst hours, and exhorting them to fight to the last moment. Feeling simply dreadful, I left them to it. One has to be practical, of course, and say there was no virtue in remaining to become a prisoner if one could manage to get away and 'live' to fight another day and fortunately I was able to do just this."

Soon after Vincent's arrival at the airfield five Hurricanes were scrambled; they were to provide top cover, in heavy cloud, for the cruisers *Perth* and *Houston* retiring from the Java Sea Battle. Several aircraft were seen to the north, but they did not approach immediately and were not engaged; however, one C5M of the 22nd Air Flotilla did succeed in evading the fighters and carried out a reconnaissance of Tanjong Priok, the crew observing two flyingboats and 14 merchant ships in harbour.

Having seen the Hurricanes off, Vincent and his party stood watching AA bursting over the harbour, when low over the airfield roared a gaggle of Japanese fighters. Everyone headed for the conveniently-placed slit trenches; Vincent continued:

> "I shouted to those around to take cover and stopped to pick up my helmet at my feet; because of this brief delay I was the last to reach the slit trenches about ten yards away. The leading Jap saw us running and as I was diving for a trench I saw his guns firing. I landed full length on top of a Sergeant as an exploding bullet hit the side of the trench, about a foot above. The pilot, evidently realising that he was attacking across these small trenches, did a circuit and came in again to fire along the length of them. Again three or four strikes came about a foot below the rim at the end of the trench, but we were almost underground by then and were only splattered with earth.
>
> "We were then able to watch the rest of the attack and were glad that the Hurricanes were away. One Hurricane did return before the 'Zeros' left and he chased them out of the area. When he came back he was fired on, and fortunately missed, by our own AA guns."

Apparently one Hurricane suffered damage during the engagement, as recalled by Sgt Dewey:

> "(Sgt) Foxwell and I took over two machine gun pits and mounted a .30 Colt machine gun in each. These had 50-round drum type magazines, side mounted.
>
> "The alert went and all the Hurricanes took off and disappeared, then a heavy bombing and strafing attack. Japs in usual 27 formation at about 2,000

feet. Foxwell and I with our guns vainly tried to pick a 'Navy 0' off the tail of a crash-landing Hurricane."

During this attack one Bofors gunner was killed, while Flt Lt Hutton of 605 Squadron was wounded in one leg by bomb splinters and 2/Lt Neil Dummett suffered temporary loss of vision caused by bomb blast and, as a consequence, his immediate evacuation was arranged. Following the raid, Vincent and his staff made their way to Tjilatjap, where they went aboard the Dutch merchantman *Zandaam*, which set sail for Colombo in the first instance, but in the event was diverted to Fremantle instead. Part of the cargo stored within this vessel were five crated Dutch Brewsters, apparently no longer required; they would see service with the RAAF on reaching Australia.

Ironically, from that direction *Sea Witch* now arrived at Tjilatjap with her cargo of 27 crated P-40Es, together with the Dutch freighter *Kota Baroe*, which was carrying six crated Douglas DB-7Bs for the Dutch Navy. But by now it was too late to make use of these aircraft, the P-40s being unloaded onto lighters in the harbour; apparently these were sunk subsequently to prevent them falling into Japanese hands. Heavy AA battery crews also arrived, but the rapidly deteriorating situation found the 180 gunners immediately impressed as infantry, being sent to join 700 Australian troops already in the area for the defence of the port. 200 more Australian soldiers together with the defence section of 258 Squadron were now ordered to leave Tjililitan and concentrate at Tjisaoek.

As a result of the worsening situation, Do 24s X-23 and X-28 of GVT-6 were flown from Tanjong Priok to a hiding place at Lengkang on the Brantas River near Modjokarta, in the Sourabaya area, leaving there next night for Broome, while the surviving aircraft of GVT-11 and GVT-12 also departed for Broome during the day.

At Tanjong Priok meanwhile, the Dutch were about to commence the systematical destruction of the Naval Base, to deny its equipment and facilities to the Japanese. Stranded here was Catalina FV-U (W8426) of 205 Squadron, which was undergoing major repairs; with it was Sqn Ldr Alex Jardine and his crew together with a detachment of ground personnel from the squadron. The aircraft was about to have its repaired starboard mainplane replaced when Jardine was advised that the hangar housing the flyingboat was to be destroyed, at which he appealed to the CO of the Naval Air Station for time to complete repairs; Jardine later reported:

> "He (*the Dutch Co*) stated that all he knew was he was awaiting instructions from higher authority to blow up the station and demolish all shipping in the harbour. He could not give me any definite information about what was to happen to the aircraft in the hangar.
>
> "I now proceeded to the Port Captain. He told me his instructions were that nothing should be left afloat in the harbour when the order was given to blow. He would not give me any guarantee that the aircraft should be left when the orders were given."

Jardine returned to the hangar and instructed that a quantity of fuel should be put in the tanks and the engines tested. The aircraft was then lowered into the water, which was covered with a film of oil. However, a serious fuel leak developed within the aircraft and before any work could be done to rectify it, the order came through that demolition of the station, the hangars, the slipway and ships was about to start. Sadly and somewhat reluctantly, Jardine and his party departed for Bandoeng.

Earlier in the day the last Dutch flyingboat — probably X-16 of GVT-8 — had departed Tanjong Priok for Ceylon. The Dornier had been abandoned as unserviceable, but by dint of last minute repairs, its pilot considered there was a chance of getting away. Passengers aboard this craft comprised mainly Dutch government officers but included a New Zealand bank official and Sgt Percy Tottle, an RAF equipment assistant. Tottle had volunteered to stay behind to carry out demolition work when his unit evacuated, but had then been wounded during a bombing attack. A sympathetic Dutch doctor arranged for him to be flown out aboard the Dornier.

When about two hours into the flight there was an unexplained explosion and the blazing flyingboat fell into the sea off the Sumatran coast. Both Tottle and the New Zealander managed to bale out — the wounded RAF man having been pushed out by the other; after many hours in the sea, supported only by his Mae West, the semi-conscious airman was plucked from the water by Sumatran natives, who had also recovered the body of the bank official. Tottle was later transferred to the hospital ship *Wu-Sueh* and eventually arrived at Bombay.

According to sketchy reports, a bombing attack on Tanjong Priok then allegedly destroyed a hangar at the flyingboat base, and with it X-16. However, it seems likely that the hangar was in fact destroyed by the Dutch themselves, as part of their denial programme, and that X-16 was actually the aircraft lost en route to Ceylon. However, a requisitioned whaler, HMS *Rahman*, was sunk/scuttled in the harbour, as was the RN's *ML1063* and a miscellany of small Dutch craft.

By noon *Perth*, *Houston* and the surviving destroyer escort, were approaching the harbour when a single-engined Japanese floatplane was seen attacking a small Dutch patrol boat, whilst above droned two Hurricanes whose pilots were obviously unaware of what was happening below. The floatplane departed but then another — or the same one — approached the cruisers from seaward just as *Houston*'s sole surviving SOC-3 scout plane was due from Sourabaya. As soon as the misidentification was realised, shots were exchanged, but the floatplane apparently escaped unscathed. However, fire from the cruisers' guns almost accounted for the Hurricane patrol, one of which was flown by Sgt Sandeman Allen of 242 Squadron, who recalled:

> "We were nearly shot down when on convoy patrol — this was the usual protection job ending as ever with a mistaken identity; she opened fire on us and the shooting was the most accurate naval gunnery we had met to that date."

Some 20 minutes later, as Lt Tom Payne arrived in the SOC-3, jumpy Dutch gunners on the shore opened fire, believing this to be another Japanese aircraft. The floatplane promptly alighted in the harbour, a Dutch patrol vessel racing to the scene; fortunately it did not open fire, allowing crew and aircraft to rejoin the mothership. However, *Perth*'s Walrus amphibian spotter aircraft (L2319) was now found to be unserviceable due to gun-blast damage to its fabric-covered wings.

At about noon the full extent of the Western Force had been realised by the Allies. One body of 11 ships, which were carrying the 230th Regiment, had left the main convoy and were heading for Eretanwetan, just to the north of Kalidjati, while the rest were heading in towards the peninsula between Merak and Bantam Bay, on the far north-western tip of Java. This force, with the 2nd Division aboard, would soon divide to land at each of these locations simultaneously.

The Eretanwetan force had been sighted while still 50 miles out, escorted by the cruiser *Sendai* and three destroyers of the 2nd Flotilla, and received the initial weight of the Allied reaction. Only two Hudsons were still serviceable and these joined with the remaining six combat-worthy Blenheims of 84 Squadron to carry out attacks on the ships. The Dutch could muster 11 serviceable Glenn Martins, seven of which were at Kalidjati, three at Tjisaoek and one at Andir.

The Blenheims took-off first, at 1830, some crews then flying three sorties during the course of the night, including Wg Cdr Jeudwine (V6093); Sgt Dave Russell, his gunner, reported:

> "With cold determination, the CO managed to squeeze in three sorties during the night. The Jap fighters came in with searchlights in their noses, pinpointing their own presence whilst illuminating their quarry, but seemingly fully aware that the Blenheim could do little against a stern attack, provided its pursuer stayed at the same altitude."

Flt Lt Wyllie's crew in Z9723 also flew three sorties, claiming hits during a low-level attack on one transport vessel. They attacked this with 11-second delay-fused 250lb bombs, and saw a night fighter on at least one occasion.

Sgt Sayer, flying the refuelled and re-armed Blenheim (Z9723), headed out to sea. He dropped down and unloaded his bombs on the bows of a large transport, but was then attacked by a fighter. The Blenheim jinked and weaved and managed to evade but, having used up all its fuel, the pilot was forced to come down in a paddy field near Rangkasbitung; neither he nor Sgt Geoff Bell, the navigator, were hurt although Sgt Ross, the gunner, fractured a bone in his back and was knocked unconscious; he vaguely recalled:

> "I cannot remember much of this incident as I was knocked out. I did not see the fighter and I do not remember the crash; only that we were covered with mud from the paddy field where we crashed.
>
>   "The sun rose and dried out our mud-caked shorts and shirts as we made our way back towards Kalidjati on push-bikes."

Another to fly three sorties during this night was Flt Lt Holland (in V6092), who later wrote:

> "We were only a couple of minutes flying time from the coast and as we approached we could see, in the brilliant tropic night, the Japanese transports and warships moored along the coast, just off the shoreline. In the bright moonlight we could see the Japanese soldiers clambering down the sides of the vessels on ladders and getting into small boats, which were moored alongside. We spent the whole of that night bombing these ships, but the anti-aircraft fire was so intense — and the Japanese also had night fighters up — that we were unable to do a great deal of damage.
>
>   "We had only a handful of aircraft left at the time but even then we were able to sink a couple of ships. However, this could be accounted as nothing compared with the vast forces that we were up against."

Flt Lt Maurice 'Dutch' Holland of 84 Squadron. *(Mrs Mary Marcon via Paul Sortehaug)*

The two serviceable Hudsons — AE506 flown by Plt Off Alex Wilson and AE553 under the command of Flt Lt B.J. Wiley (of 1 RAAF Squadron) — also departed Kalidjati, Wilson leaving first at about 1930; he subsequently reported:

> "As we were the first available aircraft we were sent to recce and bomb this new convoy. Briefing was sketchy and practically no night flying or signals information was available. We took off about 1930 hours just before dark with no precise information as regards Kalidjati's night landing facilities.
>
> "On a course of 015 degrees we picked up the enemy convoy about 50 miles off-shore, travelling south very fast. We were briefed to fly between 4,000 and 5,000 feet and could only be supplied with instantaneous nose-fusing bombs, which eliminated any chance of making a really low-level attack.
>
> "A reconnaissance was carried out however without attracting any ack-ack fire and we attacked from 2,500 feet, dropping a stick of bombs which straddled an escort vessel. My observer reported the vessel to be severely damaged. We returned to base, reported to Ops, bombed-up and took off again. The second time we contacted the convoy it was only 15 miles from the coast, and there were seven large ships 8,000 to 15,000 tons in line astern. Various other enemy units were in the vicinity including a concentration of shipping to the north-west.

"We attacked a larger ship from 1,000 feet, the safety height with instantaneous bombs. There was heavy ack-ack fire and a few seconds after the bombs had gone, there was a large explosion on the attacked ship, an area of the sea being lit up for some miles around. The ship was presumed sunk."

Plt Off H.A. Campbell Hill, Wilson's observer, added:

"We attacked the largest ship from just over 1,000 feet. By this time we had attracted some anti-aircraft fire. A few seconds after the release of our bombs there was a large explosion on the attacked ship, an area of sea being lit up for some miles around. At the same time ack-ack from other ships was increasing in intensity and we returned to base, reported to Ops, bombed up and took off again".

The Hudson was refuelled and re-armed and took off again with the same crew; Wilson continued:

"On reaching the sea, clouds had gathered and were forming over the coastal area. We were unable to locate the convoy from its original bearing, so we carried out a square search of the vicinity. We were not equipped however, with ASV and low cloud with sea mist had increased, also my crew and myself were beginning to complain of eye-strain. It was now about 0300 hrs and we had been flying since 1930 hrs. We could not locate the convoy which we presumed had begun landing operations under the cover of low cloud. We reported this to Ops, on our return to base."

On landing, AE506 was yet again re-armed and sent out to continue the series of attacks, this time in the hands of Flg Off Peter Gibbes and his crew; they reported bombing the convoy and also the presence of night fighters. The other Hudson, AE553, had returned early due to electrical failure of the bombing gear, but as soon as this was rectified, Flg Off Bob Richards and his crew replaced that of Flt Lt Wiley and set out. Richards found the convoy but his aircraft was damaged by AA fire and, with an elevator cable shot away, he was obliged to fly around until dawn, when a crash-landing was carried out at Kalidjati.

26 Blenheim and six Hudson sorties had been made when the attacks ceased with the arrival of dawn; by then the crews had almost reached complete exhaustion. It should be mentioned that Hudson sorties were undertaken only by crews familiar with the Mark III Hudson, hence the small number of person-nel involved. The weather had been bad and results difficult to assess, although it was believed that at least two ships had been sunk and others damaged. The Kalidjati-based Glenn Martins of 1-VlG-I and 1-VlG-II also made 17 night sorties: all returned safely and their crews claimed hits on a cruiser and a des-troyer but actually achieved only two near-misses.

By late evening *Perth* and *Houston* had sailed again, heading west for the Sunda Strait and Ceylon. For superstitious sailors aboard *Perth*, the fact that the ship's mascot — a tabby cat named 'Red Lead' — had repeatedly tried to leave the ship before it sailed from Tanjong Priok, was a bad omen. The cruisers were to be accompanied by the Dutch destroyer *Evertsen* but, at the eleventh hour, the captain signalled that he had not received orders to depart. An incensed Capt Waller (of *Perth*) ordered him to join them immediately but was advised it would be an hour before the destroyer could do so. The cruisers thus departed alone. At 2230 they were sighted by the Japanese destroyer *Fubuki*, which commenced shadowing, awaiting help. Before this was forthcoming, the Allied cruisers came upon those transport vessels of the Western Force, which had reached Bantam Bay, so at once opened fire. At this stage *Fubuki* launched nine torpedoes, all of which missed but apparently some exploded amongst the assembled transports!

Before the covering force could intervene, gunners aboard *Perth* and *Houston* believed they had sunk at least two transports and possibly two more, but Kurita's four cruisers and nine destroyers then came to the rescue, both Allied vessels being sunk, although they were able to inflict damage on two more destroyers before their demise; *Perth* went first — shortly after midnight — hit by shells and torpedoes, taking with her Capt Waller and 353 of his crew — and the ship's mascot, 'Red Lead'. Some 40 minutes later *Houston*, struck by at least six torpedoes and many shells, followed, Capt Rooks having been killed by shrapnel before his ship went down; 655 American sailors perished.

Evertsen had followed the cruisers as soon as she was ready, and headed for the Sunda Strait as instructed. Shortly before dawn, with the crew believing that they had made good their escape, the Dutch warship was sighted and attacked by two Japanese destroyers. Badly damaged, her captain succeeded in beaching her on the island of Sabuku, where she became a total loss.

In Bantam Bay the landings had gone ahead virtually unopposed on the ground, although much damage had been caused to the invasion force by the naval and air actions. At least two transports had been sunk — the 7,170-ton *Sakura Maru* and the 9,912-ton *Horai Maru* — as had minesweeper *W-2*, whilst General Hitoshi Imamura's HQ vessel, the 10,000-ton *Ryujo Maru* had also been severely damaged — "tons of heavy equipment on the decks sliding into the sea". The General and his staff had to swim to the shore.

As survivors of the sunken Allied cruisers reached shore in daylight, many were amazed to see the amount of damage the invasion fleet had suffered. Lt Tom Payne, one of *Houston*'s reconnaissance pilots, reported seeing a vessel which he thought to be a seaplane tender "of about 18,000 tons which had several seaplanes lashed to her deck, lying well over on her side, and beached." This was presumably *Ryujo Maru*, which had been mistaken by Allied aircrews earlier in the campaign for a small aircraft carrier, due to its 'flat-top' appearance. Another transport, the *Tatsumo Maru*, was severely damaged as was the tanker *Tsurumi Maru*; it would seem that these three vessels sank in shallow waters and were later salvaged. Three destroyers and one cruiser had also sustained damage during the naval action while, undoubtedly, one or two of the transports had been sunk or severely damaged by the Blenheims and Hudsons.

Whilst Blenheims of 84 Squadron had been in action against the invaders, one of the unit's missing crews — Flg Off Brian Fihelly with Sgts Gomm and Oliver, who had been shot down a few days earlier — had reached a small island in the Sunda Strait in their bid to return to Java, but their hopes of progressing further were rapidly fading when, as recalled by Eric Oliver, they saw in the early morning light:

"A beautiful, two-masted, yacht. It was white painted and just anchored there. We decided to make our way to it — two paddled and one baled out. We went as fast as we could — changing jobs as we became exhausted, as the boat was sinking fast — Brian could not swim, so we kept going until we came alongside.

"We saw a white chap with a beard — wearing a white shirt and shorts — and a native on board. We hollered: 'What nationality are you?' The reply came in English, enquiring who we were. He threw us a rope, helped us to board, and then instructed us to get below. Down below we found 40 Royal Naval sailors in a hell of a state, covered in oil and some wounded. Voices enquired: 'Who the hell's this?'

"Our reply provoked some humour into the situation. The sailors then went on to explain that they were originally on two Naval minesweepers which were leaving Batavia Dock for the Sumatra Straits, when they had been approached by the RAF Squadron Leader who owned the yacht — called *White Swan* — and agreed to tow it out, as he wanted to get it away from Java.

"Whilst towing it, they ran into the end of the naval battle in which the *Houston* and *Perth* had been sunk, and were themselves sunk. However, for some reason the Japs did not see the *White Swan* and it was, therefore, able to pick up survivors. They were in a right sorry situation."

One of the two sunken requisitioned minesweepers was the 350-ton *Wo Kwang*, a former tug, from which two survivors were later picked up by another vessel departing Batavia. Sgt Oliver continued:

"Further problems started when they had run into Japs and were boarded. However, a boarding party had not been left on the yacht but they had been instructed to remain there and wait for an escort to take them to Java.

"By now, we felt and looked a bit better, as the skipper had told us to help ourselves to shorts, shirts and shoes. Brian, Tommy and I had a conference — we could take the ship's small boat and some supplies, but the Japs were across the Straits. It was a chance, but we'd ask the rest of the chaps. They agreed to have a go.

"We 'upped' anchor but did not start the engine although with the sails up, we sailed all night. There was a good wind and moon — the boat was making good progress: if only we could keep this up for another one and a half to two hours we would be out of the Straits. However, by daylight it would be easy to spot us. Day broke and the wind dropped; the going was slow so we started our diesels and went full speed on our course.

"Suddenly, our look-out shouted 'ship on the port bow — ship on the starboard bow'. Things looked disastrous! We kept going at first but there was a bang and a warning shot whistled over our bows; we shut off the engines and came to a standstill. They came alongside and a Jap Marine came aboard and ordered us all over one side. He asked where we were going and we replied South Africa. He asked for all our charts and only allowed us to retain a local one and said, 'You must return to Bantam Bay or this ship is dead'. He then left.

"We turned round, to head back, and after about three quarters of an hour they left us and we entered Bantam Bay. At first the Japs thought we were Japs who had captured the boat and cheered us — then, realising we were not, sent out a boarding party."

During the day the JNAF had managed to spare the effort to attack Port

Moresby again, discouraging any attempt at aid from New Guinea — not that any had been considered, or was possible. The flyingboat base was the target this time, and three RAAF Catalinas were destroyed. This left only two Catalinas and one Hudson serviceable as the base's total air component!

The Japanese preparations could not have been more complete, thorough or effective. Virtually defenceless, Java now hung like a ripe plum, ready to fall into the invader's outstretched hand.

Chapter 7

BURMA — THE FALL OF RANGOON
1 February — 9 March

At the start of February Allied air strength could hardly be said to be vast. At Rangoon were some 25 AVG P-40s (of which 18 were serviceable) plus ten Hurricanes. At Toungoo were a dozen Blenheim IVs of 113 Squadron (although a detachment continued to operate from Zayatkwin and a new strip called 'Johnnie Walker'), four Buffaloes of 67 Squadron and six Lysanders, with more of the latter arriving. The only other aircraft available were the three Blenheims of 3 CD Flight at Bassein.

Sunday, 1 February
From Zayatkwin Flg Off Freddie Proctor departed for the first Hurricane PR sortie, although on this occasion his task was a visual reconnaissance of Tak and Mesoht airfields. During the coming two weeks the two PR Hurricanes would carry out daily sorties, Flg Offs Proctor and Ken Perkin taking turns to cover the various Thai airfields and other specified locations.

The fighter version of the Hurricane was tested during the day by Sqn Ldr Frank Carey (CO of 135 Squadron) in a mock dogfight over Mingaladon with a 67 Squadron Buffalo flown by Sgt Gordon Williams. The Buffalo's performance at 20,000 feet and above was actually found to be superior, whilst at 16,000 feet the two aircraft seemed evenly matched. Below that level the Hurricane undoubtedly had the edge. The result thereby cast an interesting light on the oft-maligned Brewster fighter.

Monday, 2 February
In a day of limited activity, five Blenheims of 113 Squadron were escorted by two Hurricanes to bomb Moulmein and Martaban Island. The escort (Plt Offs Jack Storey and Alan Kitley of 135 Squadron) became separated, so strafed an artillery post. Returning from another sortie during the day, the Blenheim (Z7680) flown by 2/Lt N.M. Russell, SAAF, crashed when a tyre burst on landing. The aircraft caught fire and, just as Russell was halfway out, the fuel tank exploded. Burned from head to waist by the flames, he managed to drag himself clear of the inferno. Not expected to survive, he did in fact recover after many weeks of intensive care.

Two of 28 Squadron's Lysanders were ordered to fly to Mingaladon to collect Lt General Sir Thomas Hutton (GOC Burma) and his Aide, Lt Nigel Chancellor, then take them to Lashio, via Toungoo and Heho. From Lashio they were to travel on to Chungking to meet Generalissimo Chiang Kai-shek. The flight proved to be a disaster. The aircraft (N1274) flown by Flt Lt E.W. Tate, in which the General was a passenger, developed engine trouble and then also became lost after darkness had fallen. With fuel exhausted, Tate undertook a force landing but one of the wings hit a tree stump and the Lysander crashed; Tate was severely injured and knocked unconscious. The aircraft began to burn and the General leapt out, endeavouring to pull Tate clear. However, the latter was jammed in his seat and Hutton was unable to free him. In desperation he beat at the flames with his greatcoat, succeeding in preventing the fire reaching the pilot until local help arrived. Part of the cockpit sides were then broken away and Tate was released, but died of his injuries six days later.

Meanwhile the second Lysander, piloted by Flt Lt A.S. Mann, had kept pace with Tate's aircraft; when it was seen to crash, Lt Chancellor bravely decided that he should bale out and assist. He successfully accomplished this, but Mann was then also obliged to force-land due to lack of fuel and was severely concussed. He was later recovered, as was his aircraft. Meanwhile General Hutton and Lt Chancellor, both shaken and bruised, were assisted by local villagers to the nearby rail-head and from here they travelled to Lashio, then on to their delayed meeting with the Chinese premier. On arrival, Hutton was handed a signal from General Wavell, ordering him back to Rangoon on the morrow.

During the evening four more Hurricane IIBs arrived at Mingaladon, flown by 135 Squadron pilots led by Plt Off Guy Underwood, who recalled:

> "The arrival at Rangoon (Mingaladon) was quite an extraordinary experience as we did not get there until it was virtually dark and the landing had to be by the use of the aircraft's landing lights with no assistance from the ground.
>
> "It was the practice of those who had already arrived at Mingaladon to remove themselves from the aerodrome every night as the Japanese were constantly bombing the area so that when we arrived, not only were there no lights to assist us on the ground but there were no persons there either!
>
> "Just to make matters worse we still had no radio communication and had left our navigating Blenheim at Dum Dum (Calcutta) where it had crashed its nose into a hangar door. Anyway, we managed to land."

The airfield and Rangoon City suffered small raids during the night by a total of seven Ki 21s and six Ki 15s, but the airfield escaped any further serious damage.

Hurricane IIB, BG843 WK-E, of 135 Squadron at Mingaladon airfield. *(Sqn Ldr W.J. Storey)*

Tuesday, 3 February

During the morning, Sqn Ldr Bunny Stone of 17 Squadron was ordered to fly to Lashio to provide an escort back to Rangoon for General Hutton and his aide, who were to be conveyed aboard Chiang's personal Sikorsky S-43W amphibian (ex NC16929) flown by the Generalissimo's American pilot, Julius Barr. With Sgt Doug Cropper as his No 2, Stone set off for Toungoo to refuel, arriving just before a Japanese bombing raid, during which the two pilots sheltered in a ditch.

Six Ki 30s of the 31st Sentai escorted by 24 Ki 27s of the 77th Sentai, undertook the raid and claimed damage to two aircraft on the ground. Indeed one Blenheim of 113 Squadron was riddled with bomb splinters and a Burma Volunteer Air Force Tiger Moth which had just landed, tipped up onto it nose in its haste to get away again immediately the attack ended. The pilot had attempted taking off without the wheel chocks having been removed!

31st Sentai Mitsubishi Ki 30 single-engined bombers at an airfield in Thailand. The nearest aircraft carries a number of victory marks on the side of its fuselage. *(Authors' collection)*

To meet the raid two Buffaloes had been scrambled, but made no contact. It seems that at least one 2nd Squadron P-40 was also up, Bob Keeton taking off in such a hurry that he failed to take his helmet and oxygen mask. Nonetheless, he climbed to 20,000 feet, where he lost consciousness due to oxygen starvation, his aircraft then falling away. As he recovered, he saw below him a Japanese bomber at which he fired, but observed no result. Apparently a member of the AVG ground crew reported seeing a bomber crash in flames near the airfield and this was credited to Keeton; this was the AVG's 100th official victory. No Japanese loss was recorded however.

With the raid over, Sqn Ldr Stone returned to his Hurricane only to find that it had developed a glycol leak. Taking Cropper's BG674 instead, he set off alone — and somewhat reluctantly — to cross the 10,000 feet high mountain range on his way to Lashio. His pessimism proved justified, for the range was covered in thick haze and he was unable to spot any landmarks. After one and a half hours, with little fuel remaining, he had no alternative but to seek a place to force-land. A small sand bar on the edge of the Irrawaddy offered a possibility, but as he touched down, the undercarriage collapsed and the nose of the aircraft dug into the sand. Unhurt, he was fortunate to find a village nearby where he was entertained by the local dignitaries — the headman, the village policeman, the doctor (an Indian) and a Chinese trader who produced several bottles of brandy! Next day Stone left for Mandalay on a paddle steamer — a three-day journey. At Mandalay he arranged for a flatboat to go upstream to collect the damaged aircraft, and he then took the train for Rangoon.

Meanwhile three Blenheims and a Lysander had been out to bomb, the former escorted by four Hurricanes and the latter by a pair of Buffaloes. The Blenheims raided an island between Pa-an and Moulmein, returning without incident. Sqn Ldr Karun Majumdar, flying 1 IAF Squadron's first operational sortie, bombed the hangar on Mehongsohn airfield, in which an aircraft was seen, and reported a direct hit.

Wednesday, 4 February

After desultory Japanese night raids on Rangoon, Pegu and Toungoo, a small-scale retaliatory daylight strike by five 113 Squadron Blenheims against Pa-an was launched, while nine Indian Air Force Lysanders, joined by two of 28 Squadron, were led by Sqn Ldr Majumdar to attack Mehongsohn again, this time without escort. Direct hits were claimed on buildings, one small aircraft was believed to have been destroyed and another damaged. The Lysanders proceeded to Heho and landed, then returned to Mingaladon the next day. Elsewhere during the day, two more of 28 Squadron's Lysanders were despatched on detachment to Port Blair in the Andaman Islands.

At around 1500, 17 Ki 30s of the 31st Sentai, escorted by 13 77th Sentai Ki 27s, raided Toungoo where they claimed four aircraft burned and five others damaged. Although 113 Squadron reported no damage to any of its Blenheims, the severity of the raid and the damage to the airfield resulted in the unit being evacuated at once to Zayatkwin. Two Hurricanes were also at the airfield, having flown in earlier, as Sqn Ldr Jimmy Elsdon recalled:

> "Had Plt Off Fuge as No 2. Air raid warnings were given by detachments sitting on top of the hills to the east. No ground R/T station so no means of calling aircraft back to base or of assisting interception. In this case warning was so good (40 minutes) that we gave up after 35 minutes thinking it must have been a recce or false alarm.
>
> "Just after we landed and dismounted, we heard ominous noises overhead — found shallow irrigation ditch near our aircraft, which we occupied! After bombing raid was over we found one of the two Hurricanes (Z5473) had been damaged by shrapnel which had passed right over our heads from near-by bomb! No point in leaving a u/s Hurricane at Toungoo, so I decided after an inspection that I would try to get it back to Mingaladon where it might be used for spares.
>
> "Actually the only complete failure was in the pneumatic system so no guns or brakes. Various chips out of the propeller did not seem to affect engine balance. Fuge escorted me back and luckily I was able to ground loop (on all three wheels) at end of the runway at Mingaladon without doing any further damage."

Friday, 6 February

Following a relatively quiet 24 hours, when only reconnaissance flights were carried out by either side, the 6th proved to be a much busier day, as the Japanese now launched an assault on Mingaladon. This began with attacks just after 0400 by four Ki 21s of the 14th Sentai, followed an hour later by six more from the 62nd Sentai. At 0700 15 Ki 30s from the 31st Sentai attacked, about 80 bombs landing within the airfield boundaries on this occasion, although little damage was done. Two 'A' Flight Hurricanes of 17 Squadron, on night readiness, were scrambled into the dawn sky — Flt Lt Allan Carvell for the fourth time that night! He and Sgt Ken Rathbone finally intercepted a number of the Ki 30s, each claiming one shot down. They obviously attacked the same aircraft for only one of the bombers failed to return.

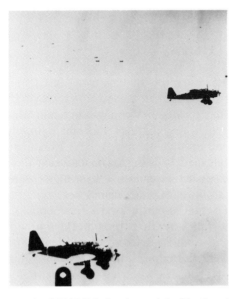

A pair of Ki 30 light bombers of the 31st Sentai en route to a target in Burma. The specks in the far distance are escorting Ki 27s of the 77th Sentai. *(Kuwabara family)*

Finally, with full daylight, came some 25 Ki 27 fighters of the 50th and 77th Sentai on a fighter sweep. A number of P-40s of the 1st Squadron and six Hurricanes were scrambled to intercept; the Japanese reported meeting 17-18 fighters, identified as 'Spitfires', Buffaloes and P-40s. Plt Off Storey was leading the Hurricanes in Z5659 WK-C, but these were jumped by three Ki 27s whilst climbing to 21,000 feet. Storey later recorded in his diary:

"What a day! Went out to 'Johnnie Walker' by lorry in early morning (dark); brought my aircraft into Mingaladon. Our runways had several bomb craters in them as a result of last night's raids. Loaded up to escort six Lysanders on a raid on Moulmein.

"Our aircraft were standing by to go off when suddenly we were ordered off to scramble to 20,000 feet to intercept a heavy wave of enemy fighters. The CO's machine went u/s so I had to lead our machines (six) into the encounter. Sgt Robertson was my No 2.

"Once airborne we climbed like Hell up into the sun. Ops kept reiterating over the R/T 'Very many bandits, very, very high' but gave no vectors — rather vague. Last section of two aircraft lost formation and we four carried on still climbing.

"Suddenly, when at 16,000 feet, I saw about 30 bandits at 10 o'clock flying at 21,000 feet and about six miles off. I then turned our section off to the right to get between the enemy and the sun and to gain more height. The distance between us closed rapidly and at 18,000 feet three enemy aircraft tried to jump us from one o'clock and 3,000 feet above.

"I immediately spiralled vertically to the left and swept up into the sun, turned and fired a burst into one enemy aircraft. A free-for-all scrap now developed: four Hurricanes against 30 Army 97s. I was fortunate to get a burst into one e/a from dead astern. It caught fire and went spiralling down vertically and crashed south-east of Zayatkwin.

"'Batchy' (Plt Off Batchelar) and 'Robbie' (Sgt Robertson) were chased down with e/a on their tails and carried out successful evasive action. The AVG joined in. Two e/a came down on my tail so I again did a violent downward spiral then pushed the throttle through the gate and swept up into the sun, came down onto the same two e/a and carried out a quarter attack on the rearmost. After two bursts it spun down to the right, crashing east of 'Z'.

"E/a again got on my tail and the same evasive action was made. By this time my radiator temperature was 135°. I subsequently carried out beam attacks on two e/a giving each a long burst as other e/a were endeavouring to get on my tail. I could not observe the results.

"Finally when having an e/a right in my sights in an astern attack I discovered that my ammunition was all gone; immediately broke away, going down from 16,000 feet to 50 feet at 430 mph and zig-zagged to base. One bullet hole was found in the starboard mainplane. Had all plugs changed in motor."

Plt Off Underwood claimed one destroyed and one probable:

"I hit one Japanese aircraft as he was climbing up — a quarter frontal attack — his aircraft bursting into flames (this was later confirmed by one of our pilots); a second dive gave me another chance and I saw bullets from my aircraft strike another fighter in a quarter attack from astern but, in this case, the pilot was either killed or took very rapid evasive action (this was claimed as a probable).

"On a further dive, however, I saw a Japanese aircraft almost head on and as I passed him in the opposite direction I could see his aircraft pulling round in a hard turn and very close to me. Almost immediately afterwards bullets hit the rear of my aircraft — presumably from that particular aircraft — and my cockpit canopy disappeared (presumably shot off) and I received what seemed to be a kick in the back of my left leg.

"With all ideas of being a hero from my initial victory earlier in the fight having disappeared in an instant, I pulled out of the fight — but that would seem to have been the end anyway as the sky which a moment before was full of aircraft, was suddenly strangely empty both of our aircraft and Japanese.

"On landing, an examination of the aircraft showed that besides the lost canopy, bullet holes were present in the rear fuselage and the top of the rudder had been shot off. My leg wound turned out to be the apparent result of an explosive bullet hitting something in the aircraft and then dispersing its bits rather like buckshot in the back of the leg."

Sgt Malcolm McRae claimed one damaged, but was hit in the shoulder when an armour-piercing bullet went straight through the armour plate behind his seat; Plt Off Eric Batchelar's aircraft was also hit. Meantime Flt Lt Barry Sutton (flying BE171 YB-B of 17 Squadron), who had been carrying out a reconnaissance sortie over the Salween River, also encountered the Japanese fighters as he was returning to base and claimed two probably shot down.

The American pilots who had joined the fight claimed a further seven 'I-97' fighters shot down and one probable to add to the RAF's three 'confirmed', three 'probables' and three damaged. Their claims were two apiece by Flt Ldrs

BE171 YB-B, a Hurricane of 17 Squadron at Mingaladon. *(Wg Cdr C.A.C. Stone)*

Robert L. Little and Greg Boyington, one each by Vice-Sqn Ldr Robert H. Neale, Robert W. Prescott and William D. McGarry whilst Charles R. Bond claimed the probable. One AVG pilot was slightly wounded, joining Underwood and McRae in sick-quarters to receive anti-tetanus injections. All three were given the afternoon off, although they were advised that they would be fit for flying next day!

For the Japanese the 50th Sentai claimed three certain and four probables, and the 77th Sentai two and two probables (Lt Kisaji Beppu one and one probable; Lt Yoshiro Kuwabara one, and Wt Off Fujinaga one probable), but

AVG pilots examine the rudder of a 77th Sentai Ki 27. *(Authors' collection)*

from the latter unit Lt Kitamura failed to return and Maj Yoshio Hirose force-landed his damaged fighter at Molulmein. No losses were recorded by the 50th. Obviously on both sides, enthusiasm had run riot.

Capt Yoshiro Kuwabara, leader of the 77th Sentai's 3rd Chutai. (*Kuwabara family*)

Following this raid Sqn Ldr Majumdar, whose Lysanders had now arrived at Mingaladon, led five aircraft from his squadron and one from 28 Squadron to bomb Moulmein railway station and dockyards, where dive-bombing was undertaken in order to obtain greater accuracy. Three large fires were reported to have started as a result of the attack.

That evening Sqn Ldr Robert J. Sandell took up his newly-repaired P-40 to test the tail unit which had been fitted to replace that damaged by the Japanese suicide pilot a week earlier. Whilst performing aerobatics over the airfield, the tail broke away and he was killed in the resultant crash. Vice Sqn Ldr Bob Neale took over the command of the 1st Squadron.

Saturday, 7 February
Japanese bombers were back four times prior to dawn. On the second occasion Sqn Ldr Carey and Plt Off Storey were on night readiness but without success; Storey:

"We were scrambled twice just after midnight. On the first raid the petrol dump of Zayatkwin was hit again, it having previously suffered in earlier raids and, on the second, our base was bombed and the flare-path and runways damaged, only three lights being left on the flare-path. We had no contacts because fighter control was very poor."

During the fourth attack, by ten 31st Sentai Ki 30s, four aircraft were claimed by the returning crews as burnt on the ground. No Allied losses were recorded.

Green-painted Nakajima Ki 27 fighter of the 77th Sentai. ((*Kuwabara family*)

As on the previous morning, 50th and 77th Sentai Ki 27s appeared in force, the 22 pilots from the latter unit reporting meeting ten P-40s near Rangoon, when Capt Toyoki Eto and Lt Jun-ichi Ogata each claimed one shot down, while Lt Kuwabara and Sgt Niino both claimed probables. The unit suffered casualties similar to the previous day; Lt Kisaji Beppu was shot down and killed and Lt Nakao was obliged to force land at Moulmein. The 50th Sentai pilots claimed two more victories and a third probable, again for no recorded loss.

Ten Hurricanes had indeed been scrambled as the sweep approached but only four had made contact, these pilots submitting claims. Sgt Tex Barrick claimed two Ki 27s shot down and a third damaged, while fellow American Flg Off Lloyd Thomas, also claimed one shot down. Two more were claimed by 136 Squadron pilots, Plt Off Eric Brown and Sgt Ting Bunting; the latter recorded:

"At 9 o'clock I relieved Bob Payne for breakfast; at 0905 we got a scramble but Maurice Cuthbert, my No 2, lost me in the dust and I lost everyone else.

Capt Toyoki Eto of the 77th Sentai, who claimed a P-40 shot down on 7 February. *(Authors' collection)*

I climbed up to 18,000 feet and saw three Hurricanes in front of me. I opened up to catch them up and about the same time saw about 15 Japs below me.

"I gave a 'Tally-ho!' over the R/T and went down in a quarter astern attack from above on the No 2 of the starboard line. I opened fire from about 400 yards and saw my bullets hitting the machine just behind the cockpit. I moved my head a little to the front and the machine hovered and then went down. I almost hit him when I broke away.

"Brown went down on them at the same time with Barrick and his No 2 (Thomas). I climbed up into sun and made four more attacks on this formation without any success as far as I could see. After my last attack I lost them but saw what I took to be a dogfight to the north. I piled in and got on the tail of a '97' but found I was the only Hurricane there and all the '97s' turned on me!

"I could see tracers coming in all directions and one chap sat on my tail while his bullets were banging against my armour plate. This was getting uncomfortable and as I had just run out of ammunition, I went over on my back and down to the deck."

Barrick reported that he had seen one RAF pilot shoot down a fighter which fell into a lake. However, a subsequent search failed to find anything, and this victory was not credited. No loss or serious damage was suffered by any of the British fighters on this occasion.

News was received during the day of Sqn Ldr Frank Carey's imminent promotion to Wing Commander and leadership of 267 Wing. Consequently Flt Lt Barry Sutton was promoted Sqn Ldr and posted from 136 Squadron to command 135 Squadron two days later. The latter squadron had lost the services of one of its more experienced pilots when Flg Off Alf Whitby, who had been decorated with the DFM for his achievements with 79 Squadron in France and the Battle of Britain, was posted away on medical grounds.

On return from his force-landing on the banks of the Irrawaddy, Sqn Ldr

Wreckage of a 77th Sentai Ki 27 at Mingaladon, from which the rudder has been removed. *(J.F. Barrick)*

Stone led a number of 17 Squadron pilots to undertake a strategic attack on Moulmein, where the railway station and ferry boat were strafed, Sgt Tex Gibson reporting that occupants of the latter were seen to jump into the river as he fired at it. Next day Stone led a mission to Moulmein when all the Hurricanes were armed with locally-designed 1lb explosive incendiaries, which were to be released via the aircraft's flare tube; however the operation proved far from satisfactory, as Stone noted:

> "Results were somewhat disappointing — damned if I could see any results at all! When I got back I asked the ALO (Army Liaison Officer) to contact the Army in Martaban and find out if Moulmein was in flames — No, Moulmein wasn't in flames — damn! Still we always carried them — it was something to drop and we had no bomb rack."

During these two days the AVG's 2nd Squadron had twice escorted Blenheims to attack Pa-an on the Salween, whilst a column moving from Moulmein had also been strafed. As a result of these actions, Sqn Ldr John V. Newkirk was recommended for a British DSO. On the 8th however, the 2nd Squadron was withdrawn for a rest, part moving to Loiwing, part to Magwe, and a few personnel to Kunming. On this date ten Lysanders of 28 Squadron landed to refuel at Toungoo preparatory to an attack on Mehongsohn. Whilst there a Japanese raid occurred and four were damaged and the mission was cancelled. Aircraft from the 10th Flying Battalion were also responsible for attacking British troops in the Pa-an area, whilst others from the 4th Flying Battalion bombed and sank two middle-sized ships and three smaller vessels at Martaban.

Monday, 9 February
As the battle on the ground raged around Moulmein and Pa-an, the 8th Sentai twice attacked British troops in the latter area, under cover of 50th Sentai Ki 27s, while three Blenheims escorted by four 135 Squadron Hurricanes and six AVG-escorted Lysanders attacked Japanese troops in the same area, before Moulmein finally fell to the invaders.

Tuesday-Friday, 10-20 February

Little was to be seen of the Japanese Army Air Force over the next ten days or so. Daily however, small RAF formations of Blenheims, Lysanders and Hurricanes bombed or strafed targets associated with the fighting on the ground. Several aircraft were lost in operational accidents or other mishaps, including a 113 Squadron Blenheim on the 10th (Sgt Webster and crew unhurt), another on the 14th (when Sqn Ldr P.R.A. Ford's V5627 suffered engine failure on take-off; the gunner was injured), and yet a third (Z7916) on the 17th (Sgt Lloyd and crew unhurt). On the 11th one of the Indian Lysanders was abandoned by its crew in the air when fuel ran out, Flt Lt N. Prasad and his gunner, Sgt E.S. Moyer, RCAF, both later returning to their unit, whilst one of 28 Squadron's machines (P1686) was destroyed on the ground on the 17th, when the American bomb it was carrying fell off; Plt Off C.C. Dickson and his gunner, Sgt E.B.G. Sedgwick, were both killed in the explosion.

It was at about this time that Air Vice-Marshal D.F. Stevenson formed 'X' Wing Headquarters, to control all fighter and bomber operations in support of the army; Grp Capt N.C. Singer was appointed to command. 221 Group was at the same time renamed NORGROUP. The three Hurricane squadrons now possessed 26 aircraft, while 67 Squadron was down to five barely serviceable Buffaloes. By now 27 Blenheims of 45 and 113 Squadrons had arrived, and there were 22 Lysanders divided between 28 and 1 IAF Squadrons. The latter had been split up, with detachments at Lashio (for reconnaissance duties on behalf of the Chinese army), at Toungoo and at Mingaladon.

On the 17th however, having carried out a number of formation bombing attacks, 28 Squadron was ordered back to India, leaving a detachment of three Lysanders and the two pilots who had converted to Hurricanes — Flt Lt Mann and Plt Off C.D.C. Dunsford-Wood (later joined by Plt Off Doug Harris) — who were to undertake tactical reconnaissance sorties in borrowed 17 Squadron aircraft. The squadron's detachment (two aircraft) in the Andamans, after surviving a bombing raid on the 13th, were burned by their own crews five days later, the personnel then being evacuated aboard HMT *Neuralia*.

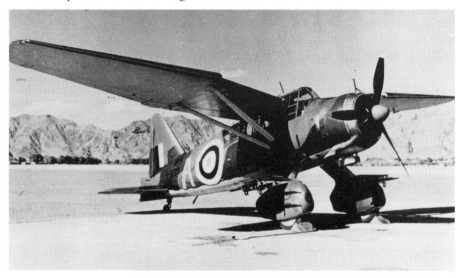

Lysander II, P9139 BF-A, of 28 Squadron, seen here at Kohat, following its return to India. *(Bruce Robertson via A. Thomas)*

Reinforcements were still gradually trickling in nonetheless. Seven more Hurricanes reached Mingaladon from India on the 14th, led by Wg Cdr C.A. Woodhouse, DFC (flying BG811). Woodhouse, a former leader of Fighter Command's Tangmere Wing, was to take command of fighter operations in Burma. He was accompanied by Flt Lt 'Bush' Cotton, RAAF, one of 17 Squadron's flight commanders, plus five pilots of 135 Squadron. Next day several more Hurricanes arrived: the pilots included Flt Lt E.J. Watson of 135 Squadron and Plt Off Ken Hemingway of 17 Squadron. They were led to the airfield by a Blenheim of 45 Squadron, which had just arrived in India from the Middle East. Five more of this unit's bombers, led by Wg Cdr C.B.B. Wallis, DFC, reached Zayatkwin next day and were in action over the Salween River within the hour.

Half a dozen American pilots of the 3rd Squadron (Flt Ldrs George B. McMillan, Charles N. Older, Thomas C. Haywood, Robert T. Smith, Paul J. Greene and Chauncey H. Laughlin), currently resting at Kunming, were flown aboard a CNAC C-47 transport to Calcutta on the 16th. There they boarded an Empire flyingboat for Cairo, from where they were to journey by C-53 transport — flown by a Pan American crew — to Accra, Gold Coast (on the west coast of Africa). Waiting for them at Accra were six brand-new P-40Es (the RAF's Kittyhawk), which were to be ferried to China for use by the AVG. More were to follow.

Bassein saw the arrival of Plt Off Les Hayton's 53 Squadron Hudson from Sumatra on the 17th (see Chapter 1), which was sent to assist the three Blenheims of 3 CD Flight based there. Also aboard the Hudson were Plt Off Tony Ayris and his 59 Squadron crew who had lost their own aircraft in an accident. Shortly after the Hudson's arrival at Bassein, Hayton was ordered by Flt Lt Hem Choudrhi (3 CD Flight's commander) to carry out a search for enemy shipping. Although they flew many miles south and carried out square searches, nothing unusual was seen.

Japanese troops had by now crossed the Salween at Martaban and tested the northern flank of the British lines, at Pa-an, bringing the invaders within 100 miles of Rangoon. Units of the JAAF began moving forward, the 31st Sentai to Lampong and the 8th Sentai to Nakhorn Sawan, whilst a detachment of the 50th Sentai moved to Chiengmai, from where the unit's fighters escorted 14th Sentai Ki 21s to raid Mandalay, Burma's second largest city; one bomber was forced down due to technical problems.

With Rangoon now threatened, part of 135 Squadron's ground party was ordered north to Akyab, to prepare the airfield there for the evacuation of Mingaladon and, on the 18th, a DC-2 of 31 Squadron arrived at the latter base to begin evacuating civilians. Next day, 67 Squadron destroyed three unserviceable Buffaloes and flew its remaining airworthy fighters up to Magwe. The new base was not popular with the squadron, as recalled by Sgt Ed Beable:

"Magwe airstrip was a very bare, dry, torrid place, situated very close to the home of the King Cobra snake. Dispersal huts were in fact large tents; food was scarce and poor. All Sergeant Pilots lived in a two-storey house on a commandeered peanut farm.

"Our breakfast was generally no more than half a soya bean sausage washed down with lashings of tea. Lunch, which we obtained from the local village, was, as a rule, water-melon followed by 'Ovaltine' (while it lasted), and the evening meal for weeks was tinned bully beef and whisky! Luckily there was no shortage of either but it wasn't what one could regard as a very wholesome diet for very long. Occasionally we supplemented this with peanuts dug from the farm on which we lived.

"There were no baths or showers — evening ablutions after a day at the airfield, where one became grimy and caked in red dust, amounted to a canvas bucketful of unheated water poured over one's head, and placing great faith in a towel to remove the dirt.

"During periods of readiness, pilots had to learn to occupy their time in some way. Sitting and waiting for hour upon hour for something to happen under conditions existing at the time, proved not only tedious and boring but also nerve-wracking. As we were in communication with Ops Rooms by telephone, a ring on this gadget indicated very often that the squadron or a section was required to scramble. Of course there were numerous telephone calls of an innocent nature, but there was a time in the operational life of almost every pilot when a ring of the telephone would make him literally jump, wake him out of a dead sleep or set up a cold sweat and palpitations.

"Whilst many pilots slept in chairs, mooched about the dispersal area, polished their aircraft, modelled small items out of perspex, wrote letters etc, others indulged in other forms of time-consuming recreation, the most popular of which were bridge, most variations of poker, pontoon, slippery sam etc. Many became quite proficient, but the game which attracted most was 'Acey Deucey', an American form of backgammon. This we learned from the AVG and it was played from dawn to dark."

Sgt Ed Beable of 67 Squadron with an AVG P-40. *(E.H. Beable)*

The Japanese were getting into their stride however, for whilst every available Hurricane was out escorting Blenheims and Lysanders, and attacking advancing

Japanese columns on this date, 31st Sentai bombers, escorted by 77th Sentai Ki 27s attacked Pyinmana station, 50 miles north of Toungoo. On the return flight heavy mist was encountered and one bomber was lost; three more were seriously damaged in force-landings.

During the final week of February the British and American aircrews were once more to be involved in sustained aerial combat, as the renewed Japanese activity once again began to make itself felt.

Saturday, 21 February

The new offensive began in the early afternoon, when 16 Ki 48s of the 8th Sentai, escorted by 15 Ki 27s of the 50th Sentai, raided Bassein airfield. The attacking crews claimed three large aircraft burned and eight damaged, in addition to bomb hits on a fuel dump, ammunition depot, the runway and nearby warehouses. Two of 3 CD Flight's Blenheim Is were at readiness, each loaded with anti-submarine depth charges, and one of these (L4915) received a direct hit and caught fire, whereupon its four depth charges exploded; a second Blenheim was damaged, whilst the bomb dump and petrol storage area were also hit.

The 53 Squadron Hudson at Bassein, which escaped damage during the attack, had however been rendered unserviceable due to an avoidable accident, as Plt Off Hayton recalled:

"On arrival at dispersal I found that my aircraft had been manhandled among the trees. There was no way out except to cut down two trees! At that stage things really went wrong. I started up and was guided forward — by an idiot — straight into the bowser, wrecking the port propeller and possibly the engine!"

"Two hours later the Japs came over in three vics of three in perfect formation, dropping their bombs from 500 to 1,000 feet between the road and the paddy field where our aircraft were parked among the trees. We dived into ditches and trenches and when all was over, it was found that the Blenheims were destroyed but my Hudson was still intact!"

Following the attack, the order to evacuate Bassein was given and a number of the Flight's personnel were flown to Dum Dum aboard the surviving Blenheim. Those remaining, including the Hudson crews, were instructed to board an old river steamer bound for Rangoon. On arrival, they realised the city was also being evacuated and therefore re-embarked; the escapees continued up the Irrawaddy to Magwe, which was reached after a seven day journey.

Five P-40s of the 1st Squadron escorted four 45 Squadron Blenheims to bomb Kawbein, 16 miles east of Martaban, where a column of over 300 vehicles was attacked. As they headed for the target, 23 Ki 27s from the 77th Sentai were seen escorting a dozen 31st Sentai Ki 21s in the other direction. Estimating the Japanese fighters to be about 40 strong, the Americans attacked, claiming four and three probables without loss, although several P-40s were damaged. Lt Kuwabara claimed one of the US fighters shot down, while probables were claimed by Lt Ogata and Wt Off Masao Hideshima. Claims for the AVG were submitted by: Flt Ldr George Burgard two, Robert H. Smith and John W. Farrell one and one probable apiece, and Flt Ldr Bond one probable; only one Ki 27 sustained minor damage.

During the raid two Blenheims were hit by ground fire and both were obliged

Top: Plt Off Les Hayton of 53 Squadron. *(Sqn Ldr L. Hayton)*. Above: "We tried all ways to manhandle the aircraft from this position. There was also a tree in front of the other wing." Plt Off Les Hayton's Hudson at Bassein. *(Sqn Ldr L. Hayton)*

to crash-land during the return flight; one crew survived unscathed but the pilot of Z7770, 2/Lt F.A.L. de Marillac, SAAF, and his observer were both wounded. During another attack on the column near Bilin two Hurricanes, flown by Sqn Ldr Sutton and Plt Off Bob Stout, were also hit by ground fire although both returned safely.

In the course of the day's attacks, troops of the British 17th Division at Mokpalin complained bitterly when they were bombed and strafed in error by some of the Blenheims, and heavy casualties were suffered. Without radios on which to contact the RAF direct, the Army was obliged to tap into the Burma Railway telephone lines and plead to be connected to RAF Headquarters! Air Vice-Marshal Stevenson, on learning of this tragic mistake, was not convinced however, expressing the belief that the Army had confused Ki 21s with Blenheims, or even that the Japanese were employing captured British aircraft!

Sunday, 22 February

The attacks on the Japanese columns were resumed at daylight without interference, but the two 28 Squadron Hurricane pilots experienced more mixed fortunes. Plt Off Dunsford-Wood, flying over the now thoroughly trigger-happy 17th Division, was shot down into the Sittang River by their fire, although he

Top: Mitsubishi Ki 15-II reconnaissance aircraft of the 1st Chutai, 8th Sentai, attacked and damaged by Flt Lt A.S. Mann of 28 Squadron (flying a 17 Squadron Hurricane) on 22 February, after force-landing at Moulmein with a wounded observer and 119 bullet holes in the aircraft. *(M. Takada)*. Above: Ki 15-II of the 8th Sentai flown by Lt Takesada Nakatani, seen here after landing at Moulmein after interception by Flt Lt Mann over the Sittang River.

135 Squadron Hurricanes. The nearest is Z5659 WK-C, flown by Plt Off (soon to be Flt Lt) Jack Storey during his successful combats in February. *(Sqn Ldr W.J. Storey)*

survived unhurt. In the same area, Flt Lt Mann encountered a single-engine reconnaissance aircraft, which he identified as an 'Army 98' and attacked; it was last seen trailing smoke. This was undoubtedly a Ki 15 from the 1st Chutai, 8th Sentai, from Nakhorn Sawan, the crew of which reported being attacked by three (sic) Hurricanes whilst over the Sittang River. Lt Takesada Nakatani, the pilot, suffered four bullet wounds to his right arm but, nonetheless, managed to crash-land the heavily damaged machine at Moulmein, where 119 bullet holes were counted in the aircraft.

Monday, 23 February

At 0930 Wg Cdr Carey, flying BM914, led a scramble by four Hurricanes on warning of the approach of enemy aircraft. Carey spotted a two-seater recon-naissance aircraft flying about 50 feet above the trees over the front line, near the Sittang River, and swiftly shot this down. His victim was a Ki 51 from the 70th Independent Chutai, flown by Capt Tadao Ohhira, who had been ordered to reconnoitre the east bank of the river. The aircraft crashed in flames, Ohhira and his observer losing their lives; their bodies were later recovered by advancing troops. Ohhira was posthumously awarded a citation.

As his leader was dealing with the reconnaissance machine, Plt Off Storey (Z5659 WK-C) noticed six fighters approaching from the east; he and his No 2 immediately engaged these, Storey selecting a straggler:

> "My man was a bit of a push-over for he was out to the right of the formation, curving around slowly, away from me, looking to see where the recce aircraft had got to, and I got him very smartly. I got in a stern attack — I don't think he even saw me — and went on fire, crashed and burned in the trees."

Somewhat later Sqn Ldr Sutton led four of 135 Squadron's Hurricanes to accompany four P-40s in a patrol over the Sittang, providing cover for a convoy leaving Rangoon. Seven Ki 27s appeared — believed to have been from the 50th Sentai — and the British fighters became involved in a dogfight over Kyaikta. Flt Lt Watson was last seen with two of the Japanese fighters on the tail of his aircraft (BG876) and he did not return.

Other Hurricanes escorted Blenheims and Indian Lysanders to bomb the Sittang Bridge, one of the latter falling to ground fire, Sgt H. Kameshwawa Dhora losing his life. The bridge was not hit during the attacks, although two spans were later demolished by British sappers before all Allied troops were across, many British and Indian soldiers being left trapped on the east bank. This conglomeration of troops and transport was heavily bombed during the late morning, many casualties and much damage being inflicted. Later in the day Toungoo was attacked by 31st Sentai Ki 30s, while from Magwe the groundcrews of 28 Squadron were now airlifted to Akyab, which was rapidly approaching operational status.

Tuesday, 24 February
The Allies hit back during the late morning, when at midday 1st Squadron P-40s strafed Raheng airfield, Sqn Ldr Neale and Bill McGarry claiming one bomber destroyed on the ground there, whilst Bob Prescott and Robert H. Smith jointly claimed a second. Flt Ldr Burgard and Bill Bartling each claimed a fighter, also on the ground. An hour or two later Wg Cdr Carey, Sqn Ldrs Stone and Elsdon and one other Hurricane pilot, accompanied by a pair of P-40s, made a similar attack on Moulmein.

Wg Cdr Frank Carey, Wing Leader of 267 Wing. *(Authors' collection)*

Carey (in BM914) spotted a transport aircraft "similar to a Dakota" taking off and quickly shot it down. Almost immediately he saw a Ki 27 just getting airborne and gave this a burst as he flashed by, claiming this shot down also. Meanwhile, Stone (in YB-X) claimed a bomber and a fighter destroyed on the ground. Japanese records indicate that a single Ki 27 of the 47th Independent Chutai was badly damaged during the strafe.

During an air raid alert at Mingaladon, an Airspeed Envoy (N9108, ex G-AFJE), attached to 60 Squadron, took off to avoid being attacked on the ground. Witnesses believed that an unexploded bomb from a previous raid blew up beneath the aircraft just as it got into the air, causing it to crash into a lake near Insein Brickworks, one mile west of the airfield, with the loss of Wt Off C.S. Gill and his navigator, Plt Off H.L. Cox.

From Dum Dum a few more Hurricanes threaded their way down to Magwe as reinforcements, of which two were flown by Plt Offs Lee Hawkins (in BM927) and John Monk (an American), both members of 135 Squadron.

Wednesday, 25 February

Constant patrols were maintained over Mingaladon all through the morning, but it was midday when a big Japanese fighter sweep approached, comprising 21 Ki 27s from the 50th Sentai, 23 more from the 77th Sentai and three of the pre-production Ki 44s of the 47th Independent Chutai, which had operated earlier over Malaya. Three P-40s were led off by Sqn Ldr Neale, together with six of 17 Squadron's Hurricanes. Plt Off Ken Hemingway in one of the latter, later recorded:

> "There was so much dust I cannot think how we failed to have a taxying prang. I know as I edged forward through the whirling clouds in order to get along to the runway allocated to us, a P-40 loomed up, just off the deck, its wheels beginning to fold up. It missed me by a matter of feet, and I was forced to wait in case there were others following. We got away well though, the CO leading us north at first to gain great height, then we came back. Ahead was a small bunch of our chaps, including 'Tex' Barrick, who had become separated during take-off."

Five pilots of 17 Squadron at Mingaladon in early February. Left to right: Sgt Jack Gibson, Sgt Al MacDonald, Sgt Tex Barrick, Plt Off Ken Hemingway and Sgt Ken Wheatley. *(J.F. Barrick via P. Clausen)*

Sgt Barrick had seen the oncoming mass of hostile fighters, which he accurately assessed to be 50 strong, and had excitedly yelled "Snapper! Snapper!" over the R/T, forgetting that this was the emergency code word used in the European theatre to indicate that they were being jumped. Consequently Sqn Ldr Stone had not reacted, and continued heading south-west, towards the position where the enemy had been reported. "Snapper! Snapper!" was then repeated with even greater urgency, at which Stone led the Hurricanes into a circle, waiting instructions, until Operations ordered them to return, having seen nothing.

Sgt J.F. 'Tex' Barrick, one of 17 Squadron's American pilots, soon to become one of the most successful RAF fighter pilots in Burma. *(J.F. Barrick via P. Clausen)*

Meanwhile Barrick, believing that the rest of the squadron were following him, had sailed into 15 Japanese fighters alone:

> "I attacked and shot down one 'Army 97' and was then jumped from above by a 'Zero' (*presumably one of the Ki 44s*). I went into a tight turn which caused one of the gun panels to fly open. This made the aircraft 'flick' and probably saved my life, because the 'Zero' was in an excellent position behind me. As it was my plane was not hit."

The AVG trio had also become engaged with the Ki 27s, claiming four shot down without loss — two by Neale and one each by Bob Prescott and Bill McGarry. Despite the five claims submitted, the Japanese fighters suffered no losses. However their own claims proved wild in the extreme, amounting to many more Allied fighters than were in the air. The Ki 44 pilots claimed two, whilst the 50th Sentai added three and two probables. No less than 11 and five probables were claimed by the 77th Sentai, one by the Headquarters flight, seven and two probables by the 1st Chutai, one and two probables by the 2nd Chutai and two, one probable and one damaged by the 3rd Chutai. Claiming pilots were: Sgt Maj Matsunaga two; Lt Kawada one; Capt Eto one and one probable; Lt Matsuo one; Lt Kuwabara one; Wt Off Fujinaga one and one probable; Wt Off Kimura one; Sgt Niino one; Lt Nakajima one; Lt Tsuguo Kojima and Wt Off Honma one shared; Lt Shinjirou Nagoshi and Sgt Ono one probable apiece.

Following this raid, Sqn Ldr Stone led 17 Squadron's six Hurricanes to attack Japanese shipping reported in the Gulf of Martaban, while four Blenheims of 45 Squadron raided Moulmein, where two riverboats were claimed sunk. The Hurricane pilots spotted two medium-sized vessels near the coast, crammed with troops, and strafed these, leaving one in flames and the other abandoned. Many soldiers were observed struggling in the sea as the Hurricanes headed back to their base.

No sooner had these two formations landed to refuel, than the Japanese returned. A dozen 8th Sentai Ki 48s, covered by all three fighter units, had flown first to Bassein, but finding no aircraft there, headed instead for Mingaladon, arriving there at about 1700. All available serviceable P-40s and about a dozen Hurricanes of 17 and 135 Squadrons were scrambled, climbing hard to 18,000 feet. Plt Off Hemingway found himself at the head of two or three other Hurricanes, and soon spotted the bombers and a mass of fighters. He managed to slide in behind one section of four bombers and saw his fire strike one before he dived away, fearful of being jumped. Pulling up, he climbed to 20,000 feet, came up behind a Ki 27 and again saw strikes before it dived away. He returned to base with one of the P-40s and was later credited with the bomber shot down, when Plt Off Frank Earnshaw reported that he had seen this go down in flames.

The AVG pilots had undertaken their favoured diving attack on the Japanese formation, and returned to submit an extraordinary 'bag' of claims: Sqn Ldr Neale two fighters; Flt Ldr Burgard one bomber and two fighters; Flt Ldr Bond three fighters; Flt Ldr Little three fighters; Robert H. Smith three fighters; Bob Prescott two fighters; Camille Rosbert one fighter and one probable; John Blackburn one fighter; Dick Rossi one fighter; Bill McGarry three fighters — to give a total of 21 fighters and one bomber!

One American pilot allegedly commented:

"I'd never seen so many fighters in the air. Some were silver. Others were camouflaged. They swarmed all over the sky like flies buzzing around a dead dog. We pitched into them and the slaughter was terrific. The fighters were blowing up all over the sky like bursts of anti-aircraft shells. Just a puff of smoke, a ball of flame, and they were gone. We knocked down 13 confirmed. We felt pretty good with a total of 24 for the day and no losses."

James D. Cross' aircraft was badly hit however, and he force-landed at the 'John Haig' strip although he was not hurt and the P-40 was soon repaired.

One section of 135 Squadron aircraft had been delayed taking off, when Sqn Ldr Sutton's Hurricane (flying Z5473 YB-J of 17 Squadron) initially failed to start. He took off about five minutes behind the rest and joined forces with a section of P-40s but soon outclimbed these and, on reaching 22,000 feet, saw anti-aircraft bursts on the horizon.

Unable to locate the raiders, he flew out over the Gulf of Martaban and was soon near Moulmein. Determined to attack something, he dived on the airfield but as he did so he encountered two bombers (presumably Ki 48s of the 8th

Sentai) going in to land. Firing at both, he saw one trail smoke as he broke away. As he attacked again, many other Japanese aircraft approached and he fired in their general direction before diving to 50 feet and heading for home. Halfway there, he met a Ki 27 head-on, opened fire and passed close by his opponent. Of the encounter, he wrote:

> "If I have missed him, I do not delude myself that he cannot whip round on my tail in that absurd little fighter of his with its perambulator-like wire wheels and pump me full of lead from behind before I have even a half-chance to follow him. Normally my tactics would be to dive away. If I dive now, as little as ten feet, I must hit the sea. If I pull up I would lose speed and be as good as a 'sitter' to the Jap behind.
>
> "He knows all this and is beginning to turn as we pass. He zooms up and behind, now standing on one wing, spreadeagled against the skyline. One minute he is there. The next he is not. He had crashed either because he spun off a very tight turn or because I had hit him.
>
> "The latter is the more likely reason, I think. I have no illusions about my ability as a marksman but it would have been hard to miss with eight Brownings and a head-on, almost point-blank shot."

Despite his denigration of his own marksmanship, Sutton had been credited with four victories during the Battle of Britain; on this occasion he returned to claim the fighter shot down, and the bomber probably so.

Sqn Ldr Barry Sutton, DFC, commanding officer of 135 Squadron. *(N. Franks)*

Only the 50th Sentai submitted any claims against the Allied fighters, claiming one and two probables for the loss of two Ki 27s, it being reported that Lt Masao Mihara had rammed an opponent (possibly the head-on attack with Sutton). The 8th Sentai lost no bombers, but claimed two aircraft destroyed on the ground. In this at least, there had been an underestimate of results, as five of 45 Squadron's recently returned Blenheims were destroyed or damaged beyond repair during the attack. Amongst those killed on the ground was one of 84 Squadron's pilots, Sgt J.C. McNamara, RAAF, who had been attached to 45 Squadron following his failure to join the rest of his unit in Sumatra.

Remains of a burnt-out Blenheim at Mingaladon, following a Japanese air raid. *(Wg Cdr G. Marsland)*

At Magwe meanwhile, 31 Squadron DC-2s and Valentias were joined by 113 Squadron Blenheims in transporting supplies and groundcrews up to Akyab. Wg Cdr H.P. Jenkins, CO of the former unit, arrived in a Lockheed 12, but flew on to Mingaladon.

Thursday, 26 February

Early in the morning a dozen Ki 30s of the 31st Sentai took off from Phitsanulok, led by Maj Kiyoshi Tojiri, for a raid on Pegu strip, rendezvousing with their fighter escort over Moulmein, and reaching their target at about 0800, where one aircraft was claimed to have been hit and set on fire on the ground. The Japanese recorded that they were followed back to Moulmein by seven Hurricanes, which were engaged by 50th Sentai Ki 27s, the pilots of which claimed three probably shot down, while a fourth was shot down by AA fire.

This report appears to accord with an attack made by six Hurricanes which were led by Wg Cdr Carey (in BM914) to strafe Moulmein following Sqn Ldr Sutton's report of the aircraft he had seen there the day before. It was agreed that Sqn Ldr Stone's section of three would provide top cover while Carey, Flt Lt Cotton and Plt Off Underwood would carry out the actual strafe. The Hurricanes were delayed in taking-off owing to a heavy ground mist and, when they did get away, they encountered a lone Hurricane over the Gulf, which turned out to be one of 135 Squadron's aircraft, flown by newly-arrived Plt Off John Monk, who was getting in some flying practice! He joined up with the formation, increasing Sqn Ldr Stone's top cover section to four aircraft. It was not until the Hurricanes were halfway across the Gulf that Carey realised they were trailing the departing raiders; he later recalled:

> "We thought we saw some stragglers over the Gulf of Martaban and during the dive down to investigate I lost one of my two Hurricanes in the dust haze."

As Carey and Underwood approached Moulmein, closely followed by Cotton, a number of the returning Ki 27s were seen making their landing circuits, while another four were seen touching down. Carey continued:

> "I picked on a likely-looking couple. These were well committed to final approach and I dived down with Underwood and picked off the rearmost of

---

279

the two. He fell in a bit of a heap on the end of the runway — which was only to be expected."

Wg Cdr Frank Carey in the cockpit of his Hurricane. *(Sqn Ldr L.C.C. Hawkins)*

Carey then immediately attacked the second, which tried to climb and turn but its port wingtip hit the ground and it crashed in flames amongst the hangars. Underwood, in BG821, claimed another off his leader's tail:

> "I noticed a fighter had just taken off and was pulling up as though it was about to fire at Frank Carey's aircraft, which was ahead of it. I succeeded in shooting the aircraft down (it crashed into the trees at the far end of the runway) but was then hit myself in the engine from something of fairly heavy calibre as I pulled away at low level over the trees.
>
> "I was virtually blind from oil and smoke so pulled the stick back, stuck my backside into the breeze and pulled the ripcord of my parachute! How it cleared the aircraft without hitting the tail I don't know but within a matter of seconds I was on the ground feeling somewhat lonely, very battered and a bit burned."

'Bush' Cotton also claimed a Ki 27 shot down and probably destroyed a second on the ground:

> "I went down on two of them and got one chap after he turned around and started to climb in the opposite direction. He was about 2,000 feet above the ground and someone must have warned him because he turned right around. I got a full beam shot into him and gave him about a one-second burst.
>
> "He flipped right over and went straight into the ground just by the edge of the aerodrome. After that I pulled up to about 5,000 feet and started getting mixed up with two of them and after getting a few bullets through my rudder did a spiral dive, got away from them, pulled out between a couple of low hills near the aerodrome and, as I zipped across the drome, shot one up as he was touching down.

"The Jap swung around, stopped, and as his aircraft was starting to burn it was enveloped in a cloud of dust. As I left I counted five columns of smoke arising on and around the aerodrome."

Wg Cdr Carey meanwhile — having accounted for two of the Ki 27s — climbed away to look for Underwood's aircraft, only to be engaged by a number of others. Manoeuvring wildly, he managed to evade serious damage and succeeded in getting in "a good burst" at one, which "spun over and dived into the ground just outside the airfield". Two of the Ki 27s also pursued Cotton's aircraft as he sped away at full throttle just above the treetops, meeting Carey's battered Hurricane on the way. Plt Off Storey, having inspected the Hurricane later, wrote in his diary:

"Wing Commander Carey landed his aircraft with dozens of bullet holes through the fuselage and wings. How he himself or a vital part of the machine escaped damage has amazed everyone."

Japanese records confirm that one 77th Sentai Ki 27 was 'burned', one badly damaged and three damaged to a lesser extent; 50th Sentai losses are unknown. When flying back from Mudon to Moulmein during the day, Maj Yasuo Makino was injured in one of the 77th Sentai's Ki 27s and was hospitalized, but whether this was due to aerial combat is not known; he may have been in one of the aircraft claimed shot down during the morning engagements in the area.

Meanwhile the downed Hurricane pilot, Plt Off Underwood, was taken prisoner:

"As I had come down relatively close to Moulmein aerodrome my obvious reaction was to get away from the local area and I headed roughly to the west which should have taken me to the estuary of the River Salween. Unfortunately, I had only gone a short way when I passed out and on coming round I found myself surrounded by rather unfriendly Burmese who were joined very shortly afterwards by several Japanese soldiers.

"My hands were tied, and, with my own scarf (which I wore when flying) tied round the worst of my leg wounds, I was marched across paddy fields to a lorry having first had my watch taken from me. Apart from a signet ring which I pretended would not come off, I had no other valuables or papers on me so there was nothing more they could have taken. I was taken to Moulmein aerodrome where my legs were bandaged and I was kept tied up to a chair in the one and only building on the aerodrome, for the rest of the day."[1]

Oddly, at around this same time the 1st AVG Squadron also recorded launching an attack on Moulmein with seven P-40s. On approaching the airfield three Ki 27s were seen standing on an auxiliary field and two of these were claimed destroyed in flames, by all seven pilots jointly. At the main airfield three more

---

[1] After three days of interrogation Plt Off Underwood received medical attention, but was then handed over to the military police at Moulmein Jail. For a further week he was subjected to repeated questioning, accompanied by beatings of varying degrees of severity. Between sessions of interrogation, he was kept in solitary confinement. Subsequently he was allowed to mix during the day with other prisoners — mainly Army officers who had endured similar treatment, although all were locked in separate cells at night. In June he was moved to Rangoon Jail, where he began three long years of captivity.

Plt Off Guy Underwood of 135 Squadron, seen here earlier in the war as a Sergeant with 605 Squadron. *(G.W. Underwood)*

Ki 27s were seen about to take off and a further 20 warming up. As the initial trio got into the air, Flt Ldr Burgard and his wingman, Dick Rossi, each claimed one shot down. Many more Japanese aircraft apparently now appeared from the south and Sqn Ldr Neale was chased out over the Gulf of Martaban with three on his tail. He escaped in cloud and returned in his damaged aircraft to claim all three shot down! Allegedly the other pilots had meantime engaged the new arrivals, Burgard claiming one more, while Flt Ldr Little claimed three, Bill McGarry two, and Camille Rosbert one!

There was subsequently much rumour about AVG pilots "buying" RAF claims due to their system of payment by the Chinese authorities for aircraft confirmed shot down. Had both Allied formations attacked at the same time, or had the Americans "acquired" this attack from the RAF? Certainly, Japanese records note only the one strafe, and identify the attackers as Hurricanes. Or had Carey's formation struck the main airfield and the AVG the satellite strip at Mudon? Much here remains unanswered.

Around midday a further raid was launched by the Japanese, this time Ki 48s of the 8th Sentai, led by Capt Sueo Yamamoto, attacking Mingaladon, escorted by Ki 27s from both the 50th and 77th Sentais. Here the bomber crews reported two aircraft destroyed and seven others damaged on the ground; apparently eight Blenheims and Lysanders were hit, several subsequently being written off, as they had been damaged beyond repair.

Nine P-40s and several Hurricanes were scrambled, the AVG pilots claiming seven fighters and one bomber shot down without loss: Flt Ldr Bond one; Flt Ldr Burgard one; Dick Rossi two; Camille Rosbert two, John Blackburn one, while Robert H. Smith claimed a 'Type 97 bomber'.

Amongst the Hurricane pilots, Plt Off Storey (Z5659 WK-C) dived to attack two Ki 27s but spotted others about to jump him, so broke away. Flt Lt Cotton encountered the bombers just after they had made their attack, and recalled:

"I was able to do one beam and quarter attack on the bomber group before the twelve escort fighters arrived on the scene, but I saw one bomber go down before they did so and this was later confirmed by the AVG. Instead of going home, I decided that I could outclimb the fighters and at about 24,000 feet was well on top and winged over to dive on their top section.

"To my eternal consternation one of them stood on its tail and squirted a burst right through the left side of my aircraft. One bullet busted my left leg just below the knee and although there were some 130 odd hits registered on my kite, I was able to do an aileron turn and dive out to nought feet and get back to the 'drome.

"All the hydraulics worked and I was able to land by jamming my right foot under the toe strap on the rudder bar and taxied back to the dispersal. Later it was found the aircraft (BD963) was beyond repair and it was blown up with a hand grenade."

Sqn Ldr M.C.C. 'Bush' Cotton, DFC, seen in India after the retreat, when he became commanding officer of 17 Squadron, following recovery from his leg wound. *(Wg Cdr G. Marsland)*

On this occasion, two of the 8th Sentai bombers did indeed fail to return, one being seen to be shot down, while one of the 77th Sentai Ki 27s was also lost. The escort fighters claimed seven and three probables, the 77th claiming three (one apiece being credited to Lts Kawada, Kuwabara and Matsuo) and one probable (Lt Shimoda). One of their victories may have been Hurricane BE171 YB-B of 17 Squadron, which Capt A.D. Penton (the Army Liaison Officer attached to the unit, who was also a trained army co-operation pilot) had borrowed to undertake a reconnaissance over the Sittang area. He was intercepted by Japanese aircraft and shot down, though he escaped injury and returned later to Mingaladon in an ox-cart.

Later in the day the Japanese reported that five British aircraft, believed to have been Blenheims, bombed Moulmein from great height, but caused little damage. Of more impact, a reconnaissance sortie flown by an 8th Sentai crew discovered Magwe airfield, previously unknown to the Japanese, counting 22 small aircraft, four medium sized and one large machine on the ground there.

These two days had brought some of the greatest over-claiming of the campaign — if not of the whole war — and for very limited actual results. On the 25th the AVG had claimed 26 and one probable, and the RAF four, for one P-40 force-landed; next day the AVG added a further 20 claims in the air and two on the ground, and the RAF six plus one probable on the ground for the loss of two Hurricanes and one P-40, with two more Hurricanes and one P-40 badly damaged. The Japanese had been almost as profligate, claiming 16 and seven probables for the loss of two Ki 27s on the 25th, followed by seven and six probables, plus one by AA gunners, on the 26th when two Ki 51 bombers and two Ki 27s were lost in the air, with one more destroyed, one badly damaged and three damaged in the Moulmein area.

Thus combined total claims by both sides for 80 aircraft shot down, plus 14 probables, had been matched by actual losses of perhaps 10 or 11, with about seven more damaged. There had obviously been some questioning at the time of the Allied claims, for Air Vice-Marshal Stevenson was later to write in his despatch:

> "There was a little feeling in the AVG on the assessment of results. Consequently I held a meeting with the AVG squadron commander, the wing leader and RAF squadron commanders, at which it was agreed that the standard of assessment should be that obtaining in Fighter Command at home.
>
> "Colonel Chennault was informed. Combat reports by pilots were initialled by squadron commanders. The claim was then admitted. Previous claims by the AVG for aircraft destroyed in the air were agreed at this meeting."

As a consequence of the claims made and accepted on these two days, Sqn Ldr Bob Neale had become the AVG's top-scorer with 12 victories plus several probables.

Friday, 27 February

Further raids were made during the day but no interceptions were achieved. Bombers of the 31st Sentai raided Pegu Station during the morning, where some 50 goods wagons were claimed destroyed, the attack being repeated in the evening. As the bombers, escorted by 77th Sentai Ki 27s, passed over Toungoo, Sgt Dildor Khan of 1 IAF Squadron climbed into the rear cockpit of a Lysander to fire at them from the ground, claiming hits on one. 8th Sentai bombers raided Mingaladon shortly before darkness fell, when one large aircraft was claimed destroyed there, whilst a night attack was made by the 14th Sentai. During one of these raids fighters were scrambled but failed to make contact. Plt Off Bob Stout of 135 Squadron crashed his Hurricane on landing and, whilst he was not hurt, the aircraft was wrecked.

Following the destruction of one of the three remaining 28 Squadron Lysanders on detachment at Mingaladon, on the 26th, the last two were now flown out to Magwe where they were taken over by 221 Group Communications Flight and evacuated to India. Only five P-40s remained airworthy at Mingaladon, others being withdrawn to Magwe, so when on the 28th Air Vice-Marshal Stevenson advised Sqn Ldr Neale that the RDF (radar) sets were being dismantled for despatch to that latter airfield, Neale decided it was time to

The wreckage of Plt Off Stout's 135 Squadron Hurricane after a landing accident on 27 February. *(Sqn Ldr L.C.C. Hawkins)*

withdraw his squadron there also. This left only four or five Hurricanes of 135 Squadron at Mingaladon, since 17 Squadron aircraft were now all at the satellite strips — 'John Haig', 'Johnnie Walker' and 'Highland Queen'. Meantime, two 136 Squadron pilots, Sgts Ting Bunting and Bob Payne, had been sent to Akyab for a week's rest, but as Bunting recalled:

"As the evacuation of Rangoon started while we were at Akyab we made our way back to Magwe, where we pinched two 17 Squadron Hurricanes and flew back to Rangoon. Here we now only had one pilot per aircraft and we were worked really hard strafing the Japs and sometimes, due to bad liaison, our own troops."

By now the operational fighter strength of 'X' Wing had dwindled to below ten, through lack of maintenance and spares, in addition to battle damage. Hurricanes were still arriving from the Middle East via India, however, and parts of the 3rd AVG Squadron had been ordered to Magwe from Kunming. As a result strength would increase over the next few days to peak at 27 Hurricanes and P-40s.

The Indian Squadron still had a lone Lysander at Toungoo which had been undertaking daily reconnaissance for the army. After the raid on Pegu on the 27th, Flt Lt Raza took off with Sgt Dildor Khan to attack Mehongsohn airfield in retaliation, firing on soldiers working there and bombing the radio station. They escaped with one bullet hole through the tailplane, and the next day they were withdrawn to Magwe.

Sunday, 1 March

Newly-promoted Field Marshal Sir Archibald Wavell, accompanied by Maj General Lewis Brereton, flew in to Magwe for a conference with Governor Sir Reginald Dorman-Smith, Lt General Hutton and Air Vice-Marshal Stevenson. Wavell then flew in a Blenheim to Lashio via Pegu, where he urged Chiang Kai-shek to move the 5th and 6th Chinese Armies into Burma.

One Blenheim of 113 Squadron (V6967) crashed on take off from Magwe when departing for a raid on Bilin, although the crew survived unhurt. From Mingaladon a pair of 135 Squadron Hurricanes strafed in the Pegu area, when newly-promoted Flt Lt Storey's BG843 WK-E was hit by two bullets in the engine oil sump, and he was obliged to force-land on return.

Monday, 2 March

For the Hurricanes, strafing was again the order of the day. Sqn Ldr Elsdon recorded:

> "We were sent to attack anything east of the Sittang Bridge as the Army had completely withdrawn to the west bank of the river. In fact Army briefing was inaccurate and some units (or parts of units) were cut off on the east bank. Unhappily they suffered some casualties from our guns in these attacks."

28 Squadron's Flt Lt Mann later set off in 17 Squadron's YB-J (Z5473) on one of his tactical reconnaissance sorties over the Sittang, where he was attacked by three Ki 27s (believed to have been 50th Sentai aircraft); the Hurricane suffered a hit in its glycol tank and the pilot was slightly wounded in one foot. With a seized engine, Mann force-landed in a paddy field near Abya, the Ki 27s following him down to strafe. He managed to avoid further injury and eventually made his way through the Japanese lines, hidden under a blanket in the ox cart of a friendly Burmese. On reaching the Burma Road, he made contact with a party of soldiers from the Burma Rifles and was conveyed to 17th Division Head-quarters, from whence he was returned to 'Highland Queen' by car.

Towards evening Sqn Ldr Sutton flew to 'Highland Queen' to confer with Sqn Ldr Stone over a proposed combined 17/135 Squadron attack on troop concentrations the following morning. Shortly before dusk however, all available Hurricanes were ordered off to search for Japanese shipping reported in the Gulf of Martaban but only three aircraft were available, Sutton joining Stone and Plt Off Earnshaw on this sortie, although he lost sight of them in the failing light. No shipping was seen and, on returning to 'Highland Queen', Sutton was obliged to land in darkness, aided by an improvised flare-path provided by the headlights of a car and a lorry, and a number of burning rag bundles, which had been dipped in rum to keep them alight! Of Stone and Earnshaw there was no sign, but both had — in the absence of a flare-path — elected to land at Mingaladon instead, the much larger airfield allowing more scope for error. Nevertheless, Earnshaw crashed on landing although he escaped injury. The proposed attack for the morrow was cancelled.

Meanwhile, the JAAF continued to build up its strength in readiness for a final push against the Allies in Burma. Units which had fought in Malaya were now being prepared for movement to airfields in Thailand and occupied Burma. Establishment of units already in the area are shown in Table 12.

Table 12

JAAF Order of Battle, Burma Theatre of Operations, 2 March 1942

Fighters:

50th Sentai	Moulmein	18 Ki 27s (6 unserviceable)
77th Sentai	Phitsanuloh	24 Ki 27s (10 unserviceable)

Bombers/Reconnaissance:

8th Sentai	Nakhon Sawan	11 Ki 15s & Ki 48s
	Bangkok	11 Ki 48s
	Mudon	3 Ki 15s, 2 Ki 46s
14th Sentai	Nakhon Sawan	11 Ki 21s
31st Sentai	Lampong	18 Ki 30s (8 unserviceable)
70th Ind Chutai		5 Ki 51s & Ki 46s

NB: 62nd Sentai was converting from Ki 21-Is to Ki 21-IIs at Phnom Penh, Indo-China.

Tuesday, 3 March

Early in the morning Sgt Tex Wisrodt, one of 17 Squadron's four Americans, departed on a solo reconnaissance sortie, but failed to return. Villagers reported having seen an aircraft, believed to be his Hurricane, dive into the Sittang; it was presumed that he had been shot down by ground fire.

Wednesday, 4 March

Four Blenheims (three of 45 Squadron, one of 113 Squadron) departed Magwe to bomb targets in the Sittang area, but were attacked by four fighters believed to be 'Zeros'. Since no A6Ms or Ki 43s were yet operating over the area, it is possible that these were the Ki 44s of the 47th Independent Chutai. Although all four Blenheims were hit, the fighters concentrated on Flt Lt F.S. Lee's Z7592, three attacking from the rear and one from head-on. The RAAF pilot was mortally wounded and the aircraft crashed 60 miles east of Pegu, the observer, Sgt K.W. Brett, RNZAF, also losing his life. Only the gunner, Sgt L. Walker, managed to struggle free of the wreckage and escape the strafing which followed. After trecking through the jungle for two days, Walker encountered a friendly Burmese who guided him to a unit of the Burma Rifles, from where he was conveyed to 'Highland Queen'.

Strafing by the Hurricanes continued, a column of tanks being attacked on the 4th and a number of river barges next day, as the Japanese Army began an encircling movement designed to take Pegu and cut the Rangoon-Mandalay road. At this critical juncture, command of the Burma Army was taken over by Lt General Sir Harold Alexander, DSO, MC, an Anglo-Irishman who had commanded 1 Corps at Dunkirk.

It was becoming clear that Rangoon must soon fall, so 135 Squadron was ordered to leave Mingaladon. The ground crews were already on their way to Akyab by ship, and now the remaining unserviceable aircraft were burned, the air party preparing to fly to Prome. 17 Squadron was also getting ready to move, the ground crews to Zigon and the air party to Magwe.

At Magwe meanwhile part of the 3rd AVG Squadron ('Hell's Angels') had arrived, led by Flt Ldr Parker Dupouy, ostensibly to relieve the 1st Squadron. However Sqn Ldr Neale refused to go, continuing to lead his unit in daily strafing sorties until the 13th, when Colonel Chennault ordered him out of

Burma. Sqn Ldr Arvid Olsen soon followed Dupouy to Magwe with the rest of the 3rd Squadron.

As more Hurricanes reached Magwe from Dum Dum, a number of 67 Squadron pilots received a brief introduction to these aircraft — varying from 20 to 50 minutes. At this stage, Air Vice-Marshal Stevenson decided that a raid should be carried out against Chiengmai airfield, using the six available 45 Squadron Blenheims, which were to be escorted by six Hurricanes (five of which were to be flown by 67 Squadron pilots), four Buffaloes and eight P-40s. Wg Cdr Carey was informed that he was to lead the mission, although he lacked maps of the target area; upon learning this, the Blenheim leader, Wg Cdr Wallis, offered to navigate the strike force to Chiengmai. On protesting to the AOC about the improbability of success for such a hastily-organized operation, Carey was threatened with a Court Martial if he refused to go. His request for the available fighter aircraft to be manned by volunteers — as was the case with the Blenheim crews — also fell upon deaf ears.

Curtiss P-40s of the AVG's 3rd Squadron, newly-arrived at Magwe in early March. *(Sqn Ldr P.M. Bingham-Wallis)*

As the fighters lacked the range to go all the way in one 'hop', it was planned that they should refuel at Namsang, an RAF airfield in the Southern Shan States, and then rendezvous with the bombers. On taking off from Magwe however, Carey's engine cut and he was forced to carry out an emergency landing. Sqn Ldr Jack Brandt took over command of the mixed fighter force and headed for Namsang where, on arrival, things began to go wrong. The strip was no more that a short stretch of ground cleared of paddy, and there was only a skeleton staff present. The brakes of one Hurricane failed as it landed and it careered straight into the thick scrub surrounding the strip. The groundcrews, unfamiliar with the aircraft, poured petrol into the glycol tank of another Hurricane! Flt Lt Peter Bingham-Wallis, who was leading the Buffaloes in W8191/H, recalled:

"The AVG and our four Buffaloes took off together. The (remaining) four Hurricanes, led by Sqn Ldr Brandt, disappeared into the haze and patrolled a little to the east and south-east of the airfield. No Blenheims were spotted and the AVG leader, Bob Neale, on reaching the Salween River, appeared to consider that he might go on alone without the bombers, although we had no radio communication with him, but he decided to return to Namsang.

"At the cracking pace he set I felt our fuel consumption would have caused us to force-land in Thailand on our return! The only Blenheim we came across was one which had landed with engine trouble and which we escorted back to Magwe the next day."

Flt Lt Peter Bingham-Wallis, 67 Squadron veteran of the Burma campaign. *(Sqn Ldr P.M. Bingham-Wallis)*

On landing back at Namsang, one Buffalo (AN168) hit a truck and was damaged beyond repair, although the pilot was unhurt. Then Sgt Ken Rutherford's Buffalo (W8245) was found to have developed oil pressure problems and had to be left behind when the others returned to Magwe. The problem was soon rectified and Rutherford followed later.

Friday, 6 March

14 Ki 27s of the 77th Sentai flew a patrol over Mingaladon during the morning and, in doing so, overflew the previously undiscovered 'Highland Queen' airstrip. Several Hurricanes managed to take off and Flg Off Lloyd Thomas was able to claim one of the Japanese fighters shot down — this was probably Wt Off Saburo Hagiwara's aircraft, which force-landed at Kyaito, the pilot returning to his unit next day. A second was claimed as a possible. In return,

Hagiwara claimed one Hurricane shot down, whilst Capt Eto's flight, together with Lt Nakajima, jointly claimed a second. On the ground one aircraft was claimed burnt by Lt Nagoshi, and several others reported damaged; one or two Hurricanes were indeed damaged beyond repair, including WK-B of 135 Squadron. As a result of this attack, 17 Squadron was ordered to withdraw at once.

General Alexander now decided to evacuate Rangoon and, next day, his mechanized column broke through the roadblock which the Japanese had managed to throw across the road, then withdrew towards Prome. 'X' Wing was ordered to Zigon to assist this retreat, as Group Headquarters in Rangoon was demolished and as much damage as possible carried out to Mingaladon.

Saturday, 7 March

During the following 48 hours, operations around Rangoon were hampered by heavy haze and by a vast column of smoke which rose up to 15,000 feet due to the demolitions which were taking place. Half a dozen fighter pilots were still at Mingaladon, and one of these, Sgt Bunting, took off at 1030 for a patrol over the docks. At about midday he was informed that Japanese aircraft were over Mingaladon and all the other strips. By then low on fuel, he headed for home, but saw eight aircraft approaching as he went in to land. One opened fire, so he pulled up the undercarriage and flaps and headed off at top speed, skidding and weaving at low level. The Hurricane was hit several times, but he managed to land with oil and glycol leaking out and his hydraulic system inoperative. When he climbed out of the badly damaged fighter, he learned that he had left his R/T on transit, treating the operating controller to some very ripe language! The damaged Hurricane had to be burnt.

Wg Cdr Carey then arrived at Mingaladon, escorting two IAF Lysanders (flown by Sgt C.H. Fox, RNZAF, and the Australian Sgt McRae) from Akyab, which were to assist with the evacuation. Sqn Ldr Sutton and Sgt Bunting departed for Prome as passengers in the Lysanders, whilst three repaired Hurricanes were flown to Akyab in the hands of Sqn Ldr Elsdon (BE290), Flt Lt Storey (BG876) and Sgt Payne. Having seen the various aircraft safely away, Wg Cdr Carey was ordered to fly to Zigon, accompanied by the last, hastily-repaired Buffalo, W8191 RD-H flown by Flt Lt Bingham-Wallis, who recalled:

> "Our instructions were to land at Zigon — an airstrip formed out of two paddy fields close to the Prome/Rangoon road and about halfway between the two towns. Frank's instructions were that we were to patrol over the army convoys which General Alexander was evacuating from Rangoon to Prome, following which we were to return to Magwe having returned to Zigon to refuel.
>
> "I took off on the second patrol — the engine started to cut out at 50 feet and cut out altogether at 100 feet. I put the nose down and kept going and fell into a pond."

The aircraft was a write-off, although Bingham-Wallis was not hurt. He and three others later evacuated from Zigon in Grp Capt Singer's staff car.

Another Lysander was despatched from Akyab, carrying aboard a 31 Squadron fitter and spares for one of the unit's DC-2s stranded at Mingaladon. The Lysander however, became lost between Rangoon and Toungoo, eventually ran out of fuel and force-landed; neither pilot nor passenger were hurt. A damaged Blenheim, which had broken its stern frame in a rough landing, was flown from Zayatkwin to Prome by Grp Capt Singer. At Akyab meanwhile, four more reinforcement pilots of 136 Squadron arrived from Calcutta in a Valentia transport (JR8328/B of 31 Squadron) — Sgts Frank Wilding, Freddie Fortune, Freddie Pickard and Jimmy Wetherall.

Waiting to go to Akyab — four reinforcement pilots of 136 Squadron: left to right: Sgt Frank Wilding, Sgt Jimmy Wetherall, Sgt Freddie Pickard and Sgt Freddie Fortune. *(F.E. Wilding)*

Sunday, 8 March
Throughout the day Hurricanes, Buffaloes, Blenheims and Lysanders flew from Zigon in support of the retreating columns on the Prome road; however several aircraft were damaged by the poor surface of this airfield and, at the end of the day therefore, all aircraft were withdrawn to a new strip north of Prome, known as 'Park Lane'. Apparently neither Zigon nor 'Park Lane' were known to the Japanese, the Hurricanes continuing to fly 12-18 sorties per day. Some were now so in need of repair that they left Zigon with wooden plugs driven into the engine blocks to seal oil leaks. Sgt Barrick of 17 Squadron recalled:

> "I flew out an aircraft that had been damaged in the strafing attack the day before. The Hurricane did not have an airspeed indicator or, in fact, any workable instruments! I reached Magwe and managed to land safely. Then, as the Hurricane rolled down the airstrip, I saw a truck come running across the runway. It ploughed into my aircraft!
>
> "Wing Commander Carey was so upset about this he threatened to Court Martial the unfortunate driver!"

Monday, 9 March
The Japanese recorded a raid on Moulmein by five Allied aircraft, just as the 8th Sentai was taking off to attack troops near Rangoon; a captured Blenheim was hit and set on fire. Next day (9th), Bunting and Fox left Zigon to fly two unserviceable Hurricanes to Magwe, but on the way Fox was obliged to bale out over Prome when his engine failed. The engine of Bunting's aircraft then failed over Magwe, but he managed to put it down safely on the airfield. At this point 'X' Wing was withdrawn to Magwe and was disbanded, its task complete. The first phase of the Japanese invasion of Burma was virtually accomplished.

Chapter 8

INVASION OF JAVA AND CLEAN SWEEP AT BROOME
1-8 March

Sunday, 1 March

The initial landings on the beaches of north-western Java began soon after midnight on the first day of the new month — a month which was to have tragic consequences for the defenders of the last bastion of the Netherlands East Indies. Dawn found the Allied air units under orders to counter-attack. The landings at Eretanwetan were the first to be reported and by 0200 the RAF's Hurricanes had been ordered to take off from Tjililitan at dawn, while the Dutch Brewsters at Andir were also made ready.

At 0530 therefore, nine Brewsters set out for Eretanwetan, one flight of four aircraft of 2-VlG-V led by Kapt van Helsdingen, the other flight — from 1-VlG-V — led by Kapt van Rest. They were joined by three Glenn Martins of 3-VlG-III, also from Andir. At about the same time, Flt Lt Julian led off a section of three Hurricanes of 242 Squadron from Tjililitan, to ascertain the exact position of the landings; they were followed by nine more led by Sqn Ldr Brooker.

The invasion fleet, when found, was estimated to comprise 11 transports in line astern, 50 yards apart and 200 yards from the shore, flanked by two destroyers with a cruiser standing a mile out to sea. The Hurricanes, which were met by intense AA and rifle fire from the transports and the shore, made their first attack on the atap huts along the shoreline in which Japanese soldiers were sheltering; these huts were left in flames. As they turned their attention to the beach itself, which was covered with men and supplies, and the barges just off shore, a voice was heard over the R/T:

"Don't strafe those barges".

Plt Off Lockwood remembered heads turning under canopies in amazement; undoubtedly someone on the ground was on the same frequency. Nevertheless, the pilots proceeded to shoot-up the barges, each attack beginning with a dive through 10/10th cloud which covered the entire area. Sgt Sandeman Allen recollected that the main landing took place "in a lovely bay 10-15 miles east of Batavia" and added:

"The set-up when we were sent out was a line of ships — nine, I think — with two destroyers. All the ships had guns and guns were already ashore.

"We attacked the barges running between the ships and shore and I think more damage was done by the gunfire from the ships and the shore than by us! As we attacked the barges we were followed by much heavier calibre fire from both sides and some barges received direct hits from shells."

During this attack the Dutch bomber crews claimed one transport sunk but one Glenn Martin of 3-VlG-III was lost, probably hit by AA fire from the ships; 2/Lt B. Groenendijk and his crew perished. On returning to Andir, one Brewster belly-landed, the pilot unable to release his undercarriage. The strafe by the Hurricanes was believed to have set fire to six landing craft and three motor vehicles.

242 Squadron carried out two more attacks during the course of the morning, when nearly all Hurricanes suffered damage, mainly from shell splinters, although none were lost. However, Sgt Young's aircraft was hit in the wing when strafing a road convoy and on attempting to land, his engine cut and he belly-landed in a swamp. Sgt Sandeman Allen was again involved:

> "We went out again and by then the troops were on the move along a long straight road between paddy fields; there was no protection anywhere and I would hate to estimate the casualties involved.
>
> "I cannot remember who, but one of the lads in this raid left his parachute behind and sat on a tin helmet as the best means of protection when all the trouble was coming up from below."

Sgt Ian Newlands also made two strafing attacks, flying BE202/R on both occasions:

> "Barges were landing troops on the beach and troops were dispersed in a clump of jungle alongside the jetty. Ack-Ack was very heavy and bursts of fire were exploding into their own barges as we kept on strafing. The small arms fire from the jungle was also very intense. If only we had some bombs the war could almost have been turned at this stage, but that was not to be!"

Aircraft from 605 Squadron also carried out attacks during the early morning and, on the first of these, Flg Off Noel Sharp's aircraft was seen to be hit by ground fire. Sgt Jim MacIntosh noted:

> "Dawn take-off. Strafing Jap landings at Cheribon, about 90 miles east of Batavia. Sharp shot down and seen to belly land in paddy field about three miles inland from landing."

Although observed to emerge from his aircraft and set it on fire, the New Zealander was not seen again and was presumed killed by Japanese troops. A second aircraft was rendered unserviceable after MacIntosh had landed his damaged Hurricane (Z5616), which had been hit in the hydraulics system.

Three F1Ms and three E13As from the floatplane tender *Kamikawa Maru* had flown to Bantam Bay in the morning, two of the F1Ms then flying on to the Eretanwetan area, where they were joined by two more from *Sanyo Maru*. During the early afternoon five Hurricanes of 605 Squadron were led off by Sqn Ldr Wright. As they approached the area they came across a lone floatplane, which all attacked. It proved very manoeuvrable and, after releasing some bombs, flew in a tight circle and opened fire on Sgt Kelly's aircraft, who hurriedly broke away. It then attacked a second Hurricane. Again all tried to hit it, attacking from various directions without success and they then held off to give Sqn Ldr Wright a chance to deal with it alone. Although he used all his remaining ammunition, he was unable to shoot down the gallant Japanese pilot, and eventually broke away, returning to Tjililitan with three of his flight.

Their opponent had been a *Kamikawa Maru* F1M flown by Wt Off Yatomaru,

Left: Flg Off Noel Sharp of 605 Squadron, who was killed on the first day of the Japanese invasion of Java. *(Sharp family)*. Right: Plt Off Mike Fitzherbert of 242 Squadron claimed two Japanese float-planes from the tender *Kamikawa Maru* off the coast of Java on 1 March. He is seen here before his posting to the Far East. *(Fitzherbert family)*

who landed to report that he had shot down three of his five opponents! Meanwhile Sgt Kelly still had sufficient ammunition left to attack the invasion forces and set off alone to do so. He observed many boats ferrying troops ashore and then saw two floatplanes in the bay. These were two of the *Kamikawa Maru* aircraft, which he attacked although under fire from AA positions, setting one on fire before returning to Tjililitan. It is possible that these floatplanes were also attacked later by Plt Off Fitzherbert of 242 Squadron, who reported destroying two 'flyingboats' just after they had alighted. In any event, the Japanese recorded that three fighters attacked in total, one F1M being burnt and the others badly damaged.

A little later another section from 605 Squadron set out, led by Flt Lt Oakden. These completed a quick sweep around the beach area and came under fire from vessels lying off-shore. The beach appeared to be clear of troops, so they headed inland and came across a troop convoy. Plt Off Harry Pettit recalled:

> "We were flying very low during this operation and in fact probably would have done better if we had used a bit more height and attacked more steeply. The Japanese were remarkably steady under fire and continued to use their rifles against the low-flying aircraft, on many occasions not even attempting to take cover. The accuracy of their fire was evidenced by a few holes in my Hurricane. I could not help admiring these troops, as I suspect I should have been looking for cover had I been shot at by eight Browning machine guns in a low-flying aircraft.
>
> "It was during this time that a seaplane, which was probably a recon-

naissance aircraft with an observer acting as a rear gunner, and fitted with machine guns firing forward, attacked. Fortunately Eddie Kuhn removed it before I even saw its approach."

Kuhn attacked the floatplane and believed he had shot it down for his fourth victory. This would appear to have been one of *Sanyo Maru*'s aircraft, Ens Kaoru Ogata reporting a ten minute fight with six fighters (identified as two-seaters!) about half an hour after the *Kamikawa Maru* F1Ms had been strafed; however, Ogata's aircraft escaped without damage.

By late afternoon, owing to the shortage of Hurricanes, 605 Squadron was ordered to stand down and its remaining four serviceable Hurricanes were handed to 242 Squadron. The pilots of the New Zealand Flight were ordered to remain however, whilst Sqn Ldr Wright was to take the rest of his men — including those of the 258 Squadron detachment — to Tjilatjap, where, he was informed, ships would be waiting to take them to Australia.

Before darkness set in, three more sorties were flown to Eretanwetan by the Glenn Martins of 3-VlG-III, but then the weather prevented further bombing attacks. Heavy rain forced a 'patrouille' from 1-VlG-II to turn back and other bombers were not sent out.

Meanwhile, disaster struck the RAF's bomber base at Kalidjati. Eretanwetan was only some 30 miles from Kalidjati but, acting on the advice of the Dutch commander, Maj General van Oyen, Air Vice-Marshal Maltby had not ordered the Blenheims and Hudsons to be evacuated, as a Dutch counter-attack was about to be made. Soon after daybreak however, the remaining Glenn Martins were ordered to Andir by Lt Col Zomer, the Dutch airfield commander at Kalidjati. Zomer had tried unsuccessfully to persuade Grp Capt Whistondale (in charge of the RAF contingent at Kalidjati) to do the same with the RAF aircraft assembled there. Whistondale had initially refused as he had different orders from BRITAIR, only agreeing at 1000 hours when it was confirmed that fighting was underway in nearby Soebang. By then it was too late. Flt Lt 'Dutch' Holland of 84 Squadron recalled:

"Dawn found us at Kalidjati taking stock of the position. We knew that the Japanese had landed for we had seen them in the moonlight and we knew that they were only about 30 miles away from our aerodrome. We phoned Air HQ in the mountains (Bandoeng) and explained to them what had happened and also the danger of our position. HQ replied that there was absolutely no danger and that all we had to do was to remain by our aircraft and await further orders.

"On coming out of the building we heard some machine gun fire. We leapt into our powerful American car and as we drove out onto the landing ground, a Japanese tank came round the corner of a hangar and opened fire on us. We shot across the landing ground at high speed to our men who were on the far side.

"We abandoned the car and leapt into a ditch just as the Japanese opened fire with their trench mortars. Most frightening. The shells seemed to fly about in all directions and explode where least expected. Often they exploded above the ground which made it practically useless to take shelter in a ditch."

Once confirmation of the landings had reached Kalidjati, Grp Capt Whistondale ordered all unservicable aircraft to be destroyed to prevent them falling into

Japanese hands. Volunteers were called for to carry out the demolitions, one of whom was LAC Chad Middleton, an 84 Squadron armourer:

"I, along with a number of my squadron colleagues, volunteered for this task although we had no idea at that time what the consequences of our action was going to be. For instance we didn't know that the Japs were hidden in the trees surrounding the aerodrome.

"However on arrival at the airfield, some time was spent in discussing which planes were deemed to be unserviceable. It must be said that all personnel who had volunteered for this task were armed.

"We had not been on the airfield very long however before all hell broke loose. The Japs who had been occupying the perimeter of the airfield broke cover and in the mayhem and confusion which followed many ground gunners and others suffered horrible deaths. We were so overwhelmed that all we could do was to try to get away from this holocaust. One of my squadron colleagues and myself spotted an army lorry crossing the drome and made a successful run for it and thus made good our escape. All the planes both serviceable and unserviceable fell into the hands of the enemy although I was told that some managed to get away. The blame for this debacle must rest fairly and squarely on the shoulders of the Dutch, who were responsible for a break down of communications."

Sgt George Dewey and his Blenheim crew (Sgts Ernie Frye and Bunny Hare) had made their way down to the airfield, where they were to take over a Blenheim from one of the night flying crews, only to find their aircraft not ready:

"So Frye and I walked about half a mile to look at some Dutch aircraft parked in undergrowth on the side of the drome. These turned out to be Ryan ST two-seater sports planes which the Dutch were going to use for training. They were brand spanking new — so I decided to start one with the thought they would make good communications planes. A Dutchman came and threatened to shoot me if I didn't get out — so I got out.

"Frye and I had just got back to the edge of the drome when firing broke out at the eastern end — so we high tailed it to nearby Bofors gun pits which were just being set up."

Plt Off Alex Wilson of the 59 Squadron detachment who, having been engaged in the night attacks, and had been resting with his crew at Soebang — about 12 miles from the airfield, where the aircrews were billeted — added:

"About 0600 hours Wg Cdr Jeudwine, CO of 84 Squadron woke us up with the information that the Japanese were entering the other end of the village and that we were to make our way to HQ Kalidjati immediately. On arrival there the position officially seemed uncertain. I repeatedly requested permission to stand-by my aircraft, but no orders were given by Grp Cpt Whistondale. It was soon obvious that mechanised units were in the vicinity, as firing including trench mortars could be heard on all sides."

Plt Off Campbell Hill, Wilson's observer, continued:

"In spite of requests Grp Capt Whistondale would not give us permission to stand by our plane, to fly it to safety or to attack the enemy. Eventually Grp Cpt Whistondale decided to leave the Ops Room and to go back to Soebang to collect his luggage. In spite of advice to the contrary Flg Off Richards, who arrived at Kalidjati during the night to relieve us, decided to accompany him. A few minutes after their car disappeared in the distance there was a prolonged burst of fire from the same direction."

The car was ambushed and both men died. It was believed by some that the main reason for Grp Capt Whistondale returning to Soebang was to enable him to retrieve his stamp collection, an abiding passion, although his parting words allegedly were: "I'm going to change my socks!" With the departure of Whistondale, Wg Cdr Jeudwine assumed command of the airfield.

Campbell Hill:

"Left without orders we decided to find our plane and to stand by for any emergency. We picked up two Australian flight lieutenants and Sergeant Scarsbrook (59 Squadron) and as our lorry entered the gate in the north east corner of the drome, Dutch armoured units passed us moving towards Bandoeng. This was significant. We 'recced' the grass strip in the north west corner of the drome assuming this to be the obvious place in which the Australian duty crew would have parked our plane, as the remainder of the drome was unserviceable due to Japanese pattern bombing.

"The Hudson (AE506), however, was not in any of the dispersal areas bordering the strip. As we turned out of the strip on to the drome proper enemy mechanised units were entering the gate in the north-east corner of the drome. We turned towards the south-west corner and 'recced' the southern boundary, eventually finding our plane in the south-east corner. The plane was in a pen with its nose jammed right up against the back of the pen."

By this time the Japanese were firing continually from the other side of the aerodrome and some shots were coming their way. They tried to pull the Hudson out of the pen but found it difficult to move, as the floor of the pen was loose and the wheels had sunk. Eventually however, they suceeded in moving it sufficiently to allow the engines to be started.

Wilson:

"There was considerable firing in our direction and at least one hit was made on the aircraft. I got the engines started and by dint of my crew lifting the wing tip over the edge of the pen, and my bursting the engine, we got the aircraft clear. My crew and Sgt Scarsbrook showed considerable courage and tenacity under fire. My observer got everyone into the plane, my air-gunner Sgt Birks got into the turret, cleared his guns, and Sgt Harrison manned the mid position guns. By this time firing was intense, and a large piece of shrapnel passed through the body of the plane (narrowly missing Harrison). In addition to this the wing tip was bent and the tail was damaged.

"It was now obvious that we could not possibly get on to the aerodrome, as there were two enemy tanks and four armoured cars within 100 yards of us, so I decided to take off from the field. There was a narrow path between the bomb-craters which my observer pointed out. I did an emergency take-off."

Campbell Hill:

"We were well level with the tanks before they recovered from their surprise and opened fire. By this time our tail was well up and we were gaining speed.

However, a heavy burst from the port side tank caught us in the port rudder and tail section and Wilson did a marvellous job of work avoiding a swing. No sooner had he got out of this difficulty than he had to start pulling off long before it was safe to do so to avoid a belt of trees. However, by extraordinarily skilful handling Wilson pulled off the plane, hopped over the trees, let her down again to gather a spot of speed, and we were away. We landed at Bandoeng."

Three further Hudsons managed to get away — A16-26 flown by Flt Lt John O'Brien and his crew; AE485 — despite a damaged fuel tank — with Flt Lt Wiley and his crew, and A16-17 which Flg Off Peter Gibbes flew unaided to Bandoeng, as recalled by Flt Lt Holland:

"In the ditch with us was a young Australian pilot from another squadron (*Gibbes*). Despite the machine gun bullets and mortar fire that was harassing us at the time, he said he was going to climb into his aircraft and take-off. He crept along on his belly towards his aircraft and, when there was a lull in the firing, he suddenly leapt up, opened the door and climbed in."

Having climbed into the Hudson, Gibbes cooly and clearly went about his business, as he later recalled:

"I did not dare to get into the pilot's seat. Bullets were still thudding into the aeroplane, cutting a swathe of holes along its side not half a metre above my head. Alone in the aircraft I lay on the floor and reached to the controls. I turned on the ignition switches, turned on the fuel cocks, set the throttles, pitches and mixtures, and pressed the starter buttons. Both engines started."

Holland:

"Apparently the Japanese hadn't seen him for the firing continued in a hap-hazard way as it had before. As soon as the engines fired he leapt into the seat and without warming up the motors, opened both throttles and the aircraft began to move forward.

"As soon as the Japanese heard the aircraft motors and saw the aircraft moving, they opened fire with everything they had got. By this time the Hudson was gathering speed and the tail was well up, but as it shot across the aerodrome it drew fire from practically all sides. He finally got airborne and the last we saw of him was as he disappeared over the far hedge amidst spurts of tracer bullets and shell bursts."

As the Hudson careered across the airfield, Gibbes spotted a Japanese motor-cyclist armed with a machine gun:

"We were away! I do not know whether I pushed the nose down or the Hudson did itself. To my astonishment I saw my bullets hit home. I saw this fellow go hurtling into the air, somersaulting wildy, and so did his bike."

None of the Blenheims succeeded in getting away although a number of crews made gallant attempts to follow the Hudsons. Unfortunately the Blenheims were dispersed at the end of the airfield infiltrated by the Japanese. However, Sqn Ldr John Tayler of 84 Squadron made a valiant effort:

"Whilst endeavouring to taxi out an aircraft from the dispersal area, the port wheel became bogged in a filled-in bomb hole. The enemy were already on

Flg Off Peter Gibbes of 1 RAAF Squadron was awarded a DFC for his many exploits. *(Authors' collection)*

the aerodrome, although not in our field of vision. A Hudson took off through a hail of fire from the ground; he had no right to get away with it, but he did.

"I realised that, as we were isolated and the remainder of the squadron had probably withdrawn according to the scheme drawn up that morning, I emptied a pan of Tommy gun ammunition into the bogged aircraft, and told Cpl Jeans to act as a driver to the flight lorry at our disposal. Flt Sgt Slee, Sgt Cosgrove, Cpl Jeans and myself began to run the gauntlet across the southern boundary of the aerodrome in our lorry.

"Midway we stopped to help an AA crew attach their gun to a lorry. This activity drew the attention of a tank and armoured car. They opened up from about 300 yards. Slee was hit in the shoulder; I told Cosgrove to put him in the first lorry — that which had the gun attached. I crawled about 30 yards to the right, and fired on the armoured car in the hope that it might distract from the army lorry which now was careering across the drome at a tangent to both of the enemy vehicles.

"It appeared to be alright when I last saw it disappear off the aerodrome. I shouted to the others to get into our lorry. An army driver took the wheel. Half-a-dozen, including Cpl Jeans, were in the back. We started off, and for a moment all went well. Two more tanks appeared on our right and opened up from approximately 200 yards. We returned fire with a Bren from the back, and I used the Tommy from the back window of the cab. We were travelling fast over bumpy ground and our fire was not very effective.

"The tank turned to bring its front guns to bear, and the next instant the lorry was riddled. Bullet holes appeared through the back of the cab, about one and a half inches from my chest and belly. The driver stopped the lot and dropped out of the open door to the ground. Another burst shattered the wind-screen and entered the engine. The lorry began to slow down. I slid across to try to revive the engine, but it was dead. I yelled to those in the back to jump out and come with me."

They came under direct attack now and their lorry, almost stationary, presented a good target. The survivors made a dash of 30 yards for cover but only Tayler and Jeans reached safety, the others falling in the effort. Tayler called out for any 84 Squadron men to join him but none did; he continued:

"There was still spasmodic fire on the drome. One of the two tanks approached the lorry. From our position on the lip of a steep gully, I fired several clips at it, but it kept coming. We withdrew then to the other side of the gully, through water up to our necks, and took cover in the bush about 75 yards off the aerodrome perimeter. From here I had a shot at a couple of Nips on the road to our right.

"Then we went deeper into the bush. We remained for the next 20 hours within a half a mile of the aerodrome expecting a counter attack, but it did not materialize. Firing ceased about 15 minutes later. We could see a good deal of activity in the form of transport aircraft landing and taking off under escort of fighters. Shortly after dawn the next day we started south through the bush for Bandoeng."

Flt Lt Wyllie had similar ideas for trying to get away:

"We ran down a road which flanked the western boundary to the lower end of the field where most of the servicing crews and many others had gathered. During this period one Hudson took off and I, with Plt Off Macdonald, went out to see if we could get one of our Blenheims off as well. I got into the cockpit and he went in under the cowling of the port engine to prime it.

"There were four Jap tanks on the road on the eastern side of the field. Three were busy demolishing a row of buildings which were occupied by a detachment who had been manning the Bofors guns intended to defend the aerodrome. The fourth tank was machine gunning anything or anyone that came in their sights who were trying to get aircraft away. They included Flt Sgt Slee, who was a tower of strength in the squadron. I saw him go down about a 100 yards away from the aircraft I was trying to get started.

"Then the right hand side of my windshield was smashed by bullets. Fortunately I had not closed the sliding hatch over my head and I made the fastest exit from a Blenheim cockpit anyone ever made. Both Macdonald and I tried to leave the field of battle with dignity but we were both at a run before we reached our objectives."

Meanwhile, Flt Lt Holland and his party found themselves the centre of attention once again:

"Three Japanese light armoured cars came half way across the aerodrome and concentrated their fire on us. One of our sergeants rolled over with blood spurting from his neck; a shell splinter had cut his head off. We retaliated with rifle fire which was, of course, of little use against armoured cars. At this point we thought it best to break off the engagement and we crept back along our ditch, and past a wood to where we had some of our squadron trucks parked."

There Holland's group met up with Wg Cdr Jeudwine and others, including Wyllie, who had escaped safely from his Blenheim; Wyllie continued:

"I rejoined Jeudwine who had ordered the evacuation and was standing a little way away, beside his car, with Flt Lts Owen and Holland. As the trucks moved off, he indicated that he had three loaded Tommy guns in the back of the car and said: 'We'll try and draw them off.' We each took a gun and Holland got on one running board of the Chevvy and I got on the other. We each had one arm round the pillars between the open windows. Owen knelt on the back seat of the car and broke the back window with the barrel of his gun. The CO drove and we came back up the road towards the Ops hut we had left earlier.

"It was not an enormously effective ruse but it did draw off two jeep loads of soldiers, who chased us for a little way, but they only had rifles which are hard to fire forwards from the back of a jeep and perhaps our return fire from the three Tommy guns and our speed made them decide to give up.

"The trucks with the rest of the squadron rejoined us as we waited at a crossing where the road they had taken rejoined the main road to Batavia. A little further on we passed through the ranks of a Dutch army contingent which had been strafed by Navy 'Zeros' and had taken cover in the ditches."

84 Squadron suffered about 20 fatalities, amongst whom were Plt Off D.W. Kewish, a newly arrived Australian pilot, and his observer, Flg Off J.W. Bott. As recorded, the squadron's Senior NCO, Flt Sgt Bill Slee, was killed as was

Sgt A.H. McBride. Observer Sgt R.D. Mohr of 211 Squadron and fellow Australian Sgt J.R. Reid, an airgunner of 84 Squadron — were both posted missing, presumed killed. Reg Mohr was a typical tough Australian, who had been awarded a DFM for his service in the Middle East; one of his countryman recalled:

> "He was noticeable because of his amazing cynical attitude regarding the general chaos. As I understand it, he walked down the road adjacent to the aerodrome and was not seen again. Perhaps John Reid was with him."

Of the 350 British troops defending the airfield, about one third were killed or captured, as were all 30 of the RAF defence personnel. Amongst the Dutch aircraft lost at the airfield was Glenn Martin M-5114 of 1-VlG-I, together with a Dutch Hurricane which had been damaged in combat a week or so earlier. A number of Ryan STMs of the Flight School were also destroyed although others had been flown to Tasikmalaja shortly before the attack. When Japanese troops entered Soebang they removed a nurse and her patients from the military hospital and massacred them, together with women and children of the civilian population (see Appendix III for Air Vice-Marshal Maltby's report on the loss of the airfield).

The dramatic events at Kalidjati were unknown to the Hurricane pilots at Tjililitan, who continued to strafe the Japanese on the beaches and approach roads. By now the larger landings of the 2nd Division at Bantam and Merak had been discovered, and during the afternoon some of the efforts of the remaining Hurricanes were to be directed here as well. Strafing continued to inflict casualties on the invaders and, of one such sortie carried out by Flt Lt Parker with Plt Offs Fitzherbert and Mendizabal, Parker later recorded:

> "I led off with Mike and 'Dizzy' in the only three aircraft available and kept the palm trees as much as possible between us and the seashore. Our first intimation that we'd reached the landing point was groups of shells exploding in the trees below and around us. We were obviously not surprising the Japs and, rather than fly straight and level at low altitude for the benefit of their gunners, I corkscrewed along a few hundred feet higher.
>
> "Then we saw the transports and a couple of warships just off-shore with three further smaller boats moving between. We each attacked a barge and then 'Dizzy' and I turned away to the shore to aim at the troops working on the beach and in the village. Mike turned out to sea and aimed at the destroyer which was banging away at us, but I doubt whether he damaged it at all. I spotted some troops dashing into a bamboo hut roofed with palm leaves and fired at it, seeing my shots breaking on the walls.
>
> "When I pulled out of my dive and round to attack again, the hut was on fire and a squad of men were lined up nearby with rifles aimed, whilst others ran out of the smoke. The riflemen had little chance to get off more than one shot at me — and none hit the aircraft — before my de Wilde was bursting on and around them, and then I'd run through my ammunition and pulled up and inland, out of effective range of the AA guns. Almost immediately I was joined by Mike and 'Dizzy' and we flew back to Tjililitan. My aircraft and 'Dizzy's were still unscathed but Mike had collected the nosecap of a heavy shell in the mainspar of his wing."

Instructions were now given for 205 Squadron at Tjilatjap to evacuate, FV-W departing for Broome at first light the following morning with Flt Lt Lowe at the controls, carrying the CO, Wg Cdr R.B. Councell, amongst its passengers. The Catalina had been condemned as unserviceable owing to a bullet hole through an airscrew; however, although a Dutch engineering officer considered it unsafe to fly it made the long flight to Australia without mishap.

The squadron's only other aircraft — FV-N — was on patrol at the time, its Australian captain, Flt Lt H. Tamblyn, being sent a signal ordering him to depart for Ceylon on his return. However, the crew failed to receive the message and Tamblyn made arrangements to follow the others to Broome. Meanwhile, the remainder of the unit's personnel were to evacuate aboard a departing ship, *Tung Song*. Before Tamblyn set course for Australia, however, he sent a message to his friend, Flt Lt Hugh Garnell, suggesting he and his crew leave the *Tung Song* and join him aboard his aircraft for the flight to Broome, which they did. In the event the departure was further delayed owing to an hour-long prayer ritual fervently undertaken by Garnell's Sikh co-pilot, Plt Off Man Mohan Singh, which was to have disastrous consequences.

Eastern Java

After joining the British aircraft in the initial attack on the Eretanwetan landings, all Dutch effort was then switched towards the larger force off the Kragan/Rembang area to the east. From their secret base at Ngoro/Blimbing, nine P-40s of the 17th Pursuit Squadron, six Hurricanes of 2-VlG-IV and six Brewsters set out, arriving just after the shipping had been attacked again by a lone B-17. At 0900 two of these bombers had set off from Madioen but one turned back with engine trouble, leaving Lt K.D. Casper to carry out a lone attack on ships anchored off the north coast of Java; eight 300kg bombs were dropped from 30,000 feet, the crew optimistically claiming direct hits on one large transport and waterline hits on another.

The Brewster pilots reported an estimated 44 transports and "hundreds" of smaller craft, before diving to strafe the ships and troops on the shore until they were out of ammunition. By the time the P-40s and Hurricanes took over the assault, the defences were well and truly ready for them and they flew into a veritable blizzard of AA and small arms fire. The Americans suffered particularly heavily; Lt Morris Caldwell's aircraft was seen to crash into the sea, while Lt Cornelius Reagan's P-40 was set ablaze. Lt McWherter attempted to lead him to where he could bale out, but Reagan was seen to open the cockpit canopy, take out a cigarette and cooly light it from the flames pouring out of the engine, and then sit back to await the inevitable crash in which he was killed.

Lt Adkins actually bounced his P-40 off the sea at the end of a power dive and carried out two strafing passes, but the aircraft was hit and he was forced to bale out over the coast, only 300 yards from the forward Japanese troops. Stopping a Javanese on a bicycle, he sat on the saddle while the owner pedalled furiously. Once the latter became exhausted, Adkins took over the bike and rode to safety. The other six P-40s landed at Djokjakarta, but every one of them had been hit and none were operationally serviceable any more.

Three of the Hurricanes were also hit and damaged; Sgt Maj Boonstoppel force-landed at Maospati airfield, while Sgt de Wilde, flying Z5664, came down in similar circumstances near Bedjonegare. 2/Lt Marinus was able to get his damaged aircraft back to Ngoro, where Lt Brunier and Sgts Dejalle and Beerling arrived with their undamaged fighters.

Refuelling and rearming began at once of those P-40s which could be made serviceable, but these were spotted by four patrolling Tainan Ku A6Ms from Bali. While two stayed up to provide cover, NAP 1/C Yoshimichi Saeki led his No 2 down to strafe the airfield, claiming one twin-engined aircraft burnt, and at least ten fighters destroyed or damaged. A report of the attack stated:

> "At about 0900 two 'Zeros' came in to strafe the field. With no opposition of any sort to hinder them, the two Jap pilots ranged back and forth till they had hunted out and destroyed every one of the parked planes."

Flg Off John David, formerly 243 Squadron's Engineer Officer in Singapore, was attached to the Dutch Hurricane unit, 2-VlG-IV at Ngoro. Of the raid, he recalled:

> "Six aircraft were refuelling and all were destroyed when the petrol bowsers brewed up. About 15 of my men were killed or seriously wounded. My life was saved by Brunier, who pushed me into a slit trench and fell on top of me just as another strafing wave came in."

All ten P-40s of the 17th Pursuit Squadron were, in fact, destroyed or severely damaged, while two LB-30s were damaged beyond repair; most of the remaining Dutch aircraft were also hit, two Hurricanes and five Glenn Martins being damaged beyond repair. For the P-40 unit it was the end. The pilots and ground crews piled into cars and trucks and headed for Malang, but this airfield had again been attacked during the morning — where a B-18 under repair was destroyed. The old bomber had been brought up to a condition which gave hope to those involved of being able to fly it to Australia, a hope that was now dashed.

The Dutch followed up the strafe of the invasion fleet by the ill-fated combined fighter force, with attacks by Glenn Martins of 1-VlG-III and four CW-22s of VkA-1 from Djokjakarta. Two transports were claimed sunk, and apparently claims were also submitted for some Japanese aircraft shot down, but three of the Dutch fighters were lost in the Rembang area. F1M floatplanes patrolling over the Eastern Force reported shooting down three 'Northrop light bombers', and it seems certain that these were in fact the CW-22s in which Lt van der Jogt, Lt Beelhouwer and Ens Beckeringh were reported killed, while observers, Lt J.L.M. Theunissen and Ens Pilgrim, were wounded.

Curtiss-Wright CW-22 Falcons were used for the first time in action to combat the Japanese landings on 1 March. CF-464 is a typical example *(via G. Zwanenberg)*

A further attack on Djokjakarta had been ordered by the Japanese meanwhile, six 3rd Ku A6Ms escorting seven Takao Ku bombers to this target. The latter claimed damage to 14 P-40s and five Brewsters, the fighters then diving down to strafe and claiming hits on seven P-40s and three Brewsters — all of which were already beyond repair.

As Dutch troops prepared to evacuate airfields near the invasion area, at Maospati a Glenn Martin, one of the Dutch Hurricanes damaged during the attack on the Japanese shipping (Sgt Maj Boonstoppel's aircraft), and two stored CW-21Bs were destroyed by the ground crews. Elsewhere, a further Dutch Hurricane (Sgt de Wilde's Z5664 with an unserviceable propeller at Bedjonegare) and another Glenn Martin were similarly destroyed. Japanese attacks during the day also wrote off two Glenn Martins of 1-VlG-II at Pasirian and one of 2-VlG-I at Wirasaba.

It was not only over the invasion beaches where action had occurred during the day. 27 Kanoya Ku G4Ms raided Sourabaya harbour again, damage being claimed to a number of vessels; three Dutch ships were severely damaged. The bombers flew into a storm of AA fire which damaged no less than 14, of which two were obliged to force-land on Bali. During the early afternoon a lone B-17E, flown by Lt Mathewson, departed from Djokjakarta to carry out what was to be one of the Americans' last bombing sorties of the campaign. The crew reported dropping their bombs on shipping at Bali, these straddling a transport and narrowly near-missing a destroyer.

The decision was now taken by Lt Colonel Eubank, commander of the USAF in Java, to commence withdrawing the American bomber force to Australia. At 1400 he advised Vice-Admiral Helfrich "that operating out of Malang would result in inevitable and unjustifiable losses on the ground." A total of 15 B-17Es, two B-17Ds, a single B-17C (which had been relegated entirely to transport duties) and three LB-30s were considered fit to make the flight to Australia, the first aircraft leaving at dusk, each carrying a dozen passengers. Those aircraft deemed sufficiently airworthy to return to evacuate more personnel were expected to be flown back the following day. In four days Capt Edward C. Teats made two further trips, spending a total of 50 hours in the air, making two trips on three engines only, evacuating 45 grateful passengers; most of the 26 evacuees on his second mercy flight were pilots of the 17th Pursuit Squadron.

The B-17 flown by Lt Clarence E. McPherson took off with a wooden tail skid in place of a broken tail wheel — and made a perfect landing at Broome. The last LB-30 departed at 0030 carrying 35 passengers and only just managed to get airborne, ploughing through the treetops at the end of the runway. The exodus now began in earnest, as the spare personnel of the 17th Pursuit Squadron — who had been despatched to Tjilatjap — were ordered to embark for Australia aboard the rusty old Dutch freighter *Abberkirk*, where they joined almost 1,500 other US air personnel. PatWing 10 did not have any serviceable PBYs left, so its personnel also began leaving, flying out the last US Naval officer at the Bandoeng Headquarters, Capt Frank W. Wagner, in one of the remaining J2F Duck liaison amphibians.

Sqn Ldr Wright's 258/605 Squadron party reached the port during the evening, in two Ford cars, after a nightmarish dash across Java in the belief that their vessel would sail at dawn on the 2nd. They were closely followed by the New Zealand Flight, released from their attachment to 242 Squadron, who had piled into a truck and set off, as Sgt MacIntosh noted:

"We waited until 12 o'clock that night in Batavia at our billets in Tanan-abang Hotel, hoping perhaps that Flg Off Sharp would turn up, but by midnight we were told that the Japs were effecting a pincer movement on Batavia from Cheribon in the east and Sunda in the west. If we delayed any longer, we may be caught."

The tension and discomfort of the journey had been heightened by lack of knowledge of how far the Japanese invaders had infiltrated; however arrival brought the appalled realisation that the port was empty. Many other units swarmed around the deserted quays, all anxiously awaiting the arrival of ships to get them away from the rapidly deteriorating situation.

At Sea

At sea there was considerable activity. The cruiser *Exeter* had departed Sourabaya the previous evening in company with two destroyers, to make a dash to Ceylon. All went well until 0400 when a merchant vessel and two warships were sighted. Capt Gordon ordered a change of course but, about four hours later, two further warships were sighted — the cruisers *Nachi* and *Haguro*. Again the course was altered but one of the cruisers had launched its spotter floatplane to investigate, which commenced shadowing. By 0930 two more cruisers were seen approaching, *Ashigara* and *Myoko* launching their spotter aircraft before opening fire. Outnumbered and outgunned, *Exeter*'s only chance of escape appeared in the cover offered by a rain squall; Capt Gordon wrote:

"Throughout the action *Exeter*'s guns were firing, whenever they got the chance, at the Japanese spotting aircraft. These were mostly single-float seaplanes but we did see one large monoplane. Later information indicated that our HA/LA armament had shot down one aircraft and damaged another."

Having launched her torpedoes without effect at two of the cruisers, *Exeter* suffered her first damage at 1120, a shell exploding in a boiler room. With her speed rapidly falling away, she became an easy target and a few minutes later Japanese destroyers closed in and fired a spread of 18 torpedoes, a number of which exploded along her hull; she rolled over and sank.

One of the escorting destroyers — HMS *Encounter* — soon followed, although the other — the American USS *Pope* — succeeded in reaching the rain squall. However, the sanctuary afforded therein was short lived, for a spotter aircraft sighted her soon after midday and, 30 minutes later, six B5Ns from *Ryujo* arrived on the scene. One bomb exploded underwater on the port side and badly damaged her plates. Almost at a standstill and abandoned by her crew, the old destroyer was bombed by the B5Ns from 3,500 feet, one salvo scoring direct hits; she sank within minutes.

When the small Dutch freighter *Siaoe* (1,573 tons) had departed Tanjong Priok, her crew had hoped to escape detection under cover of darkness but she too ran into the invasion force in Bantam Bay. A destroyer despatched her to the bottom in short time. Another fleeing Dutch vessel, the 8,806-ton *Modjokerto*, was intercepted by the cruiser *Chikuma* and badly damaged. She struggled gamely south-westwards, only to be torpedoed and sunk by *I-58*, going down with 42 of her crew. There seemed to be no escape. A third Dutchman, the 1,172-ton *Parigi*, also fell prey to one of the patrolling cruisers; survivors were later picked up but all were then lost when their rescuer was also sunk. In a desperate bid to evade a similar fate, the master of the British tanker *War Sirdar* took his vessel into unsafe waters and paid the price, the tanker becoming wrecked on Jong reef, north-west of Batavia. Although a minesweeper went to her aid and attempted to tow her free, air attack prevented rescue and the tanker was lost. Three Dutch vessels fleeing Tjilatjap also fell foul of patrolling warships, while the British *Nam Yong* was sunk by submarine *I-2*, 800 miles south of Java, her master and four of the crew surviving as POWs.

At least two of the vessels engaged in evacuating civilians and service personnel from Padang, Sumatra, were intercepted during the day and sunk. The small Dutch passenger vessel *Ban Ho Guan* (1,693 tons) went down with the loss of all aboard, while a sister craft — the 1,035-ton *Roosenboom* — carrying 150 British military personel, was torpedoed and sunk; there were only a few survivors, two of whom were picked up by another Dutch vessel, *Palopo*. Two others landed on Sipora Island after 26 nightmarish days in an open boat. Amongst those lost when the *Roosenboom* went down, was the disgraced Grp Capt Nunn, former CO of the MVAF, who nevertheless sacrificed his life whilst endeavouring to save his wife. Sadly, although Mrs Nunn survived the sinking, she died aboard the lifeboat.[1]

Off Christmas Island the American destroyer USS *Edsall* rendezvoused with the tanker *Pecos*, transferring 177 survivors from *Langley* who had been plucked from the sea. On her way back to Tjilatjap *Edsall* was attacked by two Japanese cruisers — *Tone* and *Chikuma* — and two destroyers, but managed to evade these. Vice-Admiral Kondo called up air support from the carrier *Soryu*, in response to which Lt Cdr Takashige Egusa and his wingman took off in their D3As. *Edsall* was soon located, Egusa attacking and scoring a direct hit; the destroyer slowed down, allowing the Japanese warships to close on her and she was promptly sent to the bottom. Only five survivors reached land (all of whom died later as POWs).

At about 1500 the tanker *Pecos* — heading for Fremantle with 670 men on board — was located, Egusa leading a further devastating attack. She soon followed the ill-fated *Edsall*, 232 survivors being picked up by *Whipple*, including the two injured pilots, Lts William P. Ackerman and Gerald J. Dix; their colleagues had all perished aboard *Edsall*. Nearer inshore the American destroyer USS *Pilsbury* was also sunk by Japanese destroyers, going down in the Bali Strait. Over the whole area the bombers of the Takao Ku searched for Allied ships, calling in warships to sink or capture them, while floatplanes from the various tenders hunted for the remaining Allied submarines, joining destroyers in attacking those which could be found.

Monday, 2 March

On Java little now remained — a few Dutch Glenn Martins, Brewsters, CW-21Bs and CW-22s; 1 RAAF Squadron's handful of Hudsons and the Hurricanes of 242 Squadron, plus the surviving Vildebeests of 36 Squadron. These latter had been withdrawn to Andir, as Tjikampek was rather too near the Rembang invasion area; they would later move again to Tjikembar in the south-west.

---

[1] The full story of the survivors of *Roosenboom* is graphically told in Walter Gibson's book *The Boat*.

Western Java

Before dawn three of 242 Squadron's Hurricanes from Tjililitan again set out for the Eretanwetan area. Whilst two attacked targets of opportunity, including a large group of Japanese cycle troops, Flt Lt Parker decided to try and silence one of the light AA guns firing at them. After two runs he was satisfied to receive no further reply and rejoined his companions. Plt Off Fitzherbert later reported that some of the troops he strafed dismounted and stood at the side of the road, firing their rifles at his aircraft.

The first Ki 48s of the 75th Sentai had already arrived at Kalidjati in the early morning, three Hurricanes being ordered off to strafe this airfield. As they approached out of the sun, Flt Lt Julian warned that Japanese fighters were in the air, and then proceeded to fly straight up the centre of the airfield. Sgt Geoff Hardie, flying his first sortie since being shot down over Singapore, turned to starboard and flew around the airfield, followed by Sgt Fleming. However, the latter saw three twin-engined aircraft — possibly the Ki 48s — sitting in the corner with their engines running. Disregarding the defending fighters, the Canadian opened fire, reporting strikes on all three and seeing them catch fire.

As he broke away three fighters bounced him, bullets hitting his radiator. He managed to head his aircraft in the direction of Tjililitan and had covered about 25 miles before his engine started to seize up. He then baled out, landing in a paddy field where he was immediately strafed by one of the pursuing fighters. Altogether five passes were made at him during which he was wounded in the left arm.

Help was quick in arriving however; several natives appeared and took him to a nearby Dutch first aid station and from there he was driven, by ambulance, to Batavia, arriving during the early evening. Unfortunately he became one of the first RAF fighter pilots on Java to be captured when the hospital was overrun by Japanese troops the following day. His fate was not known for some considerable time, as his two companions reported, on their return to Tjililitan, that they thought he had crashed on the airfield, having seen much fire and smoke — probably the burning bombers which Fleming had just strafed. No report of this victory or of the attack on the bombers is recorded by the Japanese, although it is believed that the Hurricanes' opponents were Ki 27s of one of the 12th Flying Battalion's sentais.

Plt Off Watson led off three more Hurricanes to the Serang area, Sgt Newlands returning early when his aircraft developed a bad oil leak. Nearing the target area, Watson's aircraft also developed engine trouble but he decided to carry on, he and Sgt Sandeman Allen attacking many troops. As with others on many previous occasions, these troops fearlessly stood their ground and fired incessantly at the Hurricanes. Inevitably, Watson's troublesome aircraft received several hits in the engine, which seized, obliging him to crash-land in a paddy field.

Shortly after Sandeman Allen's lone return to Tjililitan, a scramble of standby Hurricanes was ordered to intercept a retaliatory raid by Japanese fighters. The squadron received a reasonable amount of notice to become airborne but, once in the air, they failed to receive any further direction over the R/T. A fight occurred over the airfield at 12,000 feet, Sgt King claiming one shot down.

The RAF noted that the airfield was under frequent attack during the day, as LAC Cowle of 242 Squadron had cause to remember:

"Our airfield was soon discovered by the Japs and became untenable. The first visit by 15 bombers found me in the centre of the airfield robbing a crashed Hurricane of parts, and shook me up a bit when they unloaded all at once."

During the course of the morning Plt Off Lockwood was detailed to fly to Buitenzorg; a Japanese convoy had been reported approaching the city and he was to observe its whereabouts, sketch a map and inform the Dutch garrison. He found the convoy just west of the city — or rather they found him, as his low-flying aircraft came under fire. He completed a sketch on the inside of the hard cover of a book, flew to a golf course on the north-eastern outskirt of the city, and dropped the map to Dutch troops assembled there.

Dutch units were also active throughout the day, Glenn Martins bombing the Eretanwetan landing fleet, claiming two more transports sunk. Two F1M float-planes of the detachment from *Sanyo Maru* intercepted one bomber — identified as a 'two-engined Boeing' — but were unable to claim any results. Glenn Martins also made an attack on Kalidjati, the Japanese noting that three bombers attacked soon after the first 75th Sentai aircraft had arrived, but caused no damage. From their base at Tjikembar, CW-22s of VkA-1 were requested by the Dutch 1ᵉ Division to scout over the Sunda Strait, where Lt van Hassen bombed and strafed a road convoy near Serang — probably that also attacked by the 242 Squadron Hurricanes. The unit would continue to operate over this area for the next few days.

At Tjililitan, by early afternoon, more Hurricanes had been made serviceable and Sqn Ldr Brooker informed his men that the unit was to carry out a full-scale raid on Kalidjati. The operation was to be undertaken from the Dutch base at Andir, just outside Bandoeng, as the advancing Japanese were now only 30 miles away from Tjililitan. All available Hurricanes, seven aircraft, set off for Andir, closely following the CO, who had the only aerial map of Java available. As they approached the airfield they experienced heavy, but inaccurate fire; the Dutch had obviously mistaken them for Japanese aircraft. Brooker, realising this, calmly led the formation around the airfield until the firing stopped, then all aircraft landed safely.

Even as the Hurricanes were on their way, a Japanese bomber formation — estimated to be 50 strong — was also heading for Bandoeng, comprising aircraft from the 27th Sentai escorted by 59th and 64th Sentai Ki 43s. Most of the bombers turned back due to bad weather, but the fighters of the 59th continued. They arrived soon after the Hurricanes had landed at Andir, when an air raid warning was sounded and four CW-21Bs of 2-VlG-IV were scrambled, closely followed by the last three Brewsters of 3-VlG-V. The RAF pilots soon witnessed a short, sharp engagement and one Dutch pilot was observed floating down under his parachute. This was the CW-21B Flight's commander, Lt Boxman, whose aircraft had been set on fire at 15,000 feet. As he baled out, his petrol-soaked clothes caught alight and, in an attempt to douse the flames, he refrained from pulling the ripcord for some 5,000 feet. However, on reaching the ground, he had sustained serious burns and would spend the next two years in hospital before making a recovery.

3-VlG-V's commanding officer, Lt Tideman, reported:

"The odds were 3 to 1. We kept them busy until they had to retreat, for fuel shortage probably. When I thought they had all gone, I saw a single Jap proudly circling our base. So I attacked. Starting head-on, I got engaged in a real classic dogfight, with no other to interfere. It was a real pleasure and we both gave everything we had.

"Although I gave him a few bursts, I did not down him and at times I could see him opening fire on me. He had the advantage of a better climbing performance but he was not able to use it to his advantage. Then I tried, after a long time, to force my hand. Because I had knowledge of the terrain, I dived into a ravine hoping he would follow, there to crash into the hills. It did not work! Straightening out in that dive, he followed me at first but steered clear and withdrew. By the time I could go after him again he was too far away, gaining on me: and that was that."

The Japanese pilots identified their opponents as Buffaloes only, claiming two shot down for the loss of one Ki 43. Fortunately on this occasion the Japanese pilots did not follow the returning Dutch fighters, and therefore did not spot the Hurricanes.

During the attack on Andir, an abandoned B-18, which was under repair, was hit and caught fire; one of the few serviceable Hudsons (A16-37) received a direct hit and was burned out, while a Mark III suffered a number of bullet strikes which holed one of its fuel tanks. 1 RAAF Squadron was by now reduced to six Hudsons of which only two were operationally serviceable, and a decision was taken to retain just five crews. The others, together with surplus ground personnel, were ordered to prepare to evacuate.

Part of the 59th Sentai formation landed at Kalidjati on return from the mission, where a further attack by a lone Glenn Martin was noted during the afternoon. After a conference with his flight commanders, Sqn Ldr Brooker decided that he would lead a strike on Kalidjati that evening, enabling the Hurricanes to return under cover of darkness. At dusk therefore, six Hurricanes set off (the seventh having become unserviceable), but as they approached the target Sgt Dunn saw a single fighter diving on them and shouted out a warning. The Hurricanes immediately went into a pre-planned defensive circle. Owing to the darkness the British pilots were unable to fire effectively, whereas the lone Japanese pilot was free to attack any aircraft he could get his sights on; consequently Sgt Dovell's aircraft received a burst of fire into its starboard wing. Dunn, observing this, immediately opened fire as the Japanese aircraft disappeared into the darkness. Dovell was obviously in trouble so Dunn formated on him, but neither pilot had noted the return course. Fortune was on their side, as Plt Off Gartrell joined them and led all three back to Andir safely. On arrival Sqn Ldr Brooker made felt his displeasure that the two sergeants had not noted the course for their return to base, and had thus risked the loss of their aircraft.

Japanese records indicate yet another raid on Kalidjati by a single Glenn Martin, and note that one transport aircraft was burned during this attack. Defending fighters claimed one Martin shot down and one Hurricane damaged. Again their records appear to understate the situation, for during the various raids on this and the next day, two Glenn Martins were shot down and two damaged; on the 2nd, 2/Lt R. Belloni's 1-VlG-I bomber was lost with the crew, while M-5108 of 1-VlG-II was similarly reported shot down over Kalidjati on the 3rd, with the loss of Ens H.K.M. Haye and his crew. Six Dutch fighters were also reported to have attacked Kalidjati during the evening, these also strafing Japanese troops near Pamanoekan. A further RAF attack against Kalidjati was planned for the following morning, so the weary pilots were found overnight accommodation in the Savoy Honan Hotel at Bandoeng, which was crowded with refugees. As the water supply had been cut off, the pilots simply discarded their dirty and sweat-stained clothes and slept naked.

Many survivors of the Japanese attack on Kalidjati airfield the previous morning had by now also reached Bandoeng, as recalled by Flt Lt Holland of 84 Squadron:

> "We were told that all organized resistance was practically at an end, and that we would be formed into guerilla troops to fight in the hills. We were issued with rifles and bayonets and told to train our men how to use them. We spent the day doing this but in the evening we received an order that all aircrew were to be taken away to Australia.
>
> "That night we said goodbye to our ground troops who had served us so faithfully and got into our cars to travel down to a port on the south coast called Tjilatjap."

Eastern Java

In the east the JNAF units had again been active, though no longer facing any opposition in the air. Early in the morning nine Tainan Ku A6Ms attacked Malang flyingboat base, finding and claiming destroyed by strafing one four-engined and two twin-engined flyingboats and a single-engine floatplane. It seems likely that the twin-engined aircraft were Catalinas Y-42 and Y-46, reported destroyed during an attack on Morokrembangen. A little later six more A6Ms set off to attack Djokjakarta and Malang, claiming two twin-engined aircraft destroyed on the ground. Six 3rd Ku A6Ms attacked Pasirian, where three pilots claimed another twin-engined aircraft by strafing.

One B-17 bombed a convoy off Denpassar whilst under attack by defending A6Ms, one of which was claimed probably destroyed by the bomber's gunners; an LB-30 bombed the airfield at Denpassar, whilst the remaining combat-worthy B-17s then carried out one last effort before leaving Java; nine aircraft bombed the convoy north of Rembang and one destroyer was claimed sunk and another damaged. By the evening the evacuation of all remaining US aircraft and personnel from Java was well underway. The last aircraft took off with the advancing Japanese only 18 miles distant, and with Dutch troops standing ready to fire demolition charges.

The wholesale destruction of merchant vessels attempting to flee to safer waters continued unabated during the course of the day, two of the escorts also falling to the guns of Japanese cruisers and destroyers. Three Dutch vessels were amongst the victims, one of which was bombed and sunk. The Norwegian freighter *Prominent* was sunk by shellfire 230 miles south of Java. At 0900 the British destroyer *Stronghold*, which had been providing anti-submarine cover for departing vessels, was sighted and shadowed by a floatplane then, just before 1800, was intercepted by the cruiser *Maya* and two destroyers. The ensuing action lasted for about an hour until finally, with *Stronghold*'s captain — Lt Cdr G.R. Pretor-Pinney — fatally wounded, the order was given to abandon the doomed vessel, which blew up some time later. 50 survivors were picked up by a captured Dutch steamer, the 1030-ton *Duymaer van Twist*, from which they were transferred to *Maya*.

With his fleet a spent force, Vice-Admiral Helfrich considered there was little point in remaining and asked the Governor-General to relieve him of his command, in view of the fact that he only had submarines left! His request was granted and he too was flown out with his staff. Taking off from Lake Bagendit next morning, Catalina Y-56 of GVT-16 (captained by Lt Cdr W. van Prooyen) landed at Tjilatjap to refuel, then carried Helfrich and his party to Ceylon via Padang. Three other Catalinas followed, Y-55, Y-57 and Y-64 all arriving safely.

Broome however was the main destination for most of the longer-ranging aircraft departing the East Indies — particularly the flyingboats, which were able to make use of its harbour facilities and moorings. From Lake Grati, Dutch Catalinas and Do 24s, including the aircraft of GVT-7 and GVT-14, made the flight to Broome, although two Dorniers had to make forced descents along the Australian coast before reaching the port. GVT-7's X-36 was damaged and was subsequently destroyed by the crew; X-24 came down near Wallah and after refuelling was able to fly on to Perth.

As it filled to overflowing with refugees and aircraft, Broome was to prove no safe haven however; the Dutch boats particularly were arriving packed with women and children. Around mid afternoon a Japanese reconnaissance aircraft was seen to circle overhead, presaging an early attack on the port. Although at this time there were only three flyingboats in harbour, this alone was now enough to bring down a fighter strafe. Shortly afterwards four more 'boats landed, together with the B-17s and LB-30s, while during the night a further nine flyingboats arrived.

Lt Colonel Richard A. Legg, previously attached to the 17th Pursuit Squadron, was now at Broome, nominally in charge of the air defence of the north-western area, but here he had nothing — no radar, AA guns or fighters. All he could do was advise the captains of the various aircraft to get off the ground again as early as possible next morning. During the night one of the LB-30s flew back to Djokjakarta to pick up any remaining USAAF personnel who might have arrived there late, but seeing no signal from the ground, returned without landing.

Tuesday, 3 March

Clean Sweep at Broome

Dawn found Broome a hive of activity. In the harbour 15 flyingboats and a single floatplane (the sunken USS *Houston*'s orphaned SOC-3) were at anchor, or moored alongside jetties, whilst at the airfield nearby were five B-17s, three B-24s (or LB-30s), an RAAF Hudson, a Dutch Lodestar, and a KNILM DC-3 airliner. As quickly as the evacuees could be roused, fed and organised, they were loaded back into the aircraft preparatory to flying on to safety further south. Three B-17s, one B-24 and one flyingboat had been got away safely when, at about 0950, disaster struck.

In Broome harbour most of the nine Dutch flyingboats — Catalinas Y-59, Y-60, Y-67, Y-70 and Do 24s X-1, X-3, X-20, X-23 and X-28 — had taken on their loads of civilians, while 25 passengers were lined up on the wharf ready to go aboard two Empire 'boats present — Qantas' *Corinna* (G-AEUC) and the RAAF's A18-10 *Centaurus* (ex G-ADUT). The two RAF Catalinas of 205 Squadron were at anchor, FV-N with its crew still aboard, while two US PBYs of PatWing 10 were preparing to take off for the flight to Melbourne. At the airfield a B-24 (believed to have been 40-2374) piloted by Lt Edson E. Kester was just taking-off with 33 men aboard, including seven personnel from the 17th Pursuit Squadron, while from the harbour the SOC-3 floatplane had also just taken off. It was at this moment that the A6Ms arrived.

From Koepang (Timor) the 3rd Ku had despatched two formations about two and a half hours earlier; nine A6Ms led by Lt Zenjiro Miyano and a navigational C5M (flown by NAP 1/C Akira Hayashi) which headed for Broome harbour and airfield, while eight more fighters and another C5M made for Wyndham airfield. In the harbour A18-10 was the first to be hit and burst into flames, the crew leaping out and escaping in a dinghy. Three A6Ms quickly latched onto the two airborne machines, the SOC-3 being forced down by Wt Off Osamu Kudo, Lt Jack Lamade and his gunner surviving the unequal contest. Kudo then similarly despatched the B-24, the big aircraft falling in flames and breaking in half as it struck the sea; only two of the men aboard were able to extricate themselves from the wreckage, the other 32 perishing.

The fighters kept up the attack for almost 15 minutes, during which time every aircraft present was destroyed, including all those remaining on the airfield. On board Catalina FV-N (W8433) Flt Lt Hugh Garnell and three others were killed immediately, and Plt Off Singh drowned. The Sikh co-pilot was a poor swimmer and had been assisted until it was adjudged by his would-be rescuers that he was able to support himself by clinging on to a piece of debris; sadly, he disappeared.

When the attack started, Lt Cdr A.J. de Bruijn, captain of Catalina Y-70, ordered one of his crew to prepare the aircraft's dinghy in readiness to evacute the passengers and remaining crew. However, the untethered dinghy drifted away, obliging de Bruijn to swim after it. Whilst doing so, Y-70 was strafed, set on fire and consequently sank, taking with it a number of the passengers, which included several Dutch Naval officers and their wives. A further 11 casualties occurred when Y-59 was attacked and sunk. The Japanese pilots correctly claimed 15 flyingboats on the water and seven more aircraft destroyed on the ground, but identified them slightly inaccurately as two B-24s and five Hudsons, whereas actual losses were two B-17Es (41-2448 and 41-2454), the second B-24, Hudson A16-119 of 14 RAAF Squadron, Lodestar LT9-18 and DC-3 PK-ALO.

Apart from wild rifle fire, the only resistance offered was by a quick-thinking and brave Dutch pilot, Lt Gus Winckel, who removed the machine gun from its mounting in an aircraft under repair and, resting it on his forearm, kept up a steady fire until the ammunition ran out. He suffered a severely burned arm for his pains, caused by the overheated barrel of the gun but, by incredible luck his fire struck the A6M flown by Kudo, which was shot down. Kudo, leader of the 2nd Shotai and victor of seven combats, was killed. The gallant Dutchman's fire may also have hit Kudo's wingman, NAP 1/C Masaki Okazaki, who was slightly wounded, while five other A6Ms were later found to have been hit by bullets.

Capt Lester Brain, in charge of the Qantas operation at Broome, aided by Mr Malcolm Millar, a representative of Qantas and British Overseas Airways in Singapore, who had arrived from Java only that morning, rowed out into the harbour in a bid to help those struggling in the water; they suceeded in rescuing seven men, a young woman and her baby, and a Dutch boy.

The Australian authorities noted — to the credit of the 3rd Ku pilots — that they did not attack the refugees waiting to board the Empire flyingboats, nor did they make any attempt to strafe the many survivors in the water. The exact

number of fatalities was difficult to establish but was put at 70 at least, including 48 Dutch, of whom 32 were women and children. However, if the figure of 48 is correct for Dutch fatalities then it would seem the actual number of deaths would have been in excess of 80, as 32 Americans were lost aboard the downed B-24 and four RAF aircrew aboard the Catalina; the bodies of at least 21 Dutch nationals were recovered. A further 35-40 Dutch evacuees were reported to have been wounded. One report of the subsequent recovery of dead and injured, stated:

Lt(jg) Osamu Kudo of the 3rd Kokutai, shot down by machine gun fire during an attack on Broome on 3 March 1942

"There were very distressing scenes as the dead and wounded collected by the lugger were brought up from the jetty. Many of them were frightfully burnt. Others had seen their wives and children killed or burnt. All these women and children were Dutch. One cannot blame the Japanese for this. It was unfortunate that women and children were aboard military aircraft at this time. The reason was that the Dutch pilots were told to endeavour to fly their aircraft to Australia and if possible take their families with them."

During the return flight the A6Ms encountered another KNILM DC-3 (PK-AFV), 60 miles north of Broome. One of the last aircraft to leave Java, it was carrying a number of passengers and also a consignment of diamonds. It was shot down by two pilots from the 1st shotai, NAP 3/C Takashi Kurauchi and NA 1/C Zenichi Matsumoto, although it was successfully force-landed on a beach near Carnot Bay, where the two A6Ms strafed it, killing one of the crew.

KNILM Douglas DC-3 (PK-AFV) which was shot down by two A6Ms and crash-landed on a beach near Carnot Bay (near Broome). It was being flown by the Russian WWI fighter ace, Capt Ivan Smirnoff, who survived. *(Authors' collection)*

During the flight back to Timor however, NA 1/C Yasuo Matsumoto, third man of the 3rd shotai, was obliged to force-land in the sea near Roti. He got ashore but was not rescued until 12 March. The seven remaining A6Ms landed at Koepang shortly after 1300.

The DC-3 shot down by the A6Ms had been flown by KNILM's oldest pilot, the celebrated 49 year-old Capt Ivan Smirnoff[1]. The initial attack by the Japanese fighters, which had set his aircraft alight, had also wounded him in one leg and both arms, but did not prevent him making a successful force-landing. Next day a Japanese flyingboat dropped five bombs on the stranded passengers, this attack killing a woman and her one year-old child; Smirnoff and eight other survivors were later rescued. However, mystery surrounds the fate of the package of diamonds which had been aboard the airliner, as apparently these stones — destined for an Australian bank and valued at one million pounds sterling — were not recovered by the authorities!

Meanwhile the other eight 3rd Ku fighters, which had almost simultaneously strafed Wyndham, had got back a full hour earlier with little to report. They had been able only to claim a lone twin-engine transport biplane destroyed on the ground, although they had also set fire to a petrol dump.

It will be recalled that in the first minutes of the attack on Broome, Lt Kester's laden B-24 was shot down into the sea with considerable loss of life, including one of the original 17th Pursuit Squadron flight commanders, Lt Howard Petschel. Two members of the squadron's ground personnel, Sgts Melvin Donoho and William Beatty, had managed to extricate themselves from the wreck and had then proceeded to swim for the shore, off which, after 12 hours, they were only a quarter of a mile. However, heavy tides prevented them from reaching land, and they were forced to keep swimming throughout the night. Next day Beatty was very weak, so asked Donoho to press on alone and bring help. The latter finally managed to struggle ashore near a lighthouse, only to find it deserted, while an apparent harbour turned out to be a mirage. Having shed all his clothes whilst in the water, he finally arrived at Broome naked and exhausted, some 36 hours after the aircraft was shot down. Beatty was later found on the beach unconscious and delerious, and was at once removed to hospital in Perth, where he died soon after arrival.

Western Java

In Java meanwhile, there had seen no let-up in the fighting, most of which occurred in the west. Early in the morning all seven RAF Hurricanes set off from Andir to attack Kalidjati again, Sqn Ldr Brooker ordering Flt Lt Parker and Plt Off Mendizabal to remain above as top cover, while he led the rest of the squadron down to strafe. Their arrival over the airfield was greeted by light AA gunfire, the pilots observing large numbers of twin-engined aircraft lined up neatly and proceeded to strafe these. As no defending fighters appeared to be present, Parker and Mendizabal dived down to join in the attack, each raking a line of aircraft, at least one of which was seen to catch fire. Parker then concentrated his fire on a petrol bowser which also burst into flames.

---

[1] A Russian by birth, Smirnoff had been one of the most successful and high-scoring fighter pilots of the Imperial Russian Air Service during the Great War. He had fled to the west at the time of the Revolution in 1917, and had later become a naturalised Dutch citizen, undertaking a world famous inaugural flight to Batavia from Holland in a Fokker F.18 Pelican, carrying the Christmas mail in 1933.

Before they were able to select any further targets however, several Japanese fighters appeared and Parker spotted one on the tail of a Hurricane. Closing in from astern, he opened fire, but it turned and attempted to get on his tail. As he had built up speed when diving to attack, he was able to pull away, but Mendizabal — the victim of the attack — was not so lucky, and his aircraft was badly shot-up; he managed to get some miles from the airfield before he was obliged to bale out. A running fight developed as the Hurricanes sought to get away, during which three victories were claimed by Plt Offs Gartrell and Fitzherbert, and Sgt King. No further Hurricanes were lost, but nearly all were damaged and Gartrell was slightly wounded.

Japanese records indicated that attacks on Kalidjati were carried out by Hurricanes, a Brewster and a B-17, where a Ki 21 bomber was reported destroyed by fire, but inexplicably no combats were recorded! Three Glenn Martins and three CW-21Bs also bombed and strafed this airfield during the day.

The presence of the Hurricanes at Andir had left Batavia unprotected and, in their absence, the airfields at Tjililitan and Kemajoran had been bombed. Consequently, following the Kalidjati attack, 'A' Flight was ordered to return immediately to the former base.

Soon after 242 Squadron's attack on Kalidjati, with so little remaining to attract their attention in the east, JNAF bombers and A6Ms started taking off from Bali, to make the long flight along the length of Java and strike at targets in the west for the first time. Six Tainan Ku aircraft were first off at 0900, heading for Tjilatjap, followed ten minutes later by a dozen more heading for Bandoeng. The latter city was also target for a further dozen 3rd Ku aircraft, which left Denpassar at just about the moment that the unit's other aircraft were beginning their attack on Broome. Rather later in the morning, Ki 43s of the 64th Sentai took off from Sumatra to escort bombers of the 90th Sentai to the same destination, then to strafe the south coast airfield at Pameungpeuk. All formations approached their targets at, or just after, midday. The 90th Sentai bombed first at Andir, claiming one 'North American' destroyed of three that were taking off. At Pameungpeuk the Ki 43s strafed and claimed two aircraft in flames. Dutch accounts note a Brewster damaged beyond repair there, plus a Hawk 75A and two Glenn Martins being destroyed at Andir; the latter were M-568 of l-VlG-I and an aircraft of 3-VlG-III.

As the Navy bombers approached Bandoeng, the 3rd Ku A6M pilots saw a fighter which they attacked, but then lost sight of; they had, in fact, attacked Maj Kato's 64th Sentai Ki 43, which was badly damaged, and he was obliged to force-land at Kalidjati! The 3rd Ku pilots then joined the six Tainan fighters in strafing the airfield where considerable numbers of aircraft were claimed destroyed on the ground, including 14 twin-engined and four single-engined types. It is known that some Dutch aircraft were destroyed at Andir on this date, but numbers and types are not recorded. As the formation headed for home, NAP 2/C Kazuo Yokokawa, No 2 man in Wt Off Watari Handa's shotai of the Tainan Ku formation, spotted a fighter which he identified as a P-40 and claimed it probably shot down. This may have been a Dutch Hurricane, one of the surviving pair of the ill-fated 2-VlG-IV, which were flown from Ngoro to Bandoeng during the day piloted by 2/Lt Marinus and Ens N. Wink; the former was obliged to force-land on the way, the aircraft being wrecked.

Meanwhile the other six Tainan fighters had strafed the flyingboat base at Tjilatjap, claiming one Catalina in flames. On this date Y-48 of GVT-18 was reported destroyed in a bombing attack on Tanjong Priok, while Y-39, Y-41 and Y-73 were similarly destroyed at Morekrembangan; the only loss recorded as having occurred at Tjilatjap was Y-66 of GVT-5 — but allegedly, next day. It may however have been PatWing 10's aircraft No 3, which had been abandoned at the port due to engine failure on the previous day. During the return flight to Bali, the A6Ms — led by Lt Jun-ichi Sasai and NAP 1/C Saburo Sakai — strafed a ship, but this was to be the last operation of any note flown by the unit for over a month.

Sgt Geoff Dewey, RAAF, a Blenheim pilot of 34 Squadron who made probably the last Wirraway flight in Java. *(G. Dewey)*

A call went out for volunteers to ferry the six former W Flight Wirraways from Pondoktjabe, where they had been deposited, to Bandoeng. Only two of the pilots available (Sgts George Dewey and Howard Hough) had previously flown the Harvard, the type from which the Wirraway was derived. Dewey, who had been trained as a fighter pilot, wrote:

"We arrived at this jungle strip and found six Wirraways pushed back under the trees. While the engineer officer and fitters gradually started aircraft, Hough and I gave the other four pilots (none of whom had previously flown a Harvard or a Wirraway) a run down on controls, cockpit layout and characteristics of the aircraft — then kept our fingers crossed.

"The four, escorted by Hough, took off and set course for Bandoeng at about 200 feet. The last aircraft took about half an hour to start and, as I taxied it out, saw the engineer officer and the two fitters leaving in cars for Bandoeng.

317

"Once airborne I found the undercarriage would not retract and flat out the aircraft would not exceed 120 mph. The canopy wouldn't close and I had no helmet, no parachute. Flew at about 50 feet following the railway line (we had no charts). Lost line on several occasions as it went into tunnels. Eventually arrived at Bandoeng about 15 minutes after it had been pattern bombed. Two of the Wirraways had hit craters on landing but Hough had guided the other two in safely — so we had four aircraft which I think any of us would have been reluctant to use on ops. They were utterly clapped out. We left and never saw them again."

The movement of Japanese units to Kalidjati was now accelerating fast, the rest of the 59th and 75th Sentais arriving during the day, followed by the 64th and 90th next day, together with six A6Ms of the 22nd Air Flotilla and five A5M fighters attached to the Mihoro Ku, which had recently reached Sumatra; one of the latter was badly damaged on landing. Alarmed by the rapid deterioration of the situation, and aware of their inability to defend the port of Batavia adequately, the Dutch authorities declared it an open city during the 3rd to prevent unnecessary damage and suffering.

Following the capture of Kalidjati, the elements of the 230th Infantry Regiment responsible had moved westwards to take Tjikampek airfield, which they reached by the 3rd. Meanwhile the rest of the regiment had headed south from Eretenwetan and concentrated at Soebang, south-east of Kalidjati, where they were to regroup after the securing of Tjikampek. The 2nd Division force from the Merak/Bantam Bay area meantime, had split into two columns, one heading for Batavia, the other towards Buitenzorg and Bandoeng. The route of the latter, more southerly thrust, was barred by defending forces which included the British/Australian elements; these forces hoped to deny access to river crossings in front of Buitenzorg, while Dutch forces which had been engaged in the Merak area had now fallen back to Serang, where the invaders captured an important road junction.

In an effort to prevent a two-pronged advance on the capital, a Dutch mobile force from Bandoeng struck north, engaging the 230th Regiment at Soebang. A small force of tanks actually penetrated right into the centre of the town, but the infantry was unable to follow up and give the necessary support, and a withdrawal followed. A reserve regiment at Buitenzorg was ordered to move to Soebang in support, but when 20 miles short of its objective, it was spotted by Japanese reconnaissance aircraft, and at once came under sustained attack by the JAAF units at Kalidjati. Throughout the afternoon and evening waves of light bombers and army co-operation aircraft attacked, the column becoming completely scattered. Next day all available forces were withdrawn by the Dutch command, to concentrate on the defence of Bandoeng.

At sea

To the south of Java the majority of the fleeing merchant vessels had by now cleared the vicinity of Vice-Admiral Kondo's far-ranging task force warships, although the American gunboat *Asheville* and the RN's minesweeper *Scott Harley* were both intercepted and sunk by gunfire. Aboard the Dutch merchant-man *Siantar*, the crew were relaxing in the belief that they had escaped the fate which had overtaken so many of their countrymen, when the vessel was torpedoed and sunk by the submarine *I-1*; 21 of those aboard perished.

The RAN sloop *Yarra*, which had departed Tanjong Priok escorting the three tankers and the depot ship *Anking*, had seen two of her charges sunk (the tanker *British Judge* having been torpedoed south of Sunda Strait), came across survivors from the sunken Dutch steamer *Parigi* and took these aboard.

Wednesday, 4 March
At sea

Early in the morning the cruisers *Atago*, *Takeo* and *Maya*, together with destroyers of the 4th Destroyer Flotilla, sighted the *Yarra* convoy heading southwards, two spotter aircraft being launched to investigate. One by one the ships were attacked by gunfire, *Anking* being the first to succumb to the bombardment just after 0630. *Yarra* was badly damaged but continued to fight back, then the small minesweeper *MMS.51* was hit and abandoned, with the loss of two of her 16 crew. One of the cruisers moved in and sank her with pom-pom gunfire. The tanker *Francol* was next to be targeted, sinking at 0730. *Yarra* was still firing her guns but was then bombed by the spotter floatplanes, sinking half an hour later, taking 118 of the crew and passengers with her, including all but one of *Parigi*'s survivors.

Of the men left drifting on their liferafts in the sea, 57 of *Anking*'s crew were rescued by the Dutch steamer *Tawali*; another 26 in two lifeboats drifted for three weeks before reaching the Java coast. By then only 18 were still alive and six of these perished in the heavy sea running off the coast. Meanwhile, the survivors of *MMS.51* — having been joined by a Chinese seaman from *Anking* — were plucked from the sea after three days by another Dutch vessel, *Tjimanoek*, while a Japanese destroyer picked up one boatload (a dozen Chinese and their Chief Officer) from the tanker. That left 34 survivors from *Yarra*, including the Dutch master of the *Parigi*; sadly, by the time help fortuitously came their way in the shape of Dutch submarine *K-XI*, 21 had died including the Dutchman.

Two further Dutch vessels fell to Japanese submarines during the day, *Merkus* being accounted for by *I-62*, the larger *Le Maire* by *I-7*. It is believed there were no survivors from either ship. Far to the north, the only retribution for these devastating shipping losses occurred, when the American submarine *S-39* torpedoed the 6,500-ton Japanese tanker *Erimo* some 700 miles north-east of Batavia.

Western Java

The only sustained Allied activity in the air involved the RAF Hurricanes, four of which were sent out at first light for the Sunda Strait area, where 2nd Division troops were to be attacked. Flt Lt Julian and Plt Off Gartrell peeled off to investigate a long column of horse-drawn transport and were fired on. They called down the top cover (Parker and Fitzherbert), then all four flew up and down a straight, tree-lined road several times with guns blazing, leaving it blocked with fallen horses and overturned carts — unpleasant work. As they pulled away, Parker saw a single horseman racing towards a thicket — one burst was sufficient to cause his demise.

The RAF pilots were eating sandwiches on the airfield later in the morning, when they were ordered to fly back to Andir on a 'permanent' basis. It was decided that the ten moderately serviceable Hurricanes would carry out a strike on Kalidjati on the way, while two semi-serviceable aircraft would go direct to the new base. Those pilots not allocated aircraft were to travel by road, a 1942 Buick — recently-acquired by Plt Off Cicurel, who had attached himself to the unit — being commandeered for the trip, while Sgts Dunn and Young offered to drive a large petrol bowser to Andir — an offer which was accepted.

On approaching Kalidjati, six of the Hurricanes were led down to strafe by Sqn Ldr Brooker, while Plt Off Lockwood, 2/Lt Anderson, Sgt Sandeman Allen and one other of 'A' Flight remained above as cover. Sgt Ian Newlands (Z5691) reported:

> "I strafed various planes on the ground but missed one taking off and he opened up on me with cannons and machine guns — four red balls in my rear vision mirror was an unforgettable sight — but I didn't get hit."

Unable to observe much from the height at which they were flying, the top cover pair of Lockwood and Anderson followed the others down; Bill Lockwood recalled:

> "As Lt Anderson followed me down, I met at around 6-8,000 feet, two 'Navy 0s' climbing. As I went past them and was about to pull around, I noticed a transport of the DC-3 type below and in a landing circuit. I dove in behind this aircraft and was about to open fire when I remembered a remark made by someone before we took off about there still being a few Dutch aircraft around and not to shoot down a Dutchman. I climbed slightly and to the right of the aircraft to check. I saw the 'fried eggs' on the wings. He also saw me and turned away to port with wheels and flaps down.
>
> "I looked in my rear view mirror and saw two 'Zeros' on my tail. I made a hurried diving attack on the transport and went to tree-top level, heading I knew not where, but hoping Bandoeng. The Japs were close behind and firing. I weaved and put the throttle through the gate. I had a slight speed edge. Flying straight and very low, I flew south for some minutes and presently came over a range of mountains and there was Andir airfield. I landed and Lt Anderson did not come in. I never saw him again."

The other top cover pair also engaged the Japanese fighters, which were caught at a height disadvantage, as Sandeman Allen remembered:

> "The 'Zeros' came in underneath and we had a simple target for the first few vital moments, after which we were so heavily outnumbered that we got into serious trouble. I was credited with two 'Zeros' destroyed, one probable and one damaged but crawled back to the aerodrome with 28 cannon shell and 43 bullet holes in the machine (Z5584), and with slight wounds to my head and legs.
>
> "I remember being given a cup of tea and I was shaking so badly it stirred itself! However, I took off in a fresh plane 10 minutes later so that I was able to recover my nerve."

Most of the other Hurricanes returned with varying degrees of damage. Although saddened by the loss of the South African Neil Anderson (who was taken prisoner but died in captivity two days later), the pilots were jubilant for they believed that they had shot down seven of the intercepting fighters — two by Sgt Jimmy King to bring his score to five in three days, and one each by Brooker, Julian and Fitzherbert, to add to the pair credited to Sandeman Allen. What the Japanese losses were in the air is not known, but their fighter pilots

— apparently from the 22nd Air Flotilla — also believed that they had shot down five of the Hurricanes. On the ground one light bomber was destroyed by fire, with two more and one reconnaissance aircraft badly damaged, while one of each and one Ki 48 were damaged to a lesser extent.

By late afternoon the 242 Squadron pilots travelling in the Buick had reached Andir, where soon after arrival a message was received requiring a Hurricane to reconnoitre the road leading southwards from Kalidjati to Bandoeng, since Japanese forces had been reported advancing down this in strength. Flt Lt Parker was detailed to undertake this sortie, Plt Off Fitzherbert volunteering to act as escort. Whilst discussing the job in hand a raid by Kanoya Ku bombers occurred, the majority of the anti-personnel bombs falling in the region of the main buildings and hangars, where one of the Dutch afdeling was housed. Immediately afterwards, Parker and Fitzherbert ran out to their aircraft, started up and taxied between the bomb craters to the end of the runway.

Taking off in a cloud of dust, they headed for the west end of the valley, when Parker realised that his wingman was signalling frantically for him to turn back to Andir. A quick check of the instruments showed that all appeared to be in order, but Fitzherbert continued gesticulating, stabbing his finger furiously downwards and then he swung his aircraft round and headed back to Andir. Parker followed suit and almost immediately the cockpit filled with glycol vapour. Anticipating the vapour cloud would increase and restrict his vision, he closed the throttle and glided down just short of the runway and to one side of it. With flaps still down from his quick take-off and the undercarriage up, he hit the ground just in front of a Dutch bomber which was being re-armed.

The Hurricane thumped into the tarmac and slid past the bomber and running men, with a tremendous clatter and clouds of vapour. Fortunately Parker was strapped in tightly and the aircraft did not turn over as it came to a stop, minus its flaps, airscrew, radiator and much of its underside. He switched off the engine and jumped out smartly, to be greeted by the Dutch groundcrew who shook his hand repeatedly. He realized they were thanking him for pulling away from them before hitting the ground — when in fact he had been rather more anxious not to have crashed into their bomb trollies!

It transpired later — after the CO had collected him and driven him back to dispersal — that the Hurricane had been damaged by a bomb splinter during the raid, and that Fitzherbert had seen the radiator streaming glycol but had been unable to warn him sooner as his R/T was not working. The reconnaissance sortie was abandoned, due to the lateness of the afternoon.

The pilots again adjourned to the Savoy Honan Hotel in Bandoeng for the night, and during dinner Sqn Ldr Brooker announced that two Dutch transport aircraft were due in that night to begin evacuating pilots. In the first instance wounded pilots would accompany Wg Cdr Maguire and himself, while four more pilots would have seats — to be settled by drawing lots. On his departure, Julian was to take command of the remaining pilots and aircraft. In the event, the evacuating aircraft did not put in an appearance that night.

Meanwhile, Sgts Dunn and Young had not yet arrived from Tjililitan in the petrol bowser, but they were on the way. The bowser had been loaded with pilots' personal possessions, including a number of gramophone records. Their journey was anything but uneventful. They had set off with Gordon Dunn driving, and were shortly overtaken by an army convoy, as he recalled:

"An army sergeant enquired of our destination and on establishing this, said he would drive back from time to time to make sure we were not in trouble. We continued on our way, quite uneventfully until we reached the mountainous area, when the engine started to overheat. Pulling into the side of the road near a paddy field, we found an old tin and with this gathered water from the field and refilled the radiator.

"Within a short while of recommencing the journey we came to a steep decline, at the bottom of which was a stream with a narrow bridge. As there was a matching steep incline the other side, I decided to accelerate, aiming the vehicle at the centre of the bridge; I noted that the speed had reached 50 mph when Tom shouted a warning. An old man with a donkey and cart suddenly appeared on the bridge. There was nothing I could do, so half expecting a collision, we careered across the bridge, missing the man and his donkey but hitting the back of the cart, before shooting up the other side!"

Apart from the radiator overheating again, the rest of the trip was relatively uneventful until eveningtime. As they parked for the night a Dutch officer approached them with a request for some fuel for his car. After facilitating him, they experienced difficulty in turning off the tap and lost about 100 gallons of fuel. In return for the petrol, the officer found them accommodation and placed an armed guard on the bowser. Next morning however, they found that they could not communicate with the guard, who spoke only Javanese and would not let them enter the vehicle; they had to wait for the return of the officer before they could get underway. Andir was eventually reached without further mishap, but not before they had noticed a stencilled warning sign on the side of the bowser: "This vehicle not to exceed 15 mph". They were hardly surprised therefore, when they later learned that the bowser would no longer travel faster than 2 mph! Their main regret however, was that their gramophone records had practically melted away in the intense heat of the glove compartment, where they had been placed!

BRITAIR was now down to seven Hurricanes, a handful of Vildebeests and two operationally serviceable Hudsons. The Dutch similarly had few aircraft left, the most potent of which were the seven Brewsters and three CW-21Bs, but serviceability was low. During the day experiments had been conducted at Andir on Hudson A16-89, to establish whether the aircraft could be re-fuelled in flight by means of a pipe running from the cabin to the starboard fuel tank. Ground tests proved to be successful and permission was granted for Flg Off Gibbes to fly the aircraft to Australia that night, taking with him his crew and two sick passengers, Flt Lts John O'Brien and Colin Verco. On learning of the evacuation, Air Vice-Marshal Maltby instructed Wg Cdr Davis also to depart aboard this aircraft, but he declined to leave his men.

Gibbes took off at 2330, his aircraft crammed full with 4-gallon petrol cans to enable the in-flight refuelling operation to take place. This entailed Gibbes reducing speed to about 90 mph, following which one of the crew, gripped by the ankles by another, had to reach through the window opening to undo the filler cap, then guide the pipe into the tank. Unavoidably some petrol sprayed into the slipstream and some splashed onto the cabin floor but sufficient went into the tanks to meet the demand, and the Hudson eventually reached the coast of Western Australia, landing near the town of Roebourne.

A second aircraft crept out of Andir this same night; this was a patched-up

Wg Cdr R.H. 'Curly' Davis, RAAF, commanding officer of 1 RAAF Squadron, who refused to leave his men and was taken prisoner. He was awarded an OBE in recognition of his sacrifice. (*Grp Capt H.C. Plenty*)

B-17E, which had been abandoned. The driving force behind the effort to make the aircraft flyable was T/Sgt Harry Hayes, who had been in charge of repair and inspection at Andir. With the departure of the US bombers to Australia, he and his Dutch labour force had initially worked feverishly to repair an abandoned B-18, but this was then destroyed in an air raid. Hopes were then pinned on making one of the three abandoned B-17Es at Andir, serviceable. The lesser damaged of the three was selected although two of its four engines had to be almost completely rebuilt; the wings had to be repaired and the tail unit overhauled. A party of American civilians had gathered at the airfield, one of whom was Gerald Cherymisin, a contract pilot who had been engaged by the Dutch to fly Lodestars from Andir.

Cherymisin agreed to fly the aircraft, having once flown the type before the war, which was one time more than his Dutch volunteer co-pilot, Lt Sibolt Kok, had managed. However, on the morning of the planned departure, a fighter strafe of the airfield further damaged the aircraft but by darkness temporary repairs had been carried out. Although one engine failed to start, the aircraft nonetheless lifted off with a total of 18 escapees (including the American pilot's Dutch wife) on board, flying at 3,000 feet all the way to Australia. Another abandoned B-17 — an old C model (40-2072) — was repaired by ML personnel at Andir, and then flown by these Dutch airmen to Australia, arriving safely at Geraldton.

A second Hudson was made ready for the flight to Australia the following night, Flt Lt J.G. White departing Andir in A16-26 with Flt Lt J.G. Emerton, his crew and one other passenger; he too made a safe landfall despite coming down in a salt pan on the Australian coast. A third successful flight was made during the next night by Flg Off John Lower and his crew plus two passengers, in AE488. They ran out of fuel just as the Australian coast was reached but put down safely. The remaining RAAF air and ground personnel were ordered to head for the coastal airfield at Pameungpeuk, from where it was hoped they would be picked up by flyingboats from Australia. During the trek southwards Flt Lts Oscar Diamond and Stu Bothroyd acquired motor cycles, the former crashing his machine en route, sustaining a broken left arm and collar bone.

Meanwhile, the remaining CW-22s of VkA-1 which had been forced to leave Tjikembar for Tasikmalaja the previous day, in the face of the Japanese 2nd Division's advance, continued to scout over the fighting in the west, where RAF ground parties now consisted of the armed force led by Wg Cdr G.H. Alexander at Tjilatjap, plus 1,900 unarmed men there, and a further 600 at Djokjakarta. Following a further raid on Tjilatjap during the day by 23 Takao

Ku G4Ms, returning crews claimed damage to five merchant ships, but they had in fact achieved greater success; three small Dutch vessels — *Manipi* (536 tons), *Kidoel* (775 tons) and *Tydeman* (1,160 tons) — were sunk in the harbour. Amongst those on board the Dutch freighter *Kota Baroe* which escaped damage whilst waiting to depart, were a number of Dutch Naval cadets, including Hans van der Kop, who wrote:

> "In a small inlet a Catalina flyingboat was being repaired; on the quay huge crates were being opened. I peered and saw to my astonishment that a twin-engined bomber stood there, which had been assembled on the quay."

The twin-engined aircraft was the first of two DB-7Bs to be assembled by the persevering Dutch naval groundcrews: four others had been despatched by train to Tasikmalaja, where they too were assembled.

Later still, as the sun was setting, van der Kop watched the flyingboat depart. The pilot of the Catalina (Y-71) was Lt H.V.B. Burgerhout, CO of GVT-5 who, next day, would fly the DB-7B from the quay to Tasikmalaja, experiencing little trouble in taking-off, despite there being only some 10-12 feet clearance between the port wingtip and the warehouses! At Tasikmalaja, Burgerhout[1] handed over the aircraft to the ML, where it was ordered to be destroyed by a demolition squad to prevent it falling into Japanese hands! With time rapidly running out, the authorities ordered the remaining four DB-7Bs be 'destroyed' by punching holes through the wings with iron bars and by tearing the carburettors off the engines. However, when the Japanese arrived at Tasikmalaja they salvaged sufficient undamaged parts to assemble at least one aircraft.

Surplus American personnel had been ordered to Tjilatjap in the hope of finding a ship, but the 160 men involved were only able to join the massed groups of RAF men already there. The personnel of 205 Squadron were more fortunate, for they — together with a few members of 211 Squadron — joined a group of Dutch sailors and embarked on a pearl-lugger, *Tung Song*. One of those aboard the old vessel was Sgt Bill Sykens, a 211 Squadron pilot who had arrived with the Sea Party from Egypt; he recalled:

> "We were supposed to meet up with other vessels off the mouth of the river and proceed in convoy but due to some engine trouble, I believe, we were delayed and missed the convoy. On one night we did see distant flashes which we put down to a naval battle.
>
> "It is to Jimmy Riddle (*Flt Sgt navigator, 211 Squadron*) we owed quite a bit. It was he who did the navigation, with only a ruler, a protractor, his aircraft sextant and of all things, a school atlas which we found lying around in what had probably been the ship's lounge!"

Tung Song reached Fremantle safely after a relatively uneventful trip, although the Dutch master had been ordered to search for the crews of two flyingboats reported shot down nearby. Neither survivors nor wreckage were sighted.

The surviving Dutch flyingboats also left at this stage, Catalinas Y-45 of GVT-18, Y-62 of GVT-2 and Y-71 of GVT-5 reaching Australia with Do 24s X-5, X-7, X-8, X-9, X-10 and X-24, together with an abandoned, damaged US PBY

---

[1] Lt Burgerhout later flew his Catalina to Australia. Eventually posted to the UK, he subsequently commanded the RAF's 320 Squadron, comprised of mainly Dutch personnel, flying B-25 Mitchells over Northern Europe. On reaching the UK, Cadet van der Kop, trained as an observer, and was also posted to 320 Squadron, where he flew as a member of Burgerhout's crew.

(Bu1215) which had been made flyable by the Dutch, taken over and re-numbered Y-3. A number of Dutch aircraft, which could not be flown to safety or transported from Java, were now destroyed including a number of Ryan STM trainers which had been flown to Tasikmalaja from Kalidjati, and a damaged DC-2 (PK-AFJ) of KNILM, which had crash-landed near Sourabaya.

During the day the 3rd Kokutai again sent out a small force of A6Ms to northern Australia and, on this occasion, Darwin was the target. Lt Ichiro Mukai's nine fighters, led by one of the ubiquious C5Ms, attacked the RAAF airfield at about 1330, where they caught Hudson A16-63 of 13 RAAF Squadron as it was about to take off, and destroyed it; however, no casualties were suffered. The Japanese pilots also claimed five small bombers burned — possibly Wirraways — although no such losses were reported. It was however to be the last attack on Darwin before an effective fighter defence arrived.

Because of the rapidity of the Japanese advance, 36 Squadron was again forced to move, going now to Tasikmalaja, the main body leaving at 0800. Of the six Vildebeests remaining, two were operationally unserviceable and were to be flown directly to Tasikmalaja, whilst the remaining four aircraft were to call in at Andir, from where they were to carry out a strike against Kalidjati that night. Arriving at 2315, Sgt Bruce Appleby's aircraft taxied into a bomb crater and was irreparably damaged. Crews briefed, the remaining three aircraft took off at 10 minute intervals to avoid the possibility of colliding in the darkness; Flt Lt Ian Hutcheson reported:

> "Owing to bad visibility and rain it took me nearly two hours to find the target, and I attacked with moderate success — nothing set on fire but my air gunner reported seeing some aircraft blown over in the bomb flashes. My parachute flares failed to light, due probably to too long exposure on the aircraft. I also destroyed or killed the crew of an automatic AA gun which was firing fairly accurately, and put a round through my elevator.

> "I returned to Andir and found that neither of the other two pilots had returned. I took off again, located the target fairly quickly and attacked again with about the same degree of success as before and no opposition, save for one light automatic which was very inaccurate and never fired near me. I then proceeded to Tasikmalaja, landing at 0630.

> "The other two pilots on the attack returned about an hour later. Flg Off Callick had searched for about three and a half hours for the target, and delivered one moderately successful attack; Plt Off Lamb had been unable to locate the target."

Thursday, 5 March
Wg Cdr Maguire and Sqn Ldr Brooker spent much of the morning in Bandoeng, where they experienced great difficulties with Dutch officials. Since many of the senior officers considered that further resistance was useless, and were divided in their wish to surrender, or to assist the RAF in continuing the fight, pleas for assistance failed; however, when verbal threats were employed, supplies of fuel — but not oxygen — were forthcoming.

Having failed to carry out the reconnaissance detailed for the previous afternoon, Flt Lt Parker — on this occasion with Plt Off Lockwood as escort — took off as soon as sufficient cloud had formed to offer some refuge should Japanese fighters appear. A few miles to the west the cloud layer actually covered the tops of the hills and, seeing this, Parker signalled his escort to stay behind, having decided that he would map read his way around the valleys just under the base of the clouds. This he did until he saw Kalidjati in the distance, easily spotting the road he was to reconnoitre. Flying low over this, he was rather surprised to find no hostile traffic before reaching the foothills leading to Bandoeng. In the distance he then observed two aircraft circling a few hundred feet above ground level, and flew towards them, ready to pull into the clouds should they be fighters. Within moments he was able to see that they were twin-engined aircraft.

> "They evidently had not seen me coming from the north and below them and by the time I had closed to 400 yards I could see the Japanese insignia. I opened fire and easily followed one round without too much deflection. After a few moments his starboard engine streamed smoke, his nose came up, then he dropped over on his back and dived straight downwards. I turned away to starboard as I was then facing Kalidjati towards which the other bomber was streaking and I lost sight of the damaged bomber under my wing for a moment. When I looked again, I saw the parabola of his smoke trail in the sky and at the end of it, on the ground, a fierce fire where the plane was burning."

Having decided to return to Andir to report the results of his reconnaissance, he then encountered four Japanese fighters which approached from his port flank and above. He tried to out-run these but, with their height advantage, they were able to overhaul him rapidly, two firing whilst the other two held back. By manoeuvring violently he managed to avoid being hit and, as he was fast approaching Andir, decided to fly directly over the airfield hoping that the Bofors guns would open up on his assailants.

> "Andir came up ahead and I centred the stick and concentrated on skidding at hangar height across the airfield, frantically willing the Bofors guns to open up. Nothing happened. I pulled round the hangars to the centre of Bandoeng and found the tower of the Savoy Honan ahead. Although I was still in fine pitch and full throttle, I set the flaps 'down' and hauled the Hurricane around the tower, knowing the great risk of hitting the tower any following fighter must take in trying a deflection shot. Still I'd not heard the clang of any hits on my aircraft and, having completed 180° round the tower, I shot off back to the airfield again.
>
> "This time the gunners were ready and, as I whistled across the field at ground level, I found myself over-taken by their bright orange shells … I had nothing left but panic. Attacked at my own base by enemy aircraft and 'friendly' gunners, I'd had enough and fled. I hared over paddy fields and trees and reached the other side of the valley before I realised I was alone. Not only alone — but gradually ashamed and indignant at my own behaviour.
>
> "I'd been airborne for only 20 minutes, and had enough petrol in my tanks for another hour's flying and I knew the location of a satellite airfield at Pameungpeuk, on the south coast. I decided I could safely have a go at the 'Zeros' and laboriously climbed to 20,000 feet, the maximum I dared without oxygen. I planned to come down at them at 400-500 mph, pick off one or two, and land either at Andir or Pameungpeuk.

"Unfortunately I lost sight of the valley and mistook it when I dived between the clouds, finding neither 'Zeros' nor Andir. For more than half an hour I searched, staying just under the clouds and following all the valleys, anxiously watching the petrol gauge and worrying about the 'Zeros', but I was hopelessly lost. Finally, I pulled away to starboard on sighting another fighter approaching dead ahead. He did the same and to my great relief turned out to be another Hurricane — Bill Lockwood. Luckily, having no map, he'd patrolled a few valleys closer to Andir and he was able to lead me safely back."

His return was enthusiastically welcomed by all, including the normally stolid CO, for having seen him pursued across the airfield by the hostile fighters, coupled with his delayed return, all had assumed that he had been shot down. Even Wg Cdr Maguire telephoned his congratulations on his return and on shooting down the bomber. However he was surprised to learn that Parker had not sighted any enemy troops on the road to Bandoeng.

The bombers Parker had encountered were undoubtedly part of a force from the 75th and 90th Sentais, which had raided Andir soon after he had left to undertake the reconnaissance. Some Hurricanes had scrambled to intercept without success, but one of these (Z5691) flown by Sgt Newlands was swiftly in trouble. No sooner was he airborne when Newlands noticed glycol fumes entering the cockpit and, after a quick circuit, he landed again within five minutes of take-off. Of the incident, he later wrote:

"Some 'erk' twit had not secured my glycol cap and my windscreen fogged up and the cockpit was full of fumes. I did a circuit almost within the aerodrome and was on the deck in less than five minutes.

"I taxied at about 40 mph to the bomb bay as another wave of low level bombers approached. I parked the kite and dived into a slit trench as a stick of bombs straddled me. One hit a Dutch bomber facing my direction about 40 yards away and set it alight; each time I poked my head out of the trench, the machine guns on the bomber — due to the heat — fired over my head!"

By the time the bomber had burnt out Newland's temper had also cooled down. He had been intent on finding the person who had not secured the glycol cap on his aircraft and exacting some sort of revenge! The Glenn Martin was one of two 2-VlG-III machines (M-520 and M-521) destroyed during the raid, whilst a further bomber (believed to have been M-592), flown by 2/Lt P.E. Straatman of 1-VlG-II, failed to return from a raid on Kalidjati, where it had fallen foul of defending fighters.

During the morning the mighty Japanese 1st Carrier Fleet launched its only major attack on the East Indies when shipping and port facilities in and around Tjilatjap were hit by 180 carrier-borne aircraft — B5Ns and D3As led by Lt Cdr Egusa and escorted by A6Ms; 19 vessels were claimed sunk and one more badly damaged. Actual losses were not quite so severe as the claims would suggest, although there was now no question of the port being used for further evacuation; five small merchantmen were sunk — *Rohan* (563 tons), *Pasir* (1,187 tons), *Tohiti* (982 tons), *Barentz* (4,819 tons) and *Canopus* (773 tons) — while the 1,594-ton *Sipora* was damaged and subsequently scuttled. At least a further eight vessels sustained damage, which denied them the opportunity to escape, and they were scuttled as a result. Tjilatjap town was reduced to ruins, with about 200 buildings demolished or gutted by fire.

The 1st Carrier Fleet then drew off back into the Indian Ocean once more, joining with Vice-Admiral Kondo's battleships in bombarding Christmas Island two days later, before retiring to its forward base at Staring Bay.

The dwindling Vildebeest force was ordered to repeat its strike of the previous night against Kalidjati, four aircraft having been made serviceable for the sortie. One of these however, was prevented from taking off by a Glenn Martin which had become bogged down in mud directly in front of the Vildebeest's dispersal pen. The remaining three — flown by Flg Off Reg Lamb, Flg Off Gotto and Sgt Appleby — departed at 2200, two aircraft armed with Dutch 50 kg anti-personnel bombs, the other (Appleby's) with six 250 lb bombs. The crews reported difficulty in seeing any aircraft on the ground, bombs being released in the dispersal area. As a result, one building and four aircraft were believed to have been hit and set on fire.

Sgt Bruce Appleby had made two runs across the airfield, releasing two bombs each time, then turned back for a third run; at this stage the aircraft was hit by AA fire, the observer, Sgt Peter Atherton, receiving a piece of shrapnel in his right arm. Attempting to regain altitude to cross the 6,000 feet high mountain range which barred their way to Andir, the Vildebeest started to shake and shudder, so Appleby ordered his crew to bale out. Although having jumped out at fairly low altitude, Atherton and the gunner, Sgt John Blunt, both made safe landings, then luckily found each other in the darkness, eventually making their way back to Tasikmalaja. Their New Zealand pilot however, was killed when the aircraft crashed.

Back at Tasikmalaja three more crews were waiting to carry out a second sortie, but the only two petrol pumps broke down and the airmen were obliged to continue refuelling with buckets. This took so long that it was nearly dawn before they were ready, consequently the proposed attack was cancelled.

Friday, 6 March

In the morning Tjilatjap was heavily raided again, this time by land-based bombers, when a further three small Dutch vessels — *Mandar*, *Dajak* and *Atjeh* — were sunk, while the 696-ton *Poseidon* was set on fire. A further nine merchant vessels — incapable for one reason or another of making attempts to reach Australia or Ceylon — were also scuttled, to deny them to the Japanese. Tjilatjap was now a graveyard of sunken merchant vessels; at least 23 ships — totalling almost 23,000 tons — lay submerged within the harbour.

One of the missing Hurricane pilots returned to the fold during the morning, when Plt Off Tom Watson unexpectedly arrived in Bandoeng, with quite a story to tell following his crash four days earlier:

"I managed to crash-land, wheels up, in a rice paddy not too far away from the Japanese. Apart from a small bump on the head, I was OK. I got as far away from the scene of the crash as I could, and as fast as I could, and then started my trek back. The Japanese were between me and Batavia and I suppose I rather advanced with them, trying to keep out of sight.

"I threw away my flying helmet, put dirt on my face and tried to look as much like a native as possible. However, I had two problems. One that I have been bald since my late teens and the sun gave me hell, and the other was we had no proper flying equipment and all I had on my feet were low shoes. However, I found an old native straw hat after the first day which kept the sun off my head but at night it rained and the mud in my shoes started to wear on my flesh so that my feet became somewhat raw.

"Most of the Indonesians were afraid of me but one young boy really helped me. He could speak some English. There was no food to be had, water I drank out of any place I could find it, and I didn't dare go to sleep. Japanese patrols were about quite a bit and once I hid while they passed. I was lucky that there was something like a haystack to hide in.

"The second day the boy walked with me most of the time and was able, by talking to other Indonesians, to ascertain where the Japanese were. It soon became obvious that I could not get back to Batavia and I headed for the hills. I eventually reached the Tjililitan River and crossed it downstream from where the Japanese were repairing the main bridge that had been destroyed.

Watson then met an elderly native who helped him put together some bamboo poles to form a raft and, although it would not hold his weight, it acted as a support for him in pushing his way across the river. He decided to make for Tjililitan and shortly after crossing the river saw a horse cart and driver, which he commandeered to take him to his destination. However, he soon met a Dutch cavalry patrol that had suffered some casualties, including their officer, and therefore they had spare horses. He joined up with them, when he realised they were also heading for Tjililitan:

"My experience as a horseman was not great at any time, and galloping with them through the jungle was rather harrowing. I was dead tired and my feet were in poor shape. We finally reached this town in the hills at about the same time as the Japanese. An Australian army captain saw me and told me to get into his truck with him, which I did. He was heading for the mountains where what was left of the Dutch and Australian troops planned to put up some sort of a last stand.

"I also vaguely recall that my Australian friend had the responsibility of blowing up bridges after we crossed them to impede the advance of the Japanese. We arrived at this mountain base at night. From walking and riding horseback I was very stiff and riding in the truck had not helped. My feet were so sore that when I got out of the truck I could not stand up for a while. Here I learned that Batavia had fallen and what was left of the air force had established at Andir aerodrome in Bandoeng.

"A Dutch captain got me a car and driver and gave me a letter for his wife in Bandoeng. I must have arrived at his home about midnight. His wife took off my shoes, bathed my feet, gave me sleeping clothes and I slept the night there. In the morning she found me socks and two canvas shoes which weren't exactly a pair but were more comfortable as they were soft. I then set off to find 242 Squadron."

On locating the squadron's HQ in Bandoeng, it was arranged that he should be driven to the airfield; Watson's traumatic adventure was not yet over however, and was about to take a turn for the better, but first:

"Sandy Allen was driving me to the drome at a good clip when a truck was pushed across the road and we crashed into it. I went through the windshield and received rather bad cuts on the forehead.

"I came to with three rather beautiful young Dutch women caring for me.

I tried to have them take me to a civilian doctor, as I did not wish to be taken POW at this stage, which would most likely happen if I went to a military hospital. However, I did end up in one. I was given an anaesthetic and an Australian doctor operated on me. I was rather lucky not to lose an eye."

Undaunted by its diminishing resources, the small RAF fighter contingent continued to operate, although from Andir the pilots could hear gunfire in the hills and watched Japanese aircraft patrolling over the fighting area. A rumour rapidly spread that the remaining Dutch Brewster fighters, fitted with extra fuel tanks, were preparing to evacuate Java, their destination being Australia! The disturbing factor was that the few remaining Hurricanes were to act as decoys to allow them to get away unmolested. The rumour appeared to become reality when Wg Cdr Maguire — although totally opposed to such a plan, but having been over-ruled by the AOC — detailed newly-promoted Sqn Ldr Julian (who had just been advised by Air Vice-Marshal Maltby that he was to take command of the unit following the decision to evacuate Sqn Ldr Brooker) to carry out the operation.

Sqn Ldr Ivan Julian, RNZAF, promoted to command 242 Squadron in the closing days of the Java fighting. *(RNZAF)*

With only six Hurricanes now available it fell to the senior pilots to undertake the task. As soon as sufficient cloud had formed to provide some sort of cover, the Hurricanes took off in pairs. However, Sgt Jimmy King's engine cut just as he had become airborne and he was obliged to force-land in a swamp. His No 2 circled overhead and was relieved to see him emerge unhurt, but by this time contact with the other four fighters had been lost and his companion was forced to return to base.

Sqn Ldr Julian led the remaining four Hurricanes into cloud, the formation having evidently escaped notice by patrolling Japanese fighters. The section separated, Julian and Gartrell heading for the Lembang area whilst Parker and Lockwood flew towards Kalidjati, where they came upon three bombers; Parker gave chase to one of these, Lockwood going after the other two. The latter made a diving attack on the rear bomber, but gained no hits, then came up directly behind it and closed to 100 yards. Observing his fire hitting one engine, he concentrated on the other and both started to burn. As his windscreen was covered with oil from his victim's damaged engines, he lost sight of the bomber and returned to Andir, followed shortly by Parker. The latter also claimed a bomber shot down and confirmed having seen that which Lockwood attacked, burning in the jungle.

They were greeted by Julian, who had landed just a short time before and had accounted for a third bomber. Gartrell had not returned, but news soon came in that he had landed his damaged aircraft at Tasikmalaja, a few miles to the east. He too claimed a bomber shot down plus a second as a probable. On his return to Andir, Julian had been informed that there had been no evacuation of Dutch Brewsters after all (only two such aircraft remained serviceable in any case) and it transpired that their proposed departure was nothing more than a rumour!

That afternoon the three serviceable Hurricanes were ordered to patrol the mountain area to the north of Bandoeng, Julian leading off Parker and Lockwood. The strain was beginning to tell by now, Jimmy Parker recording:

> "I was getting a bit fed up with this. On the ground I was scared stiff of having to take-off and I was suffering from 'pink-eye', not at all happy to look up into the sun. However, I was more ashamed to appear scared in front of the others whilst we had a fair chance of survival."

Soon after becoming airborne Lockwood saw two aircraft to starboard and, receiving no reply to his R/T warning, headed off to investigate, identifying them as two-seater dive-bombers. As he approached from astern and was about to open fire, both aircraft made sharp turns to port. He turned inside one and, in a stalled position, fired a short burst as it went past, see-sawing in a vertical bank. After regaining speed he came round again, slightly above, for another attack, but now noticed the rear gunner firing at him. His Hurricane began to shake as bullets punctured the radiator and he dived away, landing at Andir safely.

Meanwhile the other two Hurricanes continued with the patrol, flying above the clouds. After about an hour, still unaware of Lockwood's combat with the dive-bombers, Julian suddenly peeled off and dived away from the direction of Andir. Assuming that his leader had spotted a target, Parker checked the sky above and then followed him down. Almost immediately he felt a tremendous thump in the midddle of his back and the clatter of bullets hitting his aircraft. He was unable to see the fighter responsible and continued in his dive, only pulling out at the last moment; he continued to fly around for some time to ascertain that he was not being followed. A quick visual inspection of his aircraft revealed that one shell had exploded in his starboard fuel tank, badly damaging the wing root although not causing a fire. The tail unit was scored and tattered, and he could feel a jagged hole in his armour-plate seat. His back began to ache so he decided to head for Pameungpeuk airfield, just in case the Japanese fighters were over Andir.

After landing and being greeted by some Dutch officers, he requested that this aircraft be refuelled, as he planned to return to Andir just before dusk. Fortunately Parker had been wearing a Dutch parachute which had thick webbing crossing in the middle of the back, which had undoubtedly saved him from serious injury. A heavy calibre shell had pierced the armour-plating of his seat; most of the fragments of this and the seat were embedded in the webbing of the parachute. However, several pieces had penetrated his back, just to the right of his spine. The damage to his aircraft prevented him returning to Andir that evening.

With the onset of nightfall three Dutch Lodestars and a KNILM DC-3 landed on a road near Bandoeng, to make one of the last evacuation flights out of Java. Again the RAF was allocated eight seats in one Lodestar; these were earmarked for Wg Cdr Maguire, Sqn Ldr Brooker, the injured Plt Off Watson, who had been collected from hospital, Sgt Sandeman Allen (who had also suffered a head injury in the motor accident) and Sgt Hardie, who was still suffering from ear trouble. Lot-drawing amongst the other pilots for the remaining seats brought allocations for Sgts King and Fairbairn, while Plt Offs Fitzherbert and Bainbridge, and Sgt Porter were to standby in case there should be sufficient room for them. The aircraft was crammed with very senior Dutch officials, together with their families, and the pilot was very anxious to get away.

Wg Cdr Maguire discovered that the cargo holds were being loaded with luggage and got out of the aircraft to try and persuade the ground crew to off-load this to let more pilots aboard. The engines were running and a crowd of people, anxious to board the aircraft, were being held back by guards with fixed bayonets. Whilst the Wing Commander was arguing with the ground crew, someone closed the door and the Lodestar taxied out and took off! Sgt Fairbairn was also left behind; having gained an allocation in the draw, he and fellow Australian Tom Young had retired to have a farewell drink and meal, but, on returning to Andir, found that the aircraft had already departed.

Meanwhile the remains of the squadron had been ordered to Tasikmalaja from Andir, but bad weather and darkness prevented them completing the flight and they landed again at Andir to await morning.

Night 6th/7th

Following the heavy bombing of shipping at Tjilatjap there was now little hope of getting away by sea, so a considerable body mostly of unarmed RAF and RAAF men (about 2,500), who had amassed at Poerwerkerta, about 30 miles inland from the port, were now to be moved westwards by rail. Their destination was Tasikmalaja airfield, 50 miles south-east of Bandoeng.

By the evening of 6th two trains had arrived at Poerwerkerta, each made up of a few carriages and a number of freight vans, the first of which was carrying a load of high octane fuel and aircraft spares. This train, under the command of Wg Cdr Ramsay Rae and packed with airmen, departed at about 1900, heading south to the junction with the main east-west line at Maos, a short distance from the Serajoe river. The second train, with Wg Cdr N. Cave in charge, followed about two hours later but soon caught up with the heavily-laden, slow-moving first train. At least 600 airmen were packed on the two trains.

At 2215 when seven miles north of the junction, near the trackside kampong at Sampang, the first train was ambushed by advanced units of the 56th Regiment, part of the Japanese force that had landed at Kragan and had infiltrated the area. Attacking with mortars, machine-guns and hand grenades, they blew several of the metal freight vans off the track, in one of which two airmen were killed while a number of others were wounded. LAC S.H. Adcock, formerly of 152 MU, recalled:

> "We had been travelling for quite a while and started to cross an embankment — the doors of the wagons were open to give some fresh air — then we ran into an ambush. A shell burst in the truck in front of ours, causing many casualties, and the young airmen talking to me in the doorway fell dead at my feet, shot between the eyes.
> "The driver and fireman jumped from the engine and let the train go. The

rear wagons were full of oil (*sic*) and were blazing furiously. In one of the leading trucks was an airman who, prior to the war was a fireman on the LMS railway, and when he saw the engine crew dive over the side, climbed along the trunks to the engine and kept it going until it ran out of steam, as it had been damaged."

Another airman recalled:

"The train kept going for a short time and then began to slow down. We opened the doors of our wagon and by the light of the moon saw the Javanese driver running across the paddy fields. Presently the train came to a halt and an officer came through to our wagon enquiring whether we had any casualties. Miraculously, our wagon hadn't been hit.

"We were then told to disembark and I then discovered the extent of the havoc that had been wreaked. One part of the train was in flames and there were many dead and badly wounded. The wounded were collected and placed in native carts obtained from a nearby kampong."

Derailed wagons of one of the two trains, carrying RAF personnel, ambushed by troops of the Japanese 56th Regiment near Maos on the night of 6/7 March. *(L.J. Robinson)*

Meanwhile the second train, forced to stop by the wrecked vans, also came under attack. The engine was hit and disabled, and there were further casualties amongst the airmen in the crowded carriages and wagons. Flg Off J. Fletcher-Cook was ordered to proceed towards Maos in an endeavour to acquire a rail car in which the wounded could be conveyed. One party of 74 under Flt Lt G. Carr, including a dozen wounded, set off towards Sampang but ran into a Japanese patrol just after midnight and were forced to surrender; five of the wounded died. The Japanese did not press home their attack and withdrew into the surrounding jungle indicating, perhaps, that only a small force was involved.

Groups of survivors made their way southwards along the track towards Maos and after a march of two to three miles arrived at a deserted trackside farm-house, where the men were assembled and were informed that not far away was a river that had to be crossed. Seven of the more seriously wounded were taken into some atap huts at the side of the track, where it was intended they should remain, with two medical orderlies, until help arrived. The five-span steel railway bridge which crossed the Serajoe river at Kesogihan had a walkway to one side. The Dutch colonial troops, whose duty it was to defend the bridge, had placed demolition charges and had orders to blow the bridge at midnight, which was by now rapidly approaching.

LAC Adcock continued:

> "When I, and my close friends reached the second span from the far end of the bridge the bridge blew-up, the centre spans going down into the river causing a large number of casualties."

About 100 men had already crossed when the bridge went up, some 30 of whom were killed or blown into the river and drowned. The defenders appeared to be under the misapprehension that Japanese troops had arrived on the eastern bank and were crossing. Two wounded airmen were found on the east bank and were taken to join the others in the atap huts, where the body of an RAF officer killed in the explosion was also taken.

Once the full horror of what had happened dawned upon the Dutch troops, attempts were made, ultimately successfully, to rig a cable from the only span left on the west side to the other side of the river.

One airman recalled:

> "When we arrived at the river we saw a large number waiting for the cable across the river to be fixed. Shortly after we were lined up and told we would have to pull ourselves across on the cable which was quite a distance. This meant being partly immersed for a while, and having seen by the light of the the moon crocodiles thrashing about, I must admit I felt a bit apprehensive, to put it mildly. Fortunately we got across without incident just as dawn was breaking."

The success of this operation was also partly due to the efforts of Flg Off Jack Abbott who, earlier, had noticed native sappers placing further charges to blow the remains of the bridge. Pleading with the Dutch officer in charge, he succeeded in delaying the second detonation until he had spoken to the local commander, who agreed to delay demolition until all survivors had got over. The last man had only just crossed when machine-gunfire was heard from the far bank and the remains of the bridge were blown.

Meanwhile Abbott had gained permission to be taken to the local Dutch HQ, established at the crossroads north of Tjilatjap. He was accompanied by Flg Off H.G. Randall and they were transported in a motor-cycle sidecar combination. On arrival, the pair were taken to see a senior Dutch officer, who admitted knowing nothing of the ambushes or of the bridge demolition, but who none-theless refused a plea to send a train to Maos to collect the wounded left at the atap huts,

> "as the sight of Europeans being evacuated would be demoralising for the Ambonese troops."

They were then dismissed.

The tragic sequel to this refusal to evacuate the wounded airmen from the farmhouse is told in the words of Cpl Bob 'Butch' Finning of 84 Squadron, one of the wounded:

> "There was a lot of blood around and fellows were moaning and some were in a very bad way and dying. We lay there for quite a time, then, as it began to get dark, I heard screams and yells from the shed next door. The Nips burst into our shed and began to bayonet the men on the floor.
>
> "I knew it was curtains for me. I wriggled close to the poor bastard nearest me and lay on my side to take the thrusts on my arse and thighs. The screams from our blokes were terrible, but the Japs were as bad every time they lunged with their rifles. When they reached me I pretended I'd snuffed it!"

Finning was bayoneted several times but miraculously sustained no fatal injuries; he continued:

> "The light was fading inside the godown, thank Christ, and I managed to pull myself among a pile of corpses. I could still hear other Japs next door, so lay on my wounded side so they could have a go at the other. Three or four of them came in and began to thrust at the people on the floor. I took another few jabs. I thought my time was up."

By the time the Japanese patrol departed, Finning had suffered 14 wounds but somehow was still alive. When he thought it was safe, he dragged himself to a window and managed to tumble out and staggered off into the bush. He passed out and when he regained consciousness it was light. Although in great pain from his many wounds and numerous insect bites, he was able to force himself further away from the scene of carnage, until he came to a river. This he managed to swim, although by now very weak from loss of blood, and lay exhausted on the bank; suddenly he became aware of half a dozen natives watching him. They dragged him to their kampong:

> "They jabbered around me, then decided to finish off what the Nips had started. They tied me up like a trussed chicken and put a rope round my neck to hang me. By that time I didn't care. They slung the end of the rope over the fork in a tree and hoisted me off the ground; I kept falling back down because I was heavy and they hadn't quite got the technique of doing the job.
>
> "This time I was convinced I'd had my chips. They got me off the ground for about the fourth time, my tongue was out and I was turning black and everything was spinning. Then I heard a car engine and they dropped me again.
>
> "There was a loud yell and I heard them scatter and I vaguely made out a strange-looking bloke waving a bloody great sword around him and I made up my mind that I was going to be beheaded instead of hung."

However the Japanese officer was his saviour. He had already picked up two other wounded airmen and now he cut Finning lose and put him in the car. All three were driven to a local POW camp full of Dutch prisoners. These, however, refused or were unable to help him and it was due only to the fact that the Japanese officer returned, saw his continuing predicament and drove him to a nearby civilian hospital, that Finning eventually recovered. There was only one other survivor of this massacre, another RAF corporal, who had managed to escape unobserved from the hut before the killing reached him.

Following the river crossing, several hundred airmen were left stranded, without transport, on the western side of the Serajoe river. Further train transport was requested to convey them to Tasikmalaja and two further trains were sent. One certainly reached its destination but according to one source the other, on reaching the bridge crossing the Djeroeklegi River near Lengkong, was blown-up together with the bridge by Dutch native troops, apparently again fearing the train was carrying Japanese troops. The engine reached the west bank but a number of freight vans full of airmen were wrecked and plummeted into the river; there were further casualties, a number of which were fatal.

Saturday, 7 March

At dawn the last five serviceable Hurricanes flew over to Tasikmalaja, finding the airfield practically deserted. The fighters were dispersed and covered with branches, the pilots then heading for the headquarters in town. Shortly after the arrival of the Hurricanes, two light bombers of 75th Sentai and six 59th Sentai Ki 43s attacked, concentrating on aircraft in pens. They claimed two large aircraft burnt and eight others damaged. Certainly they managed to destroy one Hurricane and damage a second, together with three Vildebeests. Also damaged was KNILM's DC-5 airliner (PK-ADA) plus a Grumman G-21a; this latter machine was probably PK-AKR of the Asiatic Petroleum Company, which had been flown to Tasikmalaja from Balikpapan a few weeks earlier. No orders were forthcoming for the RAF contingent. The Hurricane pilots were close to exhaustion and, when darkness came, 242 Squadron had not flown any sorties during the day; only two aircraft remained serviceable.

Kapt Jacob van Helsdingen (left) and Sgt Gerardus Bruggink, who took part in the last Dutch fighter operation on 7 March, during which van Helsdingen lost his life on his 35th birthday. *(via D. Chalif)*

The day also saw the last operation by the ML, when Kapt Jacob van Helsdingen (whose 35th birthday it was) led the four remaining serviceable Brewsters off to attack Kalidjati. Flying in two widely-spaced pairs, the Dutch pilots (all of whom had fought with the unit in Singapore) soon encountered Japanese fighters, six of these attacking van Helsdingen who was shot down and killed over Lembang; Sgt Gerardus Bruggink, who was flying 600 feet lower, escaped into cloud and returned to Andir. The second pair saw only a single fighter at which Lt Gus Deibel fired and saw strikes, before it escaped in cloud. Three more then appeared which Deibel engaged; two of these fell away under his fire but his own aircraft was hit and he too returned to Andir with his wingman, Sgt Jan Scheffer. They landed during a thunderstorm, Deibel's aircraft ground-looping due to damage to one of the wheels sustained in the fight.

Kapt J.P. van Helsdingen of 1-VlG-V in flight over Java in Brewster 339 B-396. The aircraft carries the unit's 'Java Rhino' badge forward of the cockpit. (*via P. Boer*)

The Dutch Navy now destroyed its remaining aircraft that did not have the range to escape; these included C-XIW floatplanes W-1, W-8, W-11 and W-13 of GVT-13 and GVT-14, as well as six T-IVs: T-15, T-16,T-17, T-20, T-21 and T-22 of GVT-11 and GVT-12 in their hiding place at Lengkong; the remaining Dornier Wal flyingboats and an impressed Fairchild 24, which had been 'donated' to the Dutch Navy at Sourabaya by its civilian owner were also destroyed.

Indeed few aircraft were serviceable anywhere in the remaining Allied-held parts of the island. Japanese troops had reached Lembang on the outskirts of Bandoeng by the 7th and, with the airfield now untenable, the last remaining flyable Glenn Martin (M-585) took off from Andir, flown by Lt P.J.P. van Erkel. This was followed by a single Lodestar (LT-924) flown by Lt Gus Winckel, who was accompanied by a Dutch commercial pilot, Capt Dunlop. This was the last aircraft to reach Australia safely; of the take off, Dunlop simply commented:

"What we used to call impossible is now only just difficult."

A further attempt to fly a previously abandoned aircraft to Australia was doomed to failure. At 2330 a badly damaged but hastily repaired USAAF C-47 transport took off from Andir, piloted by Maj Bill Horrigan (a B-17 pilot).

Amongst the passengers were two Australians, Flt Lts Val Morehouse (a pilot of 1 RAAF Sqn) and John Wright, an RAAF Equipment Officer; there were also two civilians. The Australians had been recouperating in Bandoeng Hospital, following bouts of malaria.

Horrigan proposed to fly to Sumbawa to refuel but, once in the air, found he was unable to retract the undercarriage. The additional drag increased fuel consumption, causing a change of plan and, instead, the aircraft was headed for Bali. However, there was insufficent fuel for the flight and Horrigan was forced to land on a beach a little east of Kendal near Semerang, running the aircraft into the sea to deny it to the Japanese. Unable to find anyone to help them, the dejected party made for Semerang, where they surrendered.

JNAF aircraft, warships and submarines continued to hunt for fleeing Allied vessels and, on this date, the Dutch liner *Poelau Bras* (9,278 tons), which had departed Wijnkoops Bay, on the southern coast of Java, on the 6th, was located by a Japanese aircraft, bombed and strafed — and sank; 33 of those embarked were killed, while two lifeboats with 118 on board reached Sumatra after many days at sea.

At 1600 Flt Lt Hutcheson, commander of the Vildebeest unit, was called to a conference convened by Air Commodore Staton and informed that he was to form the squadron into an infantry battalion, which was to fight in the mountainous area south of Garoet. When Hutcheson returned to his men with the latest news, he offered those who wished to attempt an escape in the two remaining Vildebeests the opportunity to do so, providing Staton would grant permission. Eight would be escapers came forward, permission was duly obtained and a plan formulated. Owing to the short range of the Vildebeest, it was agreed that the two aircraft would fly along the Java coast, cross the Sunda Strait to Sumatra, then fly along that coastline, looking for a likely evacuating ship alongside which to ditch. Failing this, they would continue until fuel ran out, ditch just off the Sumatran coast and work along the villages in the hope of finding a suitable boat in which to make a sea crossing of the Indian Ocean.

Sunday, 8 March

The two Vildebeests departed at 0145, K6393 flown by Flt Lt Allanson, carrying Flg Offs Gotto and Tayler, plus Plt Off Tom Lamb. The other aircraft, K6405, was in the hands of Flg Off Reg Lamb, with whom were Flg Off Callick, Wt Off Peck and Sgt S.P. Melville. They flew at 10,000 feet, Allanson's aircraft leading, and the western tip of Java was soon reached, followed by the sea crossing to a point south and west of Oosthaven. At 0615, after passing a collection of lights, Allanson decided to lose height.

Lamb's aircraft followed but then ditched about six miles out from the coast; the crew scrambled out into the aircraft's dinghy but when this developed a slow leak, Lamb decided to swim ahead and look for a boat in which to assist the others; he was not seen again. After about three hours the dinghy had almost completely deflated, forcing the occupants to swim for shore. After 18 hours in the sea, during which Melville lost sight of the other two, the coast was finally reached; Melville immediately fell asleep, completely exhausted, to be awakened by Japanese soldiers who took him to Bencoelen Hospital. Sadly, Basil Callick and George Peck were assumed to have drowned in their attempt to reach land.

Meanwhile, Allanson's aircraft had similarly ditched, out of fuel, coming down half a mile off shore in a small bay. With the aid of their dinghy his party reached the coast safely, together with a parachute bag containing clean clothes and tins of bully beef. After drying their clothes and having a meal, they set out to survey the area but quickly ran into a 20-strong, heavily-armed, Japanese patrol and were taken prisoner.

Dawn had seen the last two Hurricanes, flown by Plt Offs Lockwood and Bainbridge, undertake a road reconnaissance to Garoet, just to the north of Tasikmalaja. When they landed, their mission completed, the aircraft were destroyed on the orders of Air HQ. Flt Lt Parker's damaged Hurricane remained at Pameungpeuk and, despite his wounds, he now took off in this in an effort to reach Tasikmalaja. At 50 feet however, the controls locked, the aircraft turned over and dived into the ground — but Parker crawled out, having suffered no further injury!

There was now so little left for the Japanese air forces to do that units were already being re-assigned. On the 5th, the Kanoya Ku had left P.2 for Saigon, followed two days later by the Genzan Ku, while the detachment of A5Ms at Kalidjati left for Penang, Malaya. On the 8th, the Headquarters of the 21st Air Flotilla left the East Indies for Japan. On Java all fighting was now virtually over. In the east, Sourabaya had been entered from the west and south during the day, most of the remaining Dutch defenders withdrawing to the island of Madoera for their last stand. Tjilatjap also fell on the 7th and Bandoeng had little chance of holding on much longer.

Since 18 February, some 7,000 Commonwealth air force personnel had been evacuated but about 5,100 more still remained. At first it was intended that the Hurricane pilots should join the armed element of the British force and take to the hills, to continue resistance as a guerilla force. However at 0900 on 8 March, the Dutch GHQ agreed to surrender and, as continued resistance would have been adjudged to be banditry, the men were ordered to lay down their arms at 1430. At first the 242 Squadron survivors, with others, remained in the hills, living off the land and sleeping in abandoned tea plantations. However, food was scarce, as were medical supplies, and the Javanese natives would not help for fear of reprisals. Many men were in poor shape, so the party finally surrendered.

One small group of fighter pilots managed to avoid capture and escaped in a somewhat bizarre and daring fashion. Plt Off Mendizabal, one of 242 Squadron's Canadians who had been shot down on 3 March, had reached the Dutch airfield at Pameungpeuk, where he was befriended by two Australians, Sgts Stuart Munroe and Alan Martin, and New Zealander Sgt Doug Jones (all newly-arrived, ex 266 Wing) but, more importantly, by Dutch Brewster pilot Ens Frits Pelder, late of 2-VlG-V. All had one aim in common — to escape; Pelder was able to use his influence with Lt Cox, the commander of VkA-4, in obtaining permission to repair one of the unit's Lockheed 212s with a view to flying it to Ceylon.

Following a search amongst the abandoned Lockheeds, L-201 was found to be the only aircraft which had not had its undercarriage deliberately retracted, having had its tail section rammed by a tractor instead to immobilize it! The five men got to work, as Sgt Martin recalled:

"We found three Lockheeds, which had been damaged by the Dutch. One had its tail missing, and another its nose. We took the tail off the second plane, and fixed it on the first, patching it with ropes and pieces of bamboo. We completed the job with bits and pieces from the third plane, and filled the tanks with petrol drawn from the other two."

Plt Off Dizzy Mendizabal, RCAF, of 242 Squadron, who successfully escaped by air to Ceylon. *(F.E. Wilding)*

40-gallon wing fuel tanks were removed from an unserviceable fighter aircraft, and were installed within the cabin. Extra cans of fuel were loaded into the aircraft and a rubber tube was run from the main tanks in the wings through a hole in the side of the fuselage. This makeshift arrangement allowed fuel to be

Sgt Doug Jones, RNZAF, one the five pilots who escaped to Ceylon aboard the Lockheed 212. *(Paul Sortehaug)*

Lockheed 212, L-201, the aircraft of 4-VlG-V in which Ens Frits Pelder, Plt Off Dizzy Mendizabal and Sgts Stuart Monroe, Alan Martin and Doug Jones escaped to Ceylon on the conclusion of the fighting in Java. *(via G. Zwanenberg)*

fed into the tanks in flight, via a handpump. With machine-guns fitted in the dorsal turret and nose position, the escapers felt confident of their chances. However, there was a further problem to surmount, as Mendizabal later related:

> "The field had been thoroughly bombed, and there was blown-up wreckage strewn everywhere. We managed to clear a semblance of a path, marking it with sticks between the craters."

At 0900 on the 9th therefore, L-201 took-off with Pelder at the controls and headed for Medan, 1,200 miles distant in Northern Sumatra, which they had been advised was still in Dutch hands. During the seven-hour flight all five pilots took turns in flying the aircraft, reporting that it handled well and a safe landing was made. Following a day when the aircraft was thoroughly checked over and prepared for the the next stage of the journey, L-201 departed Medan early on the morning of the 11th for Lho'nga, on the northern tip of Sumatra, the final refuelling stop. On arrival, willing hands hastily pushed the aircraft under cover, as a Japanese reconnaissance aircraft circled above. The Lockheed's tanks were speedily topped up and Pelder took off just as nine bombers were reported heading for the airfield. As he pulled the aircraft out to sea, two bombers were seen diving down but the Lockheed was not attacked.

By late afternoon, following an uneventful eight-hour flight during which each pilot again took a turn at the controls, Ceylon was sighted. Unable to find an airfield, a Hurricane was fortuitously seen cruising by and this was followed to Colombo, where a safe landing was made at Ratmalana airfield.

They were the lucky ones.

Chapter 9

THE END IN BURMA
10 March – 22 May

136 Squadron's experienced commanding officer, Sqn Ldr Jimmy Elsdon, DFC, with the unit's mascot — a baby monkey. *(Grp Capt T.A.F. Elsdon)*

The loss of Rangoon and events further south were about to bring a disastrous change to the situation of the Anglo-American air forces in Burma. To date, the major Japanese air raids had been achieved mainly by the temporary diversion of units operating in Malaya, the total strength to support the forces driving through the southern half of the country having been relatively limited. Throughout that period the defenders of Rangoon had enjoyed a fairly effective aerial warning net, the JAAF units generally being based at some considerable distance from their targets.

Additionally, the British forces had enjoyed the great advantage offered by the port facilities at the capital city, which allowed reinforcements and supplies to be brought in by sea, with relative ease. By comparison, the Japanese had been obliged to move all their requirements via the torturous overland route from southern Thailand or Malaya, in an area of difficult terrain.

The RAF and AVG had gained greater success than had been achieved in any of the other areas under attack and had maintained and increased their strength. As has been seen, the casualties they inflicted had not been anywhere near as severe as they believed but, nonetheless, they retained a degree of initiative and remained a cohesive force.

The fall of Rangoon changed all that at a stroke. Coming as it did, immediately after the fall of Singapore, the conclusion of the Netherlands East Indies fighting and the restriction of US resistance in the Philippines to the Bataan peninsula, the Japanese had forces in abundance to spare. With their control of the sea they could make full use of Rangoon's docks, while the British were forced onto the long and difficult land route through Central and Northern Burma to Assam. Calcutta was the nearest major port available, although many hundreds of miles away.

General S. Iida's 15th Army was ordered to take the airfields at Yenangyaung and Bassein and, if possible, to seize that at Akyab. For this purpose he was to receive substantial reinforcement. The 213th Regiment of his 33rd Division had remained at Bangkok but this, together with a regiment of mountain artillery, was then shipped to Rangoon as a priority. This was to be followed, on 25 March, by the arrival of the 56th Division (less its 146th Regiment, which was still in the East Indies and would not arrive until 19 April) and then, on 7 April, the 18th Division from Singapore (less one battalion which went to garrison the Andaman Islands), together with the 1st and 14th Tank Regiments. Thus Iida's previously small army was raised effectively to the formidable strength of four full divisions.

There were two main routes from Rangoon — the Irrawaddy Valley and the Sittang Valley, which run parallel, joining at Mandalay, Burma's second largest city. Further east is the Salween Valley, reached from Toungoo on the Sittang, which provided access to the Shan States and, ultimately, the Chinese frontier.

In the Irrawaddy Valley, Lt General Alexander (the newly appointed GOC Burma) had the tired and weakened 17th Indian Division, reinforced by the highly experienced 7th Armoured Brigade, which had recently arrived from the Middle East, equipped with Stuart light cruiser tanks. In the Sittang Valley was the equally weakened 1st Burma Division, backed by the two Chinese armies, the 5th and 6th, which had been nominally under British Command. In fact, each Chinese army was equivalent in strength to a British division, the three divisions in each equating to British brigades; both were very short of supporting arms.

Alexander decided that 1st Burma Division should withdraw through the 5th Chinese Army, whose 200th Division (the best of the Chinese divisions in Burma) would take over the frontline at Toungoo. The 5th Army would then hold the Sittang Valley, to cover Mandalay, with 6th Army in the Shan States to protect the left flank. The 1st Burma Division would move to the Irrawaddy, to join the rest of the British forces in front of the oilfields. This force, named BURCORPS, was taken over on 19 March by Lt General William Slim, a tough and successful soldier, who had previously fought in East Africa.

The British had one big problem of command however. In February Generalissimo Chiang Kai-shek unilaterally removed his armies in Burma from direct British command, and appointed the American Lt General J.W. Stilwell as commander of the Chinese in Burma, but failed to raise the latter's status with the Chinese Army above Chief-of-Staff. Stilwell moved his headquarters to Burma on 21 March and soon built a good working relationship with Alexander. However, he was to find to his chagrin that the Chinese generals, ostensibly under his command, would not follow his orders unless these had been approved by the Generalissimo. The delays thus caused were to prove most damaging.

In mid March, the Japanese 33rd Division began to head up the Prome-Yenangyaung road in the Irrawaddy Valley, while the 55th set off from Pegu towards Mandalay and Meiktila, via the Sittang Valley. The 56th Division, as soon as it had arrived, moved to Yaunggyi by way of Toungoo and Meiktila, followed later by the 18th Division. Against such a push, Field Marshal Wavell, who had resumed his position as Commander-in-Chief, India, was well aware that Upper Burma could not be held with the forces available and advised the British government accordingly.

What then of the air situation? The most convenient airfield from which BURCORPS might be supported was the former civil airport at Magwe, situated on the Irrawaddy, north of Prome and the south-west of Mandalay. Almost exactly due west was Akyab, located on an island off the coast, below the base of the Arakan peninsula. On 11 March the remains of 'X' Wing moved to Magwe and was disbanded, BURWING being formed there under Grp Capt Seton Broughall (former OC Mingaladon). Under his command were 17 and 45 Squadrons with Hurricanes and Blenheims respectively, 3rd AVG Squadron with P-40s and an army co-operation flight of Lysanders from 28 Squadron. The radar set withdrawn from Rangoon was also set up, but without the established reporting infrastructure that had been available there. BURWING became operational on 18 March and was to enjoy the highest level of air transport support that India Command could offer.

At Akyab, AKWING was established under Grp Capt Singer (former commander of X Wing), comprising 136 Squadron which was beginning to reform with some elderly Hurricanes (of which more later), a flight of Hudsons and the BVAF Communications Flight which took over the remaining Lysanders of 1 IAF Squadron to add to its various light aircraft (formerly the property of the Burma Volunteer Air Force). 113 Squadron was supposed to join this wing later but, in the event, did not. Air Vice-Marshal Stevenson also set up his own headquarters there. Toungoo, while it remained in Chinese hands, continued to be a useful staging post for attacks on Japanese airfields over the border in Thailand.

To face this small air force, the JAAF 5th Air Division, by then headquartered in Rangoon, was being reinforced very substantially. During the middle part of

45 Squadron Blenheim IV at Magwe on arrival from a sortie. One of the newly-arrived American jeeps which the AVG brought with them is in the foreground. *(IWM)*

March, virtually the whole division was on the move. To Mingaladon and its satellite fields at Maubin and Mudon moved the Ki 27s of the 50th and 77th Sentais, the Ki 30s of the 31st Sentai, Ki 15s of the 1st Chutai of the 8th Sentai and the reconnaissance aircraft of the 70th Ind Chutai. The 8th Sentai's Ki 48 bombers moved to Moulmein.

Nakajima Ki 44 Shoki of the 47th Independent Flying Chutai with Capt Yasuhiko Kuroe at the controls.

Meanwhile however, from Malaya and Sumatra, the Ki 21-II bombers of the 12th and 98th Sentais, escorting Ki 43s of the 64th Sentai and supporting reconnaissance aircraft of the 51st Independent Chutai, moved to convenient airfields in Thailand (these units had appeared over Burma before, in December), while the Ki 27s of the 12th Flying Battalion (the 1st and 11th Sentais) moved in to Pegu, where they were joined by the Ki 44s of the 47th Independent Chutai. It would not be long before the 64th Sentai, also, would move to Mingaladon in order to be nearer the battle zone. JAAF strength in Burma was assessed by the RAF, at this time, as being about 400 aircraft but, in fact, amounted to about 260 — however, still a formidable force considering the opposition it faced. The Order of Battle may be seen in Table 13.

Table 13

JAAF Order of Battle, Burma Theatre of Operations
20 March 1942

Fighters

HQ 12th Flying Battalion	Pegu	3 Ki 27s
1st Sentai	Pegu	15 Ki 27s
11th Sentai	Pegu	14 Ki 27s
47th Ind Chutai	Pegu	4 Ki 44s
50th Sentai	Mingaladon	17 Ki 27s
77th Sentai	Maubin	35 Ki 27s
64th Sentai	Chiengmai	15 Ki43s, 2 Ki 27s (plus 1 Hurricane captured in Malaya)

Bombers/Reconnaissance

I/8th Sentai	Mingaladon	12 Ki 15s
8th Sentai	Moulmein	32 Ki 48s
12th Sentai	Lampang	31 Ki 21-IIs
31st Sentai	Moulmein	25 Ki 30s
98th Sentai	Nakorn Sawan	35 Ki 21s
51st Ind Chutai	Lampang	5 Ki 46s, 5 Ki 15s
70th Ind Chutai	Mingaladon	9 reconnaisance, 2 Ki 51s

Ki 43s of the 64th Sentai on an airfield in Burma with the unit's captured Hurricane in the background.

Tuesday-Monday, 10-16 March

As the retreat northwards continued, there was limited activity in the air. Reconnaissances and sweeps were flown by the remaining Hurricanes, but little was seen as the Japanese concentrated on their re-dispositions.

67 Squadron was at last relieved, Sqn Ldr Brandt leading the remaining six flyable Buffaloes (W8223, W8243, W8245, W8246, W8250 and AN214) to

Akyab, where one immediately became unserviceable; the others flew on to Dum Dum airfield at Calcutta. Meanwhile, other pilots were evacuated from Magwe in 31 Squadron's DC-2 transports. On departure, the Squadron silver was buried outside the Officers' Mess, whilst the only male bulldog in the Far East — the proud possession of the manager of one of the local oilfields — was evacuated aboard one of the departing Buffaloes. The machine left behind at Akyab was later made airworthy and flown to Dum Dum by Flt Lt Lawrence Gill of the BVAF.

Close behind came the rear party of 1 IAF Squadron, Sqn Ldr Majumdar included, carried to Asansol in a 7th Bomb Group B-17 that had been flying in personnel and supplies for the AVG. All but one of the remaining 113 Squadron Blenheims also left for Dum Dum on the 12th, carrying some members of the unit's ground crew.

During the evacuation of Rangoon, more than 70,000 Indian civilians departed by sea for Calcutta, but many thousands of others had set off by road, most travelling via Prome, over the Arakan hills to Taungup and then, by boat, to Akyab. Initially, as some of the docks and other services in Rangoon had come to a halt with their departure, the Burmese Police were ordered to stop the flow crossing the Irrawaddy. However corruption flourished; police officers charged two rupees to let people cross, plus an additional six rupees if they could not produce an innoculation certificate (at this time l6 rupees = £1 Sterling, or four US dollars). Those who managed to get to Taungup were then charged a further three rupees to board a boat to Akyab. At this latter destination better arrangements existed, one shipping line running five extra vessels to Chittagong, whilst US pilots flew out several hundreds. At least 500,000 Indians reached their homeland, while between 10-15,000 were believed to have lost their lives. US bomber crews had been particulary helpful; during March, eight B-17s (six from Java and two from the Middle East) and one LB-30 had reached India, initially being thrust into service as impromptu transports. In six days, 8-13 March, they carried 474 native troops and more than 29 tons of supplies from Asansol to Magwe, carring out 423 civilians during the return flights.

The situation facing the British in Burma was to prove somewhat different from that in Malaya and elsewhere. Here many of the population were actively hostile to their ertswhile rulers and welcomed the Japanese invaders, in anticipation of freedom. Indeed, during December the Prime Minister, U Saw, had been arrested as it was believed that he was associated with the anti-British Thakin Movement and in collusion with the Japanese.

By the latter stages of the campaign, following the fall of Rangoon, the Japanese were accompanied, to an increasing extent, by Burmese volunteer units (also by units of Thai volunteers), while the Buddist priests were to prove particularly hostile. As the retreat got fully underway, pockets of resistance fighters were encountered, some of whom attacked and killed individual British troops or small isolated units, particularly in the Irrawaddy Valley.

It was for the Indian shopkeepers, traders and money lenders that their particular wrath was reserved however. As these became refugees and fled northwards they were attacked and beaten, robbed, raped and murdered in their thousands, by roving gangs who took this opportunity to revenge themselves on these more immediate oppressors. Despite this, many Burmans did remain loyal to the British and served them well. So too did the hill tribes — the Chins,

Kachins and particularly the Karens — none of whom had any great love for the more numerous Burmese, thus remaining loyal members of the Burma Rifles and other formations throughout.

The Blenheims continued to see a little action at this time, notably on 11 March, when five 45 Squadron aircraft were despatched from Magwe to bomb railway bridges south-west of Pyuntaza, near Pegu. Z9799, flown by Sgt D.J. Smith, was hit by ground fire and the pilot was killed. Sgt D.A. Golder, the navigator, assisted by the gunner, Sgt J.J. Alt, managed to fly the aircraft back to base, where they both baled out rather than risk trying to land it. Three days later, the lone remaining 113 Squadron machine, which was attached to 45 Squadron, set off with another all-RAAF crew on a reconnaissance sortie, but failed to return. Sgt L.W.H. Conner (pilot) of 113 Squadron and his crew (Sgts L.S. Powell and J.J. Eden) were lost, their fate not having been established.

Reinforcements were gradually reaching India from various sources and, on 12 March, ten P-40Es (some of those diverted from Java) reached Karachi; most would eventually find their way to the AVG. The latter remained active during this period, seeking road targets to strafe in the area north of Kyaitko, on the 14th and 15th. As the four operating on the latter date were so engaged, six Ki 27s attempted to 'bounce' them, but Bob Moss of the 2nd Squadron was able to turn the tables, claiming one shot down 15 miles south of Nyunglobin (identified by him as a 'Navy 96').

By the end of this week of movement, BURWING and AKWING were established and ready for action. At Akyab, 136 Squadron had resumed its existence with ten of its original pilots and five newer ones. It was equipped with nine worn Hurricane Is from 10 Operational Training Unit — all reputedly marked 'fit for training only' — and a single Mark II (BG853, ex 17 Squadron).

Orders of Battle were:

BURWING – Magwe

17 Squadron	16 Hurricane IIs
45 Squadron	9 Blenheim IVs
28 Squadron Flight	3 Lysanders
3rd Pursuit Squadron, AVG	6 P-40Bs
3 PRU	1 Hurricane, 1 Tiger Moth
RDF Station (radar)	

AKWING – Akyab

136 Squadron	9 Hurricane Is, 1 Hurricane II
Hudson GR Flight	6 Hudsons (ex 53, 59 and 139 Squadrons)
3 Coastal Defence Flight	2 Blenheim Is
BVAF Comm Flight	Various
113 Squadron	No aircraft

Tuesday-Wednesday, 17-18 March

45 Squadron, escorted by 17 Squadron Hurricanes, had been out to attack the satellite fields known as 'Highland Queen' and 'Park Lane' near Rangoon, on the 17th. The next day, escorted by five Hurricanes and five P-40s, the Blenheims attacked boats on the Irrawaddy, while the fighters strafed the river banks.

Shortly afterwards, Flt Ldrs Ken Jernstedt and Bill Reed flew a pair of 3rd Squadron P-40s down to Moulmein and to a subsidiary airfield ten miles south of the town, their aircraft each loaded with 30 fragmentation and incendiary bombs. They attacked both airfields catching many aircraft on the ground at each. The results were "staggering, some blew up, other burned; 15 or 25 aircraft seen claimed totally destroyed", stated the report. Reed claimed an 'MC 20-type' transport, two 'Army 97' bombers and five 'Army type 98' fighters destroyed, Jernstedt submitted similar claims, except he claimed only four fighters.

The claims were quite accurate, though rather more prosaic. At Moulmein two Ki 21 bombers were, indeed, destroyed in flames, plus a Ki 48 and a Ki 15 badly damaged. The satellite field was Mudon, where three Ki 30s and a Ki 15 were burned, while two more Ki 30s were badly damaged; 31st Sentai, at this base, was left with only one serviceable aircraft. Obviously, the American pilots had identified the Ki 48 as a transport and the single-engined Ki 15s and Ki 30s as fighters, although they had double-claimed on these.

Saturday, 21 March

Reconnaissance over the Rangoon area, on the 20th, had brought evidence of at least 50 Japanese aircraft at Mingaladon, so Grp Capt Broughall decided that an attack should be laid on for the morrow. It was agreed that a combined Blenheim and Hurricane strike be despatched at first light.

Dawn thus saw ten Hurricanes of 17 Squadron roar into the sky and climb slowly to 25,000 feet, then circle over Rangoon, to await the arrival of nine Blenheims of 45 Squadron. As these had not appeared after some time, Sqn Ldr Bunny Stone decided to press on without them. Arriving over Mingaladon from the north, Stone (YB-C) led four Hurricanes from 'B' Flight down to attack, while Flt Lt Allan Carvell simultaneously swept in at the head of four 'A' Flight machines; Stone recalled:

> "Descending in a dive at about 400 mph, we were met by light flak. The aerodrome appeared packed with aircraft, mainly fighters and recce aircraft. I took on a fuel tanker and some recces parked wing-tip to wing-tip. Looking back as I broke to the north, there appeared to be a nice little fire starting.
>
> "I then broke to port at treetop level, having given strict instructions that on no account was a second attack to be carried out since, by then, everyone would be waiting for us. A moment later bombs from the Blenheims, now arrived on the scene, erupted on the field."

One of the 'A' Flight Hurricanes (YB-X) was flown by a Canadian newcomer, Plt Off Hedley Everard, who later graphically recorded:

> "The sun's first rays were almost parallel to the airfield runway as we made our first strafing attack. My task was to silence an ack-ack position on the northern approach. As I closed the range to 600 yards, I was able to see the half dozen members of the gun crew sitting on a low wall of sandbags. They were knocked over by my initial burst.
>
> "I performed a climbing-diving turn towards a line of fighters parked wing-tip to wing-tip along the runway, some of which were already smoking from the initial surprise attack by my fellow flyers. I carefully sighted my burst at the first machine in the line, but had obviously fired out of range since the bullets clammed short of the target.

"As I flashed overhead, I looked down into the cockpit and caught the bland curious stare of the Japanese pilot who was being helped to strap in by his crewman. It was incredible. They had ignored my murderous attack.

"I swung around for a second pass. By now the pilot had started his engine and was just beginning to move towards the runway. With deadly purpose now, my bullets riddled the engine and cockpit. The aircraft slewed up on its nose as I passed overhead. I glimpsed the pilot slumped in his seat.

"I glanced at the runway and saw my buddies picking off the fighters as they vainly attempted to take off. The Squadron Leader had spotted some Japanese fighters rising from other satellite airfields nearby and gave the order to return to base."

One of the Ki 27s was swiftly onto the tail of Sqn Ldr Stone's Hurricane, as he weaved northwards and skimmed the treetops:

"The only way to avoid him was to run for it as, if I had climbed, he would undoubtedly have shot me down. Pulling the booster plug, I weaved madly among the trees. He gave me several bursts but, thank God, he proved as bad a shot as I was!"

The final pair of Hurricanes, flown by the American duo, Sgts Tex Barrick and Jack Gibson, had been ordered to break away, skirt the area, then attack from the south after the rest of the force, to catch any fighters which were taking off to pursue them. The Japanese took these late arrivals to be "three Tomahawks" and some Ki 27s were led off by the new 50th Sentai commanding officer, Maj Tadashi Ishikawa, claiming all shot down! Barrick (flying YB-D) recalled:

"Jack Gibson and I were flying together, coming from the south. I remember seeing quite a few Jap planes burning along the runways. I did witness Gibson shooting down an 'Army 97' as it was taking off."

Barrick claimed one fighter probably destroyed and one damaged during his own strafe — both of which were later credited to him as "destroyed on the ground" — and then engaged another in the air, as it attempted to get on Gibson's tail, claiming this shot down.

Following the strafe, most of the Hurricanes returned individually or in pairs. In one of the former, Flt Lt Carvell had become separated from his section and on his way back found himself over 'Highland Queen', where he sighted more Ki 27s on the ground. These he strafed, leaving two in flames, then engaged another as it attempted to intercept his Hurricane, claiming it shot down.

The engine of Plt Off Frank Earnshaw's Z5599 had been hit by ground fire during his pass over the airfield and he was obliged to force-land during the return flight. Surviving this experience unhurt, he began the long trek northwards and was fortuitous in gaining a lift aboard a 7th Armoured Brigade tank, the crew of which were also heading for Magwe; he thus arrived back at the airfield in some style.

When claims were finally tallied, a total of 14 aircraft were assessed to have been destroyed or badly damaged on the ground during the attack, including two apiece by Sqn Ldr Stone and Flg Off Lloyd Thomas, plus three more shot down. This proved a close estimate of the results achieved, for JAAF records show that the attack by the Hurricanes had destroyed two aircraft in flames and badly damaged 11 more.

On their approach to the target area, the Blenheims — devoid of fighter protection — had been intercepted by an estimated 18 Ki 27s. Japanese accounts differ, reporting that only three fighters from the 77th Sentai's 2nd Chutai encountered the bombers whilst patrolling over Maubin airfield and claimed one shot down and three probables. The confirmed victory was credited to Lt Shinjirou Nagoshi, who was then shot down and killed in this engagement; the three probables were claimed jointly by Wt Off Togota and Sgt Maj Nagoe. The Blenheims, in fact, all fought their way through to Mingaladon, though most suffered damage and one pilot, Flg Off J.S. Muller-Rowland, was wounded, while the Blenheim gunners claimed two fighters shot down, two probables and a further two damaged. One of these was credited to Sgt K.S. Gardiner, who was slightly wounded, his aircraft being struck by 57 bullets.

On arrival over the airfield — with most of the airfield AA defences neutralized and the fighters prevented from taking off — the Blenheims were able to carry out their attacks without undue interference, a total of 9,000 lb of bombs being released during the raid, without loss.

Grp Capt Broughall was delighted with the results of the morning's attacks and planned a repeat strike for the afternoon but was pre-empted by the Japanese, who launched a devastating counter-attack. There were only 15 Hurricanes and six P-40s available at Magwe, of which only a dozen were fully serviceable. At 1300 a single reconnaissance aircraft was reported approaching and two Hurricanes were sent off, although Plt Offs Murdoch and Chadwick failed to make contact. Murdoch's aircraft then developed engine trouble and he was obliged to land at an emergency airstrip.

20 minutes later a formation of hostile aircraft was reported approaching but, as the formation was not flying from a southerly direction, it was late being spotted on the radar. All available fighters — six Hurricanes and three P-40s — were scrambled, Plt Off Neville Brooks getting airborne as the first bombs began falling. 31 Ki 27s of the 12th Flying Battalion, led by Lt Colonel Sada Okabe, the new commanding officer of the 11th Sentai, had been despatched ahead of the main formation, the pilots briefed to patrol over Magwe. They were followed by 25 Ki 21s of the 98th Sentai and 27 of the 12th Sentai, escorted by 14 Ki 43s of the 64th Sentai and a number of 51st Chutai Ki 46s, to observe results. Some way behind came ten Ki 30s of the 31st Sentai and 14 more Ki 27s. One 98th Sentai Ki 21 had crashed on take-off.

In the initial attack by the Ki 21s much damage was inflicted on the airfield buildings, with communications and services being rendered unserviceable. One trio of Hurricanes was engaged by the escorts as they attempted to get to the bombers, Plt Off Everard reporting that he had time to make only one firing pass through the formation before the Japanese fighters were upon him like a swarm of angry bees. He heard the other two pilots, Plt Offs Ken Hemingway and Brooks, call over the R/T that they had been hit and were going down: Hemingway, who claimed a Ki 27 probably destroyed, crash-landed in a dried-up river bed a few miles north of Magwe, while Brooks, who believed that he had also shot down one of the fighters, force-landed on the airfield. Within seconds of vacating his aircraft, it was totally destroyed by bombs.

Meanwhile, Sgt Al MacDonald, RCAF, reported shooting down another of the Japanese fighters. Everard meantime, saw an aircraft erupt in a fireball as the P-40s engaged. He then dived away to low altitude, where he spotted a lone Ki 27:

Left: Plt Off Neville Brooks of 17 Squadron. who force-landed at Magwe on 21 March after being attacked by Ki 27s. *(J.F. Barrick)*. Right: Plt Off Hedley Everard, RCAF, of 17 Squadron with his Hurricane. On 21 March he shot down "one of theirs and one of ours". *(Sqn Ldr H.J. Everard)*

"It was obvious that the pilot neither saw me or else thought I was a fellow friend. I eased back my speed and waited until his aircraft completly filled my gunsight, then fired. The aircraft lurched and began to trail black smoke. I pulled to one side and watched as he continued his original dive angle straight into the far side of our airfield."

The P-40 pilots reported engaging seven of the Ki 43s, Parker Dupouy diving on the rear aircraft and claiming that it blew up under his attack — probably the fireball that Everard had noted. Reed's aircraft was hit and he was wounded, although he managed to get down safely. Meanwhile the Japanese fighters had turned on Dupouy's aircraft, causing severe damage; a bullet grazed his arm and fragments wounded him in the shoulder and leg.

Three further P-40s had managed to get off by this time and attacked a formation of ten bombers, one of which was claimed damaged by Bob Prescott, while Ken Jernstedt reported that he had barely got his aircraft off the ground before the first bombs began exploding. Unable to rendezvous with other P-40s, he attacked alone and reported that he shot one bomber out of formation. Coming in for a second pass, he saw his fire hitting a second but then his windscreen, struck by a bullet, exploded in his face. Unfortunately, he had left his goggles pushed up onto his forehead and glass fragments entered his left eye. He saw the second bomber he had attacked begin to go down, so turned and flew back to Magwe where he landed safely, despite the bomb craters and his injuries.

Meanwhile, as Everard approached Magwe, he saw Japanese fighters strafing and followed one of these, opened fire and reported that it turned away, trailing smoke. He then saw another — "a dark blue aircraft which I incorrectly guessed to be a Navy Zero" — and fired at this, as it skimmed over the airfield. One of the Japanese aircraft lost was the Ki 27 flown by Lt Col Ishikawa, who was killed. Other 11th Sentai pilots claimed three victories, while 64th Sentai pilots reported engaging two P-40s but achieved no decisive results.

Almost an hour later the 31st Sentai Ki 30s — with their escorts — approached, bombed and claimed 21 large and four small aircraft destroyed or damaged on the ground. A handful of P-40s were able to scramble and pursue the retreating raiders, Cliff Groh claiming one Ki 27 shot down 15-20 miles to the south-east of the airfield.

During these two raids the Japanese claimed a total of eight aircraft burned on the ground and 27 destroyed or damaged, plus eight more shot down, at a cost of four of their own aircraft. The defenders' claims were, indeed, assessed as four and one probable — the two fighters claimed by the AVG and three by the Hurricane pilots. Jernstedt's claims do not appear to have been listed, possibly because his wounds prevented him submitting a report. Two Hurricanes and two P-40s were hit and damaged, the two former being obliged to force-land, while six more Hurricanes and two P-40s were damaged beyond repair on the ground.

The mystery surrounding Plt Off Everard's second claim — the "dark blue Navy Zero" — was soon solved: he had, in fact, attacked Flg Off Ken Perkins' dark blue PR Hurricane (Z4949) as the latter returned from a reconnaissance sortie over Yenangyaung! Perkins, who suffered only minor injuries, carried out a successful belly-landing in his badly damaged machine, under the impression he had been shot down by a Japanese fighter. Victor and victim were later to meet in the Mess, when Perkins was not at all amused to learn the truth. The downing of many drinks softened his attitude and all was eventually forgiven, Sqn Ldr Stone remarking: "Not a bad day's work, Everard — one of theirs and one of ours!"

Sunday, 22 March

The Japanese were back next morning, when a dozen Ki 48s of the 8th Sentai, together with a dozen Ki 30s of the 31st Sentai, set off to repeat the attack on Magwe, under a massive fighter escort provided by 34 Ki 27s of the 12th Flying Battalion, 13 of the 50th Sentai and 14 of the 77th. The raid showed up on the radar at 0804 but there was then a breakdown in the W/T link. Two Hurricanes, flown by Plt Off Everard and Sgt MacDonald, had earlier been scrambled after a reconnaissance aircraft was heard over the airfield; these two encountered the incoming raiders. MacDonald dived to attack the bombers and reported strikes on two before he was chased away by the fighters. Everard made repeated attempts to get through to the bombers but was frustrated by the escorts each time. When, at last, he managed to break through it was to find that the guns in his port wing would not fire, the asymmetric discharge from the starboard guns causing his aircraft to slew in that direction, destroying any chance of accurate fire. Ki 27s were quickly on his tail, their fire stripping the fabric from YB-X's rear fuselage before he was able to escape.

Meanwhile, MacDonald had attempted to land at one of the emergency airstrips, as the main airfield was under attack. However, his undercarriage failed to lock which caused the aircraft to land on its belly, the Hurricane consequently becoming a complete write-off. Everard also landed at the same strip, putting his damaged Hurricane down safely. Several other Hurricanes, which had scrambled as the raiders commenced their bombing runs, were unable to engage.

At 1300 a reconnaissance aircraft was again reported approaching and two Hurricanes, of the three that remained serviceable, took off but failed to intercept. When they returned to land, an hour later, a further raid followed them in. This attack comprised 27 Ki 21s of the 12th Sentai, 26 of the 98th, 18 Ki 43s of the 64th Sentai and 23 Ki 27s from the 12th Flying Battalion. Following this latest raid, Magwe was left shattered; the runways were rendered unserviceable and the remaining communications cut. Nine Blenheims and three P-40s were destroyed or irreparably damaged, while AVG pilot Frank Swartz was severely wounded as he dashed to his aircraft; he later died from his wounds. 3 PRU was left without aircraft, as Plt Off Doug Harris recalled:

"The Japs destroyed on the ground all our aircraft but one — a Tiger Moth. As I had instructed on Tiger Moths, I was ordered to fly over to Toungoo and search for a British unit cut off by the Japs.

"Leaving Toungoo the day before the Japs took it, I returned to Magwe only to find the RAF were retreating to Lashio, on the Chinese border, where I joined them in my Tiger Moth."

There was no option but to evacuate Magwe. The AVG ground party loaded five damaged P-40s onto trucks and departed, to follow their air party to Loiwing, while six Blenheims and 11 Hurricanes — most of them unserviceable, although flyable — were ordered to Akyab. From there it was proposed that they should be flown on to Lashio and Loiwing to refit, until Magwe could be made tenable again; in the event it was not to prove safe for use other then as a forward refuelling base. By evening two of the Hurricanes were still not ready, leaving nine to depart for Akyab, flown by 17 Squadron's 'B' Flight; en route Sgt Barrick was obliged to bale out of his aircraft when its engine failed.

Monday, 23 March
Akyab was to prove no safe haven, for this was the next target for the JAAF. Blenheim L4914 was just taking-off as the alarm went and 26 Ki 21s of the 98th Sentai, escorted by 16 Ki 43s of the 64th Sentai, swept in to attack. Rather than risk being shot down, the Blenheim pilot retracted the undercarriage and 'pancaked' the aircraft at the end of the runway. Meanwhile, 136 Squadron managed to scramble all its available Hurricanes, Sqn Ldr Elsdon leading these against the bombers, two of which were claimed shot down: one was credited to Sgt Jimmy Wetherall, the other to Sgts Vern Butler and Freddie Pickard jointly.

The Ki 43s were soon upon them however, Plt Off Eric Brown, a 33 year-old Lancastrian, being attacked from astern and baling out of Z4650 into the sea; he suffered severe burns to his face and legs but was soon picked up by a native craft. A second Hurricane was hit by the airfield's AA guns, Plt Off Freddie Goddard's legs being peppered with shrapnel splinters, while a third Hurricane suffered an engine malfunction, obliging Sgt Ting Bunting to crash-land. Flt Lt Guy Marsland, a newly arrived Battle of Britain veteran, claimed one of the Ki 43s shot down although apparently all Japanese aircraft returned safely.

At the airfield the watch office and hangar received direct hits, whilst a Hudson of the GR Flight was destroyed and two more damaged, as were two Blenheims and two Hurricanes; Sqn Ldr F.J. Austin, one of the 45 Squadron

Survivors of 136 Squadron on their return to India, seen here with replacements. Left to right, rear: Sgt Frank Wilding; Sgt T.T. Young; Plt Off Kit Kitley; Flt Lt Guy Marsland; Sqn Ldr Jimmy Elsdon; Plt Off Moorhouse; Sgt N.F. Banikhin; Sgt Ting Bunting. Front, left to right: Sgt Jimmy Wetherall; Sgt Chas Beale; newly-promoted Plt Off Biff Viens; Sgt Vern Butler. *(K. Bunting)*

flight commanders, was wounded by shrapnel. Following this attack, 17 Squadron's eight 'B' Flight Hurricanes were handed over to 136 Squadron and the pilots were ordered back to Calcutta, to which destination they were to move over the next few days. At Magwe meanwhile, Sqn Ldr Stone was ordered to evacuate the ground party and 'A' Flight pilots to Loiwing, therefore the Squadron set out in a convoy of more than 60 vehicles for their new destination.

Tuesday, 24 March

Early next morning five of the AVG 1st Squadron P-40s flew from Kunming to Namsang, close to Heho in Central Burma, where they were to be joined by four of the 2nd Squadron aircraft from Loiwing. On arrival however, no sign of the latter aircraft were to be seen, so the 'Adam and Eves' flew on to their target alone. This was Chiengmai airfield in Thailand, where an estimated 50 aircraft were seen on the ground. Sqn Ldr Bob Neale ordered an attack and the P-40s dived through heavy AA fire, made several passes and claimed 13 aircraft destroyed, all of which were identified as bombers. Neale, Charlie Bond, Greg Boyington, Bill McGarry and Bill Bartling were credited with two apiece, Neale and Bond shared another, as did Boyington and Bartling.

The four pilots from the 2nd Squadron had arrived at the rendezvous late, heading first to Chiengmai's satellite airfields, where nothing was to be seen, but they did strafe two armoured cars whilst on their way to the main airfield. It seems that at least one of these pilots, Vice-Sqn Ldr Ed Rector, arrived while the 1st Squadron were still there, as he shared in the destruction of one aircraft with McGarry and claimed two more alone, bringing the total claims to 15.

However, as the 2nd Squadron aircraft swept over Chiengmai, the P-40 flown by the commanding officer, Jack Newkirk, was seen to take a direct hit and crash in flames. McGarry's 1st Squadron aircraft was also hit and was seen to

Flt Lt Guy Marsland, newly-arrived flight commander in 136 Squadron, was a Battle of Britain veteran. *(Wg Cdr G. Marsland)*

trail smoke; he baled out 55 miles from the border and remained at large for 28 days, before being captured by Thai police. The AVG had lost two of its leading pilots. However, the attack had been about as successful as estimated, although their victims had not been bombers, but Ki 43s of the 64th Sentai. Three of these went up in flames and at least ten others were damaged beyond repair.

Despite these losses the 64th Sentai was still able to despatch 11 fighters, that afternoon, to escort 53 Ki 21s to undertake a repeat attack on Akyab. By this time, 136 Squadron had been able to make serviceable two of the Hurricanes received from 17 Squadron and, as the raid approached, a dozen fighters were put into the air in defence of the base. During the ensuing engagement Plt Off Alan Kitley and Sgt Biff Viens each claimed bombers probably destroyed, while Sgt Frank Wilding (BM927) engaged the escort and claimed one shot down and one probable:

"I had just landed from a scramble and was refuelling by hand from 5-gallon cans, helped by a couple of ground crew. Conditions were a bit rough out there and, when the Japs started bombing the strip, I got off pretty quickly and sort of flew through the bombs! I remember how interesting it was to look down and see big bursts of red flames as they hit the ground.

"I was only just off at about 400 feet when I saw Sgt Bob Payne; he flew in front of me, chasing a Jap fighter. I tried to join him but naturally I was going pretty slowly as I was climbing, so that by the time I joined in there was another Jap fighter on Payne's tail. So there was Jap-Payne-Jap-me and, afterwards I found out from the chaps on the ground, there was another Jap behind me!

"Apparently we were going round and round the airstrip. I was firing at the Jap behind Payne, when I saw Bob hit and go into the sea just off the airfield. I then hit the Jap that had hit Bob and he went into the sea. I now found myself closing up on the first Jap in the queue and knocked a few spots off him — which I claimed as a probable; he then pushed off as fast as he could go.

"The Jap behind me had only put a few holes in me, and he suddenly went. I carried on for a bit but all seemed to have gone. The airstrip had enough left in one piece for me to get down — so I got down. The ground staff had seen it all — I felt quite good!"

Sgt Frank Wilding of 136 Squadron in his Hurricane. *(F.E. Wilding)*

Sgt Payne was killed. A second Hurricane (BG858) failed to return, although a slightly injured Sgt Butler turned up the next day, on foot. Additionally, Sgt Freddie Fortune crash-landed his shot-up aircraft on the airfield and suffered minor injuries in the process. Regarding the loss of Payne, Sgt Bunting was to add:

"The biggest blow to all was losing Bob. He was a grand pilot — the best we had — and the keenest man I knew; he was mad-headed and it cost him his life."

On the ground two serviceable Blenheims and a BVAF Moth were destroyed; two other Blenheims were damaged, a hangar was demolished and there were a number of fatalities amongst the ground personnel.

During the day a Hudson of the GR Flight flew from Dum Dum on a reconnaissance over Port Blair, in the Andamans. On its return the crew reported that they had seen three transports, a cruiser and three destroyers anchored off the south-west coast. The warships fired at the aircraft but failed to hit it. Japanese marines had, indeed, gone ashore to secure the port, while a detachment of seven H6K flyingboats, from the Toko Kokutai, flew in to undertake reconnaissances over the Indian Ocean, preparatory to a planned carrier raid on Ceylon.

Wednesday, 25 March

Although there was one scramble from Akyab, early in the morning, it proved to be a false alarm. Later a DC-2 of 31 Squadron arrived at the airfield to evacuate the two wounded 136 Squadron pilots, Brown and Goddard, together with some wounded soldiers and RAF ground personnel, all of whom were flown out to Dum Dum. This unit would continue to send a DC-2[1] to the airfield each evening until it was evacuated.

Douglas DC-2 transport 'P' of 31 Squadron, seen here at Dum Dum, en route to Burma. *(Wg Cdr G. Marsland)*

Thursday, 26 March

By this time only two Hurricanes remained fully serviceable at Akyab, so AHQ India ordered that AKWING should prepare to withdraw across the border to Chittagong. Therefore six flyable, but non-combatworthy, Hurricanes were at once flown there, Sgt Wilding recording that "things were bad there — utter panic and chaos, with civilians trying to get away." A number of pilots found themselves without aircraft and they, together with some of the ground personnel, left Akyab under the command of Flt Lt Marsland, sailing

---

[1] Eight DC-2s were currently to hand, although all were very old and worn when the squadron took them over. They had only recently returned from a long detachment to the Middle East. During one of the last sorties to Akyab, one (AS755) ran into a bomb crater and was damaged beyond repair.

for Chittagong in the 3,000 ton former Yangtse coaster *Hunan*; two of 17 Squadron's remaining pilots 2/Lts Doug Bailey and Gordon Peter (both SAAF) were flown out to Dum Dum in the daily DC-2.

Friday, 27 March

The final attack on Akyab occured around 1230, when 18 Ki 43s of the 64th Sentai swept in to strafe. Despite warnings of an impending attack, the RAF was unprepared; a Valentia twin-engined biplane transport (K2807) and seven Hurricanes — three of which had just been made serviceable — were destroyed on the ground, although the Japanese pilots claimed a total of 11 aircraft destroyed or badly damaged.

Two Hurricanes had been scrambled on the approach of the raiders but, as they struggled to gain altitude, they became separated. Plt Off Lorne LeCraw was engaged immediately and his aircraft was badly damaged; he baled out and came down in the sea. Sqn Ldr Jimmy Elsdon (V7758) was also attacked but evaded and landed at the Old Angus emergency strip. Learning that Akyab had been heavily raided again, he flew directly to Chittagong and, with very little fuel left, landed on a runway which was still under construction. 64th Sentai pilots claimed one fighter shot down and possibly a second.

Meanwhile, the Canadian LeCraw had been trying in vain to inflate his Mae West life jacket but, as he tried to blow up the jacket, the air escaped through a bullet hole in his cheek! He managed to keep afloat for three hours however, at the end of which time he was rescued by some natives in a small boat.

From Chittagong the six recently-arrived Hurricanes were ordered back to Dum Dum. As Sgt Wilding took-off, his aircraft (BM927) "blew up" due to a glycol leak and he was obliged to land again. The leak was fixed and later that evening he was able to undertake the flight.

Saturday-Thursday, 28 March – 2 April

Following the evacuation of Akyab, there was little aerial activity for a few days, the centre of attention moving to the other side of the Bay of Bengal, as Ceylon came under threat (these actions are dealt with in detail in Chapter 10).

In support of the forthcoming strike against Ceylon, the H6Ks at Port Blair (Andaman Islands) had begun operations on the 26th, while Mihoro Kokutai G3Ms from Sabang, in Northern Sumatra, also undertook patrols over the Southern reaches of the Indian Ocean. 18 A6Ms of the 22nd Air Flotilla's attached Fighter Group flew from Bangkok to Mingaladon on the 30th, to operate in defence of Port Blair where, on 4 April, they would be joined by 18 G3Ms of the Genzan Ku from Bangkok.

In Burma meanwhile, the Japanese army had opened their attack on the Chinese 200th Division near Pyu on 19 March, enveloping and cutting off this force by the 23rd. Other Chinese units were ordered by Lt General Stilwell to counter-attack, but failed to do so. In the Irrawaddy Valley, the 1st Burma Division began a demonstration of force in support of the trapped Chinese but, as they did so, the Japanese advanced along this route and the British were forced to withdraw. In the event, the 200th Division was to fight a grim and determined defence, holding the Japanese at bay for nearly two weeks, although heavy casualties were suffered. They finally broke out and withdrew, but this meant the loss of Toungoo as a forward airfield. Prome was given up on the

1 April, then a slow retreat towards Yenangyaung and Akyab began. With no air support, the fatigued 17th Indian Division was becoming dispirited, also both British and Chinese forces suffered almost continual air attack once that the Japanese found a lack of real opposition in the air.

Despite the departure of the RAF, the remaining elements of the AVG at Loiwing continued to operate when possible. On the 29th JAAF bombers raided Loiwing and Namsang, claiming buildings destroyed and the runways cratered, but lost one of their number. This may have fallen to the 3rd Squadron's Flt Ldr Charles Older, who claimed one Japanese aircraft shot down ten miles from Loiwing on this date, identifying it as a reconnaissance machine.

At the end of March BURWING was established at Lashio, still under the command of Grp Capt Broughall. 45 Squadron's remaining Blenheims, under Wg Cdr Wallis, were joined there by a section of 28 Squadron Lysanders, under Flt Lt T.R. Pierce, together with the P-40s of the AVG's 1st and 3rd Squadrons; 17 Squadron was also there, awaiting aircraft. The airfield was bombed on the 31st and again the next day, but without particular damage. Meanwhile, at Asansol in India, a bomber force was again being established to support the retreating army, as far as would be possible, and on 1 April, 113 Squadron began to reform under Wg Cdr. J.F. Grey, previously a flight commander of 60 Squadron in Malaya. On the night of 2nd/3rd two B-17s and a LB-30 set out from Asansol to attack Port Blair, in the Andamans (see chapter 10), while two other B-17s had taken-off to carry out an attack on Rangoon — but the first bomber crashed and exploded just after it had become airborne, killing Capt Elmer Parsel (a veteran of the Philippines and East Indies) and his crew. The other aircraft returned soon afterwards, having suffered an engine failure.

Friday-Tuesday, 3-7 April

On the 3rd (Good Friday) more than 50 bombers of the 7th Flying Battalion flew from their bases in Thailand to attack Mandalay. The city was defenceless and the results were devastating, 60% of the houses were destroyed and many hundreds of civilians killed. A train loaded with bombs and ammunition was hit and blew up, adding to the carnage and chaos. Up to 100,000 people fled — many of them Indians, many of whom were attacked and robbed by hostile Burmans as they went. Those with sufficient means to pay an air fare of 280 rupees (which was about £20 or $80) were airlifted from Magwe and Shwebo by US aircraft. By 9 May, when this route was finally closed, over 14,000 people, including 5,000 Indians, had been flown out, thus a number of small fortunes had been amassed by certain unscrupulous airmen.

During the night of the 3rd/4th six bombers from the 7th Bomb Group raided Rangoon, inflicting only minor damage while one bomber failed to return. With daylight on the 4th nine Ki 30s of the 31st Sentai, escorted by Ki 27s of the 77th Sentai, flew up to Magwe but saw nothing to attack. However, Ki 43 pilots of the 64th Sentai reported having strafed and burnt one large and one small aircraft there. Meanwhile on 4 April JNAF aircraft moved from Bangkok to Mingaladon to support a planned carrier attack on Ceylon (see Chapter 10). 18 G3M bombers of the Genzan Ku, 18 A6Ms of the Attached Fighter Group, and a C5M flew in. Next day aircraft from these units raided Calcutta and Akyab, as the carrier airgroups attacked Colombo. A 2,000 ton minelayer was claimed sunk in the harbour at Akyab, while strafing A6M pilots claimed a Hurricane and a transport aircraft destroyed on the airfield, where bomber crews claimed a large and small aircraft destroyed by bombing. It seems that both claims, and that of the 64th Sentai pilots on the previous day, all relate to the same, unserviceable Hurricane (BM930) and DC-2 (DG474/B of 31 Squadron). The Naval units returned to Thailand after these operations.

During the day, eight Hurricanes of 17 Squadron were flown to Lashio from Calcutta (via Imphal and the Chin Hills) by 'B' Flight pilots, led by Flg Off Thomas. A Blenheim also arrived at Lashio, bringing Grp Capt Singer to take over the command of BURWING from Grp Capt Broughall.

Capt Katsumi Anma (left) commander of the 3rd Chutai, 64th Sentai, who was killed on 8th April 1942, with Capt Masuzo Otani, leader of the 1st Chutai. Otani would also subsequently be killed in action over Chittagong on 5 December 1942.

Wednesday, 8 April

Two days earlier, three of the 64th Sentai's more successful pilots had departed the unit to return to Japan. Therefore, as Capt Katsumi Anma, leader of the 3rd Chutai, headed for Loiwing, soon after midday on the 8th, several of the pilots he was leading were inexperienced new arrivals. The radar operator at Loiwing detected the raid in good time, hence eight of the new P-40Es were scrambled and gained altitude over the airfield (these aircraft had been ferried across India from the Middle East, during March, by pilots of the 2nd and 3rd Squadrons). Four more were scrambled before the attack began and, as the eight Ki 43s swept in low to strafe the airfield, a further three got off. Both sides gravely over estimated the strength of the opposition, the Americans reporting 30 'Model 0s' while the Japanese believed that they were attacked by 20 or more P-40s.

The first eight P-40s to take off, by then high in the sky, dived from the clouds to hit the Ki 43s: Flt Ldr Fritz Wolf (two), Ed Overend, Cliff Groh, Sqn Ldr Arvid Olsen, Flt Ldr Bob Little and John Donovan claimed seven shot down, one probable and seven damaged between them. It seems that the pilots who had got off later probably attacked at the same time, from lower level: Flt Ldr

Pilots of the AVG's 3rd Squadron in April in front of Flt Ldr R.T. Smith's P-40B. Left to right: Sqn Ldr George McMillan, Paul Greene, Flt Lt Duke Hedman, Flt Lt Lewis Bishop, John Donovan, Flt Ldr Bill Reed, Flt Ldr Bob Brouk, Flt Ldr Link Laughlin, Cliff Groh and Bob Raines. *(Authors' collection)*

Bill Reed claimed one (not officially allowed however) before two others shot the windscreen off his aircraft. Within five minutes, five more were claimed, two of them by Flt Ldr Robert T. Smith, who also claimed a probable and three damaged, two and a damaged by Flt Ldr Chauncey 'Link' Laughlin, and another by Fred Hodges to bring total official claims to 12:2:11. Of his victories, Smith wrote:

> "It was the most thrilling experience I've ever had. I picked a 'Zero' (*sic*) that was just completing a strafing run. I opened fire at about 300 yards. I couldn't miss, and the 'Zero' flipped over on its side and dove for the ground, crashing in a ball of flame. I spotted another 'Zero' just starting a strafing run. I could see my tracers flying wildly all around him, until I kicked the rudder and saw them finding their mark; smoke and flame poured from his engine, and that was that."

Plt Off Ricky Chadwick had led a section of three Hurricanes into the air as the raid approached, the pilots briefed to engage any bombers which might have been accompanying the fighters. As he climbed for altitude, Plt Off Everard spotted a Ki 43 skimming the treetops and heading for the airfield:

> "I was in a perfect position for a full deflection shot. Suddenly a mushroom of ground fire erupted between my streaking tracers salvo and the target aircraft. A hard yank on the elevator control and half-roll returned my Hurricane to its original heading."

Sgt Barrick was also in the air when the attack occurred but could not lose altitude fast enough to join the fight. At first he thought he could see bombs falling on the airfield, but then realised that the explosions were aircraft crashing, nearly all of which fell within the Lashio perimeter. The interception had upset the Japanese attack, which succeeded only in the destruction of two P-40s and damage to an unserviceable Blenheim.

The 64th Sentai had indeed been hard-hit, but not to anything like the degree reported by the AVG, whose claims substantially exceeded the number of Japanese aircraft present. However, half the Japanese formation failed to return; the four missing pilots included the leader, Capt Anma, plus another veteran, Sgt Maj Haruto Wada. Two of the new pilots, Lts Muneyuki Okumura and Tadao Kuroki were also lost.

Leading pilots of the 64th Sentai prepare to take-off for a sortie during April. Left to right: Lt Shogo Takeuchi, Lt Shunji Takahashi, Sgt Maj Yoshito Yasuda and 3rd Chutai commanding officer, Capt Katsumi Anma. *(Authors' collection)*

Thursday, 9 April

A small formation of Japanese fighters, identified as one Ki 43 and four Ki 27s, strafed Loiwing again early in the morning; five P-40s suffered some damage but none got off the ground. Three Hurricanes were scrambled but contact was brief, Plt Off Everard evading a Ki 43 which attempted to get on his tail before it disappeared in cloud. As the Hurricanes returned to Loiwing, the airfield was obscured by heavy cloud and they became separated and lost. Whilst Plt Off Chadwick managed to find the airfield, his fuel ran out and he crash-landed one mile short of the runway. Meanwhile, Everard and Sgt MacDonald were both obliged to force-land near a river, which turned out to be only ten miles from the airfield, so made their independent ways back to Loiwing: both Hurricanes were irretrievable; one was BM909.

Friday, 10 April

Lt Colonel Tateo Kato personally led four pilots of the 64th Sentai on an early morning strafe on Loiwing, where 23 P-40s were counted, parked side by side, prior to the attack. Nine of these were damaged before the Japanese made good their escape, without interception, and returned to their base to claim damage inflicted upon at least 15 of the American fighters.

During mid afternoon the Japanese unit carried out a repeat attack, although this time nine Ki 43s took part. Four Hurricanes and four P-40s were scrambled when "three bogies" were reported approaching, but came through cloud to find an estimated 20 plus on the other side. 2/Lt Gordon Peter, SAAF, saw Sgt Barrick shoot down one, after which the South African dived on two others, which were trying to get on the tail of Barrick's aircraft. Before he could open fire however, he was attacked by another Ki 43, which thoroughly shot-up his Hurricane. Badly wounded, Peter was able to bale out of the stricken BH121 and, as soon as he was located, was rushed to Nalmkalm Hospital. Meanwhile Barrick, having watched his victim crash, was jumped by two others (as witnessed by Peter). He managed to get some strikes on one of these before his own aircraft (BG824) was hit in the engine, which stopped. Hot oil from the damaged engine spurted into the cockpit, burning his face, chest and arms, while shrapnel splinters inflicted minor wounds.

Almost blinded by oil, and without the aid of flaps, Barrick managed to force-land the Hurricane on the side of a hill, but struck his head on the gunsight in the process. Despite the pain of his injuries, he was aware of a native shouting to him and pointing skywards. He was able to scramble from the cockpit and dive for cover just as his victor came down to strafe the Hurricane.

The other two Hurricane pilots, Plt Off Earnshaw and Sgt Gibson, both engaged the Ki 43s, each claiming one damaged. Earnshaw managed to manoeuvre onto the tail of another and opened fire from 75 yards, reporting that it fell in flames. The two 17 Squadron pilots also reported seeing a P-40 pilot finish off the Ki 43 Barrick had damaged. The American pilots claimed a total of four fighters shot down, one falling to Robert T. Smith of the 3rd Squadron: he had inflicted damage on one of the Japanese fighters (credited as a probable) before he saw three more:

"Two of them were close together, the third slightly off to one side and maybe 200 yards behind. I cut loose then with everything, and the 'Zero' immediately jerked up abruptly. I flipped over in a half-roll, and dove straight down. He went down and crashed on the side of a mountain."

Other AVG claimants were Flt Ldrs Robert Hedman and Charles Older, who shared one, while Flt Ldr Bob Brouk and Bob Keeton claimed one apiece, bringing the total claims by the Allied pilots to five shot down, one probable and three damaged, against an actual loss to the 64th Sentai of two aircraft. Although Lt Yohei Hinoki, one of the sentai's leading pilots, was hit and wounded, he succeeded in flying his damaged Ki 43 back to base. However, Sgt Maj A. Misago, his No 2, was shot down as was Sgt Maj Tsutomu Goto. Two Hurricanes were correctly claimed, one of them by Sgt Maj Yoshito Yasuda.

Meanwhile, the injured Barrick had set out on foot for Loiwing. However, he soon encountered a patrol of Chinese troops who passed him on to a missionary doctor. With his wounds and injuries treated he was then transported to Chennault's Headquarters for hospitalization, following which he was flown to India in a C-47 transport, together with his wounded squadron colleague, 2/Lt Peter.

Shortly after the raid four Blenheims of 113 Squadron arrived at Loiwing on

17 Squadron's successful American pilot, Sgt Tex Barrick, who was shot down and wounded on 10 April. *(J.C. Barrick)*

detachment, led by Capt J.L. Viney, SAAF. Another aircraft from this unit had arrived a few days earlier.

Sunday, 12 April

At first light, Capt Viney led all five Blenheims to attack targets at Nyaung-bintha in support of the Chinese; all returned safely. Later during the day two P-40s flown by 2nd Squadron pilots, Sqn Ldr Tex Hill and his wingman, Peter Wright, encountered ten unescorted bombers north of Toungoo, which they identified as 'Army 98s', one of which was claimed shot down by Wright. The

Lt Yohei Hinoki of the 64th Sentai, who was wounded during combat over Loiwing on 10 April. *(Authors' collection)*

two pilots then strafed the airfield, where Hill claimed two bombers on the ground and Wright another.

Monday, 13 April

The RAF contingent at Asansol was strengthened by the arrival of a number of Wellington medium bombers of 215 Squadron, which had travelled from the UK via the Middle East. At the same time 5 PRU was formed, partly at Karachi and partly at Dum Dum, absorbing some of the PRU pilots who had operated in Singapore and Burma, plus a number of Dutch aircrew of the Militaire Luchtvaart, under Kapt Witert van Hoogland. The unit was allocated a few camera-equipped Hurricanes, together with six B-25C Mitchell bombers; the latter were originally ordered for use by the Dutch in the Netherlands East Indies. The ventral gun turrets of the bombers had been removed and each aircraft had three cameras installed within the turret opening aft of the bomb-bay.

At Lashio only two serviceable Hurricanes remained available to 17 Squadron, both of which were loaned to 3 PRU for tactical reconnaissance duties; Flg Offs Proctor and Perkins continued to undertake sorties over Magwe, Yenangyaung, Chauk, Heho, Loilem, Hopong and Hsipaw during the ensuing two weeks, aided by Plt Off Harris in the Tiger Moth. Owing to the dire shortage of Hurricanes, Sqn Ldr Stone flew to Calcutta to try and get more, but was unsuccessful. On the 16th he returned to Lashio to instruct his pilots to prepare for evacuation; most were flown out to India during the next few days, as passengers in departing Blenheims.

Capt Viney led his 113 Squadron Blenheim detachment from Loiwing to attack two flotillas of small boats at Singbaungwe. On completion of the attack the bombers flew direct to Chittagong. From there, next day, three flew directly back to Asansol, while the remaining two undertook reconnaissances over the Bay of Bengal before following the others to their home base.

The Allies believed that up to 13 Japanese flyingboats were now located in the Andamans. The Hudsons of the GR Flight were the only RAF aircraft with the range to reach Port Blair — and then only when they refuelled at Akyab, en route — although currently there were only three serviceable aircraft available. Nonetheless, on the 14th, two of these, led by Flg Off E.F. Page, RNZAF, were despatched to attack the flyingboats at anchor and, consequently, two twin-engined and one four-engined 'boats were claimed sunk, with a further 11 believed damaged by gunfire. The other Hudson, flown by Flt Sgt F. Brown, RCAF, suffered damage from AA fire, which fatally wounded his navigator. On reaching Akyab, Brown succeeded in landing safely in bad light, only to run into an unmarked bomb crater.

Four days later, on the 18th, two Hudsons returned to this target, but this time they had to fight their way through a screen of A6Ms; they made several runs at an altitude of 30 feet over a dozen H6Ks seen, two of which were claimed destroyed and three badly damaged. The Hudson (V9221) flown by Sgt G.H. Jackson was pursued and shot down by the fighters, whilst that flown by Sgt Scott-Young suffered severe damage; there were no survivors from Jackson's aircraft. It was felt that these attacks allowed many of the 70 British merchantmen, which were in port at Calcutta, to flee to safer waters, as Calcutta was considered to be under threat from air and sea attack.

Elsewhere, on the 16th, six aircraft of the 7th Bomb Group raided Rangoon again, while six 113 Squadron Blenheims were once more detached, this time to Loiwing where, next day, V5937 was damaged beyond repair in a taxying accident; the remaining five bombed Magwe. At 1300 on the 18th, Flt Ldr Bob Brouk and his wingman, Bob Prescott, of the AVG's 1st Squadron, intercepted a "white-painted Army 98" reconnaissance aircraft — probably a Ki 46 — over the Loiwing/Lashio area and claimed to have shot this down.

Four of 113 Squadron's Blenheims were despatched from Loiwing on the 19th to attack a target near Allanmyo. Z9820, flown by Flg Off M.M. Hickey, RAAF, failed to return and was, later, reported to have crashed into the Irrawaddy River, with the loss of the whole crew. Two days later six more of this unit's aircraft arrived at Loiwing, led by Wg Cdr Grey; the four survivors of the earlier detachment then returned to Asansol.

JAAF reconnaissance aircraft were brought nearer to the front on the 19th, when the 89th and 91st Independent Chutais moved to Toungoo, but the AVG continued to gain successes against such aircraft. On the 20th Vice-Sqn Ldr Rector and Flt Ldr Hedman, of the 2nd and 3rd Squadrons respectively, jointly intercepted and shot down a Ki 15 of the 8th Sentai, which was on a recon-naissance over Pyinmana; Lt Akira Fujimori and his pilot were both killed. Next day P-40s intercepted a reported ten fighters which had just attacked Namsang airfield; one of these was claimed damaged by Flt Ldr Tom Jones south of Pyawbwe.

Another of the GR Flight's Hudsons was lost on the 23rd when V9254 crashed as it took-off from Chittagong for a reconnaissance to Rangoon; Plt Off R.M. Rice, RCAF, and his crew were killed. However, Hudsons were continually arriving for the unit, mainly 139 Squadron aircraft from the UK, 18 of which had originally set out with Singapore as their destination although none had, in fact, reached the Island.

Friday, 24 April

During the morning four Blenheims of 113 Squadron took off in pairs to make a low level attack on the Hopong-Loilem road. The first pair returned safely, but Flt Sgt W.T. Hind's Z9831 was shot down by AA fire as the second pair attacked; only Sgt Alan Bailes managed to bale out and he returned to Lashio a few days later. Flg Off G.W.N. Bassingthwaighte led three more Blenheims from Asansol to Lashio, from there bombing targets in the Sandowy-Taungup area. All returned safely, although V6333 belly-landed on the airfield.

A USAAF C-47, which had just delivered a load of fuel and ammunition for the AVG at Lashio, was intercepted on its return flight by a fighter identified as a 'Zero'. Capt Don Olds, the co-pilot, took the transport down to treetop height to frustrate the Japanese pilot's attacks, while Colonel Caleb B. Haynes went back down the fuselage to help other members of the crew attempt to ward off the attacks with sub-machine guns; on this occasion the aircraft managed to escape damage.

During the morning Sqn Ldr Tex Hill, Vice-Sqn Ldr Ed Rector, Flt Ldr John Petach and Peter Wright of the AVG 2nd Squadron, intercepted and, between them, claimed to have shot down a 'Type 98' bomber over Liolem. At Toungoo South, the JAAF had been further reinforced when the 27th Sentai had arrived with more light bombers. Following the recent loss of Capt Anma in the 64th Sentai, Capt Yasuhiko Kuroe was posted in to lead the 3rd Chutai; Kuroe had claimed three victories by this time, having flown Ki 44s with the 47th Independent Chutai over Singapore and Malaya. On the 25th however, this small unit handed its remaining pre-production examples of this fighter to the 64th Sentai and left for Japan.

Capt Yasuhiko Kuroe of the 47th DH Chutai, who saw action over Malaya and Burma flying one of the pre-production Nakajima Ki 44 Shoki fighters. He later served with the 64th Sentai, ending the war with 30 victories.

Saturday, 25 April

The AVG was to enjoy more success during the day and claimed three aircraft shot down. After lunch Flt Ldrs Robert T. Smith, John Petach, Lewis Bishop and Link Laughlin of the 3rd Squadron reported meeting an 'Army 98', some 80 miles south of Lashio, which they shared in shooting down with Peter Wright of the 2nd Squadron. Petach and Wright then joined Smith, Robert Raines and Freeman Ricketts in shooting down another, identified as either an 'Army 97' or 'Army 98', which fell in the same area. Raines made the third claim, alone, for a single-engined aircraft south of Loilem, identified as either a fighter or a reconnaissance aircraft.

Sunday-Monday, 26-27 April

On the 26th, two 3rd Squadron pilots reported an engagement with fighters, identified as 'Model 0s', south-east of Lashio, when Vice-Sqn Ldr Dupouy and his wingman, John Donovan, each claimed one probably shot down. Next day Lashio was strafed by Ki 27s, which resulted in damage to one Blenheim. Grp Capt Singer consequently ordered BURWING to evacuate the airfield, as the Japanese were getting close. Four Blenheims flew out that day, another remained to await the return of the shot-down Sgt Bailes, who was known to be on his way back. The force-landed Blenheim (V6333), a belly-landed P-40 and a damaged Lysander were all blown up by the departing troops.

Tuesday, 28 April

As 28 April was known to be the day before the Emperor of Japan's birthday, Chennault anticipated a big attack on Loiwing on this date. His prediction became a reality when, at 1030, two dozen Ki 21s of the 12th Sentai and 20 escorting Ki 43s of the 64th Sentai approached, to find the AVG already up and waiting for them in strength. As the P-40s attacked, Lt M. Kataoka was shot down and killed, while Cpl Y. Hirano was shot-up and reportedly collided with a pursuing P-40, both pilots baling out; Hirano returned to his base, on foot, six days later but there is no record of an AVG aircraft having been lost on this date, apart from that flown by Robert T. Smith, which ran out of fuel.

The Americans' enthusiasm obviously overcame accuracy in determining the results of their actions, the AVG pilots claiming no fewer than 15 'Model 0s' shot down, plus one probable and two damaged. Apparently they had all dived and attacked at once, probably all firing together at the same pair of aircraft. Their claims were: 2nd Squadron: Sqn Ldr Tex Hill two, Flt Ldr Lewis Bishop four and Flt Ldr Tom Jones one: 3rd Squadron: Flt Ldr Ken Jernstedt one, Flt Ldr Charles Older two, Flt Ldr Robert T. Smith one, Flt Ldr Tom Haywood and Vice-Sqn Ldr Parker Dupouy one shared, Ed Overend one and one damaged, Frank Adkins one, Flt Ldr Paul Greene one and one damaged, Sqn Ldr Arvid Olsen one probable.

During the month 31 Squadron had started to receive some DC-3s and, by the 20th, had three of these on strength. A detachment, comprising these aircraft and one DC-2, was then sent to Dinjan to operate from Myitkyina, while the rest of the squadron moved to Lahore, to overhaul the other DC-2s. On the 28th Wg Cdr H.P. Jenkins flew the first of the DC-3s (LR233) to Shwebo to collect 28 casualties. It had been hoped that five Curtiss Mohawks of 146 Squadron, newly-arrived at Dinjan, would be able to escort 31 Squadron's transports but difficulty was experienced in maintaining control in cloud, due to poor equipment, and the proposal was dropped.

Wednesday, 29 April

An attempt was now made by the Japanese to seize Lashio by using para-troops. Transport aircraft carrying these men, supporting bombers and close support aircraft, together with 16 escorting Ki 43s took off to undertake this operation; on take-off a Ki 46 and a Ki 51 collided at Toungoo. However, the weather was so foul over the proposed dropping zone that the whole operation had to be cancelled. During the return flight two of the transports were lost and one Ki 43 suffered a fuel leak, obliging Sgt Maj Yoshito Yasuda to crash-land in Allied territory, from where he made his way back on foot four days later.

With Lashio threatened by the advancing Japanese army, the Allied air forces began withdrawing. From Loiwing, Sqn Ldr Stone decided to lead a small convoy back to India, by road; the party eventually reached Myitkyina from where it was evacuated in DC-3s. However, five of the squadron's pilots remained at Lashio – newly-promoted Flt Lt Chadwick together with Plt Offs Everard, Warburton, Murdoch and Reid – with instructions to scrounge lifts in departing aircraft.

Following the withdrawal of 113 Squadron, two bomb-damaged Blenheims remained at Lashio, waiting to be destroyed. At Chadwick's instigation, and with the agreement of the pilot of one of the Blenheims, Plt Off MacArthur, it was decided that all should work in an attempt to render one airworthy. This involved the removal of one aircraft's damaged port engine and replacing it with a similar engine from the other aircraft. Working through the night they succeeded in this difficult task and were able to undertake an uneventful flight to Dum Dum the next day.

Other BURWING personnel also made their way to Myitkyina, but here they were divided. The aircrew were flown to Dinjan and from there left for Calcutta by rail, where 17 Squadron was to be reformed for the defence of that city. The rest of the party, 200 officers and 324 men, went into China – to Chengtu – from where they were supposed to be flown out in Hudsons. However none could be spared and, as RAFCHIN, they were to stay for the next year, helping the Chinese to develop air bases and train ground staff. They took with them the RDF set from Lashio, which was put to good use. The AVG had also gone, retreating into China to Kunming after burning 22 of their P-40s which were under repair.

Elsewhere in Burma operations continued. Bombers of the US 7th Bomb Group again raided Rangoon after dark – without loss – but with the onset of daylight, Hudson AE574 of the GR Flight was despatched to assess the damage, and was shot down near the city; Plt Off L.G. MacLeod, RCAF, and his crew perished.

Friday-Saturday, 1-2 May

On day one of the new month Mandalay fell to the Japanese and, two days later, they took Bhamo. Most active response during this period continued to be made by the AVG, from its relatively more secure bases in China, where more P-40s were still being delivered from the Middle East, both by US and RAF pilots. The newly-arrived Wellingtons of 215 Squadron undertook their first operations from Pandaveswa airfield, during the night of the 1st/2nd, when they set out to raid Magwe, but encountered a violent storm; as a consequence, BB460 ran out of fuel and force-landed in a field 30 miles from Bhagaliur, on the bank of the Ganges. A second aircraft (BB515) force-landed in a paddy field, ten miles east of Pandaveswa, after an engine had broken lose and fallen out! It was hardly an auspicious start for the new unit.

Next day the remaining Hudsons of the GR Flight at Dum Dum were absorbed into the newly reformed 62 Squadron, under Wg Cdr D. Halliday, DFC. As further aircraft and crews of 139 Squadron arrived in India from the UK, they too were absorbed into this unit, as were five 59 Squadron crews who had failed to reach the Netherlands East Indies, captained by Plt Offs J.A. Mather, P.W. Smith, P.G. Bell, D.A. Crouchen and A.C. Blythe; they were joined by three crews from 53 Squadron, captained by Plt Offs P.E. Springman, F.W. Letchford and Plt Off A.O. Hawkins, RNZAF. The squadron's Hudsons included V9178, V9189, AE508 and AE514 (all ex 59 Squadron) and AM941 (ex 53 Squadron). Two other crews posted to 62 Squadron were those of Plt Offs Les Hayton and Tony Ayris, fresh from their escape from Burma. One of the Flight's final duties, before being absorbed, had been to evacuate Governor Dorman-Smith, and his staff, from Myitkyina to the safety of India.

Sunday, 3 May

Sqn Ldr Bob Neale, of the 1st Squadron, intercepted a single-engined bomber or observation aircraft north-east of Lungling, at 1420, which he claimed to have shot down for his 13th personal victory. Meantime, Flt Ldr Jones of the 3rd Squadron flew a photo-reconnaissance to Hanoi and, on return, reported an estimated 40 'Model 0s' parked at the city's airport. A strike by four bomb-carrying P-40Es was therefore planned for the morrow.

The AVG's most successful pilot was Sqn Ldr Bob Neale of the 1st Squadron, seen here with his P-40B carrying the unit's emblem on the fuselage. *(Authors' collection)*

Meanwhile, four more P-40Es arrived at Dinjan airfield, en route for the AVG at Kunming, having been ferried from the Middle East. In mid April five such aircraft had departed Ismailia (Egypt) in the hands of three RAF ferry pilots of the Air Delivery Unit – Plt Offs Jim Pickering and Bob Brookman, together with Sgt Len Davies[1] – and two USAAF pilots, led by an ADU Blenheim. At Habbaniya one of the American-flown P-40Es became unserviceable, while at Sharjah a second one also dropped out; however, the remaining three were joined by another, flown by Lt Hans Werbke, USAAF, which had been delayed from an earlier delivery flight.

On arrival at Dinjan, Plt Off Pickering (the formation leader) was confronted by Colonel Robert Scott, USAAF, Executive Officer of the ABC (American-British-Chinese) Ferrying Command:

---

[1] Plt Off Pickering and Sgt Davies had both flown Hurricanes with 261 Squadron in the defence of Malta (see *Malta: The Hurricane Years, 1940-41* by Christopher Shores and Brian Cull with Nicola Malizia, published by Grub Street).

"He tried to commandeer one of my aircraft, but I wouldn't agree. He pulled rank on Lt Werbke and took his aircraft, so honour was satisfied all round."

Of the incident, Colonel Scott wrote:

"Number 41-1456 stayed with me. It was mine and I was proud of it. I found a painter. Buying red and white paint from the village, I had him paint the shark's mouth on the lower nose.

"Very proudly I taxied out for my first take-off. All around me on the airdrome I could feel the jealous eyes of every American and British pilot – or at least my ego thought it felt their looks."

One of the new P-40B Kittyhawks, armed with six wing-mounted .50-in machine guns, reaching the AVG from the Middle East during April and May. The recently-arrived aircraft, still carrying the US national insignia, is prepared for gun harmonisation tests. *(Authors' collection)*

Monday, 4 May

The JAAF launched an offensive against the nearest AVG airfield at Paoshan (just across the border in China), bombs from 98th Sentai Ki 21s falling mainly on the town where, amongst others, AVG pilot Ben Foshee was fatally wounded. Only two P-40s were able to get off in time to intercept, as there had been no warning of the raid. Sqn Ldr Charles R. Bond was able to break through the fighter screen, provided by the 64th Sentai, and shoot down one of the bombers before he was shot down over the airfield, baling out slightly burned. Two other bombers returned with three wounded aboard.

Tuesday, 5 May

A larger attack was launched against Paoshan, when the 27th Sentai despatched its light bombers, escorted by 11th Sentai Ki 27s and 64th Sentai Ki 43s. Intercepting at 1300, 1st and 2nd Squadron P-40 pilots claimed seven shot down and three probables – all misidentified the single-engined, fixed-under-carriage, bombers of the 27th Sentai as 'I-97s' (Ki 27s). The Japanese suffered five losses during this raid, comprising three 11th Sentai Ki 27s and two 27th Sentai bombers. One victory was claimed by the 64th Sentai and two by the

11th, one of them the first for Sgt Takeo Takahashi, a future 'ace'. One of the Ki 43s was badly damaged in a landing accident on return. AVG claims were: 1st Squadron: Flt Ldr Matt Kuykendahl one 'I-97'; 2nd Squadron: Sqn Ldr Tex Hill one 'Zero'; Flt Ldr Frank Schiel one fighter; Flt Ldr John Bright one 'I-97' and one probable; Flt Ldr Frank Lawlor two 'I-97s'; Freeman Ricketts one 'Zero' and one 'I-97' probable; Ray Hastey one fighter probable.

Both Schiel and Hastey failed to return following this engagement, the former having been forced down; after a three-day trek he reached the AVG base at Yunnanyi, which was also the home of a Chinese flight school. Hastey had run out of fuel and baled out 40 miles from the airfield, returning five days later on the back of a mule.

During the morning Lashio was visited by a lone P-40E, in the hands of Colonel Scott. As he approached the occupied airfield, he spotted a twin-engined 'Army 97' bomber parked in the north-west corner and dived to attack:

> "My first shots hit the front of the plane. I turned for a second attack. This time I did better. I saw my tracers go into the fuselage and then into the engines. It was on fire."

Wednesday, 6 May

Myitkyina was now almost in the front line. Nonetheless, two of 31 Squadron's DC-3s from Dinjan landed there to pick up casualties and evacuees. As they were loading however, aircraft were heard overhead, which were initially assumed to be reconnaissance machines, but were probably Ki 30s for, as LR230/D was commencing its take-off run, a bomb fell in front of it and destroyed the port wing which caused it to crash. The second transport (LR231/E) was also badly damaged when aircraft, identified as 'Army 98' dive-bombers, carried out strafing attacks.

Both aircraft were hastily evacuated, but two European women and a child were killed; several others were wounded, two of them − both Army doctors − critically. One of the pilots, Flt Lt David Howell, opened fire with a Thompson sub-machine gun on a low flying bomber, reporting a trail of white vapour from the engine, which led him to believe that he had hit it.

Two further DC-3s arrived shortly after this raid, LR235/J taking out the majority of the stranded passengers and crew, although Wg Cdr Jenkins and two others remained behind. LR233/H was obliged to take-off in a hurry before it had loaded, when a further air raid alarm was given. During this second attack, the damaged LR231 was hit again and set on fire. LR235 returned later to evacuate Jenkins and the remaining RAF personnel. USAAF C-47s had also been evacuating refugees from Myitkyina; one transport pilot, Lt Jack Sartz, took off with no less than 73 persons on board: when he landed the number had risen to 74 − a baby had been born during the flight!

Thursday, 7 May

During the day, Japanese armoured units reached the west bank of the Salween, the AVG being called upon to delay their crossing into China. Four P-40Es loaded with 500 lb bombs flew from Kunming to attack, protected by four P-40Bs. Four more, armed with Chinese 35 lb bombs, then repeated the strike; the Japanese force was badly damaged, which allowed the Chinese to cross the river and counter-attack. One bomb was reported to have destroyed a headquarters, while the Chinese troops estimated that they killed more than 2,000, driving the survivors back over the frontier.

Friday, 8 May

In the early hours of the morning, the Japanese recorded an attack at Mingaladon by five large aircraft – presumably US 7th Bomb Group B-17s or B-24s. Two Ki 43s attempted to intercept, aided by searchlights, but in vain.

Myitkyina was now abandoned to the Japanese, the crews of the last few fully laden DC-3s of 31 Squadron having had to hold back the mass of the refugees with drawn revolvers. Next day a flight of Curtiss Mohawks of 5 Squadron (a recently formed unit operating out of Dum Dum), led by Flt Lt D.O. Cunliffe, reconnoitred the airfield, the pilots reporting that a Japanese aircraft was already present, which was duly strafed. A Blenheim from the reformed 60 Squadron at Asansol, which now returned to operations, undertook a special reconnaissance to ascertain the position of Alexander's forces, finding them south-west of Kalewa. The Japanese were found at Ye-u by drawing their fire.

With the ending of evacuation operations, 31 Squadron was about to begin supply dropping sorties to the front-line troops – soon a regular and vital feature of operations on the Burma-India frontier. In these activities they were to be joined by 215 Squadron's Wellingtons, but the onset of the monsoon was beginning to restrict flying and make further movement on the ground difficult.

Saturday, 9 May

Five Blenheims raided Magwe, to which airfield JAAF units had now begun moving, where four Ki 27s and a Lockheed-type transport were destroyed in flames. From the opposite direction, 7th Battalion Ki 21s attacked Chittagong several times, claiming five small ships sunk in the harbour. Aircraft from Burma were also straying deeper into China and, during the afternoon, Sqn Ldr Neale and Bill Bartling of the AVG's 1st Squadron intercepted a single-engined reconnaissance aircraft, 60 miles south-west of Kunming, which Bartling reported shooting down into a lake.

Colonel Scott (in his 'private' P-40E) made four flights into Burma during the day, the first of these escorting two C-47s to Paoshan. Shortly after he had departed, Paoshan was subjected to an air raid but little damage resulted and no interceptions were made. Scott flew to Lashio and carried out a strafing run, his own aircraft sustaining a few bullet strikes. By the end of the day, having returned to Dinjan three times to refuel and re-arm, Scott had logged no less than ten hours flying.

Sunday-Thursday, 10-21 May

The RAF now began to hit back rather more frequently, as the last of the British troops pulled wearily out of Burma. On the 10th, five Blenheims of 113 Squadron set out to bomb Magwe but became separated in bad weather. Only Sqn Ldr C.W. Harper (who had flown with 34 Squadron in Malaya and Singapore) reached the airfield, where he was pursued for 30 minutes by two patrolling Ki 27s of the 77th Sentai's 2nd Chutai. Wt Off Kimura claimed to have shot the Blenheim down, but in fact it returned undamaged to Dum Dum, where the gunner, Sgt M.W. Taylor, reported that he had damaged one of the attackers.

B-25Cs of 5 PRU made their inaugural operational sorties during the morning of the 12th, when Lt P.L. Andre de la Porte (a former Brewster pilot of 3-VlG-V in Java) and Flg Off Freddy Proctor flew sorties to Mingaladon airfield: both aircraft returned safely to Dum Dum.

AVG P-40s from the 2nd and 3rd Squadrons flew south deep into Indo-China on this date, to attack Gialam airfield at Hanoi. Flt Ldrs Tom Jones, Lewis Bishop and Frank Schiel of the 2nd, together with Link Laughlin and John Donovan of the 3rd, each claimed three aircraft destroyed on the ground. 14 of these were fighters, the other − claimed by Laughlin − being identified as a transport. However, Donovan's aircraft was hit by AA fire and crashed, killing the pilot.

Next day (13th), Sqn Ldr R.W. Davy led four Hudsons of 62 Squadron to raid Akyab, where they apparently surprised the defences and claimed three of five aircraft "caught napping" on the ground. All returned safely. On the 14th it was the turn of the two Blenheims of 113 Squadron to carry the attack to the enemy, when Magwe was raided. Patrolling Ki 27s of the 77th Sentai's 2nd Chutai intercepted, five of these fighters pursuing the two bombers, which on this occasion they identified as Wellingtons. Their quarries proved to be as fast as their own aircraft were, and in fact, faster in the dive. One bomber was seen trailing smoke from an engine, apparently badly damaged, and was claimed as a probable by Lt Yatabe. He had damaged Plt Off G.W.L. Hanson's aircraft but this returned, the gunner (Sgt Taylor again) claiming one fighter probably shot down, although the 77th also suffered no loss.

That night (15th/16th) a most unusual 'bomber' headed towards Hanoi; it was in fact a US Transport Command C-47, in the hands of Lt William Grube. Aided and abetted by his co-pilot, Lt Jack Krofoed, and accompanied by Lt Dick Peret, AVG engineering officer, and Sgt Roy Hoffman, the transport aircraft set out on its unauthorised bombing sortie against Hanoi, arriving over the city at about 0400. On board were clusters of Chinese incendiary bombs, a few French 50 and 100 pounders and some Russian 250 lb bombs − all 'stolen' from the Chinese armoury at Kunming!. The bombs had to be armed individually prior to being thrown or rolled out of the cabin door, as the aircraft circled over Hanoi at 11,000 feet! Running low on fuel as he struggled to find Kunming on the return flight, Grube was forced to feather one engine to save fuel before the airfield was sighted at 0830. Two nights later they set out to repeat the raid but missed Hanoi, so bombed Haiphong instead. News of the sorties soon reached Colonel Chennault, who promptly put a stop to any further such flights.

60 Squadron despatched two of its Blenheims to raid Akyab on the 16th but on this occasion the defences were more alert and both bombers − flown by Sqn Ldr E.F. Cawdrey and Plt Off A.P.S. Wood, RAAF − were damaged, although both regained their base. Flt Ldr Tom Jones of the AVG's 2nd Squadron lost his life during the day, when his P-40E crashed while he was practising dive-bombing.

Next day (17th), another of the 2nd Squadron's 'aces', Sqn Ldr Lewis Bishop, was shot down in flames by AA fire during a bombing attack on the railway yards at Lackay. Colonel Scott accompanied the AVG pilots:

> "I saw Bishop's bombs hit dead centre on the round-house. Then I dropped
> mine. Just at that moment Bishop's fighter belched fire and smoke, and I
> saw him slide his canopy back and jump."

Bishop came down safely but landed in the occupied town and was immediately captured.

While the 77th Sentai had been protecting Magwe, the 64th now began sending detachments up to Akyab for similar duties, although noting that pilots sent there all began falling victim of dengue fever. The unit's first success here occurred on the 17th when Lt Saburo Nakamura intercepted and shot down a 62 Squadron Hudson (AM934) flown by Plt Off E.C. Corbett, RCAF, the whole crew being lost when it crashed near Mhazi. Two days later, on the 19th, two Hudsons carried out a repeat attack on Akyab, Flg Off Page's crew reporting "wrecking" two Navy Zeros on the ground, after which the Hudson was pursued by four others; Page commented:

> "My observer's aim with the bombs was perfect. After that it was a merry-go-round from cloud to cloud. The Japs chased us for a quarter of an hour but we managed to get away with it."

Three 113 Squadron Blenheims repeated the raid shortly afterwards and were also intercepted, although all three returned safely, their gunners believing thay had damaged two of their pursuers. Pilots of the 64th Sentai claimed one of the Blenheims shot down.

On the 21st however, the Japanese unit's actions were more successful when Sgt Maj Yoshito Yasuda and two others intercepted another 62 Squadron Hudson (AM941 flown by Flg Off Paul Springman, one of the 53 Squadron pilots), which Yasuda managed to shoot down after pursuing it to within 20 miles of Chittagong; the wreckage was later located by searching aircraft, washed up on the shore near Chambri. 215 Squadron lost another of its Wellingtons during the day, when Plt Off J.E.D. Brewer's aircraft (BB465) crashed in the Kabaw Valley in Upper Burma; there were no survivors and the cause of its loss is not known.

On this day Lt Colonel Kato led seven of the unit's Ki 43s on a sweep to attack Chittagong airfield, but no British aircraft were seen. During the return flight Wt Off Takeshi Shimizu's aircraft suddenly burst into flames and he baled out; he landed safely but was captured.

On the 20th meanwhile, Lt General Alexander's forces reached Imphal and the long retreat from Burma was over. A period of consolidation by both armies would now begin, prior to three years of hard and costly fighting in the jungle that would follow. BURCORPS ceased to exist; during the retreat it had lost some 13,000 troops killed, wounded or missing. By contrast the pursuing Japanese 33rd Division had lost 1,896 men killed, 108 more had died of their wounds and 438 were wounded.

At this point, Air Vice-Marshal Stevenson issued a synopsis of the air force's apparent successes and the cost thereof. Claims against the Japanese forces in the period December 1941 to May 1942 were considered to have been:

	Confirmed	Probable	Damaged	Destroyed on the ground
RAF in Burma	54	33	29	20
AVG in Burma	179	43	87	38

The cost, he said, had been 22 Buffaloes and Hurricanes and 16 P-40s shot down, plus eight bombers missing. Most of the downed fighter pilots had survived, although two had been killed whilst parachuting. At least 51 aircraft (including more than 20 P-40s) were stated to have been destroyed on the ground.

Friday, 22 May

During the morning P-40s were sent to attack Japanese emplacements near Paoshan, along the Salween. AA fire struck the aircraft flown by Flt Ldr Bob Little, shooting away the right wing, causing another of the AVG's leading 'aces' to crash to his death.

Blenheim IVs of 60 Squadron at Asansol. The nearest aircraft wears the code 'OM' of its previous unit, 107 Squadron. *(F.C. Joerin)*

From Asansol nine Blenheims of 60 Squadron flew to Dum Dum in preparation for an attack on Akyab airfield. Initially it was planned that six bombers would fly up-river to attack targets there, while three others would attack the airfield. In the event, only the latter three finally prepared for take-off, but one suffered engine trouble and did not get away, while a second returned early with other technical problems. This left Z9808 in the hands of Wt Off Martin Huggard (with Sgt John Howitt as navigator and Flt Sgt 'Jock' McLuckie as airgunner). After some deliberation as to whether they should proceed alone, they decided so to do. To improve their chances, they dived down from 10,000 feet to 1,500 feet, swung round the target to come in from the east, released their bombs and dived for sea level, heading for base a few feet above the waters of the Bay of Bengal. However, as they passed over the airfield, they had seen fighters taking off, and indeed five pilots of the 64th Sentai had scrambled individually to give chase. Although Huggard had flown throughout the opening months of the Burma invasion, this was the first time he had even seen a Japanese aircraft in the sky.

Sgt Maj Yoshito Yasuda had been first off from Akyab and he soon caught the Blenheim, diving from above to attack. However he was at once hit and wounded by McLuckie's return fire, so headed back to Akyab. Capt Masuzo Otani then attacked in the same way, but again return fire hit his fighter and he too was obliged to retire. Finally Lt Colonel Kato arrived, accompanied by two others, the commanding officer diving to attack. Those with him subsequently reported that his fire struck the bomber (actually it did not), but as he pulled up McLuckie raked the underside of the Ki 43 and saw it begin to burn.

The fighter then "wobbled", turned right over and dived straight into the sea. Kato's two shaken companions turned back at this time, returning to Akyab to report that their commander had shot down the bomber and then, obviously

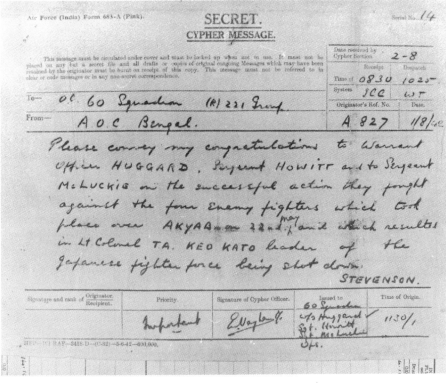

Top: Flt Sgt Jock McLuckie (left) and Wt Off Martin Huggard of 60 Squadron. McLuckie shot down the 64th Sentai's famous leader, Lt Colonel Tateo Kato, on 22 May. *(W.M. Huggard).* Above: The signal issued by Air Vice-Marshal Stevenson to Wt Off Huggard's crew (on 1 August), when British intelligence had ascertained the identity of their victim. *(W.M. Huggard)*

The 64th Sentai's famous commanding officer, Major Takeo Kato. *(64th Sentai Assoc)*

realising that he could not get back, had half-looped and dived into the sea, as he had advised his pilots to do in similar circumstances.

McLuckie had not realised that he had hit the first two fighters to attack, while Huggard's tactics (of hugging the wavetops) had been wise in the circumstances, for his Blenheim had not suffered a single hit. Their troubles were not yet over however, as the aircraft was experiencing hydraulic problems and one wheel was hanging down. Only by 'banging' it on the surface of the sea was it knocked back into place! On return to Dum Dum, Huggard had to crash-land the Blenheim with the undercarriage retracted but all survived unhurt.

The loss of Kato, the JAAF's first great fighter 'ace' and a noted leader, was a great blow to the morale of his pilots. Kato's final personal score was considered to be about 18, nine in China in 1938 and nine in the current war. While no longer a big total compared with some of the pilots who had served at Nomonhan, his position as the first Army 'ace' in China remained unassailable and his leadership beyond question. He was posthumously promoted to the rank of Major General.

The British were soon to be aware of what had happened, via the Intelligence Service, for, on 2 August, 60 Squadron received a signal from Air Vice-Marshal

Stevenson personally, which read:

> "Please convey my congratulations toward Warrant Officer Huggard, Sergeant Howitt and Sergeant McLuckie on the successful action they fought against the four enemy fighters which took place over Akyab on 22 May and which resulted in Lt Colonel T.A. Keo Kato (*sic*) leader of the Japanese fighter force being shot down."

This action effectively brought to an end the first Burma Campaign.

Christopher Shores and Yasuho Izawa were able to put Martin Huggard in touch with Yoshito Yasuda; in 1989 Yasuda visited England with a party of other Japanese veterans, met Huggard and attended an air show with him.

Chapter 10

CEYLON[1]

By the end of March 1942 most of the initial Japanese objectives had been accomplished. The Indies had fallen by the 8th of that month, on which date the valuable Burmese port of Rangoon had also come into Japanese occupation. Final resistance in the Philippines was near to being snuffed out, while the first moves into New Guinea and the Solomon Islands had been made. Following the Battle of the Java Sea, Allied naval power in the area had virtually ceased to exist, with the shattered US base at Pearl Harbour and the Royal Navy's Eastern Fleet in the Indian Ocean both far away. The China Sea was now a Japanese 'lake', and the protective perimeter of the Malay Barrier had been all-but established, with supplies of tin, rubber, and above all, oil and rice, now assured.

In only two areas did serious fighting continue. In the far south — New Guinea, the Bismark Archipelago and the Solomons, where there were signs that US and Australian resistance was stiffening — and in northern Burma. Although the British forces were reeling back in defeat in the latter country, the defence of this route into India was of the utmost importance to them. The defence of Burma was vital if India was to be held as a staging base for the subsequent re-occupation of Malaya. In any event, India was the very epitome of Empire, and its loss was unthinkable. The area was of almost equal import-ance to the Americans, for only from Assam could China still be supplied and kept in the war. Already during March the loss of central Burma meant the closure of the Burma Road from Lashio to Kunming, whence supplies to Generalissimo Chiang Kai-shek's Kuomintang armies had been despatched. Now only the air route over the Himalayas looked likely to remain, with possibly the new Ledo Road — but if these were to be lost and China fell, a major part of the Japanese army would no longer be held locked in endless conflict on the Asian mainland. From the Japanese viewpoint too, if supplies to China could be cut off and the war there brought to a successful conclusion, overwhelming forces could be deployed against India, thus greatly strengthening the 'Greater Asia Co-Prosperity Sphere'.

The occupation of Java had effectively neutralised north-western Australia, completing the process begun by the devastating attack which had been made on Port Darwin by carrier-based aircraft on 19 February. The task of neutralising New Guinea had, as has already been described, begun in the same way with carrier strikes on the Rabaul area of New Britain, and on bases on the

---

[1] Renamed Sri Lanka in 1972 following Independence in 1948

north-west coast of New Guinea itself in late January. These had been followed by the occupation of New Britain and by landings in New Guinea's province of Papua. These latter landings, undertaken during March, were giving the Allies serious fears for the safety of Australia. Such fears were in fact groundless, but the United States needed a secure Australia, as a main base for air and ground operations against the Japanese and, to these ends, great numbers of reinforcements had started arriving there.

At the beginning of April therefore, the situation on both major land fronts — Burma and New Guinea — was highly unstable. Until Rangoon fell it had been the major port concerned with the supply of China, and the Japanese were now advancing into central Burma. In New Guinea, the Japanese bridgehead on the north-east coast had been consolidated, and their army was advancing overland on Port Moresby; this important harbour and base area was being subjected to almost daily aerial attack. Neither of these campaigns required the involvement of the Imperial Japanese Navy for the moment, in the way that the Indies campaign had done; consequently the full weight of the Combined Fleet was available for "pure" naval operations, conceived in terms of grand strategy, rather than local tactics.

Following its success at Pearl Harbor and Darwin — and the attacks on Tjilatjap (Java) on 5 March — the Striking Force of the Combined Fleet had returned to the anchorage at Staring Bay, Celebes, on the 11th. The carrier *Kaga* was suffering from mechanical defects, which required repairs in a Japanese dockyard, but her withdrawal was made less serious by the return to the Striking Force of the 5th Carrier Division (*Shokaku* and *Zuikaku*). Aircraft losses had been negligible since Pearl Harbor but, during the next fortnight, the Air Groups were built up to full strength and flying exercises were undertaken preparatory to the next operation — a strike against Ceylon.

Ceylon, lying off the south-east tip of the Indian sub-continent, occupies an extremely significant strategic position in the Indian Ocean, across the main shipping routes from Singapore and Rangoon to the Red Sea and the Persian Gulf. There are two fine natural harbours at Colombo and Trincomalee, the former primarily a trade port, and the latter suitable for the development of a naval anchorage and base, with deep-water creeks leading off a huge central basin. The northern entrance to the Malacca Strait is approximately 1,000 miles to the east of Trincomalee, which could thus serve as a base for submarine, surface ship, or carrier operations against Japanese shipping proceeding to Rangoon. Colombo's main importance lay in its new function as the terminal of most east-bound merchant shipping, with the responsibility for controlling tonnage bound for destinations on the east coast of India.

Plans had been made — and some work carried out — to develop Colombo and Trincomalee, as well as to construct airfields for local defence, but by March 1942, the only usable operational airfields were at China Bay, near Trincomalee, at Ratmalana, near Colombo, at Colombo Racecourse and at a small strip at Minneriya, on the south coast. China Bay airfield was, in effect, a wide grass runway with the sea at both ends, contained between a high tree-covered ridge running along its southern edge and a lower ridge along its northern edge. Aircraft could only take-off and land in either a north-east or south-west direction dependent on wind conditions. Three large oil storage tanks stood in a facility away from the north-east corner of the airfield, forming part of the long established Royal Naval Base at Trincomalee Harbour.

Until February 1942 the air defence of the island had rested almost entirely in the hands of the Royal Navy; two fighter units had just arrived in the Colombo area after re-equipping with Fulmar II two-seat fighters, 803 Squadron under Lt Bruce McEwen and 806 Squadron commanded by Lt Robert Johnston, both of which had recently been operating from land bases in the Western Desert alongside the RAF. Flying with McEwen on the trip from Egypt as his observer was Sub Lt Roy Hinton, a veteran of the battle of Crete the previous year, who recalled:

> "We proceeded overland in four batches of six aircraft. I flew with McEwen and we had an hilarious flight out, arriving at Bangalore (southern India), which we liked so much we decided to spend a week in relaxing. Another flight lost their way and came down in the grounds of the Maharaja of Hyderabad, and became guests for several days.
>
> "All aircraft, by a miracle, arrived at Ratmalana, more or less, in flying trim. Accommodation was very poor. McEwen, myself and a few other chaps decided that the Galle Face Hotel in Colombo was more in keeping with our status, so we moved in, spending most of the daylight hours relaxing in the sea.
>
> "Sure enough, we were rudely awakened by the C-in-C, who could not find any responsible person at Ratmalana and eventually tracked us down. Back to base and work!"

As a stop-gap measure, eight Hurricanes, which had been assembled at Karachi, were also flown to Ceylon, six by pilots of 136 Squadron — who were in transit, their original destination being Burma —arriving at Ratmalana on 23 February; included in this party, although not a member of 136 Squadron, was Sqn Ldr P.C. Fletcher.

A Fleet Requirements Unit, 788 Squadron, had been impressed for coastal reconnaissance, torpedo-bombing and general duties, for which it was equipped with Swordfish biplanes; it was intended that the unit would subsequently be re-designated 839 Squadron as a fully operational formation but, in the event, this never happened. At China Bay airfield was 273 Squadron, which operated antiquated Seal and Vildebeest biplanes for general purpose duties, and a few Fulmar Is and IIs, borrowed from the Navy.

The main defence of Ceylon rested on the Eastern Fleet, which was itself maintaining a primarily defensive role in the Indian Ocean. The loss of several modern units in the East Indies was felt by the cruiser and destroyer forces, and the battle line represented all that could be spared from the Home and Mediterranean Fleets. Only one battleship, *Warspite*, had been modernised to the extent that it could match the Japanese. The cruiser situation was even more desperate, with only two relatively modern heavy cruisers — *Cornwall* and *Dorsetshire* — and a miscellany of four small, old, six-inch gun cruisers. The major strength of the Fleet lay (on paper) in the number of aircraft carriers, three of which had assembled by late March.

Of the carriers, *Indomitable* was the newest and largest in the Royal Navy. She had been intended to join *Prince of Wales* and *Repulse* at Singapore in late 1941, but an accident while working up in the West Indies had delayed her arrival in the Indian Ocean until the New Year. Proceeding to Aden to continue working-up, *Indomitable* had been ordered to disembark her Fulmar Squadron — 800 — and one of her two Albacore Squadrons — 827 — in order to make

Vildebeest II, HH-B of 273 Squadron over Ceylon. *(R.C.B. Ashworth via A. Thomas)*

room for the Hurricanes of 232 and 258 Squadrons, which were to be delivered to Java (see Volume One). For her own defence on passage, the carrier retained the nine Sea Hurricane IIBs of 880 Squadron and a dozen Albacores of 831 Squadron. Following an uneventful ferry trip, which had succeeded in flying off all the Hurricanes in two ranges on the 27 and 28 January, *Indomitable* returned to Aden to embark two more RAF Hurricane squadrons — 30 and 261, withdrawn from the Middle East Command to reinforce Java. By the time that they were on board and the ship about to leave, Java had been invaded, so their destination was changed to Ceylon.

Not until mid-March did *Indomitable* rejoin the Fleet, for she had to return to Aden first to collect her own squadrons. Although necessary, her time as a ferry carrier was wasted as far as the Fleet was concerned, for the training of her aircrews suffered while she was thus misemployed.

Hermes had been "east of Suez" for over a year, and her single squadron of Swordfish — 814 — was a thoroughly well-established unit, having taken part in the final operations against Italian Somaliland in early 1941, and then the Iraq campaign in May and June of that year. With only a dozen aircraft, her value was restricted, for she was unable to search, shadow and strike simultaneously; her complete lack of fighters was also a disadvantage.

Formidable, newly repaired after damage in the Mediterranean, did not leave the United Kingdom until mid-February, arriving at Colombo on 24 March. Her working-up had to be conducted during the fast passage out, and it was not an altogther happy process, as she had a large number of very inexperienced aircrew in her squadrons. By the time she joined the Fleet, her fighter unit — 888 Squadron equipped with 16 Martlet IIs — was reasonably well trained, but the two Albacore squadrons — 818 and 820 — had suffered a number of accidents and were barely ready for combat. Two of *Formidable*'s Martlets were flown to China Bay where four of the Naval pilots were to practice deck landings. One of these was Sub Lt Laurie Brander:

"I had joined 888 Squadron on the day before she left the UK, having never flown a Martlet or made a deck landing. It was essential for me to have some flights ashore before attempting the deck."

Indomitable's aircraft were few in number and their performance left something to be desired, when compared with those in Vice-Admiral Choichi Nagumo's Striking Force. Of the 37 fighters — 16 Martlet IIs, a dozen Fulmar IIs, and nine Sea Hurricanes — only the Martlets could be regarded as approaching an even match to the A6Ms. The Fulmars were at least as fast as the Sea Hurricanes at low levels, and were capable of taking on torpedo-bombers, but their advantage over the dive-bombers was marginal and their manoeuvre-ability was far inferior. The Sea Hurricanes were too few in number to be really effective, but their medium-level performance was such that they should have been able to break up approaching formations without suffering drastically at the hands of the escort. As none of the fighters had a high rate of climb, standing patrols would have to be maintained whenever there was a threat of air attack.

The search and strike aircraft were all biplanes — Swordfish and Albacores. The Royal Navy's air torpedo was a good, reliable, weapon and these aircraft could carry it up to 270 miles (in the case of the Albacore), but daylight attacks against opposition were out of the question. The Royal Navy's one clear advantage over the Japanese lay in the possession of radar, ship and airborne; the majority of the Albacores were equipped with Air-to-Surface Vessel (ASV) radar, enabling them to carry out night and bad weather searches and strikes. The Japanese, although partially 'night-qualified', had no such night search and strike potential and their ships had no form of reliable warning.

Vice-Admiral Sir James Somerville, who had built up a reputation for achieving much with little during his time as Flag Officer, Force 'H', in the Western Mediterranean, took command of the Eastern Fleet on 26 March. His Fleet was dispersed, with *Hermes* and *Warspite* at Trincomalee; *Formidable*, *Cornwall* and *Dorsetshire* at Colombo; *Indomitable* and the four old 'R'-class battleships at the new Fleet anchorage at Addu Atoll. No time had yet been found to weld this 'ad hoc' collection of ships into a fighting fleet, and the best course open to Vice-Admiral Somerville was the formation of two separate 'divisions' — one of the fast ships and the other of the slower units of limited value. The two armoured carriers, the two County-class cruisers, two very fast but elderly six-inch cruisers, six destroyers and the battleship *Warspite* made up Force 'A' under Somerville's own direct command. Force 'B' was very strong in theory, with four battleships, three cruisers (including the Dutch *Tromp*), eight destroyers and the one small aircraft carrier, but the heavy units were the least modern in the Royal Navy and, of the destroyers, only two were less then seven years old.

RAF reinforcements were also on their way with the setting-up of 222 Group in Ceylon, and the imminent delivery of the two fighter squadrons destined originally for Java, which as stated were diverted to this island when it became apparent that they would arrive at their original destination too late. Aircraft from both 30 and 261 Squadrons began flying off *Indomitable* on 6 March without undue difficulty. 20 of the former unit's fighters got into the air, but Sgt Whittaker, RNZAF, suffered a glycol leak and made a successful landing back on board the carrier. He did not receive quite the congratulatory welcome he was perhaps expecting, as it was pointed out that he was as close to Ceylon as to the ship when his trouble occurred, and it was suggested that his motives might have involved an element of exhibitionism! Later in the day the squadron got off its remaining six Hurricanes and, within two days, both units moved their Hurricane IIBs to their operational bases, 30 to Ratmalana, and 261 to join 273 Squadron at China Bay.

30 Squadron, commanded by Sqn Ldr G.F. Chater, DFC, had been operating for some months in the Western Desert as a night-fighter and intruder unit. It had equipped with Hurricanes after the campaigns in Greece and Crete ended in May 1941, having previously flown Blenheim IF fighters. The unit included a number of combat-experienced pilots, amongst them Flt Lt R.T.P. Davidson, a Canadian former Blenheim fighter pilot with three victories; Plt Off J.H. Whalen, another Canadian, and Flt Sgt T.G. Paxton, both of whom also had three victories, the former having claimed his over Northern Europe, the latter in the Middle East.

261 Squadron, which had been formed for the defence of Malta in late 1940, included on its establishment a number of former instructors who had flown fighter aircraft over Iraq and Syria during May and June 1941 with 'X' Flight. Apart from a brief period of operations, during the occupation of the Iranian oilfields in August, no further action had been seen since. The commanding officer was Sqn Ldr A.G. Lewis, DFC and Bar, a South African who had fought with great distinction in the Battles of France and Britain during 1940, and had been credited with 18 victories, 11 of them in just two days. He had then been shot down and badly burned, and had only just returned to a front line unit, joining 261 Squadron as it was about to go aboard *Indomitable*. On his first attempt to take off from the carrier, he had suffered an immediate engine over-heating:

> "I explained the situation on the R/T and Commander Flying suggested trying to land back on deck. The carrier was turned into wind, and 'Full Speed Ahead' ordered, achieving a slipstream of about 40 mph over the deck.
>
> "I was told to bring the Hurricane in as slowly as possible, about 80-85 mph, to a position astern of the deck, just above, and to motor her in, touching down as near the edge of the deck as possible. Having no arrester gear, I would have to rely on my brakes and the crash-barrier cables.
>
> "Somehow we touched down OK — brakes worked overtime — and we rolled to a stop, halfway up the deck. A very relieved and grateful young man climbed out of the cockpit. Needless to say, the Navy was glad to have an extra Hurricane on its strength."

After suitable refreshment, and the awarding of a specially prepared 'Line-shooting Certificate', he took off again in the same aircraft — Z4961 — and reached Ceylon without more ado. 261 Squadron was organized into three flights — 'A' under the command of Flt Lt R.B. Cleaver (who had flown with 'X' Flight in Iraq and Syria), 'B' under Flt Lt David Fulford, DFC (who had at least two victories to his credit) and 'C' (the training flight) under Flt Lt Eric Edsall, DFC, a Battle of Britain veteran with at least three victories.

Soon after arrival, Sqn Ldr Lewis was ordered to find a suitable flat piece of land which could be used as a satellite strip, and was offered a flight in one of Trincomalee's Swordfish from which to reconnoitre the area. Accompanied by one of his flight commanders, Flt Lt Fulford, and with Flt Lt John Chamberlain, a Staff pilot, at the controls, the biplane set out to survey the coastal strip

Sqn Ldr A.G. Lewis, DFC & Bar (lower) and Flt Lt D. Fulford, DFC, two experienced pilots of 261 Squadron. *(Wg Cdr A.G. Lewis)*

Pilots of 261 Squadron in front of one of their Hurricanes. Left to right, standing: Sgt G.A. Walker, Flt Sgt C.J. Gauthier, RCAF, Sgt Richmond, Sgt Buchan, Sgt Patterson, Flt Sgt J.D. Martin, Sgt Thompsett, Plt Off A.L.D. St Aubin, RCAF, Sgt P.L. Jordon, RNZAF, Wt Off J.J. Griffin. Front: Sgt Galloway, Flt Lt R.B. Cleaver, Plt Off Kershaw, Flt Sgt T.A. Quinn, Flg Off J.V. Marshall (behind), Sgt Harrison, Sgt K.A.S. Mann, RAAF. *(P.L. Jordan)*

between Mullaittivu and Jaffna Straits. Having made a couple of landings at prospective sites, Chamberlain decided to show his passengers what the old biplane could do, as Lewis recalled:

> "We were told to hang on, as we would simulate a dive-bombing attack. The 'old girl' shuddered and shook and, as we went into the second dive, I shouted above the noise: 'Will she take it?'
>
> "Chamberlain grinned and gave the thumbs up sign, but this time as we pulled out of the dive, there was a shudder and a lurch and two cylinders flew off, the conrods flopping about in a rather comical way.

Nevertheless, Chamberlain was able to throttle back and then glided down to a stretch of beach along the shore. A number of large rocks made the area less than suitable for a forced landing, and the Swordfish turned over on its back as it collided with these; Lewis continued:

> "Fulford and I had released our harnesses in the rear cockpit so, as the 'old girl' whipped over on her back, we were flung out into the surf. For one dread moment I thought I was drowning, but as the surf receded I found myself sitting up in about two to three feet of water, and felt silly.
>
> "Several yards away in a little deeper water, and still strapped in, Chamberlain hung upside down, getting redder in the face every minute. Fulford and I released the harness, and one very irate pilot fell into the water on his head."

All three, none the worse for the experience, were conveyed back to Trincomalee by various means, including ox cart, having spent the night at a nearby Government resthouse. A few days later Sqn Ldr Lewis was obliged to force land his Hurricane (BE328) in a paddy field, having run out of fuel when caught up in a violent storm; although he was knocked unconscious, he quickly recovered and was not seriously hurt.

Other opportunities had also been taken to strengthen the defences at this time and, on 1 March, a new fighter unit was formed at Ratmalana. It was known initially as 'K' Squadron. Sqn Ldr Peter Fletcher, a Rhodesian, who had arrived from Karachi with the Hurricane detachment a few weeks earlier, took command of the new unit, although six of those who had accompanied him from Karachi would be released to continue their travels eastwards to Burma. A number of pilots who had flown off *Indomitable* were posted in. These included Flt Lts Spencer Peacock-Edwards, Aubrey McFadden and James Lockhart — all Battle of Britain veterans — and three sergeant pilots; Lockhart, who had dropped rank to return to operations, had served with 80 Squadron during the Syrian Campaign of the previous year, whilst Peacock-Edwards had served on Malta (with 261 Squadron) and, at this time, had four confirmed victories to his credit.

Hurricane IIBs of 258 Squadron over Ceylon. *(Sqn Ldr A.H. Milnes)*

On 7 March a group of pilots from the now-defunct 258 Squadron, who had been evacuated from Java on the *Kota Gede*, began disembarking at Colombo. These were: Flt Lt Denis Sharp, Flg Off Ting Macnamara, Plt Offs Charles Campbell-White, Teddy Tremlett, Ambrose Milnes, Art Brown, Doug Nicholls and Jock McCulloch, and Sgts Duncan Caldwell and Art Sheerin, who were posted to K Squadron. 222 Group changed the title of K Squadron to 131 Squadron on 14 March, but it was swiftly discovered that this number had just been allocated to a Spitfire squadron in England. Consequently, on the 22nd, it became 'G' Squadron, but on the 30th was renumbered 258! This was mainly at the behest of newly-promoted Wg Cdr James Thomson, commander of the original 258 Squadron, who had also reached Ceylon and had just become Station Commander at Racecourse airfield, to which base the unit had moved on the 23rd. Fletcher remained in command of the unit, which received ten Hurricane IIBs and seven Hurricane Is as flying equipment.

Meanwhile two further units had arrived. On 15 March, 14 Blenheim IVs of 11 Squadron touched down at Ratamalana, having flown from the Western Desert via India, under the leadership of Wg Cdr A.J.M. Smyth, DFC. Then, on the 28th, the first of six Catalinas of 413 Squadron, RCAF, arrived at Koggala (a small lake on the south coast, eight miles from Galle) from the United Kingdom, to join others already based there — mostly unserviceable aircraft. These formed a composite unit comprising three aircraft from 240

Squadron, which had arrived earlier in the month from the Middle East, one from 202 Squadron and a survivor (Z2144/R) of 205 Squadron from Singapore; additionally, four Dutch machines — Y-55, Y-56 and Y-57 of GVT-16, and Y-64 of GVT-2 — which had escaped from Java, were at China Bay, although all were in poor condition.

On 24 March more Fulmars began arriving at China Bay for 273 Squadron, the first batch being flown in from RNAS Cochin — an aerodrome on the south-west coast of the mainland — by FAA pilots, led by Lt P.E.I. Bailey. Most of these pilots had served with 808 Squadron, but were now 'homeless' following the loss of their aircraft carrier, *Ark Royal*, in the Mediterranean the previous November; on arrival at China Bay the Naval pilots were attached to 273 Squadron. The Fulmars had been delivered to Cochin in crates, aboard the transport *Engadine*, and had been closely followed by the arrival from Karachi of Cdr Robin Kilroy, piloting another Fulmar, who had been instructed to supervise the assembling and testing of these fighters. Bailey recalled:

> "I had just finished assembling and testing some Fulmars. These were not the world's best fighters and my recollection is that the RAF pilots of 273 Squadron were not that keen to fly them against what we were certain would be 'Zeros'.
>
> "Anyway, I had arrived ex-*Ark Royal* with a number of pilots from that ship, and we were sent to China Bay where we were attached to 273 Squadron. I recall two very sporting RAF (ex-Army) pilots who remained with us."

With the arrival of further Fulmars, 273 Squadron had a total of 16 of these fighters on hand, ostensibly under the command of Flt Lt R.M. Pimm but, as this unit now had a larger proportion of Naval aircrew than of RAF personnel, Lt Bailey was effectively in charge.

Thus, the beginning of April found Ceylon greatly reinforced in a period of just one month. The Hurricane IIBs were reasonably competent to handle the opposition, but only a handful of the pilots could be considered to have any depth of operational experience, and some had none at all. The Fulmars could not be expected to cope with modern fighter opposition but, given the chance, would be able to deal with most bombers they were likely to meet with a reasonable chance of success; the experience of their pilots was generally comparable with that of the members of the Hurricane squadrons. So far as the bombers were concerned, a number of the Blenheim crews had adequate recent experience of bombing land targets in the Western Desert, but had received no training nor any experience in attacking shipping.

Training continued apace, the fighter pilots all being eager to learn what they could from their colleagues in 258 Squadron who had been evacuated from Java. The story got around that, due to its light construction, the 'Zero' would break up in flight if it tried to follow a Hurricane in a pull-out from a fast dive — this in fact probably stemmed from the experiences of the Hurricane pilots in Sumatra with the JAAF's Ki 43s.

One young Australian pilot in 261 Squadron, Sgt K.A.S. Mann, attempted a terminal velocity dive in his Hurricane as a practice for this tactic, but the gravity force in the pull-out unlocked the retracted undercarriage of his aircraft and tore one wheel off; as a result he crash-landed. The Station Commander, Grp Capt G.V. Howard, demanded that Sqn Ldr Lewis "make an example of the man, that is what is needed" — in other words, a Court Martial. Lewis was reluctant, having already severely reprimanded the pilot, as to put him under close arrest would prevent both the pilot and his escorting officer from carrying out further training, at a time when this was essential. Lewis therefore allowed the matter to slide a bit, a course of action which was almost his undoing, as will be related later.

In the event the reinforcement of the island with a proper air defence had occurred only just in time. Only two days after Vice-Admiral Somerville had taken up his new command, he was informed that Intelligence sources had received warning of an imminent attack on Ceylon by Japanese naval forces — two or more carriers, with cruiser and destroyer support, plus the possible addition of fast battleships. According to the same source, the attack would probably take place on 1 April. Somerville's forces were divided between Addu Atoll, in the Maldive Islands, and Colombo, with four ships at Trincomalee. Addu, 690 statute miles to the south-west of Colombo, was a recently developed Fleet anchorage, used for replenishment. Preparations were being made for the construction of a naval air station on Gan Island, where the anchorage was virtually submarine-proof. Addu's greatest security lay in the fact that the Japanese were completely unaware that it was in use by the Eastern Fleet, and indeed remained ignorant of its existence until long after the crisis had passed.

In the light of the threat of a Japanese foray into the Indian Ocean, the Admiralty ordered that the main ports — Calcutta, Madras, Trincomalee and Colombo — should be cleared of as much shipping as possible. At Calcutta alone there was in excess of 250,000 tons of merchant shipping, many of these ships having fled Singapore and Rangoon. Although more than 70 vessels departed Calcutta, some of these later fell foul of air and seaborne attacks. The first of these to be attacked was the 9,415-ton *Glenshiel*, on her way to Australia with 100 passengers embarked. Although hit by two torpedoes fired by the submarine *I-7*, all her crew and passengers were able to take to lifeboats, from which they were rescued by the destroyer *Fortune* a few hours later.

The Japanese General Staff had decided upon a raid into the Indian Ocean with the intention of neutralising any Allied fleet capable of staging a damaging attack on the barely-consolidated bases along the Malay Barrier, or of joining up with the US Pacific Fleet to the east of Australia. The idea of an invasion of Ceylon was never seriously entertained. A secondary purpose in this operation was the disruption of supply shipping in the Bay of Bengal. Reinforcements and supplies for the British forces which, together with the Chinese, were holding the Japanese 15th Army between Rangoon and Mandalay in Burma, were passing through the ports of Calcutta, Chittagang and Akyab. Although the Japanese were to break through the Prome-Toungoo line before the end of March (see Chapter 9), the ability of the Allied armies to reform and consolidate new defensive lines would depend very much upon the continuance of uninterrupted supplies, brought in in large quantities by sea.

Beyond this, the presence of a strong British naval force in the Indian Ocean posed a threat to Japanese convoys carrying supplies to the newly-captured port of Rangoon. The intention of the Japanese was therefore to deliver a crushing blow to the main base at Ceylon in similar manner to those administered at Pearl Harbor and Port Darwin. These moves would have the double advantage of demonstrating to the Indian population the might of Japan, and of persuading them to continue with the campaign of civil disobedience, sabotage and open hostility which was at this time plaguing the British authorities.

After a two-week break for training, Vice-Admiral Nagumo's Strike Force again sailed — on 26 March — passing through the gap between Timor and the southernmost tip of the Javanese islands, and heading almost due west until the afternoon of the 30th. It then altered course to the north-west, heading straight for Ceylon. The Strike Force now included five large carriers, *Akagi, Soryu, Hiryu, Shokaku* and *Zuikaku*, the 3rd Battle Squadron with four fast battleships of the *Kongo* class, the 8th Cruiser Squadron with two heavy cruisers, and a flotilla of 11 destroyers, led by the light cruiser *Abukama*. Oilers and supply vessels were to rendezvous with the fleet as necessary for refuelling and revictualling, while seven submarines were to operate in the Bay of Bengal in support of this force. In gun power, there was little to choose between the Japanese fleet — known for this operation as Nagumo Force — and the Royal Navy's Eastern Fleet, the greater speed of the former being countered by the larger numbers and the technical (radar) superiority in a number of the latter's ships. The carriers, however, were the decisive factor in the Japanese force.

Other Japanese warships were also in the area; Vice-Admiral Jisaburo Ozawa's Malaya Force was cruising off the Andaman Islands, where it had been supporting Japanese landings and, on 1 April, this force set out to prey on shipping in the Bay of Bengal, while the main attack was underway. This smaller fleet comprised the light fleet carrier *Ryujo*, the heavy cruisers *Chokai, Kumano, Suzuya, Mikuma* and *Mogami*, the light cruiser *Yura*, and four destroyers. As already recorded, *Ryujo*, the flagship of the 4th Carrier Division, had taken part in several amphibious assaults in the Philippines and East Indies, providing close support and protection for the troops and shipping. During the break from operations, her fighter unit's A5M fighters had been replaced by A6Ms. The dozen fighters were complemented by 15 B5Ns, which had bombed shore and sea targets, but not delivered any torpedo attacks as yet, nor had the chance of any intensive training in this demanding role.

As a preliminary to the dual thrust into the Bay of Bengal, Japanese forces from Burma had landed in the Andamans (as mentioned above) on 23 March, and had swiftly captured Port Blair. The Toko Kokutai — nominally 24 H6Ks, but in fact only 15-18 aircraft strong — moved to Port Blair from Sabang, Sumatra, on the 26th, and began flying long-range patrols, the main purpose of which was to protect the Japanese convoys between Singapore and Rangoon. Offensively, the flyingboats could patrol at distances up to 700 miles from base — 85 miles short of Trincomalee — while their ability to strike as far away as Akyab, 500 miles to the north, was demonstrated as early as the 28th, when a single H6K bombed (but missed) a troop transport 150 miles to the west of that port. Next day a second vessel was attacked near Ceylon, when a direct hit was claimed.

With the presence of this reconnaissance/bombing force at Port Blair now revealed, Allied air attack was feared and a number of A6M fighters from the 22nd Air Flotilla Fighter Group were moved from Bangkok, Thailand, to Mingaladon, Burma, beginning defensive patrols over Port Blair from the 30 March. At about the same time, regular reconnaissance sorties were started over the Andamans by Hudsons of 139 Squadron from India, staging through Akyab to reach the area. On 1 April three H6Ks flew the 700 nautical miles from Port Blair to Ceylon, to carry out their first reconnaissance of the approaches to the island.

Aware that the Japanese Fleet was approaching, Vice-Admiral Somerville instituted a search for it at once but, bearing in mind the vulnerability of his strike aircraft in a daylight attack, he carefully kept his distance. He hoped to discover the Japanese at sufficient range to prevent an immediate attack on his own vessels and allow him, when darkness fell, to launch a strike and to withdraw before morning. Two days of fruitless search eventually led Somerville to believe that Nagumo had abandoned the sortie and withdrawn, so he decided to return to Addu Atoll. His optimism was to go unrewarded however, for no such Japanese withdrawal had occurred!

During the morning of 2 April, three H6Ks from Port Blair had repeated the long mission to the Ceylon area, encountering two merchant vessels 20 miles from the Indian coast, one of an estimated 10,000 tons and the other of about 8,000 tons, both of which were claimed damaged by near misses. One of the vessels was the 7,748-ton *Orestes*, southwards-bound from Madras, which reported being attacked three times by a four-engined aircraft; the ship's 12-pounder gun succeeded in keeping the attacker at a distance and she escaped damage. Next day the crews of three more of these flyingboats reported sighting 13 ships anchored off the Ganges Delta and attacked these, claiming a 20,000 ton vessel sunk and two smaller ones damaged; in fact, little damage was inflicted on this occasion.

During the night of 2nd/3rd, two B-17s and one LB-30 of the US 7th Bomb Group flew from India to attack Port Blair, as detailed in Chapter 9.

During the morning of the 4th, a lone H6K was sent to reconnoitre Trincomalee harbour, the crew reporting the presence of eight merchant vessels and a destroyer. On this same date 18 Genzan Ku G3Ms, together with 18 A6M fighters and one reconnaissance C5M of the 22nd Air Flotilla Fighter Group, moved forwards to Mingaladon from Thailand, to begin operations in support of the Nagumo Force.

In the early hours of the morning of the 4th, AJ155 QL-A of 413 Squadron, piloted by Sqn Ldr L.J. Birchall, RCAF, who had arrived at Ceylon only 48 hours earlier, took off to search. Throughout the day the lookouts looked for signs of the elusive Japanese vessels then, at about 1600, when 350 miles to the south-east, they were sighted; Birchall subsequently recalled:

> "As we got close enough to identify the lead ships, we knew at once what we were into, but the closer we got the more ships appeared, and so it was necessary to keep going until we could count and identify them all. By the time we did this there was very little chance left."

The slow, lumbering flyingboat was soon spotted by the air patrol, three A6Ms each from *Akagi* and *Zuikaku* plus six more from *Hiryu*, giving chase; Birchall continued:

> "All we could do was to put the nose down and go full out, about 150 knots. We immediately coded a message and started transmission — we were halfway through our required third transmission when a shell destroyed our wireless equipment and seriously injured the operator; we were now under constant attack.
>
> "Shells set fire to our internal tanks. We managed to get the fire out and then another started; the aircraft started to break up. Due to our low altitude it was impossible to bale out, but I got the aircraft down on the water before the tail fell off."

The one-sided fight lasted just seven minutes; the A6Ms continued to strafe the wreck, seriously wounding the front turret gunner — Sgt J. Henzell — before he could vacate his post. He was lost when the aircraft sank, also taking with it the badly wounded WOp/AG, Sgt L.A. Calorossi, RCAF. As the survivors swam away from the burning fuel which had spread out over the water, bullets struck and killed the other WOp/AG, Sgt I.N. Davidson, RCAF. The six survivors — all wounded, three seriously — were eventually picked up by the destroyer *Isokaze*.

In Ceylon meantime, Birchall's signal had been picked up but was not entirely understood. Requests to amplify brought no replies and, under the impression that invasion was imminent the defences were alerted. Following receipt of this report, all shipping in harbour at Colombo and Trincomalee, including the aircraft carrier *Hermes* (her Swordfish remaining at China Bay), was ordered to scatter; up to 48 vessels of all sizes departed with much haste to the west and north-west of the island. Two of the vessels which had put to sea from Colombo, the cruisers *Dorsetshire* and *Cornwall*, steamed south-west to rejoin the Eastern Fleet 600 miles away at Addu, where Somerville, on receipt of the news, was raising steam with all speed. At Colombo 21 merchant ships and 13 Royal Naval vessels were unable to sail in time and were to remain to weather the impending storm.

Sunday, 5 April

Dawn on the 5th — Easter Sunday — thus found the defences fully alerted and ready to repel an expected invasion; at 0600 the Nagumo Force carriers began launching aircraft for a strike on Colombo from 120 miles out to sea. The formation which set course for the target comprised 53 B5Ns loaded with bombs (18 from *Soryu*, 18 from *Hiryu* and 17 from *Akagi*) led by Cdr Mitsuo Fuchida, who flew as an observer in Lt Mitsuo Matsuzaki's aircraft, 38 D3As (19 each from *Shokaku* and *Zuikaku*) led by Lt Cdr Kakuichi Takahashi, together with an escort of 36 A6Ms under the overall command of Lt Cdr Shigeru Itaya, who personally led nine aircraft from *Akagi*; other sections of fighters were led by *Soryu*'s Lt Iyozo Fujita and *Hiryu*'s Lt Sumio Nono, with a further nine from *Zuikaku* under Lt Masatoshi Makino.

Meanwhile, further Catalinas had been despatched to shadow the force, one of these establishing contact with a battleship and two cruisers at 0648, while a second was to report two battleships, two cruisers and a number of destroyers at 0830; no aircraft carriers were reported.

The A6Ms were first to arrive at 0732, the *Hiryu* element encountering a formation of six Swordfish of 788 Squadron, in two flights of three, one led by Lt Stephen Longsdon in V4413, the other by Lt Cyril Pountney in (possibly)

Pilots of *Zuikaku's* Fighter Unit seen here early in December 1941; most of the same men were involved in operations over Ceylon. Second row, second from left: Lt Yuzo Tsukamoto; third from left: Lt Masatoshi Makino; third from right: Lt Masao Sato, the unit commander; far right: NAP 2/C Tetsuzo Iwamoto. *(Sei-ichi Tsukuda)*

V4412. Only the leaders' aircraft carried observers, although each had an air gunner on board. The Swordfish had been ordered to leave China Bay and were flying to Ratmalana when they were attacked over Colombo.

When the fighters approached they were assumed to be Hurricanes and a recognition signal (two green stars) was fired by Sub Lt P.A. Meakin's TAG (N/Air George Skingley), whilst the letter of the day was flashed by Longsdon's observer, Sub Lt N.R. MacKay. The other flight leader, Lt Pountney, in fact, reported being attacked by "a Hurricane with a large red dot painted on the wings and fuselage." Although Pountney throttled back and did a very tight turn, the Japanese pilot was able to get in a telling burst, severely wounding the TAG, Pty Off(A) John Hall, shell splinters hitting both Pountney (in the left leg) and his observer, Sub Lt George Creese, in the left arm. The Swordfish glided down on to the edge of the beach and turned over, spilling its occupants into the sea. The wounded Hall, whose leg had been almost severed by a cannon shell, was dragged on to the beach. Despite the application of a tourniquet, he had lost too much blood and died shortly afterwards.

Longsdon's aircraft crashed upside down into a paddy field after the pilot had been badly wounded in the face, although his observer (MacKay) and TAG, Pty Off(A) Jock Heath, were only slightly hurt. Heath had previously been shot down whilst flying in a 205 Squadron Catalina from Singapore (see Volume One, Chapter 4); allegedly his once black beard was now streaked with white! The aircraft flown by Sub Lt Anthony Beale (possibly V4371) — who had been awarded a DSC for his attack on the German pocket battleship *Bismarck* the previous year — crashed into the sea, Beale and his TAG, L/Air Fred Edwards, losing their lives. Edwards had managed to bale out but was apparently machine-gunned during the descent, his bullet-ridden body later being recovered from the water. A further machine (possibly V4379) was forced to ditch in the sea, Lt David Carter and his badly wounded TAG, L/Air David Bolton, taking to their dinghy; sadly, Bolton died before they reached land.

Meanwhile, Sub Lt Meakin crash-landed his damaged machine (possibly V4397) on a beach, he and his TAG scrambling clear, only to be strafed by an A6M. Skingley was killed while Meakin was seriously wounded in the ankle, necessitating the amputation of his foot. The sixth Swordfish (possibly V4398) tried to force-land in the jungle, but its torpedo exploded, killing Sub Lt Charles Shaw and injuring the observer/air gunner, Sub Lt I.E. Cope. Thus, in the space of a few minutes, all six Swordfish had been shot down although the victorious Japanese pilots slightly overestimated their success, claiming eight biplanes in this engagement.

While this one-sided action was in progress, 21 Hurricane IIBs of 30 Squadron, nine Mark IIBs and five Mark Is of 258 Squadron, plus six Fulmars — three each from 803 and 806 Squadrons — were scrambling as hard as they could from Ratmalana and Racecourse. The latter airfield was not initially attacked but, at the former, the last four Hurricanes of 30 Squadron were still taxying when the first D3As from the *Zuikaku* contingent dived to the attack; one Hurricane was damaged by bomb blast which prevented it from taking off. Other pilots, for whom no aircraft were available, opened fire with Thompson sub-machine guns in support of the airfield defence Bofors crews. At Ratmalana, L/Air Bert Holt of 803 Squadron was 'Duty TAG' in the Ops Room — a thatched hut — and recalled:

"At about 0740 a large number of planes came over from the seaward side — the ones I saw seemed to be Navy 97s and 'Zeros', flying in V formation. At the same time the phone rang — it was the RAF asking if we knew of any carriers sending off aircraft. I answered: 'Yes, Japs! Get your bods airborne!' I then ran outside, screaming as loud as possible: 'Scramble! Scramble!' I don't suppose anyone knew who gave that alarm. The most vivid thing I remember then was a sub lieutenant, towel in hand and wearing only his black beard, belting out of the showers, heading for his flying gear.

"I ran into the Ops Room, grabbed my pads and other gear, then to the parachute store looking for my chute, which was missing. Someone else, no doubt, had it so I grabbed another, but by this time everyone else was on the jeep, and it was moving out; I was left behind.

"Getting the armoury open, I took one of the Vickers 'K' guns, which had only just arrived the week before, and mounted it on top of a mound, but then along came Sub Lt Peck, who took over the gun! When I pointed to a Jap coming low over the trees, he fired, but only three shots as the pans had not been wound up.

"One of the RAF Hurricanes piloted by Sgt Davies (Sgt R.L. Davies of 30 Squadron) shot down a Jap crossing the end of the field, before he had retracted his wheels."

The leader of the 803 Squadron section, Sub Lt W.H. Anderson, later recalled:

"Just as we reached the airfield perimeter by truck, the second wave of aircraft were arriving at a much lower height, dropping what appeared to be enormous bombs (which were, in fact, long-range fuel tanks made of papier-mâché), strafing the airfield, and taking an incredible toll of the Hurricanes as they scrambled ahead of us.

"One of the only TAGs (N/Air Fred Johnson) to reach the airfield in time for the scramble, jumped into the back of my Fulmar and used the only weapon available — a Very pistol and cartridges — to frighten off any Jap getting a bit too close!"

Anderson's two companions were immediately pursued as they climbed away from the airfield, Sub Lt Ian White-Smith's Fulmar (possibly DR705) diving into the sea while Sub Lt A.S. Diggens — who had fought against the Italians in the Desert (where he had been credited with shooting down a Fiat G.50 fighter) — crashed into the jungle; he too was killed; his body was later recovered from the wreck of DR729. The 806 Squadron section was marginally more successful, although Sub Lt K.J.M. Pettitt (possibly flying X8569) was also shot down and killed, his Fulmar seen to dive in flames into the jungle. Lt Mike Hordern, the section leader, recalled:

"We were caught on the ground for a start, and not many of us even got airborne. A Petty Officer with a sub-machine gun leapt in the back of my aircraft and I believe even fired it with wild abandon!

"I was on my own and saw a number of enemy aircraft circling over the sea — possibly reforming or in defensive orbit against some other aircraft. I approached through broken cloud cover, at about 5,000 feet, and made one pass before breaking off at high speed and seeing one aircraft burning on the surface of the sea.

"I was credited with one Navy 96 (sic) shot down — seen and confirmed by a Naval officer standing outside the Mount Lavinia Hotel."

The third Fulmar (possibly X8640) of the section, flown by Sub Lt John Sykes, was also shot down:

"Having seen some of our boys getting into trouble almost immediately on take-off, I thought I would do a quick, tight circuit and protect anybody who was still on the ground or in the process of getting airborne.

"This wasn't such a bright idea — I was jumped by two Nips who got on with the business of shooting me down. I was frightened, bloody frightened. Tracer bullets were hammering me from the rear, the instrument panel shattered, the right-hand side of my head — by my right eye — was blistered by a tracer which came a bit too close, and the controls of the Fulmar stiffened.

"If I cried out to God, would He hear? I cried out. I heard later that the gunners, entrenched round the airfield, shot the first Nip out of the sky. The second Nip got through their fire, but by this time I was heading for a paddy field.

"I came to a halt in the mud in the middle of the field, and was unstrapped and out of the aircraft in a matter of seconds! There was the roar of an engine. I looked up. There was this Nippon bastard coming to finish me off whilst I was up to my knees in mud! Bullet holes all round me but nothing hit me! I ran, or tried to run, for the side of the field.

"My enemy came back three times. There were bullet holes in the mud all round my foot prints, but I did not even get a scratch."

A few minutes after the initial attack by the *Zuikaku* D3As and *Hiryu*'s A6Ms began, *Soryu*'s and *Akagi*'s fighters joined the fight, and at 0750 *Shokaku*'s' D3As started their attack. The Fulmars' attackers included A6Ms from *Soryu*, their leader, Lt Fujita, personally claiming one shot down. 30 Squadron was never able to form up and became involved in a number of confused dogfights, but 258 Squadron did manage to join formation and reach the harbour, just as one of the formations of D3As went into their dive (probably *Shokaku*'s aircraft); the Hurricanes pressed home an attack for as long as possible, but were then badly bounced, probably by the *Hiryu* fighters.

Reported Sqn Ldr Fletcher:

"Having received no warning and finding the enemy aircraft overhead we took off, and climbed for the harbour as being the most likely point of enemy attack.

"When we arrived we found that the bombers had commenced their attack, and there was a strong force of enemy fighters as a top cover, and considerably above my formation. I decided to attack the bombers in the hope that it would impair the efficiency of the enemy attack, realising that this would put the enemy fighters in a strong position.

"We continued to attack the bombers for as long a period as possible though this resulted in rather heavy losses inflicted by the enemy fighters. I should like to stress that the AA fire continued in spite of our presence directly overhead".

Fletcher claimed one D3A shot down but his Hurricane (Z5680 ZT-A) was then hit by fire from the ground; he was subsequently attacked by an A6M and baled out of his blazing aircraft, covered in oil and punctured by pieces of shrapnel.

Meanwhile, Flt Lt Sharp (Z4247) and Plt Off Campbell-White were each credited with D3As destroyed, Sharp also claiming one damaged; his own aircraft was then hit and damaged by escorting A6Ms. Other dive-bombers were credited as damaged by Plt Offs Brown and Nicholls. Reported the latter:

"I was scrambling with the squadron, and once again warning was given when the enemy was almost overhead. Over the harbour I became involved with two enemy fighters and a light bomber (*a B5N*) and eventually claimed the bomber as destroyed (*although this was apparently only credited as damaged*). It was extremely unwise to mix it with 'Zero' fighters at low altitude and I had to break away from the main centre of the activity to gain height and come in at the top again.

"By this time the action had developed into a series of quick diving attacks as the Japanese force retreated out to sea."

The rest of the squadron was very badly hit, and altogether nine aircraft failed to return to base, of which two force-landed with Category II damage. Of the five which did land at 0835, two were damaged, one seriously. Flt Lt Peacock-Edwards (Z5461 ZT-B) had also been brought down after personally shooting down a D3A and probably destroying an A6M:

"We scrambled furiously and I climbed right up after them, catching them up over the sea just as they were turning back towards the harbour. I went down after them and got one from behind in the middle of the dive.

"Then their fighters, who must have been waiting up above them, came tearing down and tracer began to fly uncomfortably close round my cockpit.

"I had to give up chasing the bombers and tried to fight the Navy 'Zeros'. There wasn't much future in that, but I managed to get one of them which came straight at me and didn't seem able or willing to give way.

"Then several of them hung on to me and I was hit all over the place. So I had to come down to ground level and, with my engine gone, did a belly-landing in a paddy field outside Colombo. Both the wings came off, but I was all right, though I didn't get out until the 'Zeros' had cleared off."

Plt Off Doug Nicholls of 258 Squadron with his Hurricane. *(Sqn Ldr D.B.F. Nicholls)*

Apart from Fletcher and Peacock-Edwards (who suffered no more than a cut eye in the crash), other casualties included the experienced Flt Lt James

Left: Flt Lt Teddy Peacock-Edwards of 258 Squadron. *(Sqn Ldr A.H. Milnes)*. Right: Plt Off Ambrose Milnes of 258 Squadron views the remains of Flt Lt Teddy Peacock-Edwards' Hurricane, Z5461 ZT-B, following his crash-landing near Colombo on 5 April. *(Sqn Ldr A.H. Milnes)*

Lockhart, who was killed when BD701 crashed on the island, and Flt Lt Aubrey McFadden, who perished when Z5665 plunged into the sea. Three others were killed when their Hurricanes crashed on land — Plt Offs Teddy Tremlett (Z4227) and Robert Neill, RAAF (Z7711) together with Sgt Ray Thain (Z5385), the latter having been seen to damage a dive-bomber before being shot down himself.

Plt Off Milnes' aircraft, an old Mark I (Z4372), was also badly damaged, as were those flown by Sgt L.P. Gavin, RNZAF, (in Z4983, also a Mark I) and Sgt K.W. Morehouse, RCAF, (BG696); none of these three pilots were hurt. Both Sqn Ldr Fletcher and Flt Lt Peacock-Edwards were subsequently awarded DFCs, mainly for their involvement in the action of this day.

Meanwhile, 30 Squadron's fighters from Ratmalana fought on, not returning until 0900. By this time Plt Off Jimmy Whalen (flying BG827 RS-W) had claimed three D3As and Flt Lt Bob Davidson a D3A and an A6M, both pilots returning unscathed, while Plt Off Alan Wagner also returned safely, jubilantly claiming two further bombers shot down. Another Canadian, Plt Off D.A. McDonald, claimed a bomber — later confirmed by Flt Sgt Paxton — but he was then attacked by an A6M and his Hurricane badly damaged, both by this and by fire from the ground defences. Paxton reported shooting the fighter off his tail, McDonald then crash-landing on an area of grass in front of the Galle Face Hotel. Apparently he strolled into the hotel only to be refused a drink as all the waiters had fled, and because "the bar wasn't open at that time!"

Paxton meanwhile, claimed a second aircraft shot down, but was then forced to bale out at 1,600 feet from his flaming Hurricane and landed in a tree, being removed at once to hospital with second degree burns. Plt Off Garth Caswell, an Australian, made three dives through the bomber formation, colleagues reporting that he shot down two, but was then killed during his third attack, his Hurricane (BG795 RS-N) crashing on the island; Plt Off H.K. Cartwright was jumped by a fighter immediately after take-off, although he escaped to make a crash-landing, but hit a tree, totally writing off his aircraft and receiving slight injuries.

Plt Off Jimmy Whalen, RCAF, walks away from his Hurricane IIB, BG827 RS-W, of 30 Squadron. This pilot claimed three dive-bombers shot down on 5 April. *(Public Archives of Canada)*

Four other pilots failed to return; Flg Off Tom Allison (BM910) was taken to hospital having baled out with a bullet in his neck, but claimed to have shot down two aircraft. An officer of the Ceylon Light Infantry reported seeing Sgt A.J. Browne shoot down one before the Australian pilot was attacked by an A6M, following which his Hurricane (Z5447) dived in flames into a paddy field whilst his victim crashed at Horana, south-east of Ratmalana. Plt Off Don Geffene (BE352), an American, and Flt Sgt Louis Ovens, DFM, were both later found dead in the wreckage of their aircraft, the former near Ratmalana, while the latter had crashed into a small reservoir on the road to Kandy.

While the battle between the RAF fighters and the D3As and their escorting A6Ms was raging, the B5Ns appeared overhead, those from *Soryu* arriving first at 0756, followed by *Hiryu* aircraft at 0805 and those from *Akagi* at 0808: they were escorted by the fighters from *Zuikaku*. The first two formations suffered a total of five bombers damaged, but the final flight and the fighters saw no opposing aircraft and suffered no loss or damage; they had all left the area by 0815. By this time only *Shokaku*'s D3As had gone, having completed their attack of 0750 in three minutes and beaten a swift retreat. The A6Ms, and the last D3As of *Zuikaku*'s contingent, withdrew between 0920 and 0935.

As the Japanese formations returned to their carriers, a flight of Fulmars from 803 Squadron returned from patrol, the crews unaware of the assault on their airfield; recalled Observer Sub Lt Roy Hinton:

"We had flown down the coast at 2,000 feet to Bentota, a distance of about 30 miles, and directly across the island to Batticalo, and were on our way back for breakfast.

"About 20 minutes flying time from base we saw a number of aircraft flying out to sea. Although all aircraft were fitted with radio, no signals whatsoever were received of impending trouble. Japanese aircraft were farthest from our minds on the return flight that morning, and we dismissed the aircraft seen by thinking they were another unscheduled FAA flight.

"Arriving back at base it was so obvious that all hell had been let loose only minutes before. It transpired that all the wireless operators at Ratmalana had sought shelter as soon as the first bombs were dropped."

Japanese fighter pilots claimed a total of 33 RAF fighters shot down plus 11 probables, to which must be added claims for five more by *Shokaku*'s D3As and one by those of *Zuikaku*, against an actual loss of 21 Hurricanes, two of which were repairable, plus several more damaged. The A6Ms also claimed eight Swordfish, with two more probables and one damaged, against an actual loss of six. It is not possible to give a full breakdown of individual Japanese fighter claims, but available details are as shown in Table 14.

On the British side, apart from the claims of 258 Squadron (4:1:4) and the Naval pilots (1:0:0), 30 Squadron initially totalled its claims as 11 confirmed, seven probables and five damaged, though as wounded pilots turned up and confirmations came in, this was later revised to 14:6:5. The anti-aircraft gunners claimed a further five, for a final total of 24 confirmed, seven probables and at least nine damaged. Like the Japanese claims, these figures were well in excess of actual losses — not surprising in such confused and heavy fighting; among the A6Ms, *Soryu* lost NAP 1/C Sachio Higashi — possibly the fighter shot off Plt Off McDonald's tail by Flt Sgt Paxton — while *Hiryu* had three fighters damaged. *Zuikaku*'s D3As, the first bombers on the scene, lost five aircraft with six more damaged, while those from *Shokaku* lost one, with one damaged.

30 Squadron pilots inspect the wreckage of an Aichi D3A dive-bomber near Colombo after the action on 5 April. Left to right: Plt Off Jimmy Whalen, Sgt Grant Bishop, Sgt C.I. Nutbrown, Sgt G.G. Bate, Sgt Jack Hurley and Plt Off D.A. McDonald. *(Public Archives of Canada)*

TABLE 14

JNAF Fighter claims, 5 April 1942:

Hiryu

Lt Sumio Nono NAP 1/C Haruo Nitta	
Wt Off Yoshimi Kodama NAP 2/C Noboru Takada	11 Hurricanes and six Swordfish shot down; one Hurricane shared with *Akagi*'s fighters; two Hurricanes probably shot down.
Wt Off Tsuguo Matsuyama NAP 1/C Yutaka Chiyoshima	
NAP 1/C Masato Hino NA 1/C Kenji Kotani	
NAP 2/C Tadashi Sasaki	two Swordfish and one Spitfire shot down.

Soryu

Lt Iyozo Fujita*	one Fulmar shot down;
NAP Sozaburo Takahashi	one Swordfish damaged;
NAP 1/C Yukio Higashi	no claims.
NAP 1/C Ki-ichi Oda*	one fighter probably shot down and two shared;
NAP 2/C Jiro Tanaka*	two fighters shot down and one shared;
NAP 3/C Takeo Takashima	two fighters shot down and one shared;
NAP 1/C Kaname Harada*	three fighters shot down and one probable;
NAP 1/C Wataru Kubota	no claims;
NAP 1/C Genzo Nagasawa	one fighter probably shot down.

Akagi

Lt Cdr Shigeru Itaya	one fighter shot down;
NAP 1/C Tetsuo Kikuchi*	three fighters shot down, two probables;
NAP 2/C Yozo Kawada	two Swordfish probably shot down;
Lt Masanobu Ibusuki	four fighters shot down, one probable;
NAP 1/C Yoshio Iwaki	one fighter probably shot down;
NAP 1/C Sakae Mori	one fighter shot down, one probable;
NAP 1/C Katsumi Tanaka	one fighter probably shot down;
NAP 3/C Hiroshi Ohara	two fighters shot down;
NA 1/C Shinpei Sano	one fighter shot down, one probable.

NB: Bracketing together of names indicates the flights and sections flown; in each case the first name was the section leader. Pilots marked * either were, or later became, 'aces'.

Total Japanese losses were thus six D3As, with seven damaged, one A6M, with three damaged, and five B5Ns damaged.

One Japanese bomber fell on the playing fields of St Thomas' College, Mount Lavinia, while another crashed at Pitta Kotte, on the eastern outskirts of Colombo. About to be captured in the cockpit of his crashed aircraft, one Japanese airman had to be pinioned by soldiers to prevent him from committing hara-kiri. Explaining his conduct through an interpreter, he said that to be taken prisoner was an "insupportable shame" and since this humiliation had befallen him, his life was finished. As a prisoner, he added, he had lost his status, and there was nothing further to live for.

Although losses in the air had been heavy for the defences, the fighters had clearly had an effect on the efficiency of the attack, and the timely removal of all possible shipping had kept losses in this respect to a minimum. Harbour workshops at Colombo were seriously damaged and the Armed Merchant Cruiser *Hector* sustained at least five direct hits, which set her ablaze; the fires were fought for three hours but she settled on the bottom. The destroyer *Tenedos* was also sunk; the submarine depot vessel — *Lucia* — was damaged, as was a merchantman, the 5,943-ton *Benledi*. Personnel casualties totalled four naval officers, 35 ratings, a dozen Goanese and Lascars killed, together with 37 civilians, all inmates of a mental hospital that was hit. Japanese claims were for a destroyer and a merchant ship plus ten smaller vessels sunk; damage to Ratmalana airfield was negligible.

During the morning land-based bombers and fighters of the Genzan Ku from Mingaladon, in Burma, had raided Calcutta and Akyab by way of indirect support to the main assault on Ceylon. The G3Ms claimed to have sunk a 2,000 ton minelayer; this was in fact the Indian Navy sloop *Indus* which was bombed and sunk, her crew suffering ten casualties. They also claimed to have destroyed a large and a small aircraft on Akyab airfield, whilst strafing A6Ms claimed to have set on fire a DC3 and a Hurricane there — probably the same aircraft as claimed by the bombers (see also Chapter 9).

From Ceylon an attempt was made at retaliation, ten Blenheims of 11 Squadron being sent off at 0830 to attack Nagumo's carriers, but they were given incorrect directions and failed to find the fleet. Catalinas from the island and Albacores from the Eastern Fleet had been searching for Nagumo Force during the day and, at 0840, while the attack on Colombo was still underway, the combat air patrol which comprised three A6Ms each from *Hiryu*, *Zuikaku* and *Shokaku* chased and engaged Flt Lt J.R. Graham's Z2144 FV-R of 205 Squadron, shooting it down at 0842, though two of *Zuikaku*'s fighters were damaged by return fire; there were no survivors from the flyingboat. Another combat air patrol from *Hiryu* — NAP 1/C Masato Hino, NAP 2/C Noboru Todaka and NA 1/C Kenji Kotani — was directed onto two 827 Squadron Albacores from Eastern Fleet later in the day, and shot down one of these, T9206/5C crewed by Sub Lts R.J.F. Streatfield and T. Weston, with N/Air Ken Porter as their TAG, all of whom perished. A third combat air patrol, also from *Hiryu*, intercepted another 827 Squadron Albacore later, but then lost it in cloud. Of the attack on this aircraft — X8944/5B crewed by Sub Lts R.J. Grant-Sturgis and V.W. Jaffray, together with TAG, L/Air Gordon Dixon, who recalled:

> "We sighted the Jap fleet — we could see the outline of the carriers and the battleships. Sub Lt Jaffray gave me a signal to send. A simple message, repeated twice, indicating the sighting. It was while sending this message that the 'Zero' made the first attack. At this time we would have been flying at 3,000 feet.
>
> "At once Grant-Sturgis dived to sea level. The 'Zero' then made a frontal attack. This we evaded by swerving side to side. The pilot fired his forward gun. It then attacked from the rear. I stood up in the cockpit with the Vickers

GO, and when the 'Zero' opened fire I responded with a burst, while Grant-Sturgis did a tight turn towards the fighter.

"It was during the second attack from the rear that I was hit in the left forearm and left hip. The fighter engaged us for about 15 minutes, making four attacks from the rear and three frontal ones. All the time we were at sea level.

"The Vickers gun had a very small bag to collect the spent cartridges, and if this got too full the gun jammed. To avoid this, I removed the bag; consequently, when firing, spent cases were flying all around the cockpit. We finally arrived back at the carrier and Jaffray fired a Very pistol, and we landed straight away. The Albacore had been hit by about 40 bullets."

On the return flight to *Indomitable*, Dixon was able to extricate the bullet, which had lodged in the muscles of his left hip, by prising it out with a screwdriver!

Aboard the carrier all personnel had been at 'Action Stations' since dawn, the aircrews ready for the fight, as Sub Lt Hugh Popham of 880 Squadron recorded:

"At 1030 the fighters on deck were put at instant readiness, pilots strapped in. We sat there, sweltering, fingers on the starter button, muscles aching with the effort of waiting. There were enemy aircraft on the radar screen."

The day was young however. Scouting planes from Japanese cruisers were searching the sea south of Ceylon for signs of the fleeing ships which they had expected to find in harbour and, just after 1100, the No 4 spotter aircraft from the cruiser *Tone* discovered *Dorsetshire* and *Cornwall* to the south-east of the Japanese fleet. On receipt of this news, the carriers at once bore round in that direction and launched 53 D3As, led by Lt Cdr Takashige Egusa, Air Group Commander of the *Soryu*: this force included 18 aircraft from Egusa's own ship, 18 from *Hiryu* and 17 from *Akagi*. Off at 1250, the D3As found the cruisers, which had initially been reported as destroyers, dead ahead.

With the sun behind them, *Soryu*'s aircraft bombed first between 1440 and 1455, claiming 14 hits. The *Hiryu* bombers joined in moments later, while those from *Akagi* reported seven hits on one cruiser and eight on the other. In the initial attack, *Dorsetshire* sustained direct hits on her aircraft catapult, bridge, engine and boiler rooms; then, with her rudder jammed, she was further hit and sank at 1448. Meanwhile, *Cornwall* disappeared under a welter of bombs, suffering 15 direct hits in seven minutes; she keeled over and sank bows first, six minutes later. Of the original combined complement of the two ships of 1,646 men, 1,222 were picked up by the Australian cruiser HMAS *Enterprise* and two destroyers (HMAS *Paladin* and HMAS *Panther*) which rushed to the scene, but not before they had endured 30 hours under a tropical sun in shark-infested waters.

Surprise had been complete, conditions perfect and the bombing excellent; no Japanese losses were suffered. After recovering their aircraft, the Japanese carriers swung south-eastwards and headed away from Ceylon.

Aboard *Indomitable* the aircrews waited impatiently; Sub Lt Popham continued:

"A W/T message had been received from *Dorsetshire* and *Cornwall*: 'We are being attacked by enemy dive-bombers.' Then why weren't we airborne and on our way? A last message from the two cruisers as they went down, and we raged and blasphemed with frustration. All day it was the same; the sour anger of enforced inaction, of a sapping impotence.

"The TBR (Torpedo-Bomber-Reconnaissance) boys were equally galled. The thought of an enemy fleet just over the horizon, simply waiting to be torpedoed, was too tantalising to be borne."

Photographs taken from Japanese aircraft on 5 April. Top: HMS *Dorsetshire*, her rudder damaged by bombs, turns helplessly as bombs strike HMS *Cornwall*. Above: Last photograph of HMS *Cornwall* before she sank. 424 sailors perished in the two cruisers. *(Authors' collection)*

But it was not to be. Vice-Admiral Somerville had deliberated, and decided withdrawal to the south-west would allow his fleet to survive to fight another day.

During the afternoon Nagumo Force was again spotted, 450 miles from Ceylon and heading for Trincomalee; it was seen from a distance of 10 miles by Catalina 'L' of 240 Squadron, flown by Flt Lt W. Bradshaw. The crew had been warned that Hurricanes and Fulmars would be in the area and, at first, took a formation of aircraft flying above to be friendly. At the same time, the warships put up a barrage of shells, about a dozen falling some 50 yards behind the wave-hugging Catalina, the resultant splashes and blast almost sending the aircraft into the sea. Nonetheless, the crew shadowed the Japanese force for the remainder of the day, only returning when their fuel began to run low.

At Colombo meanwhile, stock could now be taken; the defences were perilously weakened — indeed 30 Squadron had only seven serviceable Hurricanes available, and 258 Squadron was in even worse shape, with only three Mark IIBs and two Mark Is serviceable. It appeared to the defenders that the raid had been beaten off with much heavier losses then had in fact been inflicted, but a second such attack would have been hard to combat.

When news of the attack on Colombo reached RNAS Cochin, on the mainland, 5 CD Flight of the Indian Air Force, which shared the aerodrome with the FAA, despatched one of its four Wapiti biplanes to search the coastal areas, in case a Japanese force was heading in the direction of Cape Comorin. Crewed by the Flight's commander, Flt Lt Wilf Russell and his deputy, Flg Off Derek Wood, the Wapiti departed Cochin in company with a Fulmar flown by Sub Lt Jack Pickard, RNZNVR. Operating from Willingdon island airstrip, further down the coast, Russell recalled:

> "We took it in turn to patrol the waters off the southern tip of India, each silently praying that we should be spared the sight of those wicked-looking carrier hulls with their dreaded brood of Zeros.
>
> "We flew our patrols all day and saw nothing. Back at the aerodrome on Willingdon island we slept out near the aircraft. I remember feeling apprehensive and rather gloomy. Should we be flying Wapitis and converted unarmed airliners[1] of pre-war vintage if there had been any strength in the country?"

From China Bay, on the other side of the island, amongst aircraft sent out to search for signs of the approach of Japanese warships, was Walrus L2295 — on attachment from the cruiser *Glasgow*. On coming into land at Clampalmin landing ground the amphibian crashed, killing the pilot, Sub Lt D.A. Baptie.

Nagumo Force had 'disappeared' again. At nightfall, searching Albacores from the Eastern Fleet found one carrier, but this was then lost again. Over the next few days fruitless searches were to be continued, but the Japanese were not idle, and during the five days, 5th-9th, 23 merchant vessels were attacked and sunk, mainly by units of Vice-Admiral Ozawa's Malaya Force. Indeed, the aircraft from *Ryujo*, with this force, had already been successful on the 5th. Ten B5Ns had taken off just before midday and attacked a convoy of ten vessels off Vizagapatam, scoring a direct hit on the 7,725-ton *Dardanus*, the 60kg bomb exploding in her engine room. Her skipper ordered the vessel to be abandoned, following which, 10 minutes later, two more aircraft attacked and gained another hit. However, an hour later the captain and some of the crew reboarded the ship, as there appeared to be no immediate danger of her sinking and, soon afterwards, another freighter — the British India Line's *Gandara* — arrived on the scene and took *Dardanus* in tow towards Madras.

---

[1] 5 CD Flight also had two DH86 four-engined biplanes — converted airliners ex-TATA Airways — on its strength, whilst other Indian Air Force Flights also included ex-civil Atlanta airliners amongst their establishments.

A flight of Swordfish was despatched from China Bay at dawn, escorted by a number of 273 Squadron Fulmars, including one (X8730) flown by 888 Squadron's Sub Lt Brander, but nothing untoward was sighted however.

Early in the morning the crew of a search floatplane from the cruiser *Tone* (with Nagumo Force) spotted a Catalina; three nearby B5Ns were directed to the area to try and intercept, but were unable to find it, returning to their own search missions. In the afternoon, Nagumo Force again changed direction, beginning a gentle swing which would eventually bring the ships onto a north-westerly course for Trincomalee. While the Japanese were thus moving northwards, Somerville's search was directed to the south under the impression that Nagumo would be heading for the East Indies following his apparent heavy losses.

As Nagumo Force was carrying out these moves, Malaya Force was continuing its hunt for shipping in the Bay of Bengal with great effect — virtually unhindered by Allied aerial interference — having split up into smaller elements to cover a wider area. *Chokai* claimed three vessels sunk; *Yura*, *Ryujo* and the destroyer *Yugiri* jointly claimed three more off Chotrapur and Vizagapatam. Indeed, survivors of the 3,471-ton *Taksang*, belonging to the British Indo-China Company, reported being shelled and sunk by an aircraft carrier and 15 of the crew were lost; however, her master was amongst the survivors. Floatplanes from *Chokai* inflicted severe damage on two more ships. Aircraft from *Ryujo* also sank two vessels, damaged six more and set fire to a fuel tanker and warehouses at Coringa and Vizagapatam. The cruisers *Mikuma*, *Mogami* and the destroyer *Amagiri* claimed five further ships off the south of Godavari, while south of Falaise Point, *Kumano*, *Suzuya* and the destroyer *Shirakumo* claimed a further seven.

The crew of *Kumano*'s E8N floatplane reported being attacked by three Hurricanes (sic) during the late morning off Akyab, but escaped serious damage. In fact, the attacker had been a single Curtiss Mohawk of 5 Squadron from Cuttack. Pilots of this recently-formed unit had moved to the coastal area from Dum Dum in preparation for action against the Japanese naval thrust into the Bay of Bengal. During the morning Flt Lt J.H. Iremonger had been despatched on a reconnaissance sortie over the bay to search for the warships, returning to report a cruiser and two destroyers off Akyab. A second Mohawk (BS795/W) was promptly sent out, flown by Flt Lt Keith MacEwan, RNZAF, who soon sighted the cruiser. As he approached the warship, he spotted a floatplane preparing to alight on the water about three miles ahead of the *Kumano*.

Diving down to sea level, MacEwan passed between the cruiser and a destroyer, and fired about 600 rounds at the floatplane, then climbed away when out of range of the ships' guns. He believed the floatplane had crashed into the sea, and was accordingly awarded a probable victory. In fact, Lt Motoe Itoh's aircraft suffered only 19 hits and alighted safely on the water, to be recovered by its mother ship.

A flight of Wellington bombers of 215 Squadron had recently arrived at Calcutta, but were unable to prepare and bomb-up in time to launch an attack owing to trouble experienced with the bomb loading gear. Based just inland from the small port of Vizagapatam, on the Indian east coast, 500 miles north of Madras, was newly-formed 6 CD Flight of the Indian Air Force, equipped with two Wapiti biplanes. At 0815 one of these, J9754 piloted by an Indian, Plt Off Barkar, with the Flight's commander, Flt Lt David Small, in the rear seat as navigator and observer, set out to reconnoitre the shipping lanes. When about 30 miles out to sea they observed gun flashes to the north-east then, when they drew closer, an aircraft carrier (*Ryujo*), several cruisers and destroyers were seen, all firing at a merchantman. As they flew back towards the coast:

> "A flight of three yellow radial-engined low-wing fighters flew below us in the direction of land. Miraculously the 'Zeros' didn't see our awkward old biplane wallowing along at 100 mph."

Later that day Vizagapatam was bombed by B5Ns from *Ryujo*, but the small airfield housing 6 CD Flight — in a field in a valley behind the town — was not attacked. The nearby port of Coconada was also bombed by *Ryujo*'s aircraft. Little damage was inflicted at either port, although panic amongst the populations was such that both towns were rapidly vacated.

Following the attack by the Mohawk of 5 Squadron, *Kumano* and her escorts came upon a burning ship, which they proceeded to sink. Their victim was probably the crippled *Dardanus*, under tow from *Gandara*; both ships had been attacked several times by floatplanes, but had escaped damage. At 0800 however, the cruisers appeared from astern. The tow line was slipped and her captain again ordered 'Abandon ship' as the cruisers opened fire — both ships were repeatedly hit but remained afloat. As the cruisers departed, one of the floatplanes returned and, following an inspection of the helpless vessels, undoubtedly called up *Shirakumo* to administer the coup de grace; both were torpedoed and sank, 13 of *Gandara*'s' crew being lost, although all of the crew of *Dardanus* survived and reached land safely.

The 7,621-ton *Autolycus* — in convoy with five other vessels from Calcutta — making for Madras, was spotted by a Japanese reconnaissance aircraft at 0730. An air escort had been promised for the convoy, but none had shown up. Soon after being spotted, three cruisers appeared and began shelling. *Autolycus* was promptly hit by two salvoes, following which she was abandoned with the loss of 16 of her crew, survivors reaching the coast 48 hours later. The cruisers then closed in on the other five vessels of the convoy and, in short time, sank *Indora* (6,622 tons), *Exmoor* (4,999 tons), *Silksworth* (4,921 tons), *Shinkuang* (2,441 tons) and *Malda*; survivors of the latter, the largest of the convoy at 9,066 tons, reported initially being bombed but the ship was then sunk by gunfire off Gopalpore, with the loss of 25 of the crew.

The 6,246-ton *Ganges* was bombed and sunk off Vizagapatam (15 killed), in which vicinity the Dutch *Banjoewangi* (1,279 tons) was also lost, while *Sinkiang* suffered a similar fate and a number of casualties; the Norwegian *Dagfred* (4,434 tons) went down to gunfire 60 miles east of Masulipatam, as did the Dutch *Batavia* (1,279 tons), 14 miles east of Calingapatam. An American vessel, the 5,491-ton *Bienville*, was bombed and set on fire, then sunk by gunfire, with the loss of 19 of the 42 crew. Other vessels lost during the day's slaughter were *Harpasa* (5,082 tons), *Hermod* (1,515 tons), *Van de Capellan* (2,073 tons) and *Elsa* (5,381 tons).

It was indeed a most successful day for the Ozawa's Malaya Force, a day which brought the number of merchant vessels lost, in a single series of attacks, to the highest figure ever suffered by the Allies in a similar area and period of time throughout the war — 19 ships, totalling almost 100,000 tons.

With the onset of darkness, aircraft of the Indian Air Force were instructed to carry out night sweeps, the two Wapitis of 6 CD Flight concentrating on a 30 mile radius of Vizagapatam, returning at first light with nothing to report except a burning merchantman. Further down the coast at Madras, two Atlantas of 1 CD Flight were sent out, one northwards, the other to the south. The crew of the former spotted three aircraft although the Atlanta was not attacked.

At dusk an Albacore of 827 Squadron from *Indomitable* sighted and became engaged with two aircraft which were identified as 'Navy 96' fighters (A5Ms), but succeeded in evading these in cloud. Due to the absence of fighters of this type from the area of the Indian Ocean, it is more likely that they were a pair of D3As from Nagumo Force on patrol, which the British crew incorrectly identified. Under cover of the operations around Ceylon, a Japanese convoy arrived safely at Rangoon on this date.

Tuesday, 7 April

Five Blenheims of 11 Squadron were again sent out looking for the carriers, but once again sighted nothing. Ceylon remained in a high state of tension. From China Bay, patrols of Swordfish continued searching — in vain — for signs of the Japanese task force, again escorted by 273 Squadron Fulmars, one of which (X8770) was flown by 888 Squadron's Sub Lt Brander.

261 Squadron suffered the loss of two of its more experienced pilots, Wt Off John Griffin and Flt Sgt Tom Quinn, a Malta veteran, when a Seal biplane (K4781) of 273 Squadron, which they were flying, hit a stationary Swordfish on take-off from Kokkilai. They were both killed, as was their passenger, Flt Lt J.C. Anstie, 273 Squadron's Medical Officer, when the aircraft burst into flames. Would be rescuers could do nothing but watch in horror. 261 Squadron had also lost the services of three of its Hurricanes in landing accidents during the previous few days, although the pilots concerned had survived unhurt.

Hurricane 'N' of 261 Squadron carries out a low-level pass over China Bay airfield. *(P.L. Jordan)*

30 Squadron had by this time traced all its missing pilots; Flt Sgt Tom Paxton had been visited in hospital on the 6th, when he had given a full account of his combats; his condition was not thought to be serious at this stage, so it came as a most unpleasant surprise to the squadron when he died suddenly from secondary shock the following day.

Prime Minister Churchill — ever the supreme strategist and with an eye to turning a setback into possible victory — had by now received detailed accounts of the attack on Colombo, and speedily despatched a cable to US President Roosevelt:

> "According to our information, five, and possibly six, Japanese battleships, and certainly five aircraft-carriers, are operating in the Indian Ocean. We cannot of course make head against this force, especially if it is concentrated.
>
> "Even after the heavy losses inflicted on the enemy's aircraft in their attack on Colombo, we cannot feel sure that our two carriers would beat the four Japanese carriers concentrated south of Ceylon. The situation is therefore one of grave anxiety.
>
> "As you must now be decidedly superior to the enemy forces in the Pacific, the situation would seem to offer an immediate opportunity to the United States Pacific Fleet, which might be of such a nature as to compel Japanese naval forces in the Indian Ocean to return to the Pacific, thus relinquishing or leaving unsupported any invasion enterprise which they have in mind or to which they are committed.
>
> "I cannot too urgently impress the importance of this upon you."

Wednesday, 8 April

During the day the Eastern Fleet finally abandoned the search and retired to Addu; however, the withdrawal south-westwards was more by design and decision, than lack of success. Realising that his force would stand little chance against the might of Nagumo's fleet, Vice-Admiral Somerville wisely retreated to conserve, a decision not immediately appreciated by his aircrews, as Sub Lt Popham later wrote:

> "It was natural enough that we should be angry at seeing our first chance of action in six months go by default; it was natural that we should see it as an unintelligible decision by Admiral Somerville. It was his decision, of course; but it was not unintelligible, and it must have been a bitter one to make.
>
> "While we were at Addu Atoll the first time, he learnt — as we did not — that the Japanese force consisted of five aircraft carriers, and four fast battleships, besides cruisers and destroyers. Against this fleet we could pit only two aircraft carriers and one fairly modern battleship. They had, therefore, a superiority in sheer numbers that would almost certainly have made any battle a foregone conclusion.
>
> "For the second time in six months, our Eastern Fleet might have suffered obliteration, leaving India, Ceylon and the whole Indian Ocean an open hunting ground."

Thursday, 9 April

As such things happen, the withdrawal of the Eastern Fleet to Addu coincided with the re-discovery of the Nagumo Force by aircraft from Ceylon a few hours later. At 0256, during the darkest part of the night, Catalina QL-Y (W8421) of 413 Squadron took off from Koggala, piloted by Flt Lt Rae Thomas, DFC, one of the unit's most experienced pilots; at 0716 he reported the position, course and speed of a large enemy force but, before his message was completed, was shot down by two A6Ms, which had taken off from *Hiryu* at 0600, flown by NAP 1/C Hino and NA 1/C Kotani, two of the trio who had accounted for one of *Indomitable*'s Albacores a few days earlier. There were no survivors from the Catalina, the co-pilot of which had been Flg Off Harry Leach, late of 4 AACU at Singapore. Nagumo Force had arrived at a position only 100 miles east of Trincomalee before being seen, and had already at 0600 begun flying off aircraft to attack the port and China Bay airfield.

Catalina QL-F of 413 Squadron. *(Authors' collection)*

This time no D3As took part, being held back for a counter-attack should units of Eastern Fleet attempt to interfere. 91 B5Ns led by Cdr Fuchida made up the strike force on this occasion, escorted by 41 A6Ms led by Lt Cdr Itaya. Aircraft involved were as follows:

Soryu	18 B5Ns led by Lt Heijiro Abe
	9 A6Ms led by Lt Masaharu Suganami
Hiryu	18 B5Ns led by Lt Cdr Yoshimasa Kasunoki
	6 A6Ms led by Lt Yasuhiro Shigematsu
Akagi	18 B5Ns led by Cdr Fuchida
	6 A6Ms led by Lt Cdr Itaya
Zuikaku	18 B5Ns led by Cdr Shigekazu Shimazaki
	10 A6Ms led by Lt Masatoshi Makino
Shokaku	19 B5Ns led by Lt Tatsuo Ichihara
	10 A6Ms led by Lt Tadashi Kaneko

At Trincomalee, radar was available and the raid was picked up before 0700, giving plenty of warning. Three Hurricanes of 261 Squadron's 'B' Flight were already up, having taken off at 0635 on dawn patrol, and these, flown by Flt Lt David Fulford (Z5146), Sgt L.T. Rawnsley, RAAF (BG786) and Sgt J.W. Walton (BG690), were vectored out to sea at 0655. 30 miles from the coast they spotted the first two formations of Japanese bombers, each flying in two vics of seven aircraft apiece, in line astern at 15,000 feet, above which escorting fighters

Hurricanes of 261 Squadron at China Bay in April. *(P.L. Jordan)*

were weaving; a mile behind came another similar formation. The escorts, which had apparently not yet seen the Hurricanes, were at 20,000 feet, so Fulford led his section to the north, climbing under cover of clouds until they reached 22,000 feet, leading them round behind the rear formation. They then dived on the escort — almost certainly those from *Zuikaku* — each pilot selecting a target.

Fulford closed dead astern of one and gave it a five second burst at point blank range; part of the A6M broke off and it went into a spin, pouring white smoke, down to about 12,000 feet; there it suddenly dived steeply, the starboard wing breaking off before it crashed into the sea. Rawnsley took the extreme starboard fighter and gave it a long burst whereupon it disintegrated and went down in flames. It would seem that they had shot down the formation leader, Lt Masatoshi Makino, and NA 1/C Tatsu Matsumoto, both of whom were killed.

Fulford climbed quickly after his victim crashed, but found six more A6Ms after him and was unable to lose them, so dived vertically, pulling out between 7,000 and 2,000 feet; he had by then lost the pursuing fighters and climbed back up to 15,000 feet. Meanwhile, Rawnsley observed Walton's Hurricane going down pouring smoke, but was far too low himself and climbed to 13,000 feet where he found himself alone; he then spotted 20 B5Ns 1,000 feet below him and was hit by AA bursts aimed at these. He then saw Fulford being chased by the A6Ms so attacked one of these, getting in a five second burst and claiming it probably destroyed. His own aircraft was struck by a cannon shell beneath the cockpit at this point; he crash-landed at China Bay, with a wounded left ankle and an A6M right behind, strafing him. Seeing his plight, Flt Lt Eric Edsall — whose own aircraft (Z4762) had been commandeered by the Station Commander, who intended to fly it to the satellite strip for safety — rushed to the shattered Hurricane and pulled Rawnsley out.

Fulford meanwhile, having regained altitude, saw a ragged formation of bombers at 7,000 feet with fighter cover, leaving the harbour. He dived on the rearmost fighter and fired the rest of his ammunition, closing to 100 yards. He claimed that the A6M turned on its back and dived straight into the sea five miles south-east of Foul Point.

At 0710, Flt Lt Cleaver scrambled with six 'A' Flight Hurricanes, followed five minutes later by another six led by Flg Off J.V. Marshall. The B5Ns were now approaching the area fast, those of *Soryu*, *Hiryu* and *Akagi* arriving at 0730, followed at five minute intervals by those of *Zuikaku* and *Shokaku*. Cleaver's flight reached 21,000 feet but, although they could see the bombs bursting in the harbour, they were unable to spot the Japanese aircraft. Cleaver (BG882) then took the opportunity to lead the formation out to sea and get the sun behind them and, having done this, they spotted a formation of bombers at about 12,000 feet.

The Hurricanes began diving towards these then, seeing that AA fire was heavy, they drew off and waited for the bombers on their way out. Cleaver dived steeply and fired at the third aircraft in the first formation before climbing away and losing his section. His No 2, Sgt G. Lockwood (BE227), attacked seven or eight bombers, but was then hit by fire from a pair of A6Ms and his Hurricane began to burn; he hastily crash-landed in a lake to the south-west of the airfield. Meanwhile, Flt Sgt J.D. Martin (Z5670) also attacked half a dozen B5Ns and fired a long burst at an aircraft on the starboard side of the formation, which dived away pouring white smoke; he then fired at one on the port side and this too broke away with white smoke streaming from the wing roots, however he was then bounced by A6Ms and had to carry out a force-landing near a small lake.

Cleaver meanwhile, finding himself alone, dived back at the formation he had originally attacked and opened fire on the No 2 aircraft, but was attacked by a fighter and lost his target. He evaded his assailant and spotted some more bombers making out to sea; flying parallel with them, he overtook before turning to make attacks on the second and third aircraft. The latter fell out of formation pouring white smoke and he reported that it went into the sea. He then observed a large dogfight over Foul Point and attacked an A6M, which was on the tail of a Hurricane, closing to 200 yards and opening fire. Before he could observe any results however, he was attacked by four more fighters and retired with 20 hits in the fuselage of his aircraft, returning then to base.

Four Fulmars from China Bay's ad hoc Staff Flight had narrowly avoided encountering the approaching raiders. Lt Jack Smith of 814 Squadron was flying as observer in Flt Lt Chamberlain's Fulmar, and recalled:

> "Our task was to try to locate the Jap fleet. My pilot was a former Hurricane pilot from the Middle East. To him, flying a Fulmar was like driving a London bus and he had never navigated before — steady course and speed and height were all anathema to him. But he did very well and I navigated by averaging!
>
> "The radio did not work and the compasses had not been swung for ages. Our search was unsuccessful but only three of the four Fulmars returned. We returned just in time to park in dispersal under the trees. We got to the Ops Room for debriefing when the Japs arrived."

The missing Fulmar (X8769/K) was crewed by Flg Off Arthur Gregg and Sub Lt Aubrey Mass; having apparently suffered engine trouble, it crashed into dense jungle just inland of Foul Point and both Gregg and Mass were killed.

Amongst the many who witnessed the attack on the airfield from close quarters was Flt Sgt George Mothersdale, late of 243 Squadron from Singapore:

> "A beat of engines at the south-west end of the airfield was heard and a formation of six single-engined bombers had come into view, flying in a tight

vic of five with one in the box. Against the solid blue sky and bright sunshine, with their red disks prominent on their near-white surface finish, they looked impressive! They came in over the ridge behind me — their altitude was only about 1,500 feet — crossed the airfield on a curving track in a matter of seconds and were on their way over the jungle north-eastwards. As I stood watching it seemed unreal — they had the sky over China Bay to themselves — and the Bofors guns on the airfield had not fired (the time the gunners had them in view must have been very limited).

"A short period lapsed then a fighter, followed by another, came into view from behind a headland just beyond the south-west end of the airfield. They came in from over the sea at about 100 feet and were soon recognised in their near-white finish. One came down low, banked steeply round the two refuellers and steam roller, quickly zoomed, quickly dived, firing a short burst at a refueller. The second fighter followed the first, firing a short burst at the other refueller and the steamroller. They then rapidly flew low over the airfield, searching for ground targets. One was nearing where I stood — I promptly slid down and crouched in the shelter trench amid the protests of those huddled in the bottom."

"From behind came the whistling sound of falling bombs. Down into the trench I crouched in the standard drill — steel helmet across the back of the head — teeth clenched — until the ear-stunning bangs of near bomb bursts ended as abruptly as they all began. I stood up and looked around."

A scene of devastation greeted him. Black smoke was rising with mounting flames from the M/T yard, and a corner of the RAF hangar had been hit, where two or three of 273 Squadron's remaining Vildebeests were housed; these were effectively damaged beyond repair. The Sergeants' Mess and a number of other Station buildings were also damaged.

In the meantime, up above, the second section of Cleaver's flight had not fared at all well. Flg Off C.F. Counter (BE241) had patrolled over the harbour at 15,000 feet until he saw a dozen fighters diving away 3,000 feet below. Diving, he fired on two, one of which half-rolled and dived vertically away. He then spotted another fighter attacking a Hurricane, which he recognised as that of Sgt Rawnsley from the dawn patrol. He quickly pulled behind this A6M and got in a good burst, whereupon it rolled slowly on its back and crashed into a lagoon. Three or four more were at once after him and he landed at China Bay under fire, his undercarriage collapsing as it touched the runway. Flt Sgt Mothersdale witnessed Counter's distress:

"The noise had quietened — it seemed like the raid was ending — and the first of 261 Squadron's Hurricanes was over Trincomalee Harbour heading for base. At a distance we could hear it's engine popping and banging, and it had undercarriage trouble. The pilot entered the south-westward leg of the airfield circuit when I heard a low-flying aircraft above where I stood. I looked up and saw a 'Navy 0' at about 300 feet, cruising steadily (*this was apparently an A6M from* Shokaku *flown by NAP 1/C Fujio Hayashi*).

"Each aircraft continued on its course — from the ground it seemed the pilots had not seen each other. The Hurricane passed about 50 feet under the 'Navy 0' and the Japanese pilot must have seen it after it had appeared from under his port wing. The fighter banked, its wings near vertical in a turn to port, and it cut across the airfield to close on the Hurricane which had commenced its final approach for belly-landing. It was grim to watch!

"I saw two Sergeant Pilots of 261 Squadron sprinting towards an unmanned Morris light ambulance. They scrambled into the cab, started the engine and were driving on a curving track on to the airfield. The Hurricane was about 30 feet above the airfield as the 'Navy 0' closed fast and fired a short burst. The Hurricane landed, did a six foot bounce and belly-slid to a halt, with the pilot scrambling over the side and sprinting to the ambulance, now alongside.

"The 'Navy 0' continued along the length of the airfield, slowly climbing but taking no evasive action. It pulled into a climbing turn to port, reached about 300 feet when the Bofors gun at the north-east end of the airfield fired four shells in rapid succession; the rear half of the 'Navy 0's' fuselage — from right behind the cockpit — disappeared! Its nose dropped and the front half of the fuselage went into a steep dive and struck the rim of a large oil storage tank in the Naval Base area. As I watched, grey smoke was rising from the tank, soon turning black and soon flames were flickering."

Flg Off Counter had had a narrow escape and was not hurt in the crash-landing. When later asked whether he had seen the A6M closing on his tail, he replied:

"Yes! I took my feet off the rudder bars, clamped my heels up on the seat edge, curled down as low as I could in the seat, got everything — arms, legs and head — all behind the back plate and let the aircraft land itself!"

Meanwhile, the fight continued overhead. Sgt D.D.P. Bowie (BG676) dived from 12,000 feet to attack a large number of B5Ns at 7,000 feet and opened fire on the leader; pieces flew off this and it appeared to dive straight into jungle-covered ground pouring white smoke. He was then attacked by two A6Ms, and though he was able to snap a burst at one, was shot down, managing to bale out though he had been wounded. The third pilot of the section Sgt W.E. Pearce (Z5533), an Australian, was seen by one of the pilots of the second flight to crash into the sea following a combat with six A6Ms; he was not found.

The second flight had got off from Kokkilai, one of China Bay's satellite airfields and, with Flg Off Marshall (BG967) at the head, had climbed to 16,000 feet before being warned that enemy aircraft were approaching 2,000 feet higher. Marshall saw bombs bursting in the harbour, but had great difficulty in seeing the attackers against the jungle background. However, when the formation was down to 10,000 feet Marshall saw the bombers and led an attack but, before he could fire, he was attacked by five A6Ms; one of these he claimed probably destroyed and then returned to base, low on fuel.

Marshall's two companions, Sgts A.T. Warnick (Z5600) and Mann dived with him and both saw the fighters which attacked him; Warnick, a Canadian, engaged the last of these with a short burst and saw smoke appear from both sides of the engine before it dived steeply away. He then saw at least a dozen B5Ns below and attacked three times without apparent result. Mann attacked another:

"I hit one 'Zero' in both wing tanks and he took off, heading out to sea with fuel streaming from both wings. I also damaged another 'Zero' with hits observed on fin and rudder."

He then broke away to make a second attack, but was himself attacked by an A6M from astern, part of his starboard aileron being shot away. His Hurricane

(BG909) went into a spin from which he managed to pull out, but he found himself surrounded by A6Ms with his own aircraft uncontrollable, so he baled out at 5,000 feet, coming down in the Bay of Trincomalee. While he was floating down he was circled by two A6Ms which did not attack, but he did see another of these fighters crash into the bay; he also saw another aircraft crash into the jungle and a Hurricane go into the sea. He was later credited with a probable for the fighter he had attacked.

Plt Off R.G. Hall, an American in the RCAF, attacked a dozen B5Ns which were flying in vics of three at 15,000 feet and fired at the leader, which poured smoke and broke formation. He then dived on and fired at the starboard aircraft of this vic and saw smoke from its port wing, but broke away as his Hurricane (BG232) was hit by return fire and began to lose glycol. Diving again, he encountered a straggler and fired a long burst, causing white smoke to stream out from underneath, and saw a large pillar of black smoke as it went down. Formating with another Hurricane, he joined in a short attack on six more bombers and saw petrol pour out of the wing roots of one, which broke formation, but his ammunition was by now exhausted and he landed back at Kokkilai.

Pilots of 261 Squadron at China Bay. Left to right, standing: Sgt Smith, Sgt Buchan, Plt Off E. Mayes, Sgt Bubb, Plt Off R.G. Hall, RCAF (US), Sgt P.L. Jordan, RNZAF, Sgt K.A.S. Mann, RAAF. Sitting: Sgt D.D.P. Bowie, Flt Sgt J.D. Martin, Sgt F.J. Jessop. *(P.L. Jordan)*

Plt Off E. Mayes (BG815) attacked some bombers at close range and hit two, but was hit and wounded in the face by return fire, and did not see the results. The last pilot of the second flight, a French-Canadian, Flt Sgt C.J. Gauthier (Z2573) dived on a dozen B5Ns flying in two vics — probably part of the force from *Hiryu* — and fired on the rear starboard aircraft with a short burst, white smoke pouring from the wing roots. He climbed and saw another two dozen bombers below him in two vics and dived to 12,000 feet, firing a long burst at two aircraft on the starboard side of the formation; smoke streamed from both, the inside aircraft swerving to port and colliding with a third. Breaking away, he gained altitude and dived to attack 20 A6Ms which were flying at 9,000 feet, 18 miles out to sea. In the resultant combat he blacked out, was shot down, and ended up in hospital with wounds.

261 Squadron's CO, Sqn Ldr Lewis, had been delayed in joining his mainly inexperienced pilots. As the Hurricanes were taking off, Grp Capt Howard suddenly appeared on the wing of Lewis' Hurricane. It transpired that he wanted to know, at that precise moment, what had been done about arranging the Court Martial of Sgt Mann! According to Lewis, he "seemed to be beside himself with anger".

> "I signalled him to get down, waved the chocks away, and taxied out for take off. As I did so, the old sixth sense caused a chill to go down my back, and I realised that I was a sitting duck, if I got caught on take off."

Taking off alone at 0745 in Z4961, he headed west over the jungle to avoid climbing over the harbour where he could already see aircraft swooping and diving:

> "I had barely got my undercart up, when a hail of bullets struck the armour plate at my back and the throttle lever was no longer there. I was obviously hit, as the plane was on fire and, at that moment, two planes with blood red roundels slid by, in close formation: I realised with a start — Zeros!! In less time than it takes to tell, I was reaching for the release pin in my Sutton harness and I was out. I caught the tailplane on my left hip as I fell away. The Hurricane nosed into the ground just ahead of me, continuing to burn, the ammunition going off like fire crackers. I landed a split second later, right on the edge of a shallow lagoon.
>
> "Our normal dress was khaki shorts and shirt. As a result, the burns I received for the second time of asking, smarted like mad when I fell into a couple of feet of salt water (luckily the burns were minor, compared with those I had received in the Battle of Britain). My left upper arm was aching (the muscles, near the shoulder, had been shot away), but worse still, the lower part of my left hand, below the little finger, was shot away, and I could see the sinews exposed (must have happened when the throttle was shot away). The sight of the injuries and the blood made me feel faint; I dragged off my flying helmet, as I was all hot and bothered, but deemed it wiser to replace the helmet, which had an oxygen tube attached, which I thought might act as a tourniquet to stop the bleeding.
>
> "What seemed to be shrapnel, rained down, and I was glad of the leather helmet. A Hurricane passed overhead; the awesome chatter of the 12 guns helped me to realise that the Japs weren't having it all their own way. Another thought struck me: what if my parachute should draw attention to my whereabouts? We had been informed that Japs fired on pilots when they managed to bale-out so, what with the burning plane a few yards away and a parachute to indicate my position, I knew I must move away from there."

He eventually found himself in a hutted clearing, where a number of villagers came to his aid. After being given a drink of coconut milk, he was guided to a jungle road which led towards Trincomalee, where he came across a stationary Army lorry:

"A young Marine lieutenant in shorts and shirt, accompanied by a local Ceylonese guide, was searching through the wreckage of a partially burnt-out Hurricane. He informed me: 'Not much hope there.'

"Realising the condition I was in, he invited me into the cab of the truck, telling me he would soon have me in hospital at the Base. We passed other planes that had come to grief in the action, and I became aware that a heavy toll of Hurricanes had resulted."

The Hurricanes had indeed fared badly: of the 16 which had taken off, eight were shot down and either crashed, or force-landed on China Bay airfield while still under attack; three more were damaged. Additionally, one of the unit's Hurricanes under repair in a hangar was destroyed, whilst the Orderly Room was demolished, and a petrol bowser containing 700 gallons went up in flames. It was while endeavouring to reach the bowser, in an attempt to drive it to safety, that Flt Lt Edsall — following his rescue of Sgt Rawnsley — was hit in the back by a strafing A6M and mortally wounded. Sqn Ldr Lewis commented:

"Sometime after the attack they found he had dragged himself some yards along the ground and passed out cold. They turned him over, thinking him perhaps dead, and found that he had dragged his hair down round his face in agony and he was bathed in sweat."

Sadly, Edsall died in hospital three days later. The Marine gunners had not got away unscathed either, for one Japanese aircraft literally flew down the gun barrel in its death dive, wiping out the complete emplacement and crew. Of the aftermath of this incident, Flt Sgt Mothersdale noted:

"I was surprised to see the rear half fuselage of a Japanese aircraft — it looked like a fighter — standing almost vertical out of a patch of low jungle growth across the airfield, its white surface finish and red disks prominent."

Two of 814 Squadron's TAGs, L/Airmen Norman Lauchlan and 'Darky' Holroyd — "without a pea-shooter between us" — had sat under a tree and watched the raid:

No 2 Hangar, China Bay, after the 9th April raid. *(P.L. Jordan)*

"After the raid we went to help the RAF put out the fires. In the FAA hangar a Swordfish was standing, tail to damaged wall, about 40 feet from the doors. One torpedo, on a trolley, was in position under the Swordfish's belly; a second torpedo was in a wooden cradle alongside the aircraft. Flames were licking the tailplane and rudder, which were scorched but not actually on fire. I yelled: 'Get those torpedoes out, while I warn the RAF there may be an explosion.'

'Go in there?' said someone, 'After you!'. We advanced slowly into the hangar. The torpedo in the cradle we could not move. I sent a Leading Airman to the M/T Section to get a portable crane. It took about 15 minutes for the crane to arrive. Meanwhile, we slipped the brake on the trolley and wheeled it, with torpedo, on to the airfield.

"We had quite a hunt for a fire extinguisher to put out the flame on the petrol drum. We were hampered by the fact that at the other end of the hangar an ammunition dump was in flames, and the larger bombs exploding sent a shower of splinters through the hangar."

The two 888 Squadron Martlets (including AM990) based at China Bay were not ordered off, as noted by Sub Lt Brander:

"Our Martlets did not take part in the defence of the island. I was not privy to the plans for the air defence but I could guess that the Martlets could have been held back to oppose the expected return of the Japs, maybe with an amphibious force. We were all very surprised that one day of bombing was all that Trincomalee was subjected to. The RAF were, I think, quite unserviceable after the raid, so maybe two Martlets could have made a difference but not much. Maybe China Bay had no .50-in ammunition so the Martlets would have been good for one flight only."

The A6Ms of *Akagi*, *Hiryu*, *Zuikaku* and *Shokaku* had all arrived over Trincomalee at about 0700 or shortly thereafter; the *Akagi* aircraft reported meeting three aircraft 20 miles out from the port at this time — clearly 261 Squadron's dawn patrol — and claimed to have shot down two (Walton and Rawnsley). The fighters of all four carriers then engaged Hurricanes over the port before going down to ground level to strafe; the *Zuikaku* aircraft strafed the China Bay airfield, those from *Hiryu* shot up oil tanks and cargo ships, claiming one oil tank destroyed, while *Akagi*'s fighters attacked a small ship during their return flight. *Soryu*'s aircraft were amongst the last to arrive at 0750, and engaged in no combat, strafing ships instead. Apart from the three losses already noted, no other A6Ms were lost.

The first three formations of bombers had attacked at 0730, dropped their bombs rapidly and left, the aircraft from *Soryu* leading; this particular formation had three of its aircraft damaged. Those from *Hiryu* followed, but were attacked by Hurricanes, losing one aircraft, while a second was so badly hit that it later force-landed; it seems that the crew were lost, as altogether five of the *Hiryu*'s bomber personnel were killed during the raid. Gunners in the bombers claimed one Hurricane probably destroyed. The contingents from *Akagi* and *Zuikaku* left next, the latter having bombed and claimed as sunk a large merchant vessel, but these encountered no opposition and arrived back at their carriers unscathed.

Trincomalee harboured mainly naval vessels but one freighter — the 7,958-ton *Sagaing* — was anchored in the middle of the harbour. Her deck cargo included a Walrus amphibian and three disassembled Albacores, as well as .303 ammunition for the Hurricanes; it was reputed that her holds also contained copious quantities of whisky! She had not been able to leave when the order to scatter had been sent, and paid the price. With her decks ablaze, she was beached by her crew, the flames consuming her cargo of aircraft and whisky alike. The old monitor, *Erebus*, was hit by a number of bombs, causing many casualties. The final formation of bombers, that from *Shokaku*, was attacked by pairs of Hurricanes both before and after bombing, and no less than seven aircraft were damaged, one airman being wounded.

When the final score sheet was drawn up, 261 Squadron pilots claimed eight destroyed — four bombers and four fighters (of which two had been seen to collide), plus one bomber and three fighters probably destroyed and one fighter and at least five bombers damaged. Clearly there had been an element of overclaiming by the defenders and it seems that several of the falling aircraft, claimed by the ground defences, must in fact have been Hurricanes shot down by the Japanese fighters.

However, if the British claims were on the high side, so too were those of the Japanese fighter pilots. After claiming two of the initial Hurricanes met, *Akagi*'s fighters claimed three more and one probable over the harbour, while those of *Hiryu* claimed two and two more shared with fighters from other carriers. *Zuikaku*'s A6M pilots claimed a total of 19 fighters and one floatplane shot down and one medium-sized aircraft destroyed on the ground, while those of *Shokaku* claimed 12 shot down and one probable, plus another 12 and one probable shared with other fighters; they also claimed two Hurricanes and a biplane — the latter probably a De Havilland Puss Moth belonging to the Colombo Flying Club — destroyed on the ground. Such claims as are known are shown in Table 15.

Spotter planes had been launched by the Nagumo Force to look for any attempt by the Eastern Fleet to attack but, with the arrival of the strike force, the absence of shipping in the harbour at Trincomalee was notified to the Fleet, and the spotters redoubled their vigilance in a search for vessels at sea. At 0755, the crew of the No 3 floatplane from the battleship *Haruna* reported that they had located a *Hermes*-type carrier and three destroyers to the south of Trincomalee, and at once the dive-bombers were ordered to be brought up and launched, the first getting off at 0843. No less than 85 D3As took off, under the overall leadership of Lt Cdr Kakuichi Takahashi, 18 each from *Soryu*, *Hiryu* and *Shokaku*, 17 from *Akagi* and 14 from *Zuikaku*. They were escorted by nine A6Ms, three each from *Akagi*, *Soryu* and *Hiryu*.

At this time, heading in the opposite direction were 11 Blenheims of 11 Squadron, which had been despatched from the Racecourse airstrip at 0820 for a further attempt at finding the Japanese ships; one other had failed to take off. Led by Sqn Ldr Ken Ault, this small force was further weakened when two aircraft had to turn back with engine trouble. Flying out of Kokkilai on the same heading, although independent of the Blenheim force, were six Fulmars of 273 Squadron, led by Lt Bailey:

TABLE 15

JNAF Fighter claims, 9 April 1942:

Hiryu

Lt Yasuhiro Shigematsu*
NAP 1/C Kazu-o Muranaka*
NAP 3/C Isao Tahara
NAP 1/C Kijiro Noguchi
NAP 3/C Toshiaki Harada
NAP 1/C Shigeru Hayashi

two Hurricanes shot down;
two Hurricanes shared — shot down with other A6Ms

Akagi

Lt Cdr Shigeru Itaya
NA 1/C Masashi Ishida

one Hurricane shot down;

Lt Shigehisa Yamamoto
NA 1/C Mitsumi Takasuga

one Hurricane shot down;
one Hurricane shot down and one probable;

Wt Off Suekichi Koyamauchi
NAP 2/C Masao Taniguchi*

one Hurricane shot down;
one Hurricane shot down.

Zuikaku

Lt Mashatoshi Makino (KiA)
NA 1/C Tatsu Matsumoto (KiA)
NA 1/C Tetsuzo Iwamoto*
NAP 2/C Shigenobu Nakada
NA 1/C Shichijiro Mae

one floatplane shot down;
one medium-sized aircraft destroyed on the ground

Lt Yuzo Tsukamoto
NAP 3/C Sanenori Kuroki
NA 1/C Koichi Fujii

19 fighters shot down, including 2 Hurricanes and two other fighters (later described as Hurricanes) which were credited to Iwamoto

NAP 1/C Junjiro Ito
NA 1/C Nobutaka Kurato

Shokaku

Lt Tadeshi Kaneko*
NAP 1/C Fujio Hayashi (KiA)
NA 1/C Sadamu Komachi*

12 fighters shot down and one probable;

Wt Off Takeshi Sumita
NA 1/C Shigeru Kono

12 fighters and one probable shared with other A6Ms;

Lt Takumi Hoashi
NAP 2/C Ichiro Yamamato*
NAP 3/C Yoshifuji Tanaka

plus, two Hurricanes and one biplane destroyed on the ground by these three.

Wt Off Yukuo Hanzawa
NAP 2/C Kenji Okabe*

NB: Two of the above victories are known to have been claimed by Okabe, and one by Komachi.

NB: Bracketing together of names indicates the flights and sections flown; in each case the first name was the section leader. Pilots marked * either were, or later became, 'aces'.

423

"The first intimation of excitement was when a Hurricane from China Bay landed at Kokkilai with a wounded RAF officer, who said the Japanese were attacking. I scrambled my flight, and with my No 2, 'Twinkle' Neal (Sub Lt N.A. Neal) flew off in the general direction of whence the Hurricane had come.

"I had had the back seat gear from all the Fulmars removed to save weight. We did not have enough parachutes and used engine covers to give us the necessary height in the seat.

"I climbed as fast as I could, which was not very fast in a Fulmar, and at about 18,000 feet I saw the *Hermes* ahead. As we approached, I saw more aircraft than I had ever seen in one place before and, as I had no wireless communication (none of us did), I rolled over — and believing that the best chance was to have maximum speed — kept pointing downhill into the melee.

"The Fulmar had a terminal velocity, so we believed, of about 270 knots, and at that speed I arrived in the middle of a lot of aircraft — fortunately all opposition! I remember noting that the *Hermes* was not on fire but seemed to be very full of holes. There was an escort of some sort.

"I found a '96 (*sic*) in front of me and was about to fire when there was the most almighty noise in my cockpit — I pushed the tit and to my surprise, whilst continuing to overtake the '96, it flipped over. The noise, I then discovered, had been my cockpit hood blowing off, doubtless due to the unexpected speed the thing had been doing.

"There was an extraordinary number of aircraft still about, and I was now at about 1,000 feet. I headed for land, being uncomfortable in the presence of the 'Zeros'. There were several aircraft in front of me and once again a '96 got in the way. I regret to say that I continued landwards after that as I had no ammunition and was nervous!

"Nothing pursued me and I arrived back at Kokkilai to find Major Norrie Martin, RM (CO of 814 Squadron) and his Swordfish alone on the strip. We had no refuelling facilities there so after a short stay I went to China Bay. There the armoury was on fire but nobody seemed very interested! We refuelled and headed out to *Hermes* again. On arrival there were no enemy and *Hermes* was sinking fast. We flew around and then returned to China Bay."

Bailey was credited with one D3A shot down and another damaged, whilst two probables were claimed by Sub Lt Neal and Lt Peter Nelson-Gracie (a Royal Marine pilot), and two others were claimed damaged.

Indeed, the first D3As had spotted their quarry before the Blenheims had found theirs — and it was the carrier *Hermes*; crews in *Shokaku*'s aircraft observed the carrier and the Australian destroyer, HMAS *Vampire*, at 1023, *Zuikaku*'s crews spotting them two minutes later.

Lt Cdr Egusa then led a copy-book attack on the two almost defenceless ships, all 32 aircraft releasing their bombs between 1040 and 1050 — there were numerous direct hits and some aircraft went in so low that they were in danger of blast from their own bombs; others approached hugging the wavetops, so low that lookouts, 120 feet above the flightdeck, reported that some swept in below their level; they were followed in by some of the aircraft from *Akagi* and *Hiryu* and so good was the bombing that the number of hits could only be arrived at by deducting the number of near-misses. Of the assault, a naval officer aboard the ill-fated carrier wrote:

"As soon as 'Action Stations' was sounded three planes were seen on the starboard beam. The ship's AA guns and pom-poms opened up but the Jap pilots flew through the barrage, unhooked a stick of bombs, then dive-bombed and machine-gunned the ship. Their bombs exhausted, they made off, and then the attack really developed. Wave after wave of planes in formations of six and three came over.

"Their bombing was pretty deadly. We caught fire and started blazing furiously. The one thing we expected, however, did not materialize. There were no torpedoes. Some of the raiders came in low despite our AA fire. They paid for their audacity. We reckon at least four never reached their bases — we saw them being smacked good and hearty — three staggered away and one came hurtling into the sea."

HMS *Hermes* blazes furiously shortly before sinking with the loss of 19 officers (including her captain) and 288 ratings. *(Authors' collection)*

Utterly shattered, *Hermes* went down at 1055, with the loss of Captain R.F.J. Onslow (who was killed in the bombing), 18 officers and 288 ratings, while HMAS *Vampire*, which had been torn to pieces, followed at 1102; her captain (Lt Cdr W.T.A. Moran, RAN) also went down with his ship, together with seven ratings. *Akagi*'s bombers had also spotted a cargo vessel and two destroyers further north; the aircraft of this contingent and those from *Hiryu* attacked these and claimed the cargo ship and one of the destroyers sunk a few minutes later. In fact their victims were the 5,571-ton RFA *Athelstone* and an escorting corvette, HMS *Hollyhock*, both of which sank under a flurry of bombs, about 30 miles south of Batticoloa Light; 53 of the corvette's crew perished. The D3As of the four carriers then set course for Nagumo Force, but those from *Soryu*, arriving only in time to see the carrier sinking, began a search for other targets to the north.

Just as the attack on *Hermes* got under way, the Blenheims of 11 Squadron arrived over Nagumo Force at 1048, which they had at last found; flying at 11,000 feet they surprised the Japanese sailors, who suddenly saw the water-spouts of bomb bursts around the carrier *Akagi* and the cruiser *Tone*. Although a number of near-misses were seen, no hits were achieved and, before the bombers could make good their escape, the A6Ms of the combat air patrol were upon them. 20 fighters were in the air, six from *Soryu*, eight from *Hiryu* and three each from *Akagi* and *Zuikaku*. Under their fire Blenheim Z7896, piloted by Capt C.H. Adcock, SAAF, was shot down at once, followed by Z9574 flown by Lt F.G. Knight, SAAF, which was seen to crash into the sea from low altitude. Adcock's crew included 806 Squadron's Sub Lt A. Peace, who was aboard as an observer to help with identification of Japanese warships.

Sgt H.A. Maclennan's aircraft (R3911) also went down after a fierce fight, crews of surviving aircraft reporting that Maclennan's gunner, Sgt F.J.G. Nell, appeared to have shot down two of the fighters first and in fact, it seems that he possibly accounted for *Hiryu*'s Lt Sumio Nono, who was lost in this action. A fourth Blenheim, Z7803 flown by Wt Off N.L. Stevenson, was then shot down before the remaining five shook themselves free from their tormentors and headed for home. There were no survivors from any of the downed aircraft.

A multiplicity of claims was put in by the exultant Japanese pilots when they landed, most of them shared; after sifting these, the final claim was set at six bombers shot down. Initial claims were as shown in Table 16.

The surviving Blenheims' ordeals were not yet over. At 1105 they en-countered *Shokaku*'s D3As and *Hiryu*'s A6Ms returning from the attack on *Hermes*, and these at once attacked the bombers. At the time the Japanese aircraft were believed by the 11 Squadron crews to be 60 fighters returning from the attack on Trincomalee. Almost at once Sqn Ldr Ault's aircraft (V5592) was shot down just off the coast; crashing on the beach, it burnt out and the crew were killed; included amongst those in this aircraft was Sub Lt F.W. Bonnell of 806 Squadron, who had accompanied Ault as an observer. Gunners in the remaining bombers claimed two of the attackers shot down. Three *Hiryu* A6M pilots, Wt Off Tsuguo Matsuyama, NAP 1/C Toshio Makinoda and NA 1/C Yutake Chiyoshima, jointly claimed one Blenheim, but Makinoda was shot down and killed, while the dive-bombers claimed to have shared with the *Hiryu* fighters in shooting down two Blenheims, one D3A being damaged in the exchange.

On its return to the Racecourse, the undercarriage of Flg Off H.T.L. Smith's aircraft (Z7759) collapsed on touch-down and the machine ground-looped; the crew emerged from the wreck shaken, but otherwise unhurt. Two of the remaining Blenheims — V6010 piloted by Sgt R.K. Garnham, RNZAF, and Z7506 captained by Sgt E.L.J. Anderson, RAAF, returned riddled by bullets but with uninjured crews; Anderson was subsequently awarded a DFM for his performance.

When the first D3As had appeared overhead, *Hermes* had called for aid, and orders were issued for fighters from both China Bay and Ratmalana to be sent to the defence of the carrier. China Bay was still reeling from the earlier attack and no aircraft could be sent off; at this stage, 261 Squadron had only two aircraft and two pilots available — the wounded Sqn Ldr Lewis and Sgt Mann, who had just walked back to the airfield after having been shot down! They were not ordered off.

At Ratmalana the message was not received until too late to help *Hermes*,

TABLE 16

JNAF Combat Air Patrol Fighter claims against Blenheims of 11 Squadron over Nagumo Force — 9 April 1942:

Soryu

NAP 1/C Kaname Harada*	two Blenheims shared with other A6Ms;
NAP 1/C Genzo Nagasawa	one Blenheim shot down.
NAP 1/C Wataru Kubota	

NAP 1/C Ki-ichi Oda*	
NAP 2/C Jiro Tanaka*	three Blenheims shared with other A6Ms.
NAP 3/C Takeo Takashima	

Hiryu

Lt Sumio Nono (KiA)	
Wt Off Yoshimi Kodama	
NAP 2/C Norboru Todaka	
	four Blenheims shot down,
NAP 1/C Kijiro Noguchi	including two shared with other A6Ms.
NAP 3/C Toshiaki Harada	
NA 1/C Shigeru Hayashi	
NAP 2/C Tadashi Sasaki	
NAP 3/C Haruo Nitta	

Akagi

NAP 1/C Katsumi Tanaka	
NAP 3/C Hiroshi Ohara	three Blenheims shot down.
NAP 1/C Shinpei Sano	

Zuikaku

NAP 1/C Satoshi Kano	
NAP 1/C Seiichi Tsukuda	three Blenheims shot down.
NAP 2/C Goro Sakaida	

NB: Bracketing together of names indicates the flights and sections flown; in each case the first name was the section leader. Pilots marked * either were, or later became, 'aces'.

---

due to damage suffered by the telephone system on the 5th. Notwithstanding, 806 Squadron's commander, Lt Johnston, mustered his available Fulmar pilots although he could not call upon the services of his Senior Pilot, the experienced Lt H.P. Allingham (who had been credited with two victories in the Western Desert with the RNAS Fighter Squadron), who was in hospital with a broken ankle. On this occasion, much to their chagrin, observers and TAGs were ordered to stand down; L/Air Bert Holt remembered:

> "We — that is all the TAGs — went to our planes but were sent away again by the pilots, who said it was only a top cover routine patrol, and we were just 'excess baggage'.

Finally, eight Fulmars of 803 and 806 Squadrons got off, but by the time they arrived over the east coast the carrier had already sunk. The D3As of *Soryu* which had arrived only to see *Hermes* sinking, and which had set up a search further north, had discovered a hospital ship, two cargo ships and a patrol boat at 1200, attacking three minutes later. Their victims were the tanker *British Sergeant*, which foundered off Elephant Point, her crew landing safely in boats, and the Norwegian *Norviken* (2,924 tons), which broke in two and sank. However, the hospital ship *Vita* was not attacked. Just before the attack ended around 1215, the Fulmars arrived and engaged the dive-bombers, becoming involved in a 25 minute battle; for the loss of two of their number, the Navy fighters claimed three D3As shot down, one apiece being credited to Lt Johnston, and Sub Lts Barry Nation (806 Squadron) and Paul Peirano (803 Squadron). L/Air Holt continued:

> "When the Fulmars arrived at *Hermes*' position she had already received her coup de grâce, and the Japs were there, greatly outnumbering them. In the ensuing fight two were lost including Paul Peirano, 'my' pilot; he was a fine type. He got at least one."

Left: Lt Richard Johnston, commanding officer of 806 Squadron. Fleet Air Arm, who claimed a dive-bomber shot down on 9 April. *(Authors' collection)*. Right: Sub Lt Barry Nation of 806 Squadron. He too claimed a dive-bomber shot down on 9 April. *(Authors' collection)*

The Japanese in fact reported losing four of their D3As and five more damaged in combat near the carrier; they recorded that they had been attacked by 19 fighters (the Fulmars of 803, 806 and 273 Squadrons), claiming to have shot down five, with two more probables. Apart from that flown by Sub Lt Peirano, a second Fulmar failed to return from this action, Sub Lt R.F.H. Jacob of 803

Squadron also losing his life. The remaining Fulmars landed at China Bay, ostensibly to refuel and re-arm, but the Station Commander commandeered them for defence of his own airfield, where they were to remain for a few days.

Thus ended the Nagumo Force attack on Ceylon; the fleet was now already steaming south-east, having swung through 180° onto this new track, just before the D3As were launched to seek out *Hermes*. It continued on this heading until midnight, then swung north-east. Bearing gradually southwards again during the next 36 hours, the serried ranks of warships passed through the Andaman Sea and entered the Malacca Strait. By nightfall on the 13th they had slipped between Malaya and Sumatra, passed Singapore and swept into the South China Sea, bound for home.

The Japanese were jubilant; for the first time carrier-borne aircraft had sunk an opposing aircraft carrier. Two cruisers and numerous other vessels had also been sunk and both major ports had apparently been hard hit; they also thought that they had destroyed 120 British aircraft. With the defences in no position to meet a further attack, the British were nonetheless also feeling reasonably self-congratulatory; they thought they had driven off an invasion attempt, and also believed they had severely damaged the Japanese Naval Air Force to the tune of 56 destroyed and 26 probables — *Hermes* and *Vampire* had been credited with having shot down one and probably a second during the attack.

As has been seen, actual Japanese losses were 18, although 33 more had been damaged; British losses in the air were 48, with others destroyed on the ground. At China Bay 261 Squadron had five Hurricane IIBs and one Mark I left serviceable and, with Sqn Ldr Lewis in hospital, command was taken over by Flt Lt Cleaver.

When news of the attacks on Ceylon reached Britain, the question was raised in Parliament " ... whether any military honours have been granted at the funerals of Japanese airmen brought down, in view of the attitude of Japanese airmen machine-gunning British women and children when leaving Singapore." The Secretary of State for Air replied that there was no doubt that the airmen in question would be "honourably interred."

Prime Minister Churchill, astute as ever, saw the triumph of the Japanese naval force for what it was, and for what it remained — a continuing threat to Ceylon and shipping in the Indian Ocean:

> "Japanese success and power in naval air warfare were formidable. In the Gulf of Siam two of our first-class capital ships had been sunk in a few minutes by torpedo aircraft. Now two important cruisers had also perished by a totally different method of air attack — the dive bomber.
>
> "Nothing like this had been seen in the Mediterranean in all our conflicts with the German and Italian Air Forces. For the Eastern Fleet to remain near Ceylon would be courting a major disaster. The Japanese had gained control of the Bay of Bengal, and at their selected moment could obtain local command of the waters around Ceylon. The British aircraft available were far outnumbered by the enemy, and the available carrier-borne air protection would be ineffective against repeated air attacks on the scale of those which had destroyed the *Dorsetshire* and *Cornwall*."

Although *Hermes* had been sunk, she had been the smallest and oldest carrier still in front line service; she had no fighter strength at all, and all her Swordfish had been left at China Bay when she fled from harbour. The cruisers lost on the 5 April were both rather elderly, and it would be fair to say that the Eastern Fleet was relatively unaffected by the Japanese sorties. The shattered fighter squadrons — 30, 258 and 261 — were soon back to strength, a steady supply of Hurricanes now readily available on the sub-continent, as were replacement pilots. 258 Squadron received back into its fold one of its wounded pilots from the East Indies campaign, when Flg Off Donahue was released from hospital.

After the battle — 1: A group of 258 Squadron pilots with one of their Hurricanes a few weeks after the battle. Left to right: Flg Off R. Tudor Jones (Engineer Officer), Flt Lt D.J.T. Sharp, Plt Off N.L. McCulloch, Plt Off A.H. Milnes, Plt Off D.B.F. Nicholls, Sgt H.M. Scott, Flg Off A.G. Donahue, Plt Off A.D.M. Nash, Plt Off A. Brown. *(Sqn Ldr A.H. Milnes)*

Damage at Colombo and Trincomalee was fairly easily repaired, and generally the strikes had not been anywhere near as effective, as catastrophic for the recipients, or as cheap for the attackers, as had been those on Pearl Harbor and Port Darwin; the worst loss was undoubtedly the very considerable tonnage of merchant shipping, sunk mainly by Ozawa's Malaya Force.

In a follow-up cable to President Roosevelt, Churchill prompted a more positive and aggressive response from the Americans:

> "I must revert to the grave situation in the Indian Ocean arising from the fact that the Japanese have felt able to detach nearly a third of their battle fleet and half their carriers, which force we are unable to match for several months. The consequences of this may easily be:
>
> (a)   The loss of Ceylon
>
> (b)   Invasion of Eastern India, with incalculable internal consequences to our whole war plan, including the loss of Calcutta and all contact with the Chinese through Burma.
>
> "It is most important to have some American heavy bombers in India. There are at present about fourteen, and fifty more authorised. But none of these was able to attack the Japanese naval forces last week. We are sending every

After the battle — 2: Pilots of 258 Squadron relaxing (pictured a few weeks after the 5 April action): Left to right: Sgt A.C. Roberts, Sgt H.M. Scott, Flt Lt D.J.T. Sharp. Sgt L.P. Gavin (front), Sgt Duncan, Plt Off A.H. Milnes, Flt Lt F. Land, Sqn Ldr P.C. Fletcher, unknown, Flg Off A.G. Donahue, Plt Off D.B.F. Nicholls (standing, rear), Plt Off N.L. McCulloch (crouching), unknown, Plt Off A. Brown (resting forearms on ground), Sgt D. Gregory (foreground). *(Sqn Ldr A.H. Milnes)*

suitable aircraft to the East which can be efficiently serviced out there, but without your aid this will not be sufficient."

Roosevelt's response was, as ever, immediate, and American build up of air power in India quickly began in earnest. Events would soon overtake the Japanese; the once mighty and seemingly invincible Japanese Navy and its air arm would be all but annihilated in a series of air-sea battles during the ensuing two months. As a result, Ceylon was to suffer no further attacks.

It is very difficult to measure the extent to which losses in aircraft and crews both in action and to other causes, during the Indian Ocean venture, caused *Akagi, Hiryu* and *Soryu*, which had by far the most experienced and efficient air groups, to stay longer in port after their return to Japan, taking on replacements of both aircraft and aircrews. Suffice to say that only *Zuikaku* and *Shokaku* were available to support the attempted landings in south-east New Guinea, which led to the Battle of the Coral Sea on 7 May — these vessels carrying, as has been described, the least experienced air groups of the Japanese fleet carriers. Had any or all the other carriers been in a position to take part in this battle the outcome could well have been very different. As it was, *Shokaku* was badly damaged and limped home to fight another day.

Chapter 11

CONCLUSIONS AND AFTERMATH

Air Vice-Marshal Maltby, AOC Java, was the most senior RAF officer to be taken prisoner with the fall of Java, together with a bevy of Air Commodores, Group Captains, Wing Commanders and so forth. Once the few evacuation flights to Australia had ceased, there was no escape from Java except for a handful of opportunists, although many others tried.

The 242 Squadron pilots going 'into the bag' to join those of 605 Squadron, included Sqn Ldr Julian, Flt Lt Parker, Plt Offs Fitzherbert, Gartrell, Bainbridge and Lockwood, Sgts Dovell, Young, May, Dunn, Fleming, Holmes, Newlands, Fairbairn, Porter and Isdale. Sgt Gordon Dunn was amongst those taken to Kalidjati, where they were forced to work on the aerodrome:

> "Shortly after our arrival questionaires were distributed and asked questions such as 'How many flying hours each person had?', 'Where they trained?', 'What the Allies used as aircrew diet?'. The Wing Commander in charge explained that the papers should not be filled out. Next morning about 20 of us were taken for private interrogation, one at a time, and were beaten in 3rd degree methods.
>
> "Sgt Kynman was placed on the floor during his interrogation and his wrists and ankles tied together behind him. A rope was thrown over a rafter, tied to his wrists and ankles and he was raised off the floor. A lighted candle was placed on the floor under him and he was then raised and lowered so that the flame would burn his bare chest.
>
> "As we were released, we were in turn brought out to a wall and told we were to be executed at 4 o'clock. Guards began picking up bits of personal clothing for their own use after the execution. The Squadron Leader in charge of the party devised a code we could use and advised filling in the questionaire, which seemed the only alternative. This gave no definite information and seemed to satisfy the Japs."

They would be kept in camps in Java for some months, and then most were transferred to Japan. While life was desperately hard, the mortality rate was not nearly as high as amongst those who had been captured in Malaya and Singapore and who ended up working on the infamous Burma-Siam railway; most of the Java captives survived to return home at the conclusion of hostilities — several of them having seen the explosion of the Nagasaki atomic bomb.

Two days before the end in Java, most of the remaining Blenheim aircrew, together with a few ground personnel, under the command of Wg Cdr Jeudwine, found themselves at Tjilatjap without a hope of getting away. Jeudwine

Sgt Ken Holmes of 242 Squadron, one of those taken prisoner with the fall of Java. *(K.H. Holmes)*

assembled his men and with sorrow, addressed them:

> "I'm afraid, gentlemen, it is now a case of every man for himself! I do wish we had been able to do better."

Undaunted at this stage, they searched for some means of escape and small parties dispersed to inspect any available craft which might be used. Jeudwine instructed Sqn Ldr Tayler to take a party of officers (Flt Lts Wyllie, Holland

and Owen) to search the harbour; John Wyllie:

"All the local residents of the port, black and white, have scarpered. Somebody must have pressed the panic button. Three apparently deserted, ships are lying in the stream. Tjilatjap is a long narrow inlet with a buoyed channel through a reef at the entrance.

"As we pull away from the wharf in a motor launch a Jap bomber comes over. He makes several unopposed runs at low level across the the dozen oil tanks and picks and chooses where he will drop his bombs. He is 100% accurate. Tanks blow up, other tanks burst and pour their contents out into the harbour. One explosion knocks me in a heap through the door beside the steering wheel. It also blows the windows out of the wheel house in which I am standing.

"Then the oil on the water catches fire. I head the boat out of the oil slick which is running down the harbour with the tide. Upstream there is a Dutch escort vessel. The Jap pilot has his gunner put a couple of bursts of machine gun fire into the ship which does not return his fire. We go on board to check her out. We find she has a crew — of two. Both are blind drunk. We look for navigation instruments but our two clowns have thrown them all in the sea. We find a chart of the section of the Indian Ocean which included the Timor Sea, Java and the NW coast of our destination, Australia. It is roughly a thousand miles away.

"We go down the harbour to a KPM cargo ship. We get on board and find that all the crew have also decamped. There is a large vessel, like a lifeboat only bigger, in her davits. This is a trap and I fall into it. Because the boat is bigger, and therefore able to carry more people, I think she will meet our needs best. We raid the ship's lazaret and stock up well with canned milk, bully beef and several large containers of dried apples. We add beakers of water and a bottle of whisky; just in case!

"At nightfall we go to a pier down the harbour, leaving our boat full of supplies alongside the KPM ship where it is out of sight of people on the shore. Two land; two stay with the boat. The two who go ashore return very soon. The Japanese are in the town. We hear sounds of shooting which confirms this. In the dark, careful not to use lights, we pick up our 'lifeboat' and move alongside a small coaster, again keeping on the side out of sight of the town. The coaster is also deserted; her engines are too complex for us to handle. She has some 60 gallon drums of oil on deck. Another trap, we fall into it. We get an empty drum down into the launch and fill it by siphoning the oil out of one of the barrels on the ship's deck. We sleep uneasily in the coaster.

"Spend the day in hiding, hoping the Japanese do not send anyone out to search the ships. Near midnight, cursing the 'bombers' moon, which happily has started to wane, we get under way in the launch towing the boat with the stores in it. Covertly, during the day, we had watched the town. We saw some men in khaki but they were too far off for us to be sure they were Japs. They were small and wore puttees, so we felt safe in assuming they were the enemy. No sign of any of our people.

"Identifying the marker buoys in the dark, going through the reef, is tricky. Nasty feeling that some trigger happy Jap with a machine gun might try to discourage us. At slow speeds, as we crawl circumspectly through the tortuous passage, the boat on tow yaws about like a drunken mariner with a wooden leg. I thought it might be because of the way we had loaded her, putting too much weight too far aft. Past the outer beacon we open up to full speed. At about five or six knots the tow rides more easily despite the fact that we run into long steep swells. In fact, the 'lifeboat' mounts them better than we do. The harbour launch is not designed to cope with sea conditions in the Indian Ocean. Except for the Canadian, John Tayler, who hails from the prairies and has scarcely ever seen the sea before, we are all as sick as dogs."

The original tankful of fuel lasted about 70 miles before it ran out, when they discovered the other drum had the wrong grade of diesel; as a consequence they transferred to the other boat and got under sail. The weather remained fine for a few days but they then ran into violent storms. The situation worsened until 4 April when the vessel finally sank in heavy seas just offshore. The party got ashore at Semajang and were driven to Soerabaya, where they were handed over to the Japanese.

Meanwhile, back at Tjilatjap, their companions had located two lifeboats, each about 20 feet long and equipped with mast and sail. A delighted Jeudwine was determined to use them in a bid to reach Australia! He despatched parties to round-up as much food and provisions as could be found — tins of biscuits, cans of meat, containers of fresh water and a supply of canned beer. All climbed aboard the lifeboats, while two others manned a small, flat-bottomed river launch, which was to tow them down river to the open sea, where the launch was to be abandoned. However, fumes from the launch's engines overwhelmed the occupants and it was prematurely abandoned. It was realised at this stage that one of the lifeboats was obviously unfit for sea travel, therefore an alternative plan was devised.

The two lifeboats pulled into a small, well-forested island (Noesa Kembangan) in the mouth of the estuary, the less seaworthy of the boats rendering itself useless for further travel on the sharp coral. The CO again assembled everybody and advised them that he still intended to sail the one remaining boat to Australia, with a hand-picked crew totalling one dozen. The remainder were to remain on the island, where there was fresh water. With great optimism, he promised to return with a flyingboat by night and land as close to the shore as possible to evacuate those left behind. Flg Off M. Keble-White (one of the newly-arrived Sea Party) was placed in charge and was "instructed to remain where we were for two months". Jeudwine, who believed he and his party could reach Australia in three weeks, departed on the evening of 7 March. They did, in fact, succeed in reaching Australia after 47 days at sea.

Five days after Jeudwine's departure, another small boat was seen amongst the debris floating into the estuary, and this was retrieved by Sgts Dave Russell, Lloyd Keene and Rod McLeod. After an inspection of the boat, the trio requested permission from Keble-White to attempt an escape by following Jeudwine's example and making for Australia. Permission was reluctantly given and after a number of repairs were made, volunteers were called for: Sgts Joe Morley and Eric Frye, both RAF, together with RAAF Sgts Neville Jeans (who had been turned off Jeudwine's boat at the last moment), Al Tredenick and Larry Foxwell were selected. Their provisions comprised one 10 gallon tin of fresh water, 40 packets of Marie biscuits, two dozen hardtack biscuits and 190 cans of beer! Progress was slow, and ten days after leaving Tilatjap, covered in sunsores and low on supplies, the boat was overturned by a large wave during the night.

All eight survived the ordeal and on recovery they stumbled on a small fishing village, where they were given coffee and pickled eggs. On payment of 100 guilders, the headman promised to find them food, tobacco and a boat but instead returned with a Japanese patrol.

A day or so after Russell's party had departed, another small boat drifted into view of those stranded on Noesa Kembangan, and was brought ashore. It seemed in reasonable condition but only Sgts Hugh Hough and Doug McKillop were keen to have a go; having gathered food and water, they too set out for Australia. Not far into journey they were hit by a tropical storm and the boat was wrecked on the rocky shoreline. Both were thrown into the sea and became separated, each believing the other had perished. In the event, both survived, clinging to the rocks during the night only to be captured by Japanese troops next day.

Those left behind, numbering about 50, were fated to remain on Noesa Kembangan for 44 days, sharing the desert island with inmates of a Dutch civilian prison and living off rations originally collected. They were not troubled by the Japanese, who were busy mopping up on the mainland. During the last three weeks they lived on six ounces of food a day per person, and had fixed up a big piece of canvas to catch rain water; they tried living off the sea, fishing with bent pins and trying their hand at spearing but to no avail. Foraging in the jungle brought little success, two of the airmen stumbling across an orang-utang which gave them the fright of their lives. Sgt Bill Miller recalled:

> "We had to be careful in among the trees because, along with all the coral on the rocks, it was dead easy to get deep scratches and abrasions and because of our reduced diet, injuries festered very quickly. We had no medical equipment to deal with any wounds we got. Doug Argent scratched his ankle rather badly on the coral and his leg swelled up like a balloon and really needed expert attention. We made a poultice out of soap and sugar and it drew out all the pus; we kept bathing his ankle with salt water to harden up the skin."

On 9 March Flg Off Keble-White called for volunteers to visit the mainland for food; Sgt Archie Wakefield recalled:

> "The party was led by Ron Millar and consisted of Geoff Bell, Doug Argent, Len Small, myself and one other whom I can't remember (*in fact, Sgt Allan Ross*). We climbed up through the jungle at the back of the beach until we reached a track. We turned along this until we came to a road which, in turn, led us to the civilian prison camp opposite Tjilatjap. The prison staff assumed that we wished to surrender to the Japs and took us down the river, landing us a little downstream from the town itself.
>
> "We scouted around but could find no supplies. The oil tanks were still burning fiercely and everywhere seemed quiet and deserted. After a time we reached the bottom of the road which led from the jetty to the town centre. There was some commotion up towards the centre and Geoff Bell and Len Small decided to investigate. We hid in the front garden of a house

watching their progress. As they walked up the road, a car came down towards them, stopped, and out jumped a Japanese officer pointing a revolver at them.

"We could do nothing and made off through a native kampong where either the inhabitants had fled or were keeping much under cover. Eventually we found an empty hut and sat on the floor waiting for nightfall."

Following a search of the area, a small dugout canoe was acquired and in this the survivors paddled back to the island, reaching the beach just before dawn. Wakefield continued:

"We were shocked to be told, when eventually we ourselves were in prison camp, that Geoff and Len had been treated so badly that the latter had died, and that the former was later beheaded."

Another party of four had also gone over to Tjilatjap — Sgts Bill Hare, Frank Cameron, George Sharley together with LAC Bill Northwood. When walking along the docks at 1330 they came across a Japanese sentry. Hare pulled out his .38 revolver and shot him; he fell screaming and a number of soldiers appeared from a nearby hut, armed with rifles and bayonets. Hare and Cameron ran at the double but Sharley and Northwood were last seen bending over the wounded sentry. It is believed that they were shot on the spot. Sgt Miller added:

"Bill Hare and Frank Cameron took three days to get back to the beach. They were like a couple of corpses when they got back. Their clothes were in tatters and they were covered in awful cuts and bruises, hundreds of them, all over their bodies, from crashing through the undergrowth to avoid search parties. At one time they had hidden in the water under a jetty, with the Nips hiving around just above their heads, obviously out in a posse looking for them. They kept ducking under and coming up for air; they knew the Japs would cut them to pieces if they found them. They made a wide detour, in case they betrayed our presence on the beach."

Towards the end of the six weeks, men were becoming ill and, on 1 April, Sgt Edward Daly went down with malaria — it was decided he needed urgent treatment, and he was taken by stretcher to within half a mile of the Dutch convict prison at the other end of the island, then two volunteers carried him the rest of the way, but Daly died almost immediately on arrival at a POW hospital (10 April). Help was asked of the Dutch prison officials, but warning had already been issued that the death-sentence would be administered on anyone who gave aid and succour to the enemy, and the Japanese authorities were duly notified. Miller:

"So over they came! Front-line troops! The took us across the river to Tjilatjap, to an open place like an arena. They dragged poor old Keble-White out to the front, so that he was the centre point for us and all the sodding natives who had formed a huge circle around us. They forced him down on his knees, grabbing his hair to jerk his head forward. The officer had his sword out and was practising his drill to show us how expert he was! I'll say this for Keble-White, he behaved well; didn't toss in the towel, gave plenty back with his tongue, wanted to know why the hell he should die when he had fought honourably — he showed he had guts. But they didn't do him after all. They got us into our ranks and marched us to a large Dutch barracks."

Of his terrifying experience, Keble-White later wrote:

> "I was told that I was considered a bandit because I had not given myself up at the capitulation and was to be executed on the spot! They even went so far as to get me in position with a large baulk of timber under my neck to prevent damage to the very large sword which was making swishing noises in the air, uncomfortably close to my ear. However, after a few minutes, the officer in charge told me to get up, saying that the sword was reserved only for 'honourable men' and that I would be shot in the morning.
>
> "On the following morning I was glad to find that I had met no unpleasantness in the way of a firing party, but was uneasy as I had no idea what was to become of us."

Another frustrated sea escape attempt involving aircrew concerned two Australian Vildebeest observers, Plt Offs Skip Glowery of 36 Squadron and Vic Ryan of 100 Squadron. At Pameungpeuk they had joined forces with six soldiers who had hatched a plan which called for a pooling of money to pay a native to build them a sailing boat, in which they would attempt to reach Australia. When about three miles out to sea the boat was pounded by breakers, severely damaging the craft and rendering it unseaworthy. They managed to reach the shore but next morning were taken prisoner by a patrol of Javanese militia.

Elsewhere on Java small groups of airmen were similarly frustrated in their attempts to render various abandoned aircraft airworthy in bids to escape. During early April, Flg Off Harry Siddell and Sgt Les Patrick of the 59 Squadron detachment, together with two Canadian fighter pilots of 266 Wing, Flt Sgts Howard Low and Russell Smith, and Plt Off Red Campbell of 605 Squadron, hatched a plot to escape from Boei Glodok prison camp and attempt to steal a Ki-56 transport aircraft which they had seen parked at nearby Batavia airport. At the eleventh hour however, Patrick went down with a bout of maleria and was forced to drop out, then, the day before the planned breakout (10 April), Campbell informed the others that he had seen Japanese personnel testing the engines of the transport aircraft and that one engine had developed an obvious fault. His doubts however failed to deter the other three from making an attempt to escape that night. Armed with revolvers and knives, they apparently killed a guard and managed to get one engine started before being captured.

It was rumoured that they were tortured by Kempetei in an attempt to extract information about any others who might be involved in the escape plot, then taken to a corner of the airfield and forced to dig their own graves, and were bayoneted to death. Their deaths are officially recorded as having occurred on 12 April (Siddell) and three days later for Low and Smith. Shortly after, all prisoners were ordered to sign a piece of paper to undertake formally not to attempt to escape. Wg Cdr C.H. Noble, the Senior British Officer, issued an order that no one was to sign, and was severely beaten for his pains, and ten men were thrown into solitary confinement, without food or water, until everyone had signed. Noble relented and agreed for all to sign, pointing out that as signatures were obtained under duress they were without effect.

At Andir meanwhile, a Glenn Martin WH-3 had been discovered which, according to Cpl George Dunbar of 211 Squadron:

> "Had not been extensively damaged, apart from ailerons, elevators and rudder being slashed. It did not require a lot of servicing. Its lack of range

was the big problem. However we did find an overload fuel tank, which had been used for delivery, I presume, and all the necessary equipment — pipes and pump — for fuel delivery. It was fitted to the bomb bay and operated satisfactorily on test. Obtaining the correct fuel was a problem, but we found a store of fuel drums in the jungle fairly close by and we used a 15 cwt truck to move it to the aircraft."

Sqn Ldr Jardine of 205 Squadron had agreed to fly the aircraft but Wg Cdr A.D. Groome, who was in charge of the RAF contingent at Andir, refused them permission to leave, as it was feared that reprisals would be taken against those staying behind.

At Tasikmalaja, where there were 2,000 mainly RAF and RAAF POWs, the Japanese issued warning that for every man who escaped six others would be shot, which effectively put an end to further escape bids. One group of aircrew had been busy trying to repair a damaged American bomber that had been abandoned in one corner of the airfield (possibly the DB-7). Following the Japanese warning, a meeting of senior officers called for volunteers to slash the aircraft's tyres, an action which upset the would be escapers, who threatened to have those responsible court-martialed after the war.

Apart from the many thousands of British Commonwealth prisoners, the Japanese also captured some 42,000 Dutch troops (2,522 Dutch officers and men had been killed during the fighting) and 76,000 soldiers on Bataan, including 12,000 Americans. A fair number of undamaged or only slightly damaged aircraft also fell into their hands, including a few in the Philippines, in Malaya and Singapore, but particularly in the Indies. At Kalidjati a substantial number of Blenheims had been captured during the surprise attack on this airfield[1], as had five Glenn Martins.

About 16 more of these bombers, including eight of the original WH-ls, remained undestroyed on Java on 8 March, to add to others found on Singapore. Indeed, so many Glenn Martins did the Japanese find in their possession that nine were subsequently passed to the Royal Thai Air Force to supplement their aircraft of this type. Other types included at least one CW-21B Interceptor, a number of Dutch Brewsters, one or two RAF Buffaloes and several Hurricanes, one of which was a Dutch machine.

At least one Hurricane was air tested by the 64th Sentai, Lt A. Kikuchi losing his life when this crashed. Also captured were a KNILM DC3 and a damaged DC-5 (PK-ADA), which was subsequently repaired and flown to Bandoeng. At least six of the Dutch Ryan STMs (RO-10, 26, 28, 44, 48 and 65) were also taken intact, and at least one brand-new Tiger Moth, still in its crate[2]. Subsequently, examples of many of these aircraft, together with a B-17D and a P-40E, were despatched to Japan for evaluation and to be put on display.

The Japanese employed Dutch POWs to continue work on salvaging the

---

[1] Sgt Dave Russell, former WOp/AG of 84 Squadron, commented: "I actually saw two of our Blenheims in flight over Bandoeng a couple of months after I'd been taken prisoner. The Japs had removed the turrets. I felt bad about that."
[2] Immediately following the Japanese surrender in 1945, vessels of the British Naval Invasion Force arrived off the western coast of Malaya and parties went ashore. Amongst British stores and supplies discovered in the Port Swettenham area was a brand-new, unassembled Tiger Moth in RAF colours, still in its original crate (this may have been the machine referred to above). It was taken aboard the escort carrier HMS *Pursuer*, assembled and air tested, and was ultimately taken back to the UK when the carrier completed its duties in Far Eastern waters.

Japanese photograph of captured Dutch Brewsters and RAF Buffaloes. Nearest aircraft, B-395 of 2-VLG-V, has had its 'Java Rhinoceros' markings painted out; next in line, W8163 GA-P, formerly of 21 RAAF Squadron, has had its RAF markings painted out and ML markings substituted. *(Authors' collection)*

DB-7Cs abandoned at Tjilatjap and by early May one aircraft had been made ready for testing (AL904). The Japanese were reluctant to fly it themselves from the quay, and ordered Mr Theodore de Bruyn, a director of KNILM, to supply a pilot. He in turn approached one of the company's pilots, Capt Karl Rupplin von Keffikon, who agreed to the request but informed de Bruyn that, should he have an opportunity to escape with the aircraft, he would make such an attempt. Two Dutch engineers volunteered to accompany him. On the day of the flight — to Bandoeng — a Japanese guard also accompanied them. The plan had been to make for Christmas Island, 300 miles southwest into the Indian Ocean. It was agreed that von Keffikon would fly the aircraft around for 30 minutes in order to estimate the fuel endurance and if there was sufficient fuel, he would remove his helmet from his head, at which one of the engineers would attack the guard with a large monkey wrench. Unfortunately for the would-be escapees, the aircraft was found to have insufficient range and was flown, somewhat reluctantly, to Bandoeng.

The aircraft was later flown by a Japanese pilot to Atsugi, Japan, where it was exhibited with other war prizes; the wreck of AL904 was discovered there after VJ Day.

Whilst it was almost impossible for those incarcerated on Java to escape, those imprisoned at Hong Kong were more fortunate, particularly in the early days of captivity. There had been 33 successful escapes from Hong Kong by May 1943, including two by members of the Station Flight, although one of the first to escape from the POW camp had been Lt Colonel Lindsay Ride (commander of field ambulance unit of HK Volunteer Corps) who got away with four others on 9 January 1942 and with the aid of Communist guerillas reached safety next day[1].

Another early escaper from Hong Kong (although not from the POW camp) was a Chinese-American fighter ace, Lt Art Chin, whose real name was Chin Jui-tien. Born of Chinese parentage in Oregon, where he learned to fly, he joined the Chinese Air Force in 1937. By late 1940 he had claimed six air victories and was flying a Gladiator biplane when, in a fight with A6Ms off Hainan Island, he was shot down and badly burned. He spent many months in hospital at Hong Kong, and was there when the Japanese invaded. He remained under cover for a month before escaping with his wife and two children to Canton.

On 1 February 1942, Plt Off E.D. Crossley, RNZAF, (late of the Station Flight) and two army officers escaped from the POW camp at Shamshuipo; they had bribed local Chinese to bring a junk close on to a breakwater near the camp wire. They broke camp and under fire from the guards swam for 20 minutes across Laichikok Bay to make their rendezvous. Safely across and eluding a Japanese patrol, they headed into the surrounding hills. Hiding by day and travelling by night they managed to evade patrols and reached the Chinese Army HQ at Waichow, some 18 days after the breakout, during which they had twice been attacked and beaten by Chinese bandits. From Waichow they were taken to Kukong, from where they were flown to India. Crossley was awarded a Military Cross for his escape, which was greater reward than that handed out to the other RAF escapee, Flt Sgt W.D. Beddow.

Flt Sgt Bill Beddow, also a former Vildebeest pilot with the Station Flight, arrived in India some months later with two other escapees, both army sergeants. According to Flt Lt Don Jackson of 34 Squadron, "the two army men were decorated on the spot but Beddow was reprimanded by the AOC (Air Vice-Marshal Stevenson) for being improperly dressed!"

Following the escape of Plt Off Crossley and the two army officers, four of the more senior RAF officers in captivity including Wg Cdr H.G. Sullivan, former CO of Kai Tak, and Flg Off H.B. Gray, AFM, of the Station Flight, were sent to Saigon where they were incarcerated in a small and filthy cell, already crammed full with Japanese defaulters. After about five months — during which time Sullivan had fallen ill and had been hospitalised — the quartet were returned to Hong Kong, where they were to remain until the end of the war, with the exception of Gray.

Flg Off Gray was arrested on 1 July 1943 together with two NCOs, all three charged with acting as couriers — smuggling medicine and messages internally — and of making contact with the British army aid group and Chinese resistance on the mainland. Two Chinese arrested at the same time were immediately executed. Ten days later two army officers were also arrested on similar charges and, on 18 December 1943, the three officers were shot; each would post-humously be awarded the George Cross. The two NCOs were sentenced to 15 years imprisonment; in the event they both survived the war.

With the fall of Burma the series of Allied retreats following on the initial Japanese assaults were at an end. Even as the tattered remnants of Lt General

---

[1] Lt Colonel Ride would later be recruited by MI9 to organize and operate a rescue organization within unoccupied China, which was to be successful in helping 38 shot down US airmen to reach Allied lines later in the war.

Alexander's army were crossing the frontier into India, desperate resistance was at last stemming the momentum of the assault in New Guinea.

When, on the eve of hostilities, Admiral Isoroku Yamamoto (Commander-in-Chief, Japanese Imperial Navy) had promised Prime Minister Konoe that, if Japan insisted on going to war with the United States, Britain and the Netherlands, he would "give them hell for a year and a half", he was only partly correct with his forecast. As has been seen, for six months the Japanese swept all before them in their conquest of South-East Asia but, from May 1942 onwards, Japan's sudden rise would progressively and inevitably start to decline. Admiral Yamamoto had, however, followed his confident boast to Konoe with a prophetic warning: "I can guarantee nothing as to what will happen after that."

Before May 1942 was out the Imperial Navy had been held to a draw in the Coral Sea, during the first sea battle ever to be fought principally between the carrier air groups, when the Japanese lost their newly-converted carrier *Shoho*, with *Skokaku* suffering severe damage; in return, the Americans lost *Lexington*, while a second carrier, *Yorktown*, suffered damage. A month later, in June, by a combination of luck, good tactics and sound experience, the US Navy was to inflict a crushing defeat on its opponent at the Battle of Midway (the Japanese losing *Akagi*, *Hiryu*, *Kaga* and *Soryu* while the Americans lost the hastily repaired *Yorktown*), putting a halt to further Japanese expansion and effectively changing the course of the war.

In August the United States would challenge Japanese occupation of the Solomon Islands by launching an amphibious counter-invasion of the southern island of Guadalcanal. This jungle-clad, fever-ridden island, together with New Guinea, which featured similar physical conditions, exacerbated by the precipitous mountains of the Owen Stanley range, were to remain the main war zones for many months to come, as was the India-Burma frontier area in the north.

The defeat of the Allied forces in South-East Asia and the East Indies had come as no great surprise, given Britain's involvement in the war with Germany and Italy in the western hemisphere, and the United States' chronic unpreparedness. What had been surprising perhaps, was the speed and completeness of the collapse. As was so often to be the case in this and other wars, audacity, training, experience, good equipment, good planning and concentration of force had achieved apparent miracles.

The Allies had been far weaker in real terms than sheer numbers appeared to indicate. The Dutch and Americans were devoid of actual experience, while the British Commonwealth troops, with all the best men and units long since drawn away to North Africa and the United Kingdom, were by and large undertrained, poorly equipped, ill-motivated, and above all, abysmally led. The lack of inter-service co-operation was regretable; the lack of co-operation by the civil administration was nothing short of scandalous. The arrogant, insular, over confident and self-satisfied attitudes of pre-war colonialism virtually ensured that the war was lost before it was even begun. For this, for appeasement, for lack of foresight and for government parsimony, the forces had paid a terrible price, as now did the civilian population.

What came out of this was the myth of the Japanese soldier as a superman, which proved ultimately untrue, however tough, ruthless, well trained and well motivated he might have been. What else arose was a tremendous and all pervading awe of the A6M 'Zero' fighter, which was perceived as the epitome

Top: The nose of a USAAF Curtiss P-40 (left) and a Dutch Curtiss-Wright CW-22 in Japanese hands. Middle: Repainted for test purposes in Japan, a Curtiss-Wright CW-21B fighter. Bottom: Delivered too late for use by the Dutch, one or two Douglas DB-7B light bombers fell into Japanese hands and were tested by them. This aircraft, carrying the RAF serial AL904, indicating that it had been diverted from Lend-Lease deliveries to the British, is seen at Andir airfield.

of the Japanese victory in Allied eyes, in much the way that the Spitfire had been seen as the victor of the Battle of Britain. Note however that it was the aircraft — the machine — which stuck in the Allied psyche, rather than the remarkable skill of its pilots, which was in fact every bit as important. The superior performance of the aircraft was credited with all its dashing successes. The sheer professionalism of the men involved seems as ever at that time to have passed British commanders by, obsessed as they were with the "numbers game" and the team ethos. The Americans appeared to learn this lesson a little better, and were quick to ensure that the aircrew they were subsequently to commit to battle were as well trained as it was possible for them to be. Successful fighter pilots were encouraged to increase their prowess, and although rested regularly, were frequently circulated back to the fighting zone for second and third tours of duty.

Not everywhere did the American military adopt an enlightened approach however. One of the few brighter aspects of the early fighting had been the relative success of Chennault's American Volunteer Group in Burma and China, whose better tactics and good training had allowed them to achieve satisfactory results. However, instead of ensuring the ongoing services and undoubted experience of this unique formation, the US Army Air Force handled their attempted induction into its own ranks in such a way, with a lack of tact or finesse, that few remained in China, and most were to see no further active service throughout the rest of the war.

The speed and nature of the disaster which had overtaken the Allies had been such that few fighter pilots had enjoyed much opportunity to build up sizeable personal scores. Few RAF fighter pilots had any greater opportunity to shine than their American counterparts, and fewer still would achieve great things as the war progressed. For most of the relative handful of experienced pilots sent out by the RAF, the opening of the Far East war was to be the culmination of their most active flying. Pilots such as Wg Cdr Frank Carey, Sqn Ldrs 'Bunny' Stone, 'Jimmy' Elsdon, Gerald Lewis, Barry Sutton and Tim Vigors, training and admnistrative posts beckoned for much of the rest of the war, although Sutton, Stone and Elsdon were all to command wings or squadrons without seeing further aerial combat.

Of the Hurricane pilots who had served in Singapore, Sumatra and Java, the most successful had been Sgt James 'Sandy' Sandeman Allen, credited with seven victories, whilst Sgt Jimmy King followed closely with six and one shared; and Flt Lt Edwin Murray Taylor (deceased) and Sgt Ron Dovell with six apiece. Sgt Henry Nicholls claimed five and one shared, whilst Sqn Ldr Ivan Julian and Flt Lt Jimmy Parker were each credited with five. Amongst those who flew Buffaloes, Sgt Geoff Fisken emerged as top-scorer with six; one source credited Sgt Bert Wipiti (who was later killed over Northern Europe) with eight although his score was probably nearer to the three and one shared as recorded.

Amongst the Burma pilots, Wg Cdr Carey had gained a further seven air victories (as recorded), having raised his tally to at least 28, including shares, adding a second Bar to his DFC. Somewhat surprisingly, he was not awarded a DSO in recognition of his leadership. Sgt 'Tex' Barrick had been credited with five and one shared, receiving a DFM, while Flt Lt Jack Storey had claimed four victories. The subsequent careers of many of the Commonwealth pilots mentioned here will be found in the new edition of *Aces High: Successful Fighter*

Top: The remains of Brewster B-3114, clearly showing the 'Java Rhinoceros' emblem of 2-VlG-V. *(Authors' collection)*. Above: This poor but interesting photo shows Japanese troops in a wrecked aircraft dump, inspecting the remains of Curtiss H-75A C-334 of 1-VlG-IV.

Top: Brewster despatched to Japan for test is seen here at Tachikawa Army Air Force Base, carrying the test centre insignia on its tail. Above: Badly damaged Martin WH-3, M-524, under inspection by Japanese troops.

Pilots of the British and Commonwealth Air Forces in WWII, due to be published in this series in 1994. (A list of the most successful pilots during this campaign will be found in Tables 17 & 18.)

Amongst the British and Commonwealth bomber pilots who had served in the area during the fighting, perhaps the most well known in the future would be 211 Squadron's commanding officer, Wg Cdr Bob Bateson. In February 1944 Bateson joined 2nd Tactical Air Force's No 2 Group to command 613 Squadron on Mosquito VI fighter-bombers. On 11 April he led an attack on a house near the Peace Palace in the Hague, Holland, hitting this precise target with 'pinpoint' accuracy. The immediate award of a DSO to add to his DFC followed. Posted to the Staff of No 2 Group in July 1944 and promoted Group Capt, he led another such 'pinpoint' raid by a whole wing of Mosquitos on 21 March 1945,

TABLE 17

Successful British and Commonwealth Fighter Pilots in operations over Malaya, Singapore and Netherlands East Indies, December 1941 — March 1942:

		Claims (SE Asia):
Sgt J.A Sandeman Allen	232/242 Sqn.	7
Sgt G.J. King	232/242 Sqn.	6½
Sgt G.B. Fisken, RNZAF	243 Sqn.	6
Flt Lt E.M. Taylor	232 Sqn.	6
Sgt R.L. Dovell	232/242 Sqn.	6
Sgt H.T. Nicholls	232 Sqn.	5½
Flt Lt B.J. Parker	232/242 Sqn.	5
Sqn Ldr I. Julian	232/242 Sqn.	5
Flt Lt R.D.Vanderfield, RAAF	21/453 Sqn.	4
Flg Off M.H. Holder	243 Sqn	4
Sgt S.N. Hackforth	232 Sqn.	4
Plt Off E.C. Gartrell, RNZAF	232/242 Sqn.	4
Sgt E.E.G. Kuhn, RNZAF	488/605 Sqns.	4
Plt Off J.A. Campbell	258 Sqn.	4
Sgt B.S. Wipiti, RNZAF	243 Sqn.	3½
Flt Lt M. Garden	243 Sqn.	3
Flg Off N.C. Sharp, RNZAF	243/605 Sqns.	3
Sgt G. Hardie	232/242 Sqn.	3
Flt Lt H.A. Farthing	232 Sqn.	3

TABLE 18

Successful British and Commonwealth Fighter Pilots in operations over Burma, December 1941 — March 1942:

		Claims (Burma):
Wg Cdr F.R. Carey	135 Sqn/267 Wg.	7
Sgt J.F. Barrick, RCAF	17 Sqn.	5½
Flt Lt W.J. Storey, RAAF	135 Sqn.	4

when the Gestapo Headquarters in the Danish town of Odense was similarly 'taken out'.

Bateson's opposite number in 84 Squadron, Wg Cdr John Jeudwine, escaped to Australia (as recorded) a feat for which he received an OBE; on returning to the UK, he later commanded 619 Squadron, flying Lancasters over Northern Europe, and was awarded a DSO and DFC, but was killed whilst test flying a Typhoon shortly after the end of the war. Of those who escaped from Java with Jeudwine, Sgts George Sayer and Bill Cosgrove retrained on Beaufighters and were both lost in the course of subsequent actions when flying with 30 RAAF Squadron. Within the RAAF Hudson units which had borne the brunt of the initial fighting in Malaya, most of the aircrews continued to fly on operations from Australian bases. As an example, Flt Lt Herb Plenty, who had been awarded a DFC, flew further operations with 100 Squadron, the RAAF Beaufort unit, winning a second DFC (see Table 19 for list of RAF and Commonwealth aircrew who were decorated for service in South-East Asia during the period covered by the book).

TABLE 19

Decorations awarded to British and Commonwealth Aircrew for service in Singapore, Malaya, Netherlands East Indies, Burma and Ceylon, and subsequent service where applicable:

Decorations awarded for operations over Singapore, Malaya and East Indies:

Flt Lt R.J. Allanson	36 Sqn.	DFC*
Flt Lt R.A. Atkinson, RAAF	205 Sqn.	DFC
Plt Off R.A. Barclay, RNZAF	36 Sqn.	DFC
Sqn Ldr R.E.P. Brooker, DFC	232/242 Sqns	Bar to DFC
Sgt K.R. Burrill, RAAF	34 Sqn.	DFM
Sgt G.W. Calder	62 Sqn.	DFM
Flg Off J.A. Campbell	258 Sqn.	DFC
Flt Lt T.A. Cox	34 Sqn.	DFC
Flt Lt H. Dane**	MVAF	DSO
Flt Lt O.N. Diamond, RAAF	1 RAAF Sqn.	DFC
Flg Off A.G. Donahue	258 Sqn.	DFC
Flt Lt J.K. Douglas, RAAF	1 RAAF Sqn.	DFC
Sgt R.L. Dovell	232/242 Sqns.	DFM
Flt Lt M.C. Fitzherbert	232/242 Sqns.	DFC*
Flt Sgt A. Frost, RAAF	8 RAAF Sqn.	DFM
Flt Lt M. Garden	243 Sqn.	DFC
Flt Lt E.C. Gartrell, RNZAF	232/242 Sqns.	DFC*
Flg Off P.J. Gibbes, RAAF	1 RAAF Sqn.	DFC
Sqn Ldr I.W. Hutcheson	100 Sqn.	DFC*
Flt Lt J.R. Hutcheson, RNZAF	488 Sqn.	DFC
Flt Lt J.C. Hutton	232/605 Sqns.	DFC*
Sqn Ldr I. Julian, RNZAF	232/242 Sqns.	DFC*
Sgt E.E.G. Kuhn, RNZAF	488 Sqn.	DFM
Wg Cdr H.J. Maguire	266 Wg.	DSO*
Sgt H.K. Minton, RNZAF	36 Sqn.	DFM
Flt Lt B.J. Parker	232/242 Sqns.	DFC*
Flt Lt A.D. Phillips	4 PRU	DFC
Flt Lt H.C. Plenty, RAAF	8 RAAF Sqn.	DFC
Sgt J.A. Sandeman Allen	232/242 Sqns	DFM
Sqn Ldr A.K.S. Scarf	62 Sqn.	VC***
Flg Off N.C. Sharp, RNZAF	488 Sqn.	DFC
Flt Lt K.R. Smith, RAAF	1 RAAF Sqn.	DFC
Flt Lt C.H. Spurgeon, RAAF	8 RAAF Sqn.	DFC
Sqn Ldr S.G. Stilling, RAAF	205 Sqn.	DFC
Flt Lt E.M. Taylor	232 Sqn.	DFC

TABLE 19 (Continued)

Sgt C.B. Wareham, RNZAF	4 PRU	DFM
Flt Lt R. Widmer, RAAF	8 RAAF Sqn.	DFC
Plt Off A.R. Wilson	59 Sqn	DSO*
Sgt B.S. Wipiti, RNZAF	243 Sqn.	DFM
Sgt T. Woods	36 Sqn.	DFM*
Sqn Ldr E.W. Wright, DFM	232/605 Sqns.	DFC*
Flt Lt J.V.C. Wyllie	84 Sqn.	DFC

Awards made to those marked * were announced in 1946, following their
release from POW internment.
** Died as Prisoner of War
*** Posthumously

Decorations awarded for operations over Singapore, Malaya and East Indies, and subsequent service:

Wg Cdr R.N. Bateson, DFC	211 Sqn.	DSO
Flt Lt R.E. Bell, RAAF	8 RAAF Sqn.	DFC
Flt Lt G.L. Bonham, RNZAF	243 Sqn.	DFC
Flt Lt A.H. Brydon, RAAF	1 RAAF Sqn.	DFC
Flt Lt D.L. Clow, RNZAF	488 Sqn.	DFC
Flt Lt D.W. Colquhoun, RAAF	1 RAAF Sqn.	DFC
Sqn Ldr J.M. Cranstone, RNZAF	488 Sqn.	DFC
Flg Off G.B. Fisken, RNZAF	243 Sqn.	DFC
Wg Cdr F.R.C. Fowle	27 Sqn.	DFC
Sqn Ldr B.A. Grace, RAAF	21/453 Sqns.	DFC
Wg Cdr J.R. Jeudwine	84 Sqn.	DSO, DFC
Sqn Ldr G.J. King	232/242 Sqns.	DFC
Sqn Ldr J.R. Kinninmont, RAAF	21/453 Sqns.	DFC
Sqn Ldr P.D.F. Mitchell	100 Sqn.	DFC
Wg Cdr A.K. Passmore, DFC	84 Sqn.	Bar to DFC
Sqn Ldr D.B. Pearson	4 PRU	DFC
Sqn Ldr H.C. Plenty, DFC, RAAF	8 RAAF Sqn.	Bar to DFC
Sqn Ldr D.J.T. Sharp, RNZAF	258 Sqn.	DFC
Sqn Ldr D.M. Sproule, RAAF	21/453 Sqns.	DFC
Sqn Ldr R.D. Vanderfield, RAAF	21/453 Sqns.	DFC

Decorations awarded for operations over Burma:

Sgt J.F. Barrick, RCAF	17 Sqn.	DFM
Sqn Ldr J. Brandt	67 Sqn.	DFC
Wg Cdr F.R. Carey, DFC+, DFM	135 Sqn/267 Wg.	2nd Bar to DFC
Flt Lt M.C.C. Cotton, RAAF	17 Sqn.	DFC
Flt Lt D.J.C. Pinckney	67 Sqn.	DFC

Decorations awarded for operations over Burma and subsequent service:

Plt Off C.V. Bargh, RNZAF	67 Sqn.	DFC
Flg Off G.W.N. Bassingthwaighte, RAAF	113 Sqn.	DFC

TABLE 19 (Continued)

Wg Cdr J.F. Grey	113 Sqn.	DSO, DFC
Sqn Ldr R.W. Davy	62 Sqn.	DFC
Sqn Ldr P. Duggan Smith, RNZAF	113 Sqn.	DFC
Sqn Ldr H.J. Everard, RCAF	17 Sqn.	DFC
Flt Lt K.A. Rutherford, RNZAF	67 Sqn.	DFC
Sqn Ldr G.S. Sharp, RNZAF	67 Sqn.	DSO
Sqn Ldr C.McG. Simpson, RNZAF	67 Sqn.	DFC
Wg Cdr R.N. Stidolph	113 Sqn.	DFC
Flt Lt W.J. Storey, RAAF	135 Sqn.	DFC
Sqn Ldr R.E. Stout, RNZAF	135 Sqn.	DFC
Sqn Ldr F.B. Sutton	135 Sqn.	DFC
Flt Lt L.D. Thomas, RCAF	17 Sqn.	DFC
Maj J.L.B. Viney, SAAF	113 Sqn.	DFC
Wt Off L. Walker	113 Sqn.	DFC
Flg Off F.E. Wilding	136 Sqn.	DFC

British decorations awarded to members of the AVG in Burma:

Sqn Ldr Robert T. Neale	1st Sqn.	DSO
V/Sqn Ldr Charles R. Bond	1st Sqn.	DFC
Sqn Ldr David L. Hill	2nd Sqn.	DFC
Sqn Ldr Jack V. Newkirk	2nd Sqn.	DFC
V/Sqn Ldr Edward F. Rector	2nd Sqn.	DFC

Decorations awarded to bomber/reconnaissance aircrew for operations over the East Indies and subsequent service:

Flg Off W.K. Bolitho, RAAF	20 RAAF Sqn.	DFC
Flt Lt W.D. Brooks, RAAF	24 RAAF Sqn.	DSO
Flt Lt D.W.I. Campbell, RAAF	13 RAAF Sqn.	DFC
Sqn Ldr J.A. Cohen, RAAF	11 RAAF Sqn.	DFC
Flg Off T.L. Duigan, RAAF	11 RAAF Sqn.	DFC
Wg Cdr W.N. Gibson, RAAF	20 RAAF Sqn.	DFC
Flt Lt J.B. Hampshire, RAAF	6 RAAF Sqn.	DFC
Flt Lt B.H. Higgins, RAAF	11 RAAF Sqn.	DFC
Wg Cdr J.M. Lerew, RAAF	24 RAAF Sqn.	DFC
Sqn Ldr W.A. Pedrina, RAAF	6 RAAF Sqn.	DFC
Sqn Ldr T.McB. Price, RAAF	20 RAAF Sqn.	DFC
Flt Lt C.F. Thompson, RAAF	20 RAAF Sqn.	DFC
Sgt L.M. Van Praag, RAAF	36 RAAF Sqn.	GM
Flg Off N.W. Webster, RAAF	36 RAAF Sqn	GM
Flt Lt W.V.D. White, RAAF	2 RAAF Sqn.	DFC

Decorations awarded for operations from Ceylon and subsequent service:

Sgt E.L.J. Anderson, RAAF	11 Sqn.	DFM
Sqn Ldr L.J. Birchall, RCAF	413 RCAF Sqn.	DFC
Flt Lt W. Bradshaw	240 Sqn.	DFC
Sqn Ldr C.F. Counter	261 Sqn.	DFC

TABLE 19 (Continued)

Sqn Ldr R.T.P. Davidson, RCAF	30 Sqn.	DFC
Sqn Ldr P.C. Fletcher	258 Sqn.	DFC
Flt Lt D. Fulford	261 Sqn.	DFC
Sqn Ldr J.V. Marshall	261 Sqn.	DFC
Flt Lt D.B.F. Nicholls	258 Sqn.	DFC
Flt Lt S.R. Peacock-Edwards	258 Sqn.	DFC
Flt Lt J.H. Whalen, RCAF	30 Sqn.	DFC

As with their RAF and Commonwealth counterparts, the indigenous Netherlands East Indies fighter pilots had little opportunity to gain many combat successes; for them, it was more a problem of survival. Only Kaptain Jacob van Helsdingen and Lt Gus Deibel, both of whom took part in the ML's last action on 7 March, were able to claim more than two victories (see Table 20). In July 1948 the members of this last Brewster patrol would be created Knights of the Militaire Willemssorder 4e Klasse; Van Helsdingen, who had already received this award on 12 February, was posthumously elevated to the 3e Klasse, while Scheffer's award was also posthumous as he died a prisoner of the Japanese. Sadly, Deibel was killed in the crash of a Meteor jet fighter at Uithuizen, Holland, in June 1951.

TABLE 20

Successful pilots of the Knil Luchtvaartafdeling in operations over Singapore and The Netherlands East Indies, December 1941 — March 1942

		Claims:
Kapt J.P. van Helsdingen	2-VlG-V	3
Lt A.G. Deibel	2-VlG-V	3
Lt G.M. Bruggink	2-VlG-V	2
Kapt M.W. van Poel	1-VlG-IV	2
Kapt A.A.M. van Rest	1-VlG-V	2
2/Lt J. Kingma	2-VlG-IV	2

Owing to their reported successes, the spotlight obviously fell on the fighter pilots of the American Volunteer Group in Burma. Subsequently several lists of their high scorers have been published, but in virtually every case the totals listed have included aircraft destroyed on the ground. These lists also, quite properly, include claims made over China, including some submitted during June 1942. All such are outside the scope of this book, but it has been possible to prepare a revised listing indicating who the successful members of the Group were in the skies over Burma.

In the Philippines, only Lt Boyd Wagner had been able to make five claims, though several of the pilots who subsequently served on Java added to their claims here. Again, many of these American fighter pilots will have their careers detailed in a companion volume to *Aces High*, currently in preparation for this series in the US.

TABLE 21

Successful pilots of the American Volunteer Group in operations over Burma, December 1941 — May 1942

Sqn Ldr Robert H. Neale	1st Sqn.	12	(+1 China)
Flt Ldr Robert L. Little	1st Sqn.	10	
Flt Ldr Charles H. Older	3rd Sqn.	9+2 shared	
Flt Ldr Robert T. Smith	3rd Sqn.	8+3 shared	
Sqn Ldr David L. Hill	2nd Sqn.	8+1 shared	(+2 China)
Wingman William D. McGarry	1st Sqn.	8	
Flt Ldr George T. Burgard	1st Sqn.	8	(+2 China)
Sqn Ldr Jack V. Newkirk	2nd Sqn.	7	
V/Sqn Ldr Charles R. Bond	1st Sqn	6	(+1 China)
Flt Ldr Robert T. Hedman	3rd Sqn.	5+2 shared	
Wingman Robert W. Prescott	1st Sqn.	5+1 shared	
Flt Ldr Percy R. Bartelt	2nd Sqn.	5	
Wingman Edmund F. Overend	3rd Sqn.	5	
Flt Ldr Frank L. Lawlor	2nd Sqn.	5	(+2 China)
Wingman Robert H. Smith	1st Sqn.	5	(+2 China)
Sqn Ldr Robert J. Sandell	1st Sqn.	5	
Wingman John R. Rossi	1st Sqn.	5	(+1 China)
V/Sqn Ldr George B. McMillan	3rd Sqn.	4+1 shared	
Wingman Camille J. Rosbert	1st Sqn.	4	(+2 China)
Flt Ldr Thomas C. Haywood	3rd Sqn.	3+2 shared	
V/Sqn Ldr Parker S. Dupouy	3rd Sqn.	3+1 shared	
Flt Ldr Richard N. Bacon	2nd Sqn.	3	
Flt Ldr Gregory Boyington	1st Sqn.	3*	
Flt Ldr Kenneth A. Jernstedt	3rd Sqn.	3	
Flt Ldr William N. Reed	3rd Sqn.	3	
Flt Ldr John E. Petach	2nd Sqn.	2+4 shared	(+1 China)
V/Sqn Ldr Edward F. Rector	2nd Sqn	2+2 shared	(+2 China)
Flt Ldr Lewis S. Bishop	3rd/2nd Sqns.	2+1 shared	
Flt Ldr John G. Bright	2nd Sqn.	2	(+1 China)
Flt Ldr William E. Bartling	1st Sqn.	2	(+3 China)
V/Sqn Ldr Frank Schiel	1st/2nd Sqns	2	(+2 China)
Flt Ldr Fritz E. Wolf	1st Sqn.	2	(+2 China)
Sqn Ldr James H. Howard	2nd Sqn.	1+1 shared	(+1 China)

*Includes 2 by his own report, details of which have not been found.

112

Amongst the Japanese forces most of those who had taken part in the fighting over Malaya, the East Indies, Burma and Ceylon would emerge as the most notable leaders and high-scorers of the Pacific War.

No less than 57 of the Navy pilots known to have been engaged, either had already, or would subsequently, achieve personal scores of five or more: indeed most would achieve double figures (see Table 23). 14 of these men would be amongst the top-scoring 26 JNAF pilots of WWII, and would include three of the top four — Lt Hiroyoshi Nishizawa (credited with 87 victories) and Lt Tetsuzo Iwamoto (approximately 80 victories) and Lt Saburo Sakai (64). The

TABLE 22

Successful pilots of the USAAF in operations over the Philippines and Java, December 1941 — March 1942

		Claims:
Lt Boyd D. Wagner	17th Pursuit Sqn	5
Lt George E. Kiser	17th Pursuit Sqn	5
Lt William J. Hennon	17th Pursuit Sqn	5
Capt Grant Mahony	3rd/17th Pursuit Sqns	4
2/Lt John H. Posten	17th Pursuit Sqn	3½
2/Lt Earl R. Stone	17th Pursuit Sqn	3½
Lt Andrew J. Reynolds	17th/20th Pursuit Sqns	3⅓
Lt Jack B. Donalson	21st Pursuit Sqn	3
Lt Joseph J. Kruzel	17th Pursuit Sqn	3
Lt Nathaniel H. Blanton	17th Pursuit Sqn	3
2/Lt Ben S. Brown	34th Pursuit Sqn	3

Army was nearly as well represented with 33 men of similar standing. Eight of these would be amongst the top 22 of the war, including Cpl Satoshi Anabuki of the 50th Sentai, who claimed three victories over the Philippines before moving to Burma where, by the end of 1943, he had increased his tally to at least 33; by the end of the war his total victories had reached 51. Another of the successful JAAF pilots was Capt Yasuhiko Kuroe of the 64th Sentai (formerly of the 47th Ind Chutai), with 30 victories (see Table 24).

TABLE 23

Successful Japanese Naval Air Force fighter pilots involved during the operations recorded (many of whom made their initial claims during the period December 1941 – May 1942 — although others had claimed in China pre December 1941 as indicated)

		Total Claims by end of WWII	(UK date style)
Hiroyoshi Nishizawa	4th Ku	87	KinA 16/10/44
Tetsuzo Iwamoto	*Zuikaku*	80 (14/China)	
Saburo Sakai	Tainan Ku	64 (2/China)	
Toshio Ohta	Tainan Ku	34	MinA 21/10/42
Shizuo Ishii	Tainan Ku	29 (3/China)	KinA 24/10/43
Kaneyoshi Muto	3rd Ku	28 (5/China)	KinA 24/7/45
Sada-aki Akamatsu	3rd Ku	27 (11/China)	
Junichi Sasai	Tainan Ku	27	KinA 26/8/42
Shigeo Sugio	3rd Ku	20+	
Kuzushi Uto	Tainan Ku	19	MinA 13/9/42
Sadamu Komachi	*Shokaku*	18	WinA 19/6/44

TABLE 23 (Continued)

Masayuki Nakase	3rd Ku	18 (9/China)	KinA 9/2/42
Minoru Honda	22nd Air Flot	17	
Keishu Kamihira	Tainan Ku	17 (4/China)	
Masao Masuyama	3rd Ku	17	
Kuniyoshi Tanaka	Tainan Ku	17 (12/China)	
Susumu Ishihara	Tainan Ku	16	
Zenjiro Miyano	3rd Ku	16	MinA 16/6/43
Bunkichi Nakajima	3rd Ku	16	KinA 16/10/43
Kunimori Nakakariya	3rd Ku	16	
Tora-ichi Takatsuka	Tainan Ku	16 (3/China)	MinA 13/9/42
Yoshimi Minami	*Shokaku*	15	KinA 25/11/44
Kenji Okabe	*Shokaku*	15	
Satoshi Yoshino	4th Ku	15	MinA 9/6/42
Yukiharu Ozeki	3rd Ku	14+ (3/China)	MinA 24/10/44
Masuaki Endo	Tainan Ku	14	KinA 7/6/43
Masao Taniguchi	*Akagi*	14	WinA 23/10/44
Ichirobei Yamazaki	4th Ku	14	KinA 9/7/43
Mototsuna Yoshida	4th Ku	14	MinA 7/8/42
Watari Handa	Tainan Ku	13 (6/China)	
Fujikazu Koizumi	3rd Ku	13 (2/China)	MinA 27/1/44
Gitaro Miyazaki	Tainan Ku	13 (2/China)	KinA 1/6/42
Akira Yamamoto	*Kaga*	13 (1/China)	KinA 24/11/44
Tetsuo Kikuchi	*Akagi*	12	KinA 19/6/44
Masao Sasakibara	*Shokaku*	12	WinA 4/2/43
Sada-o Yamaguchi	3rd Ku	12	KinA 4/7/44
Iyozo Fujita	*Soryu*	11	
Takeichi Kokubun	4th Ku	11	MinA 2/9/42
Kiyoshi Sekiya	3rd Ku	11	KinA 24/6/44
Ichiro Yamamoto	*Shokaku*	11	KinA 19/1/44
Kozaburo Yasui	22nd Air Flot	11	MinA 19/6/44
Yoshiro Hashiguchi	3rd Ku	10+	MinA 25/10/44
Yoshikazu Nagahawa	*Kaga*	10+	KinA 6/9/43
Yasuhiro Shigematsu	*Hiryu*	10+	KinA 8/7/44
Ken-ichi Abe	22nd Air Flot	10	WinA 6/5/43
Takahide Aioi	3rd Ku	10 (5/China)	
Jiro Tanaka	*Soryu*	10	KinA 10/12/42
Kaname Harada	*Soryu*	9	WinA 17/10/42
Hideo Izumi	Tainan Ku	9	KinA 30/4/42
Ki-ichi Oda	*Soryu*	9 (4/China)	KinA 10/12/44
Juzo Okamoto	3rd Ku	9 (4/China)	MinA 11/10/42
Aya-o Shirane	*Akagi*	9 (1/China)	KinA 24/10/44
Keisaku Yoshimura	22nd Air Flot	9	KinA 25/10/42
Tadashi Kaneko	*Shokaku*	8 (3/China)	KinA 14/11/42
Kazuo Muranaka	*Hiryu*	8 (1/China)	
Shigeru Yano	3rd Ku	8	KinFA 17/4/42
Osamu Kudo	3rd Ku	7	KinA 3/3/42

TABLE 24

Successful Japanese Army Air Force fighter pilots involved during the operations recorded (many of whom made their initial claims during the period December 1941 – May 1942 — although others had claimed in Mongolia and China pre December 1941 as indicated)

		Total Claims by end of WWII	(UK date style)
Satoshi Anabuki	50th Sentai	51	
Mitsuyoshi Tarui	1st Sentai	38+ (28/Mongolia)	KinA 18/8/44
Isamu Sasaki	50th Sentai	38	
Yasuhiko Kuroe*	64th Sentai	30 (2/Mongolia)	
Shogo Saito	11th Sentai	26+ (25/Mongolia)	KinA 2/7/44
Tomori Hasegawa	11th Sentai	22 (19/Mongolia)	
Zenzaburo Ohtsuka	11th Sentai	22 (22/Mongolia)	KinA 29/6/42
Naoharu Shiromoto	1st Sentai	21 (11/Mongolia)	
Saburo Nakamura	64th Sentai	20**	KinA 6/10/44
Shogo Takeuchi	64th Sentai	19+	KinFA 21/12/43
Takeo Kato	64th Sentai	18 (9/China)	KinA 22/5/42
Kazuo Shimizu	59th Sentai	18	
Yukio Shimokawa	50th Sentai	16	
Tokuyasu Ishizuka	11th Sentai	15 (12/Mongolia)	
Masatoshi Masuzawa	1st Sentai	15 (8/Mongolia)	
Toshio Matsu-ura	1st Sentai	15	KinFA 2/12/43
Shigeo Nango	59th Sentai	15	KinA 23/1/44
Toshio Sakagawa	47th Ind Chutai	15	KinFA 19/12/44
Tomio Hirohata	59th Sentai	14	KinFA 22/4/45
Taka-aki Minami	1st Sentai	14 (14/Mongolia)	
Hiroshi Onozaki	59th Sentai	14	
Yoshiro Kuwabara	77th Sentai	13	KinA 14/3/44
Takao Takahashi	11th Sentai	13	MinA 13/11/44
Yutaka Aoyagi	11th Sentai	12+ (10/Mongolia)	KinFA 23/6/42
Katsumi Anma	64th Sentai	12 (1/China, 6/Mongolia)	
Toyoki Eto	77th Sentai	12 (2/China)	
Yohei Hinoki	64th Sentai	12	
Yoshito Yasuda	64th Sentai	10+	
Takeomi Hayashi	59th Sentai	9	
Yoshio Hirose	77th Sentai	9	KinA 22/12/44
Katsutaro Takahashi	59th Sentai	9	KinA 14/12/42
Teizo Kanamaru	50th Sentai	8+ (3/Mongolia)	KinA 24/12/42
Takeshi Shimizu	64th Sentai	8	POW 21/5/42

NB: *Yasuhiko Kuroe had been credited with 3 victories with the 47th Independent Chutai prior to joining the 64th Sentai.

NB: **Saburo Nakamura's total includes an unspecified number of ground victories.

If there was one shock above all others to come out of the opening months of the war for the Allies, it was the discovery of the Japanese attitude to war, and above all their code of honour and conduct, and the almost complete disregard for their own lives. The Western mind was totally unprepared for an enemy to whom the concept of honourable surrender was quite incomprehensible. Indeed, it must be said that had this been brought home to all units before the fighting commenced, many might have been prepared to put-up more determined resistance, out of desperation if nothing else.

Here was a cultural divide almost impossible to bridge. Japanese servicemen had been brought up from their earliest days in a tradition of service to their emperor where death in battle was honourable, but surrender beyond contempt, bringing shame and disgrace not only to them, but on their families at home. Failure frequently brought ritual suicide by way of atonement. They had under gone some of the toughest and most rigorous training in the world, enduring severe physical punishment that taught them to be comtemptuous of their own suffering, and thereby, to that of others! Illness was not tolerated, thus, when faced with enemies who gave up, frequently after only limited resistance, these would not in their eyes be considered honourable foes but craven and disgraced cowards who were beneath contempt — and were treated accordingly.

It was not that the Japanese did not respect their adverseries. A brave foe met their approval. On occasion much Western outrage arose when airmen shot down in the course of a particularly gallant attack, were subsequently captured and executed. However, for the Japanese the execution was a reflection of respect for their gallantry, because it was felt that they did not deserve the ignominy of imprisonment. To those Westerners experiencing or aware of such treatment, raised as they had been with much greater regard for the sanctity of their own lives, inbred with the view that lives should not be squandered need-lessly and that suicide was essentially wrong, this behaviour seemed only cruel, barbaric and brutal beyond their understanding. This was further exacerbated by the Japanese practice of seeking to shoot downed pilots on their parachutes or on the ground after crash-landing. This was completely in accord with their philosophy, but totally at odds with Western notions of chivalry.

That either side should come to appreciate and accept the other's inherent position and beliefs in the short period of the war and while locked in mortal combat, is not realistically conceivable. For many who experienced the situation and, particularly amongst those who suffered as a consequence, it probably never has become possible. In any event it made the war in the Far East in many respects a far more terrible one than that in the West — worse even, in many ways, than that on the Eastern Front.

In conclusion it has to be said that, following the successes of the initial pre-emptive strike on the US Fleet at Pearl Harbor, the preponderance of strength of the Japanese Navy was such that is is unlikely that the Allies could have prolonged considerably their defence of the Philippines, the Indies or Malaya and Singapore, as it would have proved so difficult to sustain them by sea in the face of this superiority. Nevertheless, responsibility for the way in which the campaign proved so great and costly a disaster to the defenders lies firmly at the door of their leadership. This was a campaign that was lost above all by attitude. The Japanese believed that they were going to win. Within days of the opening of the war, the Allies believed that they were going to lose. At that point, the battle was already half lost.

Air Commodore J.P.J. McCauley was later called upon to report on the campaign in Malaya to ascertain the lessons which might be learned from it should an invasion of Australia follow. Extracts from this provided further insight into the problems encountered by the air forces here, which were not greatly different from those experienced subsequently in the Indies. The situation was perhaps somewhat different in the Philippines, due to the much greater initial destruction of US airpower based there.

> "From the initiation of the enemy attack our aerodromes in Northern Malaya, progressively and with amazing rapidity, were rendered untenable for our operational use and subsequently fell into enemy hands".

The cause of this, he surmised, was due to:

a)   The complete absence of/or inadequate fighter defence.

b)   Inadequate defence on the ground.

c)   Unsuitability of the conventional peacetime station to withstand air attack.

d)   Lack or inadequacy of air attack warning system.

He continued:

> "At no time in the campaign in Malaya was there adequate fighter cover on any aerodrome. This was due to the numerical insufficiency of fighter aircraft at all stages of the campaign. Over some aerodromes an attempt was made to maintain a first light to last light fighter patrol, but this eventually broke down owing to the endurance of the small number of available aircraft and pilots, becoming exhausted. The enemy, on the other hand, in both Malaya and Sumatra, invariably made their initial occupation of the aerodrome for operational use by flying in fighter aircraft. These fighters were used to provide fighter screens for bomber formations proceeding from backward bases to forward objectives, preventing aircraft making rendezvous with their bombers.
>
> "In cases where the enemy utilised a captured aerodrome in a more or less forward position for the maintenance of a bomber force, they maintained a fighter umbrella above the aerodrome. At no time during the campaign did we have sufficient fighters to afford our indulgence in the tactics which were being employed by the enemy, or to afford a proper top cover protection for our heavier types of aircraft. In fact, the provision of an adequate fighter escort for our bomber formations was a rare thing and the consequence was that daylight bomber operations were only undertaken in cases of extreme emergency."

Air Commodore McCauley went on to criticise the Army plans, which appeared to be based entirely on fighting a delaying action and which appeared to ignore the possibility of a Japanese advance down the west coast. He complained too of the lack of airfield defence troops, commenting that while airmen could, and had been trained to a degree for such duties, these had to remain subordinate to their main functions, which prevented the possibility of them becoming effective as properly trained infantry. Frequently, he commented, they had been called upon to undertake actions which were beyond their capabilities in this respect.

Newly-commissioned Plt Offs Jimmy King and Geoff Hardie, late of 242 Squadron, seen here in Melbourne, Australia, in December 1942. Although not a member of the RAAF, King appears to be wearing the darker blue uniform of that air force. *(Mrs Ida King)*

With regard to defence from air attack, he commented:

> "In Northern Malaya the anti-aircraft defences on the aerodrome were, without exception, inadequate. For instance, at Kota Bharu, the total anti-aircraft defences consisted of two 3.7" AA guns. These proved totally unsuitable against low flying attack. At Sungei Patani the AA defences consisted of four Bofors guns. These diverted the low level attacks, but once the enemy had discovered the absence of heavy AA defences they carried out medium level bombing attacks which they followed by low level machine gunning attacks after the defences had been reduced. These examples demonstrated that the AA defences of an aerodrome must consist of both heavy and light AA weapons. MMGs and LMGs are not suitable for AA defences and no great reliance should be placed on them."

Training and organisations for evacuations, provisions for repair of bomb damaged to runways and airfield buildings, dispersal and camouflage had all been inadequate. The situation at P.2 airfield in Sumatra had been very much

The war over, a gaunt-looking Air Vice-Marshal Paul Maltby (left) arrives in Chungking in August 1945, having been released from captivity. *(John Maltby)*

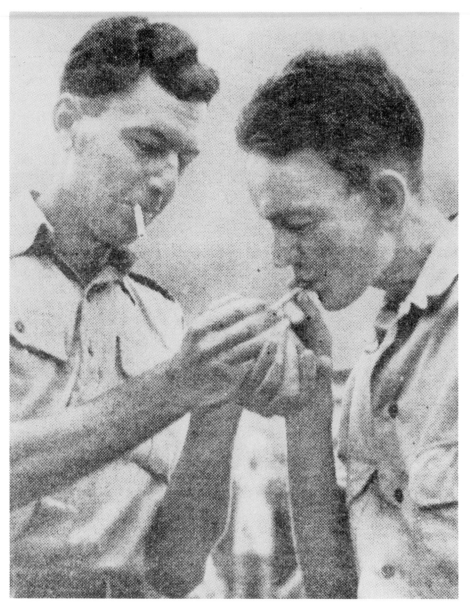

Released! Flt Lt J.W. Appleton (left), a 60 Squadron pilot taken prisoner in Singapore, with Flt Lt Maurice Holland, ex 84 Squadron. *(Mrs Mary Marcon via Paul Sortehaug)*

better in this respect, he advised, and could be used as a good example of well-planned concealment and dispersal.

Following the issue of his report, a more forthright and personal appraisal was prepared by Wg Cdr F.N. Wright, who had commanded 8 RAAF Squadron. This document provides an excellent overview of the attitudes prevailing which may probably be taken as being fairly representative of all the colonial commands at the time. This report is included in full as Appendix II, and its contents provide illuminating reading as a postscript to one of the greatest disasters in modern military history — the whole interlude being adequately summed up by many of the survivors as little short of a "Bloody Shambles".

Postscript:

In late 1945, the first of the survivors of "three and a half years of living hell" were starting to come home. Many thousands stayed behind — forever.

> "When you go home
> Tell them of us and say
> For your tomorrow
> We gave our today."

War Memorial Inscription, Kohima, Northern Burma

(A third volume dealing with the subsequent air war over Burma, June 1942 – August 1945, is to be prepared in this series.)

Appendix I

MALAYAN VOLUNTEER AIR FORCE — INVENTORY OF AIRCRAFT
(DETAILS SUBJECT TO AMENDMENT)

MVAF No:	Previous Registration:	Fate (UK date style):
1 Moth Major	VR-SBA	crashed Singapore 16/5/41
2 Moth Major	VR-RAS	
3 Moth Major	VR-RAT	
4 Moth Major	VR-SAB	
5 Tiger Moth		collided with Buffalo 7/11/41
6 Gipsy Moth	VR-SBF	collided with Buffalo 29/12/41
7 Moth Major		
8 Tiger Moth	K4273 ex RAF	
9 Tiger Moth	VR-RAM	
10 Tiger Moth	VR-RAO	
11 Hornet Moth	VR-SAN	DBR bombing Kallang 20/1/42
12 Whitney Straight	VR-SBB	reached Batavia 2/42
13 ?		
14 Gipsy Avro	VR-RAJ	
15 Moth Minor	VR-SBE	
16 ?		
17 Dragonfly	VR-SAX	w/o bombed Kallang 20/1/42
18 Rapide	VR-SAV	w/o bombed Ipoh 18/12/41
19 Rapide	VR-SAW	w/o accident Palembang 2/42
20 Moth Major	VR-SAC	w/o bombed Penang 9/12/41
21 Moth Major	VR-SAK	w/o
22 Moth Major	VR-SAZ	w/o
23 Moth Major		w/o
24 Moth Major		c/l nr Padang 14/2/42
25 BA Eagle	VR-SAP	w/o bombed Penang 9/12/41
26 Avro Cadet	VR-RAK	reached Batavia 13/2/42
27 Avro Cadet	VR-RAL	
28 Tiger Moth		reached Batavia 13/2/42
29 ?		
30 ?		
31 Hawk Major	VR-RAV	c/l Pakanbaroe 1/2/42
32 Miles Falcon	VR-RAP	reached Batavia 13/2/42
33 Club Cadet	VR-RAR	w/o bombed Pakanbaroe 7/2/42
34 Tiger Moth		reached Batavia 13/2/42
35 Tiger Moth	VR-RAU	
36 ?		
37 Club Cadet	VR-RAJ	reached Batavia 13/2/42
38 Club Cadet	VR-RAW	
39 Magister	VR-SAY	u/s Bukit Timah 5/2/42
40 Leopard Moth	VR-RAX	w/o bombed Kallang 20/1/42
41 Tiger Moth	K2590 ex RAF	
42 Avro Tutor	K3334 ex RAF	u/s Bukit Timah 5/2/42
43 Tiger Moth	L5902 ex RAF	

Key: DBR — damaged beyond repair; w/o — written off;
c/l — crash-landed; u/s — unserviceable

Appendix II
REPORT BY WING COMMANDER F.N. WRIGHT, CO 8 RAAF SQUADRON

The following report is rendered covering my service in the Far East, during the period 26 August 1940 to 21 February 1942.

On arrival in Singapore in August, 1940, as Commanding Officer 21 RAAF Squadron, it was plainly evident to me that there existed a state of affairs which was far out of line with the reports which had been received and accepted in Australia regarding the defence of Singapore. In addition to obvious shortage of aircraft and equipment, there was also an acute shortage of trained personnel. There appeared to be no prospect of obtaining additional aircraft or personnel, and neither did there appear to be any great effort made with a view to improving the efficiency of the RAF personnel who were there. Right up until hostilities broke out RAF units, with the exception of one maintenance unit, worked only from 0730 to 1230 each day, with 15 minutes break during the morning, and, although RAAF units proved that working an additional two hours per day was not detrimental but beneficial, so far as efficiency was concerned, the RAF units made no effort to follow suit, and there can be no doubt that the standard of efficiency of RAAF units was far above that obtained by any RAF unit in Malaya.

Although it is realised that there is always a tendency for units and stations to criticise higher command, it was certain that, in the majority of cases, the criticism levelled at high command in the Far East was justified. In many instances it was clear that the attitude of those responsible resulted from a general tiredness and lack of interest or determination to get on with the job. In other instances sheer stupidity and rigid adherence to Air Ministry Orders (despite obvious misapplication) prevented an improvement in efficiency. An example of this blind adherence to non-applicable orders was shown very clearly when 8 RAAF Squadron moved to RAF Station Kota Bharu. 8 RAAF Squadron was the first squadron to occupy this station, which, despite assurances from Air Headquarters, was not in any fit state to receive any unit. There existed neither accommodation nor facilities of any kind, with the exception of three inadequate barrack blocks designed to house a total of 66 personnel. Here it was found that outside labour (so essential at all Malayan stations) could not be obtained for the simple reason that Air Ministry Orders had set down fixed rates of pay, and, only by taking the matter into our own hands, were we able to obtain cooks, sweepers, etc. to feed and care for over 300 men.

Although visits were made by Headquarters Staff officers these visits were, with the exception of one made by the Air Officer Commanding (Air Vice-Marshal Pulford), so hurried that the results obtained from such visits were negative.

It might appear that this report is nothing more than a petulant outburst by a unit and station commander, but it is the only report which can adequately fit in with the general atmosphere and condition which existed in Malaya. As already stated, there was only one (Staff officer) who showed, and continued to show a practical outlook on the situation. It seemed rather strange, however, that such a senior officer should have found it necessary to cover duties which should have been the responsibility of other officers.

It is certain that the shortage of personnel in the higher command possessing up-to-date practical knowledge of the tasks allotted to them contributed to the ill-defined and half-baked schemes sent out to units and stations from time to time, and this fact, when connected with the evident lack of control exercised by senior officers at stations and units, in my opinion, resulted in the disinterested attitude which permeated the whole of the RAF in Malaya.

It can be stated that the RAF pilots were very willing to carry out tasks allotted to them but they were carried out under conditions and in accordance with instructions which could only result in inefficiency. Not only did squadron commanders lack the ability to issue clear and concise instructions to aircraft crews, but, in many instances, it appeared that they were not sufficiently interested to prepare any plan in a manner which might have increased the effectiveness and efficiency of the tasks on hand. Examples of this lack of control were most evident when RAF squadrons were operating side by side from the same station as RAAF, and engaged on similar tasks. Whereas RAAF control would prepare for captains of reconnaissance and bombing aircraft a complete brief consisting of letter of the day, map co-ordinates, Direction Finding verification, Syko cards, information covering Naval dispositions, maps and a complete written instruction covering the task, the RAF would expect their captains and crews to keep these details in their minds, and take them away on any scraps of paper which might be available. The results of these preparations were very evident, and there is no doubt but that the Far East Command placed a great deal of reliance on any reports and on the accuracy of any positions given by RAAF crews.

Not only did squadron commanders neglect their duties as far as administration was concerned, but there was clear evidence that their half-hearted interest (the shortage of spares etc. being appreciated), regarding the maintenance of their aircraft, the lack of interest was also manifest in all the pilots, and as a result many tasks allotted to the RAF squadrons were only partially successful, because of this serious fault.

An example of this can be quoted when at Palembang II (P.2) on 13 February 1942[1], 12 Hudsons of the RAAF were ordered to carry out a night attack on Kluang aerodrome, and 22 Blenheims of RAF squadrons from the same stations were ordered to attack enemy shipping concentrated at Anamba Islands. Only 10 of the Blenheims succeeded in getting off from Palembang II, three of which crashed shortly after taking off and one returned before reaching the target. On the other hand, 12 Hudson aircraft took off on time, attacked the target 400 miles away and returned safely to base. It is a fact that more than 25% of RAF crews had no knowledge of the serviceability of their aircraft on any particular day, nor did they know what bombs or fuse delays were fitted to the aircraft which they were to fly. It must be again stressed here that the RAF pilots referred to were always willing and anxious to carry out tasks allotted to them, but, as already stated, results obtained were often nullified by the manner in which the task was planned and carried out.

The attitude adopted by Air Headquarters staff concerning matters which, to us, appeared to be of great importance, was amazing. An example of which may be quoted as follows: During November 1941, strange reconnaissance aircraft were sighted and reported by 8 Squadron RAAF flying at high altitudes over RAF Station Kota Bharu. Application was made to RAF Headquarters for fighter aircraft to be stationed at Kota Bharu, but the first interest displayed by Air Headquarters was a signal asking whether we needed their help to identify the aircraft and a query as to whether we required better binoculars. In reply to this facetious signal, the CO 8 RAAF Squadron made a complaint to Air Staff, and some weeks later three Buffaloes were stationed at Kota Bharu. By this time, however, the strange aircraft (presumably Japanese)[2], had secured all the photographs they required of Kota Bharu and other aerodromes in north-west Malaya.

From shortly before hostilities commenced, 21 and 8 RAAF Squadrons were despatched to their War Stations, namely Sungei Patani and Kuantan. 1 RAAF Squadron was already at their war station — Kota Bharu. 8 RAAF Squadron was despatched despite the fact that three weeks previously I had rendered a report to Headquarters stating quite plainly that RAF Station Kuantan was not in a fit state to receive 8 RAAF Squadron or any other operational squadron (it was discovered later that the report rendered wandered through the usual channels, and was never acted upon until two days before war broke out, and when the situation at Kuantan was obvious to everyone). 21 RAAF Squadron was placed in a position similar to 8 RAAF Squadron, but perhaps,

---

[1] Should be the night of 11/12 February (see Chapter 1)
[2] This was so (see Volume One, Chapter 1)

slightly more difficult, in that the control of the station to which they were posted was perhaps less efficient than at RAF Station Kuantan.

Just prior to being despatched to their war station, 21 RAAF Squadron had been completely disorganised owing to (a) change over in command, (b) change over from Wirraway to Buffalo aircraft, (c) change over of more than 50% of their pilots, (d) the remaining 50% of Squadron pilots detached from the squadron and engaged on instructional flying at RAF Station Kluang. These changes, coupled with the fact that they were transferred to Sungei Patani and came under a hurriedly formed group control, which apparently knew very little of the application of fighter aircraft, no doubt contributed largely to the failure of the Squadron to give its best. Much has been said regarding the low standard of morale obtained from 21 RAAF Squadron during the early stages of war with Japan, but it is certain that bad organisation and poor administration by higher command were the factors which governed this low standard.

As with 21 RAAF Squadron, 8 RAAF Squadron, then under the temporary command of Squadron Leader A.D. Henderson, moved to its war station, and came directly under the control of a station which was obviously not prepared to meet the emergency which arose. As previously mentioned a report on the conditions and preparedness of this station was submitted to Air Headquarters through Group Captain McCauley some weeks prior to the move of 8 RAAF Squadron. There was no Defence Scheme drawn up for Kuantan, and no orders to cover emergencies which even the simplest person could foresee, would be necessary in the event of an attack on the station. There was no Operations Room equipment with the exception of that prepared by 8 RAAF Squadron during the inspection referred to above. The station Duty Pilot's Office consisted of an office and one pencil. No attempt had been made to obtain the equipment or manufacture and display the signs which are so necessary at the control centre of any aerodrome. The only explanation which could be given by the station commander for the lack of such facilities was that he expected pilots to exercise common sense. As with 21 RAAF Squadron, much was said regarding the morale of 8 RAAF Squadron personnel when subject to air attack. This matter was the subject of a Court of Inquiry with Group Captain McCauley as President, and full reference as to the reasons for the disorganised control and subsequent hasty evacuation from Kuantan can be gauged by the fact that the station commander who made the derogatory statement concerning the squadrons at his station, was recommended for trial by Court Martial.

When, as was to be expected, 1 and 8 RAAF Squadrons suffered heavy aircraft losses after one day's operations, at their war station, they were recalled to RAAF Station Sembawang, and re-organised as a composite Squadron until such time as serviceability and additional equipment allowed for separate control. Here, with strict control and proper supervision, and a refusal by the station commander to allow the aircraft to be engaged on tasks which were obviously beyond the capabilities of the aircraft, the Squadrons carried out very valuable work — work which received the approbation of the AOC, who despatched a signal complimenting the Hudson squadrons on the fine work which contributed to the safe passage of valuable convoys entering Singapore. With the forward approach of the enemy, Air Headquarters repeatedly asked for maximum bombing efforts from the Hudson aircraft in addition to the full reconnaissance and search patrols which these aircraft were carrying out. On these bombing attacks without fighter cover, the Hudsons and crews acquitted themselves very creditably, but the full effort was not always possible, owing to the extensive damage sustained by aircraft on the ground during enemy bombing raids. Raids were carried out daily with little or no opposition from our fighter and AA defence. AA defence was, in my opinion, ineffective and certainly did not provide any measure of confidence.

Similarly did this apply to fighter aircraft. It is admitted that the number of fighter aircraft available was totally inadequate to deal with the opposing forces, but there seems to be no reason why such large numbers of aircraft should have been destroyed on the ground.

In one case, 46 replacement Hurricane aircraft were rendered more or less ineffective for the simple reason that they were brought right forward to the battle area with guns packed with grease and in a condition which took at least two days to render them serviceable, and I have been given to understand that, when this work was complete, some individual had removed an essential part of the guns, which resulted in the aircraft being grounded, and then suffered much damage by raiding or enemy aircraft.

At Sembawang the effectiveness of Nos 21 and 453 RAAF Squadrons were increased beyond measure due simply to the very firm and definite control exercised by Group Captain McCauley. He refused to allow them to be misused by Fighter Control, which was definitely being run by incompetent personnel. At this stage, however, both 21 and 453 RAAF Squadrons had suffered losses of both aircraft and personnel and at times were unable to put more than 14 aircraft into the air at any one time. Despite this serious disability, these squadrons carried out excellent work against odds which were never in their favour, and any criticism levelled at 21 and 453 RAAF Squadrons were by personnel who never understood and never tried to understand for obvious reasons the difficulties with which these two squadrons had to contend.

It appears to be an accepted fact that personnel who had been in the Far East for any considerable time develop a general apathetic outlook, and, whilst there seems to be no doubt that personnel who have been in the East a long time are affected by the climatic and other conditions prevailing, there is no doubt whatsoever in my mind, that in many cases, the condition of tiredness and disinterestedness is one of adoption. There is also no doubt in my own mind that this adopted attitude resulted in a great loss of efficiency, and that many of the unfinished jobs could have been completed, and completed ones made more efficient, had the personnel concerned really tried. As already stated, the squadrons under my command worked comparatively long hours each day for the 20 months I was in Malaya, (as was proved after war commenced) without detriment to themselves or the Service. The foregoing is perhaps one of the reasons why 21, 1 and 8 RAAF Squadrons were able to carry out so much training, and yet maintain a high state of serviceability.

Whilst dealing with the question of serviceability, I wish to refer to a stated impression given or made by an Air Headquarters senior officer to the effect that the RAAF Control was not prepared and showed a disinclination to accept full risks. This, in my opinion, was the statement of one who was not prepared to study closely practical results, and I can state quite definitely that it was not a matter of "not taking risks" — rather was it a case of careful preparation and well considered judgement. An example of risks and results was illustrated by the ill-timed despatch of RAF Blenheims and RAF Hudson aircraft from Palembang on the occasion when the enemy landing force at Endau was attacked. The Blenheims and Hudsons were despatched from Palembang at a time which did not permit for even a fighter cover over the well defended target area, and at a time which did not permit relatively untrained crews to return to a strange aerodrome before dark, the result of which was that one Hudson aircraft was shot down over the target and two crashed with a loss of all crew, in the vicinity of the aerodromes to which they were returning. It is fully appreciated that there are circumstances which demand full sacrifice of aircraft and equipment, but there are many occasions when the results obtained are not commensurate with the risks and subsequent damage incurred. It is my considered opinion that there was a large proportion of aircraft and equipment which was completely lost and never ever used against the enemy, simply because the aircraft were thrown away on useless tasks.

When it was decided that 1 and 8 RAAF Squadrons should proceed to Sumatra, difficulties in operations similar to those at Malayan up-country aerodromes were experienced, but to a more marked degree. Palembang II, to which these Squadrons were posted, had no facilities of any kind, other than accommodation sufficient for perhaps one and a half–two squadrons. Eventually 1,400 personnel were dumped at this station. There were eight squadrons all possessing aircraft in various stages of repair

— the total number of aircraft being about 80, of which at any one time a maximum of 40 could be put into the air. For the 80 aircraft, there existed one 400 gallon refuelling unit, no repair equipment or facilities of any kind, and, because of the shortage of squadron equipment and tools, the matter of aircraft repair became an acute problem.

Perhaps the most difficult problem of all was the shortage of transport, there being in existence about one quarter of the transport needed to efficiently cope with the station and squadron needs. The transport problem became even more acute when, owing to additional personnel, it was necessary to house and therefore transport three complete squadrons some six miles each way daily.

The shortage of transport was also one of the main reasons which prevented transfer and salvage of valuable stores and equipment during the various hurried movements of squadrons in Malaya and Sumatra.

The above report has been rendered with the idea of disclosing weaknesses which came to notice during my service in Malaya, and it is submitted with a hope that some lessons may be drawn therefrom.

Appendix III

REPORT BY AIR VICE-MARSHAL P.C. MALTBY ON THE JAPANESE ATTACK ON KALIDJATI AIRFIELD, 1 MARCH 1942

On hearing of the capture of Kalidjati we (*Maltby and Van Oyen*) both considered the incident unsatisfactory, and ordered an immediate enquiry with a British Army and Air Force Officer to sit as a Court and take such evidence as they could collect. On this evidence they were to produce a joint report. The report shows clearly that, whilst mistakes were admittedly made, the allegation that British troops fled from the aerodrome cannot be substantiated. Subsequent evidence that has since come in shows that those that were in a position to fight did so.

The attack came as a complete surprise, and the responsibility for this must rest with the higher command, in that there were no protective troops between the aerodrome and the coast. There were small parties for warning purposes, but this warning was never received. The aerodrome in question was about 50 miles from where the landing took place, and the speed with which the enemy could land tanks and reach a point so far inland in so short a time was not appreciated.

The evacuation of the aerodrome was under consideration early in the morning by the RAF Station Commander, Group Captain Whistondale, who unfortunately went to investigate the report of enemy approach in person and did not return. His senior Squadron Commander, Wg Cdr Jeudwine, after waiting a while for the former's return, quite rightly ordered both squadrons and the aerodrome and AA defences (which it had been agreeed should move together) to evacuate from Kalidjati and move to Andir. In most cases the order to cease fire had been given to the guns and ground defence detachments were packing up preparatory to moving off with RAF ground staff and this was under way when the attack was made by the enemy. In consequence they were completely unprepared and the little opposition being met which came from the few detachments and guns still in action and patrols, was entirely due to this surprise.

The British troops for the defence consisted of light AA battery with ground defence troops; a total of about 350 all ranks and about 30 RAF personnel who were manning some pill boxes. Of the Army personnel, about 110 all ranks are still missing including the Commander of the ground defence troops and most of the detachment of the missing Bofors guns. Evidence which has since been received indicated that the Commander of the ground defence troops was killed or captured while endeavouring to organise an adequate defence which does not appear to have been fully deployed at the time of the action. RAF personnel manning pill boxes are still missing being last seen engaging the Japanese from the pill boxes.

In addition, there were various contributary circumstances namely, the multiplicity of command, the difficulty of co-operation between two nations working on different organisations and the fact that the British ground defence troops had only come in early the same night when the Dutch aerodrome guard was withdrawn on relief.

The chief mistakes appear to have been:

a) Lack of adequate covering troops to give either warning or protection against a surprise attack. For this the responsibility must lie with the Dutch Divisional Commander, who, under the Dutch organisation, is responsible for all aerodrome defence in his district. It must be remembered that in view of the very few troops available to the Dutch, this would have been very difficult to arrange.

b) The Battery Commander, who was in command both of the light AA battery and the ground defence troops covering the battery, was undoubtedly at fault in moving both guns and ground defences at the same time. He should have arranged to cover his retirement and has been censured for this.

In fairness to the personnel concerned, it should be borne in mind that, though organised and partially armed as infantry, the ground defence troops were actually personnel of a Heavy AA battery whose guns were left in Sumatra, and that officers and men had had very inadequate training in their new role. They would never have been deployed had there been anybody else available.

The matter was subsequently discussed between Air Vice-Marshal Maltby, as the senior, and Maj General Van Oyen as a result of the report submitted, and it was then agreed that whilst the whole incident was admittedly far from satisfactory, there was no evidence of fleeing from the aerodrome and, in view of the present situation, it would be better to let the matter drop since further enquiry could only lead to recrimination between two nations. The Governor General's wire was sent without our knowledge, and the fact that the matter had been referred outside Java at all came as a complete surprise.

We understand that the Commander-in-Chief, Lt General Ter Poorten, proposes to cable the British Government to the effect that the report that British troops had fled was based on unconfirmed rumours, which have since turned out to be false, and in this event we recommend the matter should not be pressed further, since additional enquiries must tend to cause further recrimination at a time when all our energies are needed to fight the enemy. Lt General Ter Poorten has seen this Report and agrees with it.

JAPANESE NAVY AIR FORCE – SOME STATISTICS:

A)

JNAF Air Strength, Production and Wastage, December 1941 to March 1942:

	On Hand 1 December 1941	Dec 1941 – Mar 1942 Produced	Expended	On Hand 1 April 1942
Fighters	660	316	300	676
Attack & Bombers (Shipboard)	330	123	146	307
Attack & Bombers (Land-based)	240	219	182	277
Reconnaissance & Patrol	10	0	0	10
Floatplanes (Reconnaissance)	270	64	93	241
Flyingboats	55	29	22	62
Transports	45	18	20	43
Trainers	510	212	92	630

Note: Number of aircraft on hand included those in storage

B)

JNAF aircraft expended in Greater East Asia War, December 1941 to April 1942
(first figure = combat losses: 2nd figure = other operational losses)

	Dec	Jan	Feb	Mar	Apr	Total
Fighters	44/32	34/34	31/38	26/60	36/35	171/199
Torpedo & Dive Bombers	19/24	11/23	15/26	8/20	19/10	72/103
Medium Bombers	25/18	11/21	40/25	5/37	11/14	92/115
Reconnaissance & Patrol	0/0	0/0	0/0	0/0	0/0	0/0
Floatplanes	2/11	15/9	13/15	13/15	6/10	49/60
Flyingboats	1/5	0/5	0/6	1/4	1/2	3/22
Transports	0/4	0/5	0/5	0/6	3/2	3/22
Trainers	0/18	0/21	0/27	0/26	0/24	0/116

Appendix V

ACCOUNT BY GROUP CAPTAIN H.S. 'GEORGE' DARLEY, DSO

In June 1941 I was posted as Wing Commander Fighter Operations to AHQ, Singapore, responsible for all fighter operations in the entire Far East which entailed continuous travel including the design and construction of fighter ops rooms in Singapore and Rangoon; also to redesign and extend Kai Tak airfield in Hong Kong as a fighter base, although no fighters were available. (Post war it was used by four-engined jet transports). I also briefed Dutch and American fighter pilots during these travels.

I was then attached to Colonel Chennault's 'Flying Tigers' at his request to Toungoo (then a vacant RAF base in Burma) to teach them fighter operational tactics, rather complicated because he had three mercenary squadrons, US Army, Navy and Marines, all with different concepts of operations against bomber raids. Firstly I had to demonstrate that an approach speed of 85 knots on their P-40s was quite safe instead of overshooting into the jungle at 140 knots. After that they listened. Eventually I arrived back at Singapore just as HMS *Prince of Wales* and *Repulse* were sinking. I will not go into details of RAF resentment of no naval advice upon the proposed movements except to emphasise that the resultant delay in our attempts to assist them was not in any way due to any fault in our air defence system. In any event we had only a third of the fighters demanded from the UK by the Singapore Chiefs of Staff.

Over this period the RAF and RAAF squadrons at Alor Star and Sungei Patani suffered from bombing attacks and were withdrawn south. So shortly after my return I was posted to command Ipoh with the remains of two RAAF squadrons. Thence we moved south to Kuala Lumpur but all fighters were then withdrawn to Singapore to protect shipping bringing Army troops. I retained the RAAD staff of the Ops Room.

On 16 January 1942, 225 (Bomber) Group formed in Sumatra on an airfield known as P.2 some 15 miles south of Palembang. On 1 February 1942, 224 (Fighter) Group reformed in Palembang town which had a nearby airfield, P.1. When the Japanese reached Johore Straits I was posted to 224 Group as Wing Command Fighter Operations and as in Singapore I had to set up an Ops Room from scratch, so I called upon the Dutch army garrison for help. Having found me a suitable house, they connected it by telephone to P.1 where there were a few ex-Singapore Hurricanes, later reinforced by some more from Java, ex-carrier HMS *Indomitable*. I was supplied with R/T receivers commandeered from shops but transmitting was a problem until I realised that oil tankers on the river Moesi connecting Palembang oil refinery with Banka Straits, some 40 miles north, were controlled into single lane traffic by R/T transmitted by the refinery. I found that it could transmit on our fighter frequencies, so I was then connected to it by telephone, and when I wished to transmit, I asked the operator to switch me over to 'transmit'. Such were the *ad hoc* arrangements, but our 'shop' worked and we were able to maintain a 24 hour shift by living and eating over the shop.

On 14 February 1942, Japanese paratroops dropped on airfield P.1 to initiate the capture of the refinery and I ordered all fighters then airborne to divert to P.2. I found the telephones to P.1 to be cut and I was ambushed as I tried to reach them by road. The Dutch garrison then took over. Eventually, after supervising the transfer of all our hospital patients by ferry across the river dividing Palembang, having commandeered the ferry by arms, I was able to ensure their eventual arrival at P.2. Few ambulances were available and so I had many service vans unloaded of kit and detailed fit airmen to act as medical assistants. When all airmen were safely across I then left myself, withdrew the armed guard from the ferry and thanked the Captain for his valuable help. I reached P.2 late afternoon and found a quiet corner from fighter operations in the bomber operations room and briefed the pilots.

On the next morning, 15 February, reconnaissance aircraft reported aircraft carriers in the Banka Straits and then many troops in open launches moving up river. The weather was low cloud, so I briefed my pilots to also keep low and to attack launches from the rear as no escorting fighters were reported. The first sorties created absolute carnage. The Hurricanes were quickly turned round, with fresh pilots, after a collective briefing between them and the first pilots. The second sorties were equally successful and any survivors were probably drowned in the deep marshes on both sides of the river. All these actions in some way revenged the capitulation of Singapore which also occurred on 14th and 15th February.

The next day P.2 was abandoned, all serviceable aircraft flying to Java. Personnel travelled south to Oosthaven, a port in south Sumatra, where we boarded SS *Yoma*, laden with Army stores. Thence we sailed to Batavia in Java where surplus personnel were sorted out and destined for Australia, but our Captain, after reaching the south coast of Java, decided to sail west for India instead. So all alone *Yoma*, with me as O/ C all troops of all services, eventually reached Karachi, via calls at Colombo and Bombay.

Further comments of Flt Lt T.P.M. Cooper-Slipper, DFC, of 232 Squadron:

Too late for inclusion in the main text, Mike Cooper-Slipper advised that during the later stages of the operations of 232 Squadron from Palembang, he undertook two sorties on an unrecorded date (probably 14 or 15 February 1942). On the first of these he attacked three bombers, reporting that when his fire hit that in the middle, it exploded and took the other two down with it. His second sortie of the day was a strafing attack on troop-laden barges on the Moesi River.

During the paratroop attack on P.1, he was captured:

> "I was treated well by the Officer in charge of the unit, who spoke very good English. They never took my Leica (*camera*) away. Just before dark I saw the road to town and when it got dark I ran away and walked into Palembang. At first light I crossed the river, and after an argument with a Dutch officer, I led about 20 officers and airmen and three nurses, to the south. After several days a few of us made it to the southern tip of Sumatra where a coaling ship took us across to Java, from where we eventually made our way to Batavia.
>
> "In Batavia I got too near a falling bomb, and I woke up in a Chinese river boat which had been converted to a hospital ship. The Japanese gave us a safe conduct and we sailed to Colombo in Ceylon. From there to Bombay, and thence by rail to No 3 British General Hospital in Poona."

MAP 1: EAST INDIES AREA
FEBRUARY — MARCH 1942

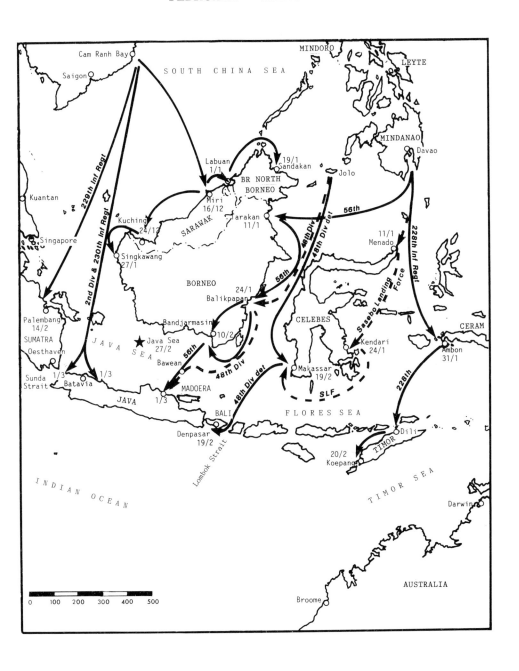

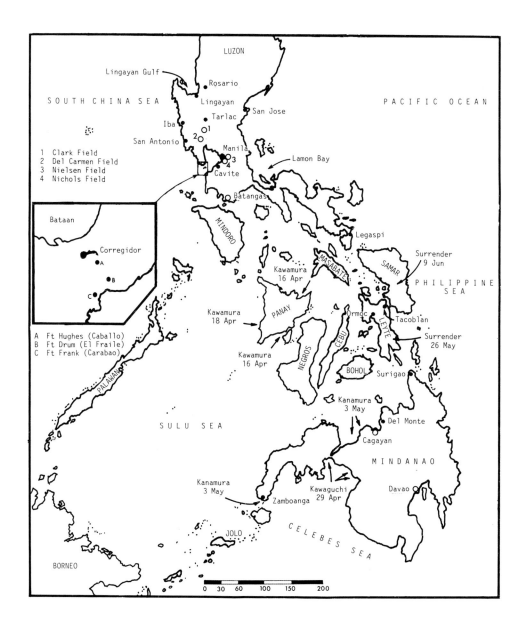

LUZON

Lingayan Gulf

Rosario

SOUTH CHINA SEA

PACIFIC OCEAN

Lingayan

San Jose

Tarlac

Iba

San Antonio

2 O 1

Manila

3

4

Lamon Bay

Cavite

1 Clark Field
2 Del Carmen Field
3 Nielsen Field
4 Nichols Field

Batangas

Legaspi

Surrender
9 Jun

MINDORO

MASABATE

SAMAR

PHILIPPINE
SEA

Bataan

Corregidor

A

B

C

Kawamura
16 Apr

Kawamura
18 Apr

PANAY

Ormoc

Tacloban

LEYTE

Surrender
26 May

A Ft Hughes (Caballo)
B Ft Drum (El Fraile)
C Ft Frank (Carabao)

NEGROS

CEBU

Kawamura
16 Apr

BOHOL

Surigao

PALAWAN

Kanamura
3 May

Del Monte

SULU SEA

Cagayan

MINDANAO

Kanamura
3 May

Kawaguchi
29 Apr

Davao

Zamboanga

JOLO

CELEBES SEA

BORNEO

0   30   60   100   150   200

MAP 3: JAVA
MARCH 1942

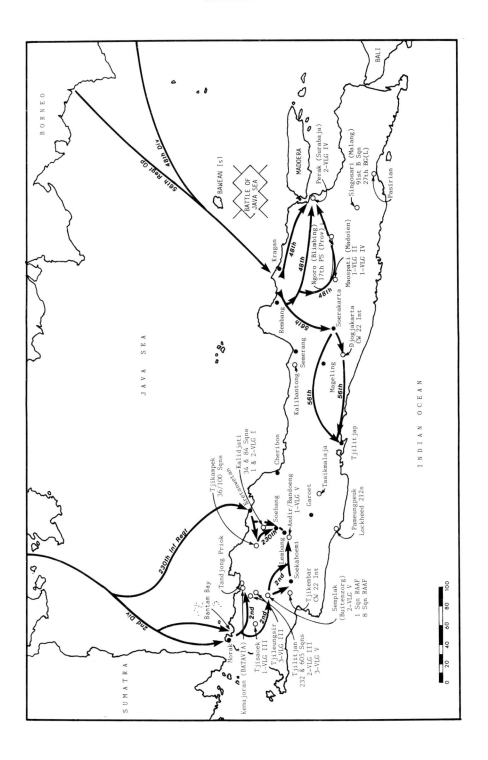

MAP 4: BURMA
FEBRUARY — MAY 1942

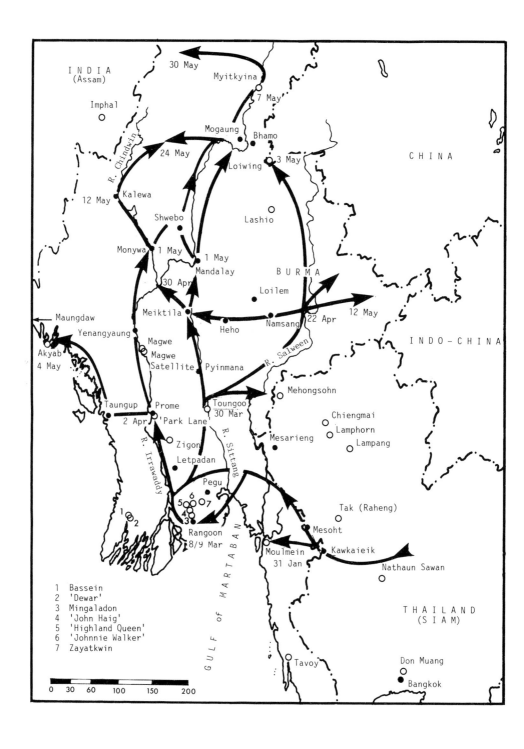

INDIA
(Assam)

30 May

Myitkyina

7 May

Imphal

Mogaung

Bhamo

24 May

CHINA

Loiwing

3 May

12 May

Kalewa

Shwebo

Lashio

Monywa   1 May

1 May

Mandalay

BURMA

30 Apr

Loilem

Meiktila

Maungdaw

Heho

Namsang

22 Apr

12 May

Yenangyaung

Magwe

INDO-CHINA

Akyab
4 May

Magwe
Satellite

Pyinmana

R. Salween

Taungup

Prome

2 Apr   'Park Lane'

Toungoo
30 Mar

Mehongsohn

Chiengmai

Zigon

Lamphorn

Letpadan

Mesarieng

Lampang

Pegu

6

Tak (Raheng)

5   7

4

Mesoht

3

Rangoon

Kawkaieik

8/9 Mar

Moulmein

31 Jan

Nathaun Sawan

1

2

GULF OF MARTABAN

R. Irrawaddy

R. Sittang

R. Chindwin

THAILAND
(SIAM)

1   Bassein
2   'Dewar'
3   Mingaladon
4   'John Haig'
5   'Highland Queen'
6   'Johnnie Walker'
7   Zayatkwin

Tavoy

Don Muang

Bangkok

0   30   60   100   150   200

MAP 5: INDIAN OCEAN AND CEYLON; ROUTES OF JAPANESE FLEETS
3-9 APRIL 1942

Nagumo Force ——————
Malaya Area Fleet _ _ _ _ _ _

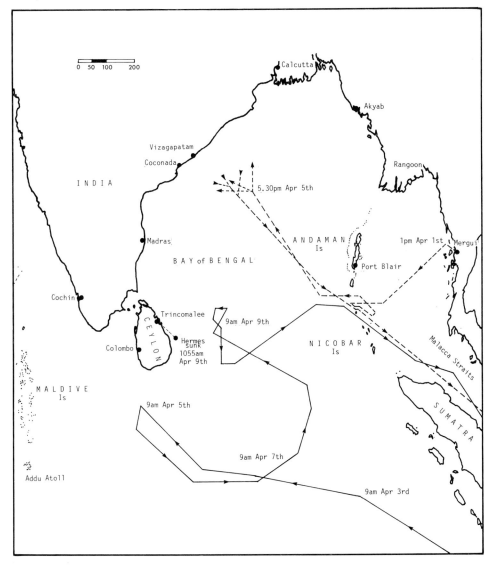

BIBLIOGRAPHY

Publication	Author	Publisher

A Flying Tiger's Diary Charles R. Bond (Texas Univ Press)

A Mouse In My Pocket Hedley Everard (Valley)

Army Air Forces in World War II, The (Vol 1) W.F. Craven & J.L. Cate (University of Chicago)

Australia's Pearl Harbour Douglas Lockwood (Cassell)

Battle of the Java Sea David Thomas (Andre Deutsch)

Battle for Palembang Terence Kelly (Robert Hale)

Battleship Martin Middlebrook & Patrick Mahoney (Allen Lane)

Bataan: The Judgement Seat Allison Ind (MacMillan NY)

Behind Bamboo Rohan Rivett (Elmfield)

Black Cats, The Richard C. Knott (Patrick Stephens)

Boat, The Walter Gibson (W.H. Allen)

Brereton Diaries, The Lewis H. Brereton

British Naval Aviation Ray Sturtivant (Arms & Armour)

But Not in Shame John Totland (Gibbs & Phillips)

Caged Eagles Vern Haugland (Airlife)

Canadian Flying Operations in South-East Asia T.W. Melnyk (Ministry of Supply & Services Canada)

Chasing After Danger Terence O'Brien (Collins)

Course for Disaster Richard Pool (Leo Cooper)

Chronology of the War at Sea J. Rohwer & G. Hummelchen (Ian Allan)

De Luchstrijd rond Borneo Peter C. Boer (Van Holtema & Warendorf)

De Luchstrijd om Indie Peter C. Boer (Van Holtema & Warendorf)

Destination Corregidor Robert Underbrink (US Naval Institute Press)

Dictionary of Disasters at Sea, 1824-1962 Charles Hocking (Lloyds Register)

Down in the Drink Ralph Barker (Chatto & Windus)

Dyess Story, The W.E. Dyess (Putnam NY)

Eagle Squadrons, The Vern Haugland (Ziff-Davis)

Emperor's Guest, The J. Fletcher-Cooke (Leo Cooper)

Epics of the Fighting RAF Leonard Gribble (Harrap)

Fall of the Philippines, The Louis Morton (US Army)

Fall of Singapore, The Frank Owen (Michael Joseph)

First Team, The John Lundstrom (Naval Institute Press)

Flying Cats Andrew Hendrie

Flying Elephants, The Chaz Bowyer (Macdonald & Janes)

Flying Fever AVM S.F. Vincent (Jarrolds)

Forgotten Skies W.W. Russell (Hutchinson)

Frontline Airline E. Bennett-Bremner (Angus & Robertson)

Ghost That Died At Sunda Strait, The Capt W.G. Winslow, USN (US Naval Institute Press)

Glory in Chaos Grp Capt E.R. Hall (Sembawang Association)

God is my Co-Pilot Robert L. Scott

Gordon Bennett Story, The Frank Legg (Angus & Robertson)

Hunting of Force Z, The Richard Hough (Collins)

Hurricane at War 2 Norman Franks (Ian Allan)

Hurricanes over the Arakan Norman Franks (Patrick Stephens)

Hurricanes over Burma M.C.C. Cotton (Titania)

Hurricane over the Jungle Terence Kelly (Robert Hale)

Japan's War at Sea David Thomas (Andre Deutsch)

Japanese Naval Aces & Fighter Units in WW II Ikuhiko Hata & Yasuho Izawa (US Naval Institute Press)

John Grey Gorton Alan Trenlove (Cassell)
Jungle Pilot Wg Cdr Barry Sutton (MacMillan)
Last Flight From Singapore A.G. Donahue (MacMillan)
Lasting Honour, The Oliver Lindsay (Hamish Hamilton)
Lion in the Sky Neville Shorrick (Federal Singapore)
Lowststawkee David Russell (unpublished)
Malayan Climax Carline Reid (Mercury Press)
Malayan Postscript Ian Morrison (Faber & Faber)
Mohawks over Burma Gerry Beauchamp (Midland Counties)
Most Dangerous Moment, The Michael Tomlinson (Kimber)
New Zealanders with the Royal Air Force Wg Cdr H.L. Thompson (War History Branch, New Zealand)
None More Courageous Stewart Holbrook (MacMillan)
Of Death But Once Roy Bulcock
Old Friends, New Enemies Prof A.J. Marder (Oxford UP)
Out in the Midday Sun Kate Caffrey (Andre Deutsch)
Pacific Sunset G.W. McCabe
Pacific War John Costello (Collins)
Percival and the Tragedy of Singapore Sir John Smyth (Macdonald)
Ragged Rugged Warriors, The Martin Caidin (Severn House)
Return to Freedom Samuel Grashio & Bernard Norling (MCN Press)
Retreat in the East O.D. Gallagher (Harrap)
Royal Australian Air Force 1939-42 Douglas Gillison (Australian War Memorial)
Royal New Zealand Air Force J.M.S. Ross (War History Branch, New Zealand)
Samurai Saburo Sakai (Kimber)
Sea Flight Hugh Popham (Kimber)
Second World War: Vol IV, The Sir Winston Churchill (Cassell)
Seek and Strike Andrew Hendrie (Kimber)
Shenton of Singapore Brian Montgomery (Leo Cooper)
Singapore James Leasor (Hodder & Stoughton)
Singapore 1941-42 Louis Allen (Davis-Poynter)
Singapore Slip Herb Plenty (private)
Singapore's Dunkirk Geoffrey Brooke (Leo Cooper)
Singapore: The Japanese Version Masanobu Tsuji (Constable)
Singapore Story, The Kenneth Attiwill (Muller)
Sinister Twilight Noel Barber (Collins)
SOE Singapore Richard Gough (Kimber)
Spotlight on Singapore Denis Russell-Roberts (Tandem)
Suez to Singapore Cecil Brown
Tale of a Tiger R.T. Smith
Their Last Tenko James Home (Quoin)
These Eagles Australian War Memorial
They Also Serve Dorothea Bourne (Winchester)
They Fought With What They Had Walter D. Edmonds (Little, Brown & Co)
They Never Surrendered Jesus Villamor & Gerald Snyder (Vrea Reyes Press)
Uncle's War in the Fleet Air Arm Lt Cdr Cyril Pountney (United Writers)
War against Japan, The (Vol I) Maj-Gen S. Woodburn-Kirby (HMSO)
War in Malaya, The Lt Gen A.E. Percival (Eyre & Spottiswoode)
War Without Glory J.D. Balfe (MacMillan)
Wings over Burma Kenneth Hemingway (Quality Press)
With General Chennault Robert B. Hotz (Zengler)
You'll Die in Singapore Charles McCormac (Robert Hale)
70 Days to Singapore Stanley Falk (Robert Hale)

Supplement to the *London Gazette* (20 February 1948) 'Report on Air Operations in Malaya and Netherlands East Indies, 8 December 1941 — 12 March 1942', by Air Vice-Marshal Sir Paul Maltby.

Supplement to the *London Gazette* (5 March 1948) 'Air Operations in Burma and the Bay of Bengal, January to May 1942', by Air Vice-Marshal D.F. Stevenson

Article entitled *Batavia's Big Sticks* by Gerard Casius ('Air Enthusiast/22'); article entitled *The St Louis Lightweight* by Gerard Casius ('Air Enthusiast/16'); article entitled *The 90-Day War* ('Air Combat'); articles entitled *Luck to the Fighters* by George Weller; unpublished article entitled *Where? And Back* by John Wyllie, DFC; unpublished memoirs of Flt Lt B.J. Parker, DFC; unpublished journal of Flt Lt G.C.S. Macnamara; various issues of Flight', 'American Aviation Historical Society Journal', 'Air Combat', 'Fighter Pilots in Aerial Combat', 'Flyer', 'Airpower', 'Air Force Museum Friends'

INDEX

Personnel — British and Commonwealth

Hornabrook, Sgt R.S. RAAF 36 Sqn 30, 35, 244
Hough, Sgt H.H. 84 Sqn 48, 51, 101, 121, 317
Howard, Grp Capt G.V. OC China Bay 391, 419
Howell, Flt Lt D. 31 Sqn 374
Howell, Sqn Ldr F.J. 243 Sqn/Air HQ 85
Howis, Sgt G.S. RAAF 36 Sqn 30
Howitt, Sgt J. 60 Sqn 378, 381
Huggard, Wt Off M.H. 60 Sqn 378, 379, *379*, 380-1
Hughes, Flg Off D. RAAF 1 RAAF Sqn 26, 204
Hunter, Air Cmdre H.J.F. 225 (B) Grp 57, 118
Hurley, Sgt J. 30 Sqn *403*
Hussey, Capt H.B. Qantas 180
Hutcheson, Flt Lt I.W. 100/36 Sqns 30, 36, 39, 245, 325, 338, 448
Hutcheson, Flt Lt J.R. RNZAF 488 Sqn 98, 448
Hutton, Flt Lt J.C. 232/605 Sqns 192, 225, 235, 248, 448
Hutton, Lt Gen Sir Thomas GOC Burma 256, 257, 258, 286
Hyatt, Sgt J.M. RAAF 84 Sqn 48, 74

Iremonger, Flt Lt J.H. 5 Sqn 409
Irvine, Sgt D.E. RAAF 84 Sqn 48, 74
Isdale, Sgt D.J.B. 266 Wg./242 Sqn 60, 204, 432

Jack, Sgt A.D. 266 Wg./605 Sqn 60, 192
Jackson, Flt Lt D.J.G. 34 Sqn 57, 58, 100, 120
Jackson, Sgt G.H. GR Flt 368
Jacob, Sub Lt R.F.H. RN 803 Sqn 428
Jaffray, Sub Lt V.W. RN 827 Sqn 405
James, Sqn Ldr T. 84 Sqn 46, 48, 68
James, Sgt W.H. RCAF 266 Wg 60
Jardine, Sqn Ldr A.M. 205 Sqn 54, 248, 249, 439
Jay, Flg Off A.B. RAAF 1 RAAF Sqn 63
Jeans, Sgt N.R. RAAF 211 Sqn 53, 435
Jeans, Cpl A.D. 84 Sqn 300
Jenkins, Wg Cdr H.P. 31 Sqn 279, 370, 374
Jensen, Sgt H. RNZAF 266 Wg 60
Jessop, Sgt. F.J. 261 Sqn *418*
Jeudwine, Wg Cdr J.R. 84 Sqn 38, 45, 46, 48, 50, 53, 54, 57, 58, 61, 72, 74, 75, 112, *113*, 114, 193, 220, 250, 296, 297, 301, 432, 433, 435, 447, 449, 468
Joerin, Flt Off F.C. 211 Sqn 47, 53, 73, *73*
Johnson, N/Air F. RN 803 Sqn 398
Johnson, LAC J. 258 Sqn 102
Johnson, Plt Off R.A.C. 62 Sqn 91
Johnston, Lt R.L.RN 803 Sqn 384, 427, 428, *428*
Jones, Sgt D. RNZAF 266 Wg 60
Jones, Sgt I.R. RAAF 36 Sqn 30
Jones, Flg Off R. Tudor 258 Sqn 78, 104, 121, *430*
Jones, Sgt Taff 59 Sqn 110
Jordan, Sgt P.L. RNZAF 261 Sqn *389*, *418*
Julian, Sqn Ldr I. RNZAF 232/242 Sqns 55, 99, 120, 191, 211, 292, 319, 320, 321, *330*, 331, 432, 444, 447, 448

Kallick, Flg Off B. 36 Sqn *31*
Kameshawa Dhora, Sgt H. IAF 1 IAF Sqn 273
Keble-White, Flg Off M. 84 Sqn 435, 436, 438
Keedwell, Sgt R.B. RCAF 258 Sqn *56*, 66
Keene, Sgt J. RAAF 34 Sqn 435
Keeping, Sgt J.B. RAAF 211 Sqn 53
Kelly, Sgt C.T.R. 258/605 Sqns *56*, 97, 120, 192, *193*, 228, 293, 294
Kelly, Sgt H.A. RAAF 36 Sqn 29, 31, *32*, 33, 41
Kendrick, Sgt G.M. 211 Sqn 53, 78
Kennedy, Wt Off J. 27 Sqn 108, 114
Kershaw, Plt Off 271 Sqn *389*
Kewish, Plt Off D.W. RAAF 84 Sqn 301
Khan, Sgt D. 1 IAF Sqn 284, 285
Kilpatrick, AC 1H 232 Sqn 100
Kilroy, Cdr R.A. RN RNAS Cochin 391

King, Sgt G.J. 232 Sqn/242 Sqns 211, 225, 308, 316, 320, 330, 332, 444, 447, 449
King, Sgt J. 84 Sqn 48
Kinninmont, Sqn Ldr J.R. RAAF 21/453 Sqns 449
Kite, Sgt 211 Sqn 53, 74
Kitley, Plt Off A.J.H. 136 Sqn 256, *356*, 357
Kleckner, Plt Off C. RCAF (US) 258 Sqn *56*, 63
Knight, Lt F.G. SAAF 11 Sqn 426
Koch, Capt A. Qantas 181
Kuhn, Sgt E.E.G. RNZAF 488/605 Sqns 192, 219, 225, 295, 447, 448, *458*
Kynman, Sgt D. 232/242 Sqns 120, 211, 432

Lamb, Flg Off. R.R. 100/36 Sqns 21, 244, 245, 328, 338
Lamb, Plt Off T.R. 100/36 Sqns 30, 35, 39, 245, 325, 338
Lambert, Sgt H. 258/605 Sqns *56*, 97, 120, 192, *193*, 224, 229, 235, 236
Lamond, Sgt H.J. RAAF 211 Sqn 53
Lamont, AC1 P. P.1 121
Land, Flt Lt F. 258 Sqn *431*
Lauchlan, L/Air N. RN 814 Sqn 420
Laverick, Lt Gen Sir John OC 1st Australian Corps 61
Leach, Flg Off H.D.T. 205 Sqn 413
LeCraw, Plt Off L.H. RCAF 136 Sqn 360
Lee, Sgt D.B.S. RNZAF 100 Sqn 21, 23, 24, 41
Lee, Flt Lt F.S. RAAF 45 Sqn 287
Lerew, Wg Cdr J.M. RAAF RAAF Hudson Flt 172, 173
Letchford, Plt Off F.W. 53/62 Sqns 371
Lewis, Sqn Ldr A.G. 261 Sqn 387, *388*, 389, 391, 392, 419, 420, 429, 444
Lewis, Sqn Ldr C.R.G. 4 PRU 166
Leys, Sgt R. RAAF 21/453 Sqn 27
Lilly, Sqn Ldr L.W.G. 62 Sqn 107
Linton, Flt Lt K. 211 Sqn 45, 51, 53, 64
Lister, Sgt K. 84 Sqn 48, 68, 75, 115
Llewellin, Sqn Ldr A.J.A. 232 Sqn 55
Lloyd, Sgt 113 Sqn 267
Lockhart, Flt Lt J. 258 Sqn 390, 400-1
Lockhart, Sgt J. RAAF 36 Sqn 30
Lockwood, Sgt C.H. RAAF 36 Sqn 30, 31, 40
Lockwood, Sgt G. 261 Sqn 415
Lockwood, Flt Lt J.M.H. RAAF 1 RAAF Sqn 74, 91, *92*
Lockwood, Plt Off W.M. RCAF 232/242 Sqns 66, 95, 111, 235, 292, 309, 320, 325, 327, 330, 331, 339, 432
Logan, Wt Off 211 Sqn 53
Longmore, Sgt A.C. RAAF 84 Sqn 48, 50
Longsdon, Lt S.M.de L. RN 788 Sqn 395, 396
Longworth, Sgt A. 59 Sqn 90, 117, 118
Lovegrove, Sgt J.A. RAAF 211 Sqn
Low, Sgt H.P. RCAF 266 Wg 60, 102, 438
Lowe, Flt Lt J.C. 205 Sqn 216, 303
Lower, Flg Off J. RAAF 1 RAAF Sqn 110, 220, 323
Lyall, Flt Sgt E. 36 Sqn 30, 34
Lynas, Sgt J.N. RAAF 211 Sqn 53

McAlister, Plt Off B.A. RNZAF 258 Sqn *56*
MacArthur, Plt Off 113 Sqn 371
McArthur, Sgt N. RAAF 100 Sqn 21, *39*
McBride, Sgt A.H. 84 Sqn 302
McCabe, Sgt G.W. RAAF 100 Sqn 19, 20, 21, 23, 24, 41
McCauley, Air Cmdre J.P.J. RAAF OC P.2 72, 109, 110, 120, 457, 465
McCulloch, Plt Off N.L. 258 Sqn *56*, 63, 67, 98, 104, 121, 390, *430*, *431*
McCulloch, Plt Off W.L. RAAF 232 Sqn 98
MacDonald, Sgt A. RCAF 17 Sqn 275, 352, 354, 364
MacDonald, Sgt C.J. RAAF 100 Sqn 21, 22, *39*, 234
McDonald, Sgt A RCAF 17 Sqn 275, 352, 354
McDonald, Plt Off D.A. RCAF 30 Sqn 401, 403, *403*
McDonald, Sgt I. RNZAF FE Pool 82

McDonald, Sgt M.D. RAAF 211 Sqn 53
Macdonald, Plt Off M.S. RAAF 84 Sqn 48, 50, 74, 108, 120, 121, 223, 301
McEwan, Flt Lt K.A. RNZAF 5 Sqn 409
McEwen, Lt B.S. RN 806 Sqn 384
McFadden, Flt Lt A. 261 Sqn 390, 401
McGrath, Father John Catholic Mission 177
McInerney, Plt Of T.T. RAAF 211 Sqn 53, 78
MacIntosh, Sgt W.J.N. RNZAF 488/605 Sqns 192, *218*, 219, 225
Mackay, Flg Off G.G. RAAF 211 Sqn 53, 78
MacKay, Sub Lt N.R. RN 788 Sqn 396
McKechnie, Plt Off J.K. RCAF 232 Sqn 75
McKeller, Plt Off T.C. RAAF 36 Sqn 30
McKern, Wg Cdr R.N. 62 Sqn 107
MacKillop, Sgt D.J. 84 Sqn 48, 108
Maclennan, Sgt H.A. 11 Sqn 426
MacLeod, Plt Off L.G. RCAF GR Flt 371
McLeod, Sgt R. RAAF 34 Sqn 100, 435
McLuckie, Flt Sgt J. 60 Sqn 378, 379, *379*, 380-1
Macnamara, Flg Off G.C.S.(Rhod) 258 Sqn *56*, 62, 77, 96, 97, *97*, 98, 100, 104, 121, 122, 390
McNamara, Sgt J.C. RAAF 84 Sqn (att'd 45 Sqn) 278
McRae, Sgt M.A. RAAF 135 Sqn 261, 262
McRae, Sgt RAAF 1 IAF Sqn 290
Maguire, Wg Cdr H.G. 266 Wg 59, 60, 75, 76, 78, 99, 102, 105, 106, 247, 321, 325, 327, 330, 332, 448
Majumdar, Sqn Ldr K. IAF 1 IAF Sqn 259, 263
Maltby, AVM P.C. Air HQ/AOC Java 42, 70, 75, 107, 191, 194, 227, 295, 302, 332, 330, 432, *459*, 468, 469
Mann, Flt Lt A.S. 28 Sqn 257, 267, 272, *272*, 273, 286
Mann, Sgt B.J. RAAF 36 Sqn 21
Mann, Sgt K.A.S. RAAF 261 Sqn *389*, 391, 417, *418*, 419, 426
Marillac, 2/Lt F.A.L. de 271
Markham, Sqn Ldr R.F.C. 36 Sqn 29, 31, *32*, 33, 40
Marra, Plt Off T.B. RNZAF 243 Sqn 22
Marshall, Flt Lt J.H.R. RAAF 8 RAAF Sqn 90
Marshall, Flg Off J.V. 261 Sqn *389*, 415, 417, 451
Marsland, Flt Lt G. 136 Sqn 355, *356*, *357*, 359
Martin, Sgt A. RAAF 266 Wg 60, 339, *342*
Martin, Flt Sgt J.D. 261 Sqn *389*, 415, *418*
Martin, Maj W.H.N. RM 814 Sqn 42
Mass, Sub Lt A. RN 273 Sqn 415
Mather, Plt Off J.A. 59/62 Sqns 371
Matson, Plt Off F.C.R. 62 Sqn 38
Maurice, Plt Off G. 84 Sqn 48, 223
May, Sgt A.W. 232/242 Sqns 442
Mayes, Plt Off E. 261 Sqn *418*, 418
Mayhew, Plt Off S.D. 62 Sqn 119
Maynard, Flt Lt A.K. RAAF 8 RAAF Sqn 90
Meaclem, Sgt V.E. RNZAF 488 Sqn 8
Mead, Flg Off J.D. MVAF 126
Meakin, Sub Lt A. RN 788 Sqn 396, 397
Meharry, Sgt H.J. RNZAF 488/605 Sqns 98, 192
Melville, Sgt S.P. 36 Sqn 338
Mendizabal, Plt Off A.R. RCAF 232/242 Sqns 29, 30, 302, 315, 339, *340*, *342*, 342
Menzies, Sgt N.G. RAAF 8 RAAF Sqn 27
Menzies, Sgt S.K. RAAF 211 Sqn 53
Mercer, Sgt J. 62 Sqn 91
Middleton, LAC C. 84 Sqn 296
Millar, M. BOAC 303
Miller, Plt Off R.D. RNZAF 84 Sqn 48, *103*
Miller, Sgt W. 84 Sqn 48, 74, 101, *103*, 108, 436, 437
Miller, Sgt, 258 Sqn *56*
Mills, Sgt H.A.H. 100 Sqn 30, 35
Milne, Flt Lt W.L. RAAF RAAF Hudson Flt 173
Milnes, Plt Off A.H. 258 Sqn *56*, 63, 66, 103, 390, *401*, 401, *430*, *431*
Milson, Flg Off G.W. 84 Sqn 48

Personnel — American:

Personnel — Dutch:

Prooyen, Lt Cdr W. van GTV-16 312

Rest, Kapt A.A.M. van 1-VIG-IV *146*, 146, 292, 451
Roumimper, Sgt O.B. 2-VIG-IV 222
Rupplin von Keffikon, Kapt K. KNILM 440

Senerpont Domis, Kapt R. 1-VIG-I 147
Schaftlein, 2/Lt 1-VIG-III 233
Scheffer, Ens J.F. 2-VIG-V 202, *203*, 337
Simons, Lt H.H.J. 3-VIG-V 208, 215, *216*

Smirnoff, Capt I. KNILM *314*, 315
Straatman, 2/Lt P.E. 1-VIG-II 327

Ter Poorten, Lt Gen H. C-in-C, NEI 469
Theunissen, Wt Off Masao 77th Sentai 270
Tideman, Lt P.G. 3-VIG-V *146*, 208, 215, 309
Tukker, Lt J.J. 3-VIG-V 208

Verhoeven, Lt J.W. VkA-1 147
Vonck, Ens C.A. 1-VIG-V 243
Vossen, Ens L.A.M. van der 2-VIG-IV 161, 171

Vries, Lt A.J. de 3-VIG-IV 147

Weijnschenk, Ens C.H. 3-VIG-IV 169
Wilde, Sgt F.J. de 2/1/3-VIG-IV 169, 171, 305
Winckel, Lt A. ML 313, 337
Wink, Ens N. 2-VIG-IV 316
Wolff, Lt A.B. 3-VIG-III 147

Zomer, Lt Col OC Kalidjati 295

Personnel — Other Allied:

Chiang Kai-shek (Chinese) Generalissimo, Head of State 257, 258, 286, 345. 382
Chin, Lt Art (Chinese) Chinese Air Force 441

Quezon, Manuel (Filipino) President of Philippines 138
U. Saw (Burmese), Prime Minister 348

Villamor, Capt Jesus (Filipino) 6th Pursuit Sqn 133, 134
Zosa, Capt Ramon (Filipino), Filipino Air Force 143

Personnel — Japanese:

Abe, Lt Heijiro Soryu 176, 413
Adachi, Lt Jiro Takao Ku 241
Aioi, Lt Takahide Ryujo/3rd Ku 72, 454
Akamatsu, Wt Off Sada-aki 3rd Ku *154*, 159, 163, 453
Anabuki, Cpl Satoshi 50th Sentai 134, *134*, 453, 455
Anma, Capt Katsumi 64th Sentai 64, 208, *362*, 362, 364, *364*, 369, 455
Aoyagi, Sgt Maj Yutaka 11th Sentai 223, 228, 455
Arita, NAP 2/C Yoshisuke Tainan Ku 129, 150, 201, 211
Asai, Lt Masao Tainan Ku 150, 201, 210, 211

Baba, NAP 2/C Tokiharu 4th Ku 186, 187
Beppu, Lt Kisaji 77th Sentai 262, 264

Chihaya, Lt Takehiko Akagi 176
Chiyoshima, NAP 1/C Yutaka Hiryu 404, 426

Egusa, Lt Cdr Takashige Soryu 176, 307, 327, 406, 424
Endo, Lt T. 64th Sentai 64
Eto, Capt Toyoki 77th Sentai 264, *264*, 277, 290, 455

Fuchida, Cdr Mitsuo Akagi 176, 182
Fujii, NA 1/C Koichi Zuikaku 423
Fujimori, Lt Akira 8th Sentai 368
Fujimoto, NAP 2/C Takaji 4th Ku 186
Fujinaga, Wt Off 77th Sentai 262, 277
Fujita, Lt Iyozo Soryu 176, 395, 399, 404, 413, 454
Fukuoka, Lt Norio 1st Ku 214
Fukuyama, NAP 3/C Kiyotaki Tainan Ku 214
Furukawa, NAP 3/C Nobutoshi 3rd Ku 167
Furukawa, Wt Off Wataru Tainan Ku 149
Fusetari, NAP 1/C Noburo 4th Ku 186

Goto, Sgt Maj Tsutomu 64th Sentai 365

Hagiwara, Wt Off Saburo 77th Sentai 289, 290
Handa, Wt Off Watari Tainan Ku 231, 316, 454
Hanzawa, Wt Off Yukuo Shokaku 423
Harada, NAP 1/C Kaname Soryu 404, 427, 454
Harada, NAP 3/C Toshiaki Hiryu 423, 427
Hashiguchi, Lt Cdr Takashi Kaga 176
Hashiguchi, NAP 3/C Yoshiro 3rd Ku 168, 454
Hasuo, Lt Takaichi 3rd Ku 159, 163
Hatakeyama, NAP 1/C Yoshiaku 3rd Ku 159
Hayashi, PO 1/C Akira 3rd Ku 313
Hayashi, NAP 1/C Fujio Shokaku 416, 423
Hayashi, Wt Off Kiyoshi Yokohama Ku 184
Hayashi, NA 1/C Shigeru Hiryu 423, 427
Hayashi, Wt Off Takeomi 59th Sentai 208

Hidaka, NAP 2/C Yoshiri Tainan Ku 155, 161
Hide, NAP 1/C Motabuki 3rd Ku 159, 161
Hideshima, Wt Off Masao 77th Sentai 270
Higashi, NAP 1/C Sachio Soryu 370
Higashi, NAP 1/C Yukio Soryu 404
Hino, NAP 1/C Masato Hiryu 405, 413
Hinoki, Lt Yohei 64th Sentai 64, 215, 365, *367*, 454
Hirano, Cpl Y. 64th Sentai 370
Hirata, NAP 3/C Yasuo Takao Ku 158
Hiromura, NAP 1/C Tsutomu Sanuki Maru 142
Hirose, Lt Nobutaka 2nd Parachute Regt 106
Hirose, Maj Yoshio 77th Sentai 263, 454
Hoashi, Lt Takumi Shokaku 423
Homma, Gen Masaharu OC 14th Army 136
Honda, NAP 3/C Toshiaki Tainan Ku 161, 167, 211, 220
Honma, Wt Off 77th Sentai 277
Hori, Capt Sadao 74th Ind Chutai 128
Hoshi, Col Komotaro 10th Ind Hikotai 130, 137

Ibusuki, Lt Masanobu Akagi 404
Ichihara, Lt Tatsuo Shokaku 413
Ichikawa, NAP 1/C H. Sagara Maru 149
Ide, NA 1/C Suehara 22 Air Flot 228, 229
Iida, Gen S. 15th Army 334
Ikeda, Lt Masai Soryu 182
Imamura, Gen Hitoshi GOC Invasion Force 253
Irisa, Lt Cdr Toshiie Kanoya Ku 150, 176
Ishida, NA 1/C Masashi Akagi 423
Ishihara, NAP 2/C Susumu Tainan Ku 150, 201, 220, 231, 454
Ishii, NAP 3/C Shizuo Tainan Ku 129, 161, 167, 238, 453
Ishikawa, Maj Tadashi 50th Sentai 351, 354
Ishizaki, NAP 2/C Goichi 4th Ku 186
Itaya, Lt Cdr Shigeru Akagi 176, 395, 404, 413, 423
Ito, NAP 1/C Junjiro Zuikaku 423
Ito, Lt Cdr Takuzo 4th Ku 184, 186, 189
Itoh, Lt Motoe Kumano 409
Iwaki, NAP 1/C Yoshio Akagi 404
Iwamoto, Wt Off Seiai 1st Ku 165
Iwamoto, NAP 2/C Tetsuzo Zuikaku 396, 423, 452, 453
Izumi, NAP 2/C Hideo Tainan Ku 201, 454

Jimbo, Capt Susumu 47th IF Chutai 36

Kamihira, NAP 1/C Keishu Tainan Ku 161-2, *162*, 217, 454
Kaneko, Lt Tadashi Shokaku 413, 423, 454
Kano, NAP 1/C Satoshi Zuikaku 427
Kasai, NA 1/C Haruo Tainan Ku 231
Kasunoki, Lt Cdr Yoshimasa Hiryu 413
Kataoka, Lt M. 64th Sentai 370

Kato, Lt Col Tateo 64th Sentai 16, 62, 99, 202, 214, 215, 316, 364, 377, 378, 379, *379*, 380, 381, 455
Kawada, NAP 2/C Yozo Akagi 404
Kawada, Lt 77th Sentai 277, 284
Kawamorita, Lt Col Shojiro 10th Ind Hikotai 136
Kawamota, Lt Katsutoshi Tainan Ku 226
Kawasaki, Wt Off Masao 4th Ku 186
Kawazoe, Lt Toshitada 3rd Ku 167
Kikuchi, Lt A. 64th Sentai 439
Kikuchi, NAP 1/C Tetsuo Akagi 404, 454
Kikuchi, NAP 1/C Toshio Tainan Ku 9
Kimura, Wt Off 77th Sentai 277, 375
Kitamura, Lt 77th Sentai 263
Koba, Gen 18th Division 18
Kobayashi, NA 1/C Kyoji Tainan Ku 155-6
Kobayashi, Lt Michio Hiryu 176
Kodama, Wt Off Yoshimi Hiryu 404, 427
Kogiku, NAP 2/C Ryosuke 4th Ku 186, 189
Kojima, Lt Tsuguo 77th Sentai 277
Komachi, NA 1/C Sadamu Shokaku 423, 453
Kondo, Vice-Adm Nobutake C-in-C 2nd Fleet 233, 307, 318
Kono, NA 1/C Shigeru Shokaku 423
Konoe, Prince Fumimaro Prime Minister 442
Kotani, NA 1/C Kenji Hiryu 405, 413
Koyamauchi, Wt Off Suekichi Akagi 423
Koyanagi, Capt Takejiro 11th Sentai 20
Kubo, Wt Off Kazuo 3rd Ku 159
Kubota, NAP 1/C Wataru Soryu 404, 427
Kubotani, Lt Toshiru 1st Sentai 197
Kudo, Wt Off Osamu 3rd Ku 313, *314*, 454
Kume, Colonel Sei-ichi 2nd Parachute Regt 107
Kume, NAP 3/C Takeo Tainan Ku 211
Kunii, Lt Masabumi 64th Sentai 77
Kurato, NA 1/C Nobutaka Zuikaku 423
Kurauchi, NAP 3/C Takashi 3rd Ku 314
Kurita, Rear-Adm Takeo Western Invasion Force 231. 253
Kuroe, Capt Yasuhiko 47th IF Chutai/64th Sentai 20, 22, 29, 36, *346*, 369, *369*, 453, 455
Kuroki, NAP 3/C Sanenori Zuikaku 423
Kuroki, Lt Tadao 64th Sentai 364
Kurosawa, Lt Takeo 3rd Ku 159, 217
Kusuhata, Lt Yoshinobu Takao Ku 201
Kuwabara, Lt Yoshiro 77th Sentai 262, *263*, 264, 270, 277, 284, 455

Mae, NA 1/C Shichijiro Zuikaku 423
Maeda, NAP 1/C Koji 4th Ku 186, 187, 188, 189
Makagune, Wt Off Yukii Sagara Maru 118
Maki, Lt Yukio Tainan Ku 241
Makino, Lt Masatoshi Zuikaku 395, *396*, 413, 414, 423
Makino, Ens Motohiro Yokohama Ku 184, 189

Makino, Maj Yasuo 77th Sentai 281
Makinoda, NAP 1/C Toshiro *Hiryu* 426
Masuyama, NA 1/C Masao 3rd Ku *157*, 159, 212
Matsumoto, NA 1/C Tatsu *Zuikaku* 414, 423
Matsumoto, NA 1/C Yasuo 3rd Ku 315
Matsumoto, NA 1/C Zenichi 3rd Ku 314
Matsunaga, Sgt Maj 77th Sentai 277
Matsuo, Lt Yoshihide 77th Sentai 277, 284
Matsuyama, Wt Off Tsuguo *Hiryu* 404, 426
Matsuzaki, Lt Mitsuo *Akagi* 395
Mihara, Lt Masao 50th Sentai 278
Minato, NAP 3/C Kosaku Tainan Ku 211
Minematsu, Lt *Kamikawa Maru* 197
Misago, Sgt Maj A. 64th Sentai 365
Mitani, Lt Akira 4th Ku 186, 189
Miyano, Lt Zenjiro 3rd Ku 313, 454
Miyazaki, 211, 220
Mizotani, Lt 1st Sentai 29
Mori, NAP 1/C Bin 4th Ku 186, 187
Mori, NAP 1/C Sakae *Akagi* 404
Morisawa, Lt Ryo 2nd Parachute Regt 122
Morita, NAP 2/C Akira 4th Ku 186
Morita, NA 3/C Masaru 3rd Ku 157, 159
Morita, NAP 1/C Minoru 3rd Ku 156
Motoyoshi, NA 1/C Yoshio Tainan Ku 150, 201, 211, 220
Mukai, Lt Ichiro 3rd Ku 325
Mune, Lt Noburu 50th Sentai 131, 132
Muranaka, NAP 1/C Kazu-o *Hiryu* 423, 454
Muto, NAP 2/C Kaneyoshi 3rd Ku 159, 453

Nabara, NAP 3/C Yasunobu 3rd Ku 159, 161
Nagahama, NAP 1/C Yoshikazu *Kaga* 177, 180, 454
Nagasawa, NAP 1/C Genzo *Soryu* 404, 427
Nagoe, Sgt Maj 77th Sentai 352
Nagoshi, Lt Shinjirou 77th Sentai 277, 290, 352
Nagumo, Vice-Adm Choichi C-in-C 1st Carrier Fleet 175, 182, 386, 393
Nakada, NAP 2/C Shigenobu *Zuikaku* 423
Nakagawa, 4th Ku 185, 186, 189
Nakahara, Ens Tsueno 3rd Ku 159, 213, 217
Nakajima, NAP 1/C Bunkichi 3rd Ku 159, 163, *164*, 454
Nakajima, Lt 77th Sentai 277, 290
Nakakariya, NAP 2/C Kunimori 3rd Ku 160, 454
Nakamura, Lt Saburo 64th Sentai 377, 455
Nakano, NAP 2/C Katsujiro 3rd Ku 159
Nakao, Lt Kikuo 2nd Parachute Regt 95
Nakao, Lt 77th Sentai 264
Nakase, NAP 1/C Masayuki 3rd Ku 159, 161, 168, 454
Nakatani, Lt Takesada 8th Sentai *272*, 273
Niihara, Maj Parachute Flying Unit 93
Niino, Sgt 77th Sentai 264, 277
Nikaido, Lt Yasushi *Kaga* 176
Nishido, NAP 2/C Masami Tainan Ku 149
Nishimura, Rear-Adm Eastern Invasion Force 232
Nishiura, NAP 2/C Kunimatsu Tainan Ku 209
Nishiyama, NA 1/C Shizuyoshi Tainan Ku 150, 220, 231
Nishizawa, Lt Hiroyoshi 4th Ku 173, *173*, 452, 453
Nitta, NAP 1/C Haruo *Hiryu* 404, 427
Noguchi, NAP 1/C Kijiro *Hiryu* 423
Nomura, NAP 3/C Shigeru 3rd Ku 159
Nonaka, Lt Cdr Taro Takao Ku 150
Nono, Lt Sumio *Hiryu* 176, 395, 404, 426, 427
Nozawa, NAP 3/C Saburo Tainan Ku 129, 155, 161, 167, 211, 243

Oda, NAP 1/C Ki-ichi *Soryu* 404, 427, 454
Oda, NA 1/C Toru 3rd Ku 159, 163, 217
Ogata, Lt Jun-ichi 77th Sentai 264, 277
Ogata, Ens Kaoru *Sanyo Maru* 295
Ogawa, Lt Shoichi *Kaga* 176
Ogawa, NAP 1/C Takegoro 4th Ku 186
Ohara, NAP 3/C Hiroshi *Akagi* 404, 427
Ohhira, Capt Tadeo 70th Ind Chutai 273
Ohshoya, NAP 3/C Muneichi Tainan Ku 231
Ohtsuka, Wt Off Zenzaburo 11th Sentai 56, 455
Ohtsuki, NA 1/C Tanekichi 3rd Ku 161, 212
Okabe, NAP 2/C Kenji *Shokaku* 423, 454
Okabe, Lt Col Sada 12th Flying Brigade 352
Okazaki, NAP 1/C Masaki 3rd Ku 313
Okazaki, NAP 3/C Shigeo 3rd Ku 159
Okumoto, Lt Minoru 2nd Parachute Regt 99
Okumura, Lt Muneyuki 64th Sentai 364
Okuyama, Sgt Maj Choichi 64th Sentai 66, *67*
Ono, NAP 1/C Kosuka 4th Ku 186
Ono, Ens Shin 4th Ku 186, 189
Ono, Sgt 77th Sentai 277
Onozaki, Sgt Maj Hiroshi 59th Sentai 62, 64, 455
Otani, Capt Masuzo 64th Sentai *362*, 378
Ozaki, Lt Cdr Takeo 1st Ku 150, 160, 176
Ozawa, Vice-Adm Jisaburo OC Malaya Force 109, 393, 408, 430

Saeki, NAP 1/C Yoshimichi Tainan Ku 161, 167, 304
Sakaguchi, Capt Fujio 50th Sentai 8
Sakaguchi, NAP 1/C Otojiro Tainan Ku 220
Sakai, Lt Noboru Yokohama Ku 184
Sakai, NAP 1/C Saburo Tainan Ku 161, 167, 201, 210, 242-3, *243*, 317, 452, 453
Sakai, NAP 3/C Tadahiro 3rd Ku 167
Sakai, NAP 1/C Toyo-o Tainan Ku 219, 220, 241
Sakaida, NAP 2/C Goro *Zuikaku* 427
Sano, NAP 1/C Shinpei *Akagi* 404, 427
Sasai, Lt Jun-ichi Tainan Ku 150, 201, 217, 231. 317, 453
Sasaki, NAP 2/C Tadashi *Hiryu* 404, 427
Sato, Lt Masao *Zuikaku* 396
Seto, Lt Masuzo Tainan Ku 129
Seto, Lt Yogono 4th Ku 185
Shibuya, Lt Kiyoharu Tainan Ku 209, 220
Shigematsu, Lt Yasuhiro *Hiryu* 413, 423, 454
Shimada, NAP 1/C Kin-ichi Takao Ku 201
Shimazaki, Cdr Shigekazu *Zuikaku* 413
Shimizu, Kazuo 59th Sentai 377, 455
Shimoda, Lt 77th Sentai 284
Shimono, NAP 2/C Kiyonori Takao Ku 201
Shingo, Lt Hideki Tainan Ku 150, 161, 167, 211, 220
Shinohara, NAP 2/C Yoshie Takao Ku 201, 211
Shoji, NA 3/C Sho-ichi 3rd Ku 157, 159
Sonoyama, NAP 3/C Masakichi 3rd Ku 163, 231
Sudoh, Lt Naohiko 98th Sentai 95
Suganami, Lt Masaharu *Soryu* 413
Sugio, NAP 1/C Shigeo 3rd Ku 159, 231, 453
Sumita, Wt Off Takeshi *Shokaku* 423
Suzuki, Lt Tetsutaro 3rd Ku 156

Tada, Vice-Adm OC 21st Air Flotilla 160
Tahara, NAP 3/C Isao *Hiryu* 423
Takada, Maj Katsushige 76th Ind Chutai 137
Takada, NAP 1/C Noboru *Hiryu* 404
Takagi, Vice-Adm Takeo Java Invasion Force 232, 233
Takahashi, Lt Cdr Kakuichi Nagumo Force 395, 422

Takahashi, Lt Shunji 64th Sentai *364*
Takahashi, NAP Sozaburo *Soryu* 404
Takahashi, Sgt Takeo 11th Sentai 374, 455
Takahashi, Vice Adm, Cdr Java Invasion Force 231
Takashima, NAP 3/C Takeo *Soryu* 404, 427
Takasuga, NA 1/C Mitsumi *Akagi* 423
Takayasu, NA 1/C Saburo Sanuki Maru 141, 227
Takenaka, NAP 1/C Yoshihiko 3rd Ku 167
Takeuchi, Shogo 64th Sentai *364*, 455
Tanaka, NAP 2/C Jiro *Soryu* 404, 427, 454
Tanaka, NAP 1/C Katsumi *Akagi* 404, 427
Tanaka, NAP 1/C Kuniyoshi Tainan Ku 161, 167, 211, 220, 454
Tanaka, NAP 3/C Yoshifuji *Shokaku* 423
Tanaka, Col Palembang Invasion Force 119, 122
Taniguchi, NAP 2/C Masao *Akagi* 423, 454
Tatewaki, NAP 1/C Hiromichi 4th Ku 186
Todaka, NAP 2/C Norboru *Hiryu* 405, 427
Togota, Wt Off 77th Sentai 352
Tojiri, Maj Kiyoshi 31st Sentai 279
Tojiri, NA 1/C Seiji 3rd Ku 159, 163
Tokuji, NAP 1/C Yoshihisa 3rd Ku 159, 163, 212
Touyama, Lt Yasushi 60th Sentai 138
Toshima, NA 1/C Hajime *Hiryu* 179, 182
Tsukahara, Vice-Adm Nishizo CinC 11th Air Fleet 231
Tsukamoto, Lt Yuzo *Zuikaku* 396, 423
Tsukuda, NAP 1/C Seiichi *Zuikaku* 427
Tsuru, Wt Off Katsuyoshi *Kaga* 178

Uchikado, NAP 1/C Musashi Kaga 178
Uchiyama, NAP 1/C Susumu 4th Ku 186, 187
Ueda, NAP 3/C Makoto Tainan Ku 226
Uehara, NAP 3/C Sadao Tainan Ku 211

Wada, Sgt Maj Haruto 64th Sentai 364
Watanabe, Wt Off Chuzo 4th Ku 185, 189

Yahata, NAP 3/C Isaburo 3rd Ku 159, 212, 217
Yakamoto, NA 1/C Suehiro 3rd Ku 159, 163
Yakomizo, Lt Koushirou Takao Ku 201
Yamada, Ens Hisao Takao Ku 201
Yamagami, NAP 2/C Tsunehiro Tainan Ku 161, 167, 211, 238
Yamaguchi, NAP 1/C Sada-o 3rd Ku 159, 454
Yamamoto, NAP 2/C Ichiro *Shokaku* 423
Yamamoto, Admiral Isoroku, CinC IJN 442
Yamamoto, Lt Shigehisa *Akagi* 423
Yamamoto, Capt Sueo 8th Sentai 282
Yamashita, Lt Michiji *Hiryu* 182
Yamaya, NAP 2/C Hatsumasa 3rd Ku 157, 159
Yanase, C/O, 10th Ind Hikotai 136
Yano, NAP 1/C Shigeru 3rd Ku 159, 163, 454
Yasuda, Sgt Maj Yoshito 64th Sentai 64, 208, *364*, 365, 370, 377, 378, 380, 455
Yasui, NAP 2/C Kozaburo 22nd Air Flot 92, 454
Yatabem Lt 77th Sentai 376
Yatomaru, Wt Off *Kamikawa Maru* 293
Yokoi, Sgt Akeshi 64th Sentai 64, 208
Yokokawa, NAP 2/C Kazuo Tainan Ku 129, 161, 316
Yokoyama, NAP 3/C Kazuo Tainan Ku 211
Yokoyama, Tak 167, 20
Yokoyama, Lt Tamotsu 3rd Ku 150, 159, 241
Yoshida, Wt Off Mototsuna 4th Ku 221, 454
Yoshimura, NA 1/C Keisaku 22nd Air Flot 92, 454
Yoshino, NAP 1/C Satoshi 4th Ku 173, 454

Air Units — British & Commonwealth:

221 Group 267, 285
222 Group 386, 390
224 (Fighter) Group 471
225 (Bomber) Group 19, 45, 57, 59, 95, 109, 118, 471

226 (Fighter) Group 57, 58, 60, 63, 70, 93, 95, 100, 121, 191
BRITAIR 227, 295, 322
RAFCHIN 371
266 (F) Wing 59, 75, 102, 379, 438

267 (F) Wing 265, *274*
270 (B) Wing 47
X Wing 267, 285, 290, 291, 345
AKWING 345, 349, 359
BURWING 345, 349, 361, 362, 370, 371

5 Squadron 375, 409, 410
11 Squadron 390, 405, 411, 422, 425, 426, 427
17 Squadron 258, 260, 262, *262*, 266, 268, *273*, *275*,
  275, *276*, 277, *283*, 284, 285, 286, 287, 290,
  291, 345, 349, 350, *353*, 355, 357, 359, 361,
  362, 365, *366*, 366, 371
27 Squadron 19, 38, 50, 57, 108, 114, 115, 124,
  193, 222
28 Squadron 256, 259, 263, 266, 267, *267*, 272,
  273, 274, 285, 286, 345, 349, 361
30 Squadron 55, 385, 386, 387, 399, *402*, 403,
  403, 408, 412, 430
31 Squadron 268, 279, 290, 291, 348, 359, *359*,
  362, 370, 374, 375
34 Squadron 50, 54, 57, 58, 64, 100, 108, 120,
  124, 126, 193, 204, 212, *317*, 375
36 Squadron *18*, 19, 20, 25, *26*, 29, 30, *32*, *33*,
  34,
  39, 40, 147, 193, 243, 307, 325, 438
41 Squadron 65
45 Squadron 267, 268, 270, 277, 278, 288, 345,
  346, 349, 355, 361
53 Squadron 78, 268, 270, *271*, 371, 372, 377
59 Squadron *52*, 52, 57, 68, 78, 110, 199, 268,
  296, 371, 372, 438
60 Squadron 275, 361, 375, 376, *378*, 379, 380,
  461
62 Squadron 19, 37, 50, 54, 57, 61, 64, 74, 79,
  91, 95, 107, 119, 194, 200, 212, 214, 219,
  234, 371, 372, 376, 377
67 Squadron 256, 267, 268, *269*, 288, *289*, 347
79 Squadron 265
80 Squadron 390
84 Squadron 38, 45, 47, 49, *49*, 50, 51, 53,
  54, 55, 57, 58, 61, 63, 64, 68, 71, 73, 74, 89,
  92, 101, *103*, 103, 108, 112, *113*, 114, 115,
  117, 120, 121, 122, *123*, 125, 193, 204, 214,
  217, 220, 222, 233, 250, *251*, 278, 296, 301,
  302, 311, 334, *461*
92 Squadron 172
100 Squadron 19, 20, *24*. 29, *39*, 148, 193, 234,
  438
108 Squadron 49, *49*, 50
113 Squadron 45, 256, 258, 259, 267, 279,
  286, 345, 348, 349, 361, 365, 367, 368, 371,
  375, 369, 376, 377
131 Squadron 390
135 Squadron 256, 257, *257*, 265, 266, 268,
  273, 273, 275, 277, *278*, 279, *282*, 285, *285*,
  286, 287, 290

136 Squadron 264, 265, 285, 291, *291*, *343*,
  345, 349, 355, *356*, 356, *357*, 357, *358*, 359,
  384
139 squadron 368, 371, 393
146 Squadron 370
202 Squadron 391
205 Squadron 54, 79, 148, 194, 197, 216, 248,
  302, 312, 324, 391, 405, 439
211 Squadron 45, *46*, 47, 46, 51, *52*, 53, 57, 58,
  61, 62, 64, 65, 71, 73, *73*, 78, 89, 108, 110,
  112, 114, 115, 121, 122, 193, 204, 214, 217,
  234, 302, 324, 438
215 Squadron 367, 371, 375, 377, 409
232 Squadron (including 232(P) Squadron)
  19, 20, 54, 55, 56, 57, 58, 59, 61, 63, 66, 70,
  75, *76*, 77, 78, 89, 98, 100, 104, 111, 117,
  119, 120, 191, 192, 385
240 Squadron 390-1, 407
242 Squadron 70, 99, 158, 170, 191, 204, 211,
  221, 224, 228, 229, *230*, 235, 249, 292, 293,
  294, *294*, 305, 307, 308, 309, 316, 321, 329,
  330, 336, 339, 340, 432, 433, *458*
243 Squadron 19, 20, 78, *84*, 192, 304
258 Squadron 54, 55, *56*, 57, 58, 61, 62, 63,
  66, 67, 70, 75, 78, *89*, 89, 92, 98, 99, 100,
  102, 103, *103*, 105, 107, 111, 112, 119, 120,
  121, 191, 192, *229*, 305, 385, *390*, 390, 391,
  397, 399, *400*, *401*, 403, 408, 430, *430*
261 Squadron 385, 386, 387, *388*, *389*, 390,
  391, *407*, 411, *411*, 413, *414*, 416, 417, *418*,
  419, 422, 429, 430
273 Squadron 384, *385*, 387, 391, 409, 411,
  416, 422, 428
320 Squadron 324
413 Squadron, RCAF 390, 394, *395*, 413, *413*,
  466
453 Squadron, RAAF (as 21/452 Squadron)
  19, 20, 192, 212
488 Squadron, RNZAF 19, 20, 61, 98, 191,
  192
605 Squadron 70, *89*, 99, 192, 200, *218*, 219,
  221, 222, 225, *225*, 228, *229*, 235, 236, 248,
  282, 293, 294, *294*, 295, 305, 432, 438
611 Squadron 172
G Squadron 390
K Squadron 390

1 RAAF Squadron *18*, 19, 27, 50, 57, 58, 63,
  74,
  91, *92*, 107, 109, 110, 119, 194, 212, 214,
  219, *229*, 307, 310, *323*, 464
2 RAAF Squadron 176

8 RAAF Squadron 19, 27, 57, 58, 73, 79, 89,
  107,
  110, 111, 194, 199, 212, 460, 463, 464, 465
11 RAAF Squadron 172
12 RAAF Squadron 176
13 RAAF Squadron 176, 235
14 RAAF Squadron 313
20 RAAF Squadron 172
21 RAAF Squadron *see* as 21/452 Squadron
  until *440*. 463, 464, 465, 466
24 RAAF Squadron 172
36 Squadron, RAAF 451
1 IAF Squadron 259, 267, 284, 345, 348

BVAF 258, 345, 348, 349, 359
BVAF Comm Flt 345, 349
MVAF 44, 49, 57, 59, 67, 68, 70, 80, 82, 103,
  126, 194, 307, 462
MVAF A Flt 59, 103
MVAF 1 Detached Flt 126
MVAF 2 Detached Flt 44, 57, 67, 126
4 AACU 20, 413
3 PRU 349, 355, 367
4 PRU 166
5 PRU 367, 375
1 CD Flt 411
3 CD Flt 256, 268, 270, 349
5 CD Flt 408
6 CD Flt 410, 411
W Flt 387
Hudson GR Flt 349, 359, 368, 371

152 MU 332
AMES 511 42
RDF Unit, Burma 349, 371
10 OTU 349

Royal Navy:

788 Squadron, FAA 384, 395
800 Squadron, FAA 384
803 Squadron, FAA 384, 397, 428
806 Squadron, FAA 384, 397, 426, 428, *428*
808 Squadron, FAA 391
814 Squadron, FAA 385, 415, 420, 424
818 Squadron, FAA 385
820 Squadron, FAA 385
827 Squadron, FAA 384, 405, 411
831 Squadron, FAA 385
839 Squadron, FAA 384
880 Squadron, FAA 54
888 Squadron, FAA 385, 409, 411, 421

Air Units/Formations — American:

USAAF:

3rd Attack Group 142
7th Bomb Group 49, 148, 150, 154, 166, 172,
  221, 348, 361, 368, 371, 375, 394
19th Bomb Group 49, 109, 111, 142, 148, 172,
  195
24th Pursuit Group 128, 144
35th Pursuit Group 160
3rd Pursuit Squadron 10
3rd Pursuit Squadron (Provisional) 168, 170,
  171, 176, 241
13th Pursuit Squadron (Provisional) 171, 195
17th Pursuit Squadron 10, 127, 128, 133, *144*
17th Pursuit Squadron (Provisional) 148, 151,
  152, 155, *156*, 158, 164, 165, *165*, 166, 167,
  168, 170, *171*, 172, 195, 197, *198*, 199, 200,
  210, 212, *213*, 213, 217, 219, 220, *221*, 231,
  234, 303, 304, 305, 312, 313, 315

20th Pursuit Squadron 10, 139
20th Pursuit Squadron (Provisional) 160, 164
21st Pursuit Squadron (Provisional) 174
33rd Pursuit Squadron 176, 196, 241
34th Pursuit Squadron 133
91st Bomb Squadron (Light) 168, 195, *196*,
  209, 212

Provisional Mobile Depot Unit 141

US Navy:

PatWing 10, 129, 154, 160, 180, 182, 226,
  231, 238, 305, 312, 317
VS-2 (USS *Lexington*) 184, 185, 189
VF-3 (USS *Lexington*) 184, 185,
  188, 189, 190
VP-22 177

AVG:

1st Squadron 260, 270, 274, 281, 287, 356,
  361, 368, 372, *372*, 373, 374, 375
2nd Squadron 258, 266, 349, 356, 362, 366,
  368, 369, 370, 373, 374, 376
3rd Squadron 268, 285, 287, 288, *288*, 345,
  349, 350, 361, 362, 365, 368, 369, 372, 376

Philippines Air Force:

6th Pursuit Squadron 133

Civil Airlines:

BOAC 43, 44, 313
CNAC 268

KNILM 44, 114, 169, 203, 204, 228, 312, 314,
  314, 315, 325, 336

Qantas 43, 86, 180, 181, *181*, 241, *241*, 312,
  313

Air Units/Formations — Dutch:

Netherlands East Indies Army Air Force

1-VlG-I 147, 169, 222, 252, 302, 310, 316
2-VlG-I 43, 52, 305, *440, 445*
1-VlG-II 43, 44, 67, 148, 252, 295, 305, 310, 327, *445*
2-VlG-II 50
1-VlG-III 147, 233, 304
2-VlG-III 147, 169, *169*, 228, 327
3-VlG-III 147, 196, 292, 293, 295, 316

1-VlG-IV 50, *147*, 148, *148*, 151, 171
2-VlG-IV 148, *149*, 151, *151*, 153, 161, 171, 194, 222, 235, 303, 304, 209, 316
3-VlG-IV 147, 168, 169, *202*
1-VlG-V *146*, 146, 147, 202, *216*, 292, *337*
2-VlG-V 147, 169, 202, 292, 339
3-VlG-V *146*, 147, 171, *202*, 208, 215, 309, 376
VkA-1 147, 194, 304, 309, 323

VkA-2 147, 195
VkA-3 147, 169
VkA-4 147, 339, *342*

WH-1 Patrouille 43, 52

Dutch Volunteer Flying Club 194, *195*

Netherlands Naval Air Service:

GVT-1 153
GVT-2 194, 237, 324, 391
GVT-3 154, 163, 194
GVT-5 153, 155, 161, 241, 317, 324
GVT-6 162, 166, 170, 220, 234, 248

GVT-7 162, 166
GVT-8 226, 249
GVT-11 248, 337
GVT-12 248, 337
GVT-13 337

GVT-14 312, 337
GVT-16 194, 312, 391
GVT-17 165, 168, 312
GVT-18 194, 199, *199*, 221, 316, 324

Air Units/Formations — Japanese:

IJAAF:

3rd Flying Division 49
5th Flying Division 130, 345

3rd Flying Battalion 200, 228, 231
4th Flying Battalion 130, 266
7th Flying Battalion 50, 361, 375
10th Flying Battalion 266
12th Flying Battalion 18, 200, 237, 308, 346, 347, 352, 354, 355
10th Independant Hikotai 130

1st Sentai 20, 29, 30, 37, 197, 207, 346, 347
8th Sentai 130, 266, 268, 270, 272, *272*, 273, 277, 278, 282, 283, 284, 287, 291, 346, 347, 354, 368
11th Sentai 20, 29, 56, 118, 197, 200, 207, 223, 228, 346, 347, 352, 354, 373, 374
12th Sentai 45, 346, 347, 352, 355, 370
14th Sentai 130, 268, 285, 287
16th Sentai 130, 131, 132, 136, 137, 139
24th Sentai 130, 131
27th Sentai 200, 309, 369, 373
31st Sentai 258, *258*, 259, 260, *260*, 264, 268, 270, 274, 279, 284, 287, 346, 347, 352, 354, 361
50th Sentai 9, 130, 131, *134*, 134, 136, 140, 260, 262, 263, 264, 266, 268, 270, 273, 275, 276, 278, 279, 282, 286, 287, 346, 347, 351, 354
59th Sentai 44, 61, 62, 64, 76, 77, 93, 200, 202, 207, 208, 214, 221, 224, 225, 228, 230, 309, 310, 318, 336
60th Sentai *94*, 137, 138, *138*, 139, 141
62nd Sentai 137, 138, 139, 140, 260, 287
64th Sentai 45, 61, 64, 66, *67*, 76, 77, *85*, 93, 95, 96, 97, 98, 202, 208, 214, 221, 225, 309, 316, 318, 346, 347, *347*, 352, 354, 355, 357, 360, 361, 362, *362*, 364, *364*, 365, *367*, 369, *369*, 370, 373, 377, 379, *380*, 439

75th Sentai 44, 61, 62, 222, 225, 308, 309, 318, 327, 336
77th Sentai 258, 259, 260, *260*, 262, *262*, *263*, 264, 264, *265*, 266, 270, 275, 276, 281, 282, 283, 284, 287, 289, 346, 347, 352, 354, 361, 369, 375, 376
81st Sentai 49, 216
90th Sentai 44, 61, 64, 69, 95, 202, 214, 222, 224, 316, 318, 327
98th Sentai 50, 93, *94*, 346, 347, 352, 355, 373

11th Transport Chutai 130
12th Transport Chutai 93
47th Independent Chutai 20, 29, 56, 275, 287, *346*, 346, 347, 369, *369*
51st Independent Chutai 346, 347, 352
52nd Independent Chutai 130, 131, 136, 141
70th Independent Chutai 273, 287, 346, 347
74th Independent Chutai 128, 130, 131, 136
76th Independent Chutai 130, 136, 137
84th Independent Chutai 140
89th Independent Chutai 368
91st Independent Chutai 368

Parachute Flying Unit 93, *94*
96th Airfield Battalion 21

IJNAF:

11th Air Fleet 231

21st Air Flotilla 148, 160, 175, 183, 190, 220, 339
22nd Air Flotilla 90, *92*, 92, 168, 184, 200, 221, 225, 226, 227, 228, 247, 321, 360, 361, 393, 394

23rd Air Flotilla 148, 158, 160, 175, 200, 210, 241
24th Air Flotilla 172

1st Kokutai 128, 150, 158, 160, 165, 175, 176, 190, 214
3rd Kokutai 150, *151*, 153, 154, *154*, 155, 156, 157, *157*, 158, 159, 160, 161, 163, *164*, 167, 168, 183, 212, 213, 217, 219, 221, 226, 231, 241, 305, 311, 313, *314*, 315, 316, 325
4th Kokutai 172, *173*, 184, 186, *188*, 190, 221
Genzan Kokutai 79, 88, 123, 184, 199, 227, 228, 230, 233, 339, 360, 361, 394, 405
Kanoya Kokutai 80, 88, 124, 150, 158, 163, 176, 190, 227, 233, 235, 238, 305, 318, 321, 339
Mihoro Kokutai 45, 50, 79, 88, 124, 233, 318, 360
Tainan Kokutai 9, 129, 140, *149*, 150, 155, 156, 157, 160, 161, 162, *162*, 166, 167, 200, 201, 209, 210, 213, 216, 217, 219, 220, 226, 231, 238, 241, 242, *243*, 243, 304, 311, 316
Takao Kokutai 137, 138, 150, 158, 163, 200, 217, 226, 231, 233, 241, 305, 307, 323-4
Toko Kokutai 174, 175, 221, 359, 393
Yokohama Kokutai 184

(See also Air Units operating from Aircraft Carriers and Seaplane tenders, listed under Naval Units)

Army Units/Formations — British & Commonwealth:

ABDA 19, 45, 57, 59, 70, 155, 227
BURCORPS 345, 377
BURGROUP 47
NORGROUP 267
WESTGROUP 70, 191, 227

I Corps 287
1st Australian Corps 61
III Corps 17

1st Burma Division 344, 345, 360
17th Indian Division 272, 286, 344, 361

7th Armoured Brigade 344, 351

Burma Rifles 286, 287, 349
Ceylon Light Infantry 402
19th Machinegun Regiment (Australian) 178

Army Units/Formations — American:

I Corps, Philippines 132

45th Infantry Regiment 133
57th Infantry Regiment 133

131st Field Artillery 155
Philippine Scouts 132

Army Units/Formations — Dutch:

1e Division 309

Army Units/Formations — Chinese:

5th Army 286, 344, 345

6th Army 286, 344, 345

200th Division 345, 360

Army Units/Formations — Japanese:

14th Army 136
15th Army 344, 392
16th Army 107

48th Division 201, 232
55th Division 345
56th Division 344, 345

2nd Parachute Regiment 93
1st Tank Regiment 344
14th Tank Regiment 344

2nd Division 231, 250, 302, 318, 319, 323
4th Division 139
18th Division 18, 344, 345
33rd Division 344, 345, 377
38th Division 231

56th Regimental Group 232, 332, *333*
20th Infantry Regiment 133
146th Infantry Regiment 344
213th Infantry Regiment 344
230th Infantry Regiment 231, 249, 318

Kawaguchi Detachment 141, 143
Kawamura Detachment 143

Naval Units/Formations — British & Commonwealth:

Eastern Fleet 384, 386, 392, 395, 405, 408, 412, 413, 422, 430
Force H 386

Aircraft Carriers:

HMS *Ark Royal* 391
HMS *Formidable* 385, 386
HMS *Hermes* 16, 385, 386, 395, 422, 424, 425, *425*, 426, 428, 429
HMS *Indomitable* 14, 54, 384, 385, 386, 387, 390, 406, 411, 413

Battleships:

HMS *Prince of Wales* 13, 384
HMS *Warspite* 384, 386

Battlecruiser:

HMS *Repulse 13, 384*

Cruisers:

HMS *Cornwall* 16, 384, 386, 395, 406, *407*, 429
HMS *Dorsetshire* 16, 384, 386, 395, 406, *407*, 429
HMS *Danae* 59, 234
HMAS *Enterprise* 406
HMS *Exeter* 109, 123, *124*, 124, 233, 238, 239, 306
HMS *Glasgow* 408
HMAS *Hobart* 109, 233
HMAS *Perth* 233, 239, 240, 247, 249, 252, 253, 254

Destroyers:

HMS *Electra* 239
HMS *Encounter* 239, 306
HMS *Fortune* 392
HMS *Jupiter* 238, 239, 240
HMAS *Paladin* 406
HMAS *Panther* 406
HMS *Stronghold* 311
HMS *Tenedos* 405
HMS *Thanet* 38, 40, 41
HMAS *Vampire* 38, 40, 424, 425, 429
HMAS *Waterhen* 182

Sloops:

HMIS *Indus* 405
HMAS *Swan* 174
HMAS *Warrego* 174
HMAS *Yarra* 319

Sub Chaser:

HMAS *Warrnambool* 183

Requisitioned Minesweepers:

HMAS *Ballarat* 82, 200
HMS *Chengteh* 82, 83
HMAS *Gunbar* 177
HMS *Hua Tong* 77
HMS *Klias* 77
HMS *MMS.51* 319
HMS *Scott Harley* 318
HMS *Wo Kwang* 254

Requisitioned Gunboats:

HMS *Grasshopper* 83
HMS *Sylvia* 40

Requisitioned Auxiliaries:

HMS *Giang Bee* 82
HMS *Kuala* 82
HMS *Li Wo* 82
HMS *Mata Hari* 118
HMS *Rahman* 249

Requisitioned Launches:

HMM/L *Hung Jao* 82
HMM/L *105*(ASR) 85
HMM/L *301* 80, 81
HMM/L *1063* 249

Miscellaneous Naval Vessels:

HMS *Anking* (depot ship) 319
RFA *Athelstone* (oiler) 425
HMT *Athene* (aircraft transport) 158
HMT *Engadine* (aircraft transport) 391
HMS *Erebus* (monitor) 422
HMS *Hector* (armed merchant cruiser) 405
HMS *Hollyhock* (corvette) 425
HMS *Lucia* (submarine depot ship) 405
HMT *Neuralia* (transport) 267

Merchant Vessels — Allied:

(N.B. List of vessels lost leaving Singapore, pages 86-7)

Convoys:

BM-12 59
MS-5 240

Transports:
Autolycus 410
Barossa 178
Benledi 405
British Judge (tanker) 319
British Motorist (tanker) 178, 182
British Sergeant (tanker) 428
City of Canterbury 60, 158
Dagfred (Norwegian) 410
Dardanus 408, 410
Derrymore 81
Deucalion 192
Elsa 410
Empress of Asia 59
Empress of Australia 158
Exmore 410
Felix Roussel 59
Gandara 408, 410
Ganges 410
Glenshiel 392
Harpasa 410
Hermod 410

Indora 410
Loch Ranza 59
Malda 410
Neptuna 178, 180
Norah Moller 58
Norviken (Norwegian) 428
Orcades 192
Pinna (tanker) 59
Prominent (Norwegian) 311
Sagaing 421
Sea Witch 219, 240, 248
Shinkuang 410
Silksworth 410
Sinkiang 410
Taksang 409
War Sirdar (tanker) 307
Warwick Castle 158
Yoma 121, 473
Zealandia 178

Coasters:

Bintang 219
Hosang 77
Hunan 359
Katong 58
Kelat 178
Larut 50, 219
Lee Sang 41
Nam Yong 307
Raub 50, 219
Relau 85
Rentau 85
Sungei Pinang 83
Tulagi 174, 178
Tung Song 303, 324
Vyner Brooke 84

Miscellaneous:

Malvie (lugger) 178
Manunda (hospital ship) 178
Vita (hospital ship) 428
White Swan (yacht) 91, 254
Wu-Sueh (hospital ship) 249
Yu Sang (ammunition vessel) 139

Naval Units/Formations — American:

Task Force II 184, 190

Aircraft Carriers:

USS Enterprise 175
USS Langley 15, 171, 175, 195, 219, 233, 240, 241, 307
USS Lexington 15, 184, 185, 189, 190, 442
USS Yorktown 442

Seaplane Tender:

USS William B. Preston 176, 178, 181

Cruisers:

USS Houston 156, 158, 160, 174, 175, 216, 239, 240, 247, 249, 252, 253, 254, 312
USS Marblehead 156, 158, 160
USS Phoenix 240

Destroyers:

USS Alden 240
USS Barker 124
USS Bulmer 124
USS Edsall 240, 307
USS John D. Edwards 240
USS John D. Ford 240
USS Paul Jones 240
USS Peary 174, 176, 178, 181
USS Phelps 185
USS Pilsbury 307
USS Pope 306
USS Whipple 240, 241, 307

Submarines:

S-37 168
S-38 239
S-39 81, 319
USS Sea Raven 184
USS Sea Wolf 213

Transports/Merchantmen:

Admiral Halstead 178
Anhui 141
Bienville 410
Don Isidro (supply vessel) 182
Florence D. (supply vessel) 177, 183
Lanakai (schooner) 213
Mauna Loa 174, 175, 178
Meigs 174, 178
Pecos (tanker) 307
Port Mar 174, 178

Miscellaneous:

Asheville (gunboat) 318
Legaspi (Filipino coaster) 137

Naval Units/Formations — Dutch:

Cruisers:

De Ruyter 109, 156, 160, 201, 211, 239, 240
Java 109, 211, 239, 240
Soerabaja 201
Tromp 109, 156, 211, 386

Destroyers:

Banckert 109
Evertsen 252, 253
Kortenar 239
Piet Hein 211
Van Ghent 109, 199

Submarines:

K-XI 319
K-XIV 81

Transports/Merchantmen:

Abberkirk 234, 305
Atjeh 328
Ban Ho Guan 307
Banjoewangi 410
Barentz 327
Batavia 410
Canopus 327
Dajak 328
Duymaer van Twist 311
Kota Baroe 248, 324
Kota Gede 192, 219, 234, 390
Kota Radja 226
Le Maire 319
Mandar 328
Modjokerto 306
Palopo 307
Parigi 306, 319
Pasir 372

Phrontis 81
Poseidon 328
Rohan 327
Roosenboom 307
Siantar 318
Siaoe 306
Sipora 327
Sloet van Beele 199
Tawali 319
Tjimanoek 319
Tjinegara 194
Tohiti 327
Tydeman 324
Van de Capellan 410
Zandaam 248

Miscellaneous:

Cheribon (minesweeper) 82
Poelau Bras (liner) 338

Coasters:

Hanne 219
Kidoel 324
Manipi 324

Togian 59
Van Lansberge 59

Naval Units/Formations — Japanese:

Combined Fleet 383
Malaya Force 393, 408, 409, 410, 430
Nagumo Force 386, 393, 394, 405, 407, 408,
   409, 411, 412, 413, 422, 425, 426, 427, 429
1st Carrier Fleet 175, 190, 327, 328

4th Carrier Division 393
5th Carrier Division 383
3rd Battle Squadron 393
7th Cruiser Squadron 231
8th Cruiser Squadron 393
2nd Destroyer Flotilla 201, 232, 250
3rd Destroyer Flotilla 21, 231
4th Destroyer Flotilla 319
5th Destroyer Flotilla 231

Yokosuka Naval Landing Force 183

Aircraft Carriers:

Akagi 175, 176, 178, 179, 180, 182, 393, 394,
   395, 398, 402, 406, 413, 415, 421, 422, 424,
   425, 426, 431, 442
Hiryu 175, 176, 178, 179, 180, 182, 183, 393,
   394, 395, 399, 402, 403, 405, 406, 413,
   415, 421, 422, 424, 425, 426, 431, 442
Kaga 175, 176, 178, 179, 180, 182, 383, 442
Ryujo 72, 79, 80, 88, 90, 93, 123, 124, 142,
   199, 231, 306, 393, 408, 409, 410
Shoho 442
Shokaku 175, 383, 393, 395, 398, 399, 402,
   403, 405, 413, 415, 416, 421, 422, 424, 426,
   341, 442
Soryu 175, 176, 177, 178, 180, 182, 307, 393,
   395, 398, 402, 403, 406, 413, 415, 421, 422,
   425, 426, 428, 431, 442
Zuikaku 175, 383, 393, 394, 395, 396, 397,
   398, 402, 403, 405, 413, 415, 421, 422, 424,
   426, 431

Battleship:

Haruna 422

Seaplane Tenders:

Chitose 172
Kamikawa Maru 75, 197, 293, *294*, 294, 295
Kiyokawa Maru 189
Mizuho 9
Sagara Maru 76, 118, 149
Sanuki Maru 137, 141, 142, 226
Sanyo Maru 226, 293, 295, 309

HQ Vessel:

Ryujo Maru 253

Cruisers:

Ashigara 306
Atago 319
Chikuma 306, 307
Chokai 123, 393, 409
Haguro 232, 238, 240, 306
Jintsu 235, 239
Kinu 246
Kumano 393, 409, 410
Maya 311, 319
Mikuma 393, 409
Mogami 393, 409
Myoko 306
Nachi 232, 238, 240, 306
Nagara 201
Naka 232, 239
Sendai 21, 250
Suzuya 393, 409
Takeo 319
Tone 307, 406, 409, 426
Yura 246, 393

Destroyers:

Abukama 393
Amagiri 409
Amatsukaze 234
Asagiri 38
Asagumo 240
Fubuki 38, 253
Hatsukaze 235
Hatsutaka 109
Hatsuyuki 197
Isokaze 395
Natsushio 168
Shirakuno 409, 410
Shirayuki 38
Yagiri 409

Minesweepers:

W-1 38
W-2 253
W-34 38

Submarines:

I-1 318
I-2 307
I-7 319, 392
I-55 59, 82
I-58 253
I-62 319

Transports/Merchantmen:

Erimo (tanker) 319
Horai Maru 253
Inabasan Maru 92
Johore Maru 246
Kanbera Maru 21, 24, 26, 33, 28
Kansai Maru 21, 37, 38
Otawa Maru 109, 110, 112
Sakura Maru 253
Sugami Maru 209
Tajima Maru 115
Tatsumo Maru 253
Tokushima Maru 246
Tsurumi Maru (tanker) 253